PHILADELPHIA ON STONE

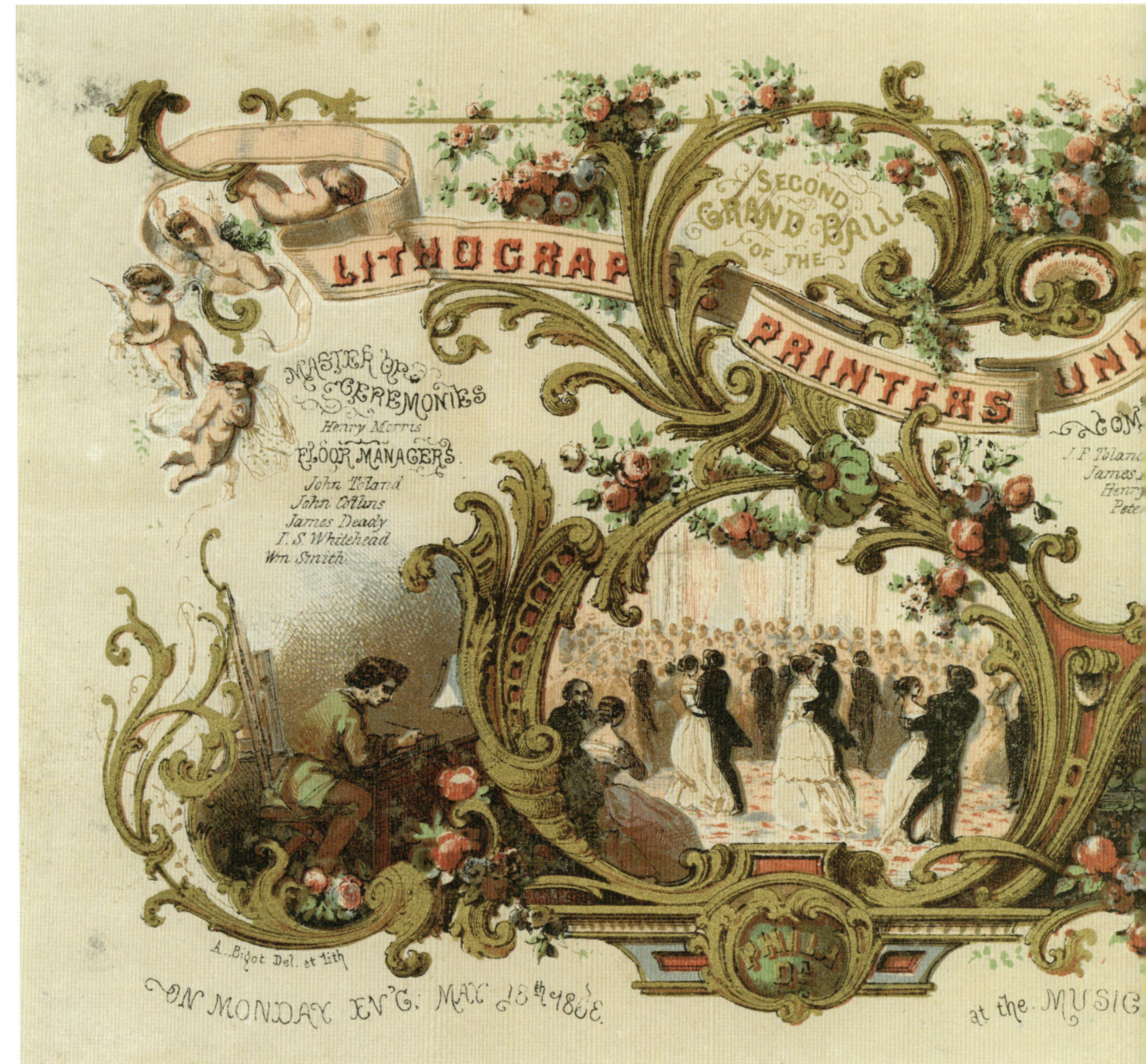

LITHOGRAP
MASTER OF CEREMONIES
Henry Morris
FLOOR MANAGERS
John Toland
John Collins
James Deady
T. S. Whitehead
Wm. Smith
SECOND
GRAND BALL
OF THE
PRINTERS UNI
COM
J. F. Toland
James
Henry
Peter
A. Bigot Del. et Lith
ON MONDAY EV'G. MAY 18th 1868.
at the MUSIC

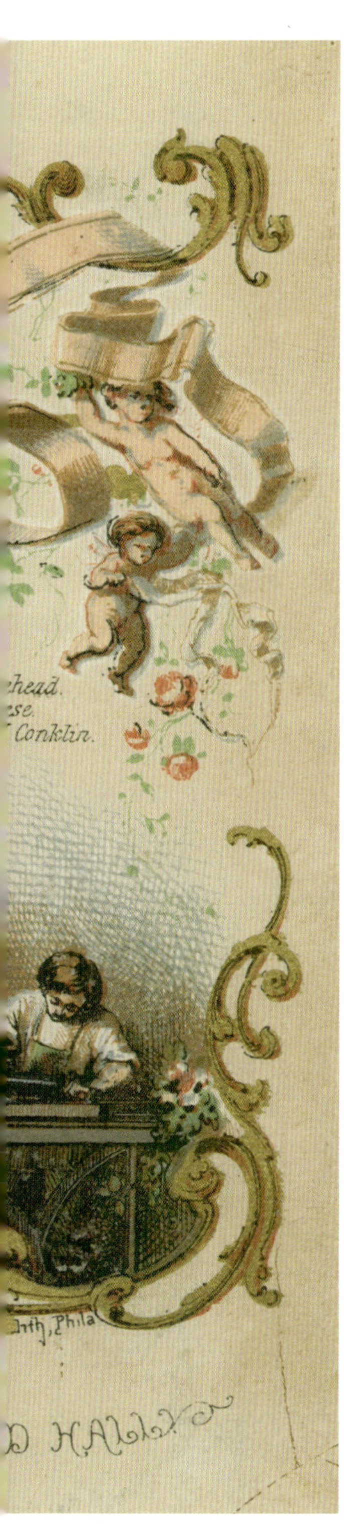

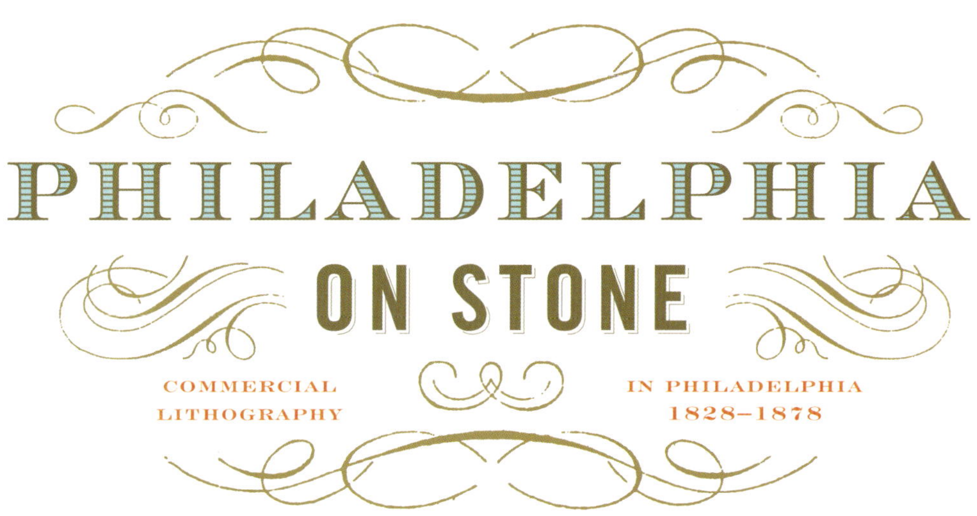

PHILADELPHIA ON STONE

COMMERCIAL LITHOGRAPHY IN PHILADELPHIA 1828–1878

EDITED BY ERIKA PIOLA

PUBLISHED BY THE PENNSYLVANIA STATE UNIVERSITY PRESS IN ASSOCIATION WITH THE LIBRARY COMPANY OF PHILADELPHIA

Published with the assistance of the William Penn Foundation

Library of Congress Cataloging-in-Publication Data
Philadelphia on stone : commercial lithography in Philadelphia, 1828–1878 / edited by Erika Piola.
         p.   cm.
Includes bibliographical references and index.
Summary: "A collection of essays examining the history of nineteenth-century commercial lithography in Philadelphia. Analyzes the social, economic, and technological changes in the local trade from 1828 to 1878"—Provided by publisher.
ISBN 978-0-271-05252-6 (cloth : alk. paper)
1. Lithography—Pennsylvania—Philadelphia—19th century.
2. Commercial art—Pennsylvania—Philadelphia—History—19th century.
I. Piola, Erika, 1971– .
II. Title: Commercial lithography in Philadelphia, 1828–1878.

NE2311.P5P49 2012
686.2'315097481109034—dc23
2011043001

Copyright © 2012
The Library Company of Philadelphia
All rights reserved
Printed in China by Everbest Printing Ltd., through Four Colour Print Group, Louisville, KY
Published by The Pennsylvania State University Press, University Park, PA 16802-1003
The Pennsylvania State University Press is a member of the Association of American University Presses.

It is the policy of The Pennsylvania State University Press to use acid-free paper. Publications on uncoated stock satisfy the minimum requirements of American National Standard for Information Sciences—Permanence of Paper for Printed Library Material, ANSI Z39.48–1992.

FRONTISPIECE: Alphonse Bigot, *Second Grand Ball of the Lithographic Printers Union. On Monday Ev'g, May 18th 1863 at the Musical Fund Hall* (Philadelphia: T. Sinclair's lith., 1863). Chromolithograph. 12 × 17 cm (4 ¾ × 6 ¾ in.). POSP 205, LCP, P.9349.277.

ADDITIONAL CREDITS: page 48, figure 35; page 78, figure 44, page 96, figure 64; page 118, figure 75; page 176, figure 118; page 202, figure 126.

Designed by Regina Starace

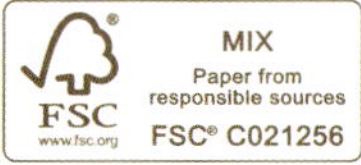

This book is dedicated to the memory of my mother,
Irene,
the true author in the family.

1 THE FIRST FIFTY YEARS OF COMMERCIAL
LITHOGRAPHY IN PHILADELPHIA
An Overview of the Trade, 1828–1878

2 PUTTING PHILADELPHIA ON STONE
An Introduction to the Techniques Used

3 JAMES QUEEN
Chronicler of Philadelphia

4 PETER S. DUVAL
Philadelphia's Leading Lithographer

CONTENTS

Over fifty years ago, Nicholas Wainwright wrote *Philadelphia in the Romantic Age of Lithography,* the most complete work of its time about the history of lithography in Philadelphia. The book, described by the author as "fancily" entitled, examined the trade from the inception of the first commercial press in the city, in 1828, until the Civil War, when, according to the author, the "flavor" of the earlier era was lost by modern technology such as the steam press and chromolithography. Wainwright provided an overview of the trade that focused on the major lithographic establishments active during those years, as well as a descriptive inventory of almost five hundred lithographs documenting the built environment of Philadelphia and held predominantly at Philadelphia repositories. A romantic, in the sense of simpler, element may have pervaded the techniques, motives, and structure of the shops of the early lithographers, but little did it pervade the majority of the imagery that dominated the Philadelphia market, or the daily lives of the artists, lithographers, and printers involved in the first fifty years of the trade. Building upon the groundbreaking work of Wainwright, *Philadelphia on Stone* reexamines this "romantic" period of Philadelphia lithography as part of a three-year collaborative survey project funded by the William Penn Foundation. By placing a greater focus on the role of the smaller artisans who sustained the industry, examining specific genres of prints, and extending the time period analyzed by Wainwright to 1878, this work seeks to document the evolution of the lithography trade in Philadelphia from a different perspective and with more comprehensive consideration of social, cultural, and economic influences.

The collections of the Library Company of Philadelphia, the Historical Society of Pennsylvania, the Free Library of Philadelphia, the Philadelphia History Museum at the Atwater Kent, the Athenaeum of Philadelphia, the American Antiquarian Society, the Library of Congress, and the Smithsonian Institution that were surveyed for the creation of the *Philadelphia on Stone* Digital Catalog (http://www.librarycompany. org/pos/poscatalog.htm) provide the content and most of the images in this book. The catalog, derived from surveys conducted between May 2007 and May 2010, contains over 1,300 lithographs, related ephemera, and prints documenting Philadelphia commercial lithography between 1828 and 1878. Lithographs listed in Wainwright, separately issued lithographs not listed in Wainwright but portraying Philadelphia, and advertisements for and printed views of Philadelphia lithographic establishments form the core content of the records and images contained in this catalog.

As did Wainwright's, our surveys for the project focused on lithographs document-ing the built environment of the city, such as storefronts, churches, landmarks, celebra-tory and disaster scenes, and panoramas or views. We extended the scope of Wain-wright's survey to include lithographers of Philadelphia views who were not local and advertisements for Philadelphia lithographers, views of their printing shops, and por-traits of the tradesmen. Although the bulk of the prints were issued from 1828 to 1878, in accordance with the parameters of the project, prints dated to about 1900 and of a more aesthetic nature have also been included in the catalog. These works serve as points of reference because of unique content, exceptional graphic design, or the lithographer. The prints frequently depict Philadelphia cityscapes but also broadly represent the visual culture of the city. Prints beyond our stated scope and not included in the surveys have also been discussed by the contributing authors in support of their arguments.

Although nongraphical primary sources are few for the Philadelphia lithographic trade, these materials also composed a part of the study. No known complete com-pany archive survives, but a scattering of invoices, business correspondence, and credit reports remain to provide evidence of the financial practices of the lithographers. The diaries of Matthias Weaver (compiled 1840–43) and George D. Shubert (compiled 1866), the only known by Philadelphia lithographers, also help us to comprehend the daily existence of the journeyman lithographer. In addition, newspaper and periodical accounts and census and other government records present additional windows onto the industry for which so few primary documents remain other than the prints the firms produced.

Neither this book nor Wainwright's would have been possible if not for two other important figures: the inventor of lithography, Alois Senefelder (1771–1834), and local collector Charles Augustus Poulson (1789–1866). Senefelder, a Bavarian playwright turned amateur printer, conceived the planographic process around 1798, when, ac-cording to folklore, he dropped a sheet of limestone marked with his specially devised ink into a bucket of greasy water and observed that it was not effaced. Lithography was the first new printing method to be introduced in more than three centuries. The revolutionary printing process transformed the printed landscape, giving rise to a pop-ular visual culture that continues to influence American society today. It was the first cost-effective method for printing in color, allowed long print runs and larger sizes, and facilitated design innovation because text and images could easily be combined.

Charles Augustus Poulson also proves a pivotal figure for *Philadelphia on Stone*. A local antiquarian and son of Library Company librarian Zachariah Poulson, Poulson amassed a large collection of antebellum Philadelphia iconography, including litho-graphic advertisements that he bequeathed to the Library Company. With this bequest, the Library Company became the public repository of the largest collection of lithographic images of Philadelphia, many inscribed with dates and notes in Poulson's hand. Given the extent of the Poulson collection, and the scores of other lithographs acquired in subsequent years, the Library Company is well positioned to update Wainwright's seminal work.

The succeeding chapters illuminate and augment this narrative and examine the history of the trade, the lives of two seminal lithographers, and specific genres of lithographs. Erika Piola and Jennifer Ambrose provide the introductory chapter, "The First Fifty Years of Commercial Lithography in Philadelphia: An Overview of the Trade, 1828–1878," and discuss the social, cultural, and economic influences that affected the Philadelphia trade between 1828 and 1878, as lithographic establishments evolved from printing shops to plants in concert with improvements to the printing process. Piola and Ambrose use the prints reviewed during the survey as a base for their insights about the production and consumption of Philadelphia lithographs, in addition to providing an analysis of the demographics of the trade. Michael Twyman, in "Putting Philadelphia on Stone: An Introduction to the Techniques Used" (chapter 2), discusses the technical process, tools, and equipment used by the local trade, with reference to European influences. Through detailed observations of lettering styles and tinting methods used by Philadelphia lithographers and their European counterparts, as well as the technological innovations they pursued, Twyman draws parallels and differences between their drawing and printing techniques.

Chapters 3 and 4 focus on the careers of eminent Philadelphia lithographers James Queen (1820/21–1886) and Peter S. Duval (1804/5–1886), collaborators and innovators in the field. In "James Queen: Chronicler of Philadelphia" (chapter 3), Sara W. Duke profiles the life of James Queen, an artist active from the early era of commercial Philadelphia lithography to the era of the predominance of chromolithography, during the 1870s. Trained under the apprenticeship system, Queen undertook work of every description and, unlike many of his peers, worked primarily for one shop, that of Peter S. Duval, his whole career. In "Peter S. Duval, Philadelphia's Leading Lithographer" (chapter 4), Sarah J. Weatherwax provides the most comprehensive biography to date of this printer, known as the premier Philadelphia lithographer of the nineteenth century. Duval can deservedly be called the father of Philadelphia lithography. During a career spanning more than thirty-five years, he produced lithographs of every genre, from book and periodical illustrations to maps to parlor prints, while cultivating many of the city's premier lithographers, including Queen. He also pioneered American chromolithography, introduced steam printing presses to the country, and served as the city's emissary to the trade.

Chapters 5 through 8 focus on specific genres of Philadelphia lithographs. In "Lithographed Plates for Books and Periodicals: A Mainstay of Philadelphia Lithographers" (chapter 5), Christopher W. Lane provides a detailed overview of the commercial importance of the production of lithographic plates for books, magazines, and government reports to the establishment of the lithographic trade in Philadelphia and later to the growth and stability of local firms. He provides an engaging account of the exceptional work produced by premier firms such as John T. Bowen for natural history publications, including McKenney & Hall's *History of the Indian Tribes of North America,* John James Audubon's multivolume works on birds and quadrupeds, and other ornithological publications. In "Commercial Architecture in Philadelphia Lithographs" (chapter 6), Dell Upton explores the depiction of commercial architecture in antebellum advertising prints and how it reflected the city's "transformations of . . . architecture and geography of commerce." His study perceptively interweaves excerpts from contemporary written commentaries on the city's architecture with deconstructions of the storefront imagery that dominated the large-format advertisements issued to promote the local business community. In "Drawn on the Spot: Philadelphia Sensational News-Event Lithographs" (chapter 7), Erika Piola provides insight into the niche market of sensational Philadelphia news prints, from inception to dissemination, with a particular focus on the interrelationships between the visual and textual accounts of the events. Piola argues that these lithographs have been unduly overshadowed by engraved periodical illustrations in the study of spectatorship and graphic journalism. Donald H. Cresswell, in "Philadelphia Lithography and American Landscape" (chapter 8), examines the artistic evolution of Philadelphia landscape imagery in lithographs and by Philadelphia lithographers over the first fifty years of the trade. Cresswell uses a range of genres for his analysis, including portraiture, sheet-music covers, and commercial atlases, to show how landscape imagery not only documented the natural beauty of the region but served as political propaganda, promoted consumerism, and evoked the demographic changes of nineteenth-century America.

The survey work for the project did more than shape the content of these chapters. Mention must be made of two other facets of *Philadelphia on Stone:* an online biographical dictionary and an exhibition. In lieu of a biographical appendix to this volume, the illustrated *Philadelphia on Stone* Biographical Dictionary of Lithographers is accessible through the Library Company's digital-collections catalog ImPAC (http://www.lcpdigital.org). The online dictionary contains the biographies of more than five hundred artists, lithographers, printers, and publishers who worked in commercial lithography in Philadelphia during the first fifty years of the trade. Historically prominent lithographers, such as Childs & Inman, P. S. Duval, Thomas Sinclair, and

Wagner & McGuigan; lesser-known figures, such as Alphonse Bigot, John F. Finkeldey, and Thomas Hunter; and journeyman who sustained the trade are included among the men and women described. The entries provide a demographic overview of the Philadelphia trade, illustrated by portraits of premier lithographers, views of their establishments, and advertisements for their businesses. The majority of the images represent materials held in the collections of the eight collaborating institutions. Based on the most comprehensive scholarship to date, the biographies are searchable by name and keyword and, unlike conventional printed dictionaries, can be readily revised with any further information provided by readers or discovered by staff.

In addition, a 2010 exhibition provided another venue to disseminate the scholarship resulting from the project. The exhibition included an overview of the history of lithography and the local trade in addition to sections documenting the lives of Philadelphia lithographers, their work, and their influence on the visual culture of nineteenth-century and modern-day society. The exhibition demonstrated how lithography allowed speedy production and a variety of imagery, as shown in the lithographs displayed, thus altering the conception, content, and consumption of prints produced for the commercial and domestic consumer in Philadelphia. Sections of the exhibition examined the change of the establishments from collaborative printing shops in the antebellum era to factories with specialized departments after the Civil War; the influence of the innovations of chromolithography (the process of printing lithographs in multiple colors) and steam printing on this transformation; and the later industry's focus on advertising, particularly trade cards, to remain viable. The online exhibition can be accessed at http://www.librarycompany.org/pos/exhibition.htm.

This book represents the capstone to this multifaceted collaborative project and hopes to show that although the romantic age of lithography in Philadelphia should be reevaluated, the romance of the research of this local trade should be infinite.

ACKNOWLEDGMENTS

This book and the project that spurred its creation relied on the ingenuity, generosity, knowledge, and graciousness of several people, organizations, and institutions. Former curator of prints and photographs Ken Finkel first pursued an update of the Wainwright book in the mid-1980s with funding from the Pennsylvania Council of the Arts. His planned "Wainwright Project" to publish a revised and expanded edition of the text served as a guide for *Philadelphia on Stone*. In 2002, in the era of the Internet, the first steps to create a digital catalog of Philadelphia lithographs began when Back Stage Library Works digitized the Library Company's collection of "Wainwright" lithographs. By 2006 former associate curator Jenny Ambrose had revived the "Wainwright Project" and redesigned it to combine both traditional and emerging methodologies. Generously funded in 2007 by the William Penn Foundation and Independence Foundation, *Philadelphia on Stone* would entail a digital catalog, online biographical dictionary, a book, and an exhibition. Following the departure from the library in 2008 of Ambrose, who fostered my knowledge and appreciation of lithography, I assumed administration of the project, for which the following words of recognition are most sincerely extended.

Project assistant Linda Wisniewski assumed, without skipping a beat, the survey work originally begun by me. She also researched and wrote the majority of the biographical dictionary entries, completed and coordinated the digitization of the image files and catalog records for the digital catalog, and served as a touchstone throughout the project. My colleagues in the Print and Photograph Department provided professional support in every sense. Curator Sarah Weatherwax contributed an essay for the text and kindly allowed me the time to complete the project. Print room assistant and digital collections manager Nicole Joniec handled rights and reproductions for the book with the utmost efficiency and made the publication process run all the more smoothly. Volunteers Louise Beardwood, Ann Condon, and Selma Kessler and interns Erica DiBenedetto, Samantha Kulp, and Casey Near provided research support for the biographical dictionary by combing through city directories and other genealogical resources and drafting entries.

The curators and rights and reproduction staff of the collaborating institutions enthusiastically provided access to their collections in our common goal of expanding our understanding of Philadelphia lithography and its importance to the study of visual culture. They include Gigi Barnhill, Lauren Hewes, and Jaclyn Penny at the American Antiquarian Society; Jeffrey Ray and Susan Drinan at the History Museum of Philadelphia at the Atwater Kent; Bruce Laverty at the Athenaeum of Philadelphia; Karen Lightner at the Free Library of Philadelphia; Lee Arnold, Matthew Lyons, R. A. Friedman, and Dana Lamparello at the Historical Society of Pennsylvania; Helena Zinkham and Sara W. Duke at the Library of Congress; and Vanessa Broussard, Kaye Peterson, Jennifer Strobel, and Helena E. Wright at the Smithsonian Institution.

Although institutions served as our official collaborators for the surveys, private collectors and descendants of Philadelphia lithographers John F. Finkeldey and Alphonse Bigot graciously shared their personal collections. The lithographs, printers' trade cards, and family artifacts of David Doret, Jeremy K. Finkeldey, Joe Friedman, Jane Stephenson, and Elizabeth Dayton helped to round out our knowledge of a number of lithographers researched for the project.

I wish to thank contributing authors Jenny Ambrose, Don Cresswell, Sara Duke, Christopher Lane, Michael Twyman, Dell Upton, and Sarah Weatherwax. Their insightful, engaging, and eloquent essays provide fresh perspectives on nineteenth-century commercial lithography in Philadelphia that inspire continuing research into the subject. In addition, Michael Twyman served not only as a contributing author but as my personal consultant regarding the history and technical aspects of lithography. The breadth of his knowledge of this printing process inspires awe and respect.

My utmost gratitude must also go to Library Company director John Van Horne, who provided unwavering support and his skills as an editor. In addition, Chris Van Horne cannot be thanked enough for her invaluable editorial assistance on the many drafts of the book and compiling the index.

I would be remiss if I did not also extend my appreciation to Penn State Press executive editor Eleanor Goodman, managing editor Laura Reed-Morrisson, production coordinator Patricia Mitchell, editorial assistant Danny Bellet, the peer reviewers of the manuscript, designer Regina Starace, and copyeditor Keith Monley.

My husband, Nick Crosson, and my friend Jessie Betts, who kept me grounded and read drafts of my essays and listened to my trials and tribulations, were also essential to the completion of the book and project.

Philadelphia on Stone was truly a collaborative process from beginning to end. My appreciation for all those involved is immeasurable.

EP

Several authors make reference to lithographs described in the *Philadelphia on Stone* Digital Catalog (http://www.library-company.org/pos/poscatalog.htm). References to these images are identified by one of three acronyms signifying POS categories followed by the number (e.g., POS 321):

POS
Lithographs cited by Wainwright and those not cited by Wainwright that document the built environment of Philadelphia dated 1828–78.

POSA
Advertisements in all graphic mediums for Philadelphia lithographers.

POSP
Lithographs and ephemeral materials that document the built environment of Philadelphia after 1878 or that serve as points of reference due to their content.

The digital catalog is also fully searchable by artist, title, date, subject, and keyword.

AAS
American Antiquarian Society, Worcester, Massachusetts

APS
American Philosophical Society, Philadelphia, Pennsylvania

Carson Collection
Marian S. Carson Collection, Prints and Photographs Division, Library of Congress, Washington, D.C.

Democratic Art
Peter C. Marzio, *The Democratic Art: Pictures for a 19th-Century America: Chromolithography, 1840–1900* (Boston: D. R. Godine; Fort Worth: Amon Carter Museum of Western Art, 1979)

FLP
Free Library of Philadelphia, Philadelphia, Pennsylvania

HSP
Historical Society of Pennsylvania, Philadelphia, Pennsylvania

LCP
Library Company of Philadelphia, Philadelphia, Pennsylvania

LOC
Library of Congress, Washington, D.C.

PMHB
The Pennsylvania Magazine of History and Biography

R. G. Dun & Co.
R. G. Dun & Co. Collection, microfilm, Hagley Museum & Library, Wilmington, Delaware

Smithsonian
Smithsonian Institution, National Museum of American History, Washington, D.C.

Wainwright
Nicholas B. Wainwright, *Philadelphia in the Romantic Age of Lithography* (Philadelphia: Historical Society of Pennsylvania, 1958)

Warshaw Collection
Warshaw Collection of Business Ephemera, Archives Center, Smithsonian Institution, National Museum of American History, Washington, D.C.

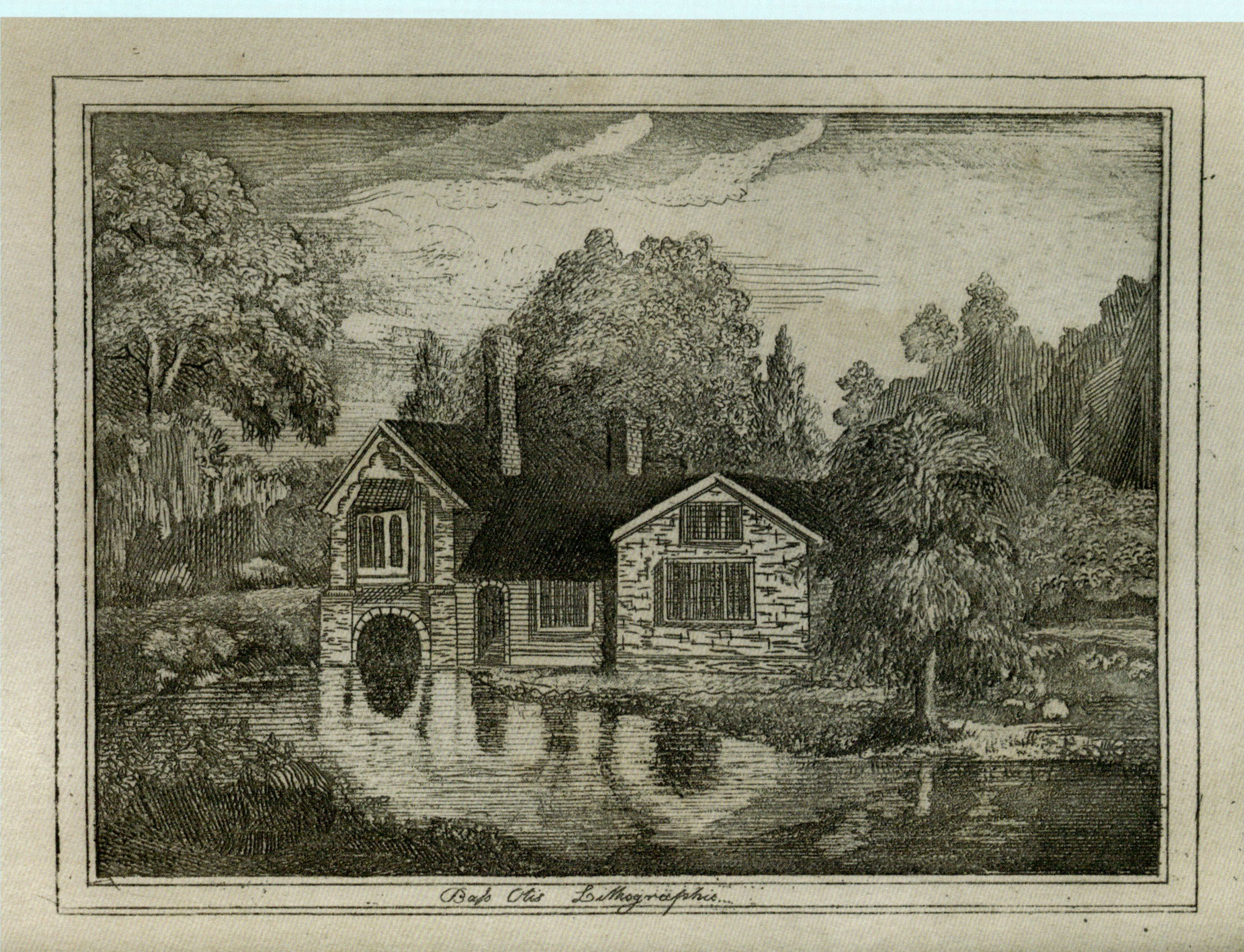
Baß Ölis Lithographie.

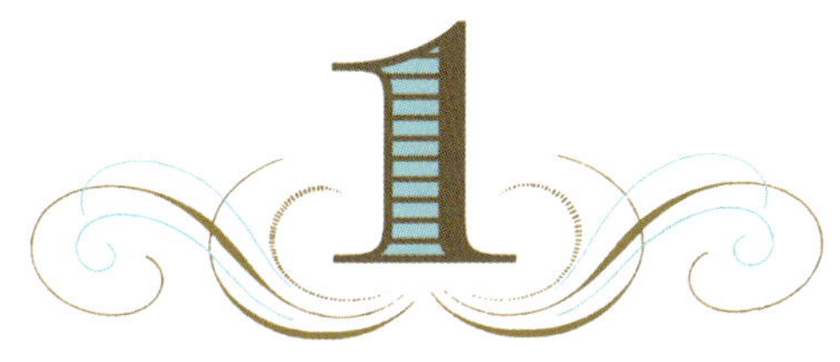

THE FIRST FIFTY YEARS OF COMMERCIAL LITHOGRAPHY IN PHILADELPHIA

An Overview of the Trade, 1828–1878

ERIKA PIOLA &
JENNIFER AMBROSE

"SPIRIT AND FREEDOM OF EXECUTION": THE FIRST DECADES OF THE PHILADELPHIA LITHOGRAPHIC TRADE

After more than a decade of experiments in the United States, the Philadelphia periodical *Analectic Magazine* published the earliest surviving American lithograph in July 1819. Bass Otis, "an ingenious and enterprising artist of Philadelphia,"[1] drew and printed a modest image of a mill that accompanied a six-page descriptive account of the lithographic process by University of Pennsylvania chemistry professor Thomas Cooper (fig. 1). The lithograph was drawn on Bavarian limestone, borrowed by Otis and Dr. Samuel Brown, a physician and chemist, from the American Philosophical Society for conducting "experiments in the art of lithographic engraving."[2] Early lithography in America was characterized by experimentation and involved practical scientists and artists with broad interests in new technologies and the natural world. They saw the potential of this new printing medium to spread knowledge, particularly scientific knowledge, more broadly and at a more reasonable cost. An active center for scientific inquiry and the printing trade, Philadelphia provided the ideal environment for artists, scientists, and publishers, like Otis, Brown, and naturalist Charles Alexandre Lesueur[3] to promote this new printing process.[4]

In conjunction with the American scientific community, European practitioners of the new print process expedited the establishment of lithography in the United States. Lithographers across the Atlantic not only published technical treatises that

FIG. 1
Bass Otis, *Lithography,* from *Analectic Magazine* (July 1819). Engraving on stone. 18 × 24 cm (7 × 9 ¼ in.). LCP, Per A 192.

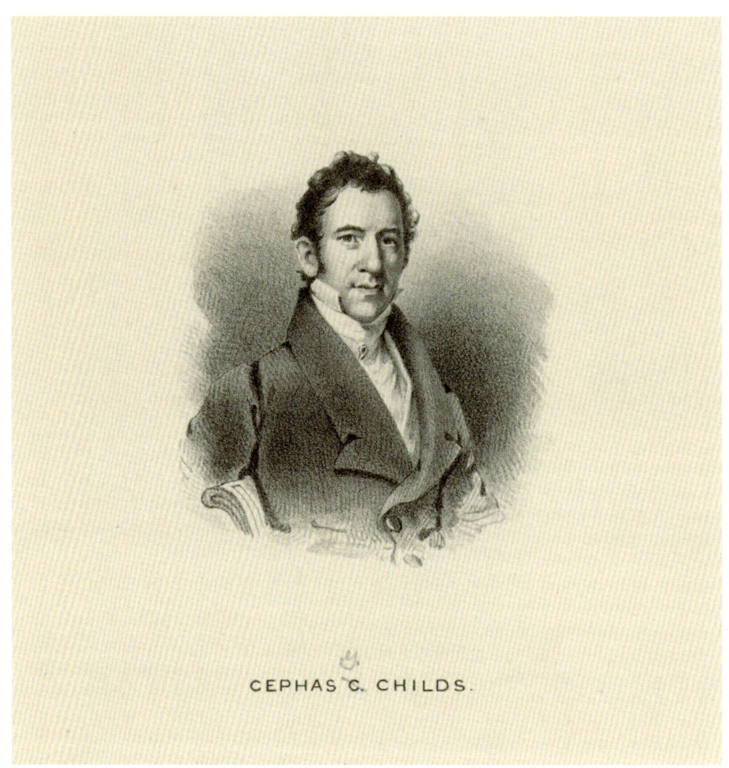

FIG.2

"Lithography," *National Gazette,* December 10, 1828. HSP, DL A-20-18.

FIG.3

Cephas G. Childs (United States, ca. 1830?). Lithograph. 30 × 28 cm (12 × 11 in.). Courtesy of the American Antiquarian Society, Graphic Arts Lithf ChilC.

instructed their American colleagues, but also sent stones, inks, presses, and examples of lithographic prints.[5] French commercial lithographer Charles Hilbert Lasteyrie sent Samuel Latham Mitchill, a New York physician and naturalist, lithographic stones and inks in 1808 so he could "ma[k]e some experiments with the new technology,"[6] and his fellow premier tradesman Godefroy Engelmann donated a collection of lithographs to the Pennsylvania Academy of the Fine Arts in 1818 to promote local interest.[7] In addition, several early American lithographers, such as the Pendletons of Boston, Philadelphian Cephas G. Childs, and Barnet & Doolittle, the New York proprietors of the first commercial establishment in the country, in 1821, traveled to Europe to receive training in lithography, purchase supplies, and solicit the services of skilled practitioners.[8]

American periodical and book publishers, several in Philadelphia, also supported early efforts to promote lithography in the United States. Scientific journals issued accounts of the process and some very early lithographic illustrations. In 1808 the *Medical Repository* published one of the first descriptions of planographic printing available in the United States.[9] In 1821 and 1822 the Philadelphia *Journal of the Academy of Natural Sciences* and the *American Journal of Science* published, between them, the first

American lithographed map, lithographs of technological machinery, and lithographs of fish by Lesueur. Around a dozen entries about the process appeared in the *Franklin Journal, and American Mechanics' Magazine* between July 1827 and August 1830, including eight "Essays on Lithography" between 1827 and 1828, translated from the original articles by Lasteyrie. In addition, early lithographs appeared as illustrations in about 150 American books published in the 1820s, primarily in scientific and technical works with relatively small print runs.[10]

Beginning with Barnet & Doolittle in New York in 1821, attempts (some successful) were made in American cities in the Northeast to establish commercial lithographic firms in the 1820s.[11] In Philadelphia, the earliest firms grew logically out of related commercial enterprises and were initially subsidized by other business interests. Philadelphia's first commercial lithographic firm, Kennedy & Lucas, dealers in "looking glasses and pictures,"[12] ventured into printing their own images in 1828 (fig. 2).[13] Practitioners of other, more directly allied trades entered the field as well. Cephas G. Childs (fig. 3) actively continued in the business of engraving while attempting to launch his fledgling lithographic business in 1829. He formed several brief partnerships with other engravers and artists before selling out in 1834 to Peter S. Duval, a lithographic printer he brought back from Paris and who was to become the premier Philadelphia lithographer of the nineteenth century.

The lithographic trade in Philadelphia increased steadily in its first decade. However, the growth in the actual number of establishments does not reflect the constant fluidity of the trade in the early years or the number of lithographers who moved in and out of local firms. In 1829 three lithographic establishments were active in the city—Kennedy & Lucas; Pendleton, Kearny & Childs; and the one-man shop of artist Edmund Brewster.[14] After M. E. D. Brown opened his Philadelphia shop in 1831, there were eight lithographic presses in operation in the city.[15] A decade later, in 1839, the city supported six lithographers: Duval (who became the proprietor of what was once Pendleton, Kearny & Childs), John T. Bowen, John Collins, Thomas Sinclair, John Frampton Watson, and the partnership of Wild & Chevalier. During the same ten-year period, half a dozen other proprietors, as well as numerous artists and pressmen, were briefly involved in the Philadelphia trade before leaving it altogether or moving to practice the profession in other cities.[16]

The changing composition of the staff employed by C. G. Childs's partnerships between 1829 and 1834 illustrates the flexible nature of the trade. The original partnership of Pendleton, Kearny & Childs included John B. Pendleton, who trained in his family's lithographic firm in Boston, and Philadelphia engraver Francis Kearny. In addition to the three partners, the firm employed as artists Rembrandt Peale and Moses

Swett, who had both worked with Pendleton in Boston, and C. Blonde as printer.[17] In 1830, after Kearny and Pendleton withdrew, Childs continued on his own but by the end of the year took on a new partner, the New York artist Henry Inman, to form Childs & Inman. The Childs & Inman partnership, noted for lithographs eliciting the "spirit and freedom of execution, which no merely imitative art can ascertain,"[18] provides further evidence of this adaptability. During the first year of the partnership, active 1830–33, Inman remained in New York and through correspondence coordinated with Childs in running the business. Although outside Philadelphia, Inman acted not only as the head artist but as a business agent. He interacted with print sellers to gauge the state of the market for lithographs; purchased and shipped supplies, including $218.50 worth of large stones (10 cents per pound); and suggested artists such as James Clonney[19] for employment.[20]

During their first year, Childs & Inman advertised the services of six artists in their employ: George Lehman; landscape artist Thomas Doughty; noted caricaturist E. W. Clay; deaf-mute artist Albert Newsam; W. H. Hay; and H. E. Sauinier.[21] This partnership dissolved in April 1833, and Childs took on artist Lehman as a partner. The new firm of Childs & Lehman relied on the artistic talents of the new partner, while it continued to retain the services of Newsam and added George Becker as draftsman[22] and P. S. Duval as printer.[23] At the end of 1834 Childs sold his interest in the firm to Duval, and the firm of Childs & Lehman became Lehman & Duval. In the brief five-year period from 1829 to 1834, individuals moved in and out of the role of proprietor, a variety of different artists were affiliated with the establishment, and the size and composition of the staff continually altered.[24]

During the early years, lithographic artists and pressmen trained and entered the profession through various channels. As in other trades, practicing lithographers took as apprentices young men, often their own sons, to learn the profession. Noted Philadelphia lithographer James Queen's apprenticeship agreement with Lehman & Duval in 1835 established the period and terms of his training, in which he was in "four years, five months, and six days . . . to be taught or instructed in the art, trade, or mystery of a Lithographic Draughtsman."[25] He trained as an apprentice with Duval between the ages of around fourteen and eighteen, before being hired as a paid member of Duval's staff. Lithographers seeking apprentices also used personal connections or advertised in the local newspapers for "stout, active boy(s) almost 16 years of age, to learn the Lithographic Printing Business."[26]

Many of the artists employed in the early lithographic trade, such as Henry Inman and Hugh Bridport, trained as traditional artists in drawing and painting, studying under experienced artists or in art schools. Some lithographic artists, like Childs and Kearny, originally trained as engravers on copper and wood occasionally turned their skills to working on stone.[27] Others, immigrants to the city, like Duval, previously received training in lithographic establishments in Europe. Instruction in lithography was also offered by some Philadelphia schools and cultural organizations. The Mercantile Library Association had a lithographic press workshop in 1831.[28]

As a consequence of Philadelphia's position from the eighteenth century as a transatlantic center of the printing trades, early lithographers initially struggled to gain a foothold in the competitive local printing market and experienced fluctuations and changes similar to those of their predecessors.[29] European and American prints of all varieties and in other media were already available in "fancy" and stationery shops and from picture dealers in the city.[30] Engravers provided illustrations for Philadelphia's book and periodical publishers. Letterpress printers produced circulars, broadsides, labels, price lists, and billheads for local businesses. From the earliest days of the trade in Philadelphia, willing lithographers took on all manner of work to sustain their businesses. Local establishments, self-described "general" or "practical" lithographers, responded to the multiplicity of needs of publishers, businesses, and artists by furnishing their customers cheaply and quickly with a variety of lithographically printed materials. Some firms specialized in particular genres, developing an aspect of the general trade or taking advantage of the talents of artists affiliated with their shops. However, with few exceptions, firms that became well known for work in a particular genre continued to take in and advertise for a wide range of services throughout most of the period studied.

To sustain their establishments, Philadelphia lithographers undertook a great deal of routine jobbing work for merchants and businessmen. It is extremely difficult, if not impossible, to estimate the scope of this work for individual lithographers or the industry as a whole in the early decades of the trade. Only a very small portion of this material has survived, and most cannot be attributed to particular lithographers. Extant invoices from lithographers from the 1830s suggest the large volume of ephemeral material produced. The invoices themselves document lithographic print jobs that averaged one to three hundred impressions (fig. 4). (Print runs up to five hundred and one thousand would be common by the early 1860s.)[31] The printing of everyday items needed for the transaction of business, often printed as transfer lithographs,[32] remained a consistent part of the services offered to the public throughout the nineteenth century. John Frampton Watson, one of only a handful of lithographers practicing in the city in the early 1830s, advertised that he could furnish business cards, "transfer circulars, price currents, and everything connected with the Mercantile and Exchange business" within a few hours.[33] Watson remained in the lithographic trade

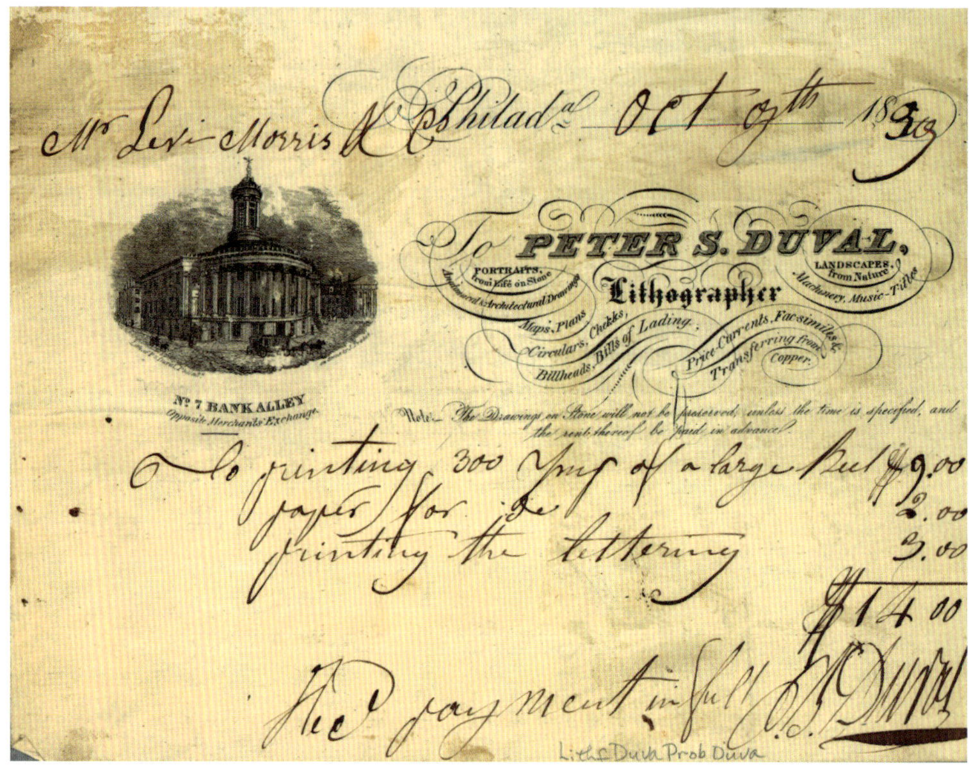

in the city for more than thirty years; however, very little of his work has survived.[34] Much of what was produced by Watson's press and the presses of many local lithographers consisted of printed ephemera necessary for the routine, daily use of businesses.

In addition to job printing, book and periodical illustration provided lithographers with steady commissions from the beginning of commercial lithography in the city. Early local lithographers created images particularly for books on natural history, as well as lithographically illustrated periodicals and sets of prints sold by subscription on a variety of subjects, including ecclesiastical portraits, city views, and the cultivation of fruit.

During the 1830s Philadelphia lithographers started to claim a place in the local printing trade. In addition to serving as job printers and producing illustrations, lithographers printed separately issued graphics including views, advertisements, and political cartoons. No longer did the "fancy" and stationery shops and picture dealers display and carry only engravings. Lithographers such as Childs & Inman, John T. Bowen, and P. S. Duval used the local press to promote their work by having columnists visit their shops and forwarding specimens to their newspaper offices.[35] Lithographs, announced in dozens of newspaper advertisements, also entered the market

through auction houses, picture-frame and looking-glass dealers, and street peddlers, with the latter often offering up the
more sensational and newsworthy prints to the daily pedestrian traffic on the major thoroughfares.[36] Lithographs, such as
the 1838 Wild & Chevalier cityscape prints commissioned by
the *Saturday Courier,* also served as premiums for the typically
more well-to-do subscribers of the newspaper (see fig. 127,
POS 241.1 and 2).[37] The display of lithographs during the early
decades of the trade also occurred at unexpected locations, no-
tably the reading table at the Merchants' Exchange, a haven
for the Philadelphia businessman. On October 30, 1835, the
Pennsylvania Inquirer and Daily Courier noted that a "specimen number" of McKenney and Hall's *History of the Indian
Tribes of North America* would be on display at the financial institution in the next few
days. Newspaper advertisements promoted lithographs new to the market as well as
the lithographers themselves.

In October of 1829, in one of the earliest known newspaper advertisements for a
Philadelphia lithographer, Pendleton, Kearny & Childs informed the public that they
were "prepared to execute Historical subjects, Portraits, Landscapes, Buildings, Bills
of Exchange, Cards, Plans, Maps, Fac-Similies, &c. for which Lithography is so well
calculated both as regards cheapness and expedition."[38] The extant lithographic work
produced by Childs and his various partners reflects a varied output—city views, pictorial advertisements, caricatures, maps, sentimental prints, images of ships, dogs and
horses, fashion plates, and illustrations (fig. 5).[39]

In conjunction with this broad range of work, Childs and his partners developed
a commercially viable specialization in portraits and produced lithographic likenesses
from life or from oil paintings as early as 1829. Childs assisted in the training of
Newsam, who became the principal draftsman, and he used Newsam's prodigious talent for portraiture to develop a popular specialty. In the early years, the portrait work
"was the main branch of the business."[40] In April 1830 Childs advertised that he would
furnish "twenty-five impressions and the stone, of any portrait, at the moderate price
of twenty-five dollars. The copy is exact and beautiful."[41] Prominent citizens of the
city, actors and actresses, singers, politicians, authors, scientists, and nationally and
internationally renowned public figures, royalty, and celebrities were drawn on stone.
The firm published portraits they believed would be popular, of both the famous and
the infamous. For example, the firm issued three different lithographic portraits of
the popular actress Fanny Kemble during her debut on the Philadelphia stage (fig. 6)

FIG. 5
Edward W. Clay, *Roper's Gymnasium. 274
Market Street, Philadelphia* (Philadelphia:
Childs & Inman's Press, ca. 1831). Litho-
graph. 24 × 39 cm (9 ½ × 15 ½ in.). POS
659, LCP, P.2181.

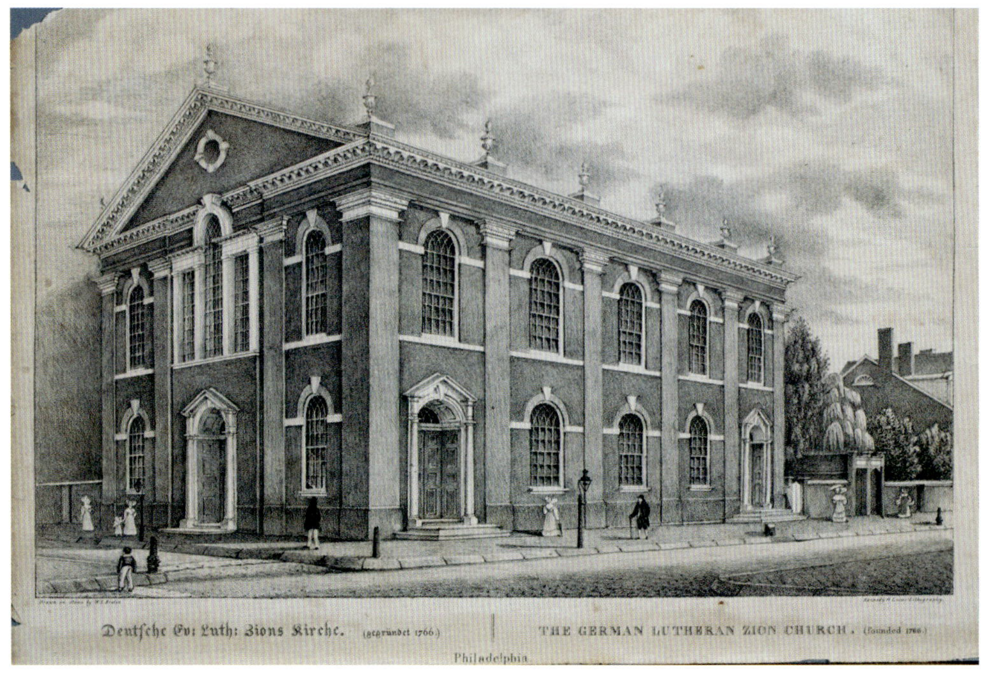

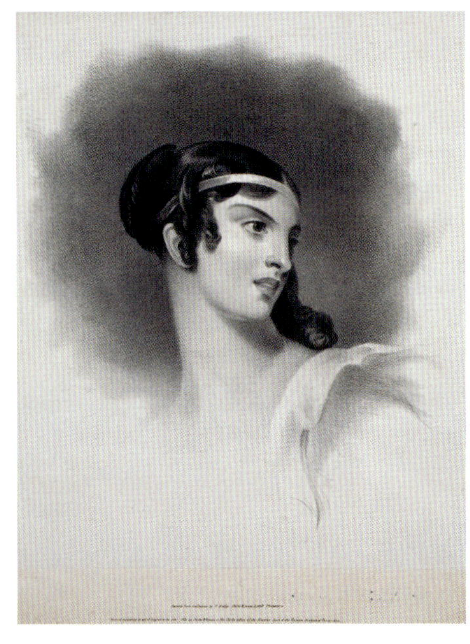

and also published an image of a murderess awaiting trial at Doylestown.[42] They also accepted commissions from individuals, usually the more prominent members of society, who wanted oil paintings copied for distribution among friends and family or from groups who wanted to honor one of their members, like Rev. George Boyd, the rector of Saint Johns Episcopal Church in the Northern Liberties. The parishioners of this laboring-class neighborhood church most likely commissioned and purchased the print as a fund-raiser for Saint Johns.

Portraiture remained an important genre to all lithographers in the early decades of the trade, and by the late 1840s the printing fees for such work were about one-quarter the price of 1830.[43] From the early 1840s lithographers copied daguerreotype and ambrotype portraits, photographic positives that could not be easily reproduced by photographers. When local photographers during the 1850s adopted new technologies that allowed portraits to be printed in multiple copies from photographic negatives, the business in lithographic portraits declined. By the 1860s portraiture faded as a mainstay of the industry, as competition from other media greatly reduced the number of lithographic portraits printed by local firms.

Churches and the area of Fairmount provided two other subjects of separately issued lithographs produced in significant numbers before 1840. Kennedy & Lucas specialized early in architectural views of churches, which would continue to be a steady part of the lithographic trade. In 1829 and 1830 the firm printed views of Philadelphia churches and meetinghouses by artist William L. Breton, depicting a broad range of local religious institutions, including Unitarian, Catholic, and Episcopal churches, two Friends' meetinghouses, and two African American churches (fig. 7).[44] Often commissioned by local congregations or church architects in celebration of new construction, dozens of church views were produced by local lithographers throughout the nineteenth century.[45] A related specialty of John T. Bowen's was "views of public buildings," which he advertised in 1838 when he reissued J. C. Wild's twenty lithographic plates from *Views of Philadelphia and Its Vicinity.*[46]

The lovely, soft tones that could be achieved with lithographic crayon also made lithography particularly well suited for the production of landscape views. As they had been for other artists working in a variety of media, Fairmount waterworks, gardens, and parklands on the Schuylkill River, a popular destination for both locals and tourists, were favored subjects for early Philadelphia lithographers. One of the first lithographs issued in 1828 from the recently established press of William Lucas, that is, Kennedy & Lucas, shows the Pagoda and Labyrinth Garden pleasure resort built in Fairmount the same year (POS 538). Over the next ten years, the early major firms— such as Pendleton, Kearny, & Childs; Childs & Lehman; Wild & Chevalier; and John T. Bowen—would issue advertisements, book illustrations, sheet-music covers, and landscapes capitalizing on the bucolic beauty of the local landmark.[47]

None of these lithographs would have been possible without the system of collaborative work between the artist, lithographer (draftsman), and printer that characterized the lithographic establishments of the nineteenth century. However, the period from 1828 until the early 1860s was not one of specialization: workers performed multiple tasks. This was an era when most lithographers operated workshops, not factories; handpresses, not steam presses. Color printing did not dominate, and apprentices still served a purpose.[48] Kennedy & Lucas had three lithographic presses of different sizes, two small tabletop presses, one standing press, and eight thousand pounds of lithographic stone when they closed their business, after William Lucas's death, in 1833.[49]

These years also required more in-house production and modification of supplies and tools used by the establishment. Initially lithographers, but by the 1830s more often the shop workers and apprentices, made the crayons and inks, prepared the stones and paper, and maintained the tools and equipment. Stones were ground to the proper polish or grain through hours of preparation with a smaller stone. Printing ink was made by the dangerous procedure of heating linseed oil to ignition and later mixing in house-made lampblack (fig. 8). Plate (sheet) paper required calendering and sizing, that is, passage through rollers to be made glossy and then coated with a glue to reduce stretching. Occasionally tools would have to be devised, particularly

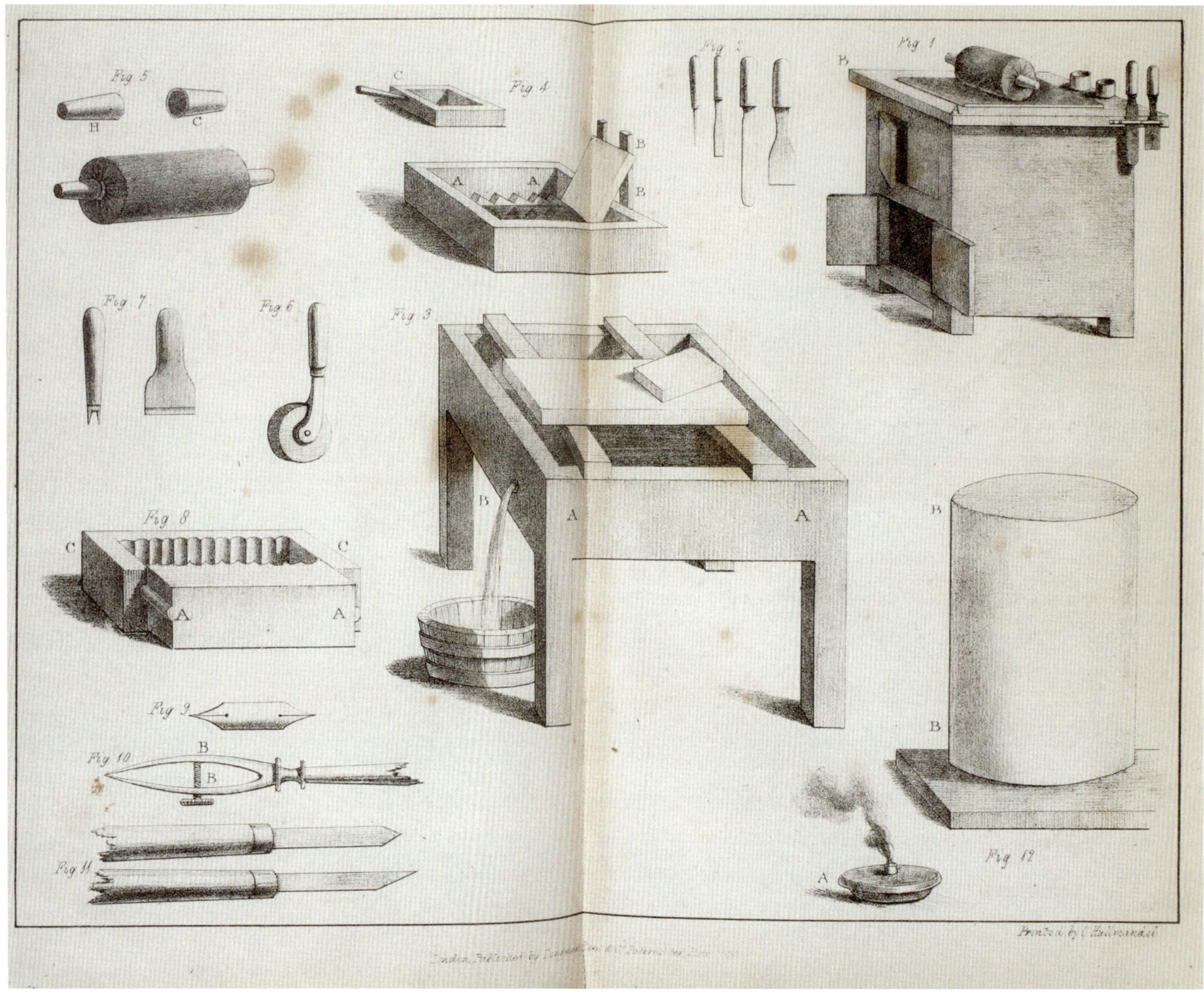

FIG. 8

Plate published in Antoine Raucourt, *A Manual of Lithography; Clearly Explaining the Whole Art, and the Accidents That May Happen in Printing, with the Different Methods of Avoiding Them* (London: Longman, Rees, Orme, Brown, Green & Longman, 1832). Lithograph. 23 × 32 cm (9 × 12 ½ in.). HSP, Dc. 8366.

lithographic pen nibs from watch springs made thinner by nitric acid, rounded by a hammer, and slit with a small pair of scissors. The crayons and writing inks were produced in the shop by cooking different combinations of soap, shellac, wax, tallow, and lampblack in pots, then pouring the mixture into molds (fig. 9).[50]

Information on the prices, amounts, and vendors of the supplies used by Philadelphia lithographers is nearly nonexistent. However, there is some information about the two largest yearly capital expenses for the antebellum establishments: the stones and paper. Bavarian limestone, like that used by Otis, was the lithographic stone preferred by American lithographers through the 1870s.[51] By 1831 lithographers such as Inman could purchase stone from a New York dealer instead of directly from Germany. In addition, local advertisements show that lithographers occasionally acted as brokers themselves, as when J. T. Bowen advertised in 1847, possibly as a result of an overshipment, "To Lithographers—Just received a large quantity of Lithographic stone, of all sizes and good quality, for sale."[52] By 1852 local middlemen had apparently taken over the market to such an extent that major German dealers such as Jegel & Schwarz, who claimed "the largest quarries of stone in Solenhofen," began to advertise in Philadelphia lower rates than those offered by dealers who had to "buy second hand themselves."[53]

Into the early 1860s prices for large stones (more than 26 inches in width) remained at about the price Inman paid earlier, 10 cents per pound.[54] Whereas in 1830 lithographers like Childs offered to sell printed stones to those who commissioned them, by the late 1830s establishments owned, maintained, and reused their stones.[55] Thomas Wagner, the proprietor of one of the larger establishments in the trade for about twenty years, held almost twenty-five thousand pounds of stone at his death, in 1863.

Like lithographic stone, the proper quality lithographic paper was available only from Europe before around 1837. According to the reminiscences of Duval, Thomas Gilpin's Brandywine Mills was the first of the local manufactories to produce suitable paper, followed by James Wilcox, and then Charles Magarge & Co., which advertised the sale of "lithographic paper" by 1841.[56] Unlike lithographic stone, the actual prices for paper before the Civil War cannot be easily deduced, although it had to be a major expense given the weights of plate paper and the amounts required. Lithographic commissions required reams of paper, each approximately five hundred sheets and weighing between 40 and 120 pounds, which by 1866 cost 33 to 37 cents a pound. Further evidence of the expense of paper can be gleaned from the R. G. Dun & Co. credit reports, which noted judgments for money owed to Magarge against a number of Philadelphians in the trade, including Alphonse Brett in 1857 and Thomas Sinclair and P. S. Duval in 1866. Sinclair owed $29,200 at the time of his judgment.[57]

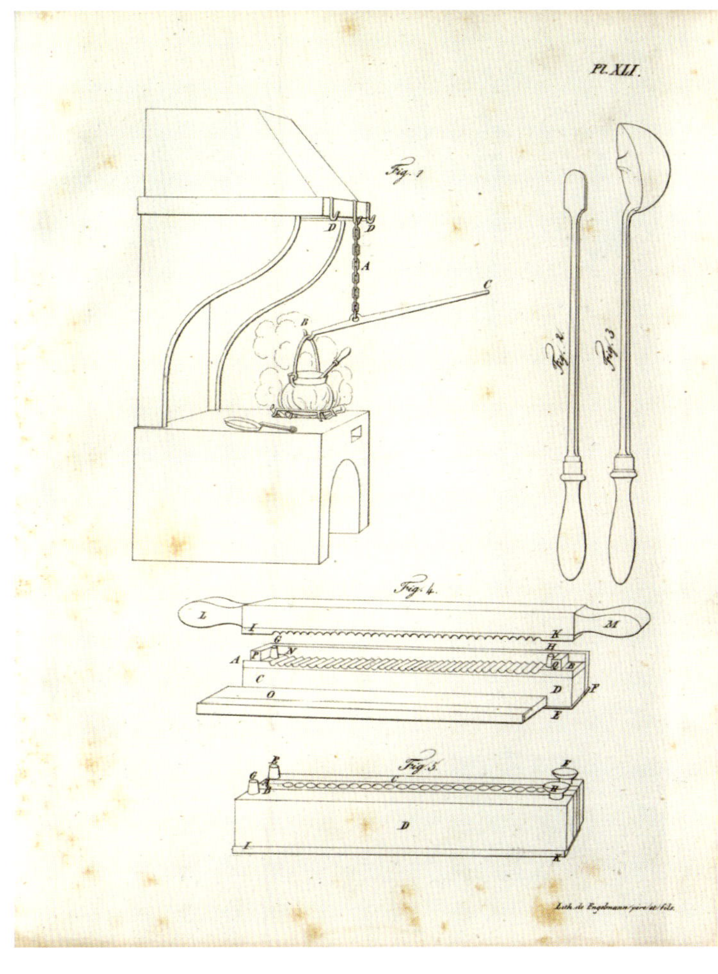

FIG. 9

Plate XLI in Godefroy Engelmann, *Traité de lithographie* (Mulhouse: P. Baret, 1839). Lithograph. 27 × 20 cm (10 ½ × 8 in.). HSP, Dc. 8395.

By midcentury Philadelphia lithographers had captured a considerable niche for themselves in the local printing market, having continued to grow in conjunction with the overall printing and publishing trade. By 1850 there were eleven lithographic establishments in the city, almost double the number in 1840.[58] By 1858 lithographic establishments running "two hundred and thirty-five lithographic presses" received mention in the industry treatise of Edwin Freedley, *Philadelphia and Its Manufactures*.[59] The trade included between twenty-five and thirty establishments in 1860[60] and had increased to about thirty-five by 1867.[61] Most establishments clustered in the area bounded by Chestnut, Walnut, Third, and Fifth Streets, with the highest concentration in the blocks from Third to Fourth Streets, all near where Kennedy & Lucas had operated on Third Street above Walnut Street.

Once local lithographers had established themselves within the broader printing industry, their proportion of the trade remained constant during the handpress era, and they failed to make further inroads until the widespread adoption of steam presses at the end of the century. In 1850 lithographers made up 12 percent of the printing and publishing establishments reported in the U.S. Census of Manufacturers.[62]

Philadelphia's earliest firms were small in scale. The proprietors owned and operated a few presses[63] and employed a small number of draftsmen and artists. While there was explosive growth in a few large firms in the 1840s and 1850s, smaller lithographic shops continued to make up a considerable portion of the industry throughout the entire pre–Civil War period. By the mid-1850s, the two largest firms—P. S. Duval and Wagner & McGuigan, a partnership between Thomas S. Wagner and James McGuigan, two Pennsylvania-born lithographers in business from 1846 to 1858—operated about forty presses each.[64] At the same time, "a number of Lithographers in the city . . . [had] but one or two presses, and [were] engaged principally in doing plain work, such as views of buildings, ships, caricatures, &c."[65] This situation prevailed in other Philadelphia industries, with a majority of small operators of relatively fixed size and a few large ones expanding their facilities and adopting new machinery. By 1860 Philadelphia had approximately 3,600 artisan shops with fewer than six employees each, making up 58 percent of the city's industrial firms.[66]

Evidence documenting small and mid-sized lithographic firms remains elusive. In 1850 lithographers with mid-sized printing shops included John H. Camp, John Childs, Norman Friend, William Hart, Alfred Hoffy,[67] and Augustus Kollner.[68] Lithographic artists such as William H. Rease and Robert F. Reynolds advertised their own lithographic businesses, accepting commissions from other lithographers or directly from customers and contracting out their printing to other shops.[69] Auctions of equipment from several smaller firms provide brief glimpses into the scale of their operations. In addition to lithographic presses and supplies, lithographers often owned other types of presses and machinery for preparing or finishing paper and did not necessarily confine their work to lithographic printing. In 1852, when an "extensive" and "active" lithographic establishment was sold, the proprietors owned seven lithographic printing presses in addition to other basic supplies, such as stones, inks, varnishes, sponges, and gum arabic. The studio also contained two embossing presses, a calender press, a cutting machine, a screw press, and a copperplate printing press.[70] In 1861 the estate of lithographer Frederick Pilliner, who had originally trained as an engraver on copper and wood, included "2 superior lithographic printing presses, with all the necessary apparatus," and five thousand pounds of lithographic stone. He also owned cutting machines and a letterpress.[71]

By the mid-1840s the three large firms that dominated the Philadelphia lithographic trade for most of the remainder of the pre–Civil War era were well established: P. S. Duval, Wagner & McGuigan, and Thomas Sinclair, a Scottish-born lithographer who took over John Collins's small lithographic printing shop around 1838. In the early 1850s a Russian lithographer, Louis N. Rosenthal, assisted by his brother Max, added a fourth firm. These four establishments spearheaded the transition in the Philadelphia lithographic trade from small printing shops to large-scale manufacturing. They owned or occupied large spaces in newly designed industrial buildings, were awarded large projects for publishers and on government contracts, took in commissions from outside the local area, and were able to garner the capital resources necessary for innovation and experimentation. These firms were the first to adopt steam power and were Philadelphia's earliest experimenters in color printing during the handpress era.

An examination of the trade as it existed during the height of this era, in 1856, provides some rough estimates about the number of workers the industry employed. The *Public Ledger* claimed that there were sixteen establishments operating 177 presses that year,[72] and, as recorded by trade analyst Freedley, P. S. Duval operated thirty-four of those presses and employed seventy to eighty people, excluding his 100–150 colorists.[73] If the ratio of the number of presses to employees (one to two) holds for other lithographers, approximately 375 people, excluding colorists, worked in lithographic establishments in the city. In the same year, the four largest firms—Duval, Thomas Sinclair & Co., Wagner & McGuigan, and the Rosenthals—employed a total of between fifty and sixty artists.[74] Among them they controlled more than half the

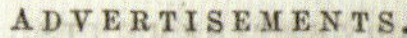

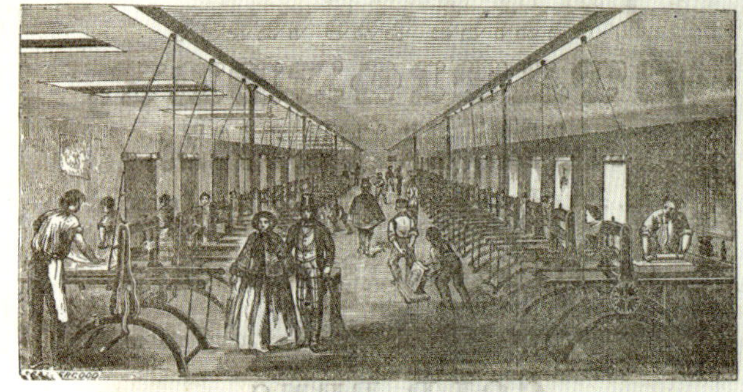

David Scattergood, "Wagner & M'Guigan's Lithographic Drawing, Engraving, and Printing Establishment," in *Catalogue of the Twenty-Fourth Exhibition of American Manufactures . . .* (Philadelphia, 1854). Wood engraving and letterpress. 26 × 20 cm (10 × 7 ½ in.). POSA 112, LCP, Am 1854 Exhib 13701.O.2.

presses in the city[75] and presumably employed at least half the lithographic artists, bringing the total for the trade to approximately 100–120 artists. Illustrated advertisements for Wagner & McGuigan's lithographic shop depict long rows of lithographic handpresses operated by one printer for each press (fig. 10).[76] Although lithographers were not always running at full capacity and some presses would have been reserved for proofing, the trade would have employed roughly 150–75 printers. As mentioned, other employees would have taken on a variety of tasks that supported the firm's operations. Foremen, clerks, printers' assistants, apprentices, and workers involved in the preparation of the stones, inks, and drawing materials, as well as others who cut, trimmed, and packed the finished work for shipment, would have swelled the number of workers on the payroll. To summarize, very rough totals for 1856 suggest that there were approximately 375 workers in the trade, including about 150–75 printers, 100–120 artists, and as many as 80–125 other employees.[77]

Researchers compiling data for the Biographical Dictionary of Philadelphia Lithographers have identified and documented approximately 150 people working in the trade in 1856. If the estimates above are accurate, the names of more than half the employees working for local lithographers are still unknown. What do we know about those who have been identified?

The employment of workers remained very fluid throughout the first fifty years of the industry. Lithographic establishments took on artists and printers on a temporary basis to work on large projects. A trade report stating that Frederick Bourquin employed six to twenty lithographers "according to the exigencies of trade"[78] was characteristic of the industry. While some lithographers worked full-time for one establishment, many took work where they could find it or transitioned back and forth as proprietor and employee, as in the case of John H. Camp. He partnered with Lewis Brechemin and Augustus Kollner during the 1840s and early 1850s and then operated his own lithographic studio for several years before serving as the director of printing at the joint establishment of Theodore Leonhardt and Ferdinand Moras from 1857 to about 1861. After another near decade of sole proprietorship, he again associated with Moras in 1870.[79] A contrast to this fluidity of employment was the career of James Queen, one of Philadelphia's most important and versatile lithographic artists. He worked primarily for Duval for his whole career. An exceptionally large body of his work—approximately one thousand lithographs—is extant and available for analysis.[80]

While the numbers of lithographic artists and pressmen in the trade grew steadily between 1840 and 1860, there were some interesting consistencies and trends in the composition of the group in these two decades. Lithographers drew most heavily on local talent to staff their establishments, whether native or foreign born. Snapshots of the trade in 1840, 1850, and 1860 show that workers remained fairly evenly divided between those born in America and European immigrants—fully one-third of all workers were born in Pennsylvania.[81] As in other American cities, immigrants employed in the Philadelphia lithographic trade were overwhelmingly German.[82] German representation in the industry remained far greater than their proportional representation in the general population. In 1850, 15 percent of known lithographers were German born, while German immigrants made up only 5.6 percent of the population of Philadelphia.[83] Some of these workers, such as Theodore Leonhardt, had been trained in lithographic establishments in Germany. While there was a small increase in the percentage of German immigrants in the city in 1860,[84] German-born workers made up 25 percent of known lithographers, representing slightly less than half of all the immigrants employed in the local trade. The other two largest groups of new arrivals were those born in the British Isles (Ireland, Scotland, and Great Britain), who made up about one-third of the immigrant lithographers between 1840 and 1860, and French-born lithographers, who represented about 15 percent of the nonnative workers. In 1850 and 1860, the predominant age of identified lithographers was twenty-one to thirty, comprising about 40 percent of the trade at the start of each decade, and most lived in the Northern Liberties, Southwark, and central Philadelphia (figs. 11a–c).

The large German presence in the trade was evident when Philadelphia's lithographic pressmen in 1854 instituted the earliest known union organization for the profession. The Lithographic Printers Union of Philadelphia was "composed of acknowledged practical Lithographic Printers, working in the city of Philadelphia," willing to pay annual dues and comply with rules regulating prices for piecework.[85] The constitution and bylaws were printed in English and German and provided for the secretary "to translate all motions or other business into the German language."[86] The local newspaper published notices of union meetings from 1857 to 1868.[87] By 1862 the Union not only sought to regulate prices but, in response to the inflation from the Civil War, began to advocate for wages higher than the "average . . . about eight to ten dollars weekly."[88]

Place of origin, age, and number of lithographers active in the trade between 1830 and 1880. Source: Sample of 321 of 500 of the lithographers identified through the Philadelphia on Stone project. Data analysis by the Greater Philadelphia Cultural Alliance.

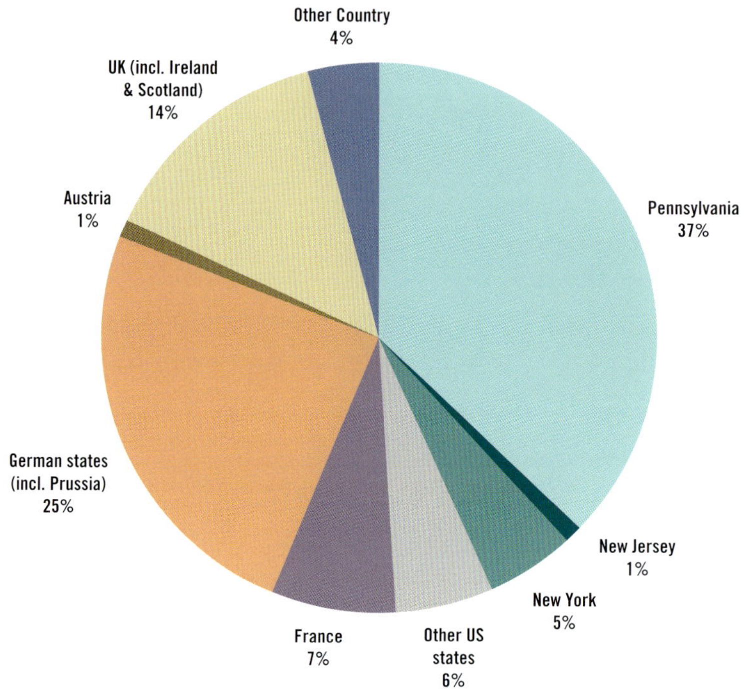

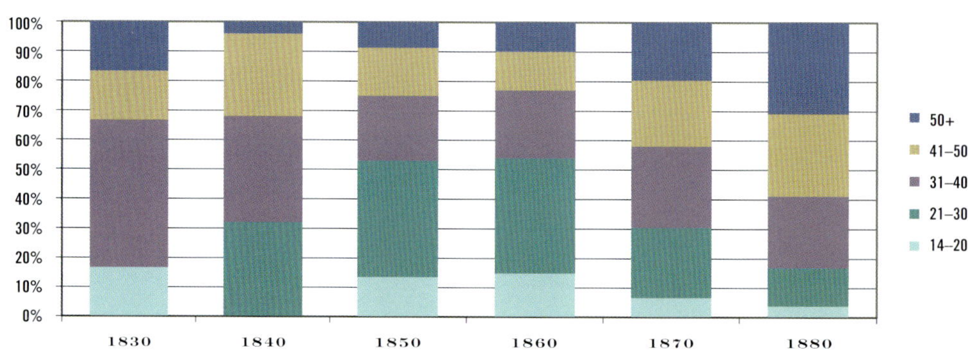

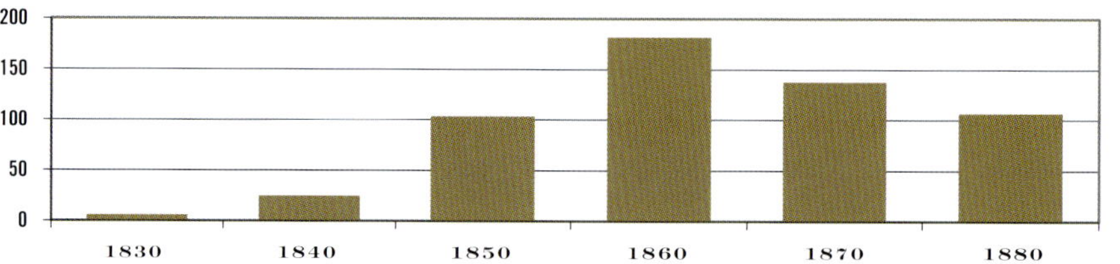

Residency of lithographers active in the trade in 1860, by ward. Source: Sample of 321 of 500 of the lithographers identified through the Philadelphia on Stone project. Data analysis by the Greater Philadelphia Cultural Alliance.

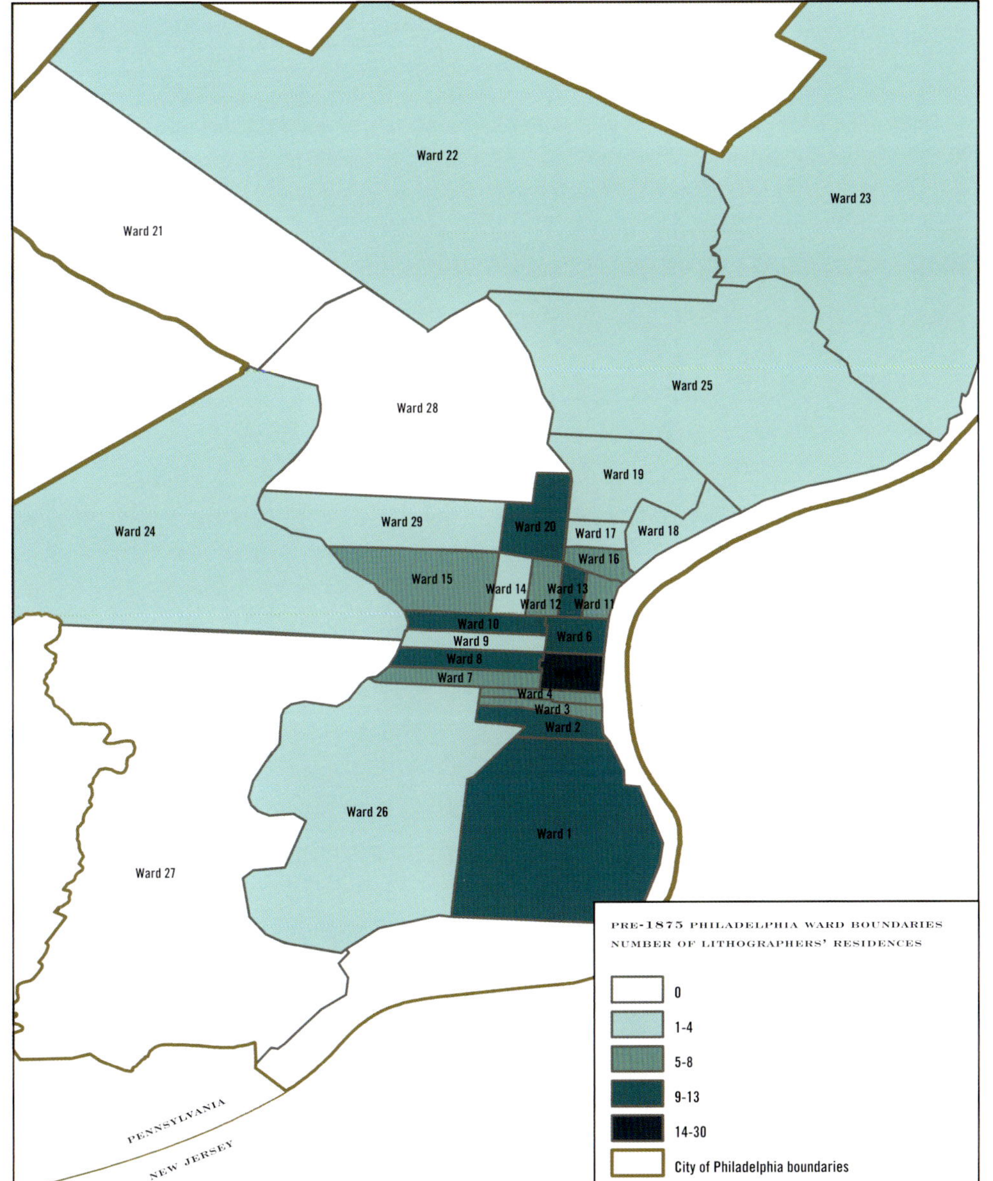

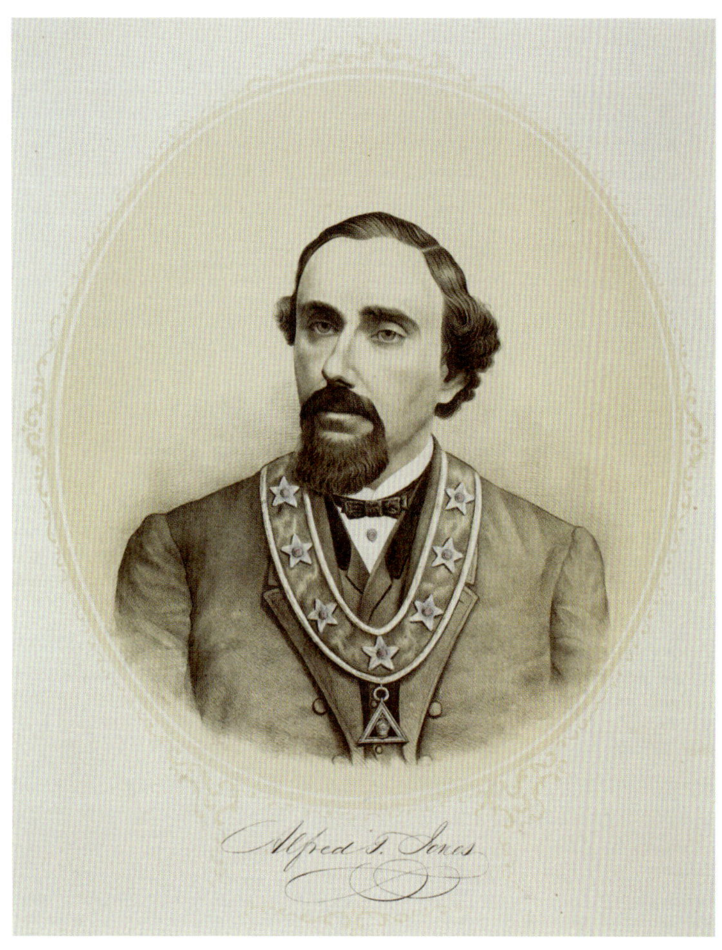

FIG. 12

Max Rosenthal, *Alfred T. Jones* (Philadelphia: Stein & Jones, 1865). Lithograph, tinted with one stone. 43 × 34 cm (16 ¾ × 13 ¼ in.). LCP, P.9349.84. Jones wears the regalia of his Masonic lodge, the Shekinah Lodge.

In addition to union activities, members gathered together to socialize, as evident from the diary of lithographic printer George Shubert, who became the secretary for the organization in April 1866. His diary includes entries recording his regular attendance at monthly union meetings, mainly at a bar called Jolly's, and a document listing fifty-seven men that may be an attendance record for an 1866 meeting.[89] Several years earlier a member had suggested that meeting at "a lager beer house was objectionable" and tended "to retard business,"[90] but apparently his complaint was ignored. Although the tavern served as the main venue of meetings for 1866, at least once they met at the Washington Hose Company, of which Shubert was a member.[91] Shubert's diary also chronicles his participation on the union's excursions committee, which arranged at least one outing for the members that year.[92] In addition to excursions, the union also held "grand" balls, including their second one, in 1863.[93]

The union was not the only fraternal outlet for social activities for lithographers; they also became involved in benevolent and fraternal organizations related to their nationalities, ethnicities, religions, or other social and cultural interests. Several premier and journeyman lithographers were members of the Freemasons, the Independent Order of Odd Fellows, and the Improved Order of Red Men, including James Queen, John F. Finkeldey, and Louis Flick, a lithographer at the Duval firm in the late 1850s. Jewish lithographers Alfred Jones (fig. 12) and Harvey Ibbotson participated in Shekinah Lodge Ancient York Masons, the Knights of Pythias, and B'nai B'rith. A number of German lithographers associated with organizations such as the German Society and Junger Maennerchor. Scotch and Irish artisans in the trade had memberships in the Hibernian Society, the Friendly Sons of St. Patrick, or, as did Sinclair, the Society of St. Andrew, which he served as treasurer in the early 1860s. Others were involved in the Artisans Order of Mutual Protection, the Zoological Society, and the Academy of Natural Sciences.[94]

The only other known diary of a Philadelphia lithographer is that of Matthias Weaver (active 1840–45).[95] Both his and Shubert's show that younger lithographers joined educational institutes and libraries such as the William Wirt Institute and the Philopatrian Society. In addition, these men visited the Pennsylvania Academy of the

Fine Arts, Walnut Street Theatre, Musical Fund Hall, and the Chinese Museum during their leisure hours.

When at the workplace, the range of printed material undertaken by Philadelphia lithographers in the antebellum period remained consistent over time. The two main staples of the commercial trade throughout the handpress period were job printing and illustration. Duval's long and successful career spanning half a century is a microcosm of the trade. In an 1838 business directory Duval claimed the ability to print "likenesses drawn from life on stone, maps, charts, plans, bill heads, bills of exchange, cheques, professional and visiting cards, labels &c. &c."[96] The advertisement contained in an 1846 directory added only "landscapes from nature," "anatomical & architectural drawings," "music titles," and "machinery" to the earlier list.[97] Some years later Duval's lush chromolithographic advertisement emphasized his work in color, the application of steam to his operations, and the skill of his transferrers, but the list of materials printed could have been from the 1830s and did not include any new genres (see fig. 65).[98] The same still held true in 1860, when his firm of Duval, Williams & Duval listed their services with almost no changes from their earlier periods of operation.[99]

Comparisons with the advertisements from other lithographers surveyed reflect the similarities among the larger firms operating in the city between the 1840s and 1860s. One of Duval's biggest competitors in the 1850s, L. N. Rosenthal, one of only a few known Jewish lithographers, produced an advertisement in 1856 that provides a fairly comprehensive list of printed materials available from his shop:

> Show Cards of any size required. Illuminated Frontispieces for Books, Music Titles, Geological, Anatomical and Botanical drawings. Illustrations of all kinds for Books and Magazines, Labels for Druggists, Perfumers, Patent Medicines and Manufacturers. Portraits, Landscapes from nature, Architectural drawings, Views of Buildings, Churches, Factories, Stores, Hotels, Ships and Steamboats, Locomotives drawn either in plain black or in their natural colors. Machinery and Mechanical drawings of every description. Engraving on Stone aided by new machinery just imported from Europe for Checks, Notes, Certificates of Stock, Diplomas, Bonds, Coupons, Commercial Blanks, Bill Heads, Price Currents, Fac Similes, Circulars, Bills of Lading, Maps, Plans, Charts, &c. &c.[100]

In the extant advertisements for Philadelphia lithographers issued before the Civil War, the materials they offered to the public remained consistent in their variety over time. When lithographers did deviate from long rote lists it often reflected their specializations. The lithographic artist Augustus Kollner promoted his particular ability to produce lithographs of "animals taken from nature" (fig. 13). He also offered "portraits of horses, correct and in every position," and "portraits of ladies and gentlemen on horseback."[101] The firm of Eugene Ketterlinus, which specialized in and received awards for the production of labels, described in greater detail than other lithographers the types of packaging labels available to its customers.[102] The lithographer's advertisements promoted gilt, embossed, and illuminated labels for manufacturers, physicians and druggists, wine and liquor dealers, perfumers, and fabric makers.[103]

Lithographers also advertised their services as printers of maps, plans, and charts and were commissioned to document the physical landscape for government reports and survey projects; railroad, canal, and coal companies; real-estate transactions and auctions; and users of roads and waterways.[104] Because of the relatively low cost and efficiency of producing maps lithographically, local lithographers were able to capture a portion of the well-established mapmaking trade from local engravers. Some specialized mapmakers expanded their facilities to work in both media. Two important lithographer-mapmakers in midcentury were Robert Pearsall Smith and Frederick Bourquin. Smith's main business focused on the production of county maps and atlases, and he partnered from 1857 to about 1863 with Frederick Bourquin, former foreman for P. S. Duval. Bourquin succeeded his former partner as the main producer in this branch of the trade after Smith's sudden retirement from the field in 1865.[105] According to Bourquin's promotions, he offered "every facility for engraving, printing, coloring and mounting state and county maps, of the largest size."[106]

Evidence shows that some lithographers expanded into other areas of printing beyond flat work. For example, a few local lithographers became involved in the manufacture of window shades, lampshades, and puzzles. A visitor to Duval's establishment in 1849 described his presses in operation: "One branch of art, to aid which lithography has been called, is printing of window shades, many of which, of very large size and beautiful designs, were printed for the gratification of the company."[107] Thomas Wagner's 1863 will documented his involvement in the production of lampshades: his inventory listed "cutting machine for shades," "shade designs," and "materials for shades."[108] Other lithographers—including Victoria Quarre; her second husband, Gustave Wedekind; and associates E. P. & L. Restein—manufactured lampshades midcentury.[109] Philadelphia lithographers were also engaged in the picture-puzzle business in the 1850s and 1860s and printed images that were mounted on wood and cut into shapes to be used as learning tools for children but often enjoyed by the whole family.[110] A later example printed by the Brett Lithographing Co. consists of a series of five puzzles depicting buildings at the Centennial Exhibition in 1876.[111]

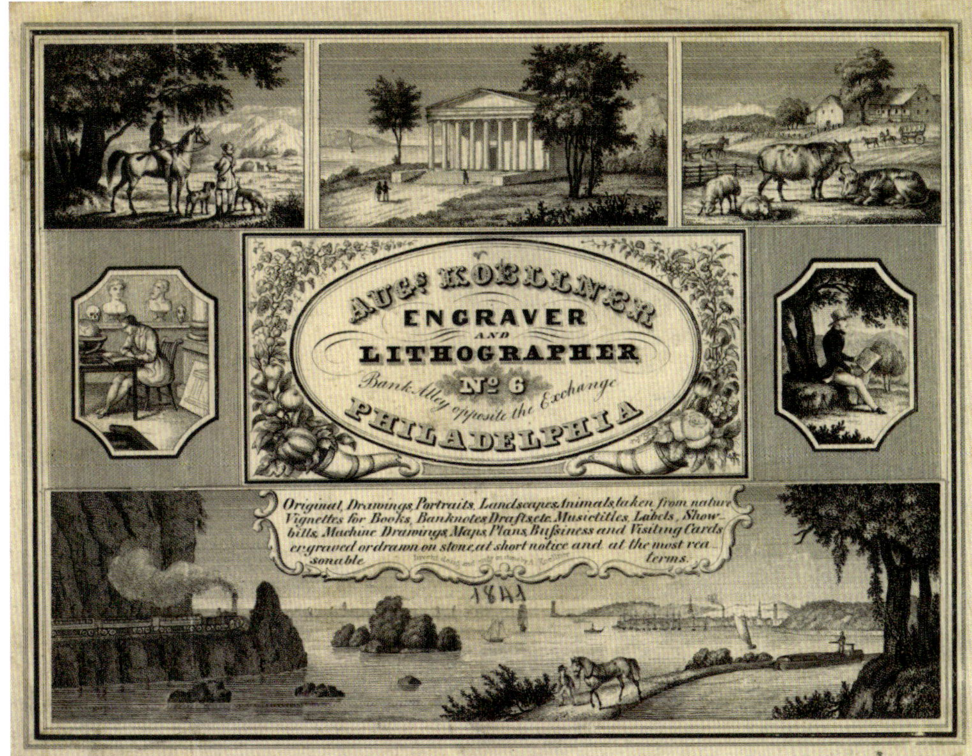

Augs. Koellner: Engraver and Lithographer. No. 6 Bank Alley Opposite the Exchange Philadelphia (Philadelphia: A. Kollner, 1844). Lithograph. 10 × 14 cm (4 × 5 ½ in.). POSA 4, Courtesy of the American Antiquarian Society, Graphic Arts Lithf Koll Koll copy 1.

Like the lampshades Victoria Quarre produced, female lithographers constituted a small but important segment of the trade during the mid–nineteenth century. She and Lavinia Bowen (wife of John T. Bowen) of Bowen & Co. are the only definitively identified women lithographers active in Philadelphia during this period. Although knowledge of their lives and careers stems primarily from circumstantial evidence, their listing in city directories as proprietors of their establishments speaks to their significance in a male-dominated field.

Victoria Quarre immigrated to the United States about 1848 with her husband Ferdinand. By 1856 city directories listed both of them with the trade "lampshades." Within a few years, Quarre was taxed solely for income from lampshade manufacturing and lithographic printing under the firm name V. Quarre & Co. By the time of her death in 1870, this successful printer was able to bequest thousands of dollars to several Catholic organizations. Her professional reputation was such that her establishment continued to operate under her name until at least 1890.[112]

Lavinia Bowen, like Quarre, entered the lithographic trade through her husband. Bowen was married and a mother when she relocated with him to Philadelphia from New York circa 1838. She assumed his business, worth more than $5,000, after his death, about 1856, and received favorable credit reports through the early 1870s.[113] Although not named in directories as part of her husband's firm like Quarre, Lavinia Bowen was a significant partner in her husband's Philadelphia career and was perhaps partly responsible for his reputation as the leading American lithographer of natural history. John Cassin, an ornithologist who had worked with John T. Bowen and was Lavinia's first partner in Bowen & Co., noted in 1858, "Nearly all plates in Ornithology published in th[e] city within the last twenty years, and many others in every department of zoology, have been prepared under the supervision and direction of this lady." Cassin so admired her skills that he also acknowledged her "highly creditable" work in his 1858 atlas *Mammalogy and Ornithology,* as well as named a bird in her honor.[114] Described by Wainwright as "earning money on the side as a 'print colorist'" when she took over her husband's business, Bowen must have been more than a colorist to evoke such sentiment from her professional partner.[115] She expanded the range of work on which the Bowen firm had focused in the preceding decades and published newspaper-carriers greetings, landscape views, and maps. She continued the business until about 1872, almost two decades after her husband's death. The professional careers of Bowen and Quarre are almost solely defined by the work left behind with their imprint and thereby contrast sharply with the careers of myriad female colorists whose anonymous work is described below. Their prints allow these two women to emerge from the shadows cast by their comparable male counterparts to round out our understanding of the composition of the trade.

Although the nature of Bowen's and Quarre's training cannot be definitively ascertained, other women of their period trained in lithography at the Philadelphia School of Design for Women (now Moore College of Art). Instituted in 1844 by socialite Sarah Peter to educate women in the arts as a means of employment, the school, by the early 1850s, trained women as lithographers and as periodical illustrators. Between 1852 and 1853, the school (now under the administration of the Franklin Institute) issued a statute that forbade students to hand-color lithographs, declaring this a misuse of their education, and a number of plates in the short-lived botanical periodical the *Florist* contained the imprint "on stone at the School of Design."[116]

Although the plates in the periodical were never attributed to the school's individual female lithographers, the Franklin Institute publicly acknowledged their abilities. In 1852 the women's "large variety of designs for . . . lithographic drawings and stones" received a first premium as "very beautiful and the highest order of merit" at the Exhibition of American Manufactures.[117] Although some nepotism most likely influenced this award and male superintendent Thomas Braidwood represented the entry, such recognition helped open the door a crack for women to enter the trade. However, Quarre and Bowen appear as the only two to be recognized by name in published records of that time. While women lithographers and their work form a significant, smaller area of study about the production end of the trade, certain genres of lithographs serve as the focal point.

Surveys of separately issued lithographic prints by Philadelphia lithographers in the period from the 1840s to 1860s show the prevalence of three notable types of commissioned prints: pictorial advertisements, large-format fashion plates, and certificates.[118] Ordered by a variety of commercial customers and local organizations—hat manufacturer Charles Oakford (see fig. 102); the Guardians, Physicians, and Surgeons of the Philadelphia Alms House (see fig. 58); patent-medicine dealer George Stuart; and fashion-plate publishers S. A. & A. F. Ward (fig. 14), to name a few—these prints reflect the broad spectrum of pictorial work lithographers produced to meet the needs of the community.

Advertisements depicting local factories and storefronts constitute the largest surviving body of separately issued views.[119] Manufacturers and shop owners commissioned lithographers to create poster-sized views of their establishments that depicted the architecture, the signs adorning their buildings, busy factory yards, and displays of merchandise in shop windows and on the sidewalks out front.

The production of these pictorial advertisements[120] was limited almost exclusively to local firms and was concentrated in the hands of a few lithographers and artists. The lithographic artist William H. Rease drew the majority of known views of Philadelphia stores, hotels, and manufactories. He was responsible for almost half of the known pictorial advertisements produced before the Civil War, and his output greatly exceeded any other artist's.[121] Rease's great success as an advertising artist can be traced to the skill with which he incorporated details of daily life, street activity, and human interaction in his views of structures (see figs. 98, 100, and 101).

The foregrounds of his prints, occasionally laid out to convey comic situations, depict city dwellers as active participants and forces in street life. Men, women, and children, blacks and whites, contributed to the liveliness of the businesses and industries being advertised. Rease often portrayed black laborers—one of the two primary occupations of black men in the antebellum era[122]—as an inherent segment of the visual landscape of Philadelphia (see fig. 98). Predominantly a marketing device, these lithographs depicting all segments of society, including black peddlers, porters, coachmen, and horse handlers, frequenting the commercial sections of the city also served to mirror Philadelphia's population during the mid–nineteenth century.

To produce these engaging advertisements that documented daily life, Rease worked closely with Philadelphia's most prolific printer of lithographic advertisements, Wagner & McGuigan, a main rival to Duval in the production of these commercial prints. Rease usually served as the artist for their pictorial advertisements. Another

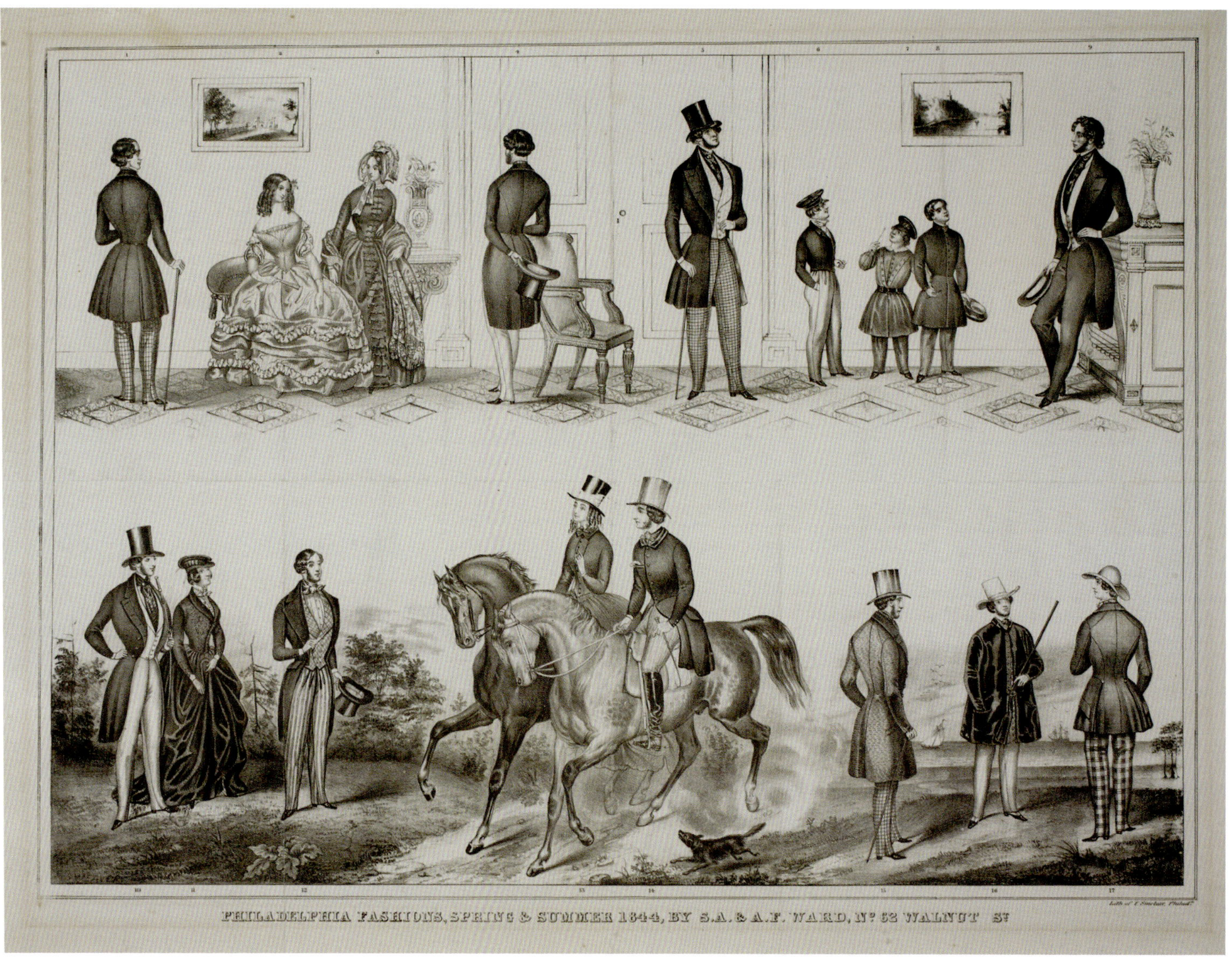

FIG. 14

Matthias S. Weaver, *Philadelphia Fashions, Spring & Summer 1844, by S. A. & A. F. Ward, No. 62 Walnut St.* (Philadelphia: Lith. of T. Sinclair, 1844). Lithograph. 56 × 71 cm (22 × 28 in.). POSP 178, LCP, Gift of David Doret, P.2002.61.1.

more surprising competitor for whom Rease worked was the much smaller printing establishment run by Frederick Kuhl,[123] who operated a small lithographic printing shop from 1840 to 1854. Kuhl specialized almost exclusively in the printing of advertising lithographs and slightly exceeded Duval's much larger firm in the number of known works produced (see fig. 39).[124]

Philadelphia fashion publishers' need for large-format fashion plates, or "tailors' archetypes," for distribution to tailors and clothing retailers provided lithographic shops with steady commission work between the early 1840s and mid-1860s. Intended for wall display in shops, these images were issued semiannually to show spring/summer and fall/winter fashions. These plates were sold separately or accompanied reports on the seasonal changes in dress and instructions on how to measure and sew the clothing depicted.[125] The advertisements show two rows of figures, often in both indoor and outdoor settings to feature different types of clothing, and primarily depict men's fashions (fig. 14).[126] Publisher F. Mahan claimed he had "near Six Thousand regular subscribers" to his plates in 1848.[127] Matthias Weaver drew the earliest known seasonal fashion plates for S. A. & A. F. Ward during his residency in Philadelphia between 1840 and 1845. He records in his diary shortly before the publication of the fall/winter 1842 plate: "Wards are getting ready for a grand splash in the way of a plate. Will try what can be done."[128] This type of work proved the most profitable for antebellum artists. Weaver's single most lucrative project in 1843 was the drawing for the spring/summer plate, for which he received $55 in payment, far more than for his work on certificates ($30), book plates ($2–$3), and advertisements ($20).[129]

In addition to producing prints for commercial purposes, lithographers responded to the needs of voluntary organizations in the city. Certificates for such organizations and events were printed in steady numbers during the mid–nineteenth century and provided lithographers with the opportunity to create some of their most original artistic designs through scenes, vignettes, and finely and elaborately drawn pictorial details. A Pennsylvania Agricultural Society certificate printed by lithographer Thomas Sinclair in 1851 received praise for such creativity in the local press: "The design is a very happy one, representing the kind of farm that an industrious and intelligent farmer usually possesses, the various implements of his industry and the products of his toil arranged in artistic groups" (fig. 15).[130]

These "diplomas" presented as prizes to fair participants were just one category in the wide array of certificates issued predominantly by the larger lithographic establishments. Marriage, birth, and confirmation certificates marked personal rites of passage often through depictions of the ceremonies. Membership certificates for charitable institutions, schools, and voluntary organizations depicted the exteriors of institutions or, occasionally, more unique designs, like the certificate for the Wagner Free Institute, printed about 1855 by P. S. Duval & Co., with a montage of plants, animals, minerals, and fossils (fig. 16). Certificates for fire companies contained vignettes of fires, fire stations, and firefighting equipment and make up a significant segment of this genre of lithograph, with most printed by P. S. Duval & Son, later Duval & Hunter, between the end of the Civil War and 1870 (fig. 17).[131] These volunteer-firefighting-company certificates carried the visual heroics and patriotism of the Civil War era's lithographs into the late 1860s.

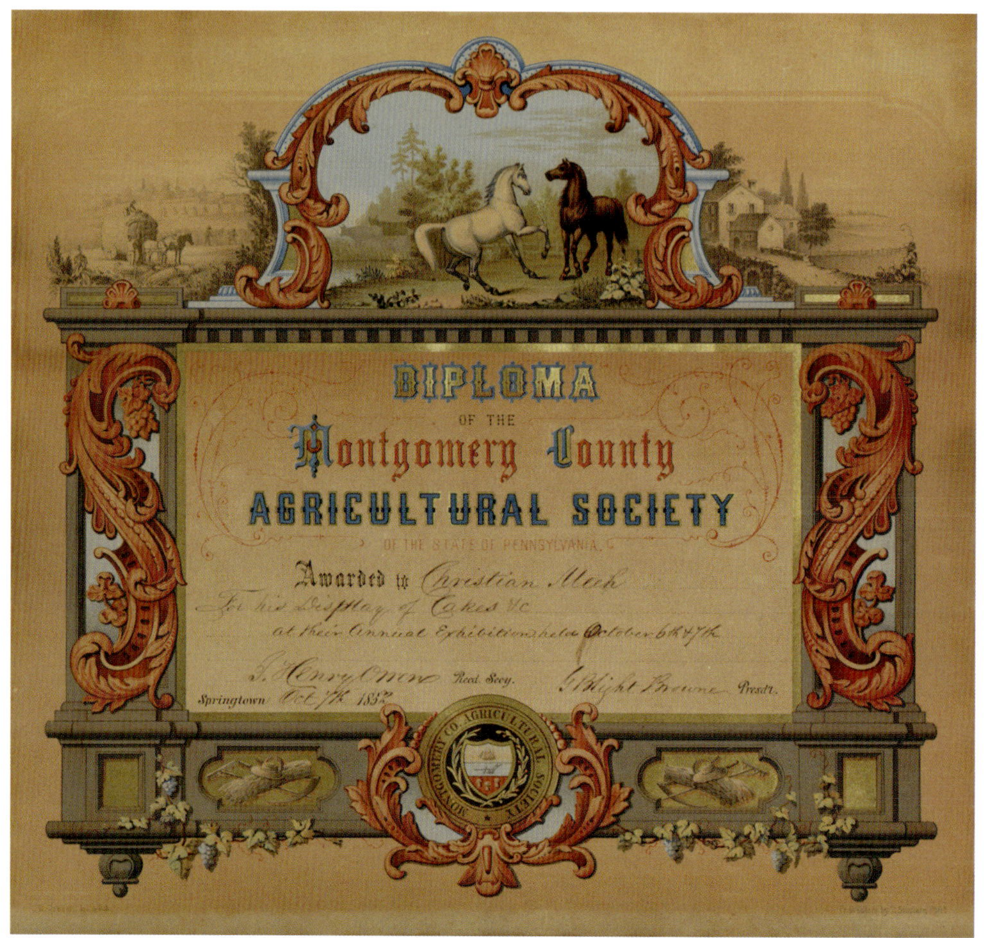

An overview of the first fifty years of commercial lithography in Philadelphia cannot overlook the impact of the Civil War. Between 1861 and 1865 prices for lithographic supplies increased, the purchasing power of printers' wages lessened, those involved with the trade enlisted, and the content of the pictorial lithographs surveyed began to include sites and patriotic imagery important to the war effort.[132] Local camps, hospitals, armories, patriotic fairs and parades, and especially the volunteer refreshment saloons—Union and Cooper Shop—were depicted in large-format, usually color-printed lithographs. In addition, the new need for patriotically themed stationery, billheads, handbills, and circulars provided many lithographers with ample work for the job-printing branch of their businesses. For many, this increased business appears to have offset the higher prices of supplies. Lithographers Thomas Sinclair, James Queen, William Boell, and Duval, who produced the large-format work described above, as well as the more specialized lithographers Stein & Jones, V.

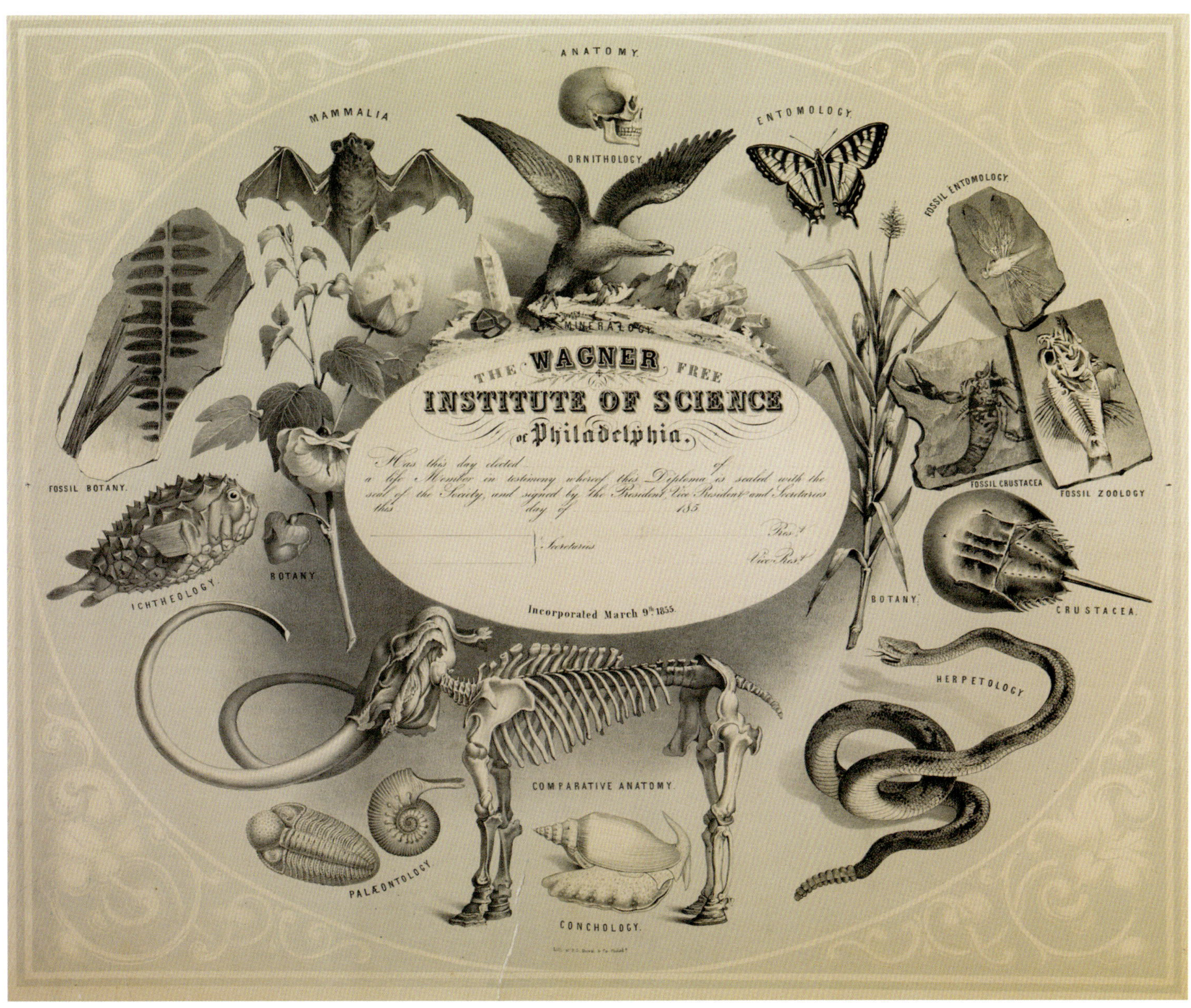

Quarre, and George Worley, all earned enough income to be taxed by the I.R.S. during the war.[133]

Although the job work by these printers probably provided much of the income that was taxed, prints commissioned for fund-raising also provided lithographers with large and profitable print runs. An example is the 1863 print *Union Volunteer Refreshment Saloon, of Philadelphia* (fig. 18), commissioned by the volunteer organization's

FIG. 16
The Wagner Free Institute of Science of Philadelphia. Incorporated March 9th 1855 (Philadelphia: Lith. of P. S. Duval & Co., ca. 1855). Lithograph, tinted with one stone. 49 × 58 cm (19 ¼ × 22 ¾ in.). POSP 266, HSP, Certificates—Wagner Free.

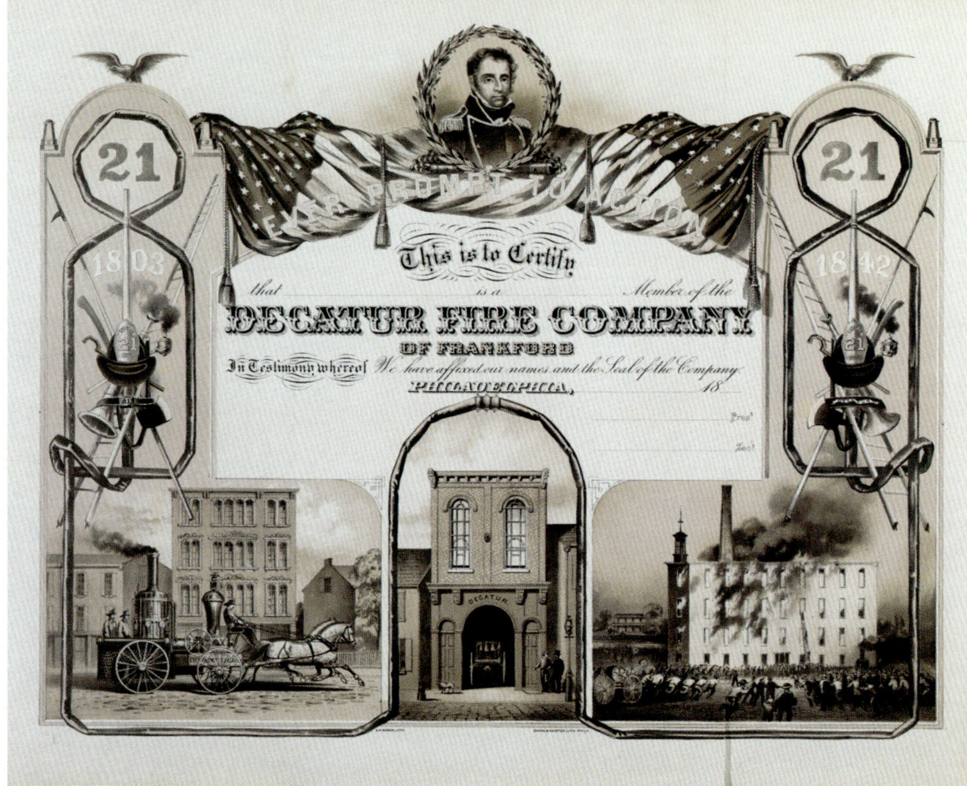

Picture Fund Committee. Printed at the establishment of Thomas Sinclair between 1863 and 1865, the lithograph provided the printer with more than $1,100 (about $15,000 current value) in income. The drawing for the color print, larger than two feet square, cost $75 and showed "a true exterior view of the institution," as described by the committee in their annual report. The initial run of about 1,600 copies cost 40 cents for each impression; the lithograph was reprinted four times until August 1865, with a total of 3,500 impressions being taken.[134]

Although Sinclair produced this print through a commission, other lithographers printed for the speculative market, often as tributes and possibly as fund-raisers. In 1861 William H. Rease advertised, as a memento and "Encouragement to our Blue Jackets," a 28 × 20-inch three-tinted lithograph after his painting of the U.S. battleship *Hartford,* which was "printed to order" for $1.[135] Max Rosenthal traveled with the Army of the Potomac and created drawings for a series of more than one hundred hand-colored lithographs of camp and battle scenes printed by his brother L. N. Rosenthal between 1861 and 1863.[136] John L. Magee diverted from his usual subject of sensational news-event prints (described in chapter 7) and issued with William Boell a *View of the*

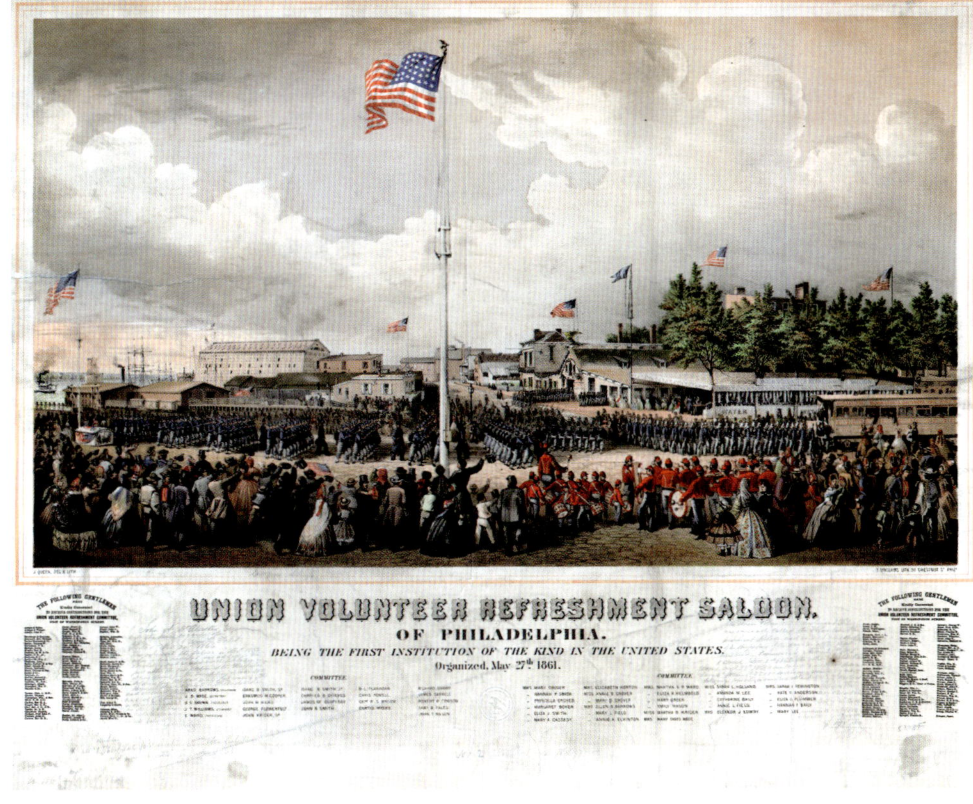

FIG. 18

James F. Queen, *Union Volunteer Refreshment Saloon, of Philadelphia. Being the First Institution of the Kind in the United States. Organized, May 27th. 1861* (Philadelphia: T. Sinclair's Lith., 1863). Chromolithograph with hand-coloring. 66 × 81 cm (26 × 31 ½ in.). POS 771, LCP, 5778.F.

Encampment of the Corn Exchange Regiment 118th Penn. Vols. Near Falls of Schuylkill (see fig. 34), which they dedicated to "The President and members of the Corn Exchange and the officers and men of the Regiment."

Prints not commissioned for fund-raising also contained imagery supporting the war to attract the patriotic consumer. For example, the fashion advertisements of F. Mahan included celebrated Union generals, such as Maj. Gen. Nathaniel Prentiss Banks, as models, and the trade-card advertisement for M. Shoemaker's Children's Central Clothing Emporium showed children promenading at the recruitment camp at Independence Square (see fig. 37). Lithographers' advertisements also included patriotic imagery. During the war, Eugene Ketterlinus included on his trade card an American flag, created through tints (POSA 21), that he did not depict in later printings, and Stein & Jones issued their 1865 calendar with vignettes depicting a battle scene and the figure of Columbia surrounded by flags and soldiers (POSA 91).[137]

The war also inspired uniquely designed prints. *View of the Reception of the 29th Regiment, P. V., at Philadelphia,* printed and copyrighted by Charles Baum in the last days of 1863, depicted the December 23, 1863, procession in honor of the 29th

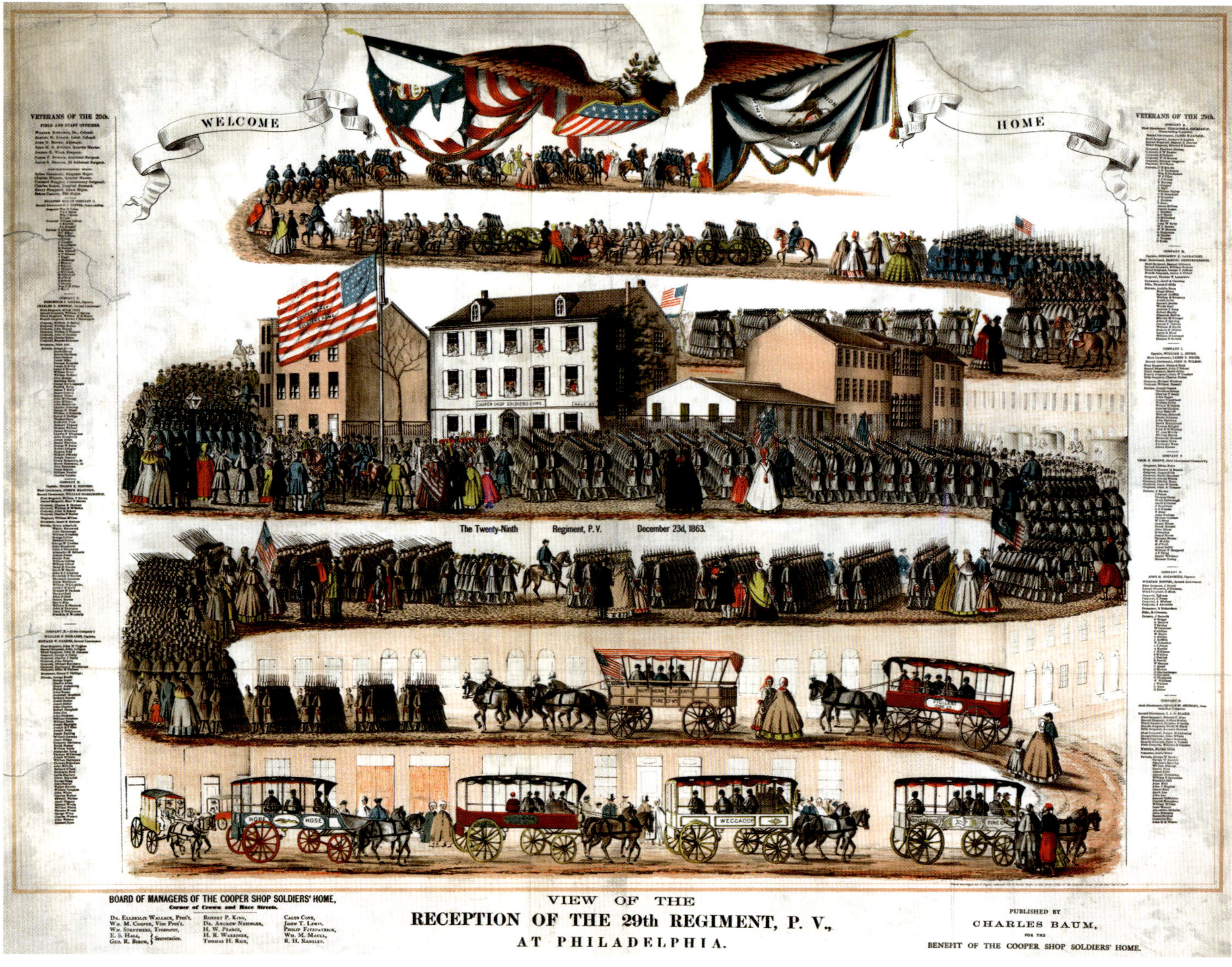

View of the Reception of the 29th Regiment, P. V., at Philadelphia (Philadelphia: Charles Baum, for the benefit of the Cooper Shop Soldiers' Home, 1863). Chromolithograph. 76 × 101 cm (29 ¾ × 39 ¾ in.). POS 807, LCP, P.2262.

Pennsylvania Volunteer Regiment and was issued for the "benefit of the Cooper Shop Soldiers' Home" (fig. 19). As in most event imagery, a series of moments has been condensed into a single scene, but, unlike in most prints, the narrative flows vertically as opposed to horizontally. Baum shows in a single bottom-up view the procession that commenced at about one o'clock from Market Street Bridge and ended after dinner at the National Guards Hall at 518–20 Race Street.

Despite the increase in work necessitated by the war, establishments needed to manage with smaller staffs and occasional slow periods. "Many artists and printers have gonne [*sic*] to the war. . . . Business had been very brisk for several months, but it is very slow now, there is scarcely anything to do," wrote Duval to his longtime artist friend Albert Newsam in August 1864.[138] Unfortunately, the exact number of craftsmen who went to the battlefront cannot be determined. Nonetheless, given the biographical data available, we do know a few of the individuals, both premier and journeymen lithographers, who did. James Queen served with the Pennsylvania Militia in 1862 and 1863. Jerome Bastian, a lithographer at Wagner & McGuigan, served as a private in the 23rd Regiment of the Pennsylvania Infantry, and Joseph Bottles served in the U.S. Navy. These men certainly represent just a small number of the "many artists and printers" who formed the approximately ninety thousand enlistments from Philadelphia (about 90 percent of the city's eligible male population) during the war.[139]

Duval's sense of "scarcely anything to do" in the late summer of 1864 was probably occasioned by comparison to his role in the Great Central Fair of June 1864. Duval printed, as a technological novelty and fund-raiser, in color, and probably by steam, hundreds of copies of *Buildings of the Great Central Fair, in Aid of the U.S. Sanitary Commission* (see fig. 133) on the fair's main avenue, daily for three weeks.[140] Numerous visitors to the fair purchased the chromolithograph, but probably few realized the print represented the future of the trade. It heralded the defining influence that steam and color printing, which had begun more than a decade earlier, would have on the production and dissemination of lithographs for the rest of the century.

The introduction of color printing and the use of steam-powered machinery were spearheaded by Duval and Wagner & McGuigan, Philadelphia's two largest firms, which had highly skilled workers, resources, and capital to devote to experimentation in new technologies.[141] The gradual shift away from the production of black-and-white lithographs colored by hand to the use of printed color created profound changes in lithographic establishments in the city.

From the early 1840s Philadelphia lithographers experimented with a variety of new methods for coloring. Throughout the midcentury, local printers used hand-coloring, tinting, and printing in multiple colors to create images, sometimes combining multiple techniques in one lithograph. Plain black-and-white lithographs issued from the same presses as complex multicolored chromolithographs, as lithographers made use of traditional and emerging technologies to meet the demands of the trade. Before color printing became commercially viable, many lithographers and other printmakers offered their customers the option of having their images colored by hand. Lithographic firms incorporated facilities for hand-coloring in their own shops or contracted out the work. Patrons would pay about twice as much for these prints.[142]

The coloring of lithographs by hand was an important part of the trade throughout the antebellum period. Philadelphia produced the finest hand-colored lithographic book illustrations of any American city in the nineteenth century, exemplified by work produced by John T. Bowen and his colorists for natural-history and scientific publications. While Bowen's shop was unusual in that it specialized in the production of high-quality, hand-colored illustrations, other lithographers also employed dozens of colorists in their shops. In 1856, after Philadelphia lithographers had been experimenting with color printing for more than a decade, Duval was still employing 100 to 150 colorists.[143] Concurrently, the coloring rooms associated with Frederick Bourquin's lithographic map-printing offices employed thirty-five women colorists to hand-color the maps issued from his twenty presses.[144]

Coloring was largely done by girls and women, working in coloring rooms attached to lithographic establishments or in more informal settings.[145] Virginia Penny in her book *Five Hundred Employments Adapted to Women,* published in the 1860s, describes a group of twenty women colorists employed by one Philadelphia lithographer: "Some associate in companies, and take their work to the house of one of their number; but the greater part are educated women, who do not wish it known that they earn money by their labor: these carry the plates to their own homes (and even have them sent to the fashionable places of resort in summer), so that many a fair damsel trips along Chestnut street with a roll of something, which seems to be music, but is, in fact, work."[146] Some lithographers advertised specifically for "girls to color lithographic prints."[147] Girls as young as ten to twelve years of age worked as colorists and could be employed at minimal wages.[148]

Philadelphia's largest lithographic establishments began adopting color-printing techniques in the 1840s, and chromolithography steadily became an increasing part of their businesses over the next twenty years.[149] The complexity of creating chromolithographs, which required printing from multiple stones, one for each color, altered lithographic shops, causing an increase in the size of facilities, the number of presses and stones required, and the specialization of workers in all areas of the shop. Chromolithographs involved collaboration, not just between a single lithographic artist and a printer but among many workers, including designers, *chromistes* (color specialists who selected colors and determined the order in which they were printed), and multiple pressmen and draftsmen.

Lithographers who were early experimenters in color like Rosenthal and Duval often used the medium in their own advertisements during the 1850s to promote chromolithography. Rosenthal advertised his shop's ability to "reproduce every object in all its original and varied tints,"[150] while Duval emphasized the use of color "for all kinds of fancy & ornamental printing."[151] Color printing became an increasingly important part of the separately issued print market in the 1860s. Between 1850 and 1870 the proportion of separately issued pictorial lithographs printed in color grew steadily from approximately 15 percent to 30 percent.[152] For job and other advertising work not surveyed for the project, this proportion would probably have been considerably higher.

Philadelphia lithographers availed themselves of steam-powered presses more enthusiastically than printers in any other American city. Duval and his workers first began experimenting with steam power in their operations in the late 1840s, with Wagner & McGuigan performing similar trials around the same period (fig. 20). By 1849 Duval had adapted his handpresses to use steam engines to lessen the work of the press operators in moving the stones through the press. Duval's innovations also provided for "the application of steam to the printing and preparation of the stones from which the lithographs [were] printed, a matter which [would] greatly expedite and cheapen the process."[153] By the mid-1850s Duval had adapted twenty-four of his thirty-four handpresses for steam, and other large lithographic establishments in Philadelphia followed his lead.[154]

The adaptation of handpresses for the use of steam heralded more profound changes in the industry when steam-powered presses with automated inking and dampening devices began to replace adapted handpresses in the later decades of the century (fig. 21). By 1870 thirty of the 450 lithographic presses in use in the city were steam powered.[155] The change to fully mechanized presses greatly increased production speeds from about one hundred imprints an hour to eight hundred to one thousand an hour,[156] enhanced specialization among press operators, and fundamentally altered the role of the skilled lithographic printer. Steam power and chromolithography spurred the transformation of the lithographic establishments from printing shops into printing plants, the increasingly dominant mode of operation for lithographers after the Civil War.

AFTER THE WAR: RECONSTRUCTION OF THE PHILADELPHIA LITHOGRAPHIC TRADE, 1866–1878

Following the Civil War, the lithographic trade in Philadelphia, along with the country as a whole, began an era of reconstruction. The overall collaborative workshop system gave way to an increasingly compartmentalized factory arrangement. Edwin Freedley reflected these changes when he again provided a commentary on the state of Philadelphia industry in 1867. Ten lithographic establishments garnered specific

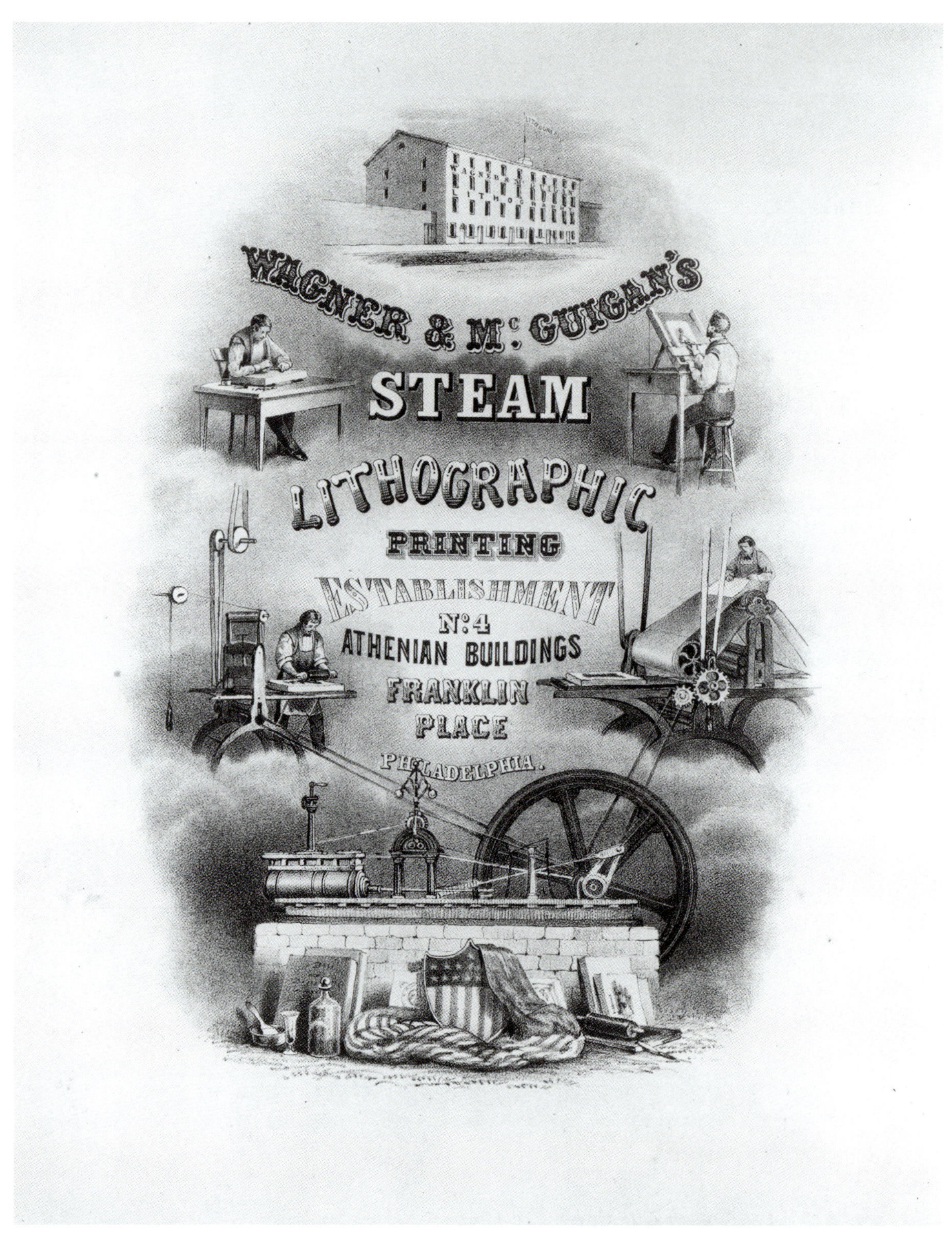

WAGNER & Mc GUIGAN'S
STEAM
LITHOGRAPHIC
PRINTING
ESTABLISHMENT
No 4
ATHENIAN BUILDINGS
FRANKLIN
PLACE
PHILADELPHIA.

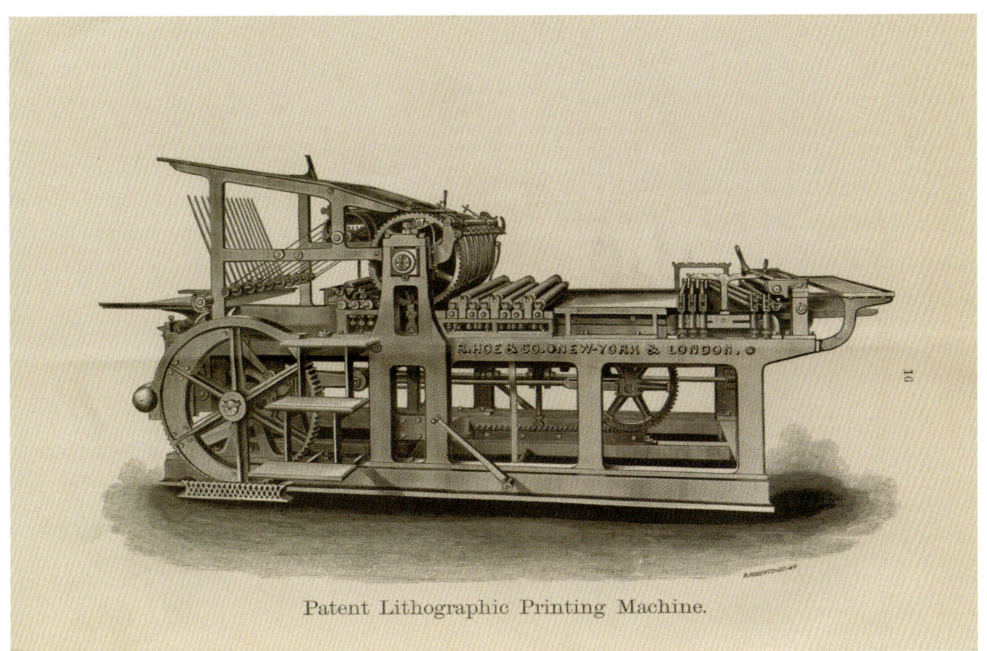

Patent Lithographic Printing Machine.

FIG. 20 (OPPOSITE)
Wagner & McGuigan's Steam Lithographic Printing Establishment No. 4 Athenian Buildings, Franklin Place Philadelphia (Philadelphia: Wagner & McGuigan, ca. 1855). Lithograph. 26 × 20 cm (10 × 7 ¾ in.). POSA 115.1, LOC, Unprocessed in PR 13 CN 1997:105.

FIG. 21 (LEFT)
Patent Lithographic Printing Machine, from *R. Hoe & Co., Printing Press, Machine & Saw Manufacturers* (New York: [R. Hoe & Co., 1876]), 16. Wood engraving. 21 × 31 cm (8 ¼ × 12 ¼ in.). LCP, *AM 1876 Hoe, 5065.F.3.

mention in this edition of *Philadelphia and Its Manufactures.* Names familiar from the earlier era, including Duval, Bourquin, Leonhardt, Ketterlinus, and McGuigan, remained, but new firms such as Breuker & Kessler, Edward Herline, Jacob Haehnlen, and H. J. Toudy had now also made a mark on the industry. These newer lithographic establishments were no longer compact printing shops run mainly with handpresses, but multilevel specialized factories powered by steam, as epitomized by the Haehnlen firm (fig. 22), described by Freedley as "the most extensive in Philadelphia, and probably in the United States."

> Mr. HAEHNLEN has purchased the extensive six-story brown stone building, known as Goldsmith's Hall, and occupies all except the lower floors, for the purposes of his business; the second floor being appropriated for the sales-room and offices, with a Machine shop and Drying room in the rear; on the third floor are the Lithographic Presses; the fourth floor is devoted principally to Card Printing; and the fifth and sixth stories to printing Pamphlets, Hand Bills, and other similar work. The machinery is propelled by a sixty-horse power engine.[157]

Although Freedley focused on ten firms, particularly Haehnlen, these did not constitute the entire industry. By 1871 the city supported around fifty-five establishments

Jacob Haehnlen's Steam Power Lithographic & Letterpress Printing Rooms, from Edwin Freedley's *Philadelphia and Its Manufactories: A Hand-Book of the Great Manufactories and Representative Mercantile Houses of Philadelphia in 1867* (Philadelphia: Edward Young & Co., 1867). Lithograph, tinted with one stone. 21 × 14 cm (8 ¼ × 5 ¼ in.). POSA 47, LCP, Uy8, 55213.O.

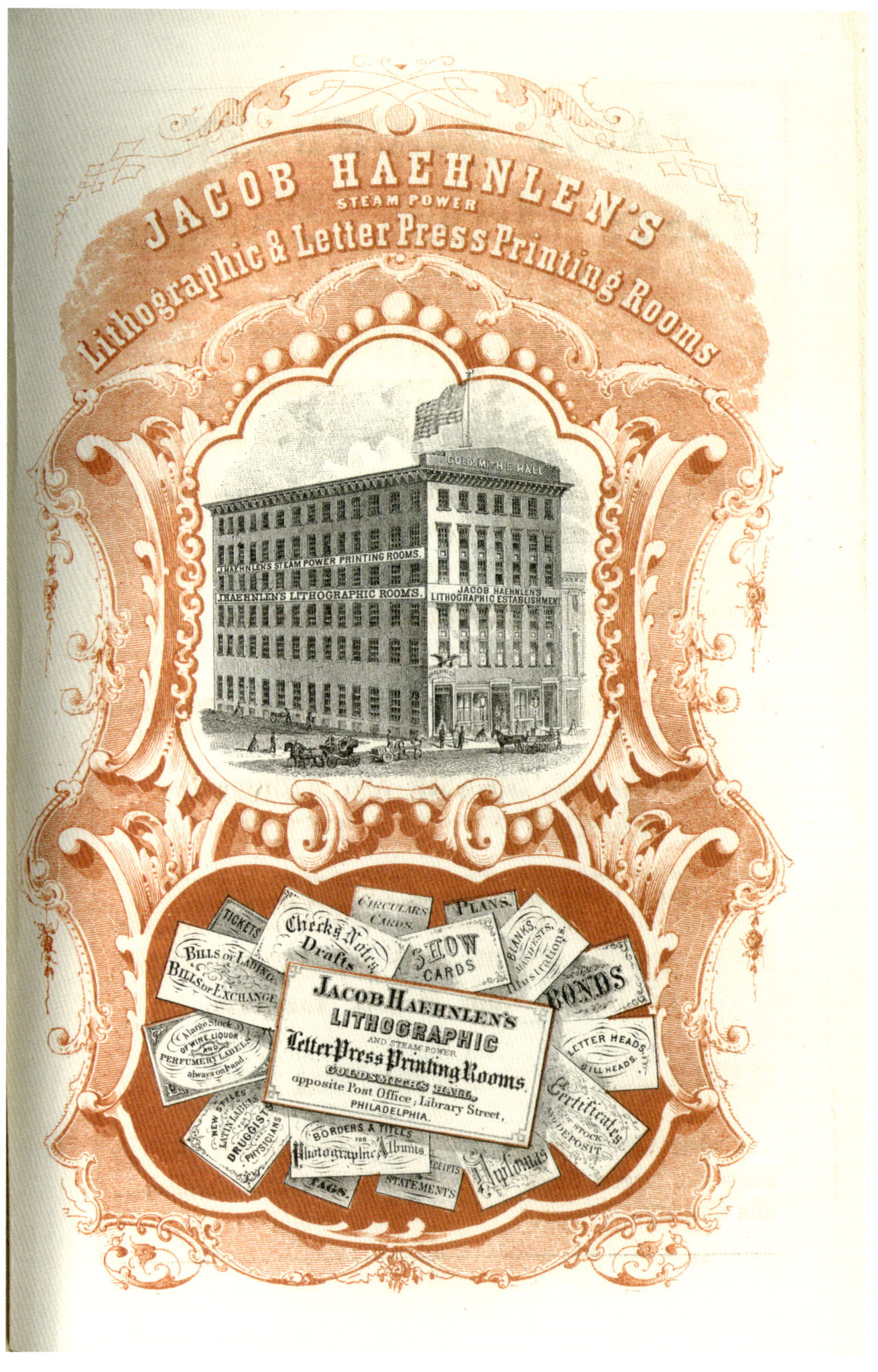

that used around thirty steam presses and included thirty firms that produced "over $500 each in value of manufactured articles." The number of establishments had nearly doubled from the mid-1850s, and the thirty most productive establishments alone employed nearly three hundred men, women, and "youths," that is, persons under sixteen years of age.[158] By 1882 the number of those employed in the trade had nearly doubled in size since 1850. However, the lithographic trade continued to account for only a fraction of Philadelphia's printing and publishing business. In the early 1880s lithographers made up only 11 percent of that business, slightly less than the 12 percent in 1850.[159]

The major firms, many of those cited by Freedley, still clustered east of Fifth Street, near and along Chestnut and Walnut Streets, especially in the 300 block of each street. A few of the stalwarts had moved north of Market Street, and a small number still further north on Arch and Vine Streets. Thomas Sinclair, for instance, relocated to the 500 block of North Street in 1867. At this location, in 1872, he promoted his work in chromolithography and his operation of the largest steam press in the city.[160] As of 1878 the "chroma factory" of E. P. & L. Restein, a major producer of chromolithographs and advertising novelties established in 1868, remained the sole establishment in South Philadelphia—despite Edmund Restein's hope to develop the industry south of Washington Avenue.[161]

The era proved a time of reconstruction for the Philadelphia lithographic trade in other ways as well. Fire affected at least seven major establishments, including those of Ferdinand Moras in 1866, Thomas Sinclair in 1870, Louis Rosenthal in 1872, Craig, Finley & Co. in 1877, and H. J. Toudy & Co. in 1878.[162] All but Toudy were able to rebuild their businesses. The combination of relative youth (the firm was established in 1866), lack of adequate insurance, complete destruction of its building (owned by colleague and real-estate magnate Eugene Ketterlinus),[163] and specialization in large-format lithographs of maps, atlases, and city views requiring more financial overhead doomed the business.[164] Although fire had always been a threat to lithographers due to the combustibility of printing materials, the clustering of industries in multistoried buildings now opened firms to even more risks of fire and water damage, and not necessarily of their own making.

The 1870s saw the Panic of 1873, in addition to the waning of some stalwart firms, the reconfiguration of others, and the emergence of new firms that would dominate the trade over the next decades. Apprenticed sons assumed partnership roles or took over as proprietors for their lithographer fathers, culminating in the firms of T. Sinclair & Son in 1870, Duval & Hunter in 1871, Geo. S. Harris & Son in 1872, and Theo. Leonhardt & Son in 1874.[165]

Where there was no son to succeed in the business, firms were reconstituted or sold in spite of the economic recession.[166] In 1873 Haehnlen, recently returned from a trip to Europe for his health, sold his "extensive establishment," that is, his business and equipment, but not the building that housed them, Goldsmith's Hall, to Lehman & Bolton.[167] The successor firm continued to thrive in the chromolithographic label business until the 1940s, despite major fires in 1882, which razed Goldsmith's Hall, and in 1886.[168] In 1874 John Reyenthaler, Eugene Ketterlinus's brother-in-law and a silverware manufacturer, bought and briefly acted as proprietor for the Ketterlinus Printing House, which remained in business until around 1970.[169] That same year the Duval name began to fade from the trade when Thomas Hunter, an 1874 American Manufacturer Exhibition silver-medal winner,[170] assumed the business of his partner, S. C. Duval, son of P. S. Duval. (The senior Duval had retired in 1869 and handed over forty presses and fifty employees to his son.)[171] The partnership between former Haehnlen foreman George W. Breuker and bookkeeper Harry Kessler, established in 1866 and thus fairly new to the industry, specialized in "all kinds of commercial engraving," including chromolithographic labels, advertising posters, and trade cards. By 1876, having "quite good credit" and having grown so large in spite of the recession, the firm relocated from a floor in the Press Building to a multistory establishment in the 500 block of Chestnut Street.[172]

By the early 1870s the procurement of stones, papers, inks, and artists' tools had become more centralized and localized, and lithographers themselves no longer needed to make their own supplies.[173] Suppliers like Otto Martin & Co., importers and dealers in lithographic materials; J. K. Wright & Co. and Grey's Ferry Ink Works, ink manufacturers; and R. S. Menamin's Printers Furnishing Warehouse (successor to Philadelphia lithographic-printing-press manufacturer F. Bronstrup) were just a few of the Philadelphia firms from which lithographers could buy their printing necessities. In many cases these supplies had dropped in price by half or remained steady since the late 1860s, a situation that was prolonged by the economic effects of 1873 and continuation of import tariffs on foreign goods.[174]

As the number of establishments increased, so too did the base salaries for seasoned lithographic pressmen. As of 1871 printers working on steam-run presses that cost about $3,000 each a year to operate could earn up to $25–$30 per fifty-four-hour, six-day work week, about $454 a week in current value.[175] Lithographic artists fared even better, earning up to $150 per week, while transferrers could earn up to $50 per week.[176] In 1871, perhaps in response to these higher salaries and the waning of the apprenticeship program, the night school for artisans at the Central High School included training for lithographers.[177]

Men still dominated the field as lithographers, but a few more women, other than Lavinia Bowen and Victoria Quarre, had progressed beyond the acknowledged position of colorist by the 1860s.[178] By 1871 women trained in lithography at the Philadelphia School of Design reportedly made up to $21 a week for their work, about on par with male lithographic printers, but far less than lithographic designers.[179] The 1870 census provides evidence that thirty-six youths and women occupied positions in the trade at that time. Although advertisements by lithographers looking for "stout" boys of sixteen years of age still prevailed, by the 1880 census at least five females, including Eliza H. Thomas, about fifteen years of age, and Ellen Jones, about twenty-six years of age, indicated their occupation as lithographer.[180] Jones may very well have been one of those thirty-six women and youths recorded ten years earlier who was not a colorist. Despite women's growing documented foothold in the trade, John Godver (b. ca. 1841), sometimes Godber, would be the only nonwhite lithographer identified as active in the industry in the nineteenth century.[181] By 1880 the Pennsylvania Institute for the Deaf & Dumb had well-equipped lithographic classrooms available to their students for learning and practicing the trade.[182]

Most known lithographers from 1870 through 1880 were twenty-one to fifty years old; by 1880 the number of those aged over fifty was double the number of those aged twenty-one to thirty. As lithographers over fifty years old increased, those aged fourteen to twenty dropped more than 50 percent, reflecting the decreasing number of boy apprentices and increasing average age of those in the profession. Most of the lithographers of the 1870s continued to be native Pennsylvanians, of German ethnicity, who lived east of Broad Street, predominantly in North Philadelphia and near the printing district (figs. 11a–c).[183] The apprentice system of the antebellum era had also undergone a reconstruction due to the compartmentalization of the factory system and the increasing unionization of the lithographic trade following the war. Youths hired to work specific jobs at low wages, about $8–$10 a week,[184] as opposed to learn a trade, had become more the norm (a trend criticized by some) than four-year apprentices, who earned less until their fourth year.[185]

One source of this criticism was the *Printers' Circular,* which began publication in Philadelphia in 1866 and provides another window on the business practices of the Philadelphia industry about which so few primary documents remain. The journal provided lithographers, such as early subscribers Edward Herline and W. F. Geddes,[186] not only articles about the state of the printing trade but advertisements for inks, papers, and other furnishings required for the industry; bargain pages for secondhand presses; as well as a forum where lithographers could acknowledge the elites in their field. Lehman & Bolton, George S. Harris, Ketterlinus, and Haehnlen were recognized for their superb specimens of printing by the editor R. S. Menamin, and they served as respected endorsers in the advertisements of allied trades.[187]

The invoices of Philadelphia lithographers provide another means by which to understand how these businesses operated during the period. Often adorned with vignettes and ornamental lettering and not infrequently addressed to customers beyond the local region, the bills predominantly listed envelopes, billheads, cards, and letterheads with runs of five hundred to one thousand copies. Small orders usually amounted to about $5–$10, with an extremely large order invoiced by established lithographer William Boell in July 1867 for $1,000, including the designs for more than a dozen chromolithographs at $20 each.[188] Invoices also reveal that it could take a year or more to receive payment and that lithographers would fill orders on credit, despite the professional advice of the day.[189] By 1880 Potsdamer & Co., a prolific printer of trade cards since the 1860s, when operated as Stein & Jones,[190] noted on their billhead "Prompt Cash 2 percent discount 30 days nett" to induce quick payment.

Later-nineteenth-century lithographers also sent correspondence to long-standing customers to request and thank them for payment, suggest design changes, make business deals, or lament the state of their business.[191] In 1876 the Ketterlinus Printing House notified the Riehlé Brothers, manufacturers of scales, "Have no use at present for anything in your line but will bear it in mind, should there be any chance to make trade."[192] In 1879 William Boell actually did "make trade" with the firm—a beam scale for a lithographic stone, presumably with a Riehlé design.[193] Theodore Leonhardt signaled the financial distress of his business when he wrote in the summer of 1877 to patron John M. Miller of Pottsville, "The times are with us the same way, collections very hard and trade dreadfully dull."[194] Despite the dire tone, probably reflecting the residual economic stagnation from the Panic of 1873, Leonhardt survived the rough period and within a few years corresponded with Miller about his expansion.[195]

By the mid-1870s, the changed framework of production and the Panic of 1873 had affected the level of both "general" and job printing executed by Philadelphia lithographers. For the period 1866–78, the number of known separately issued pictorial lithographic prints, that is, "general" work in the scope of this study, decreased to less than half of the known number from the period 1851–65.[196] Only about five different lithographs containing a Haehnlen imprint appear to survive. This figure proves telling. If the "general" work of the most "extensive" firm of the 1860s has become virtually invisible in the surveys of work from the 1870s, the more ephemeral job work at the premier lithographic firms must by then have accounted for an even more significant portion of their total workload. Trade cards, labels, scraps, bank checks, and other small ephemeral lithographs, often chromolithographed and absent an imprint, predominated.[197] Indicative of this decreasing demand for larger-format pictorial lithographs, stationers and letterpress and job printers, such as William F. Christy, W. F. Geddes & Son, and John D. Avil, who usually produced small-format work, began to market themselves and succeed as lithographic printers as well.[198]

The shift in the types of prints produced after the war occurred hand in hand with the rise of chromolithography. Despite the promotion of this print process by Duval in 1850, chromolithography did not have a real impact on production in the separately published print trade until more than a decade later, as exemplified by the predominance of firms like Ketterlinus, Leonhardt, Breuker & Kessler, and Lehman & Bolton. These establishments specialized in forms of advertising that suited increasingly visually receptive consumers—chromolithographed labels, trade cards, and poster advertisements—and thrived.[199] Whereas these firms, like their predecessors, were dependent on commercial patrons to survive, the Philadelphia lithographer Joseph Hoover focused on chromolithographed parlor prints, a branch of lithography not based on commissions. Although chromolithographic fine-art prints are not a focus of this survey, their publication and distribution enhance understanding of the trade.

Joseph Hoover, originally a manufacturer of frames, began advertising his large stock of "chromos" in 1865. Within a few years, he evolved from distributor to publisher and finally to printer of chromolithographs, with a plant built about 1876 at North Thirteenth and Buttonwood Streets. A prolific advertiser in the newspapers, he employed lithographers Duval & Hunter and James Queen in the 1860s and 1870s and, as a result of the explosion in demand for parlor prints, operated one of the most productive chromolithograph factories in the country by 1893.[200]

Hoover capitalized on a continuing tradition of the interrelationship between the trades of lithography and frame making started by Kennedy & Lucas. From the early decades of local commercial lithography, framers marketed lithographs in the more elite, predominantly subscription newspapers *Philadelphia Inquirer* and *North American*. By the 1860s longtime glazier and frame dealer James S. Earle & Sons continually advertised in these papers, which had expanded their readership into the middle classes.[201] Lower single-copy prices, newsboys, and delivery routes allowed merchants who advertised in the *Philadelphia Inquirer* to market their wares to the artisan (and more casual reader) as well as to the ardent subscriber from the professional classes. Often using brief declarative statements such as "Great Novelties and Looking Glasses, Picture Frames, New Chromos" and "Chromos and engravings at the lowest prices for reliable goods . . . Frames equally cheap," Earle promoted bargains to both types of

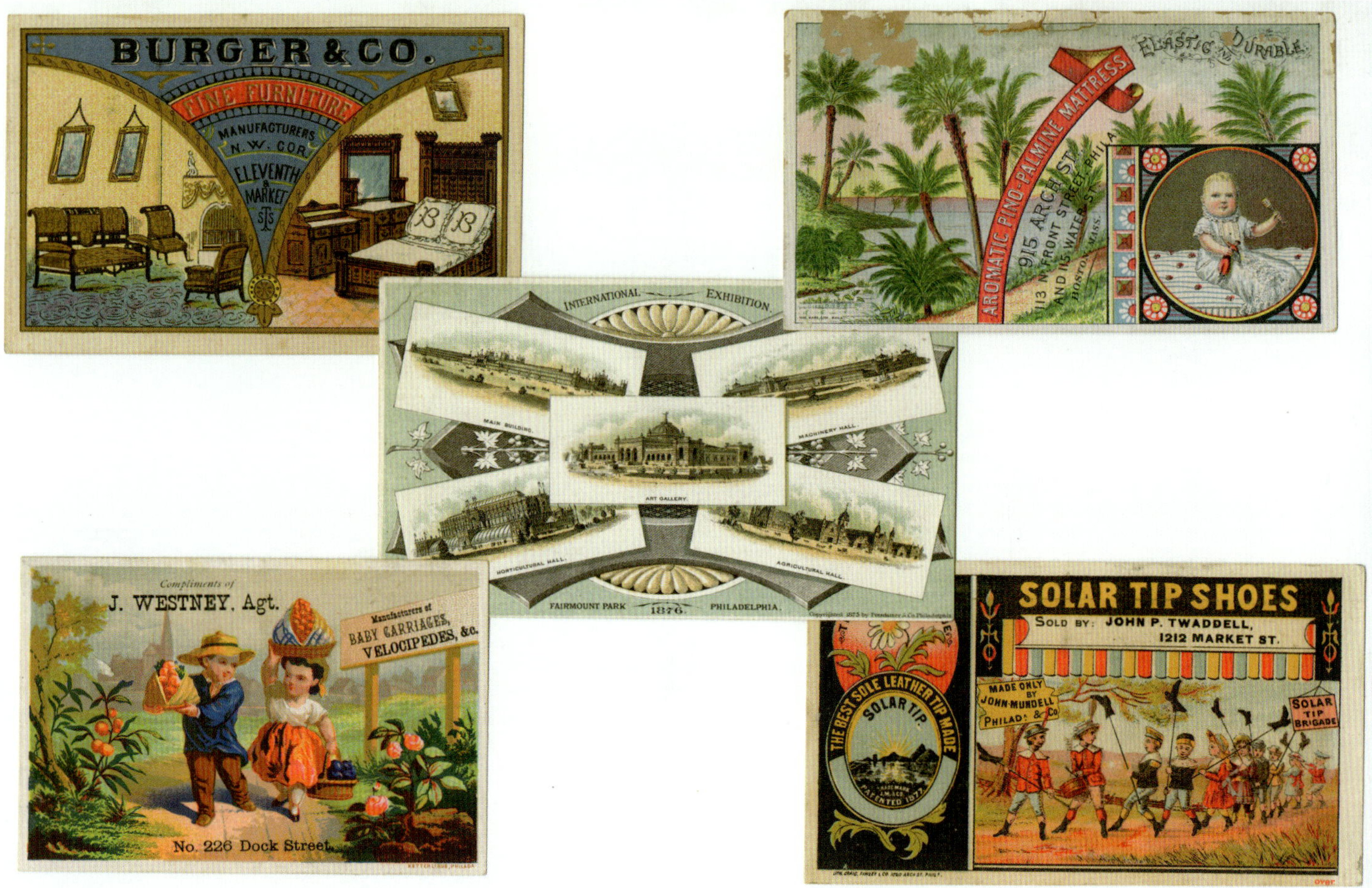

readers. Depending on the patron, they visited Earle to purchase reasonably priced or inexpensive quality parlor prints and matching frames of their choice, to adorn their walls as with a solitary piece of "art," or only one of many, that turned their houses into homes.[202]

In addition to the frame stores, printshops, auctions, and peddlers long used to sell lithographs, catalogs also now served as a way to market the prints. Duval & Hunter and the National Chromo Company (established in 1875)[203] issued catalogs that not only provided prices, descriptions, and occasional illustrations but also promoted the "artistry" of the work, while soliciting for child canvassers who could "earn $2–3 a day in their own neighborhoods," where their primary customers would presumably be their mothers and the other "ladies of the house."[204] Still described as "new art" in the 1860s, chromolithographic parlor prints sold for 50 cents to $30. By the 1870s, pervasive marketing and promotional giveaways (known as "chromo dodges")[205]

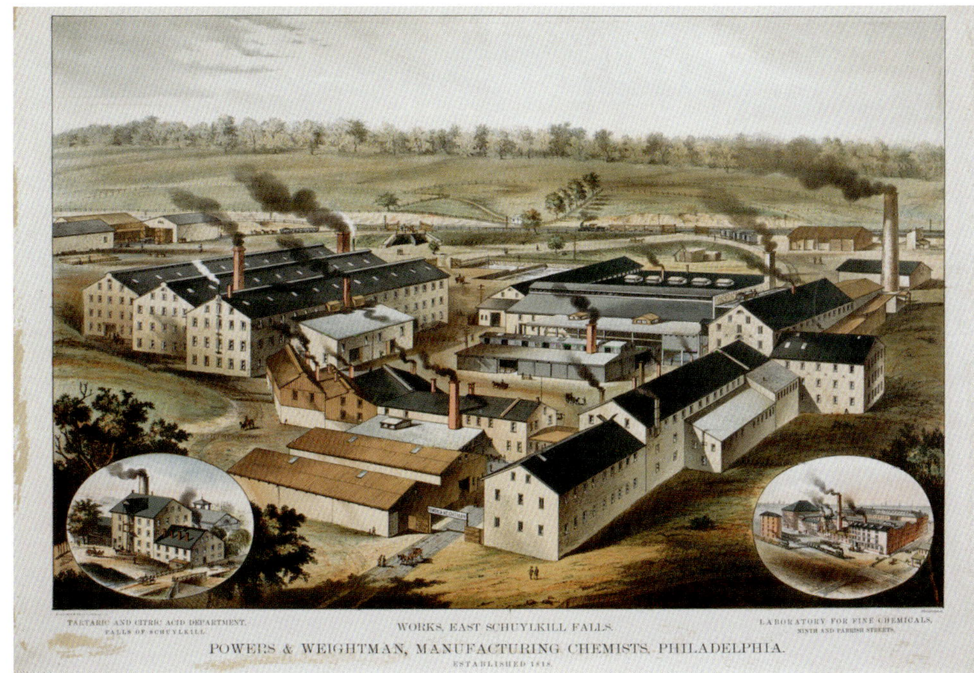

Albert Blanc, *Works, East Schuylkill Falls. Powers & Weightman, Manufacturing Chemists, Philadelphia. Established 1818. Tartaric and Citric Acid Department, Falls of Schuylkill. Laboratory for Fine Chemicals, Ninth and Parrish Streets* (Philadelphia: [Longacre & Co., ca. 1870]). Chromolithograph. 37 × 51 cm (14 ½ × 20 in.). POS 867, LCP, Gift of David Doret, P.2008.24.23.

had increased demand and volume to such an extent that they could be bought for a few cents to a few dollars each.

Between 1860 and 1878, as the overall number of lithographs within the scope of this project decreased, the number of chromolithographs in the survey doubled from the previous two decades.[206] Trade cards[207] epitomized this shift in production at the local establishments. Advertising prints like those designed by William H. Rease had evolved. In addition to custom-designed and stock trade cards (often genre scenes) that promoted the storefront businesses (fig. 23), industrial businesses ordered large-size prints that provided more of an aerial view than a front elevation of the factory complexes (fig. 24) and posters and labels that showcased their products.[208] These prints, all predominantly printed as chromolithographs, accounted for *a,* if not *the,* major share of the work produced by Philadelphia lithographers by 1880.

Advertisements for the lithographers themselves also evolved in step with the ones lithographers provided for their clients. Pre-1855 advertisements contained specimens of their work as vignettes, such as the 1844 Kollner print (fig. 13) or Duval's clever trompe l'oeil design of 1840 (see fig. 64). The allegorical and patriotic imagery that dominated in the 1850s and 1860s gave way to genre scenes on smaller-scale advertisements, such as trade cards, bookmarks, and circulars, or, to the other extreme, on large wall calendars.[209] Depictions of establishment exteriors also became more prevalent,

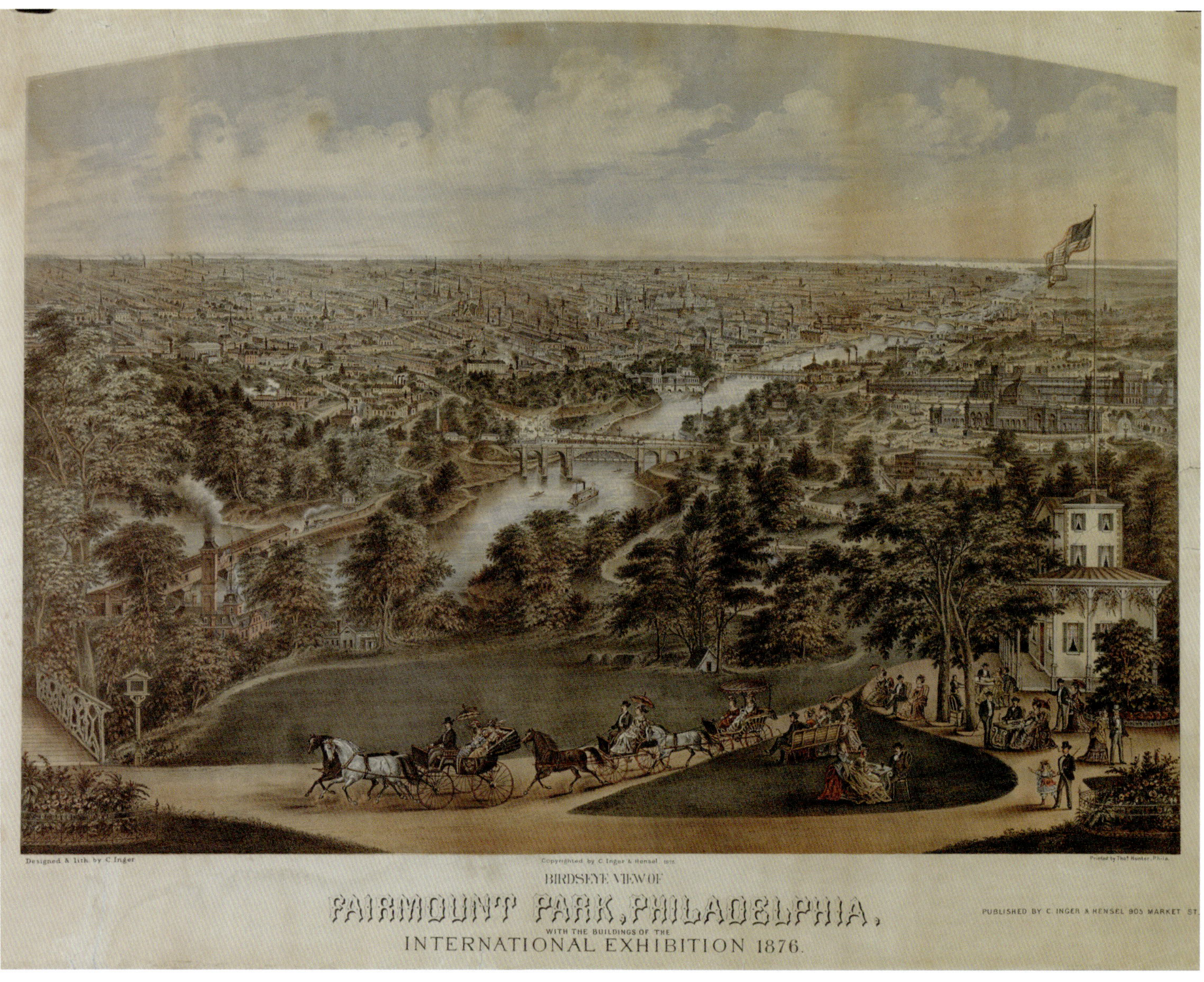

as evident from the advertisements of Haehnlen (fig. 22), Ketterlinus, and Breuker & Kessler.[210]

Despite local firms' increasing focus on the production of advertisements following the Civil War, certificates and church views, staples of the past decades, also remained relevant for the trade. Theodore Leonhardt & Son produced several membership certificates for German organizations during this period. Duval & Hunter dominated the printing of such certificates, particularly for firefighting organizations, which showcased much more elaborate imagery—costing up to $60 for the design alone—for which the firm was known.[211] Church views issued as souvenirs and fund-raising devices continued as well, and by 1880 the firm of Packard & Butler had become the Kennedy & Lucas of their day for this genre.[212]

The city's commercial lithographers also continued to produce beautiful landscapes of Philadelphia, none more so than the prints displaying the grounds of the Centennial Exhibition of 1876. Centennial views, with a built-in market, made up a large segment of this genre in the last twenty years studied (fig. 25). From May 10 to November 10, 1876, the city of Philadelphia was the site of an international exhibition of industry, agriculture, and art to celebrate the hundredth anniversary of the nation. Planning for the five-month-long celebration consumed the city for years before the actual event. By 1872 the Centennial Commission, a planning committee of prominent local citizens, businessmen, and government officials, and several subcommittees had been organized. Lithography played a role from the beginning to the end. The report by the Committee on Classification compiled in 1872 included lithographic stones as eligible for display in the "Raw Materials" Department, the Centennial Horticultural Society used lithographs of the Vienna Exhibition of 1873 as models for the design of their buildings,[213] and lithographs of the grounds were issued during the planning stages and as souvenirs during the fair. H. J. Toudy & Co.[214] and Thomas Hunter[215] dominated the publication, but a few others, such as Breuker & Kessler, also issued the panoramic and bird's-eye views, which were later often transformed into advertisements when stamped with the names of commercial exhibitors and distributed at the fair.

Lithographs not only showed the grounds but were used in greater numbers for more ephemeral items such as train schedules, trade cards, advertising circulars, and handbills. Several Philadelphia firms that specialized in this type of work thrived during the Centennial, including Ketterlinus and Geo. S. Harris & Sons.[216] The Centennial also provided a venue for the display and marketing of the work of Philadelphia lithographers. Joseph Hoover received an award for excellence in chromolithography, and Lehman & Bolton and Potsdamer & Co. were honored with awards for commercial lithography.[217] Theodore Leonhardt & Son used the Centennial as an opportunity to capitalize on the concurrence of the firm's silver anniversary and the nation's hundredth anniversary. The partnership issued elaborately illustrated progress-themed circulars, including the promotional text, "Our experience in this quarter of a century enabled us to Study the Wants of the Commercial World at large, and as we have always been striving to produce the Best Work, we leave it to your own judgement to convince yourself by personal inspection. We remain Respectfully Yours, Theo. Leonhardt & Son. Philadelphia, May 1st 1876."[218]

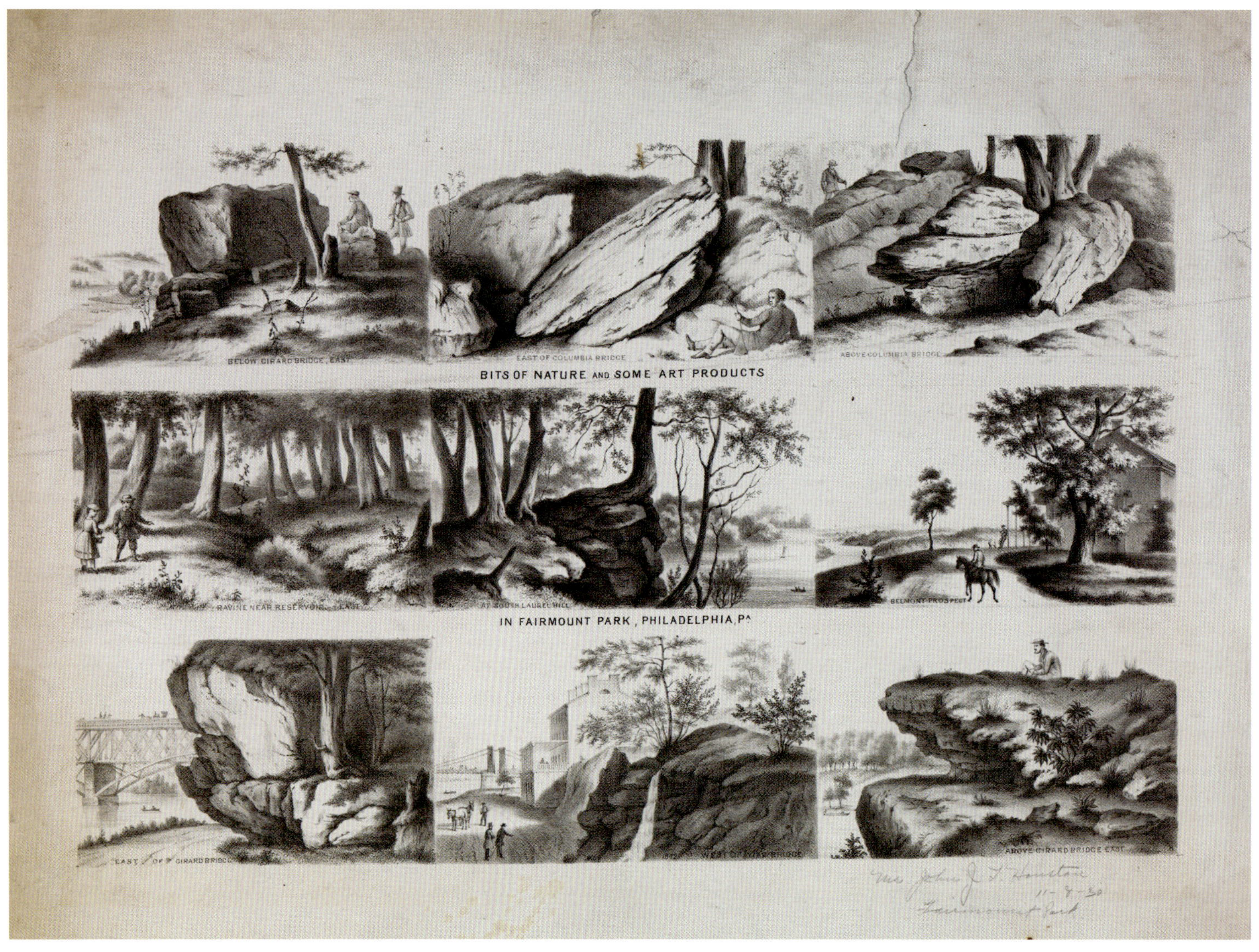

Augustus Kollner, *Bits of Nature and Some Art Products in Fairmount Park, Philadelphia, Pa.* (Philadelphia, ca. 1878). Lithograph. 42 × 53 cm (16 ½ × 20 ¾ in.). POS 56, HSP, Bc 81 Z 99.

Although by 1878 colored-printed lithographs dominated the speculative print market, uncolored prints still had a place, and well-established, traditional lithographer Augustus Kollner issued a series of uncolored views of Fairmount and the Wissahickon entitled *Bits of Nature and Some Art Products in Fairmount Park* (fig. 26).[219] Occasionally tinted, the prints highlighted why many early-generation lithographers entered the field—for the artistic advantages that work on stone provided. The landscapes, some originally sketched in the 1840s, show the waterworks, bridges spanning the Schuylkill, ravines, rock formations, and babbling brooks, with park visitors and wildlife often added for more atmosphere. Although such prints were somewhat rare, and the trade focused more on commercial—in the truest sense of the word—than on general lithography, these prints provide an ironic twist. Views of the iconic park that so dominated the first years of commercial lithography had cycled back fifty years later, as a stark reminder in a sea of color that Philadelphia lithography started with a black-and-white landscape on stone.

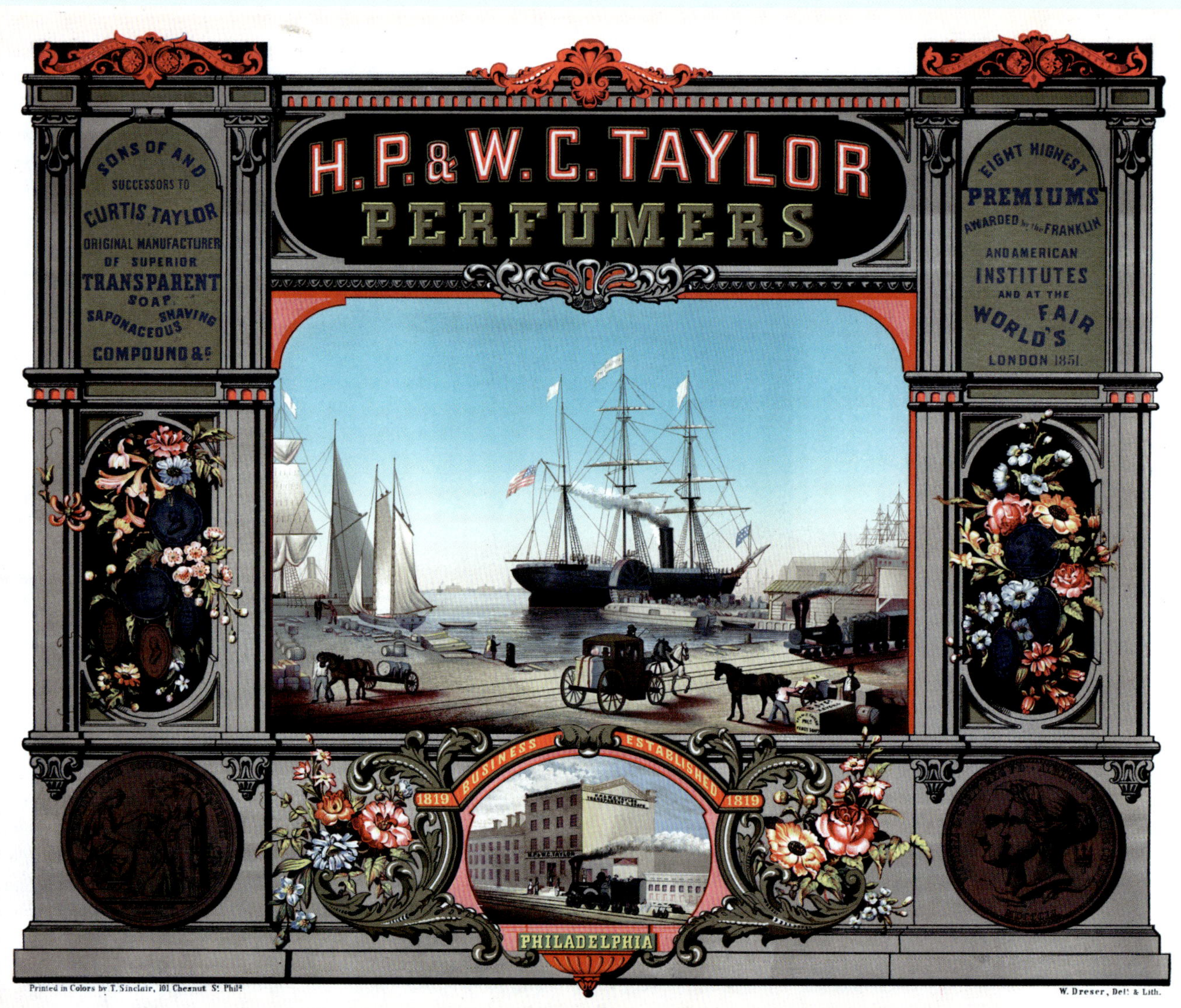

H. P. & W. C. TAYLOR
PERFUMERS
SONS OF AND
SUCCESSORS TO
CURTIS TAYLOR
ORIGINAL MANUFACTURER
OF SUPERIOR
TRANSPARENT
SOAP.
SAPONACEOUS
SHAVING
COMPOUND &c
EIGHT HIGHEST
PREMIUMS
AWARDED by the FRANKLIN
AND AMERICAN
INSTITUTES
AND AT THE
WORLD'S
FAIR
LONDON 1851.
1819
BUSINESS
ESTABLISHED
1819
PHILADELPHIA
Printed in Colors by T. Sinclair, 101 Chesnut St. Phila
W. Dreser, Del. & Lith.

PUTTING PHILADELPHIA ON STONE

An Introduction to the Techniques Used

MICHAEL TWYMAN

WHAT LITHOGRAPHY OFFERED THE ARTIST

Lithography gave artists and letterers the opportunity to multiply their own marks more easily than they could when using any other method of printing.[1] This was one of its main selling points in the first few years of the nineteenth century and continued to be so for several decades. The range of effects lithography offered those who worked on stone was, and remains, unparalleled in its diversity, ranging from vigorous crayon marks to meticulous crayon hatching and lines drawn in ink with a steel pen or a fine sable brush. Later on, techniques were developed that allowed artists to draw with graded washes of ink comparable to those of the watercolor painter.

In addition, there was the option for artists to have their work interpreted by specially trained lithographers, either because they had no access to lithographic facilities or because they lacked the skills or interest to work on stone. This became increasingly the case as the process developed in complexity and as the marketplace demanded more refined images. From the 1840s, the use of such professional lithographic artists gained momentum from the pressure to produce images based on photographs, particularly portraits and town views. It is not always possible to identify when professional lithographers worked as interpreters; they were sometimes identified at the foot of the print, but not always. In any case, a lithographic artist may have used assistants to undertake some of the more tedious parts of a drawing on stone, such as flat tints in skies, and specialists may also have been brought in to add figures to a view and provide lettering.

Another major feature of the process was the facility with which pictures and words could be combined. Lithography was not unique in this respect, but it was exceptional in attaching equal importance to the work of the pictorial artist and that of the writer and letterer. The professional lithographic writer gradually replaced the engraver of lettering as the nineteenth century progressed, and most large lithographic establishments would have had craftsmen undertaking this kind of work, if only to add imprints to pictorial lithographs. As we shall see, the combination of words and pictures was to become one of the features of lithographed advertising views produced in Philadelphia in the middle of the century.

THE LITHOGRAPHIC PROCESS

The printing process known as lithography takes its name from the use of stone as a printing surface. The stone, a compact calcareous limestone the components of which had been deposited in the mud flats of shallow lagoons when dinosaurs roamed the earth, consists primarily of calcium carbonate (usually around 97 percent).[2] The finest such stone came from quarries around Solnhofen in Bavaria, where it existed—and still exists—in vast quantities.[3] The stone from these quarries had been in use since ancient Roman times for a variety of purposes, including sculpture and inscriptions, but only a small proportion of the total output was ever used for lithography. Stone from the Solnhofen region had a virtual monopoly in the lithographic trade for a century or so because it was easily extracted (in later years in very large sizes), unequaled in quality, and relatively free from impurities. Paradoxically, though these quarries supplied the world's lithographers with fossil-free stone into the twentieth century, they are probably best known for providing some of the finest surviving fossils, including that of the earliest known bird form, *Archaeopteryx lithographica*.[4]

Calcareous limestone's suitability for lithographic printing rests on its fine grain and its ability to absorb water and greasy substances with equal ease. In the simplest form of lithography, marks are made on the stone with a greasy ink or crayon. These marks appear black on the stone, though the black simply allows the artist to see what has been drawn. What really matters is the penetration of the grease into the surface of the stone. The greasy marks are absorbed by the stone and, after a certain chemical treatment, which has varied slightly over the years, become bound inextricably with it. This treatment involves applying a solution of gum arabic with just a few drops of nitric acid.

At the heart of the lithographic process lies the fact that water and grease do not readily mix.[5] Taking a print from a drawn stone involves dampening its surface and then applying greasy printing ink with a roller. The greasy marks on the stone tend to reject the water, whereas the bare areas attract it. By the same token, the greasy drawn marks attract the greasy printing ink, while the moistened stone rejects it. The basic principles of lithography are easy enough to explain in this way, but a little harder to believe. Even today the principles underlying the process have an almost magical simplicity, which we acknowledge whenever we use the expression "it's like water off a duck's back." There is much more to the process than this, and as early as the mid–nineteenth century it had developed its own scientific basis. But initially such a simple idea seemed just as incredible as digital imaging does to many of us today.

Traditionally, stones were "dressed" at the quarries and then, at the printers, either polished (to produce a surface not unlike that of prepared marble) or given a fine grain, the texture of which could be varied according to the kind of drawing required. The difference in surface was achieved by grinding two stones together with water and sand of different degrees of fineness or by using a levigator (a flat, round metal device) as an alternative to the upper stone. Drawings made with greasy crayon had to be done on grained stones, though ink marks could be made on either grained or polished stones. When drawings on stone were no longer needed, they could be ground away using methods similar to those described here.

THE EUROPEAN LEGACY

Lithographic methods were established surprisingly early on and almost twenty years before the first lithographs were made on United States soil by Bass Otis for the *Analectic Magazine* in Philadelphia in 1819.[6] Initially, lithographic methods were discussed in brief journal articles, some of which relied on second- or thirdhand information and have to be treated with a degree of suspicion.[7] But books on the subject had already appeared before Alois Senefelder, the inventor of lithography, published his own account of the process in 1818. A few years earlier Heinrich Rapp had issued a reliable monograph on the subject, *Das Geheimniss des Steindrucks,* which was published anonymously in both Tübingen and Schweinfurt in 1810 (curiously in two versions in the same year, both with specimen plates, but one with its text in black letter, the other in antiqua type). An English-language monograph on lithography was also published well before the inventor's treatise. This was Henry Bankes's *Lithography, or The Art of Making Drawings on Stone* (Bath, 1813), which initially appeared anonymously, but with the author's name and a modified title in London in 1816. Eventually, the inventor was goaded into publication and produced a comprehensive and detailed account of his invention with the title *Vollständiges Lehrbuch der Steindruckerey* (Munich and Vienna, 1818). Its impact was immediate, and in the following year English and French editions appeared, with a reduced Italian edition following in 1827.[8]

No other printing or printmaking process had attracted such a body of writing as lithography did in the period 1810 to 1840, when scores of books were written in England, France, Germany, and Italy explaining the process. Most of the early ones concentrated on methods of drawing on stone; later ones covered both the making of marks on stone and the printing from them. Nearly all include illustrations, and many of them specimens of some of the methods described. Books of this kind—along with the earliest trade journal of lithography, *Le lithographe* (Paris and Rotterdam, 1838–48), and of course the prints themselves—provide us with our principal sources of information about the methods of early lithographers.

Curiously, no books on the practice of lithography appear to have been published in the United States in the first half of the nineteenth century. If existing or potential lithographers in Philadelphia and elsewhere in the country had read useful descriptions of the process, they would have had to come from overseas.[9] It would be good to know which of the many European manuals on the subject did manage to find their way across the Atlantic in that early period. We might assume that some were included among the treasured possessions of the numerous trained lithographers who left Europe to start a new life or escape from an old one, particularly at the time of the revolutions of 1848. Others may have come from recruiting or fact-finding trips to Europe undertaken by master lithographers. But for the most part, it seems that lithographic methods and techniques would have been passed on by example or by word of mouth, in many cases, no doubt, in halting English. In general, though there were some differences, the lithographic methods practiced in Europe were taken over lock, stock, and barrel in Philadelphia, as they were in other parts of the United States.

INK DRAWING ON STONE

The simplest and most robust lithographic method involved drawing with greasy ink on stone. A stick of greasy material consisting of wax, soap, tallow, shellac, and lampblack was coaxed into liquid form by dissolving it in distilled water, the resulting ink usually lasting in a good state for a day or two. In theory such greasy ink could be applied by any means, but in practice the tools used were either a steel pen or a fine sable brush. The quill, which was still in general use when lithography was introduced to Philadelphia, would not normally have been appropriate, since it became soft when used with lithographic ink and would have worn badly when in contact with the stone. The sable or similar brush was capable of producing finer marks than the pen, especially when it was trimmed down to all but a few hairs, as it sometimes was. But whether a pen or brush was used, the ink had to be applied in concentrated form, since it was not possible in the early days of lithography to produce washes of ink in varied tones. This was a real limitation for many artists because it meant that tonal effects had to be produced optically by hatching or stippling. Corrections could be made to ink lithographs relatively easily by scraping away the offending marks and adding new ones. If all went well, an ink drawing on stone could produce thousands of impressions,[10] far more than would have been needed in most situations in which lithography was used in Europe or the United States in the first half of the nineteenth century.

Aside from Bass Otis, very few early Philadelphia artists produced ink lithographs. The major exception was Augustus Kollner, who was trained as an engraver in Germany and lithographer in Paris before leaving for the United States in 1839.[11] He was to become something of a specialist in ink lithography. In his set of plates published in 1856 as *City Sights for Country Eyes,* he used the pen much as an etcher would an etching needle, though in this instance he supported each drawing with a light straw-colored tint stone (fig. 27), a technique to be explained later in this essay. Ink drawing with a pen or brush was generally of little interest to artists as an independent medium, but it was widely used by letterers, music writers, and cartographers. It was also used in conjunction with crayon drawing to define forms more clearly and to produce rich blacks, as in many Philadelphia advertising views.

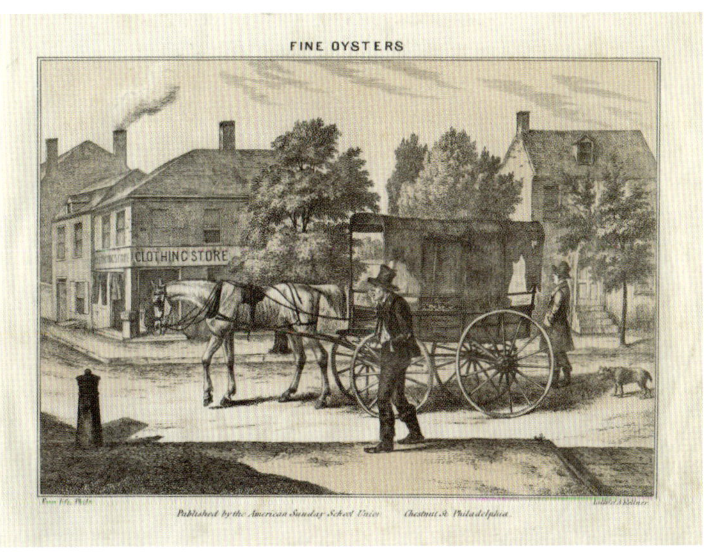

FIG. 27

Augustus Kollner, *Fine Oysters,* from *City Sights for Country Eyes* (Philadelphia: American Sunday School Union, ca. 1856). Ink lithograph with tinted background. 23 × 29 cm (9 × 11 ½ in.). POS 249, HSP, Bd 61 K8343.17

CRAYON DRAWING ON STONE

The technique that most attracted artists who made monochrome lithographs, in both Europe and the United States, was drawing with greasy crayons. When lithography was first introduced, it was claimed that all artists had to do was to sketch on stone much as they would have done on paper. But within the first decade of the nineteenth

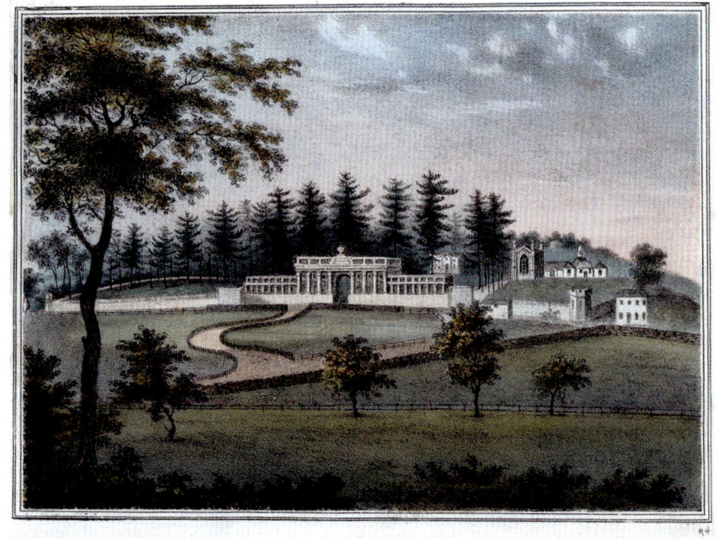

John Caspar Wild, *Laurel Hill Cemetery*, from *Views of Philadelphia and Its Vicinity* (Philadelphia: Lith. of Wild & Chevalier, 1838), plate 20. Hand-colored crayon lithograph. 14 × 18 cm (5 ¼ × 7 in.). POS 430.1, LCP, 6626.F.

century in Germany, and by the mid-1820s in Britain and France, it was realized that the process was capable of great refinement and that certain techniques were essential if a drawing was to stand up to long runs. In any case, the process had also to be capable of producing tonal images that would allow it to compete with mezzotint in portraiture and aquatint in landscape and topography.

The methods of drawing on stone that were designed to achieve these ends were described in some of the early lithographic manuals, particularly in Godefroy Engelmann's *Manuel du dessinateur lithographe* (Paris, 1822) and Charles Hullmandel's book *The Art of Drawing on Stone* (London, 1824).[12] Hullmandel went into these methods in great detail. The crayon was not to be held in the bare hand, as there would have been a real danger of greasy finger marks being transmitted unintentionally to the stone. Various kinds of *porte-crayon* were devised to obviate this, but for the finest tints any tool had to be as light as possible if its own weight was not to leave too dark a trace when the crayon was applied to the stone. Hullmandel recommended a *porte-crayon* made of cork or goose quill instead of the common metal version, and this alone provides some indication of the extreme delicacy of the tints he had in mind. The crayon was sharpened to a very fine point and applied in a series of parallel lines, each of which began thin, swelled in the middle, and then tapered. Series of short strokes of this kind were to be applied end-on to one another with their thin parts overlapping so as to produce the effect of a single line of equal thickness. This procedure was to be repeated in several different directions over the same area so that the initial linear structure of marks was lost in an overall tonal effect. Additional stages ensured that no trace of the crayon lines remained, only a flat tonal area. Such techniques were used in Europe to lay in tints (for example in skies and similar flat areas), and by the middle of the century assistants were being employed to undertake such tedious work.[13]

Artists who turned to lithography in Philadelphia followed similar methods of laying in tints but made no real attempt to hide the linear structure of their crayon marks, producing instead less refined tints, sometimes with the lines laid in one direction only. Among the early lithographers working in Philadelphia in the late 1820s and 1830s, W. L. Breton, G. Lehman, and C. G. Childs produced tints of this kind on their delicately drawn images, which were technically broadly similar to European crayon lithographs of the period. Later, J. C. Wild produced twenty crayon lithographs in much the same carefully rendered way for his *Views of Philadelphia and Its Vicinity,* which were published in five monthly numbers in plain and hand-colored versions by Wild & Chevalier in 1838 (fig. 28), to be followed in the same year by four panoramas under the title *Panorama of Philadelphia. Views Taken from the State House Steeple.*[14]

Lithographic crayons came in different degrees of hardness, according to the proportion of their ingredients, the harder ones producing silvery gray marks and the softer ones coarser but richer marks. Harder crayons would have been used for the lines that defined the edges and major parts of buildings, which nearly always seem in Philadelphia lithographs to have been drawn with a straightedge. This is a method much more commonly associated with American than with English and French lithography and may stem from the fact that many of those making lithographs in Philadelphia were essentially draftsmen. Softer-grade crayons were normally used for foregrounds; in landscapes, for example, for freely drawn clumps of grass and vegetation. An outlet for such marks in Philadelphia views was offered by its cobbled streets and sidewalks, which William H. Rease in particular rendered with naïve graphic enthusiasm.

Once drawn on stone, positive marks and tints could be modified in several ways, either by scraping with a knife or point to produce negative lines or, from the late 1830s, by rubbing down areas with coarse cloth to reduce their tone. The use of the scraper to produce negative effects was put to particularly good use in Rease's 1860 print *Franklin Iron Works,* where the name of the factory is shown in "Tuscan" letters (that is, with bifurcated serifs) and reads white against a threatening dark sky (fig. 29). In this case numerous finely scratched lines appear side by side to form solid-looking white letterforms. The technique was normally employed much more subtly to suggest highlights and, in Philadelphia views, the bonding of brickwork. In his 1833 print *Fairmount Waterworks* (POS 240.1), George Lehman made use of it to pick out white railings in the middle distance and reflections on the water. Marks that read as lights on a darker ground could also be produced by drawing on stone with a solution of gum arabic before any ink or crayon work was applied, since gum acts as a resist and prevents any greasy drawn marks from being absorbed by the stone. This was a technique frequently used in views of Philadelphia, sometimes in combination with scraper work, to produce signs on buildings that show white lettering on a black ground.

The laying-in of overall tints with crayon of the kind Hullmandel described could take many days, even weeks, and in 1819 Godefroy Engelmann came up with a less tedious but rather unpredictable means of producing light tints that he called *lavis lithographique* or *aquatinta lithographique,* both terms suggesting the effect of washes on stone.[15] The method was discussed by Hullmandel, who called it the dabbing style, since the subtle tones associated with it were produced by striking a dabber coated

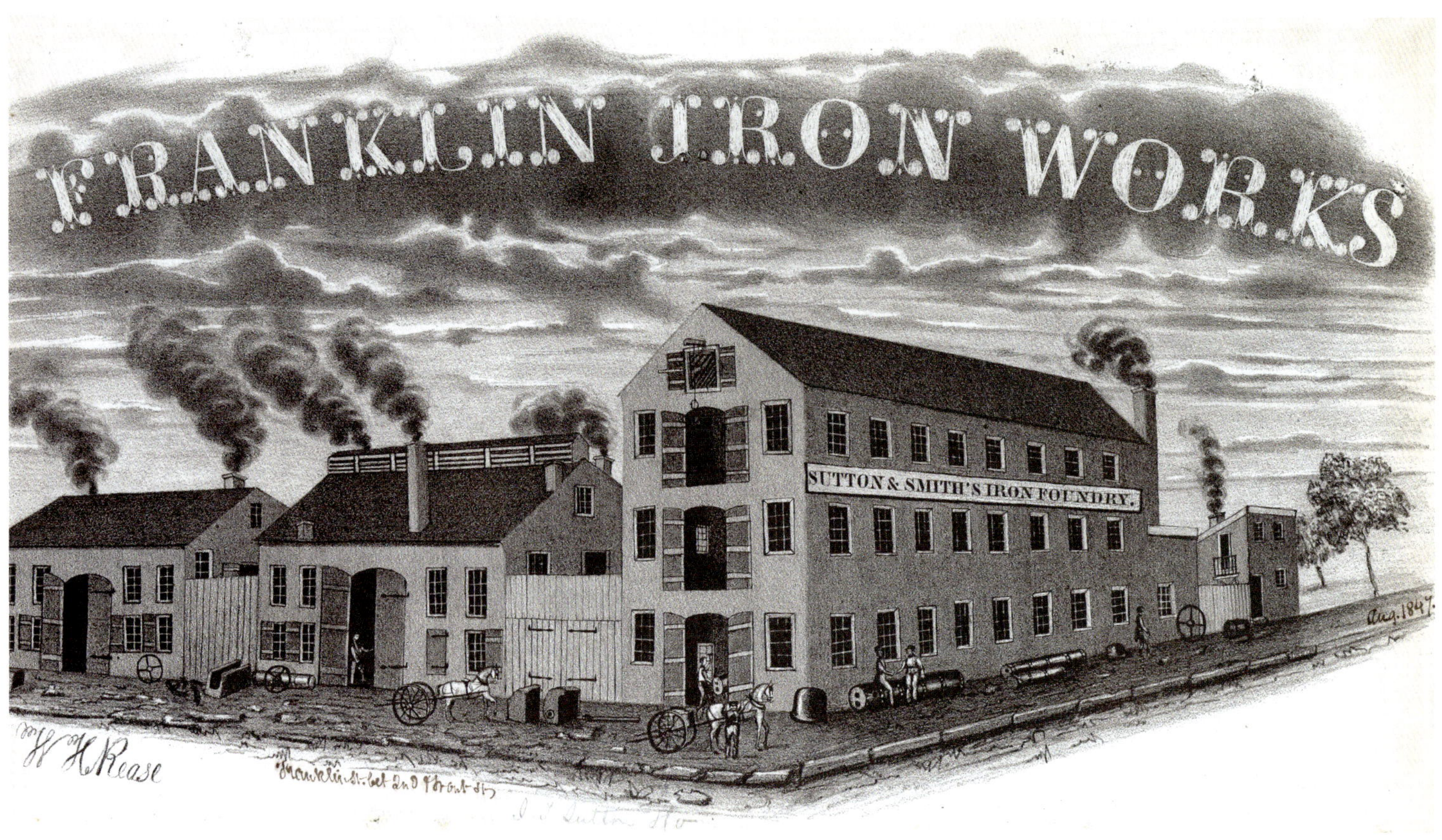

with lithographic ink (mixed to the consistency of honey) against the surface of the stone. In the hands of talented executants the method worked remarkably well, but by around 1825 it was regarded as so unreliable that it fell out of use. It was abandoned in Europe by the time lithography had gained a foothold in the United States, and no obvious examples of its use have been found in early Philadelphia lithographs.

Corrections were much more difficult to make in crayon lithography than they were when using ink, as scraping away unwanted parts of an image removed the carefully grained surface of the stone. Parts of a drawing could be removed entirely, but for a couple of decades it was not possible to add work to stones that had already been prepared for printing. And it was not until 1827, when Godefroy Engelmann came up with the idea of removing unwanted parts of an image chemically, that additions could be made to crayon-drawn stones once printing had begun. He kept his methods secret, but it was soon revealed that he must have used acetic acid to remove the offending parts: unlike nitric acid, it allowed for the redrawing of the stone; unlike scraping, it did not destroy its grain.[16]

The finest crayon lithographs needed to be printed on appropriate paper, the ideal being India paper (often referred to as *papier de Chine*).[17] This was laid down onto the inked-up printing surface, having already had its nonprinting side coated with paste. A larger sheet of damp plate paper was then laid across the India paper, and as the two sheets of paper passed through the press in the course of printing, they became one. Several examples of Philadelphia lithography from the 1830s show the use of this method of printing on India paper, with its telltale evidence of printing that extends, unintentionally, across the two different surfaces. The first two editions of Wild's *Views of Philadelphia* were printed on India paper (fig. 28), whereas later issues and editions were not. Copies of W. L. Breton's print *North-East View of St. Peter's Church,* printed by Kennedy & Lucas in 1828 (POS 511), are also found on both India and plate paper. Crayon lithographs were much more difficult to print than ink-drawn ones, and in the 1820s several failures to print crayon-drawn stones satisfactorily were reported in Britain.[18] In a letter to a client in 1820 Hullmandel admitted that a crayon drawing would be worn out after five hundred impressions had been taken.[19] But this number was soon to be exceeded, and a couple of years later Hullmandel was recorded as having printed a crayon lithograph for the *Gentleman's Magazine* in some thousands of impressions.[20]

Some early crayon lithographs in Philadelphia, as elsewhere, would have been published plain and also, more expensively, colored by hand. Most surviving separately issued lithographs from Philadelphia appear without hand-coloring, though some exist in both versions, such as George Lehman's *Eastern Penitentiary of Pennsylvania,* published in 1833 (POS 202). Hand-coloring was an integral part of the printmaking trade throughout the first half of the nineteenth century, and in some places long afterward. J. T. Bowen, best known for his hand-colored octavo edition of Audubon's *Birds of America* (1839–44), worked in Philadelphia from 1838 as a lithographer specializing in print coloring, employing whole teams of hand-colorists.[21]

TINTED LITHOGRAPHY

Lithographs that have one or more tint stones added to a black impression to introduce a modicum of color are normally called tinted lithographs.[22] In the early days of lithography artists found that the drawings they made on stone looked somewhat bleak when printed on white paper, and for this reason they occasionally had them printed on tinted paper or the printer added a solid impression in a stone, buff, or straw hue to compensate for the loss of color of the stone. This explains why, initially, the predominant color of tinted lithographs lay within this range of hues. It was not long, however, before artists realized that they could imitate drawings touched up with white by introducing light areas on the tint stone, either by reserving them with gum arabic in advance of drawing a solid area in lithographic ink or by scraping them away afterward.[23]

All this began within the first decade of lithography in Germany,[24] but in 1837 Charles Hullmandel in Britain, with the assistance of the artist James Duffield Harding, developed ways of producing a wide range of tones within the tint stone to capture all the subtleties found, for example, in cloudy skies.[25] The methods they used were both positive and negative. Positive methods included the use of the stump, a piece of wood covered in chamois leather, which was charged with lithographic crayon and worked across the surface of the stone by the artist to produce a range of subtle tones. Negative methods included reserving with gum arabic areas that were intended to appear white and partially removing the surface of others that had already been drawn. This partial removal of drawn areas went far beyond scraping them away with a knife, point, or similar tool: and areas that had been drawn in ink on grained stones were rubbed down with rough cloth and wire brushes to produce a wide range of tones. Positive and negative methods could be used in more than one sequence, and it was not uncommon for those who drew on stone to reserve parts of a drawing with gum arabic before establishing a range of tones positively (using the stump for light tones and the brush for solid areas); they might then rub down some of the solid areas to produce an additional range of tones and, finally, work over them with ink to produce further positive marks. Tonal effects could be produced by such means that defy precise analysis in the finished print.

These enhanced methods of tinted lithography were an immediate success in Europe and were soon to be equally popular in the United States. They were applied most frequently to skies, where artists had considerable license to exploit special effects of a kind that would normally have been unacceptable in other parts of topographical prints. Furthermore, cloud and atmospheric effects could be produced entirely on the tint stone, which meant that hand-colored versions of a print could retain their freshness and clarity of hue in these areas.

Lithographers in Philadelphia took full advantage of the possibilities of tinted lithography. A fine and relatively early example is a large print, *Philadelphia, from the State House Steeple, North, East and South* of 1849, which was lithographed by Leo Elliot after a sketch by Joseph Thoma and printed by T. Sinclair (fig. 30). Its skies show a full range of tones that must have been produced by the techniques described above, and unlike many tinted lithographs of Philadelphia, its tint was printed in the characteristic

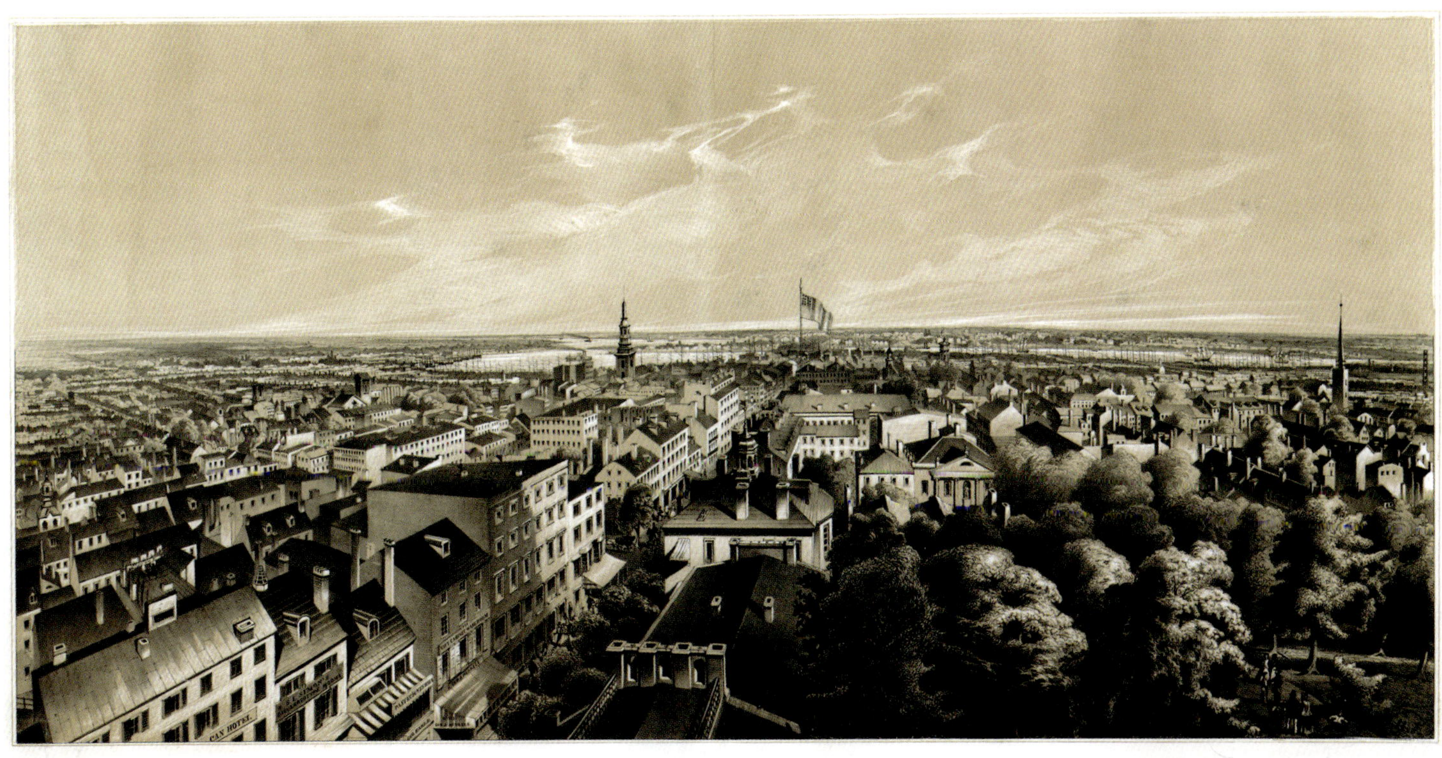

FIG. 30
Leo Elliot after Joseph Thoma, *Philadelphia, from the State House Steeple, North, East and South* (Philadelphia: J. C. Sidney, printed by T. Sinclair, 1849). Single-tint lithograph. 45 × 89 cm (18 × 35 ½ in.). POS 587, LCP, P. 2125.

beige or stone color normally associated with the process in Europe. Tint stones had to be registered accurately with their related black image, and several views of Philadelphia show at two of their corners the characteristic pinholes used for this purpose.[26]

The idea of combining a tint stone with a black printing led to other ways of adding color at little extra cost. There were two main ways of doing this: inking up a single tint stone in several colors and increasing the number of tint stones, each in a different color.

The first approach, called rainbow printing, involved charging a roller with ink in a limited range of colors so that they fused with one another where they met. The roller had to pass across the stone consistently in one direction to keep the integrity of the colors, which meant that the effects produced were somewhat limited. In rainbow-printed landscapes the conventional approach was to have a blue or gray color at one end of the roller and a buff color at the other. The printer P. S. Duval used this method when printing James Queen's *Shad Fishing* in 1855, its tint stone having been rolled up in inks that range from a gray-blue in the sky through light orange to buff for the

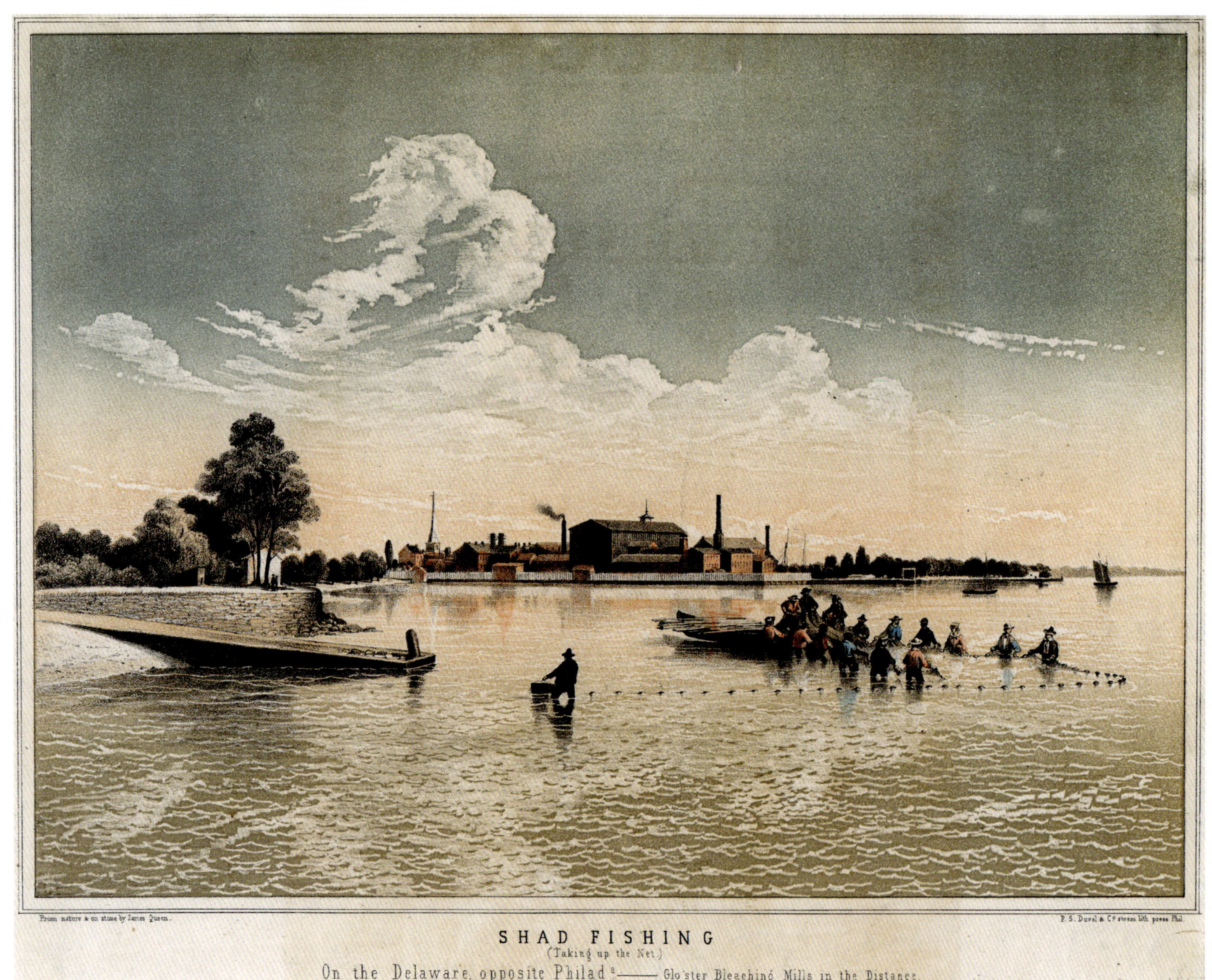

FIG. 31

James F. Queen, *Shad Fishing* (Philadelphia: P. S. Duval & Co., 1855). Single-tint lithograph, the tint inked in a range of colors. 28 × 34 cm (11 × 13 ¼ in.). POS 691, LCP, P. 2189.

water (fig. 31). At the close of our period the plates of Augustus Kollner's *Bits of Nature and Some Art Products in Fairmount Park,* 1878, include a range of rainbow-printed support stones, each chosen to meet the needs of the particular image.

A more common approach to producing color prints at a reasonable cost was to add several tint stones to a black, usually crayon-drawn, foundation drawing. Such lithographs might be referred to as double-, treble-, or multi-tinted, but when more colors were added, they moved imperceptibly into the realm of color printing and might be called chromolithographs. Double-tinted lithographs, normally with a gray-blue stone for the sky and a beige or stone color for the foreground, were common in Europe in the 1840s, mainly for topographical work.[27] In Philadelphia, the double- or treble-tinted lithograph became the favored method for town views, though the muted color values of European lithographers were abandoned in favor of relatively bright blues for skies and strong, warm pinks (almost coral in color) for buildings. Though in America the combination of such colors was not limited to Philadelphia,[28] it became the norm for its city views in the middle of the century and led to the production of some striking tinted lithographs. The choice of such distinctive colors appears to stem from the desire to show buildings in their finest light, with clear blue skies and in bright sunlight, the latter producing the coral-like glow on Philadelphia's characteristic red-brick buildings. Two good examples, both printed by Wagner & McGuigan around 1851, are R. F. Reynolds's *Robert Wood's Railing, Architectural & Ornamental Iron Works* (fig. 32) and an anonymous view of the Louis L. Peck manufactory (see fig. 90). Not all double-tinted lithographs produced in Philadelphia were of this kind, and an alternative approach is seen in Rease & Schell's *Steam Tugs, Columbus and Alert,* which was printed by T. Sinclair around 1855, with a blue impression in varied tones appearing over most of the print and a stone color reinforcing the form of the principal tug (fig. 33). Other tinted lithographs kept the familiar blue and warm-pink colors but added one or two more neutral printings. This was the approach of Rease & Schell in *Wm D. Rogers' Coach & Light Carriage Manufactory,* which was printed by Wagner & McGuigan around 1854 with a peach color added to its black, blue, and warm pink (POS 855).

CHROMOLITHOGRAPHY

Though chromolithography (printing lithographs in color) was first practiced elsewhere in the United States, Philadelphia can be regarded as its main commercial test bed.[29] P. S. Duval, Thomas Sinclair, and Wagner & McGuigan were all pioneer color printers in the city, producing a wide variety of work in association with several artists of distinction. All three produced chromolithographed book illustrations in the 1840s or early 1850s, Duval with his specialist chromolithographic artist Christian Schussele, and Sinclair with William Dreser and Alphonse Bigot. Duval, who had arrived in the United States from France, and Sinclair, from Scotland, were heavily influenced by European lithography, and their chromolithographed book illustrations reflect this. But diversity has to be seen as the major characteristic of early chromolithography in Philadelphia, which developed in different ways according to the type of work under-

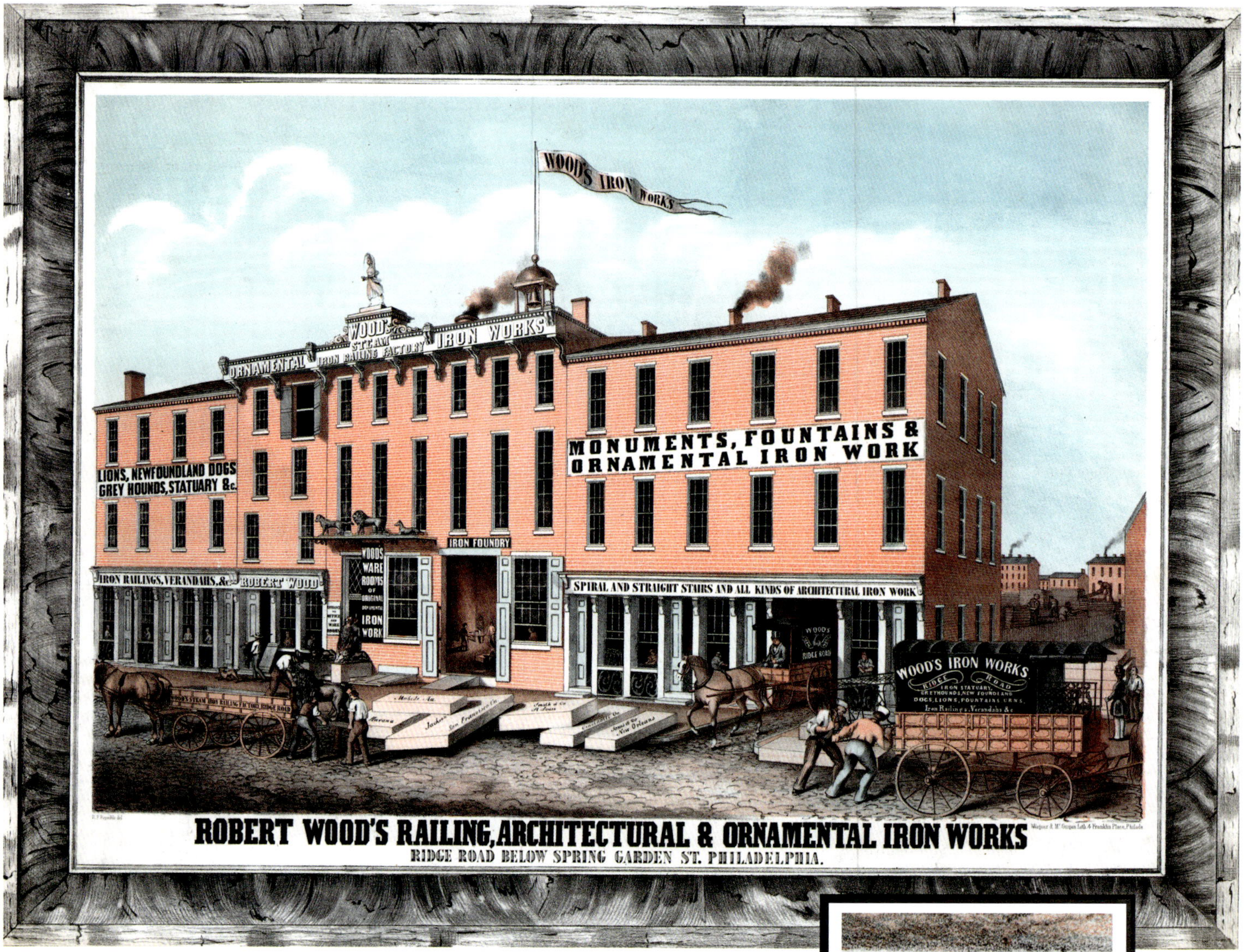

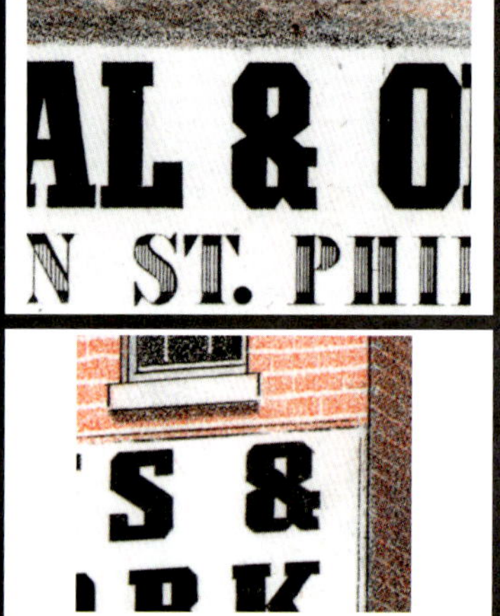

FIG.32
Robert F. Reynolds, *Robert Wood's Railing,
Architectural & Ornamental Iron Works*
(Philadelphia: Wagner & McGuigan, ca.
1851). Double-tinted lithograph. 53 × 68
cm (21 × 27 in.). POS 655, LCP, P. 2253.

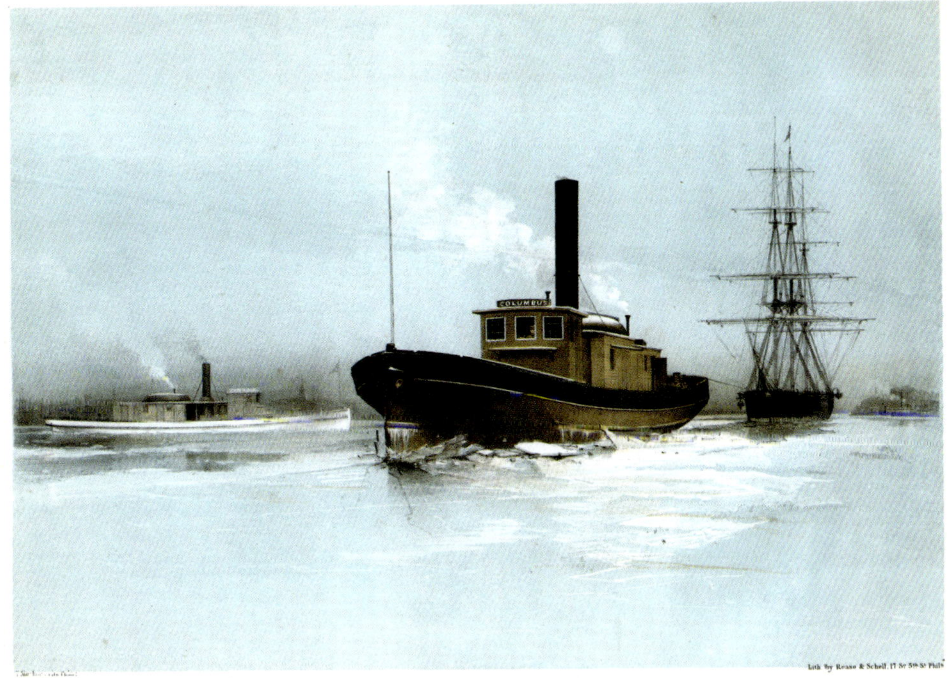

taken. In general, the book illustrations printed by the three lithographers referred to above were very different stylistically and technically from their city views, which adopted one of two approaches.

The most common approach was a further development of tinted lithography in which several color printings, rather than just one or two, were added to a foundation drawing. This was a more or less inevitable technical development given the strong local tradition in tinted lithography. In some cases artists and printers made tentative attempts to produce additional hues by overprinting (such as blue over yellow to produce green); but by and large further printings were added without much thought having been given to such matters. In all such prints the foundation drawing would have made some sense if it had been printed without the addition of color. An example of this approach is the view of the Eagle Hotel (POS 196), which Sinclair printed around 1855 from the drawings of an unacknowledged artist, with blue, green, light-brown, and stone colors added to a foundation crayon drawing. Another is the large membership certificate James Queen drew with a medley of images for the Citizens Volunteer Hospital (see fig. 53), which was "printed in colors by P. S. Duval & Son" in 1861 using ochre, stone, vermilion, green, and blue over a foundation crayon

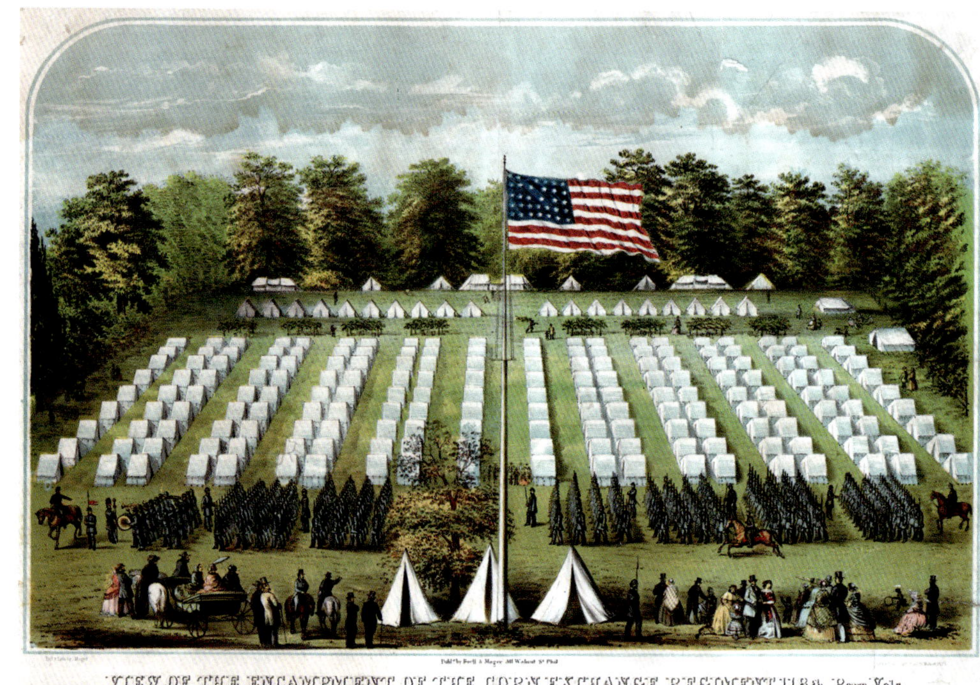

drawing. Some prints of this kind go a little further in making use of overprinting to produce additional hues, as does John L. Magee's *View of the Encampment of the Corn Exchange Regiment 118th Penn. Vols.,* which was printed by William Boell in 1862 with four colors added to a black foundation drawing (fig. 34). In this case, yellow was used in combination with blue over large areas of the image to produce the green of the grass and trees, and crimson lake was combined with yellow to produce touches of orange on a few figures in the foreground.

The other approach, which began to make an impact in the 1850s, relied less, if at all, on a foundation drawing. It is best exemplified by William Dreser's large chromo-lithograph for the perfumers H. P. & W. C. Taylor of the early 1850s (fig. 35), which carries the imprint "Printed in colors by T. Sinclair." The print features a docked ship on the Delaware Riverfront in a central panel, which is surrounded by an architectural border that includes garlands of flowers, a view of Taylor's factory, and medals awarded to the company. Dreser, who had worked regularly for Sinclair for some years, did the original drawing and was also responsible for the work on stone, which involved at least ten color stones, all drawn in ink. The print has no obvious foundation drawing, and Dreser must have followed the chromolithographic practice of the day, which meant

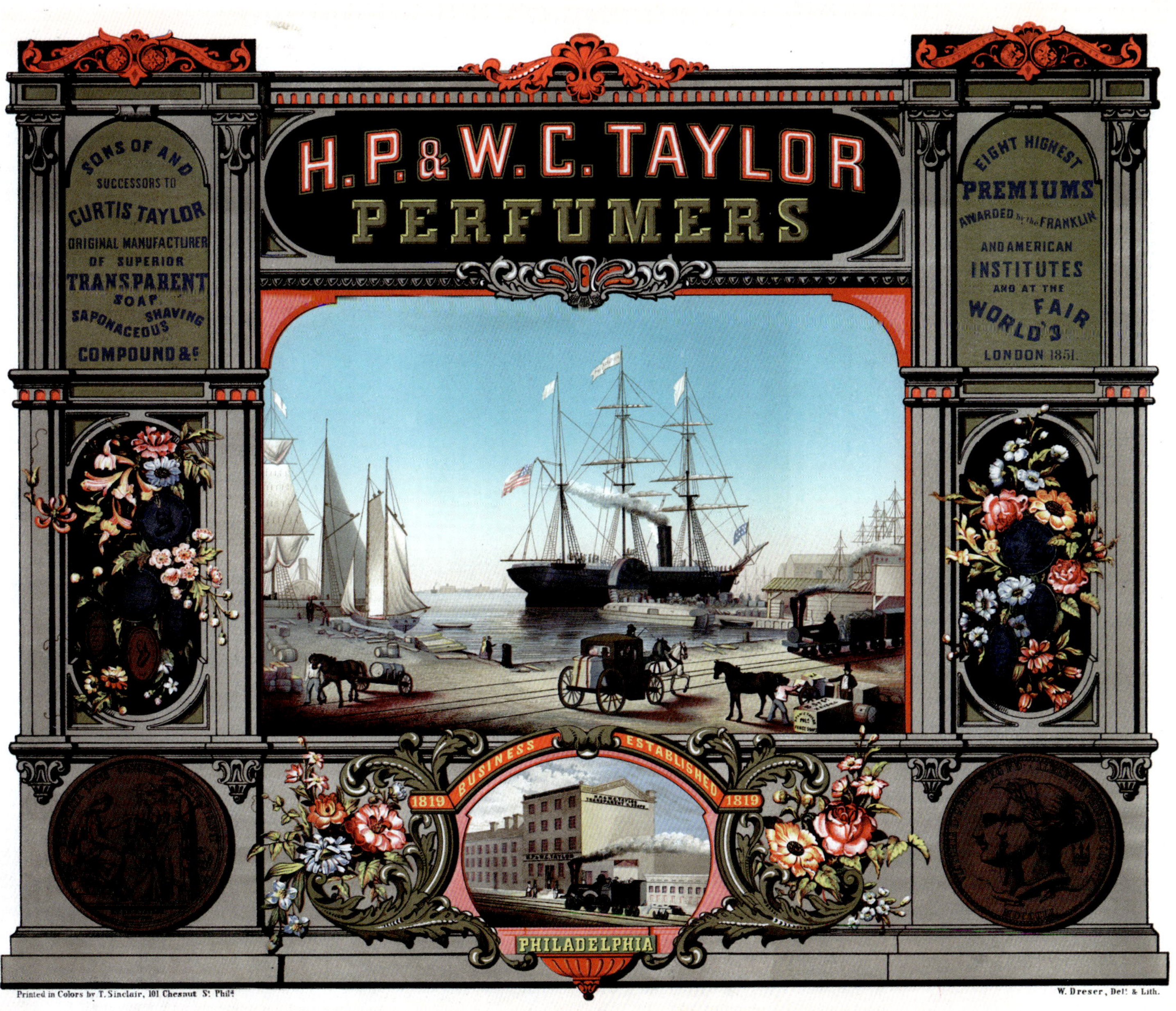

William Dreser, *H. P. & W. C. Taylor, Perfumers* (Philadelphia: T. Sinclair, ca. 1851). Ink-drawn chromolithograph in at least ten colors. 45 × 59 cm (17 ¾ × 23 ½ in.). POS 338, LCP, P.2074.

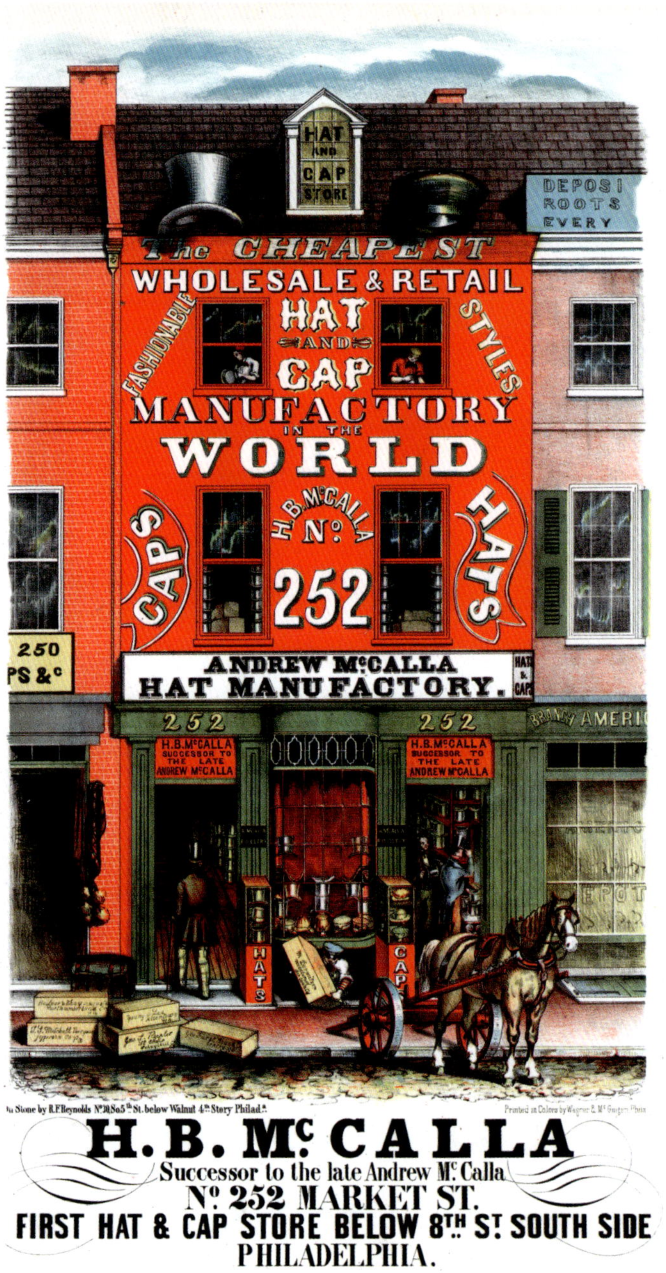

making a key-line drawing that identified the color values of the original so that appropriate parts of the drawing could be allocated to each of the ten or so color stones.

The variety of technical approaches to chromolithography in Philadelphia in the middle of the century is evident from several disparate examples. A sheet music cover for *The Oakland Schottisch* takes tinted lithography in an unusual direction. It was printed by P. S. Duval & Co. in 1852 and includes at its head a pictorial vignette of the Oakland Female Institute together with a railroad scene.[30] Technically, the image can be classed as a tinted lithograph, as it includes an underlying background tint and a black crayon-drawn stone, but in addition—and most unusually—two crayon-drawn stones have been added in purple and emerald green.

Even more remarkable is a view of H. B. McCalla's hat and cap store, by R. F. Reynolds, which was "Printed in colors by Wagner & McGuigan, Phila," ca. 1852 (fig. 36). Whether intentional or not, the print has all the appearance of having been produced as an experiment in the use of Godefroy Engelmann's method of printing in four colors (blue, red, yellow, and black), which he patented in 1837 and called *chromolithographie*.[31] Though Reynolds's print has a black working that defines its image, it would not have stood on its own by any stretch of the imagination. What makes it remarkable is its use of the three primary colors. Whereas Engelmann blended his colors and rarely used them as solids in his *Album chromolithographique* (1837)[32]—the publication through which he demonstrated and promoted his process—Reynolds introduced solid areas for all of them, including red, which he used with great bravura for the façade of the building. In addition, he combined yellow and blue in solid forms to make green, used crayon hatching to modify the tones of both red and blue, and produced extra color effects by adding black crayon work to the primary colors. It is tempting to suggest that Wagner & McGuigan had some knowledge of Engelmann's process and that they encouraged Reynolds to work in this way. The experiment does not seem to have been repeated or taken further in Philadelphia views, though the artist and printer returned to a similar use of bold areas of solid color a few years later with the print *Jones & Co. . . . One Price Clothing Store* (see fig. 99). Here red, blue, and a deep green were added to a rather coarse black impression, the major impact stemming from the solid green of the store's façade.

A decade later James Queen drew and P. S. Duval & Son printed a remarkable small advertising trade card in seven colors (fig. 37). Unlike most of the examples discussed above, all the work on stone was done in ink, including a light tan foundation image that must have been used to position the color drawings on their stones. The print also makes good use of overprinting to create additional effects of hue and tone. It is lettered at its foot "Independence Square Recruiting Camps," but ambitiously reversed out from several stones in an area of dark foliage at the top of the image are the advertising lines "Childrens Central Clothing Emporium / M. Shoemaker / No. 2 North Eighth Street / Philadelphia." This lettering forms an integral part of the image, which confirms that it was intended as a trade card, or may have been substantially modified to become one. This must make it one of the very earliest chromolithographed advertising trade cards to have been produced in the United States.

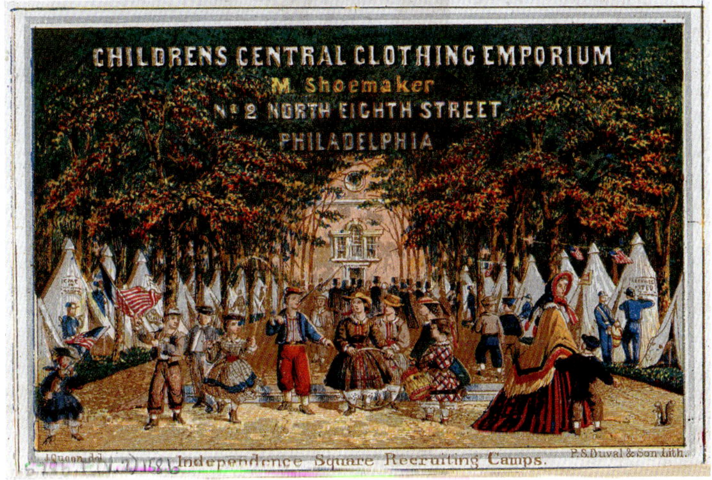

FIG. 36 (OPPOSITE)
Robert F. Reynolds, *H. B. McCalla, Successor to the Late Andrew McCalla, No. 252 Market St. First Hat & Cap Store Below 8th St. South Side, Philadelphia* (Philadelphia: Wagner & McGuigan, ca. 1852). Chromolithograph printed in four colors. 53 × 34 cm (21 × 13 3/8 in.). POS 337, LCP, P.2076.

FIG. 37 (ABOVE)
James F. Queen, *Independence Square Recruiting Camps* (Philadelphia: P. S. Duval & Son, 1862). Chromolithograph printed from ink-drawn stones in seven colors. 9 × 12 cm (3 1/4 × 4 3/4 in.). POS 380, LCP, (2) 5786.F.138b.

ENGRAVING ON STONE

What was generically called engraving on stone was not widely used in the first half century of lithography in Philadelphia, but it had some practitioners. The process is impossible to describe in a few words, since it covers a spectrum of methods from pure planographic printing to ones that depended on the production of hollow marks of different depths, as in intaglio printing.[33] The stone was inked differently according to where the work on stone lay within this spectrum, the main common factor being that it was damped before inking. This gave it an edge over etching and engraving on copper, since the dampened parts of the stone rejected the ink, which meant that one very time-consuming stage in intaglio printing (wiping the plate clean) could be avoided.

Engraving on stone was practiced from the outset of lithography and primarily where great precision was required. It was only rarely used by artists and would find little place in a discussion of early Philadelphia lithography were it not for the work of Augustus Kollner, who came from Germany with a background in intaglio engraving, and M. H. Traubel, who issued a trade advertisement with specimens of machine-engraved borders and patterns, one of them using the process of anaglyptography (commonly known as medal engraving) to simulate three-dimensional decoration. Engraving on stone is normally found on small-scale work, but a large lithograph of the Masonic Hall, which was produced by D. Chillas in 1853 after an intaglio engraving of 1813, had its sky engraved on stone somewhat coarsely with a ruling machine (POS 460).

WORDS AND LETTERFORMS

Lettering played a significant role in views of Philadelphia, and particularly in what might be described as the advertising views of shop fronts drawn by William H. Rease. Though images of the kind he produced may not have been exceptional in the United States, they do not seem to have survived in quantity elsewhere and are not known in Europe. As so often has been the case with ephemeral printed matter, we owe the survival of many of these Philadelphia prints to a contemporary collector, in this case Charles Augustus Poulson (1709–1866).[34] Their purpose and place of display are not at all clear, but many of them feature words and letterforms very strongly and were clearly meant to promote the particular store while remaining essentially pictorial views.

The most distinctive of these prints are the ones that show a shop front parallel to the picture plane. There is no reason whatsoever to doubt the general accuracy of such depictions,[35] but in many cases the wording has been given the strongest possible contrast, such as appearing white against a solid black ground. Judged by contemporary artistic canons, such contrasts would have been regarded as unusual, if not unacceptable. The shop fronts of the day in Philadelphia must have led to the kind of "street reading" discussed by D. M. Henkin in relation to nineteenth-century New York,[36] but when recorded on paper, the signs on them become particularly dominant and seem to echo the punch lines of typographic broadsides of the period. Whether the particular letterforms of the prints accurately follow the styles of those on the original buildings or not, they include examples of all the major display letterforms of the period that were used on broadsides of the day (fat-face, shaded, Egyptian, black-letter, gothic or sans serif).[37] And in nearly every case the artist has made sure that essential words are kept in their entirety, rather than cropped for pictorial reasons. Not every shop front drawn by Rease and others is quite as word oriented as the one depicted in *Charles Gilbert's Stove Manufactory* (fig. 38), but lettering was certainly one of the most characteristic features of these illustrated shop-front prints, and more generally of Philadelphia views.

Displayed lettering also appears at the foot of many Philadelphia views in the form of titles, a custom that goes back to the early 1830s, when a few Philadelphia lithographs

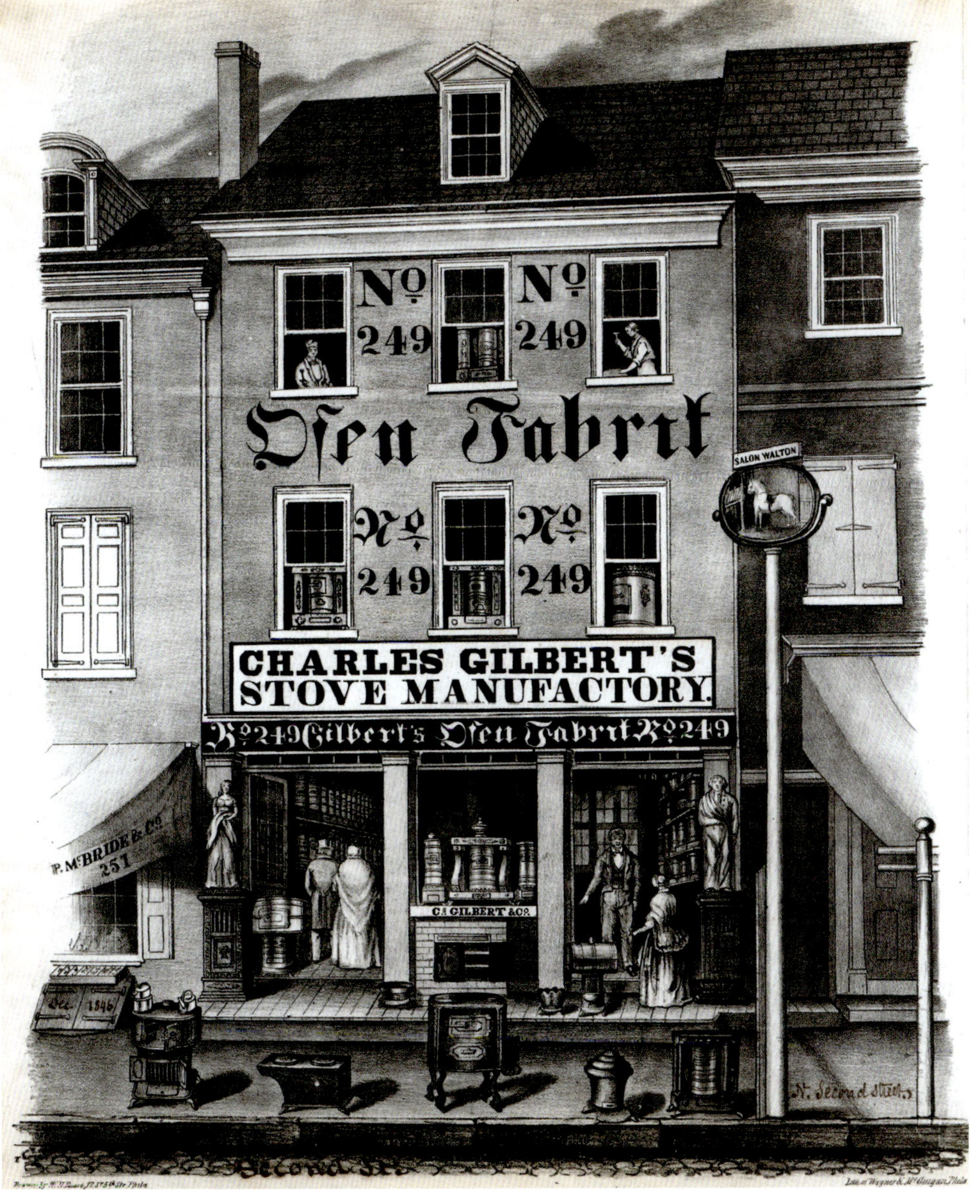

FIG. 38

William H. Rease, *Charles Gilbert's Stove Manufactory, 249 North Second Street, Philadelphia* (Philadelphia: Wagner & McGuigan, ca. 1846). Combined crayon-and-ink-work lithograph. 39 × 31 cm (15 ¼ × 12 ¼ in.). POS 105, LCP, P.2021.

were overprinted with letterpress titles, set rather prominently in shaded characters (POS 15.2, POS 574). This practice continued into the middle of the century (POS 499), and at least one example has displayed wording transferred to stone from type (POS 626). But in this later period the lettering beneath the prints was normally done by hand and fairly prominently on the stone, presumably by a professional letterer.

All this begs the question whether the lettering that appears as part of the artist's rendering of a shop front was generally executed by the person who provided the lettering beneath the print. The answer is probably that practices varied. But both categories of lettering served precisely the same overall advertising purpose, and sometimes we can be reasonably sure on stylistic grounds that the same person was responsible for both. Stylistic evidence is all we have to go by, but the forms of letters and their spacing along the line often appear highly personal and occasionally can be credited to particular, though usually anonymous, workers.

Traditionally in Europe, the role of the lithographic letterer has been distinct from that of the pictorial artist; writers and letterers would normally have worked in-house, whereas artists were generally self-employed and often worked away from the printer. Unfortunately, little is yet known about William Rease and his training, but his prints survive in sufficient quantity for some tentative conclusions to be drawn about the lettering on them.

In his lithograph of the manufactory of Hart, Montgomery & Co., which was printed by F. Kuhl around 1852 (fig. 39), it seems likely that the same person was responsible for both the wording in the picture and the wording beneath it. If we allow for the need to compress the lettering on the building, the similarity is most obvious when we compare the word "Manufactory" on the building with the same word on the first line of the title. The capital letters *C* and *R* show precisely the same features in the two locations, and the letters *A* and *M* in both have decidedly heavy serifs. Similarly, Rease's 1847 drawing of *Robert Wood's Steam Iron Railing Works* includes a highly distinctive capital *G* in the word "railing," both on the building and beneath it (fig. 40). Comparable similarities can be seen in R. F. Reynolds's *Robert Wood's Railing, Architectural & Ornamental Iron Works,* which was printed around 1851 by Wagner & McGuigan (fig. 32). Here the letterforms are consistently similar in the two different sets of wording, and the unusual ampersands in particular must surely be the product of the same craftsman. It is possible that both Rease and Reynolds were accomplished letterers. However, this hypothesis is undermined by Rease's lithograph *Garden & Brown, Silk & Fur Hat Manufactory,* which was printed in 1847 by Wagner & McGuigan (fig. 41). Here the lettering on the façade of the building is shown with all its thick and thin strokes in the right (i.e., conventional) places, whereas the display units for hats in the foreground have letters with thicks and thins the wrong way round. This is so in all four instances of the letter *A,* which on the façade of the building is shown correctly formed. This suggests that Rease was not familiar with the process of lettering backward on the stone, and therefore makes it rather unlikely that he would have been responsible for the much more accomplished lettering depicted on the building. Unless documentary evidence is forthcoming, we cannot be certain of who did what, but it seems likely that one or more specialists of the kind normally responsible for lettering the titles beneath prints would also have lettered the signs that appear on the buildings in Rease's prints, and also perhaps those of others. Rease seems to have produced so many of these advertising views that he may even have had his own assistant who put in the lettering for him as and when the occasion arose.[38]

STONES AND PRESSES

Limestone from the Solnhofen region of Bavaria continued to be the major printing surface used for lithography throughout the nineteenth century, and invoices survive that show stone being transported from Solnhofen to Philadelphia via Hamburg in the 1890s.[39] Metal plates, though used for inferior work from time to time in this period, are unlikely to have been used for many, if any, of the crayon-drawn views of Philadelphia discussed here.[40] What changed as far as the printing substrate goes was not the material but the sizes and categories of stones available. When the Philadelphia firm of Kennedy & Lucas went into liquidation in 1834, its stones ranged in size from 8 × 10 inches to 23 × 34 inches[41] (the latter being among the largest stones available commercially at the time). By the late nineteenth century stones were being sold in sizes up to 42 × 62 inches in various shades (yellow and gray), single and double sided, and in several qualities (the best often being referred to as "American quality").[42]

Every effort was made to find stone in North America so as to reduce transport costs, but despite discovering several promising locations and even exploiting some quarries commercially, particularly in Kentucky, Bavarian limestone remained virtually unchallenged.[43] This was so even after a variety of stone thought suitable for lithography was displayed at the Philadelphia Centennial Exhibition[44] and despite the fact that taxes had been imposed on imported stone, as they had been on many other materials. In April 1867, for example, a shipment of eight crates of lithographic stone to James McGuigan of Philadelphia incurred duty at the rate of 20 percent.[45] Stones were sold by the pound and bought by printers through local agents. They represented a major capital expense, and printers retained ownership over them so that they could keep control of images on them and their printing.

Lithography required presses that were different from those used in relief and intaglio printing, the amount of pressure needed being greater than that for relief printing but less than that for intaglio work.[46] The solution adopted for lithography was to apply pressure progressively across the surface of the stone, not normally with a cylinder, which tended to break stones, but with a scraper. Senefelder came up with the idea of using a scraper when he designed his first successful press, the pole press,

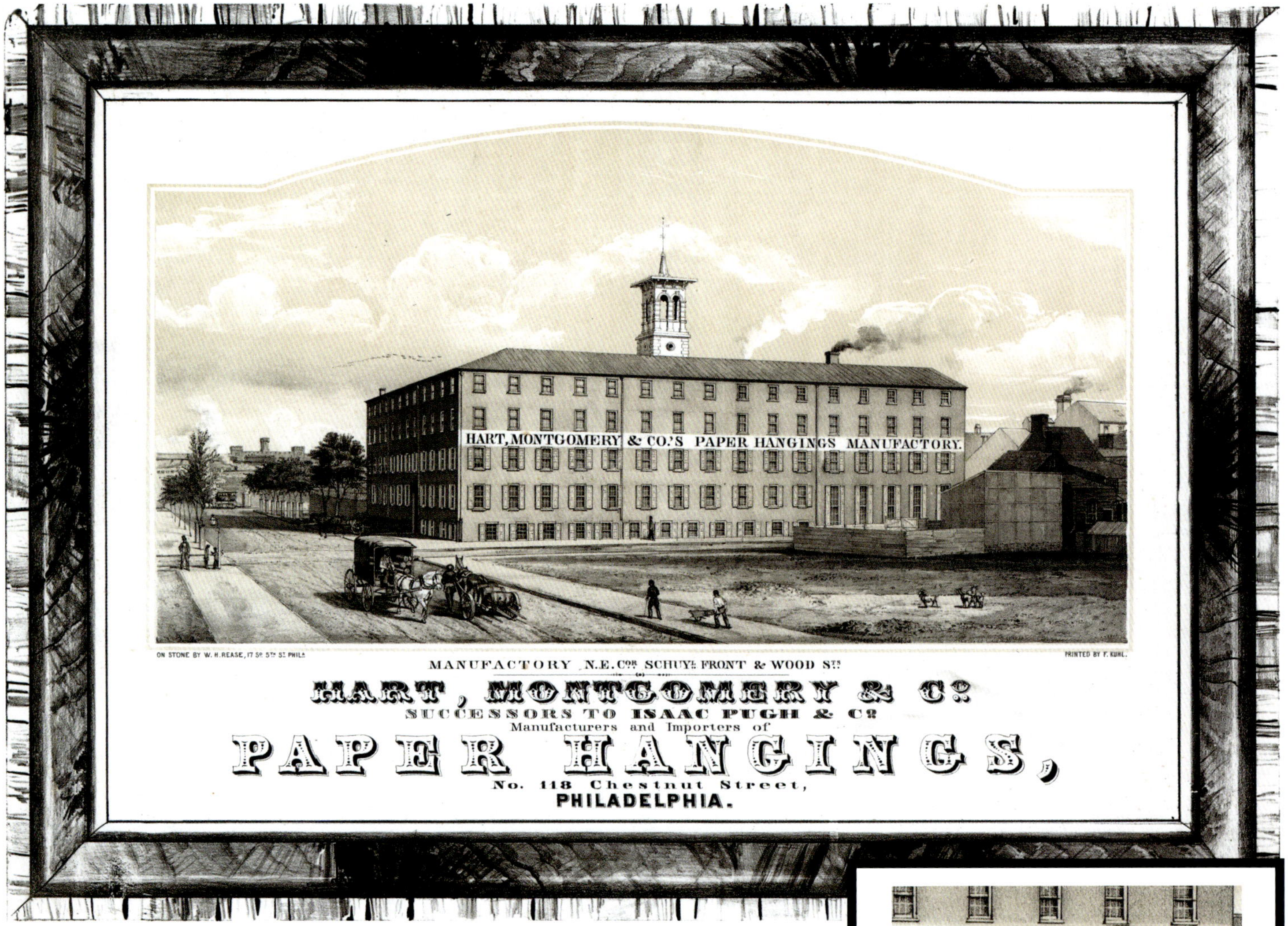

FIG. 39

William H. Rease, *Hart, Montgomery & Co. Successors to Isaac Pugh & Co. Manufacturers and Importers of Paper Hangings* (Philadelphia: F. Kuhl, ca. 1852). Single-tint lithograph. 49 × 67 cm (19 ¼ × 26 ¼ in.). POS 344, LCP, P.2072.

FIG. 40 (OPPOSITE)

William H. Rease, *Robert Wood's Steam Iron Railing Works* (Philadelphia, ca. 1847). Combined crayon-and-ink-work lithograph. 60 × 45 cm (23 ¾ × 18 in.). POS 656, LCP, P.2254.

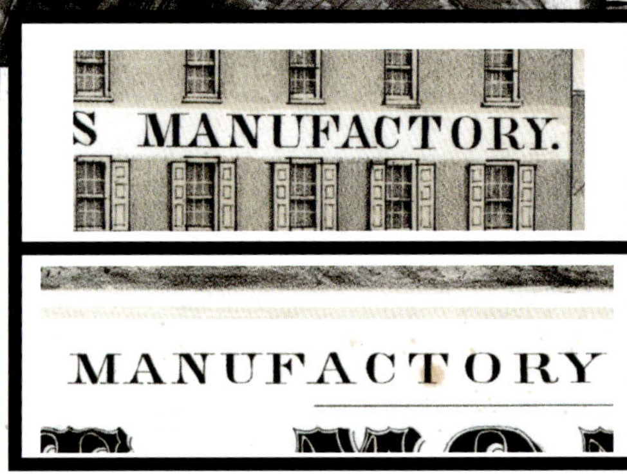

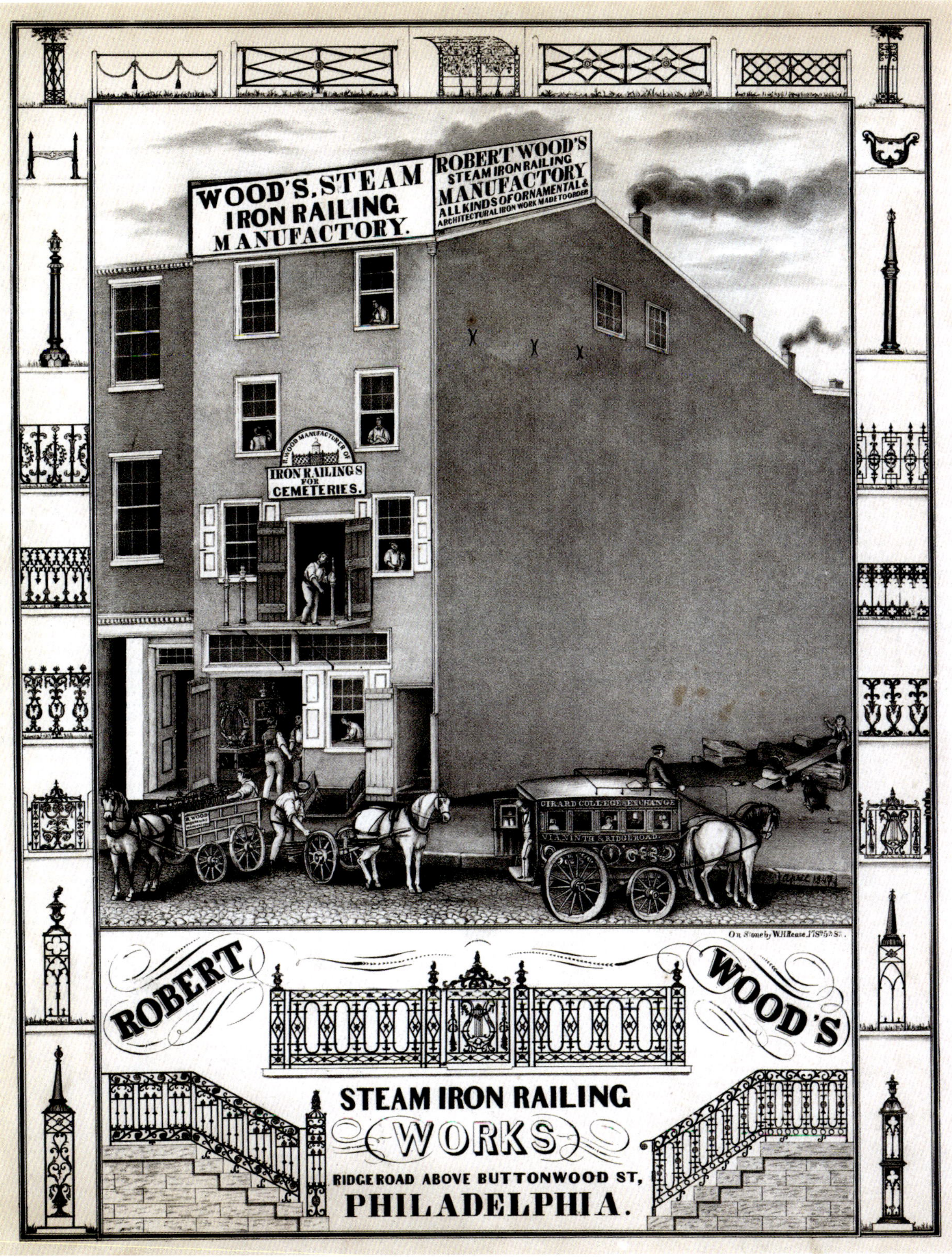

WOOD'S, STEAM IRON RAILING MANUFACTORY.
ROBERT WOOD'S STEAM IRON RAILING MANUFACTORY ALL KINDS OF ORNAMENTAL & ARCHITECTURAL IRON WORK MADE TO ORDER
IRON RAILINGS FOR CEMETERIES.
GIRARD COLLEGE EXCHANGE
VIA NINTH & RIDGE ROAD.
On Stone by W.H.Rease. 17S & 5th St.
ROBERT WOOD'S
STEAM IRON RAILING
WORKS
RIDGE ROAD ABOVE BUTTONWOOD ST,
PHILADELPHIA.

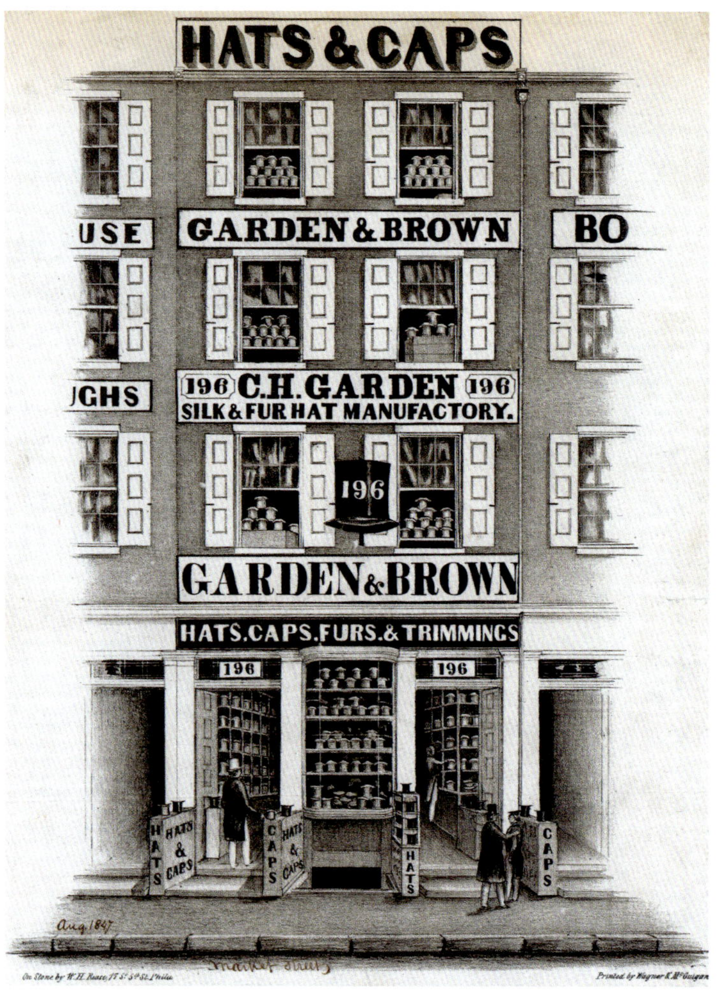

William H. Rease, [*Garden & Brown, Silk & Fur Hat Manufactory, 196 Market Street, Philadelphia*] (Philadelphia: Printed by Wagner & McGuigan, 1847). Combined crayon-and-ink-work lithograph. 29 × 21 cm (11 ½ × 8 ¼ in.). POS 291, LCP, P.2050.

which required the printer to pull the scraper under pressure across the surface of a stationary stone. But the kind of press that gained ground more or less everywhere worked on the opposite principle and incorporated a fixed scraper and a mechanism for moving the bed of the press under pressure beneath it. In essence its design goes back to 1805 and can be attributed to Hermann Mitterer of Munich; by the time a lithographic trade had been established in Philadelphia, the basic structure of the lithographic handpress had been settled along such lines. Numerous "improvements" continued to be proposed, but no major changes were made to the lithographic handpress after around 1830. Despite the best efforts of printers and engineers, the output of the most efficient presses of this kind was never to exceed 120 impressions an hour, even for the simplest ink work, and complicated crayon drawings were printed at only a fraction of this speed.[47]

Traditionally the scraper of the lithographic handpress was made of boxwood and covered with leather. It was held in a beam that either was fixed or could be made to pivot upward or swing sideways. Various kinds of pedals, or levers attached to eccentric members, were introduced to apply pressure to the stone by forcing it against the beam. There were also various methods of adjusting the amount of pressure that was applied to the stone, and of pulling the bed of the press, with the stone on it, beneath the scraper (the paper on the stone being protected by a metal or leather tympan). Numerous kinds of scraper presses were developed in the first half of the nineteenth century, but two broad categories can be identified, both of which had many variants. There was the wooden press, which had a stationary scraper beam (either pivoting or swinging) in which the bed was pulled along runners by means of strong webs, using a star wheel attached to an axle as a winch. There was also the iron press with a fixed scraper beam that used either a handle attached to a friction cylinder or a series of cogwheels to drive the bed along beneath the scraper. French lithographers, and to a lesser extent German ones, used wooden presses with a stationary, pivoting, or swinging scraper beam and a star wheel. British lithographers, on the other hand, used iron presses with a fixed scraper beam, which were normally driven by handles attached to a friction cylinder. Curiously, given the preponderance of lithographers from France and Germany working in the United States, it was the British model that appears to have been broadly followed in this country, though the use of cogwheels to move the bed of the press appears to have been an American innovation.

Information about handpresses used in the United States in the early days of lithography is extremely hard to come by. But probably the earliest representation of such a lithographic press appears under the heading "Lithographer" in Edward Hazen's *Panorama of Professions and Trades* (Philadelphia: Uriah Hunt, 1837). Though badly drawn, it depicts a pressman moving the bed of the press beneath a scraper beam by turning a handle attached to a cogwheel. Over the following decades several other illustrations of handpresses in use in the United States appear to show similar devices.[48]

With the exception of a couple of presses shown on an advertisement of the Philadelphia printers Wagner & McGuigan around 1856,[49] all lithographic handpresses illustrated in contemporary American publications that I have seen follow the British pattern and appear to have been made of iron.[50] The two presses of Wagner & McGuigan just referred to are shown in the foreground of a scene depicting a large bank of iron presses (see fig. 10). Each has a strong wooden base, which supports a fixed scraper beam made of iron, a lever to apply pressure, and a handle to drive the bed beneath the scraper. In several respects they resemble a press, likewise made of wood and iron, devised by Naumann of Frankfurt sometime before 1840, though this was specifically designed to be operated by two men and was supplied with a pressure lever and handle on either side.[51]

Once the design of the lithographic handpress had been resolved, attention turned to the application of steam power to lithography, spurred on by advances that had already been made in letterpress printing. As early as 1818 Senefelder had pointed to the need to mechanize lithographic printing,[52] and in the 1830s and 1840s, particularly in England and France, numerous patents were taken out for powered lithographic machines, a few of which were made to work, at least experimentally.[53] The problem of mechanizing the lithographic process was much greater than it was for letterpress printing, since dampening the stone introduced an additional stage in the operation. Eventually a few workable machines were manufactured and put to commercial use, beginning with one designed by the Austrian engineer Georg Sigl, which was patented in Austria and France in 1851.[54] It applied pressure by means of a cylinder and included devices for automatic dampening and inking. The progress of the lithographic industry toward mechanization in Europe is still not clear, but there is reliable evidence that Sigl's powered machines were used in both Vienna and Britain by 1854.[55]

In the United States, Philadelphia was at the forefront of moves to apply steam power to lithography. P. S. Duval refers to his own use of steam in 1850 but only, he writes, "so far as to save muscular labor,"[56] by which he must have meant that it was only the pulling of the stone through the press that was mechanized, a process that would have been relatively easy given that the beds of his presses seem to have been moved by means of cogwheels. Not to be outdone, Wagner & McGuigan went a step further, claiming that they were a "Steam lithographic printing establishment" on an advertisement of around 1851,[57] though judging by the machines they illustrated they may not have done much more than Duval. Handpresses are shown being driven by webs from a steam engine, one of them using the press's cogwheel for this purpose. This particular press suggests that Wagner & McGuigan may have made some small advance over Duval, as it has an impression cylinder clothed with a continuous belt of leather (or similar material), which also served as a simple feeding device. But at this stage neither Duval nor Wagner & McGuigan can be said to have printed from powered machines in the normally accepted sense of the term, since the dampening of the stone and the rolling up of the image on it would still have had to be done by hand.

By the mid-1860s four powered lithographic presses had been patented in the United States, two by W. H. Stübbe of Boston in 1859 and 1864,[58] and one each by Bernard Ackermann of New York in 1861[59] and E. Reynolds of Mannsfield, Connecticut, in 1864.[60] All these presses applied pressure by means of a scraper, as did a machine based on drawings brought over from Germany that was constructed and demonstrated in New York in 1859.

Most of the first powered presses in the United States came from overseas. Duval, referring to the late 1860s, wrote that the most common type of powered lithographic machine in the United States was constructed by Hughes & Kimber of London, who had bought the right to use the machine from Huguet in France and then made improvements to its design.[61] The first such machine was introduced to the United States in 1866, and, like most other true powered machines, it dampened and inked the stone automatically and applied pressure by means of a cylinder.

The trade in European powered machines was so significant by the late 1860s that the New York printers Major & Knapp (earlier Sarony, Major & Knapp) went as far as to claim—falsely as it happens—exclusive rights over all such imported machines.[62] A little later, R. M. Hoe of the firm of Robert Hoe & Co., having met the Paris press manufacturer Marinoni while on a European trip, managed to obtain the rights over a press for which he was granted a United States patent in 1869.[63] The machine, which Duval illustrated in 1871,[64] worked on principles very similar to those of many earlier ones. It applied pressure to the stone by means of a cylinder, and its dampening and inking were fully mechanized; it also incorporated elaborate feeding and delivery mechanisms. This and other Hoe/Marinoni machines were a great success in the United States and for a while cornered the market. Support for home-produced lithographic presses in the United States was sufficient for a French journal to report—no doubt with a trace of bias—that an Alauzet powered machine, which the French firm displayed at the Philadelphia Centennial Exhibition in 1876, was entirely ignored until the emperor of Brazil was seen to take an interest in it.[65]

How frequently powered machines would have been used for quality work is difficult to establish with certainty. Crayon drawings on grained stones were not to be printed effectively on powered machines for some time to come because of their limited rolling power as well as their inability to produce sufficient pressure. In addition, large stones would have presented problems in the early days of lithographic machine printing. When it is also borne in mind that powered lithographic machines (in contrast to the power-assisted presses of Duval and Wagner & McGuigan of the 1850s) would only have been economically run when editions were large, we have to conclude that they would not often have been used for the sorts of views discussed in this publication.

AFTERWORD

This chapter focuses on the methods used by lithographers to produce views of Philadelphia. It covers a period of forty years and traces the development of the lithographic process from prints drawn primarily in crayon, some of them intended for hand-coloring, to chromolithography. In between these two approaches, and to some degree running parallel to both, were various kinds of tinted lithographs, some of the most striking being double-tinted prints, the colors having been chosen to highlight bright-blue skies and the sun-drenched red-brick buildings of the city. Unusually, many of these lithographs put emphasis on the letterforms of the urban scene, picking them out in stark contrasts of white and black. Other methods used for putting images of Philadelphia on stone include pen-and-ink lithography and, occasionally, what was called engraving on stone; there is even one recorded example of the use of the litho-tint process for a genre scene.[66] But even this range of methods does not cover all the ways in which the process was used, and one of the principal methods of producing routine commercial work, the transfer process, is excluded from this account.[67] With these exceptions, however, the lithographed views of Philadelphia discussed here and elsewhere in this book allow us to appreciate the extraordinary range and capabilities of the process, which the United States came to adopt as its own in the course of the second half of the nineteenth century.

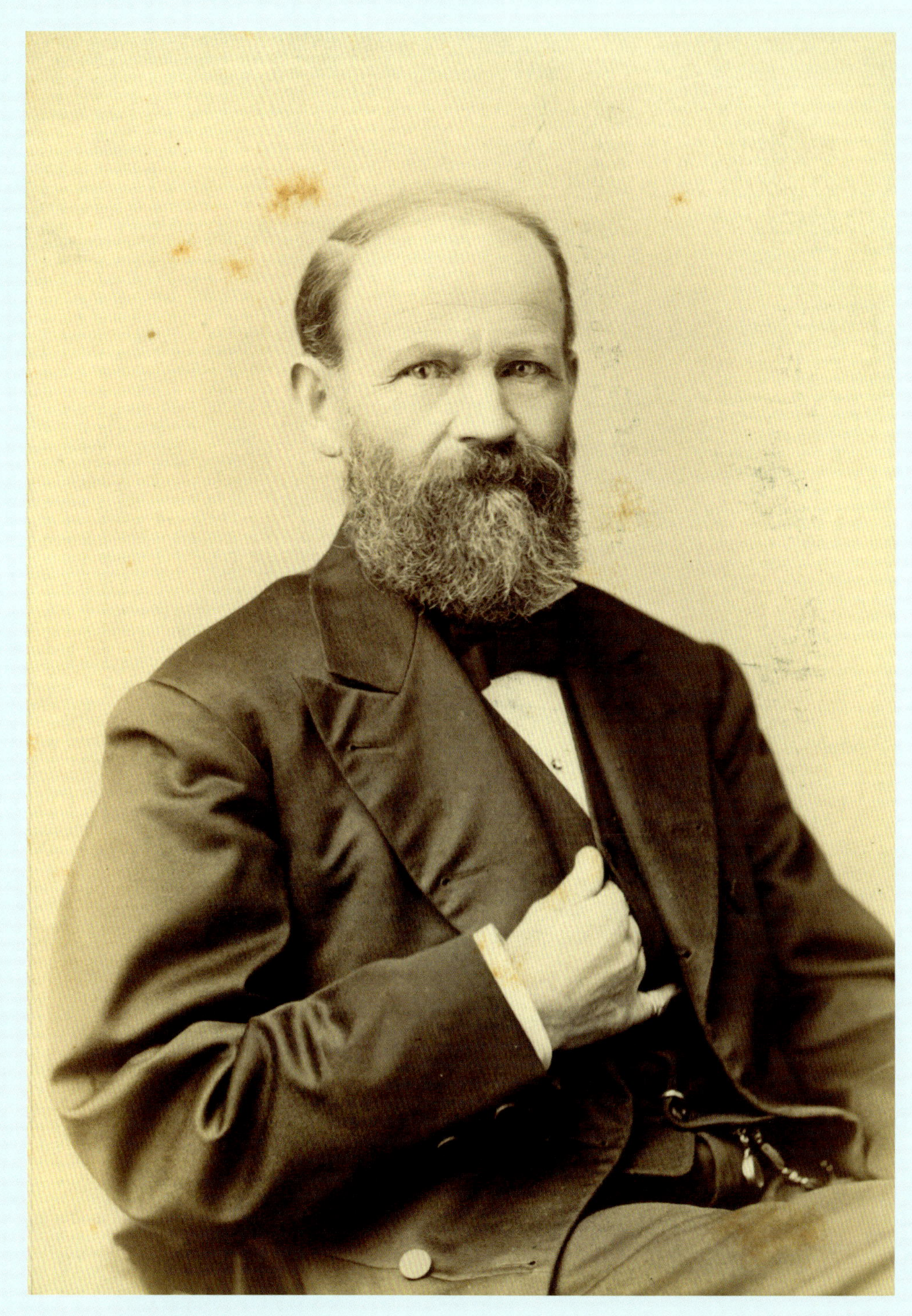

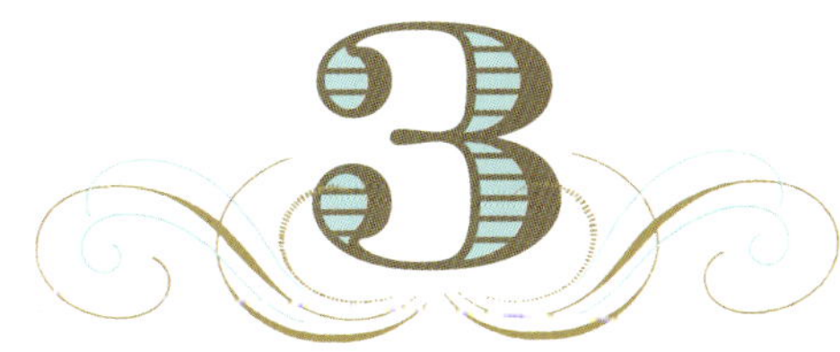

SARA W. DUKE

JAMES QUEEN

Chronicler of Philadelphia

In January 1856 the artist James Queen stood on the frozen ice of the Delaware River, sketching the frenzy about him. The river had frozen solid during one of the coldest winters on record. While the ice cutters labored hard, many of the citizens of Southwark, the Philadelphia neighborhood (near the Navy Yard) where Queen lived and worked, exploited the opportunity for winter recreation.[1] In the drawing and lithograph for *Scene on the Delaware River at Philada. During the Severe Winter of 1856* (figs. 42, 43),[2] Queen provided a lively scene of ice-skaters, a vendor, and a crowd around an amusement ride that included a sledge and men pushing a large turnstile, all taking place on the glittering surface before the ice-bound ships of the Navy Yard. The bustling scene that Queen composed was not a generic sentimental image of skaters on the ice; one can sense the crowded neighborhood of artisans, laborers, and merchants unleashed onto the boundless expanse of ice, still jostling for elbow room. A pulse of energy seems to move through the throng, anxious to escape the claustrophobic indoors, despite the severity of the cold. In his depiction of the vitality of city life Queen makes the "souvenir of the coldest winter on record" something truly memorable.

James Queen (1820/21–1886) was a professional artist and lithographer who began his career with an apprenticeship to George Lehman and P. S. Duval on November 24, 1835, around his fourteenth birthday. Queen produced lithographs for several other Philadelphia printers, including Thomas Sinclair and Wagner & McGuigan until shortly before his death, on January 18, 1886.[3] A prolific artist, his long

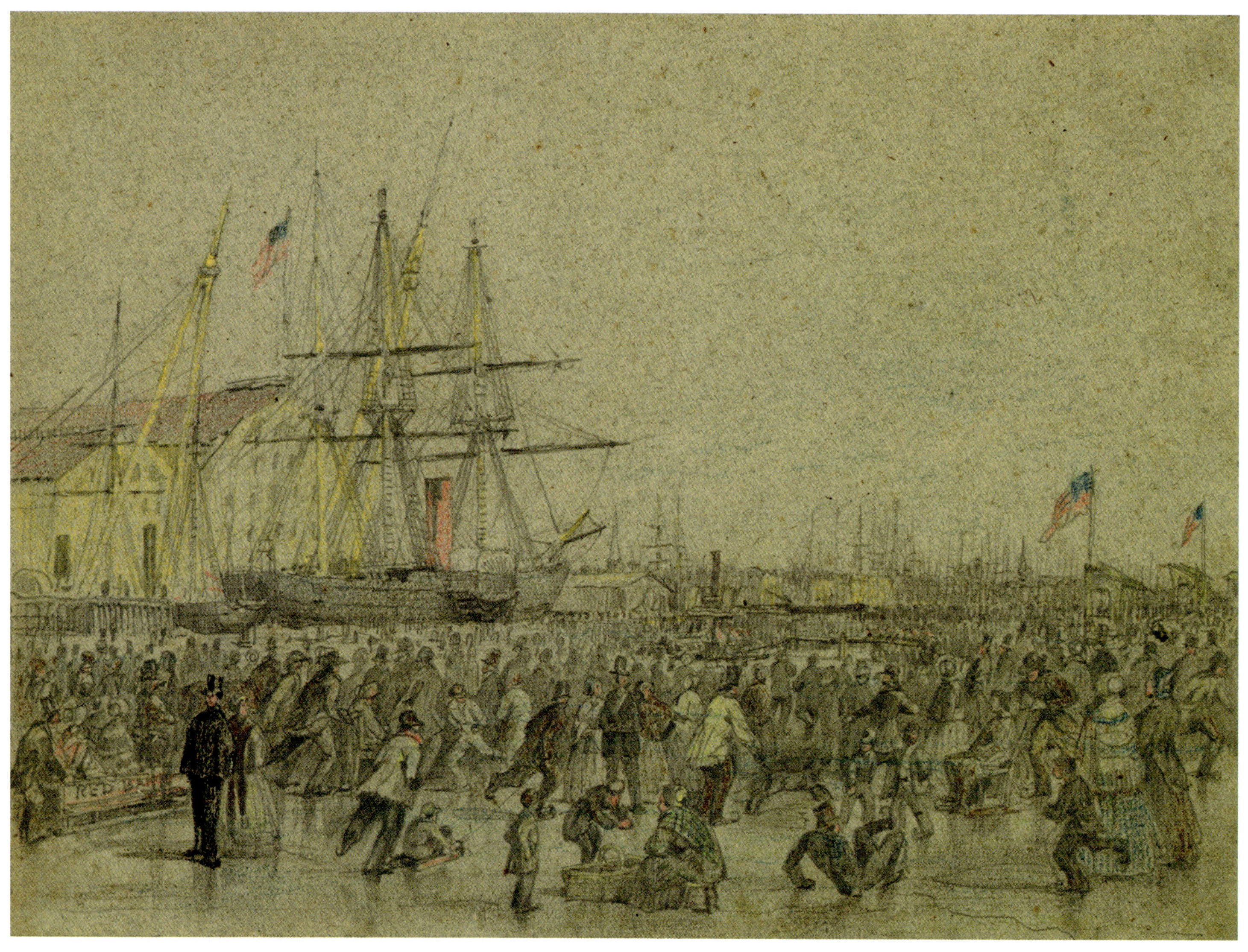

FIG.42
James F. Queen, [*Scene on the Delaware
River at Philada. During the Severe Winter
of 1856*]. Crayon and graphite drawing on
blue-gray paper. 25 × 33 cm (9 ¾ × 12 ¾
in.). Cochran 15, LC-DIG-ppmsca-19643.

career paralleled the development of the art of lithography in Philadelphia. During
the course of his life he produced a variety of work that included advertising, art reproductions, and documentation of events. He recorded the social life of Philadelphia,
the city's architectural and engineering achievements, and its businesses. He created
lithographs depicting disasters and natural beauty. He also made chromolithograph
reproductions of European paintings for the parlor walls of Philadelphia's middle class.

The Library of Congress has the largest collection of art by James Queen. An estimated 450 drawings, watercolors, and lithographs, acquired from several sources, are
available to researchers in the Prints and Photographs Division. There is sheet music

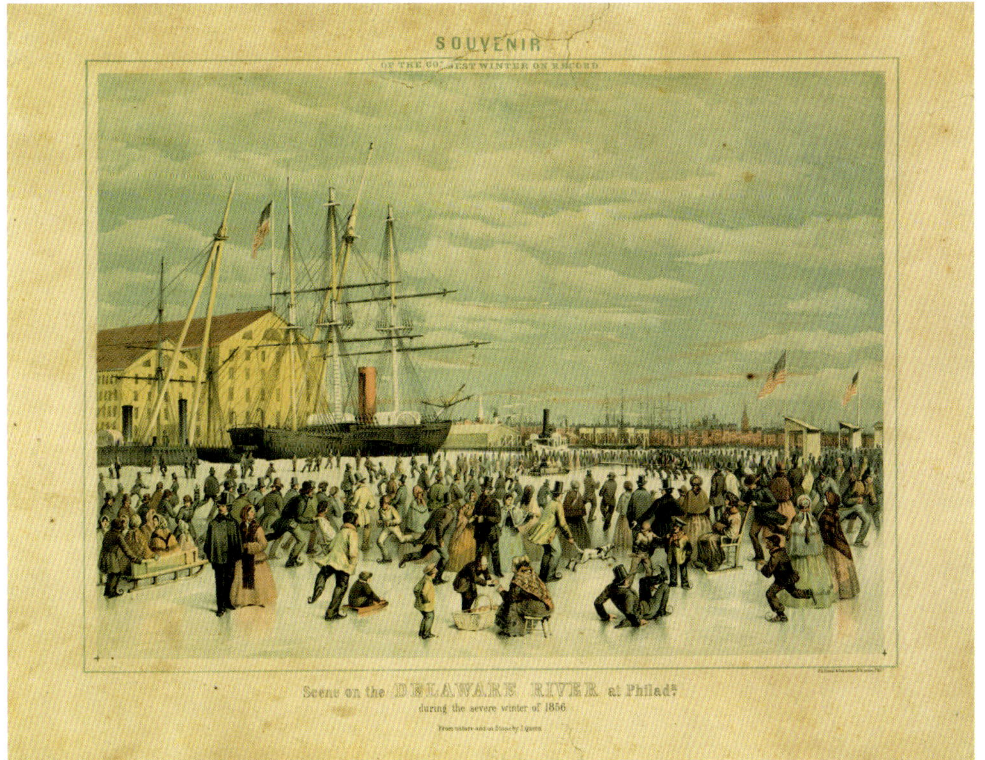

FIG. 43
James F. Queen, *Scene on the Delaware River at Philada. During the Severe Winter of 1856. Souvenir of the Coldest Winter on Record* (Philadelphia: P. S. Duval & Co., 1856). Lithograph, printed in colors with some watercolor. 33 × 43 cm (13 × 17 in.). Cochran 306 (POS 704), LC-DIG ppmsca-19644.

created early in Queen's career and deposited for copyright in 1840. Chromolithographs published by Duval & Hunter arrived through copyright deposit in 1875 and represent Queen's later prints.[4] The core body of images, dating from 1839 through the 1860s, with the majority from the mid-1850s through the mid-1860s, is in the Marian S. Carson Collection.[5] Philadelphia collector Marian Carson obtained the Queen pictures from his family and later recalled, "I realized it was a whole collection and ought to be kept together." She ordered a stamp and marked each piece to denote that it came from the James Queen archive.[6] In 1996 her collection came to the Library of Congress, through a combination purchase and donation.[7] The presence of original drawings and finished prints for the same images makes the Carson Collection a valuable research source for any study of nineteenth-century art and lithography and a critical resource for understanding James Queen.

Queen was born into a middle-class artisan family in the suburb of Southwark, next to the Delaware River (fig. 44). His father, William Queen, was a cordwainer, a shoemaker, as opposed to a cobbler, who repaired shoes. William may have lived at the edge of poverty during tough times, but all three of his sons learned to read and write and pursued middle-class occupations. His daughter Henrietta was literate as well.[8]

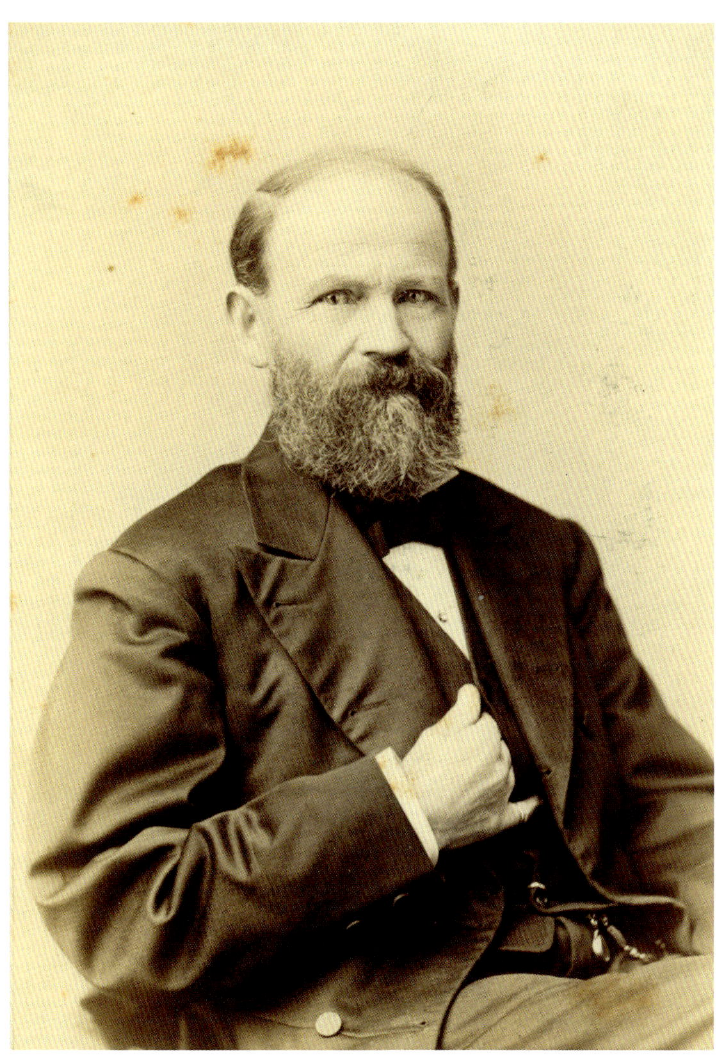

He arranged for his sons to be apprenticed to men engaged in publishing, whether text or artistic.[9] His sons all married in their early twenties, indicating that they earned sufficient income to live independently once they completed their training.[10] James's older brother, John, became a newspaper reporter while his younger brother, Francis, was initially apprenticed to a printer and eventually became a newspaper publisher who divided his time between Philadelphia and New York.[11]

Recent studies of the Southwark of Queen's childhood and young adulthood have focused on working-class employment and the neighborhood's tendency toward violence.[12] This focus neglects the reality that in the nineteenth century the middle class, whose hold on economic stability could be tenuous, occupied the same urban neighborhoods as the working class. As an educated artisan, Queen had more resources than many of the unskilled laborers in his neighborhood. By 1860 he owned his own home and personal property worth $400. In 1864 he paid federal income tax on his annual salary of $542 and his exceptional personal property.[13] He volunteered as a firefighter in Southwark, worshipped in a Southwark church, and was employed by a Southwark business. A middle-class man, he continued to reside in Southwark and to take pleasure in sketching the denizens of the community, as documented in the Carson Collection.

Both James Queen and his younger brother, Francis, belonged to the Weccacoe Engine Company, a Protestant fire company, whose members frequently clashed with the Catholic members of the Weccacoe Hose Company in the 1840s.[14] Queen created at least sixteen documented images of firefighters and firefighting equipment. His work parallels that of John Rubens Smith, Currier & Ives, and other artists and printmakers who glorified the work of firefighters.[15] In his watercolors of firefighting scenes, Queen romanticizes the life of the young, strong firefighters who dashed from their firehouses to put out blazes in the neighborhood. In a nighttime scene of the Weccacoe Engine Company, Queen depicts his fellow firefighters pulling an engine from the house toward the cobbled streets of Southwark while others run toward the firehouse, pulling on boots and retrieving clothing from interior lockers (fig. 45). The palette is muted, and Queen uses light from unseen lamps inside the firehouse to

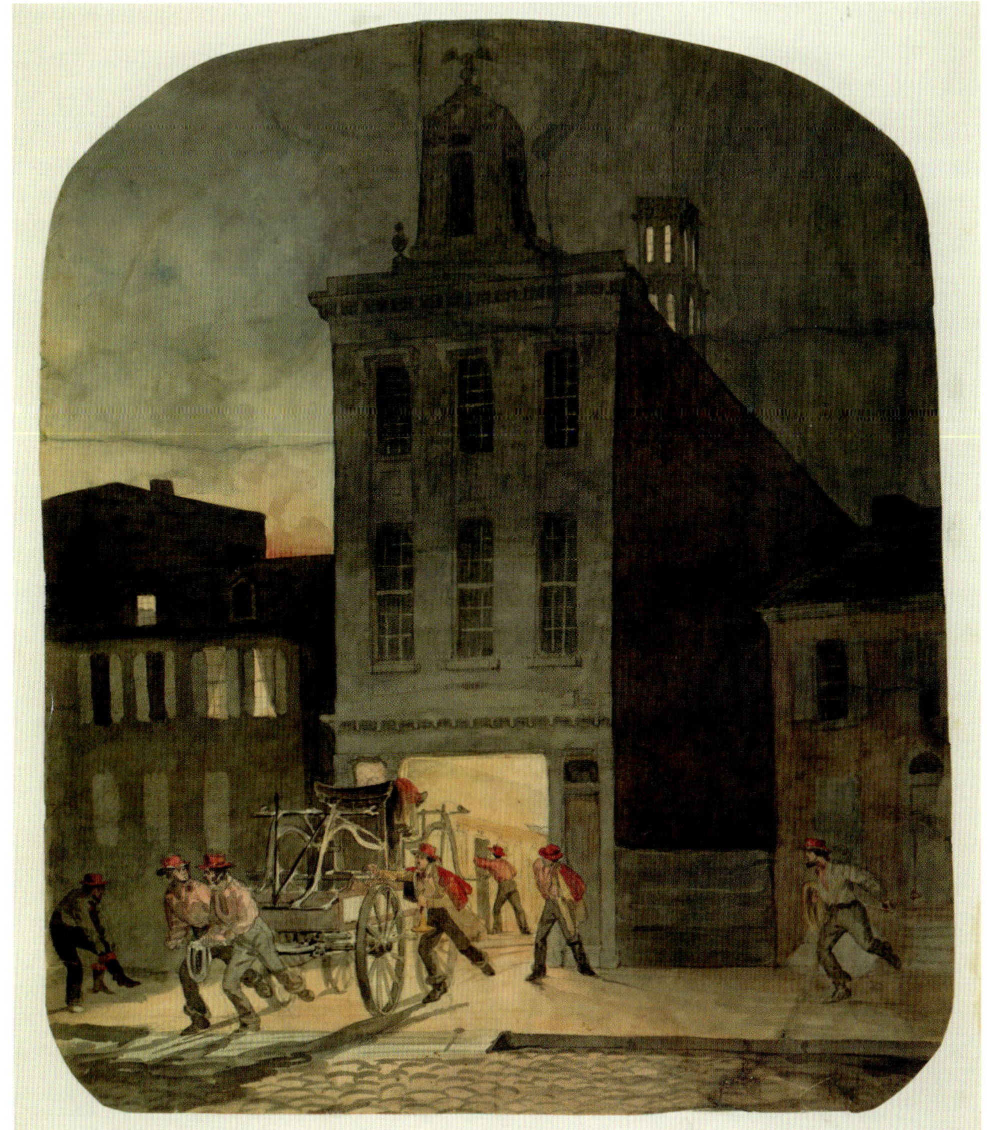

James F. Queen, [*Firehouse Scene in Phila-delphia Showing Firemen from the Weccacoe Engine Company Pulling a Hand-Drawn Fire Engine as Other Firemen Scramble to Readiness*], ca. 1857. Watercolor over graphite underdrawing. 56 × 48 cm (22 × 18 ¾ in.). DRWG/US Queen (J. F.), no. 3 (C size), LC-DIG-ppmsca-19656, LC-USZC4-6029.

illuminate the firefighters as they head off into the night to extinguish the fire, whose orange glow and smoke fill the nighttime sky. Queen avoids depicting the internal tensions that contemporary newspaper accounts emphasized, but rather shows the company's collective energy summoned to respond to disaster within the neighbor-hood. He focuses on the brotherhood and the elevated role of the firefighter in the community in an image that is not intended to be documentary but yet provides historical evidence of the equipment firefighters used, the uniforms they wore, and the nature of their work.

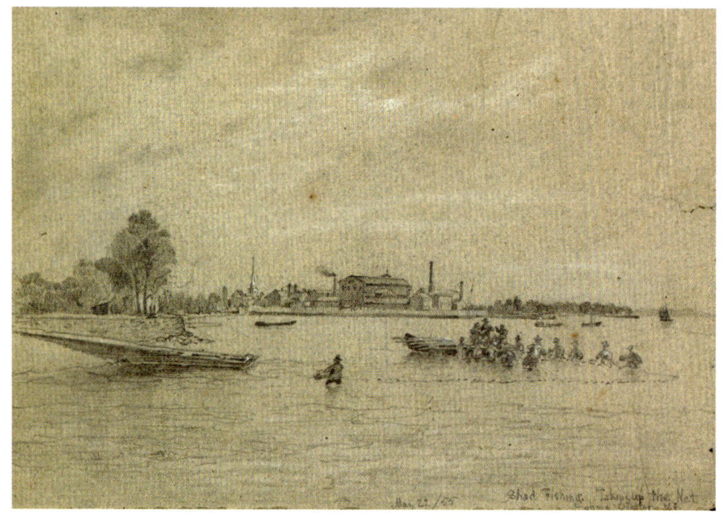

FIG. 46

James F. Queen, *Shad Fishing. Taking Up the Net Above Chester N.J.,* May 22, 1855. Drawing, graphite and black chalk heightened with white chalk on gray-blue paper. 23 × 33 cm (9 1/8 × 13 1/8 in.). Cochran 11, LC-DIG-ppmsca-19640. See fig. 31 for the lithograph after the drawing.

Queen's depiction of the community in which he lived was not limited to personal experiences. He captured life on both the Schuylkill and Delaware Rivers in all seasons, from ice-skating in winter's cold to shad fishing in the spring (fig. 46). In one delicately drawn scene of fishermen standing waist-high to haul their shad catch in the Delaware River south of Philadelphia, the top of the seine net is nearly indistinguishable from the surface of the river. Faint yet broad lines indicate the gentle ripple of the river, while strong lines delineate the bleaching mills, smokestacks, and church spires of Gloucester, New Jersey, at the water's edge on the opposite shore. White and black chalks indicate the pattern of clouds in the sky. Queen subtly depicts the contrast between man's interaction with nature, fishing at a time when shad ran thick in America's rivers, and the built environment and its smokestacks. The genre lithograph that resulted from this sketch, *Shad Fishing (Taking Up the Net.) On the Delaware, Opposite Philada.—Glo'ster Bleaching Mills in the Distance,* printed in 1855, exhibits the three-color background that Queen favored in many of his works, from dusky blue to a rose-tan horizon and a gray-green river (POS 691).[16] He created an image of water, men, factories, and sky peacefully coexisting.

Due to his proximity to the Delaware River, Queen appears to have used his leisure time to record life at the water's edge. The Navy Yard that had played a prominent role in his childhood[17] continued to provide a boundless source for his personal and professional artistic output. He sketched people enjoying walks, drew the rowboats on the river, and in one instance illustrated a disaster in his own neighborhood. Queen must have run to the Delaware, if he was not there already, when a wharf collapsed on the night of July 1, 1856 (fig. 47). There is no evidence that the drawing became a published lithograph, but clearly Queen felt a need to document the catastrophe. According to newspaper accounts, the Reed Street Wharf extended far into the river south of the Navy Yard and had become a favorite destination for the residents of Southwark on hot summer evenings. When a large section of the wharf collapsed into the river, the victims were struck by pilings. Most of the victims were women, children, and teenagers.[18] Queen used paper prepared with a lithographically tinted background fading from dark blue at the top to evoke nightfall, when the event occurred, to pale blue and then brown. He placed the Navy Yard at the horizon of the drawing; the masts of the ships and the large buildings are highlighted by the pale blue tint behind them. The collapsing wharf, on the other hand, is in the beige-brown-tinted area,

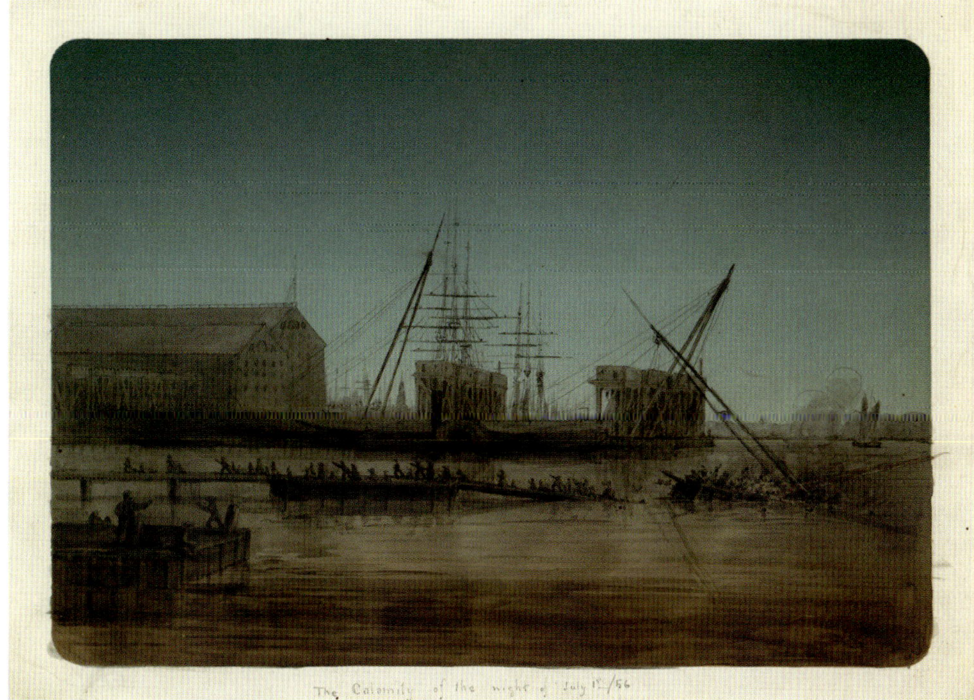

FIG. 47
James F. Queen, *The Calamity of the Night of July 1st / 56,* 1856. Drawing, graphite and ink wash on prepared lithographic paper fading from dark blue to brown. 25 × 32 cm (9 5/8 × 12 ½ in.). Cochran 107, LC-DIG-ppmsca-19639.

which serves to emphasize the terrifying chaos in the dusky night. The roughness of the sketch is a product of the immediacy of the event and the dynamic reaction of the artist to the disaster in his own neighborhood.

Queen's career intertwined with that of Peter Duval. While Queen created prints for other firms during the course of his life, Duval remained his most steady and consistent employer, accounting for about 90 percent of the lithographs in the Carson and other collections. Duval felt that Queen was one of the best lithographic artists in the country.[19] A notation from "Steve" to "Jim" on a lithograph in the Carson Collection indicates that not only Peter Duval but also his son Stephen had a personal relationship with Queen.[20] The short inscription reads, "Dear Jim, This is the best proof I have taken—you had better keep it, Steve," suggesting that the majority of Duval collaborations in the Carson Collection may have been proofs pulled and given to Queen for his personal portfolio. In 1861 Duval, in an advertising print, announced Queen as the "superintendent" of the drawing department of his firm.[21] Carl Cochran, in his master's thesis on Queen, argues that Queen sought for years to break his professional relationship with Peter Duval, but no source is cited for this statement, and it is not evident in the published work.[22]

Duval relied on Queen for a variety of custom prints, whether the lithographs ordered were plates to illustrate a book on Pennsylvania or a certificate for a county fair.

James F. Queen, *Mount Pisgah, Mauch Chunk,* 1855. Drawing, graphite and charcoal heightened with white on gray-blue paper. 25 × 33 cm (9 ¾ × 12 7/8 in.). Cochran 14, LC-DIG-ppmsca-19642.

James F. Queen after ambrotype by H. P. Osborn of Bethlehem, *Bird's Eye View of Mauch Chunk, from Mount Pisgah [Showing] [Le]high Gap in the Distance* (Philadelphia: P. S. Duval & Son, ca. 1860). Lithograph with tint stones. 16 × 26 cm (6 3/8 × 10 ¼ in.). Cochran 436, LC-DIG-ppsmca-19633.

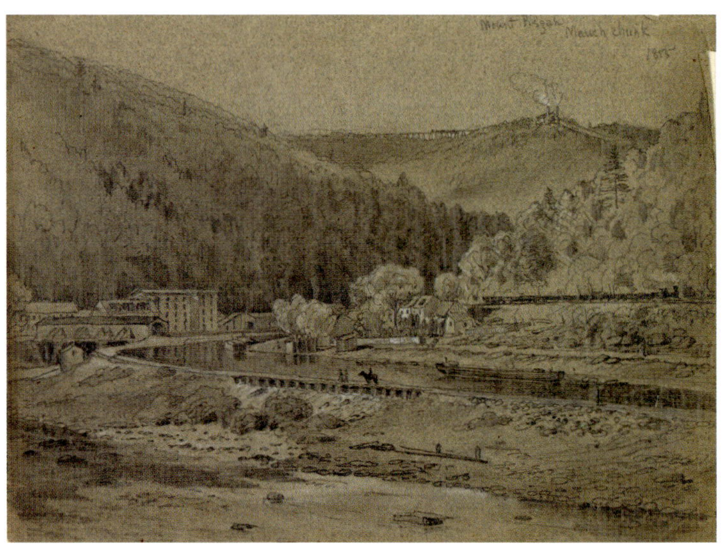

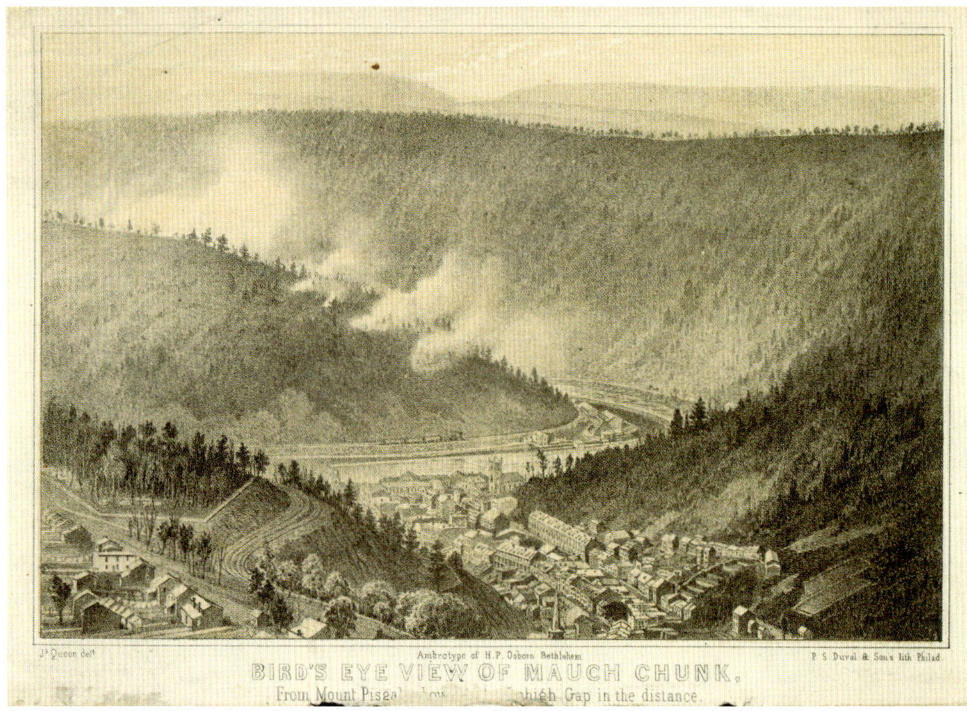

In some instances, Queen's sketches and the resulting lithograph remain together in the Carson Collection. For Mathew Henry's *History of the Lehigh Valley,* published in 1860, Queen made his images from photographs taken by H. P. Osborn of Bethlehem, as in the case of *Mount Pisgah, Mauch Chunk* (figs. 48, 49). He did not draw first on lithographic stone but rather with graphite on paper, occasionally

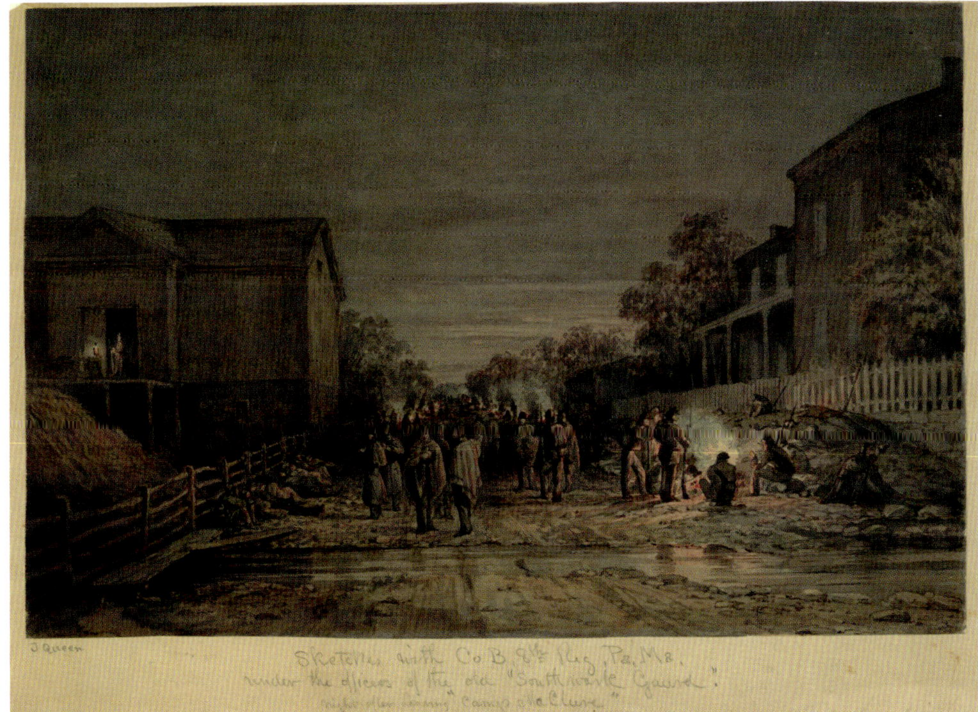

FIG. 50

James F. Queen, *Sketches with the Co. B 8th Reg., Pa. Ma. [Militia]. Under the Officers of the Old "Southwark Gaurd" [sic] Night After Leaving "Camp McClure,"* ca. 1862. Drawing, watercolor, crayon, and graphite on white wove paper, mounted on brown paper. Image: 27 × 40 cm (10 ¾ × 16 in.); mount: 34 × 45 cm (13 ¼ × 17 7/8 in.). LC-DIG-ppmsca-19645.

enhanced with watercolor, preferring to create his own impressions of place and to give his own interpretation of the image on paper. He then took care with making the drawing on stone so that the resulting lithograph conveyed specific information about individual structures in the village. There are in the Carson Collection many drawings of the Lehigh Valley, including images of the old Delaware River bridge in Easton. Sketching on paper before drawing on lithographic stone was his modus operandi. In addition to those for the Lehigh Valley, the Carson Collection contains several preparatory sketches for the Delaware Water Gap,[23] Civil War fund-raising prints, and other lithographs.

A diversion from his life in Southwark occurred during the Civil War. Then in his forties, Queen served double duty during the summers of 1862 and 1863, as a member of the Pennsylvania Militia, protecting the state from incursions by the Confederate Army, and as an artist, documenting both his military service and the life of his company.[24] He returned home from service in 1862 to create a series of eleven finished watercolors depicting Company B of the 8th Regiment of the Pennsylvania Militia. There is no drama in these images—no sense of urgency—but rather a sense of duty, of chilly nights under blankets (fig. 50), muddy streets, and long hot marches in the summer sun. When Queen returned to the militia during the summer of 1863, he

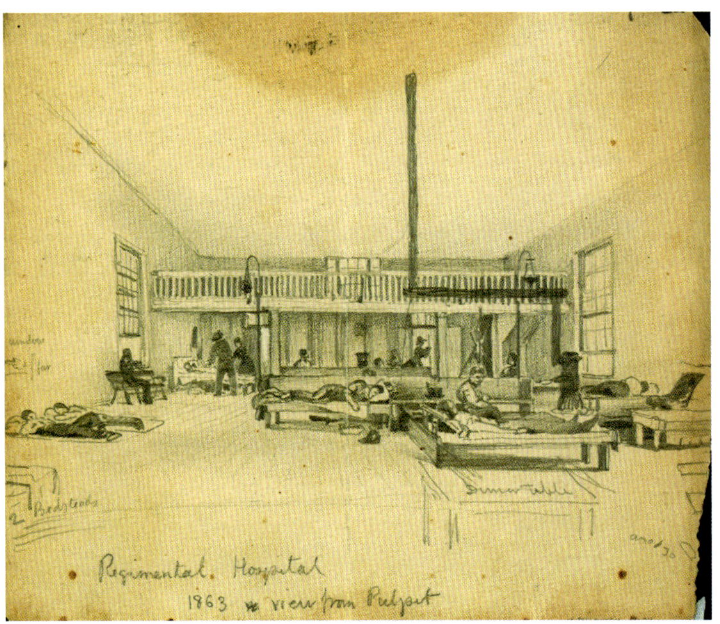

FIG. 51
James F. Queen, *Regimental Hospital 1863—View from Pulpit.* Graphite drawing on tan layered paper. 18 × 20 cm (7 1/8 × 7 5/8 in.). LC-DIG-ppmsca-19634.

made more sketches that described his experience, but no watercolors followed (fig. 51). Although there is no evidence that Queen or his state militia company ever saw battle, his service consumed two summers and gave him an opportunity to use his talents to document life on the road during wartime.

Queen's war efforts were not limited to his short tenure as a soldier. He also worked in an official capacity as a professional artist to document the effects of the Civil War on the city of Philadelphia, and he became the most prolific producer of prints for local charities. Union troops from further north were constantly on the move through the city, as they took the train to Camden, New Jersey, and then ferried across the Delaware before continuing south to the front. Southwark established refreshment saloons to feed southbound soldiers. Some of the severely wounded came back to Philadelphia for treatment, and volunteers established several hospitals. In response to the first flood of casualties coming from the Battle of Antietam, Queen designed several fund-raising prints and certificates for the Citizens Volunteer Hospital, which opened in September 1862 at the corner of Washington Avenue and Broad Street, conveniently close to the Philadelphia, Wilmington & Baltimore Railroad terminus.

Established by Thomas Tasker and run by a cadre of men and women volunteers, the Citizens Volunteer Hospital, before closing in August 1865, treated more than fifty thousand of the most severely injured men who passed through Philadelphia.[25] Queen created an initial fund-raising print, with interior and exterior views, although the accompanying design drawing in the Carson Collection lacks the lower vignette, showing the hospital ward, that appeared in the lithograph printed by Duval (figs. 52, 53). Queen's composition is balanced with graphic elements that direct the viewer's eye from one vignette to the next. From the kitchen to the dining rooms, bathing and wash rooms, the stores of clothing, and the pharmacy, he focuses not only on the wounded but also on the female volunteers and their activities. An exterior view of the hospital occupies the central vignette. Queen made repeated use of his initial print in later fund-raising certificates. Both the main interior and exterior scenes appear in a certificate in the Carson Collection inscribed with the name of Miss K. Souder, who had donated $1,422.55 to the hospital.[26] This completed certificate is an example of Philadelphia charity during the Civil War and the use to which Queen's art was put. Another certificate designed by Queen celebrated the closure of the hospital in 1865

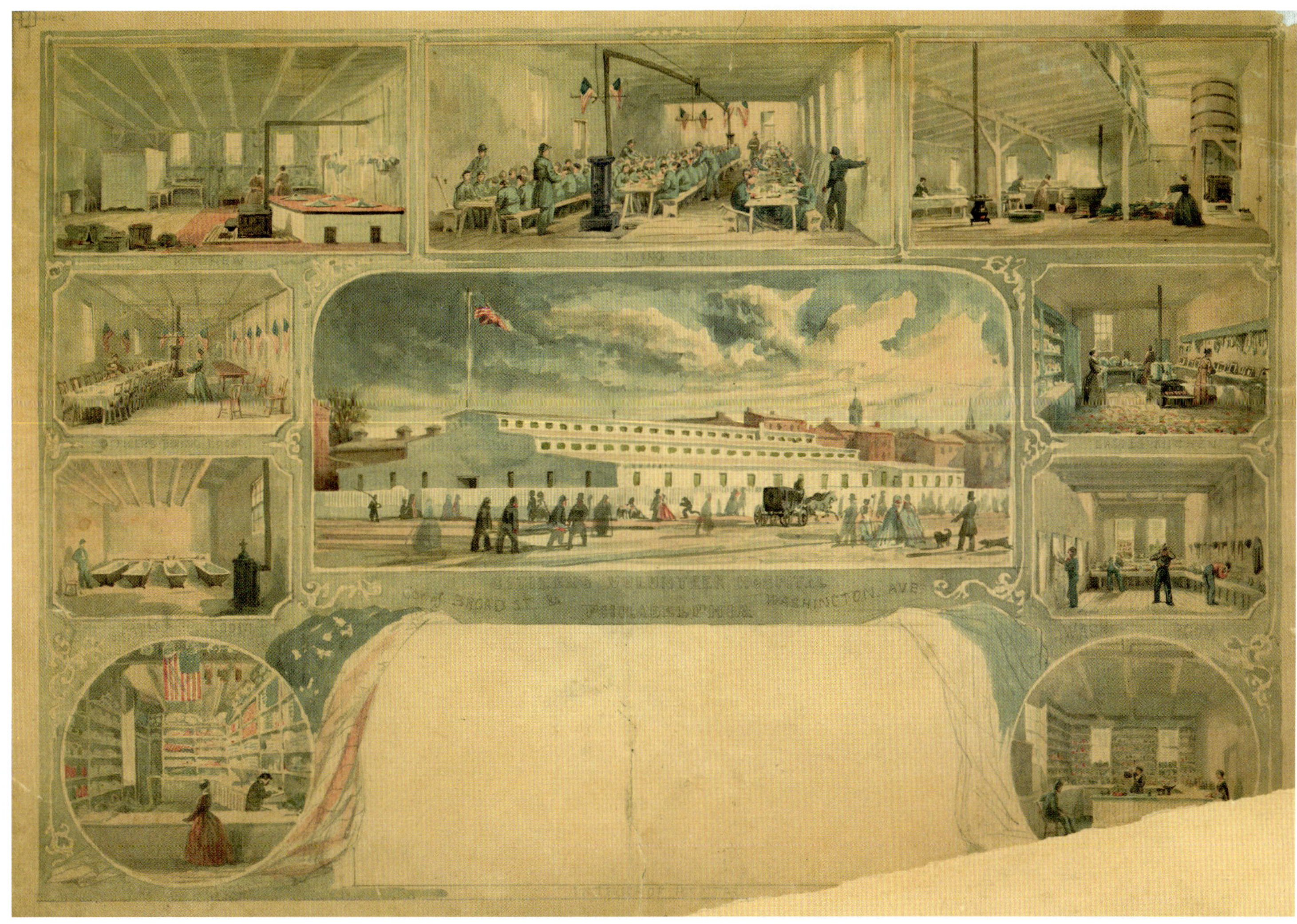

with a simple image of the building exterior, enhanced with tint stones to give it an almost photographic quality (POS 129).[27]

The Civil War provided Queen with a wealth of subjects that he depicted in his lithographs and chromolithographs, from the sentimental (Lookout Mountain, Tenn., and the Union drummer boy John Clem) to the patriotic (Ulysses S. Grant, Lincoln paired with Washington as "Champions of Liberty").[28] His depictions of wounded soldiers recovering in local hospitals were used in several ways—to advertise local druggists, to decorate sheet music, to fill out small portfolios, and to serve as fund-raising prints for local hospitals.[29] Combining prewar and wartime subjects, Queen made a design drawing for a lithograph memorializing the service of the Weccacoe firefighters in the Civil War, *War Roll for the Weccacoe Fire Company, Always Useful—Fireman in*

James F. Queen, *Citizens Volunteer Hospital Philadelphia, Corner of Broad St. & Washington Avenue,* 1862. Drawing, watercolor over graphite underdrawing on tan paper. 32 × 53 cm (12 ½ × 20 7/8 in.). Cochran 110, LC-DIG-ppmsca-19655.

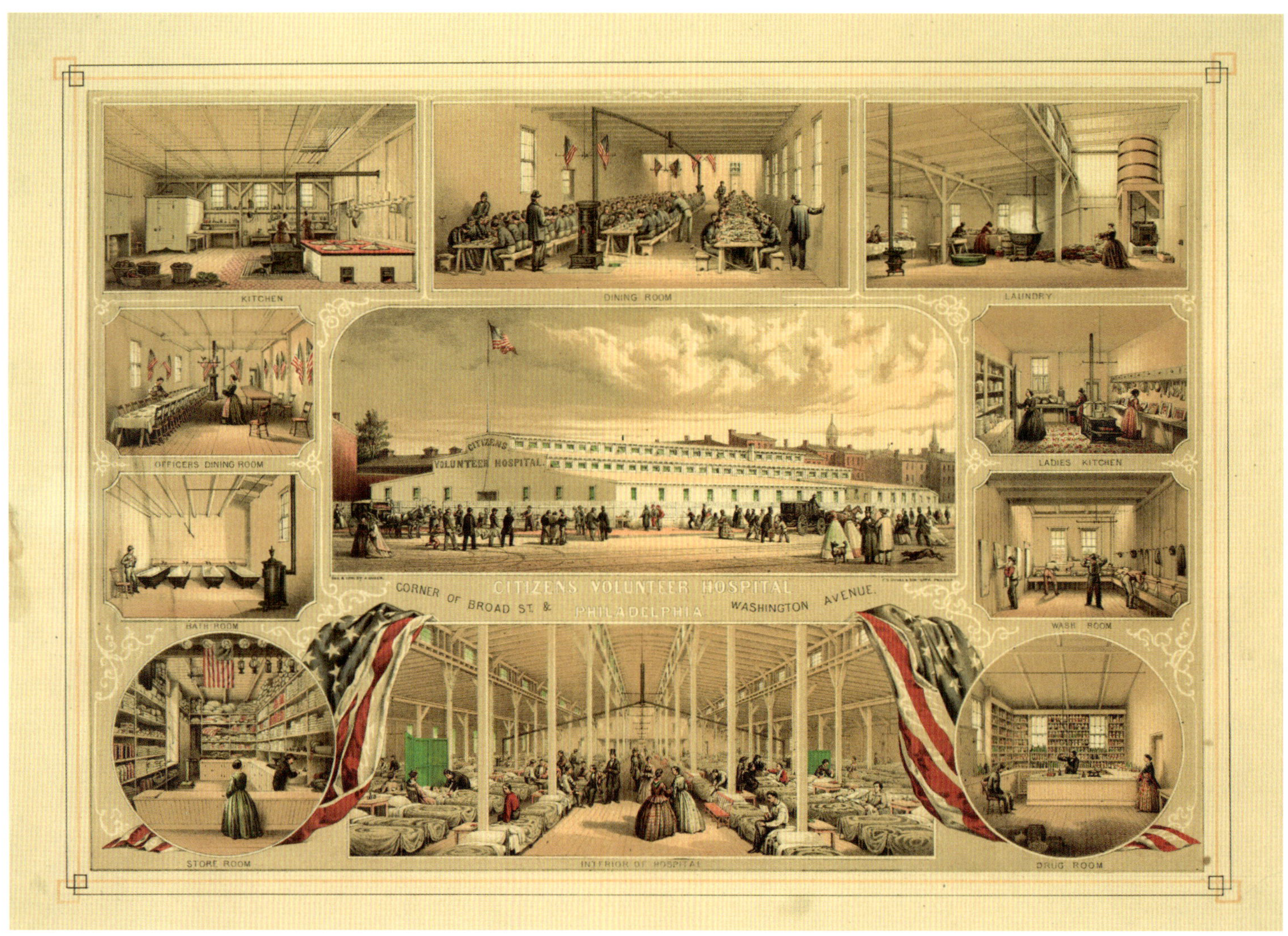

FIG.53

James F. Queen, *Citizens Volunteer Hospital Philadelphia, Corner of Broad St. & Washington Avenue* (Philadelphia: Printed by P. S. Duval & Son Lith., [1862]). Chromolithograph. 48 × 61 cm (19 × 24 in.). Cochran 310 (POS 131), LC-DIG-ppmsca-19654.

Peace—Soldiers in War. The allegorical drawing, in addition to marking out space for the honor roll of Weccacoe Engine firefighters who had served in the war, depicted firefighters in their dual role of protecting Philadelphia from fire and defending the Union.[30]

Peter Duval considered Queen to be at the height of his career during the war years. Writing to his retired portraitist Albert Newsam, Duval noted, "James Queen is still with us and is now one of the best artists in the country. He is very useful to us and we have more work for him than he can do."[31]

Queen also produced beautiful and highly narrative chromolithographs during the Civil War. The Carson Collection has the design watercolor *Armory of First City*

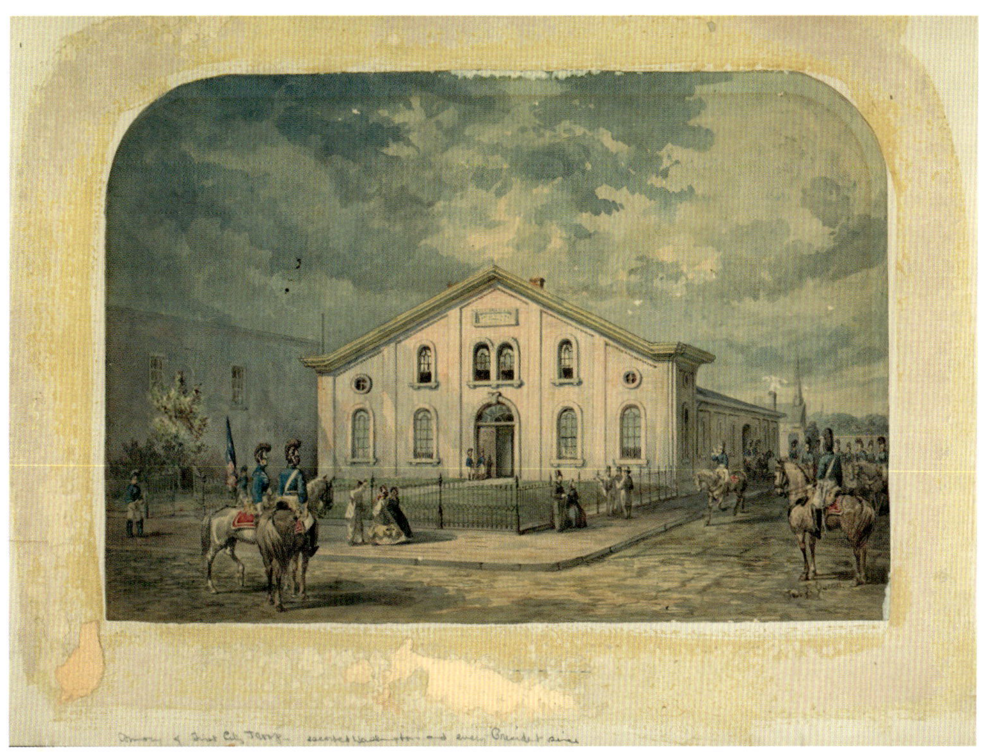

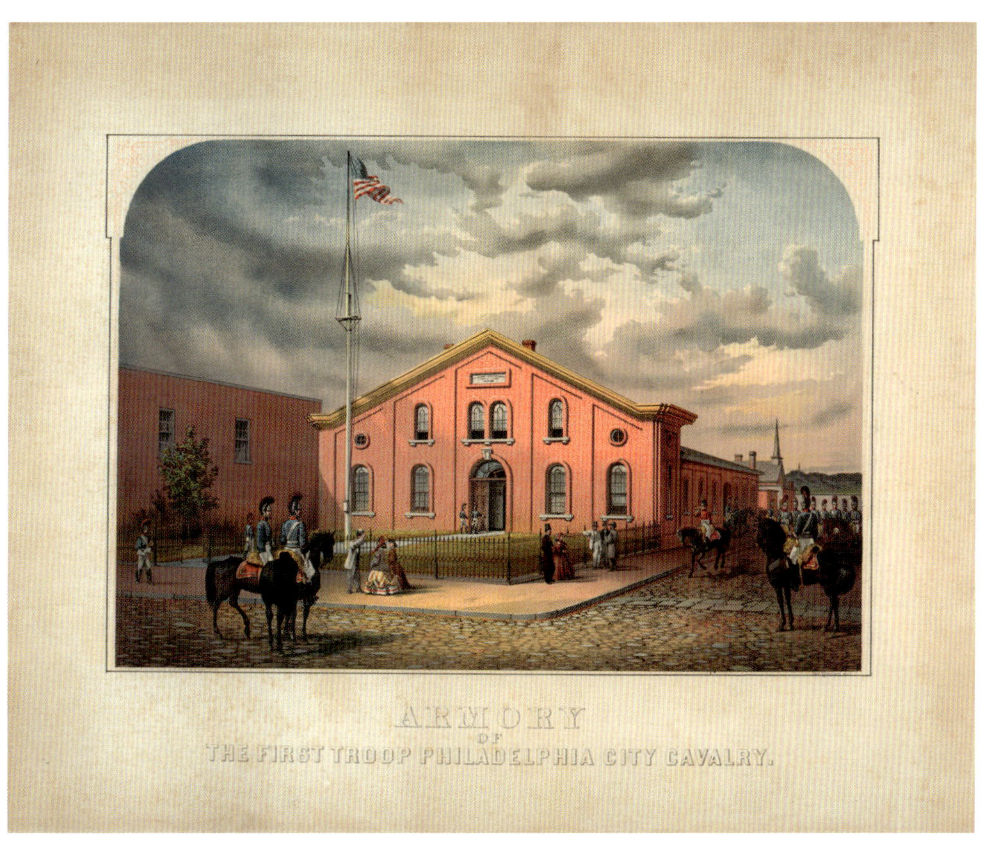

James F. Queen, *Armory of First City Troop—Escorted Washington and Every President Since,* ca. 1863. Drawing, watercolor over graphite on paper mounted on board. Paper mount: 37 × 50 cm (14 3/8 × 19 ½ in.). Cochran 121, LC-DIG-ppmsca-19650.

James F. Queen, *Armory of the First Troop Philadelphia City Cavalry* (Philadelphia: Lithd & printd in oil colors at P. S. Duval & Son, ca. 1863). Chromolithograph. 43 × 53 cm (17 × 20 ¾ in.). Cochran 204 (POS 24), LC-DIG-ppmsca-19651.

Troop—Escorted Washington and Every President Since and the chromolithograph that followed (figs. 54, 55). This large-format view documents the newly erected building at 21st and Ash (now Ludlow) with narrative touches, like the gentleman tipping his hat to the two women passersby, and the cavalry guard in their blue uniforms well placed in groups around the building. In the watercolor Queen evokes details with the slightest of brushstrokes—the brick on the armory, the shadow from the adjoining building, the dappled horses, and the wrought-iron fence. The resulting chromolithograph conveys detail without losing the narrative touch of the guards and ordinary citizens around the structure.

While Queen tended to create works of a serious nature for Peter Duval and even for himself, he had a sense of humor that came out in a few collaborative works with other publishers. For Wagner & McGuigan he created a sentimental Independence Day image, *Done Up,* depicting a boy exhausted from the day's celebrations.[32] The series of trading cards that Henry Louis Stephens drew and his brother William Allen Stephens published were put on stone by Queen. These are dynamic and humorous cards, especially *The Adventures of a Conscript as Told by Himself,* in which a rabbit attempts to avoid the draft into the Civil War but, once compelled to fight, does so victoriously and wins the woman, the female rabbit, of his dreams. Stephens and Queen combined forces for other trading-card sets relating to the Civil War and to the natural world.[33]

Queen's family life is reflected in the Carson Collection through a few drawings that show some quiet moments in his home and outdoors. The verso of the design drawing *War Rolls for the Weccacoe Fire Company* has a lovely family image of his daughters and nephew gathered around a game board, probably playing draughts, or checkers, as it is now more commonly known (fig. 56). Queen probably drew his family around 1858 or 1859, when his youngest daughter, Elizabeth, shown seated on the floor, was an infant. His eldest daughter, Emma, plays the game with the nephew Queen raised, Albert Henry, while his middle daughter, Mary, watches.[34] The calmness of the scene is enhanced by the sleeping animal, perhaps the family cat or dog, under the table. Unfinished in graphite, the drawing gives the sense that Queen depicted his children during a rare quiet moment for him away from Duval's presses, perhaps a Sunday afternoon in the parlor. Another image, dated December 11, 1857, shows an interior domestic scene with a woman ironing on a large table under gaslight or candlelight from a wall fixture, a basket of laundry on a chair by the door, and another woman seated at the table, opposite her.[35] The women might be Queen's wife, Sally, and her sister, Elizabeth, who lived with them. The charcoal-and-ink-wash drawing is more carefully rendered than that of Queen's children playing draughts. While these two drawings provide only the slightest glimpse into Queen's home life, they do give a sense of Queen as an attentive family man, catching his middle daughter's desire to play draughts with her cousin and older sister, and his wife and sister-in-law doing domestic chores in the evening, when the rest of the house was quiet. Perhaps they also suggest the middle-class lifestyle that his prodigious output made possible, one that was not unduly interrupted by the disastrous 1856 fire that destroyed the printshop of Duval.

By 1870 Queen had amassed real estate worth $7,000 and personal property worth $1,000. His wife, Sarah, had passed away, but his sister-in-law, Elizabeth Harvey, continued to keep house for him and his daughters Emma and Lizzie.[36] By 1880, when his former employer was boarding with others, Queen continued to prosper.[37] Instead of experiencing economic decline in the last years of his life, Queen's income stabilized when his brother Francis, publisher of the *New York Clipper,* passed away in 1882 and bequeathed him $60,000 out of an estate worth $350,000.[38] At the time of his death, in 1886, Queen owned real estate worth $20,000 and personal property worth $12,500. The size of his estate permitted his sister-in-law and his daughter Emma to continue living in their home, something that single women rarely could afford to do in the nineteenth century.[39]

By the end of his career, James Queen had shifted from producing images of predominantly local interest to high-quality chromolithographs of sentimental images for national retail. He found employment not only with Duval & Hunter (Stephen Duval's short-lived attempt to run his father's business with Thomas Hunter) but also with Joseph Hoover and then with Thomas Hunter when he succeeded the Duval family. The chromolithographs at the Library of Congress from the last decade of Queen's career come not from the Carson Collection but from copyright deposits and select purchases that the Library of Congress has made since 1869, the year in which Peter Duval retired.[40] As late as the 1880 U.S. Census, James Queen listed his occupation as "chromo artist," evidence that he continued working, navigating changes in popular printmaking.[41] Queen had honed his sense of what was needed for the popular market as it shifted, and he created such religious images as *The Baptism of Christ,* which were popular for the nursery and church school.[42] He created chromolithographs from

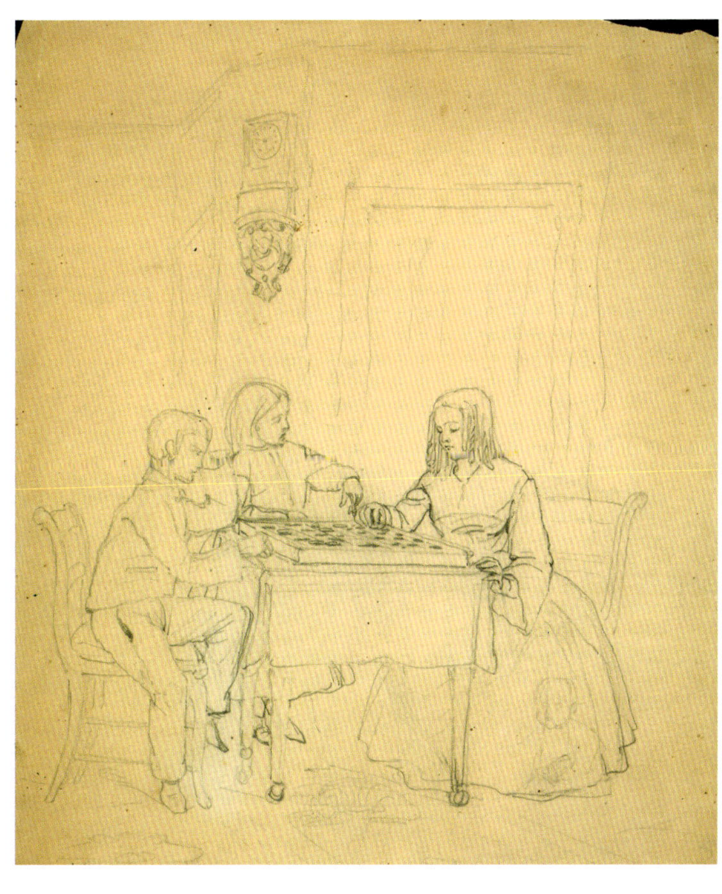

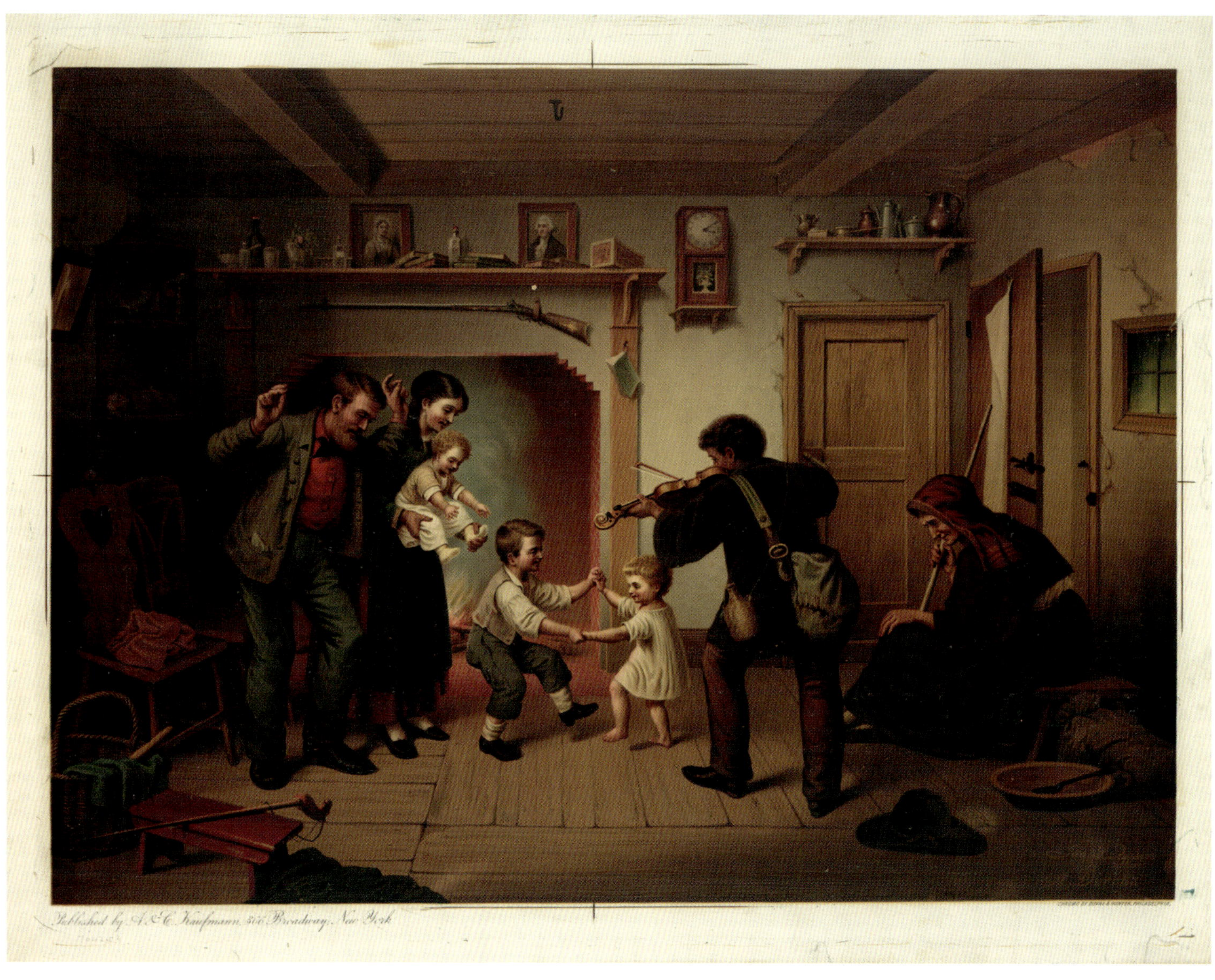

sentimental European paintings, including *Home Sweet Home* by Anthonie Jacobus van Wyngaerdt (Dutch, 1808–1887), perhaps for the growing numbers of middle-class European immigrants, hungry for images of home.[43] His genre scene after German painter Auguste Durcks's *Power of Music,* printed in 1872 and depicting an itinerant fiddler entertaining a family that dances before their rural fireplace in the middle of the night, is variant enough to stand as a work of art on its own (fig. 57). These chromolithographs were embossed to resemble oil paintings and were undoubtedly matted and framed to hang as fine art in the parlors of American homes.

James Queen began his apprenticeship during the first decade of active lithography in Philadelphia and, over the course of his career, adapted his artistic skills to the changing market for popular prints, making the best use of what lithography had to offer as it evolved from basic black-and-white advertisements to full-color chromolithographs for parlor walls. His ability as an artist stood out in an era when mass production of sentimental images dominated the market.[44] When he died of multiple sclerosis in 1886,[45] he left behind prints and drawings that represent the transformation of an art form from single-color lithographs to complex color prints in oil colors, just as he himself had transformed from lower-middle-class artisan to middle-class artist.

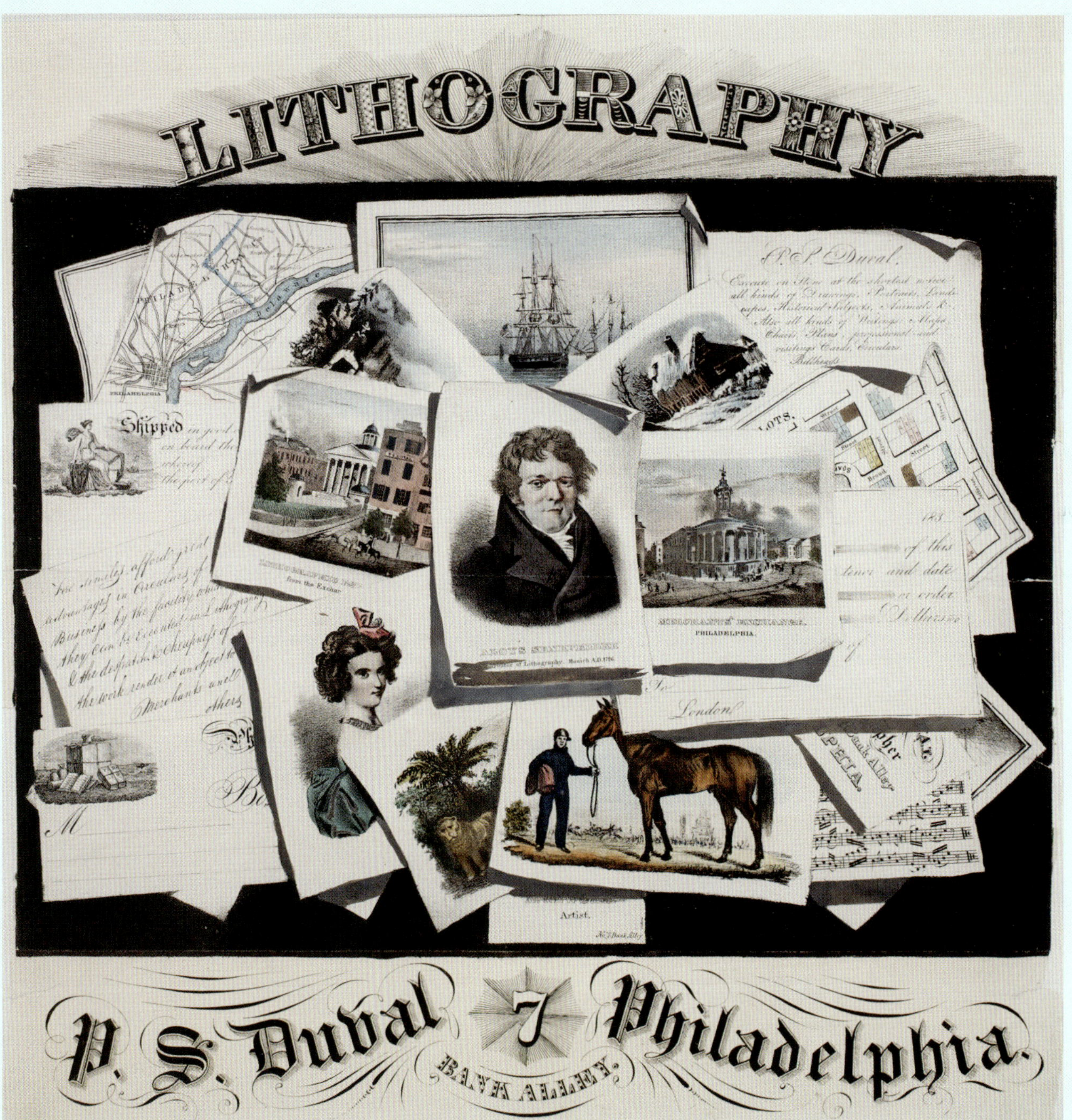

LITHOGRAPHY
P. S. Duval 7 Philadelphia.
BANK ALLEY.

PETER S. DUVAL, PHILADELPHIA'S LEADING LITHOGRAPHER

SARAH J. WEATHERWAX

When editor John Luther Ringwalt approached Peter S. Duval (ca. 1804/5–1886) around 1870 to write an extensive entry on lithography for his *American Encyclopaedia of Printing,* he turned to an expert, a man who probably had more lithographic experience than anyone then living in America.[1] Duval had been prominent in the field for forty years, working in both France and the United States. He had quickly progressed from working for others, to partnering in a firm, to serving as the sole proprietor of a flourishing business. His retirement in 1869 may have given him more time to focus on his encyclopedia entry, a project in which he could display his extensive technical and historical knowledge of lithography.

Duval divided his ten-page entry into sections describing different lithographic processes, including crayon, transfer, and chromolithography. Given Duval's important role in introducing color lithography to America, it is not surprising that he declared that "chromos are without exception the finest products of the art of lithography."[2] Duval's entry also provided historical information on the development of lithography, with a keen eye to European advances in the field. Born in France and fluent in both French and English, Duval was not parochial in his essay's overview. Nor did he unduly promote his own contributions, but Duval's significance in shaping the direction of American lithography is obvious in his descriptions of adding steam power to his handpresses, hiring well-known European artists to work for his Philadelphia firm, and searching for top-quality domestic stones and paper. Through his own life and professional experiences, Duval, Philadelphia's leading lithographer, was uniquely qualified to write the definitive entry on lithography.

In late September 1831 Peter Stephen Duval, a young man in his midtwenties, arrived in New York City's harbor on board a ship from France.[3] He had accepted a job offer from Philadelphia engraver and publisher Cephas G. Childs (1793–1871), who had been traveling through Europe learning more about lithography. Duval, who had trained as a lithographic printer in France, would bring some much-needed expertise to the new printing firm run by Childs and Henry Inman (1801–1846). In the early 1830s lithography was just beginning to establish itself in America. When Duval arrived in Philadelphia in the fall of 1831, the city was home to only eight lithographic presses.[4]

Most likely due to the skill of Duval, the firm of Childs & Inman quickly earned praise for the work they produced. "The lithographic establishment of Messrs. Childs and Inman, is conducted with unremitting diligence and success," declared the *National Gazette* in the fall of 1832. "It furnishes constantly new and fine specimens of art, which is daily found to be one of the most valuable improvement[s] of our times."[5] Childs's opinion of his own business, however, was quite different, according to lithographic artist Albert Newsam (1809–1864), who worked for Childs and later for Duval. Childs told Newsam that he "did not make one cent at lithography" and considered the business a failure.[6] Childs, who in 1833 had entered into a partnership with artist George Lehman (d. 1871), sold off his half of the business to Duval in late 1834 to repay a $750 debt.[7] Peter Duval and George Lehman remained partners until 1837, when Duval took over sole proprietorship of the business.

During the three-year partnership of Lehman and Duval, lithography gained a firmer footing in Philadelphia, at least partially because of the quality of the work produced by the firm. The *Pennsylvania Inquirer and Daily Courier,* for example, described their portraits of politicians Henry Clay and John Calhoun as "admirable likenesses, and creditable specimens of the Fine Arts of this country."[8] In addition to portraits, separately issued advertisements, certificates (fig. 58), maps, views, and book illustrations—including many of the magnificent plates in McKenney and Hall's *History of the Indian Tribes of North America* and John Edwards Holbrook's *North American Herpetology*—all came off the firm's presses.[9]

The firm of Lehman & Duval served as the training ground for a talented group of men who remained associated with Peter Duval throughout much of their careers.[10] In November 1835 fourteen-year-old James Queen (1820/21–1886), for example, entered into a four-and-a-half-year apprenticeship with Lehman & Duval to learn lithography.[11] From a lowly apprentice whose work undoubtedly included sweeping

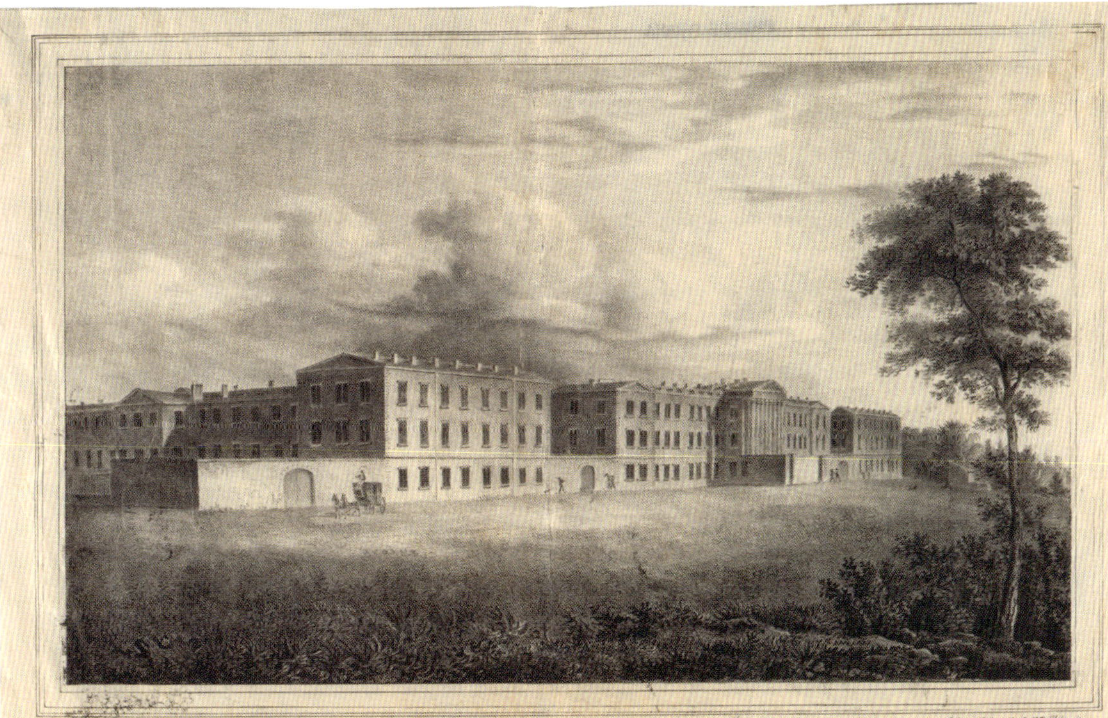

We

the Guardians Physicians and Surgeons of the

PHILADELPHIA ALMS HOUSE

Do certify that ______________________________ of
______________________________ of the said Alms House

and Public Hospital for ______________________________

In testimony whereof we have hereunto

affixed our names in the year of our Lord one thousand Eight hundred and ______________________________

Number of Patients during the current year

Medical ______________________________   ______________________________ President of the board of Guardians

Surgical ______________________________   ______________________________ President of the board of Physicians & Surgeons.

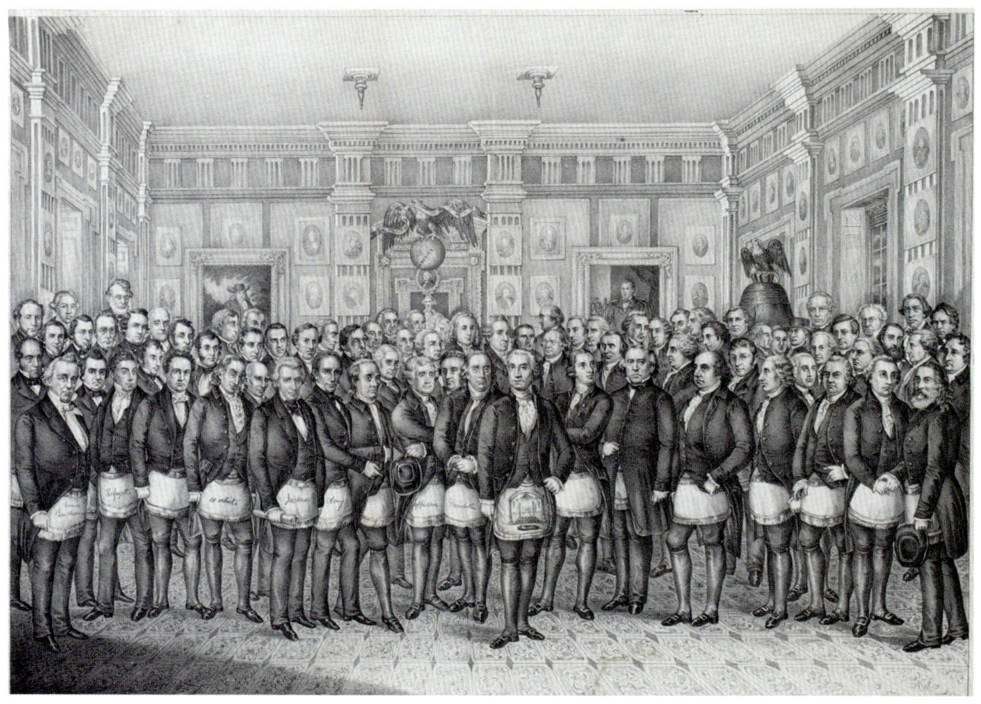

up the shop, grinding, graining and polishing stones, and making tracing paper, lithographic crayons, and varnish, Queen rose to the position of superintendent of P. S. Duval & Son's drawing department in the early 1860s.[12] Similarly, deaf and mute artist Albert Newsam, who began his career as an apprentice to Cephas G. Childs, stayed with Duval until deteriorating eyesight and failing health in general forced him into retirement in the late 1850s.

The year 1837 was momentous for the United States as well as for Duval. Financial instability rocked the nation, and during the economic panic of 1837 hundreds of banks across the country failed.[13] Meanwhile, Duval and George Lehman dissolved their business partnership, and Duval, although it may not have been a good year to launch one's own business, did just that, accepting the challenge of running a business in an English-speaking country where he had resided for only six years. Perhaps to mark his commitment to a new life in the United States, Duval in 1837 also officially declared his intention to become an American citizen.[14]

Although Duval may have been willing to give up his French citizenship, he established and retained close ties to the French community of Philadelphia throughout his life.[15] By 1839 Duval had joined the Société française de bienfaisance de Philadelphie (the French Benevolent Society of Philadelphia), an organization composed of approximately one hundred members who offered assistance to needy members of the local French community.[16] The society's 1839 treasurer's report lists Duval as paying his $3 subscriber's fee and records his occupation as "lithographe." With the exception of a physician, Duval was the only member to have his profession specified, perhaps an indication of the pride he took in his work.[17] Duval remained an active member of the society throughout the 1840s and 1850s. He periodically served on the Comités distributeurs, which dispensed coal, footwear, wood, and groceries to the poor, participated on committees that organized the society's annual ball and other fund-raising events, and held positions on the elected Bureau d'administration.[18] Duval also belonged to another Philadelphia French charitable organization, the Société française de secours mutuels (the French Association for Mutual Assistance).[19]

While it is not known if Duval ever returned to France after leaving his native country in 1831, he remained interested in European affairs. Philadelphia's *Public Ledger* noted that in the spring of 1848, as political and social upheaval rocked Europe, P. S. Duval was among the speakers who addressed a large crowd in French during a demonstration for "liberty for Europe" held at Independence Square.[20] Even in his midseventies Duval remained active in French causes, serving on a committee of the city's French citizens who in March 1880 greeted Ferdinand de Lesseps, the French developer of the Suez Canal, during his brief visit to Philadelphia.[21]

Duval's social network was not confined, however, to Philadelphia's French community. In 1838 he joined the Freemasons as an apprentice in Philadelphia Lodge No. 72.[22] Around the same time, he also joined the Robert Morris Lodge No. 29 of the Independent Order of Odd Fellows, quickly becoming their treasurer, a position he held for at least twenty years. Membership in these organizations may have helped anchor Duval to his new life in America but also proved useful for his business. Duval's shop printed invitations to I.O.O.F. balls and membership certificates for the fraternal order.[23] About 1860 he printed a group portrait of an imaginary gathering of seventy-seven distinguished Masons. Drawn by Christian Inger, the august group includes many signers of the Declaration of Independence and American politicians and clergy, all portrayed as standing in Independence Hall wearing their Masonic aprons (fig. 59). General Lafayette, the French hero, is prominently placed in the front row. Masonic brethren could purchase the lithograph, along with a key and descriptive brochure, for $2.[24]

Duval's bilingual ability was called into service by Philadelphia's justice system when in June 1844 a violent incident took place at the Dock Street "French boarding house" of August Esmoil, where Duval boarded. Duval gave sworn testimony to a jury that two other residents, Mr. and Mrs. Jules Lesueur, had lived at the boardinghouse for about a month and that he knew them only casually, having shared an occasional meal with them during that time. Upon hearing shots fired early in the morning hours

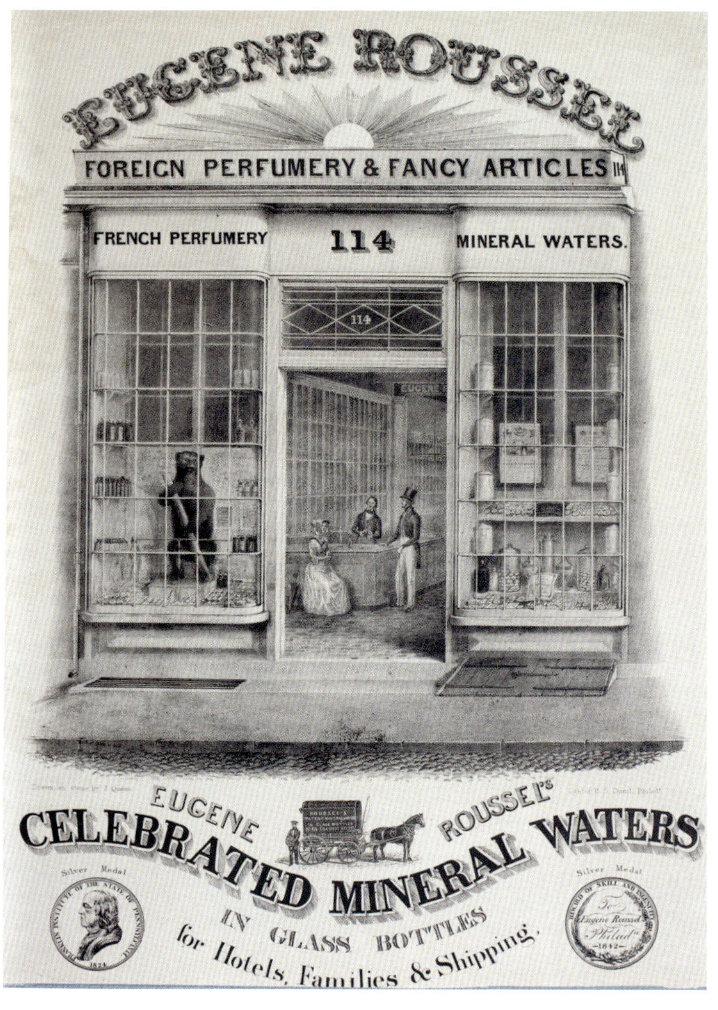

James F. Queen, *Eugene Roussel's Celebrated Mineral Waters in Glass Bottles for Hotels, Families & Shipping* (Philadelphia: P. S. Duval, ca. 1843). Lithograph. Trimmed. 45 × 33 cm (17 ½ × 13 in.). POS 212, HSP, Bb 38 Q32.

of June 1, Duval, as he reported to the jury, rushed into the couple's room and found their dead bodies. After this testimony Duval then translated into English the note left by the husband, leading the jury to conclude that the deaths were caused by a murder/suicide.[25]

Just as Duval's ties to the world of fraternal orders had brought work to his establishment, his connections to the French community also generated commissions. Eugene Roussel, who sold perfume and mineral water in the city during the 1840s, knew Duval as a fellow member of the French Benevolent Society of Philadelphia.[26] About 1843 Duval printed an advertisement, drawn by James Queen, of Roussel's shop. Roussel's products are handsomely displayed in large windows, while through the shop's open door well-dressed customers can be seen (fig. 60). About seven years later Duval printed another lithographic advertisement for the business after ownership transferred to Xavier Bazin, who was also a member of the French Benevolent Society of Philadelphia.[27]

The years immediately following the breakup of Lehman & Duval found Duval immersed in a whirlwind of projects, some fairly successful and others only short-lived. The *Parlour Review, and Journal of Music, Literature, and the Fine Arts,* a weekly magazine issued in both French and English, began in January 1838 and featured lithographic portraits of musicians and performers drawn by Albert Newsam and printed by Duval, but lasted for only ten weeks.[28] Duval also provided lithographic illustrations for the *United States Ecclesiastical Portrait Gallery,* another short-lived periodical that featured portraits by Newsam. In 1841 artist and publisher Alfred Hoffy (1796–1872) chose Duval's press to print the illustrations for the *Orchardist's Companion,* the first illustrated American journal devoted to fruit cultivation. The accuracy and beauty of the illustrations were essential to the magazine's appeal, and the publisher assured readers that the cost of the illustrations, each "richly coloured and designed from nature and of full size," was only 14 ½ cents per image.[29] Despite the *Pennsylvania Inquirer and Daily Courier*'s assertion that "no friend of agriculture, no lover of fruit, no patron of the Fine Arts, should be without it,"[30] the magazine only survived for two years. The magazine may not have been a success, but Duval received praise for the high quality of his work.

Hoffy probably chose Duval as his printer for the *Orchardist's Companion* because he was pleased with the work they had done together on the *U.S. Military Magazine*. Debuting in March 1839, each issue of the *U.S. Military Magazine* contained text describing the uniforms and activities of Philadelphia's volunteer militia groups, accompanied by an illustration; most of these illustrations were drawn by William M. Huddy (1807–1846), lithographed by Hoffy, and printed by P. S. Duval. Subscribers could order the entire year of monthly issues in advance for $5, while individual colored prints could be obtained for 75 cents. Black-and-white prints cost half that amount.[31] Within two months Huddy and Duval became partners in this venture, although Duval continued to pursue work under his own name as well. The magazine was successful enough that Huddy and Duval felt no compulsion to distribute complimentary copies, a decision they clearly stated in a letter to an unidentified inquirer.[32]

Even after the demise of the *U.S. Military Magazine* in 1842, Alfred Hoffy continued to collaborate with Duval on work. *The Artillery Corps of Philadelphia Greys* (fig. 61) resembles the work Hoffy did for the *U.S. Military Magazine,* although in this print there is less attention to the details of the troop uniforms. On September 25, 1845, Hoffy received a $75 payment for his work sketching Captain Cadwalader and his troops drilling in West Philadelphia, and later drawing on the stone. The stone and paper for the lithograph came from Duval's shop, and his employees lettered the stone and printed 310 copies. Employee P. C. Hollis recorded on November 22, 1845, that Duval's shop received $38.30 in payment for the materials and work they provided for the lithograph.[33] Peter Duval's relationship with Hoffy expanded into the personal in 1860 when Duval's son Stephen (1833–1907) (fig. 62), whom Duval took on as a partner in the lithography business in 1857, married Hoffy's daughter Emma.[34]

The Artillery Corps of Philadelphia Greys is a hand-colored lithograph, although by the time of its publication in the mid-1840s Duval had already experienced some early success with printing in color. The April 1843 issue of *Miss Leslie's Magazine* printed what the editor described as a lithotint, entitled *Grandpapa's Pet,* produced by Peter Duval and artist John Richard after a series of experiments (fig. 63). Lithotinting was a lithographic process using different strengths of ink applied to the printing stone to create the appearance of a watercolor, but bright colors still had to be applied to the print by hand. Duval continued his experimentations, and by 1846 he felt confident enough to advertise that his shop printed in colors.[35] True success in printing in color, however, was still a few years away.

As the firm's owner, Duval worked hard to promote his business.[36] The large first-floor display windows and bold signs advertising his lithographic establishment on

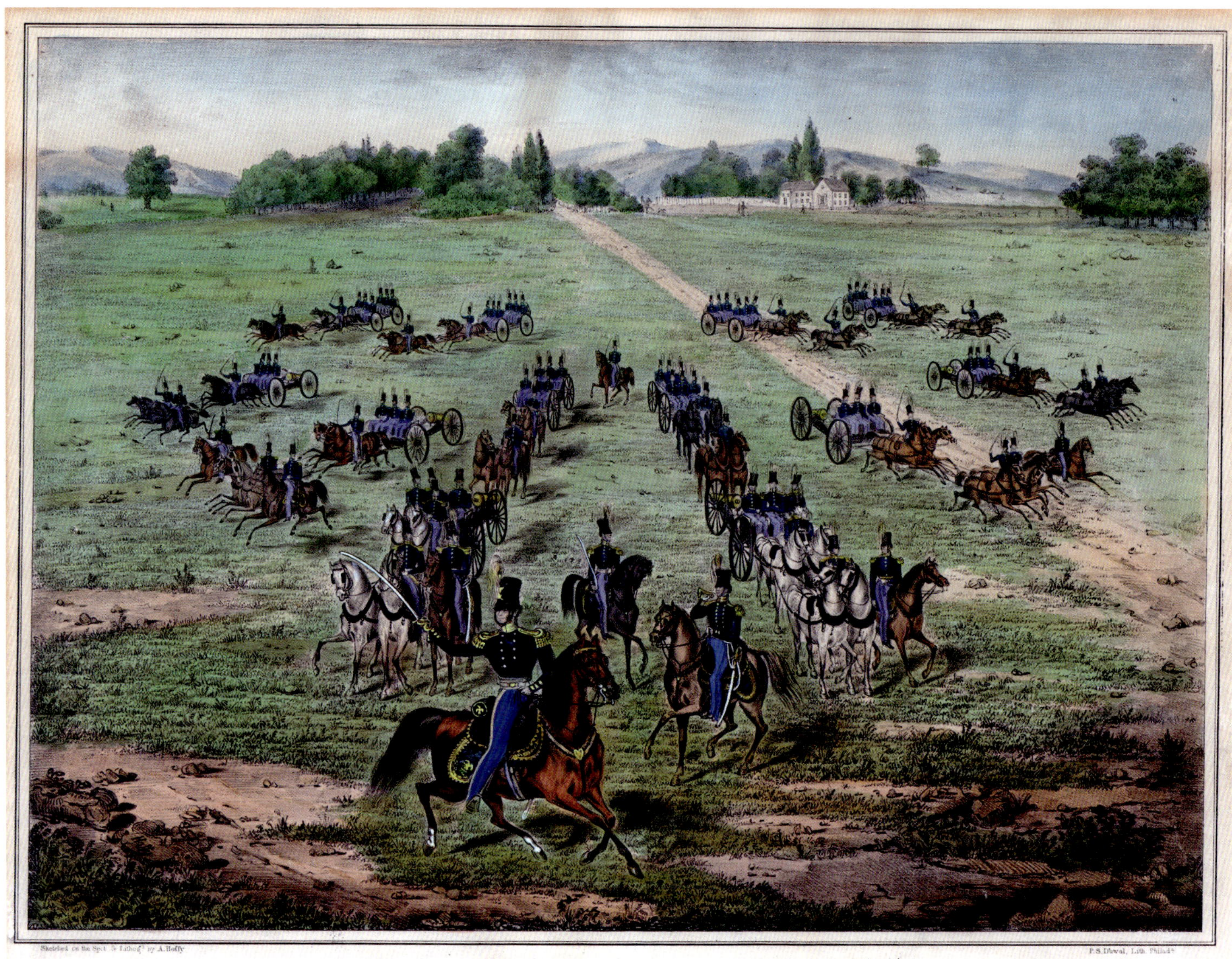

the building's façade surely caught the eye of the hordes of businessmen bustling in and out of the Merchants' Exchange building across the street.[37] Duval's proximity to the Merchants' Exchange played a part in much of his advertising. A billhead dated 1839 for Duval's business included a view of the Merchants' Exchange, rather than his own building, with his address, "No. 7 Bank Alley Opposite Merchants' Exchange," printed below (see fig. 4). Duval included textual references to the Exchange in city-directory advertisements and occasionally in imprint information on prints.[38] His most clever use of the Merchants' Exchange in his advertising appears in a circa-1840 trompe l'oeil print (fig. 64) that incorporates a lithographic view of Duval's shop from the Exchange paired with a view of the Exchange from his shop. With scattered prints and documents, Duval visually and succinctly advertised the scope of his work, which included maps, sheet music covers, portraits, views, and billheads; paid homage to Alois Senefelder (1771–1834), the inventor of lithography, with a portrait; and acknowledged the contribution of artist Albert Newsam by including one of Newsam's business cards.

Although the 1840s found Peter Duval successfully establishing his own lithographic business, the early years of the decade were marked by tragedy in his personal life. In July of 1840 his youngest son and namesake died just before his first birthday.[39] Two years later, almost to the day, Duval's twelve-year-old son drowned in the Delaware River. He had been fishing with a few others in a boat near the Navy Yard when the boat capsized.[40]

Success can be measured at least in part by outgrowing one's space, and in 1848 Duval moved into more spacious accommodations in the recently completed Artisan Building on Ranstead Place. Hoping to rent his No. 7 Bank Alley facility, Duval took out a notice in the *Public Ledger* advertising the availability of a fourth-floor room seventy feet in length with north and west exposures, as well as a large fifth-story room with north and south exposures.[41] In his new accommodations, Duval more than doubled his space. He occupied the entire second floor of the Artisan Building, filling his six-room suite with equipment and sixty to seventy artists, draftsmen, and workmen. Nearly thirty lithographic presses filled the main room, 150 feet long by 30 feet wide. The *Public Ledger* described his business as "probably the largest in the lithographic branch of art in the United States."[42]

Within his new space, Duval continued to experiment with improvements to lithography. In 1849 Frederick Bourquin (1808–1897), Duval's foreman and soon-to-be partner in the business known as P. S. Duval & Co., developed a cost-effective technique for transferring images onto zinc plates, which were sturdier than stones.[43] Throughout the 1850s Duval's advertisements promoted his ongoing work with color printing and touted the introduction of steam-powered presses to his establishment. On a Saturday afternoon in February 1849, Peter Duval opened his establishment up to about two hundred guests to celebrate his new use of steam in the lithographic process. Guests observed the presses in action, drank, sang, ate, and listened to speeches by local dignitaries.[44] Michael Twyman in chapter 2 concludes, however, that it was not before the late 1860s that steam power was used in any of the lithographic processes in Duval's

FIG.61 (OPPOSITE)
Alfred M. Hoffy, *The Artillery Corps of Philadelphia Greys, (Company D), Comd. by Capt. Geo. Cadwalader, First Regiment of Artillery, 1st Brigade, 1st Division, P. M.* (Philadelphia: P. S. Duval, 1845). Lithograph with hand-coloring. 33 × 42 cm (13 × 16 ¾ in.). POS 27, LCP, P.9504.6.

FIG.62 (BELOW)
S. C. Duval ([Philadelphia], ca. 1860). Lithograph. 21 × 18 cm (8 × 7 in.). LCP, (I) 5750.F.142g.

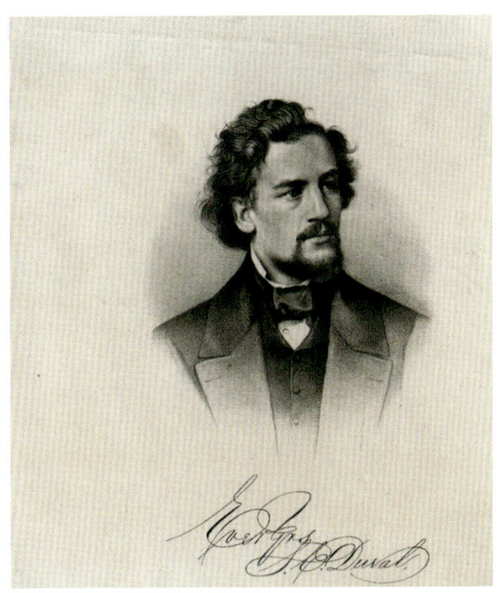

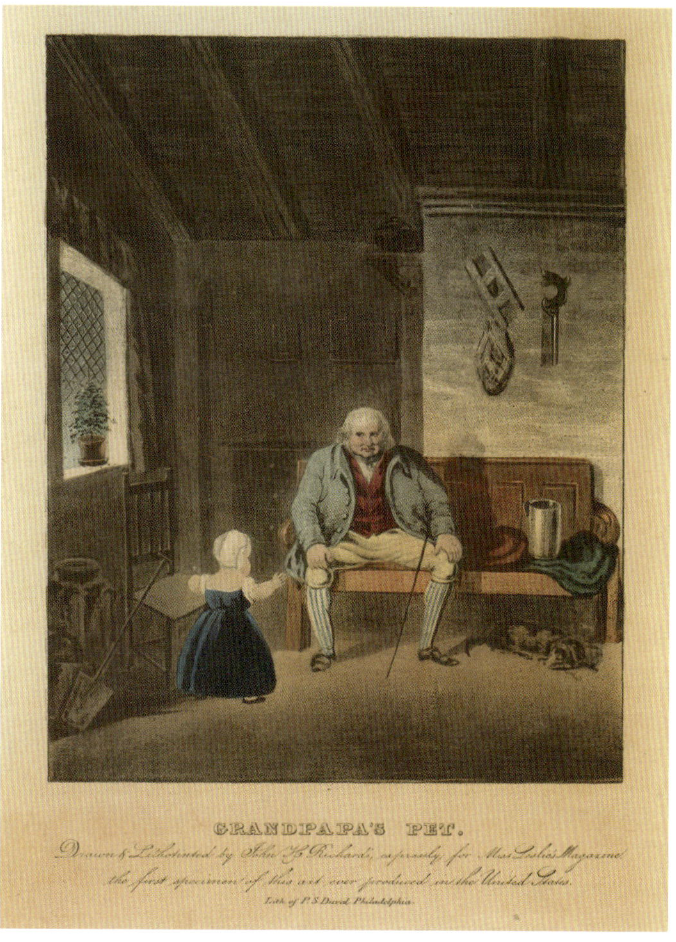

John H. Richard, *Grandpapa's Pet, Drawn & Lithotinted by John H. Richard's, Expressly for Miss Leslie's Magazine. The First Specimen of This Art Ever Produced in the United States* (Philadelphia: P. S. Duval, [April 1843]). Lithotint. 24 × 16 cm (9 ½ × 6 ¼ in.). POSP 99, LCP, Gift of David Doret, P.2005.18.39.

Albert Newsam, *Lithography: P. S. Duval, 7 Bank Alley, Philadelphia* (Philadelphia: P. S. Duval, ca. 1840). Lithograph with hand-coloring. 28 × 37 cm (11 × 14 ½ in.). POSA 60, HSP, Albert Newsam Print Collection, V-100, Box 10, Folder 3.

shop other than to pull the stone through the press. Dampening the stone and rolling up the image were still done without the assistance of steam power.[45]

Even if Duval exaggerated his use of steam-powered presses, his printed advertisements provided tangible proof of his success with color printing, as is evident in figure 65. Made to resemble an illuminated manuscript, this advertisement, done in a rich palette of colors, set classically inspired figures within Gothic-style architectural details. Its artist, Christian Schussele (1824–1879), had been brought to Philadelphia by Duval in 1849 because of his experience working with chromolithography at Godefroy Engelmann's Paris establishment.[46] Schussele's mastery of chromolithography is well displayed in the large portrait prints he executed around 1849 of George Washington and the Marquis de Lafayette, each using thirteen different stones. Both of the portraits are full-length depictions of the men gazing heroically off into the distance. Washington stands on a quiet spot on a battlefield while in the background clouds of smoke from musket fire billow in the air and men and horses charge forward in battle (fig. 66). In 1852 the *Public Ledger* referred to the "chrome lithographic pictures" of Washington and Lafayette as "the most perfect specimens of this new art issued in this country." The newspaper urged readers to see the prints on exhibition at the Art Union.[47] Although not copyrighted until 1851, Duval wrote that the portraits had won silver medals at the Franklin Institute in 1849, the American Institute of New York in 1850, the Maryland Institute of Baltimore in 1851, and the Metropolitan Fair in Washington and the Massachusetts Charitable Association in 1852. According to Duval, the portraits also won a bronze medal at the London World's Fair in 1850.[48] Perhaps once they had won widespread recognition, Duval decided to copyright the images.

The decade of the 1850s, which had started so promisingly with Duval's recent move to a new, larger space and his continuing artistic and technical improvements to the lithographic process, saw Duval by the later years of the decade struggling to weather severe blows to his business. His personal circumstances also seem somewhat cloudy during this time. In *Philadelphia in the Romantic Age of Lithography,* Nicholas Wainwright wrote, "Comfortably settled in his house on the corner of Second and Cox streets in Southwark, Duval led a patriarchal family life, his home crowded with a dozen children, relatives, and servants. Soon he was to move to a more fashionable

LITHOGRAPHY

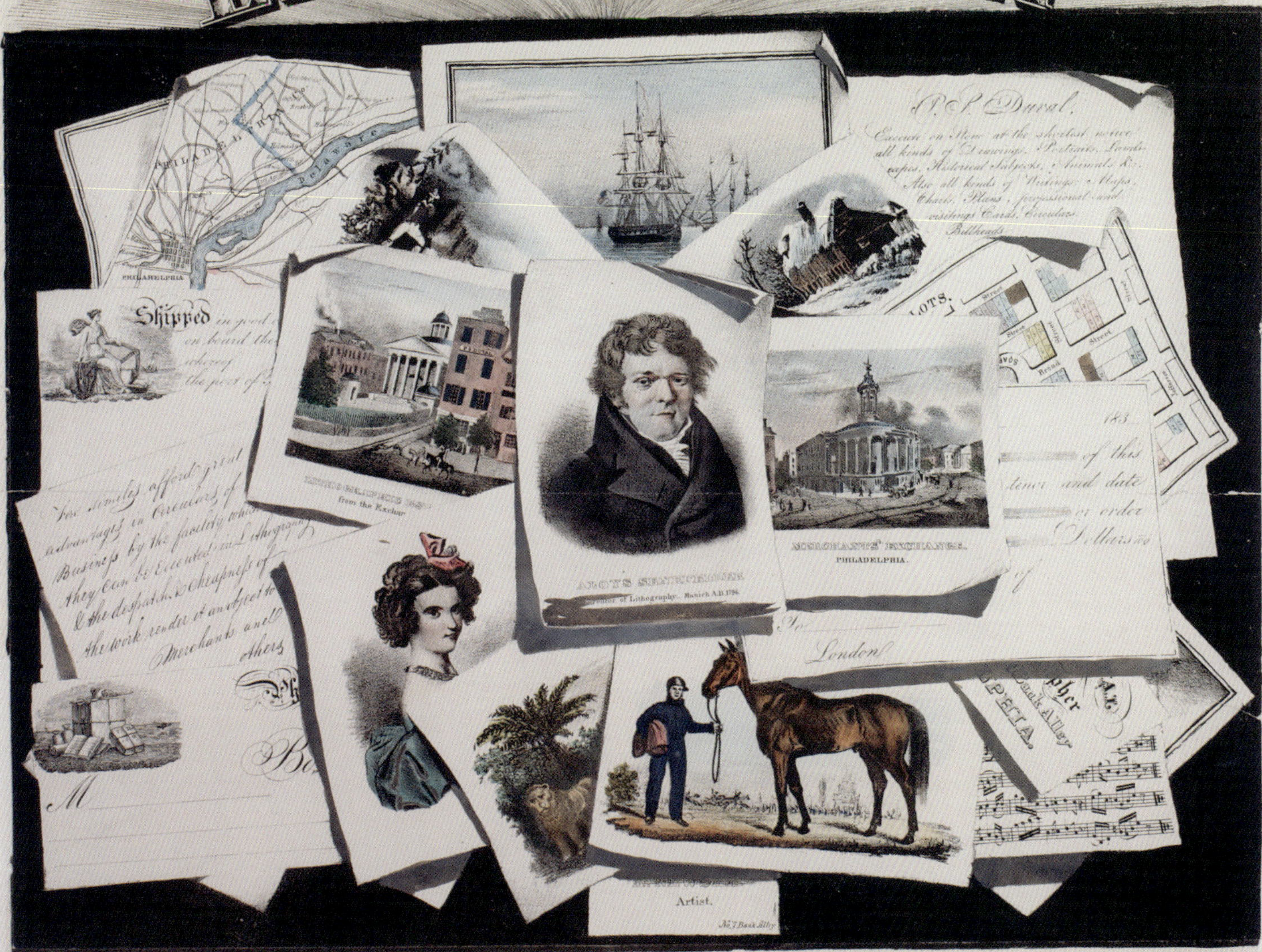

P. S. Duval 7 Philadelphia.
BANK ALLEY.

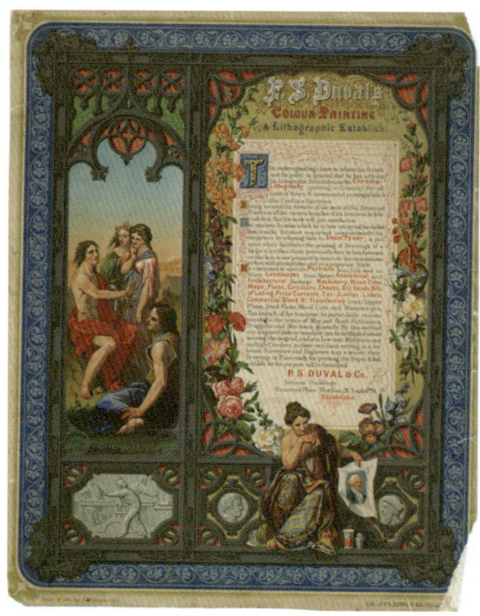

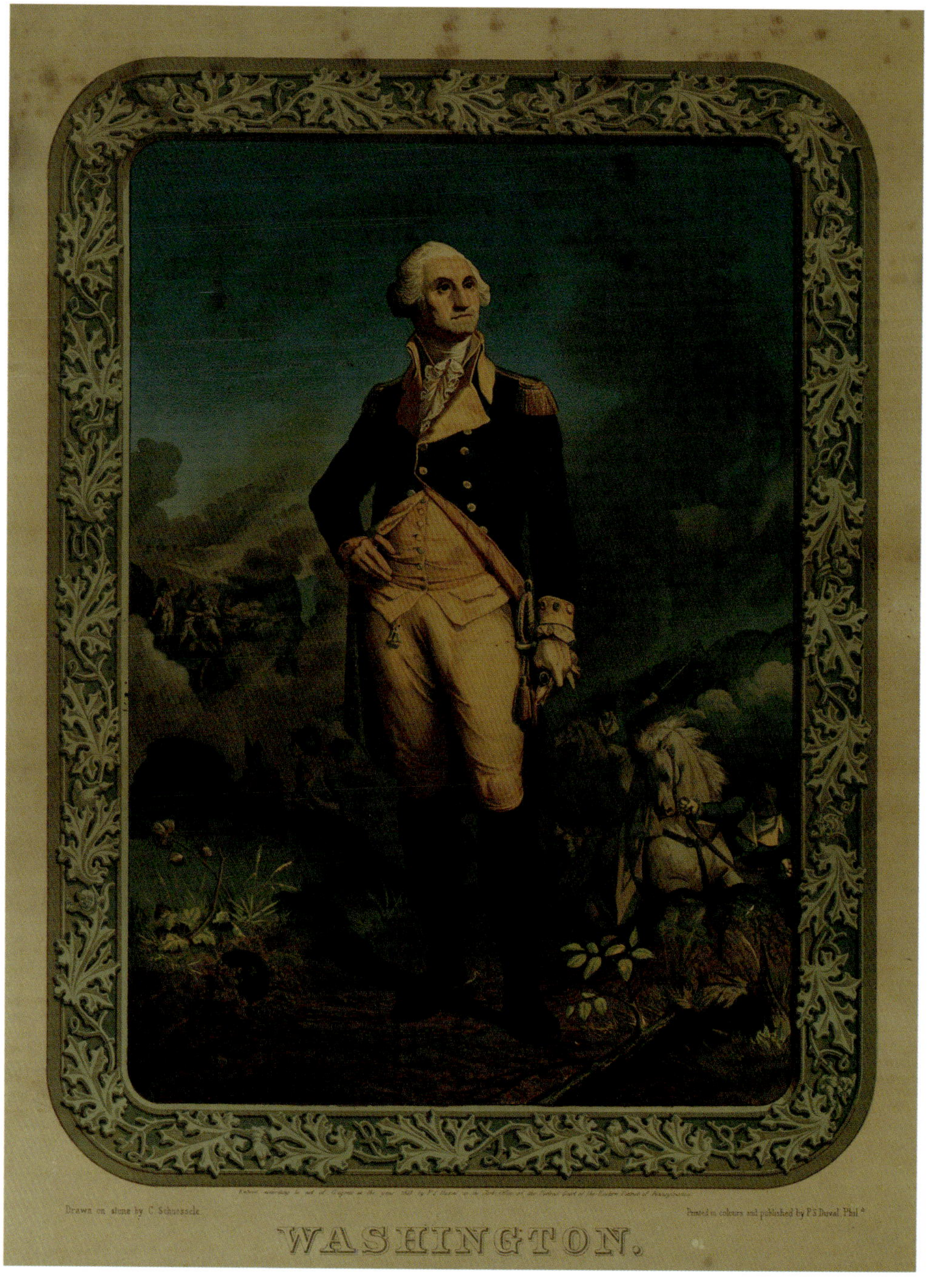

FIG. 65 (ABOVE)

Christian Schussele, *P. S. Duval's Colour Printing & Lithographic Establish[ment]: P. S. Duval & Co. Artisan Building Ranstead Place, West from 26 South 4th St. Philadelphia* (Philadelphia: Lith. of P. S. Duval & Co., ca. 1849). Chromolithograph. 32 × 26 cm (12 ½ × 10 in.). POSA 75, Print and Picture Collection, FLP, Philadelphiana—Lithographers.

FIG. 66 (RIGHT)

Christian Schussele, *Washington* (Philadelphia: P. S. Duval, 1851). Chromolithograph. 57 × 43 cm (22 ½ × 17 in.). HSP, Bc 983 S395.

residence on Walnut Street near Tenth."[49] Duval's personal life during this time, however, seems much more unsettled than Wainwright's description. Duval was living at Second and Cox when his sons died in the early 1840s, but by the mid-1840s he lived in a boardinghouse run by Mr. Esmoil that catered to the French community. By 1850 he had moved to Walnut and Tenth Streets, where he remained for more than a decade. In the 1850 and 1860 censuses, Duval is listed as living with almost completely different household members in each of the census years. Only his son Stephen is listed as part of his household in both censuses.[50]

Regardless of his personal circumstances, Duval's business flourished during the first half of the 1850s. Advertisements, certificates, sheet music covers, fashion plates, and views poured off the presses carrying the imprint of P. S. Duval & Co. Duval's shop accounted for approximately 25 percent of all the 1850–55 prints surveyed for the *Philadelphia on Stone* project. The view of Commissioners' Hall in the Northern Liberties section of Philadelphia proudly proclaimed on its imprint line that it was produced by P. S. Duval & Co.'s steam-powered lithographic presses (fig. 67). Lithographed by Swiss immigrant artist Charles Conrad Kuchel (1820–1864), who had worked for Duval since the mid-1840s, the print included both a detailed rendering of the building's architectural elements and a lively genre scene of Philadelphians going about their daily business while enjoying a newly fallen snow. Editors at the *Public Ledger* received a copy of the print, presumably from Duval, and declared it "a very fine and correct winter scene."[51]

Success and public acclaim, however, gave way to disaster when in the early morning hours of April 11, 1856, fire destroyed Duval's establishment in the Artisan Building. Duval's business on Bank Alley had survived a small fire in April 1842,[52] but this time he was not as lucky. The fire began on the building's top floor, occupied by another firm, and soon engulfed the entire structure, destroying almost $400,000 worth of property. Duval's firm suffered the greatest loss, with the damages estimated at $100,000. The fire destroyed thirty to forty presses and a large number of stones and images, including about $6,000 of work commissioned by the U.S. government. Duval's insurance only covered $30,000 of his loss. Other victims of the destructive fire included lithographer John H. Camp (1822–1881), who had purportedly worked for Duval between 1840 and 1848.[53] His business sustained an $8,000 loss, only a quarter of which was covered by insurance.[54]

One of the stones known to have been destroyed in the fire at Duval's establishment was Rembrandt Peale's (1778–1860) portrait of George Washington (fig. 68). In an 1859 letter, Peale recalled that "whilst at the Printers his premises were destroyed by fire and my Lithograph reduced to powder."[55] Peale's initial disappointment with circumstances

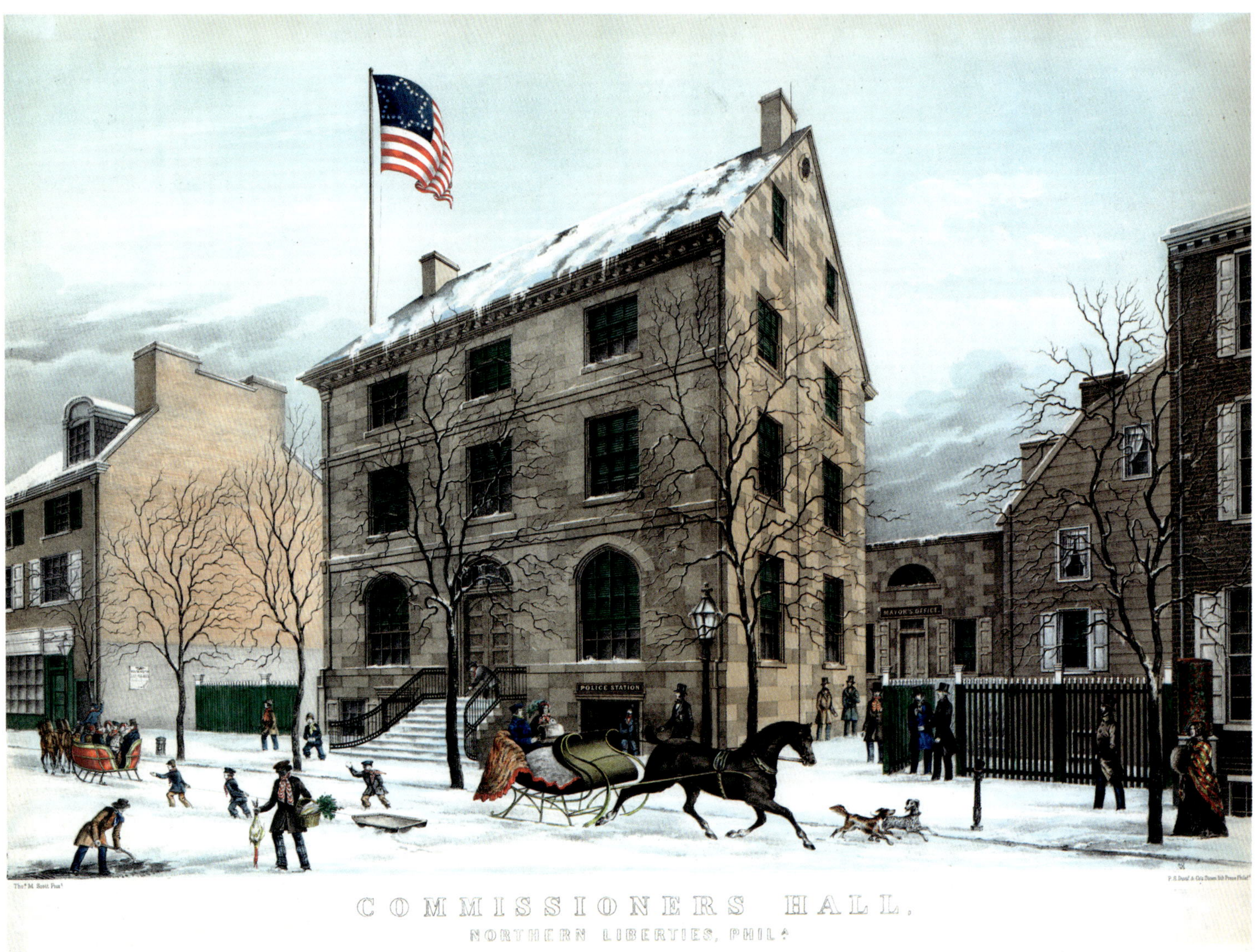

FIG. 67

Charles Conrad Kuchel after Thomas M. Scott, *Commissioners Hall, Northern Liberties, Phila.* (Philadelphia: P. S. Duval & Co.'s Steam Lith. Press, 1853). Lithograph, tinted with two stones and hand-colored. 50 × 66 cm (19 ¾ × 26 in.). POS 151, LCP, P.2034.

beyond Duval's control later turned to dissatisfaction with Duval's work. According to Peale, the use of too strong an acid at Duval's shop ruined the next stone, and the next attempt to print also yielded disappointing results because of "the Printer's inexperience in treating so large a work."[56] Duval's establishment, however, did have experience printing maps and advertisements the size of Washington's portrait, which measured 30 × 24 inches. Although the portrait retained Duval's name, the dissatisfied Peale apparently acquired the prints from Duval's shop and changed their appearance to meet his standards. Peale finished them with "Italian crayon," creating what he called monochromic drawings.[57]

Only two months after the utter destruction of his establishment by fire, Duval pulled together his resources and opened a new shop at the corner of South Fifth and Minor Streets. He placed an advertisement in the *North American* announcing that he had hired additional "artisans and engravers" who were prepared to fill any orders without delay. Anyone whose drawings had been destroyed in the fire would receive a 25 percent reduction of the original price if reordering the work.[58] In this time of need, Peter Duval turned to his son Stephen, who had trained as a lithographer, and in 1857 made him a partner in the firm.[59] Within a year, P. S. Duval & Son moved a few doors down the street to 22 South Fifth Street, where Peter Duval would finish out his lithographic career.

Physically reestablishing the shop, hiring new talent, and actively seeking out customers, however, were not enough to save the business. In November 1859 Peter Duval appeared before the Court of Common Pleas of Philadelphia County to declare his insolvency and ask for relief from his creditors. He laid the blame for his financial woes on the devastating 1856 fire. Even after receiving money from his insurance company, Duval declared that his loss amounted to more than $30,000, a smaller figure than what was reported in newspaper accounts at the time of the fire. According to Duval, he was "obliged to recommence business upon very limited means and compelled to borrow largely in order to purchase new apparatus and start his affairs. . . . This present insolvency," concluded Duval, "was a consequence of his first great loss by the fire which deprived him of the means of carrying out his business."[60]

The court documents relating to the insolvency hearing are a rich source of information about P. S. Duval & Son's business network and practices. At the time of his court appearance, Duval declared that the firm's assets totaled $44,554.71, but he faced creditors who sought to recover $62,326.34. Excluding real-estate property assets, stock shares, and a note owed to Duval as part of a previous court settlement, the largest asset of the firm listed by the court was receivables: $785 owed by a J. C. Powers of Peoria, Illinois; $550 owed by a Thomas Hurley of Perth Amboy, New Jersey; and more than $660 owed by John Desbordes, a Philadelphia tassel maker. An unspecified group of "P. S. Duval & Son, Agents" owed the business nearly $300.[61] Debtors from as far away as Nashville, St. Paul, New Orleans, San Francisco, Washington, D.C., and Hinsdale, Massachusetts, all owed Duval varying amounts, but mostly relatively small sums. Of the one hundred people or businesses that owed Duval money, almost half owed $25 or less, with about one-third owing less than $10.[62]

In contrast to the relatively modest sums owed by individuals to the firm, P. S. Duval & Son owed large sums of money to many people. Excluding property mortgages owed by Duval, eleven of the 113 businesses or individual creditors listed in the

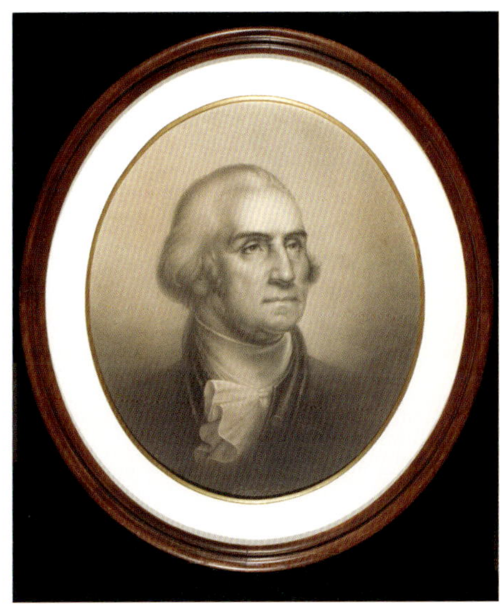

Rembrandt Peale, *G. Washington* (Philadelphia: P. S. Duval & Co., 1856). Lithograph. 69 × 59 cm (27 × 23 in.). LCP, Gift of Donald Neiman, P.2007.19.

court documents were owed more than $1,000 each. The firm's largest creditor was Stephen C. Duval, who was owed more than $6,000. Other large creditors included Charles Magarge & Co., a Philadelphia paper manufacturer; J. B. Lippincott, a Philadelphia bookseller; William Pelletier, identified in Philadelphia directories as a gentleman; and John Desbordes, the Philadelphia tassel maker who also owed money to P. S. Duval & Son. Not surprisingly, Duval owed money to numerous local businesses involved in the printing trade, including stationers and card, ink, and paper manufacturers. Five individuals, all identified through other sources as lithographers, appeared on the creditor list as being owed wages in amounts ranging from $25 to more than $200.[63] P. S. Duval & Son owed money to other artists and lithographers, but not in the form of wages, indicating that those men had forged a different type of working arrangement with Duval. For example, the firm owed long-term lithographic artists James Queen $117.67 and Albert Newsam $250 for their work.[64] Perhaps because of Peter Duval's more than twenty-five years in the lithographic trade and good reputation, the court declared that he would have seven years of freedom from creditors in order to reestablish his business.[65]

While declaring insolvency in 1859, after decades as a successful business owner, was certainly a professional low point, Peter Duval also experienced other setbacks that year. Early in the year Duval, along with Philadelphia lithographer Thomas S. Wagner (1813/14–1863) and engravers William H. Van Ingen and Richard Major, traveled to Washington, D.C., to testify before Congress during an investigation into the late superintendent of public printing's awarding of government contracts. Duval, along with many other printers, had benefited from the government's need for illustrations and maps to accompany reports about territorial exploration and other governmental affairs. Duval, for example, produced nineteen lithographs for the first volume of Henry R. Schoolcraft's six-volume *Historical and Statistical Information Respecting the History, Condition, and Prospects of the Indian Tribes of the United States,* a project authorized by Congress in 1847 (fig. 69).[66] The committee found that Duval and others who had received government work had been pressured to employ certain agents who directed work toward particular firms. The engravers and lithographers stated that "they made provision in their bills for the allowance which they were expected to make to the agents." The printers were not cited for any wrongdoing, but the committee commented harshly on the bookkeeping and general business practices of the former superintendent.[67]

Just before Duval's declaration of insolvency, his firm experienced a smaller, more personal setback with the loss of its longtime artist Albert Newsam, who fell victim to a paralyzing stroke in the fall of 1859. Despite Duval's own financial woes,

he and a group of men raised money to place Newsam, who
was no longer able to support himself, in a home for inva-
lids near Wilmington, Delaware. Duval characterized his relationship with Newsam as focused "altogether on business
matters,"[68] but correspondence between the two men reveals
a mutual respect and kindness not confined to business. A
lengthy unsigned note, most likely written by Duval in the
early 1850s, for example, offered Newsam advice about his living and working arrangements.[69] In letters exchanged during
Newsam's last years of life, Newsam inquired about the health
of James Queen and other artists working for Duval, asked
about the items he still had stored in "the artists' room" at
Duval's shop, and requested Duval to write to him as soon as
possible.[70] Duval in turn offered to send Newsam copies of
the firm's most recent portrait prints and apprised Newsam of
changes occurring in the lithographic trade.[71]

   As Duval built up his firm after declaring insolvency, he
realized the importance of staying abreast of technological improvements and changing tastes in the marketplace. "Lithography do[es] very little now in the portraits," he reported in
an 1864 letter to Albert Newsam; "they are nearly all donne
[*sic*] by photographs or massetints [mezzotints]."[72] Duval may

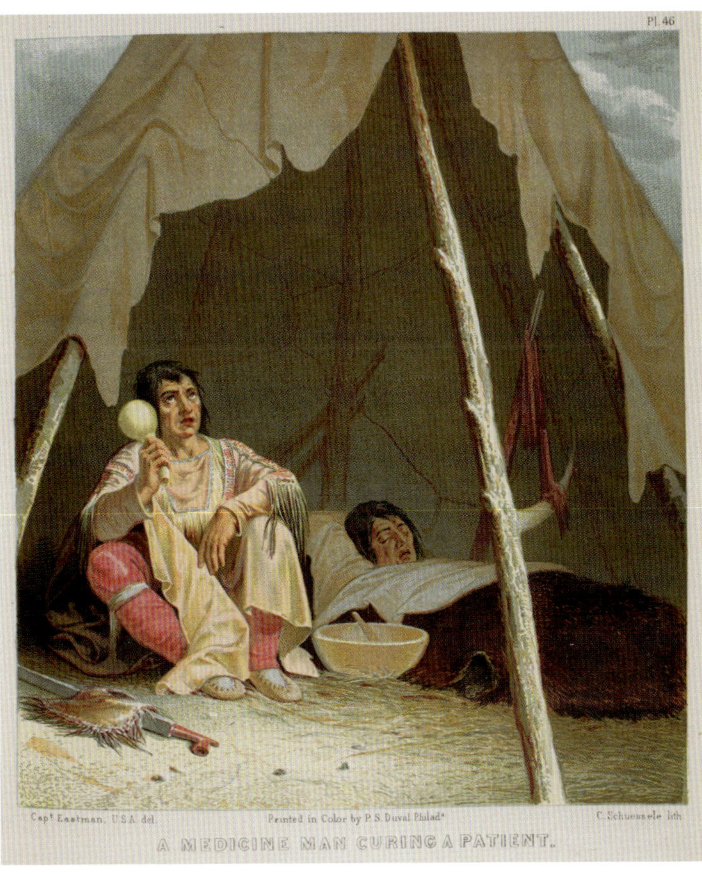

FIG. 69
Christian Schussele after Seth Eastman,
A Medicine Man Curing a Patient, from
Henry R. Schoolcraft, *Historical and
Statistical Information Respecting the His-
tory, Condition, and Prospects of the Indian
Tribes of the United States* (Philadelphia:
Lippincott, Grambo & Co., 1851), pt. 1,
plate 46. Printed by P. S. Duval. Chromo-
lithograph. 41 × 32 cm (16 × 12 ¼ in.) LCP,
*Am 1851 Sch 2580.Q.

have viewed photography as depriving lithographers of business, but he also took
advantage of photographic technology to expand his lithographic business in new
directions. While artists like Newsam had long relied on daguerreotypes as sources
for lithographic portraits and some land and cityscape views, by the 1860s Duval was
probably experimenting with using photography more directly by photographically
reproducing images, rather than drawing them, on stones. An 1860 billhead for Duval,
Williams & Duval declares that "a photographic room is attached to this establishment."[73] Duval's entry about lithography in the *American Encyclopaedia of Printing*
includes several paragraphs describing photolithography, clearly indicating Duval's
familiarity with the process.

   In the same 1864 letter to Newsam, Duval also noted the impact the Civil War
was having on his business, declaring that "a great many artists and printers have
gonne [*sic*] to the War" and bemoaning the vicissitudes of business during the unsettled times.[74] The upsurge of patriotic fervor in the country, however, gave Duval
and other printers new subject matter to illustrate and created consumers eager to

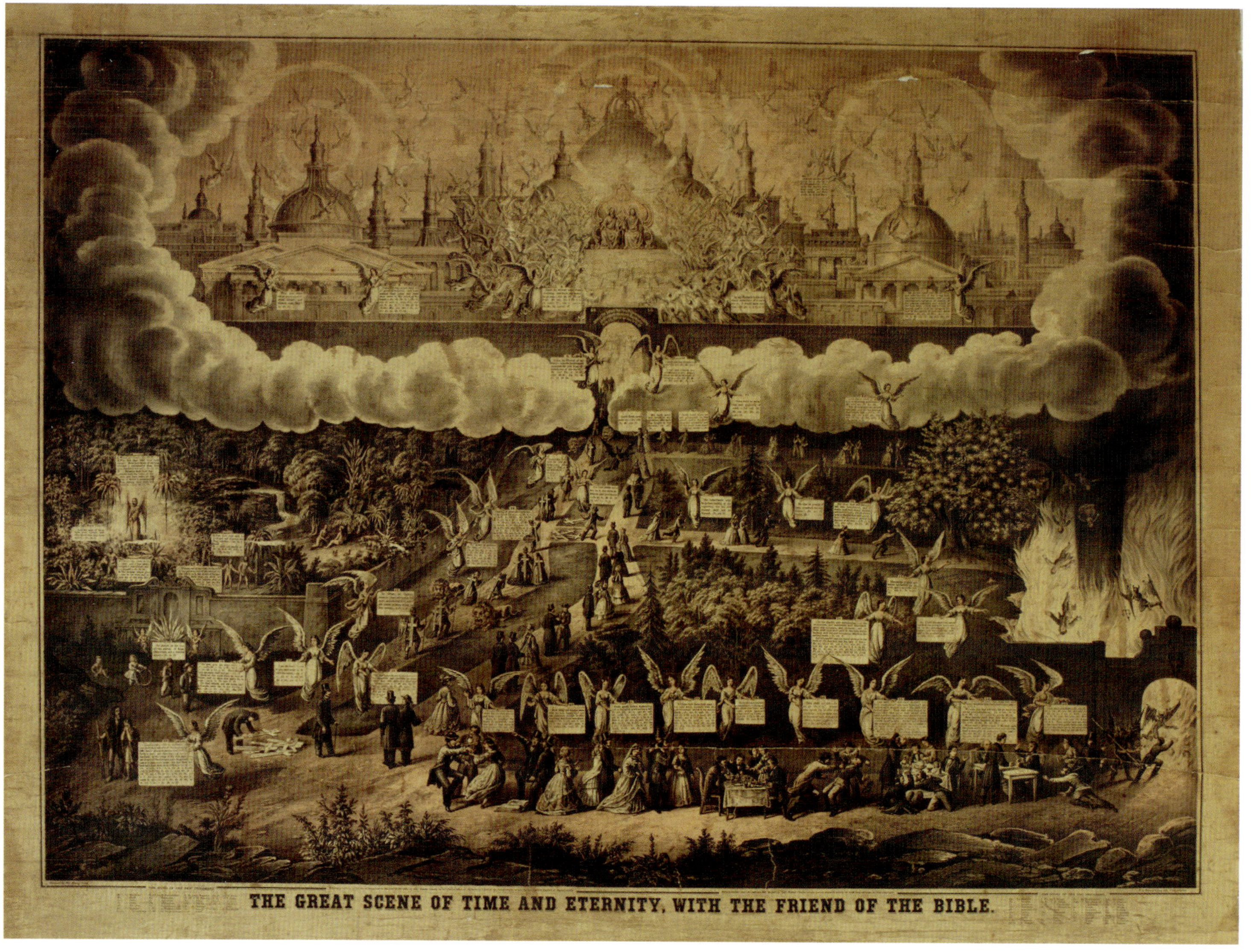

The Great Scene of Time and Eternity with the Friend of the Bible (Philadelphia: P. S. Duval & Son, 1864). Lithograph, tinted with two stones. 101 × 131 cm (40 × 51 ¾ in.). LCP, P.2007.30.

display their feelings about the conflict. Duval's shop produced membership certificates for patriotic organizations, sheet music covers depicting the war, military maps, and views of hospitals and campgrounds. The Duval firm also played an active role in Philadelphia's Great Central Fair, a three-week-long display of art, crafts, and historical exhibitions held in June 1864 to raise money for the Union soldiers' relief organization, the U.S. Sanitary Commission. Among the Central Fair contributors listed in the *Philadelphia Inquirer*, P. S. Duval & Son donated the largest amount of goods (more than $315 worth of lithographs), as well as $50 in cash.[75] The lithographs were most probably copies of Duval's view of the buildings of the fair (see fig. 133), which he printed there and sold for $2 apiece.[76] This view was also reproduced as a small souvenir card.

During the early 1860s Peter Duval and his son labored to reestablish their business on solid financial ground, a process described in R. G. Dun & Company's credit report as "up hill work."[77] Duval's overall professional reputation, however, seems to have survived despite his financial problems. It was Duval, rather than any of his growing number of competitors, whom delegates from the Japanese embassy chose to visit while touring Philadelphia in the summer of 1860.[78] Peter Duval had had little competition when he entered the lithographic field in the 1830s, but by the middle of the century he was attempting to reestablish himself in a city increasingly crowded with lithographic establishments. In 1856 sixteen lithographic firms supported 177 presses. By 1870 the number of establishments had nearly doubled, having increased to thirty, with almost three hundred presses in operation.[79]

Duval needed to set his firm's work apart from that of his competition. His firm continued to produce pictorial prints, including membership certificates for fire companies and fraternal organizations, in greater quantities than other Philadelphia lithographic businesses, which began focusing on more ephemeral lithographic needs such as trade cards, bank checks, and labels.[80] Duval's ability to produce enormous pictorial prints also directed attention to his firm. In 1861 he printed *Washington's Triumphal Entry, New York, Nov. 25th, 1783,* a heroic historical scene of George Washington entering New York City immediately after the British evacuation, which measured approximately 34 ½ × 47 inches. The accompanying descriptive pamphlet declared the print to be "the largest specimen of Chromolithograph ever executed."[81] P. S. Duval & Son produced an even larger lithograph with the completion in 1864 of *The Great Scene of Time and Eternity with the Friend of the Bible* (fig. 70). Based on the genre of prints known variously as "The Two Ways," "New Jerusalem," and "The Broad and the Narrow Way," the print depicted dozens of men and women traveling along various paths on their way to heaven or hell. The lithograph, more than three feet high and four feet wide, made an impressive statement both in subject matter and size.

Throughout the seven years Peter Duval had to reestablish his business, the firm took in various partners for brief periods of time. Prints carrying the imprint Duval, Williams & Duval appeared about 1860, and in the middle of the decade a print was published with the imprint of Duval, Swander & Co.[82] In 1867 the firm added Isaac L. Miles as a partner (although he was not named in the firm's title), forming P. S. Duval, Son & Co. R. G. Dun & Company in their credit assessment described Isaac Miles as a young man of good character and in possession of a patent for printing on glass.[83]

The firm, regardless of its partners, continued both to print and to publish a wide variety of commercial lithographs.

When Peter S. Duval retired from the firm in 1869, he may have left behind the day-to-day cares of running a lithographic business, but he certainly did not leave the lithographic field. In the summer of 1871 Duval's peers elected him president of Philadelphia's Lithographers' Association. The association resolved to celebrate the upcoming centennial of Alois Senefelder's birth by holding a banquet and chose Duval to serve as the organizing committee's chairman. Donations for the banquet from more than two hundred lithographers totaled $750, but plans for the celebration changed at the last moment, when the Lithographers' Association decided to donate the money to fire victims in Chicago, Wisconsin, and Michigan.[84]

As the 1870s began, the firm that Peter S. Duval launched more than thirty years earlier was now under the management of his son Stephen, who quickly took on Philadelphia lithographer Thomas Hunter (born ca. 1828) as a partner. Duval & Hunter paid homage to the firm's long and illustrious history in its promotional material. The back cover of its 1873–74 catalog, for example, proudly declared that Duval & Hunter and its predecessors had won nineteen first premiums and medals from exhibitions around the country and abroad between 1841 and 1872. The catalog also emphasized the firm's continued interest in producing chromolithographic art reproductions.[85] Soon after that catalog was issued, Stephen Duval left the firm, an action that, according to R. G. Dun & Company, "rendered the house stronger in the opinion of the trade."[86] Duval may then have moved to Richmond, Virginia, but by 1877 he had returned to Philadelphia and had begun his own lithographic firm, establishing his new business at the Fourth Street and Ranstead Place location of his father's old firm.[87] Although Thomas Hunter continued in the lithographic business on his own until a disastrous 1886 fire, Stephen Duval's lithographic career seems to have been less successful. By 1880 he had apparently left Philadelphia, and in 1900 he and his wife, Emma Hoffy Duval, lived in New York City with their adult daughter and her family.[88] Stephen Duval and his wife both died in New Orleans in 1907.

Peter Duval died in Philadelphia of "enlargement of the heart" on February 9, 1886, seventeen years after retiring from his lithographic firm. His former shop superintendent James Queen had passed away only a few weeks earlier. Duval was buried in Philadelphia's Monument Cemetery, modeled after Paris's Père Lachaise.[89] Early in his career Duval and his partner Lehman had printed a plan of Monument Cemetery, in which they had been shareholders from the time of its 1838 incorporation.[90] By the mid-1950s Philadelphia's insatiable need for land encroached upon the once-rural Monument Cemetery, and Duval's remains, along with those of approximately twenty-eight thousand others, were relocated to a suburban cemetery.[91]

Although the lithographic firm he headed for more than thirty years did not survive long without him, Peter S. Duval surely realized that his accomplishments in the field of lithography would long outlast his shop. The expertise he brought with him from France when American lithography was in its infancy allowed lithography to gain respect as a printing process equal to engraving. His commitment to pursuing technological improvements, whether experimenting with color lithography and photolithography or adding steam-powered equipment to his shop, not only created interest and excitement in his firm's activities but also advanced the field of lithography as a whole. Duval's firm weathered crippling setbacks but persevered to stand as a leader in Philadelphia lithography, as well as become one of America's most preeminent lithographic establishments.

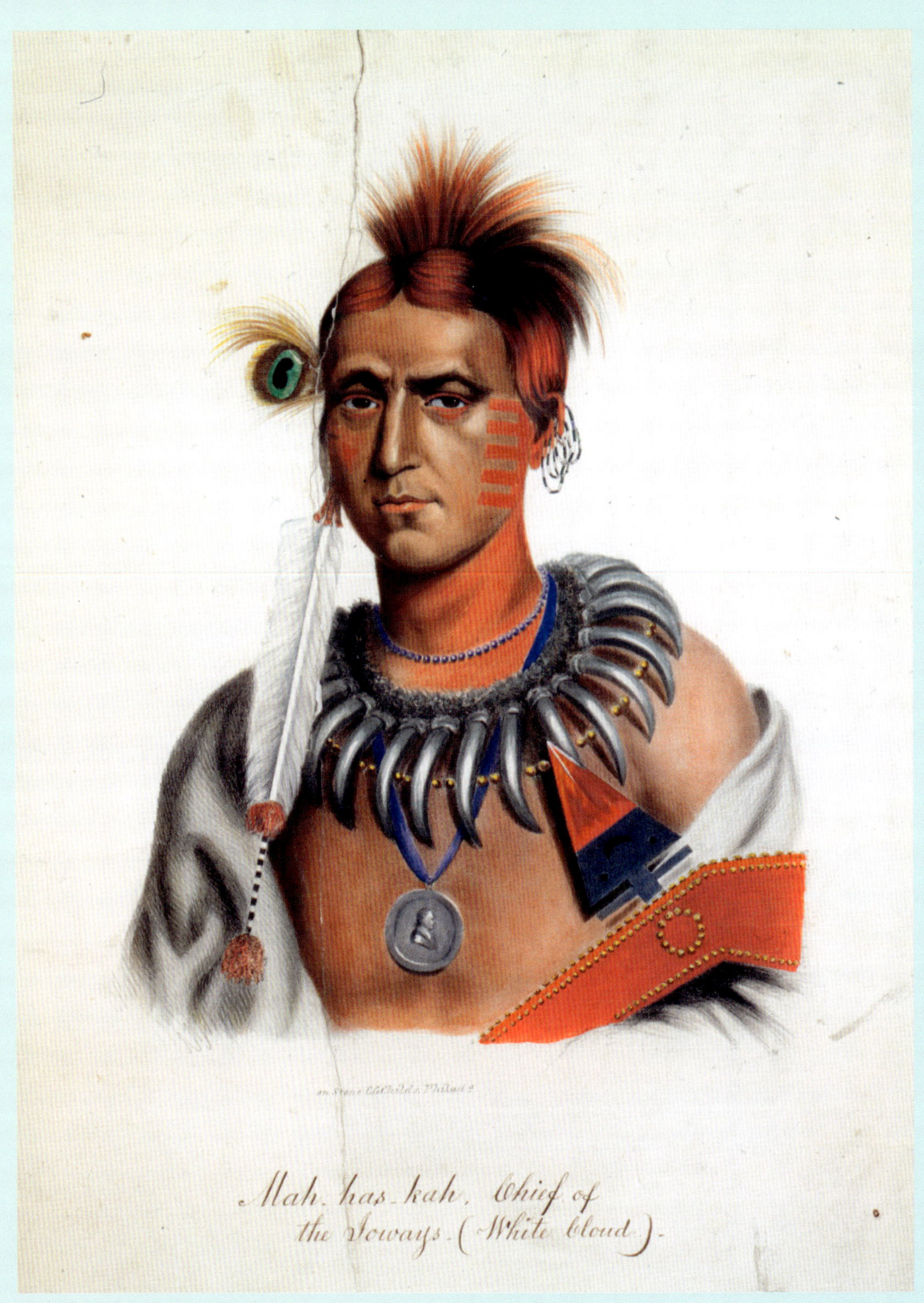

Mah-has-kah, Chief of
the Ioways. (White Cloud).

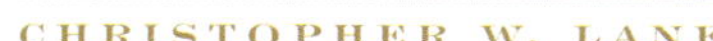

LITHOGRAPHED PLATES FOR BOOKS AND PERIODICALS

A Mainstay of Philadelphia Lithographers

American lithographers[1] in the nineteenth century generally had to produce prints for a wide range of purposes and clients.[2] Especially in the early days of the 1820s and 1830s, it was not easy for a lithographer to find enough work to stay in business. There was already a thriving industry of metal and wood engravers available to those seeking to have a print made, and at first it was not easy for lithographers to grab a significant share of that business. Lithography did offer some practical and economic advantages,[3] but it was still necessary for lithographers to be flexible and diversified in their work.

A staple for most nineteenth-century American lithographers was job-order prints, where a customer hired the lithographer to produce a specific type of print for a particular need. These included such items as menus, tickets, checks, billheads, labels, plans, circulars, and many other prints of an ephemeral nature. Other commissioned prints included individual and group portraits and views of buildings or landscapes, ordered by private customers or civic and commercial organizations. As the industry matured, some lithographers began to issue speculative prints, as discussed in chapter 7, creating prints without commission, in hopes that they would find a market for them. But for most lithographers, the majority of their business consisted of commissioned prints.

Many of these were issued as separate prints, but many others were illustrations for some sort of larger publication.[4] As early as 1819 lithography was seen as a potentially useful means of illustrating scientific reports, an article on the subject in

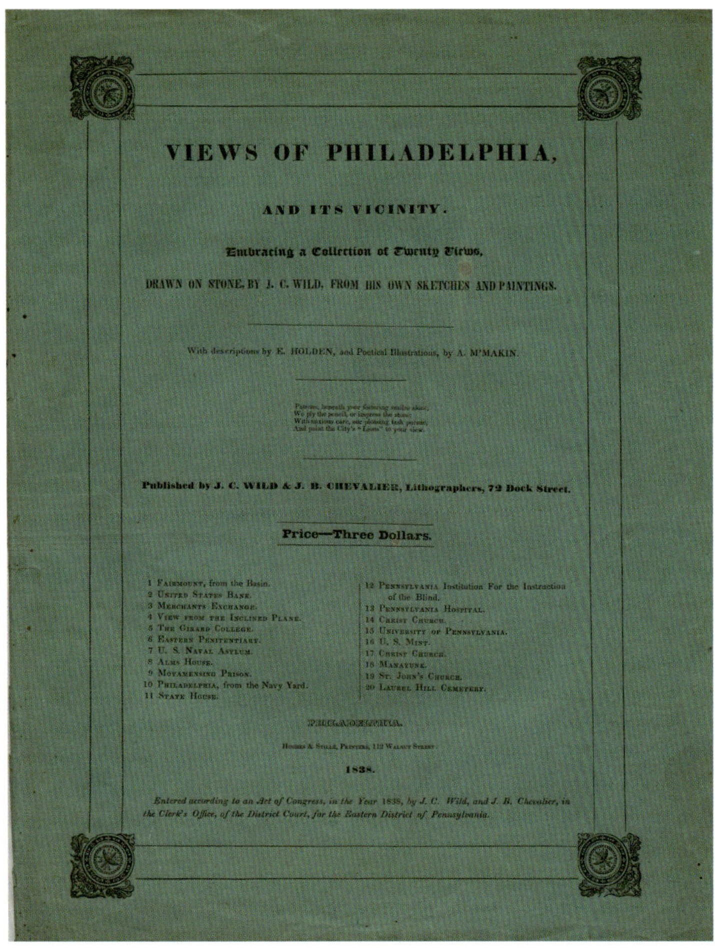

VIEWS OF PHILADELPHIA,

AND ITS VICINITY.

Embracing a Collection of Twenty Views,

DRAWN ON STONE, BY J. C. WILD, FROM HIS OWN SKETCHES AND PAINTINGS.

With descriptions by E. HOLDEN, and Poetical Illustrations, by A. M'MAKIN.

Patrons, beneath your fostering smiles alone,
We ply the pencil, or impress the stone;
With anxious care, our pleasing task pursue,
And paint the City's "Lions" to your view.

Published by J. C. WILD & J. B. CHEVALIER, Lithographers, 72 Dock Street.

Price—Three Dollars.

1 FAIRMOUNT, from the Basin.
2 UNITED STATES BANK.
3 MERCHANTS EXCHANGE.
4 VIEW FROM THE INCLINED PLANE.
5 THE GIRARD COLLEGE.
6 EASTERN PENITENTIARY.
7 U. S. NAVAL ASYLUM.
8 ALMS HOUSE.
9 MOYAMENSING PRISON.
10 PHILADELPHIA, from the Navy Yard.
11 STATE HOUSE.
12 PENNSYLVANIA Institution For the Instruction of the Blind.
13 PENNSYLVANIA HOSPITAL.
14 CHRIST CHURCH.
15 UNIVERSITY OF PENNSYLVANIA.
16 U. S. MINT.
17 CHRIST CHURCH.
18 MANAYUNK.
19 ST. JOHN'S CHURCH.
20 LAUREL HILL CEMETERY.

PHILADELPHIA.

HUGHES & STILLE, PRINTERS, 112 Walnut Street.

1838.

Entered according to an Act of Congress, in the Year 1838, by J. C. Wild, and J. B. Chevalier, in the Clerk's Office, of the District Court, for the Eastern District of Pennsylvania.

FIG. 71

Cover of the fifth part of *Views of Philadelphia and Its Vicinity* (Philadelphia: J. C. Wild & J. B. Chevalier, printed by Hughes & Stille, 1838). 37 × 27 cm (14 ½ × 10 ¾ in.). LCP, 6626.F.

Analectic Magazine stating: "All works of science may now be freed from the prodigious expense attending numerous engravings."[5] And, indeed, it has been argued that the "first impetus toward lithography in America came from physicians and scientists who wished to have a cheap, easy means of illustrating their writings on natural history."[6] Soon lithographic images were used as illustrations for magazines, lithographic maps and charts were included in the reports and pamphlets of various businesses and organizations, and it was not long before the illustrations on the covers of music sheets were almost all lithographed (see chapter 8).

Books also shortly began to appear with lithographic title pages and illustrations, especially specialized books such as scientific or travel works. Lithographs tended not to be used in books as illustrations within the text, for lithographs had to be printed from a press different from that used for the text; for text illustrations it was therefore cheaper and more convenient to use wood engravings.[7] However, where the publisher wanted a better-quality image, to be inserted as a plate[8] in a book, lithography was often used. By the 1830s, lithographs, especially hand-colored ones, were used to produce the more elaborate "plate books."

Plate books are publications in which the plates are as important as the text, or more so. In the nineteenth century, plate books were issued with elaborate illustrations, and they tended to be expensive publications meant for an elite audience. Hand-coloring, which added to their expense but also made these works more luxurious, gave these plate books a cachet that appealed to the wealthy.

The cost of these works was high, both to produce and purchase, and in order to spread out the expense over time, plate books were often sold by subscription. In such cases, the publisher would issue the work in "parts," containing some text and a number of plates that the subscriber would then pay for, providing the publisher with the funds to produce the next part. These parts were usually issued with paper covers (figs. 71, 82), and when the work was complete, the parts could then be bound into a book proper, though sometimes these publications would be kept as a portfolio.[9]

Many types of plate books were issued in the nineteenth century, including view books, the first American example of which was William Birch's *City of Philadelphia,* a volume containing twenty-eight engravings issued in 1800.[10] Other plate publications included children's books, drawing and pattern books, architectural-plan books, travels, and natural-history volumes. At the start of the nineteenth century these were composed primarily of engraved plates, but beginning in the 1830s and then in greater numbers in the 1840s and 1850s, lithograph plate books became ever more common, with increasingly elaborate and artistic plates as the printmakers perfected their techniques.

Lithographic illustrations for publications were produced in all American cities that had lithographic businesses, but this type of production was especially important for the Philadelphia lithographic industry. Indeed, plates for books and periodicals were a mainstay for much of the Philadelphia lithographic trade from early in the nineteenth century. Separately issued, frameable prints and large colorful advertisements are generally more flashy and collectible than plates from some publication, so the former often receive more notice than the latter. However, for many Philadelphia lithographers in the nineteenth century, plates for books and periodicals were equally important to or more important than separate-sheet prints, forming a large percentage, if not the majority, of their output.

The significance of lithographic plates intended for books and periodicals for Philadelphia printmakers resulted from a number of factors, foremost of which was the fact that for much of the nineteenth century Philadelphia was the leading center of book and magazine publishing in America. Ever since the eighteenth century, Philadelphia had developed a thriving publishing industry, along with the related businesses of printing-press manufacturing, type founding, papermaking, binding, ink production, and, of course, printmaking. It was natural that Philadelphia lithographers would take advantage of the opportunities offered by local book and magazine publishers, though they also worked for firms from elsewhere. Antebellum-era lithographers also worked during a period when the periodical market exploded in size to reach the increasingly literate mass market. The number of publications increased nearly sixfold between 1825 and 1850,[11] an interval dubbed a "Golden Age of the Periodicals" by journalism historian Franklin Mott. Several of the numerous new periodicals emerging were published in Philadelphia, which became an epicenter not only for books but for the production and consumption of periodicals with captivating illustrations best delineated as lithographs.[12]

Kennedy & Lucas,[13] the first commercial lithographic business in Philadelphia, was founded by William B. Lucas in 1828, about seven years after the first American commercial lithographic firm Barnet & Doolittle appeared in New York City. This firm, which continued until 1833, when Lucas died, was typical of early American lithographic printmakers, producing a relatively small number of several different types of prints. They invited local artists and amateurs to make their own lithographs, did job printing, produced sheet music covers, and issued separate-sheet views. They also became involved in producing illustrations for publications.

Among their first prints were more than a half dozen lithographs, ca. 1829–30, of Philadelphia churches taken from drawings by William L. Breton.[14] This series was likely commissioned by Breton, who had an additional lithographic church print produced by another Philadelphia lithographer, Cephas G. Childs. Though these do not appear to have been bound, the similar size and format indicate that Breton may have intended these prints for a plate portfolio or book. Kennedy & Lucas also produced a similar series of five views of Niagara Falls, drawn on stone by Lucas and Hugh Bridport after drawings by W. Vivian.[15] These are copies of the lithographs in Vivian's 1825 *Views of the Great Falls of Niagara,* produced in London, and it is likely they were intended for an American edition of that portfolio.

In 1830 Kennedy & Lucas did produce sixteen book illustrations for antiquarian John F. Watson's *Annals of Philadelphia* (fig. 72). These lithographs were also based on drawings by Breton, as were seven more plates that were included the next year in Thomas Porter's *Picture of Philadelphia.* Kennedy & Lucas lithographs appeared in a number of other publications between 1830 and 1833, including six plates for Jean Frédéric Lobstein's *Treatise on the Structure, Functions, and Diseases of the Human Sympathetic Nerve* (1831) and plates for a number of railroad-company reports. The firm also lithographed magazine illustrations. Breton was the artist for their print *Comly Ville near Frankford—Philadelphia Co.,* from *Godey's Lady's Book* in 1830, and two botanical plates by Kennedy & Lucas were included in the July 1832 issue of *Floral Magazine and Botanical Repository.*

The firm of Kennedy & Lucas did not depend solely on their lithographs, for they continued to operate a shop that sold frames and mirrors, but in terms of their print production, it is clear that illustrations for various publications formed a major part of their business. They are known to have produced only three sheet music covers and twelve prints that clearly were separately issued, as well as the near dozen prints that were from series that might have been intended to be part of portfolios. For publications, they produced at least seven magazine and report plates and thirty-five book plates, well over half their known prints.[16]

Another early Philadelphia lithographic firm that depended substantially on illustrations for publications was Wild & Chevalier, which operated in 1837 and 1838. John Caspar Wild was a Swiss artist who had studied in Paris before moving to Philadelphia in 1832.[17] J. C. Wild produced the lithograph *Bunch of Grapes* for Cephas G. Childs shortly after he arrived, and he also partnered in a lithographic firm with another Swiss artist, Charles Fenderich, whom he may have known from Paris. As Fenderich & Wild, they issued a number of lithographs, six of which are recorded, before Fenderich moved to Washington about 1835.

In that year Wild also left Philadelphia, moving to Cincinnati, because he did not feel he could find sufficient work as an artist and lithographer and hoped to have better luck elsewhere.[18] In Cincinnati Wild began to paint a series of views of the city, which he intended to be turned into lithographs.[19] No prints after these Cincinnati drawings have been discovered, so it is likely Wild continued to face a lack of support for his lithographic ambitions. It appears, however, that in the meantime he was receiving encouragement from Philadelphia, for in 1837 Wild returned to that city and began work on an ambitious plate book of views of Philadelphia.

On July 15, 1837, Andrew M'Makin and Ezra Holden, publishers of the Philadelphia *Saturday Courier,* announced in their paper that they intended to produce a volume of engraved prints of Philadelphia: "The architectural beauty of many of the PUBLIC BUILDINGS of this city is proverbial. Believing it will be acceptable to our numerous patrons to be presented with Engraved Illustrations of these edifices, we are engaged in bringing out a complete series . . . that may well be termed THE LIONS OF PHILADELPHIA."[20]

This series was never realized, but later that same year the endeavor to produce a series of views of Philadelphia buildings was taken up by J. C. Wild, partnered with another Philadelphia lithographer, J. B. Chevalier. It seems likely that Wild was encouraged in this by his old supporter M'Makin,[21] for certainly Wild & Chevalier at least had the tacit support of publishers, as not only did they set up their shop at the same address, 72 Dock Street, as the *Saturday Courier,* but on December 2, 1837, the paper ran this announcement: "Splendid Views: Messrs. Wild and Chevalier (at 72 Dock Street) are engaged in bringing out a beautiful series of views, forming 20 in all, for the very low price of $2.50, less than half price of any thing of the kind ever published. We are much gratified that the specimens of the publication have thus far yielded them unparalleled encouragement."[22]

This was to be a typical view book, consisting of twenty lithographed views of Philadelphia and its vicinity, with text, and to be sold by subscription (fig. 71). As described on the cover of the first part, issued in January 1838:

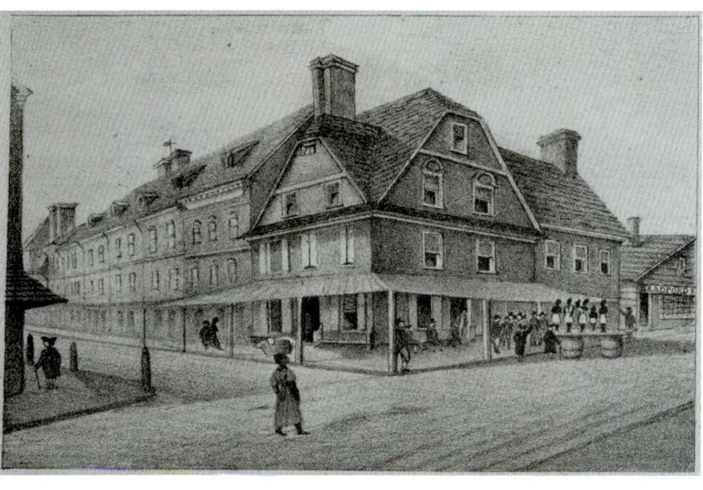

William L. Breton, *London Coffee House,* from John F. Watson, *Annals of Philadelphia* (Philadelphia: E. L. Carey & A. Hart, 1830). Printed by Kennedy & Lucas. Lithograph. 14 × 23 cm (5 ¾ × 9 in). POS 442, LCP, 9245.Q.20.

These Views will be published in five monthly numbers, beginning with January, and will be on fine paper, of the size of the *New York Mirror.* Each number will contain four Views, printed on Chinese paper, and embellished with a beautiful cover. . . . The subscription price is $2.50 in advance, after the issuing of the first number: or 50 cents for each number, payable on delivery, which will be less than half the price of any view of the kind that has ever been given to the public, and will form an object of attraction for every centre table, or for the ladies' album.[23]

It is clear that from the beginning Wild & Chevalier intended this series of prints to be issued as a plate book. Typical of plate books sold by subscription, not all the impressions of the prints in the series would have been bound, for some would inevitably have been framed for decoration or, as the prospectus suggests, used as pages "for the ladies' album." As soon as the prints were all completed, in May 1838, Wild filed for a copyright for the publication *Views of Philadelphia and Its Vicinity,* with a sale price of $3.00, and Wild & Chevalier announced that they were also going to publish a *Panorama of Philadelphia,* to consist of a set of four views showing the city as seen looking in the cardinal directions from the steeple of the State House.

Throughout the publication of *Views of Philadelphia,* Wild & Chevalier received support from the publishers of the *Saturday Courier.* Holden provided a page of text and M'Maken a stanza of poetry for each print, and the paper also advertised that it would offer the entire series as a subscription bonus. It may have been the support of the newspaper that allowed Wild & Chevalier to purchase their own press[24] and announce that "the subscribers take pleasure in informing the public that they are now fully prepared to execute every description of Lithography: such as Drawings, Writings, Maps, Bills, Cards &c. on stone, in the fine style of the art; and respectfully solicit a share of public patronage."[25]

The support of M'Maken and Holden continued, for appearing in June 1838 were two larger views of Philadelphia published by Wild & Chevalier and commissioned by the *Saturday Courier*—views of Fairmount Waterworks and Girard College (see fig. 127) that were offered by the paper as subscription bonuses. On each lithograph was printed text indicating that a subscription for the paper was "two Dollars a year in advance" but would include "two Engravings of this Kind Yearly." The paper also ran advertisements to this effect from June 2 through the end of November 1838.

Despite Wild & Chevalier's offer to "execute every description of Lithography," the artistic success of their views, and the support of the *Saturday Courier,* the firm did not appear to receive many orders for new work. Besides the twenty views of

Philadelphia, the four panorama lithographs, and the two subscription bonus prints, fewer than ten other lithographs by Wild & Chevalier are known. This lack of success seems to have soured Wild once again on Philadelphia, and before the end of 1838 he had sold out to Chevalier and moved to St. Louis.

It is interesting that while Wild had not achieved financial success with the series of views he had embarked on either in Cincinnati or in Philadelphia, he still saw the production of lithographic plate publications as a promising foundation for his future. While in St. Louis he produced two other plate books,[26] neither of which was completely successful. Wild's lithographic career lasted from his arrival in America in 1832 almost until his death, on August 12, 1846. Like Kennedy & Lucas, Wild was heavily dependent on plates for various publications, for about two-thirds of the lithographic prints he was involved in were from such works.[27]

Later in 1838, after Wild left Philadelphia, Chevalier decided to combine the four panorama prints with the twenty views of Philadelphia and issue them together as a single volume, *Panorama and Views of Philadelphia and Its Vicinity.* However, Wild had been the firm's artist and apparently its prime mover, for almost immediately after Wild left Philadelphia, Chevalier's lithographic career all but ended. Not only did the planned yearly pair of premium prints for the *Saturday Courier* never materialize, but in that same year Chevalier sold the stones and rights for the *Views* to J. T. Bowen, who brought out a third edition at the end of 1838 and then a fourth edition ten years later.

Chevalier did make one more attempt to produce a publication illustrated with lithographic plates. In November 1838 he filed a notice that he intended to edit a book, *The Ornithology of the United States,* with text by John Kirk Townsend and "drawings, from nature by J. C. Wild."[28] Wild did not end up participating in this venture, but about a year later, in the September 4, 1839, issue of the *United States Gazette,* the following notice appeared: "Ornithology: Mr. J. B. Chevalier, No. 85 Dock Street, has commenced the publication, in numbers, of the 'Ornithology of the United States,' the description by J. K. Townsend. The illustrations are large, done in lithograph, and richly colored from nature. We have had occasion to mention the plan of the work already, and are happy to observe that the proprietor is encouraged to carry it into execution."

The first part of this work, which was to be sold by subscription, included twelve pages of text and four hand-colored lithographs of birds, drawn by T. Delarne and lithographed by "J. B. Chevalier & Co. Lithographer" (fig. 73). The preface explained that the book was being published because "it is considered desirable to offer the public a work of portable dimensions and generally accessible form, containing a particular account of the birds of the United States. . . . No one has yet completed this task

T. Delarne, *Caracara Eagle,* from John K. Townsend, *Ornithology of the United States of North America* (Philadelphia: J. B. Chevalier, 1839). Lithograph with hand-coloring. 16 × 26 cm (6 × 9 ¾ in.). The Academy of Natural Sciences, Ewell Sale Stewart Library, QL696.A2.T7.

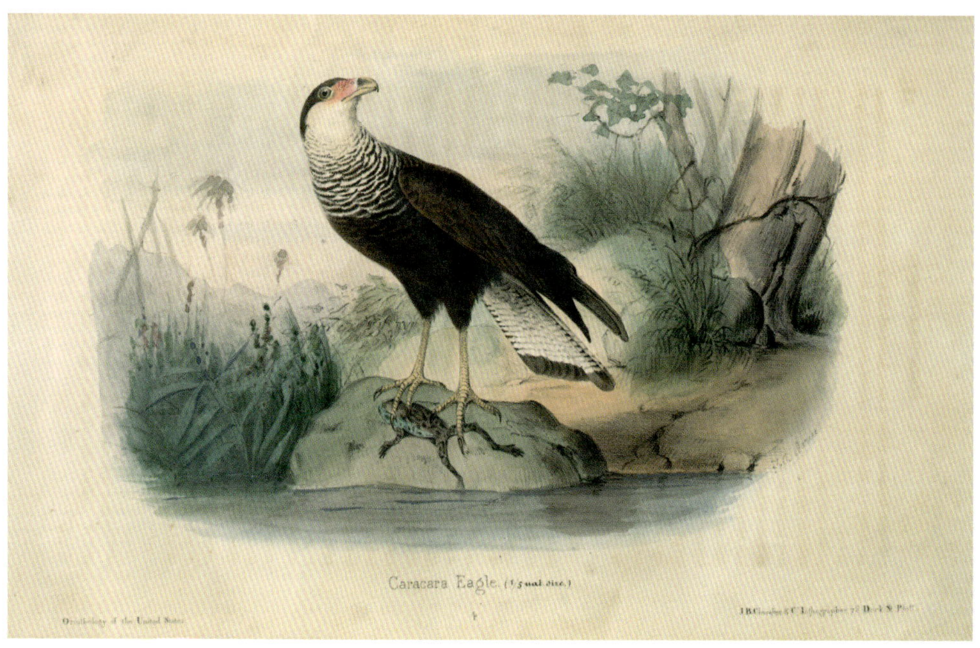

except the indefatigable Audubon, the high price of whose splendid work confines it to the libraries of the affluent."

This last sentence refers, of course, to John James Audubon's double-elephant folio *Birds of America* (1827–38), which was both massive and expensive. Audubon, however, intended to produce his own portable and affordable edition. Chevalier and Audubon decided it was mutually beneficial to join forces, so they forwent the publication of *The Ornithology of the United States* and filed a joint copyright for an octavo edition of *Birds of America* in 1839. Both Chevalier and Audubon were listed on the title pages of the first five volumes, published from 1840 to 1842. Chevalier disappeared from the scene after that, and the final two volumes (1843 and 1844) were published by Audubon alone. Overall then, Chevalier's lithographic career was, like J. C. Wild's, primarily involved with the production of plates for various publications.

Wild's first lithograph, *Bunch of Grapes,* had been printed by Childs & Inman, a firm that had its roots back in 1829, when Cephas G. Childs[29] founded the second lithographic business in Philadelphia. Childs began his printmaking career as an engraver in the early nineteenth century, and around 1825 he conceived the idea of producing a view book with engraved scenes of Philadelphia and its vicinity, to be sold (typically) by subscription. The parts appeared between 1827 and 1830, and when completed, the book had twenty-four engraved views. Childs intended to produce two other series of engraved views, but neither one came to fruition.[30]

At about that time, Kennedy & Lucas were producing their views of Philadelphia churches for W. L. Breton, and Childs, who knew of these prints—and later himself lithographed one of this series for Breton—realized the potential for lithography and decided to expand his printmaking business in that direction. In 1829 Childs formed the lithographic firm of Pendleton, Kearny & Childs, announcing in the *United States Gazette,* on September 9, 1829: "It is the intention of Mr. Childs, and the gentlemen connected with him, to present to the public specimens of lithographic drawing that shall tend to beget a taste for the arts and introduce some of its pleasing products at a price within the command of almost every person."

Childs saw this lithographic business as an extension of his engraving work, with an emphasis on taking advantage of the fact that lithography was a less expensive and time-consuming process than engraving. In the October 5, 1829, issue of the *National Gazette,* the firm stated that they were "prepared to execute Historical subjects, Portraits, Landscapes, Buildings, Bills of Exchange, Cards, Plans, Maps, Fac-Similies, &c. for which Lithography is so well calculated both as regards cheapness and expedition."

Pendleton and Kearny soon left the firm, and Childs was on his own until the end of 1830, at which time he persuaded New York artist Henry Inman to form the partnership Childs & Inman. In 1831 Childs went on a trip to France to learn more about lithography. It is possible he met J. C. Wild at that time and encouraged him to immigrate to Philadelphia, for as mentioned above, the first lithograph Wild is known to have produced was *Bunch of Grapes,* published by Childs.

While Childs did produce a wide range of lithographs similar to that listed in the *National Gazette* announcement, he saw a particular opportunity to have a successful business specializing in lithographic portraits. He was fortunate to have in his employ the talented lithographic artist Albert Newsam, whose skill at rendering portraits on stone was unsurpassed.[31] Also, one of the reasons Childs partnered with Henry Inman was likely Inman's renown as a portrait artist.[32] Childs & Inman produced portraits of famous individuals based on Inman's drawings, as well as those of other artists, such as Thomas Sully, in addition to keepsake portraits for regular Philadelphia citizens (fig. 6).[33]

Childs, as a smart businessman, saw the potential of lithographic plates for books and magazines, and he was one of the first American lithographers to produce plates for publications. As early as October 1829, Pendleton, Kearny & Childs produced a plate for *American Turf Register and Sporting Magazine.* Also in 1829, the firm provided the title-page illustration and three portraits for the *Cabinet,* a small book about President Andrew Jackson and his cabinet, and in the following years lithographs by Childs and his various partners appeared in books such as *History of the Schuylkill Fishing Company* (1830), *The American Portrait Gallery of Distinguished Individuals* (1832), *The*

Lives of George Washington and Thomas Jefferson (1833), and *New Fresh Water Shells of the United States* (1834). Childs's firm also produced maps and views for a number of reports between 1832 and 1834.

In 1830 Childs became involved in John and Thomas Doughty's *Cabinet of Natural History and American Rural Sports, with Illustrations,* a publication "designed to embrace the higher and more interesting branches of *Zoology;* viz: Ornithology and Mammalogy, together with an account of the sports and pastimes of North America."[34] The Doughtys' *Cabinet of Natural History* was issued in monthly parts, each containing illustrations, from 1830 until 1833, when it abruptly ceased after the publication of the fourth part of volume III. The first print in this work was an engraving by John Sartain, but almost all of the rest of the illustrations were lithographs, a total of fifty-three in all (fig. 74). The second and third plates were hand-colored lithographs by C. G. Childs, and these were followed in volume I by twenty-one prints by Childs & Inman, who added five further plates for each of the next two volumes.

This book was the first important American publication illustrated with hand-colored lithographs, the majority of which were by Childs & Inman. Though *The Cabinet of Natural History* was halted before its intended completion,[35] it still was successful enough to demonstrate that publications with hand-colored lithographs were both feasible and desirable, and it began a period when lithography became the dominant printmaking process used to produce American plate books. The lithographs by Childs in this work were important not just for American lithography in general but also for his business. They were not, however, Childs's most significant publication illustrations, for in 1830 he became involved in an even more ambitious lithographic plate book, Thomas McKenney's *History of the Indian Tribes of North America.*[36]

From 1824 to 1830, Thomas McKenney, as head of the Bureau of Indian Affairs, created a magnificent "Indian Gallery" of paintings of Native Americans for the government. Toward the end of his tenure, McKenney conceived of the idea of a plate book containing prints of the portraits from the gallery, so in September 1829 he signed an agreement with Philadelphia publisher Samuel F. Bradford to produce such a work in twenty parts, each to contain text and six hand-colored lithographs. This was the start of what would become the most complex lithograph-plate publication ever produced in America.

The project began simply enough, however, when Bradford borrowed six of the Indian Gallery paintings and took them to Childs to copy as lithographs. By April 1830 Childs had Newsam produce at least one lithograph, based on Charles Bird King's portrait *Mah-has-kah, Chief of the Ioways—(White Cloud)* (fig. 75). McKenney had

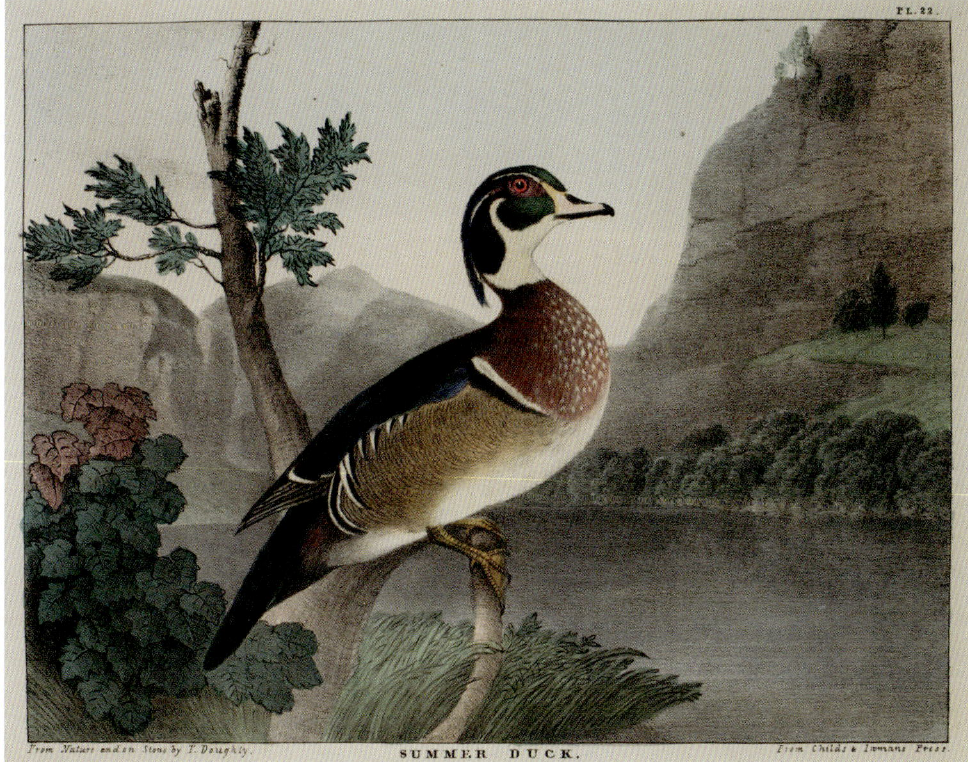

FIG. 74

Thomas Doughty, *Summer Duck,* from *The Cabinet of Natural History and American Rural Sports, with Illustrations* (Philadelphia: J. & T. Doughty, 1830). Printed by Childs & Inman. Lithograph with hand-coloring. 17 × 21 cm (6 ½ × 8 3/8 in.). LCP, Per C 3,13824.Q.

examined the proof and was delighted, writing in the margin of the print, "I consider the above copy, perfect; a perfect likeness of the man, who is known to me—and an exact copy of the original drawing by King, now in the office of Indian affairs." When Inman joined Childs at the end of 1830, the project continued, with Inman called on to make copies of the portraits borrowed from the government and Childs & Inman to produce lithographs after these copies.[37] The publication was not a financial success, however, and Bradford was forced to declare bankruptcy by the end of 1832.[38] A new publisher was found when John Key and Edward C. Biddle bought out Bradford's interest in the publication.

The financial and logistic difficulties of the project likely proved too much for Inman, for by the end of 1833 he had dissolved his partnership with Childs, returning to New York City.[39] Childs immediately took on a new partner, George Lehman, an artist who had previously worked for Childs & Inman. Childs & Lehman produced at least six more lithographs for the publication, but the project was still not a financial success, and by the end of 1834 Childs was heavily in debt. In order to pay off a large debt to his employee P. S. Duval, Childs sold Duval his interest in the partnership, thus leading to the formation of the lithographic firm of Lehman & Duval.

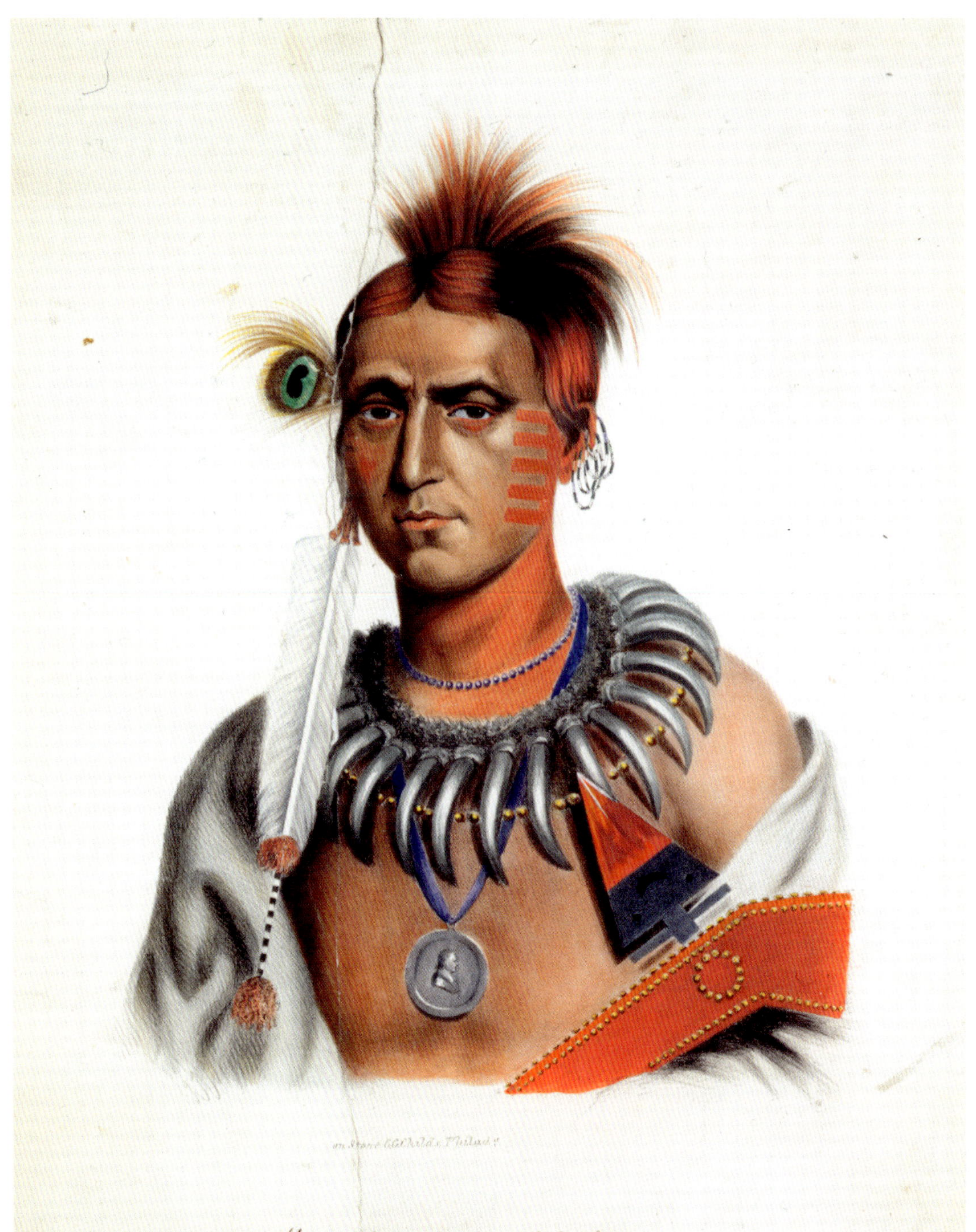

Mah-has-kah, Chief of
the Ioways. (White cloud.)

Childs had five partners in just five years as a lithographic printmaker, and, despite a reasonable output, he "had not made a penny out of his lithographic career and considered it a flat failure."[40] Childs, by himself and with partners, was responsible for thirty-three prints for *The Cabinet of Natural History*, a dozen portraits for McKenney's *History of the Indian Tribes*, and dozens more plates for various other publications. It would seem that about half of Childs's lithographs were plates for books or magazines, but despite being involved in two of the earliest significant American lithographic plate books, his lithographic career was not ultimately a success.

Besides the wonderful plates for the Doughtys' and McKenney's important publications, Childs's greatest legacy might have been bringing Peter S. Duval to Philadelphia (see also chapter 4). During his 1831 trip to France, Childs hired Duval, a twenty-six-year-old Frenchman who was an expert printer and eventually would become one of the foremost lithographers in the country. Duval's importance to Childs's business, both as pressman and creditor, led to his becoming a partner in the firm when Childs left in 1834. Duval remained as the principal in various eponymous lithographic firms until his retirement in 1869.

In 1834, after Childs retired, work on the McKenney publication ground to a halt, but Lehman & Duval picked up a new commission for a competing plate book of Indian portraits. This was the work of James Otto Lewis, who had painted a number of the images in the original government Indian Gallery. Apparently angered at what he perceived to be a lack of recognition and proper remuneration from McKenney, Lewis decided to issue his own rival volume, *The Aboriginal Port-Folio* (fig. 76), hiring Lehman & Duval to do the lithographs.

Lewis's portfolio was to be published in ten monthly parts, beginning in May 1835, each part to include eight hand-colored lithographs. The images were produced with neat lithography and bright hand-coloring, but Lewis's images were fairly crudely drawn,[41] which, combined with the expense of this lavishly illustrated work and the competition from the already printed McKenney lithographs, meant that sales of the parts were slow. By the time the tenth part was prepared, in 1836, only a very few examples were printed, perhaps just salesmen's sample parts. While Lehman & Duval did produce eighty lithographs for the work, not many impressions seem to have been made, and the project was not a success for the firm.

Not putting all their eggs in one basket, Lehman & Duval continued their relationship with the McKenney project, reissuing some of the Childs & Lehman prints as well as providing new images. Unfortunately, in 1836 the publishing firm of Key & Biddle was dissolved, but luckily McKenney, who had by then taken on a partner of his own, James Hall, to help with the text and finances, was able to get E. C. Biddle

Albert Newsam after Charles Bird King, *Mah-has-kah, Chief of the Ioways—(White Cloud)*. Unpublished proof plate; note dated April 29, 1830. Printed by C. G. Childs. Lithograph with hand-coloring. 58 × 35 cm (23 ¼ × 13 ¾ in.). LCP, 5750.F.118.

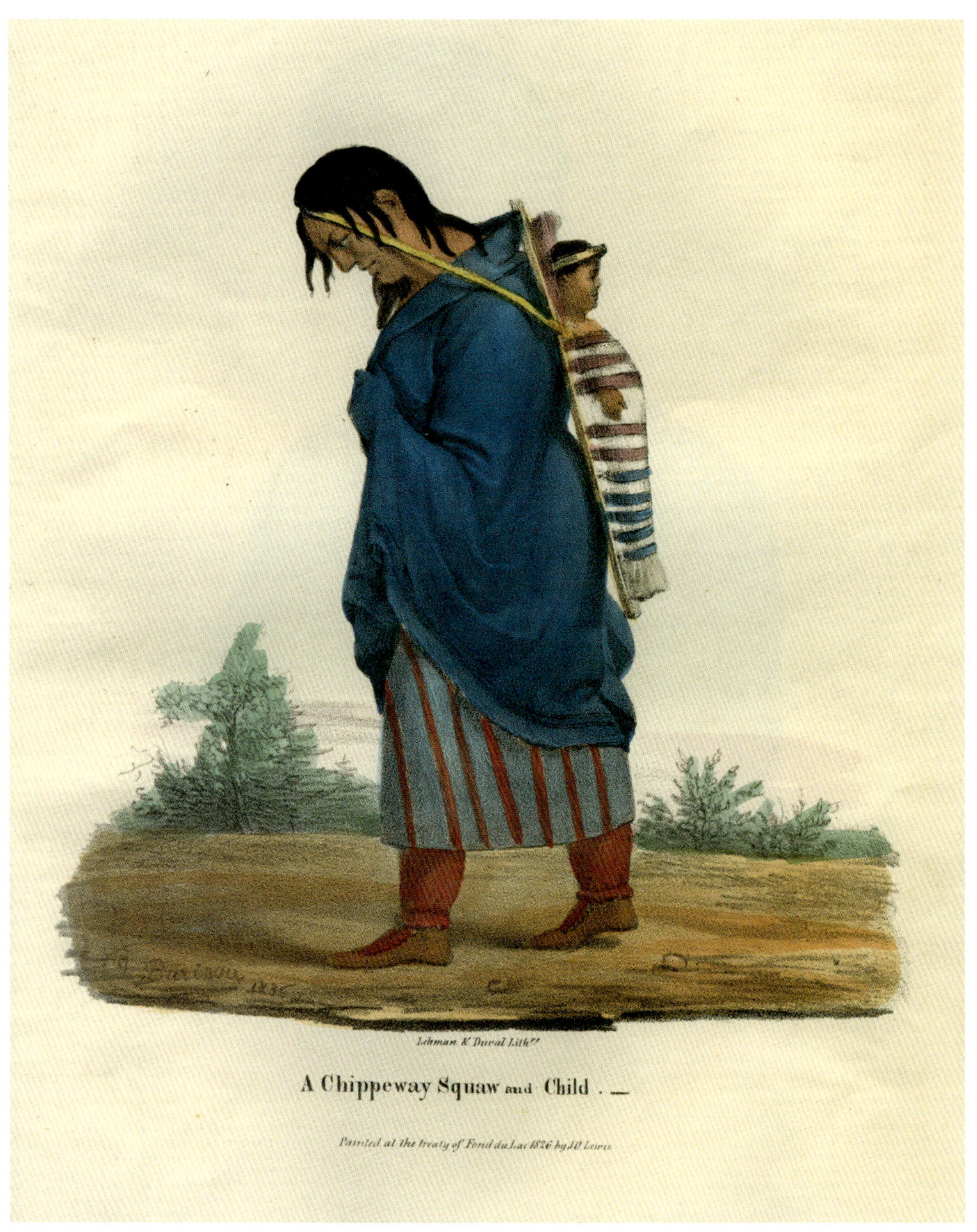

to stay as sole publisher of the *History of the Indian Tribes.* Lehman & Duval continued to produce new portraits, but by August 1837 the firm ended its association with McKenney and Biddle.

About the time they stopped their work on the *History,* Lehman left the firm and P. S. Duval continued on his own. In its short existence of about three years, Lehman & Duval did produce a variety of lithographs, such as portraits, music sheets, and views, but the majority of their output consisted of plates for various sorts of publications. Besides the portraits for the J. O. Lewis and Thomas McKenney volumes, Lehman & Duval provided plates for Timothy A. Conrad's *Monography of the Family Unionidae* (1836) and John Edwards Holbrook's *North American Herpetology* (1836–38), not to mention a significant body of maps and plates for various reports and pamphlets between 1835 and 1837.

Duval continued as a lithographer for over thirty years more; he was one of the most prominent of Philadelphia's lithographers and produced a wide range of prints, from job-order checks and billheads to separately issued portraits and views. He lithographed advertisements, certificates, large views, commissioned prints, maps, song sheets, sporting prints, and even designs for window shades. He also continued to produce plates for various publications, which, while perhaps not making up quite so significant a percentage of his output as such plates did for Kennedy & Lucas, J. C. Wild, or C. G. Childs, still remained a crucial part of his business through the next several decades.

Duval provided the illustrations for a number of periodicals, including the *Parlour Review* (1838), Benjamin Silliman's *American Journal of Science and Arts* (1839), and fellow lithographers Thomas S. Wagner's and Alfred Hoffy's *United States Ecclesiastical Portrait Gallery* (1841) and the *Orchardist's Companion* (1841–42), respectively. Duval even used a periodical to showcase his foray into color-printed lithography, for in the April 1843 issue of *Miss Leslie's Magazine* appeared a fashion plate "Printed in Colours by P. S. Duval expressly for Miss Leslie's Magazine." Edwin T. Freedley wrote in his *Leading Pursuits and Leading Men:* "In 1834 Mr. Duval, on becoming proprietor of his present establishment, made every effort to increase the demand for the productions of his art, . . . and to this end he published several periodicals, with lithographed illustrations."[42] The periodical Duval published that did the most "to increase the demand for the productions of his art" was what became known as the "U.S. Military Magazine."

This magazine was originally the creation of Philadelphia artist William M. Huddy, who was also a major in the Philadelphia militia and conceived the idea of a magazine with text and illustrations about the Philadelphia volunteer corps. The first issue appeared in March 1839, with plates printed by Duval and lithographed by Alfred Hoffy usually after paintings by Huddy.[43] Within two issues Duval had become a partner in the publication of *Huddy & Duval's U.S. Military Magazine,* which soon expanded in scope to cover volunteer companies from around the United States.

The magazine continued until September 1842, by which time an impressive body of hand-colored lithographs of military portraits and scenes, by Hoffy and

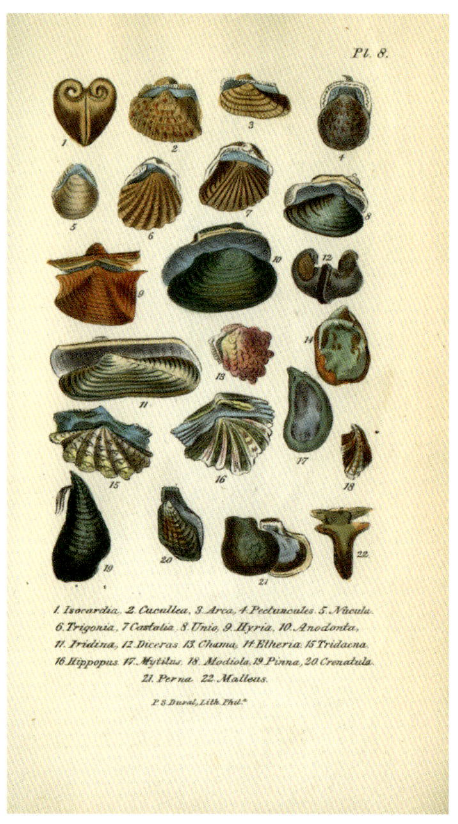

1. Isocardia. 2. Cucullea. 3. Arca, 4. Pectuncules. 5. Nucula.
6. Trigonia. 7. Castalia. 8. Unio, 9. Hyria, 10. Anodonta.
11. Iridina, 12. Diceras. 13. Chama, 14. Etheria. 15. Tridacna.
16. Hippopus. 17. Mytilus. 18. Modiola, 19. Pinna, 20. Crenatula.
21. Perna. 22. Malleus.
P. S. Duval, Lith. Phil.ᵃ

FIG. 77
After Thomas Brown, plate 8 in *The Conchologist's First Book* (Philadelphia: Haswell, Barrington & Haswell, 1839). Printed by P. S. Duval. Lithograph with hand-coloring. 19 × 12 cm (7 ½ × 4 ½ in.). LCP, Am 1845 Poe 68207.D.

other Philadelphia lithographer-artists, such as Albert Newsam, James Queen, and Augustus Kollner, had been included in its issues. These handsome images of local military units, which often included actual portraits of prominent Philadelphians, proved very popular. This spurred Huddy & Duval to issue some of the prints as separate publications for members of the corps pictured, and led as well as to private commissions for other military prints.

Meanwhile, Duval continued to produce lithographic plates, and later chromolithographic plates, under his own name. These included illustrations for pamphlets and reports, as well as plates for scientific publications like Thomas Wyatt's *Manual of Conchology* (1838), Edgar Allan Poe's *Conchologist's First Book* (1839) (fig. 77), and John Edwards Holbrook's very rare *Ichthyology of South Carolina* (1860). Duval produced plates also for a wide variety of other publications, including a number of gift books, such as *The Iris: An Illustrated Souvenir* in the years 1851 to 1853. This charming work was very popular, and even Queen Victoria, who had ordered a number of copies for her household, remarked that "it was the prettiest book she had seen from America, and reflected great credit on the city of Philadelphia."[44]

One of the largest parts of Duval's work in the late 1840s and 1850s was plates made for the reports from the many government-sponsored explorations of the period (fig. 78). In 1856 Freedley reported:

> The government of the United States became one of [lithography's] patrons by intrusting to it the illustrations of numerous reports of expeditions sent out to explore its vast domain, and as these reports were generally accompanied by maps, views, and subjects of natural history and botany, they furnished a vast amount of work for the lithographic press. Mr. Duval has always obtained a large portion of this work, and has at this time a large contract on hand to furnish the illustrations accompanying the report of Lieut. [Lardner] Gibbon on the Amazon River, and also those for Lieut. Gilles' [James Melville Gilliss's] Astronomical expedition to Brazil.[45]

The federal government published dozens of copiously illustrated reports of its expeditions, including many prints by lithographic firms from Baltimore, Washington, New York, Buffalo, and, of course, Philadelphia. Print scholar Ron Tyler has calculated that for just the eighteen government reports between 1843 and 1863 dealing with expeditions to the American West, more than 1,600 unique images were produced, totaling almost twenty-six million separate impressions![46] The government's large orders for these plates had an enormous impact on the business of the lithographic firms that

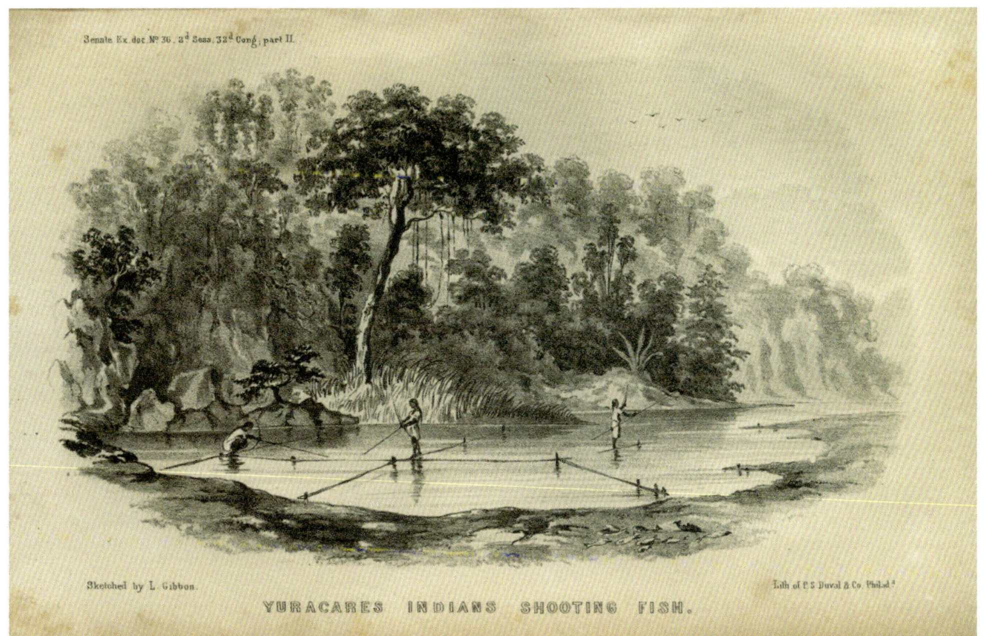

FIG. 78
After L. Gibbon, *Yuacares Indians Shooting Fish,* from William Lewis Herndon, *Exploration of the Valley of the Amazon: Made Under Direction of the Navy Department* (Washington, D.C.: Robert Armstrong, Public Printer, 1853). Printed by P. S. Duval & Co. Lithograph. 15 × 23 cm (5 ¾ × 9 in.). LCP, Am 1853 Her 74133.O.

were awarded the contracts, and Duval got a good share of the work. He produced plates for more than half a dozen reports of government explorations, providing his firm with steady work for about a decade.

Duval's name appeared on the many prints that were issued in the government publications, but for another, very important part of his business—the unattributed lithographic transfer and printing of atlas maps for Philadelphia's cartographers—he got no printed credit. Philadelphia was the leading American center for map publishing from the end of the eighteenth century to well into the nineteenth century, first with engraved and later with lithographic maps. Beginning with S. Augustus Mitchell's 1846 edition of the *Universal Atlas,* Duval received steady and important work producing atlas plates.[47] A decade later Freedley commented on the importance of this aspect of business for Duval:

> Another source from which this art receives a great supply of work is in the printing of copper plate engravings transferred to stone, as a very large proportion of all the maps now published in this country are printed by the lithographic press. The method of doing this has already been described, but as transferring may be considered an art in itself not universally understood, even by Lithographers, it is proper to mention the name of Mr. F. Borquin, who first introduced it into Mr. Duval's establishment, and who to this day

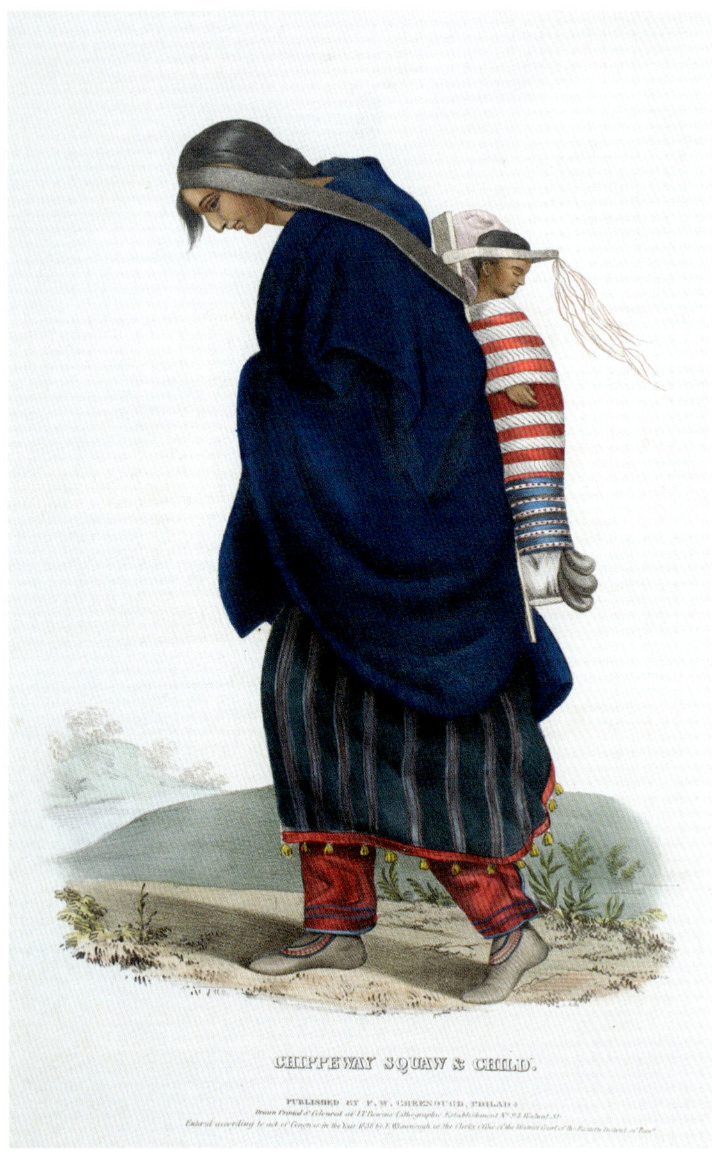

FIG.79

After James Otto Lewis, *Chippeway Squaw & Child,* from Thomas McKenney, *History of the Indian Tribes of North America,* vol. 1 (Philadelphia: F. W. Greenough, 1838). Printed by J. T. Bowen's Lithographic Establishment. Lithograph with hand-coloring. 51 × 36 cm (20 ¼ × 14 in.). LCP, Am 1838 M'Ken, 2955.F.

has but few if any equals. The rapid increase of the business will be at once perceived, when we state that Mr. Duval now runs thirty-four presses, and employs from seventy to eighty hands constantly, besides furnishing work to a hundred and sometimes one hundred and fifty print colorists.[48]

Over the years, a significant portion of Duval's business consisted in the production of plates for books and magazines. He had initially become involved in this when an employee of C. G. Childs; he began his own plate publishing with the two great North American Indian volumes of J. O. Lewis and Thomas McKenney, and he continued his work in this area over the next decades, taking advantage of new opportunities for plate books to enable his firm to grow and prosper. However, one of the plate books that proved less than successful for Duval was McKenney's *History of the Indian Tribes,* the production difficulties of which probably led to the dissolution of his partnership with Lehman in 1837.[49] Still, Duval did survive and indeed thrive as a lithographer after breaking his connection with McKenney, who also was able to continue with his project when he found a worthy successor to Lehman & Duval, a lithographer and colorist from New York City named John T. Bowen, the most important American publisher of plates for publications.

Bowen began as a print colorist in New York City in 1834 and expanded into lithography in 1835.[50] Apparently the potential for the lithographing and coloring work needed on McKenney's *History of the Indian Tribes* was sufficient inducement for Bowen to move to Philadelphia sometime after August 1837, where he immediately set to work on the Indian portraits (fig. 79). Bowen printed and colored eight plates that Lehman & Duval had already prepared and then produced three new images drawn by Alfred Hoffy, who probably came to Philadelphia with Bowen.[51] By the end of 1837 or the very beginning of 1838, Biddle completed volume 1 and soon thereafter resigned as publisher for the project but remained as its business agent.

Biddle was replaced as publisher by F. W. Greenough, who came into the project with fresh vigor. On the cover of his reissue of part 8, he wrote:

The publisher of the Indian History and Biography, feels pleasure in announcing to the public, that the liberal patronage, already bestowed on this
great National Work, places its continuance to completion beyond all doubt.
. . . The daily increase of the subscription list enables him to say that, instead
of allowing the work to decline in merit, as is frequently the case with similar
undertakings, additional efforts will be made, without regard to expense, to
render it yet more worthy of favor.

This pledge of "additional efforts" was good news for Bowen, for it generated a
large amount of work for his firm. For Greenough, Bowen produced new, redrawn
stones for most of the prints already published, as well as thirty-six new images. However, despite Greenough's enthusiasm and this burst of activity, financial problems
continued to plague the publication of the *History.* Thomas McKenney, completely
discouraged, withdrew from involvement with the project, and in 1841 Greenough
declared bankruptcy and was forced to withdraw as publisher.

Bowen briefly attempted to publish the *History* on his own, but by April 1842
Daniel Rice and James G. Clark took over as publisher. Rice and Clark, along with
Hall, who remained as author, and Bowen, who remained as lithographer,[52] pushed
the *History* through to completion. In all, it took six publishers before the *History of
the Indian Tribes of North America* was finally completed in 1844, fifteen years after
Bradford and McKenney first agreed to begin the project.

This mammoth undertaking not only brought Bowen to Philadelphia but allowed
him to build his business and ultimately made him financially successful. Within
months of Bowen's arrival in Philadelphia, in early March 1838, the following advertisement appeared, "To Print Colorers—Wanted immediately, several good hands to
color lithographic and other prints. . . . Apply to J. T. Bowen 94 Walnut St."[53] Later
that year, on December 8, the *Saturday Courier* reported that "there are busy, daily,
upon this Indian work [McKenney's *History*], some thirty or forty persons, about
twenty-five of whom are females. In this way, whilst the work itself promises to make
ample returns for the intellectual labour and research bestowed upon it, a large number of persons draw from it a comfortable subsistence."

Bowen received universal praise for his work on the prints for the *History.* For
instance, the same *Saturday Courier* article remarked:

Mr. Bowen having been put in charge of the lithographic and coloring divi-
sions, gave, at once, proof that, in his hands, the Indians would lose none of
the spirit and expression of their unique countenances; nor their costume any

of its striking peculiarities. The public, both in Europe and America, or far as this work has reached it, speak in terms of unqualified praise of the skill of this distinguished artist. Col. M'Kenney, and those who are associated with him in this monument to Aboriginal character, feel the benefits of Mr. Bowen's skill, and put upon it appreciation.

This work established Bowen's reputation as one of the best lithographers and colorists in the nation, and it also set the course that Bowen's firm would follow until his death, in 1856.

When Bowen first arrived in Philadelphia, besides the work for McKenney's *History,* he pursued a variety of other jobs typical of lithographic firms of the period, filling job orders and publishing separate prints of events, landscapes, political cartoons, and a series of beautiful Philadelphia views. However, it was the production of plates for a book that brought Bowen to Philadelphia, gave him his start and ultimate success, and formed the core of his business for the next two decades. His early focus on publications with lithographic plates is evidenced by the fact that within months of coming to Philadelphia, Bowen purchased the rights to Wild & Chevalier's *Panorama and Views of Philadelphia and Its Vicinity,* which he reissued at the end of 1838. A decade later, Bowen published a fourth edition of this book, this time without the panorama and with Wild's name removed from the prints themselves.

Also in the first three years or so of being in Philadelphia, Bowen produced plates for works such as Mrs. A. Walker's *Female Beauty* (1840?), which included elaborate overlaid color plates to show the effect of a variety of clothes on those with different complexions. He also published his own plate publications, such as his artists' copybooks, *The United States Drawing Book* (1839), *My Own Sketch Book* (1839–43), and *The Child's Drawing Book* (1839–43). Bowen even became involved in publishing a magazine, as announced in the *United States Gazette* on June 29, 1839: "Architect's Magazine—Mr. J. T. Bowen 94 Walnut has published in large quarto form, the first number of a monthly series of engraving and letter contribution towards architectural science entitled 'The Architect's Magazine and Book of Designs.' . . . The work is to consist of ten numbers and the first number gives proof of interest and instruction."

Bowen's reputation for high-quality lithography and coloring soon led to a business relationship that further solidified him as the most important American lithographer of plates for publications, for at the end of 1839 Bowen began work on the reduced version of John James Audubon's *Birds of America* (fig. 80).[54] This octavo edition was to be sold in one hundred parts of five plates each for just $1 per part, totaling a reasonable $100. Audubon selected J. T. Bowen to produce the lithographs, probably,

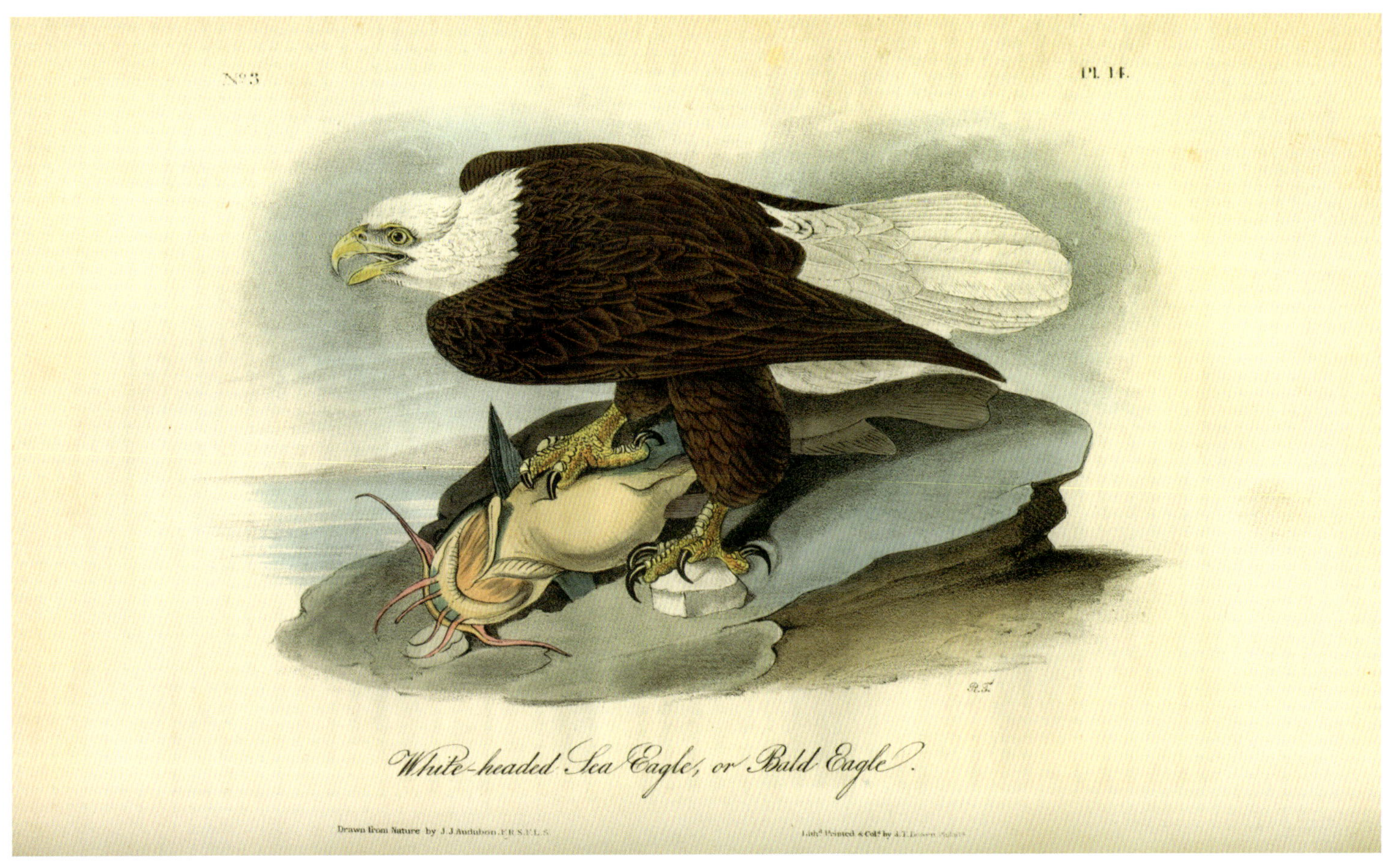

as stated in the *Saturday Courier,* January 4, 1840, because he had been impressed with the plates from McKenney's *History of the Indian Tribes:* "Audubon was truly fortunate in placing his great work in such hands [i.e., Bowen's], but he had seen the Indians and their admirable execution."

The octavo edition of Audubon's *Birds* was a huge success, the original projected issue of three hundred copies ultimately increased as the number of subscribers climbed to more than one thousand. The large number of different prints, which had to be printed in those very large runs and then each hand-colored, put a considerable strain on Bowen's business. He faced financial difficulties from lack of payment for his work on the McKenney *History,* so Audubon and others had to provide a loan in order to keep Bowen going.[55] Audubon later complained that Bowen had simplified some of the backgrounds for the prints in order to save expense and that Bowen threatened to take the seventy employees he had working on the *Birds* off the job unless Audubon would help him meet his weekly payroll.[56]

FIG. 80
Ralph Trembley, *White-Headed Sea Eagle, or Bald Eagle,* from John James Audubon, *The Birds of America* (New York: J. J. Audubon; Philadelphia: J. B. Chevalier, 1840), plate 14. Printed by J. T. Bowen. Lithograph with hand-coloring. 17 × 27 cm (6 ½ × 10 ½ in.). LCP, Am 1840 Aud, 78817.O.

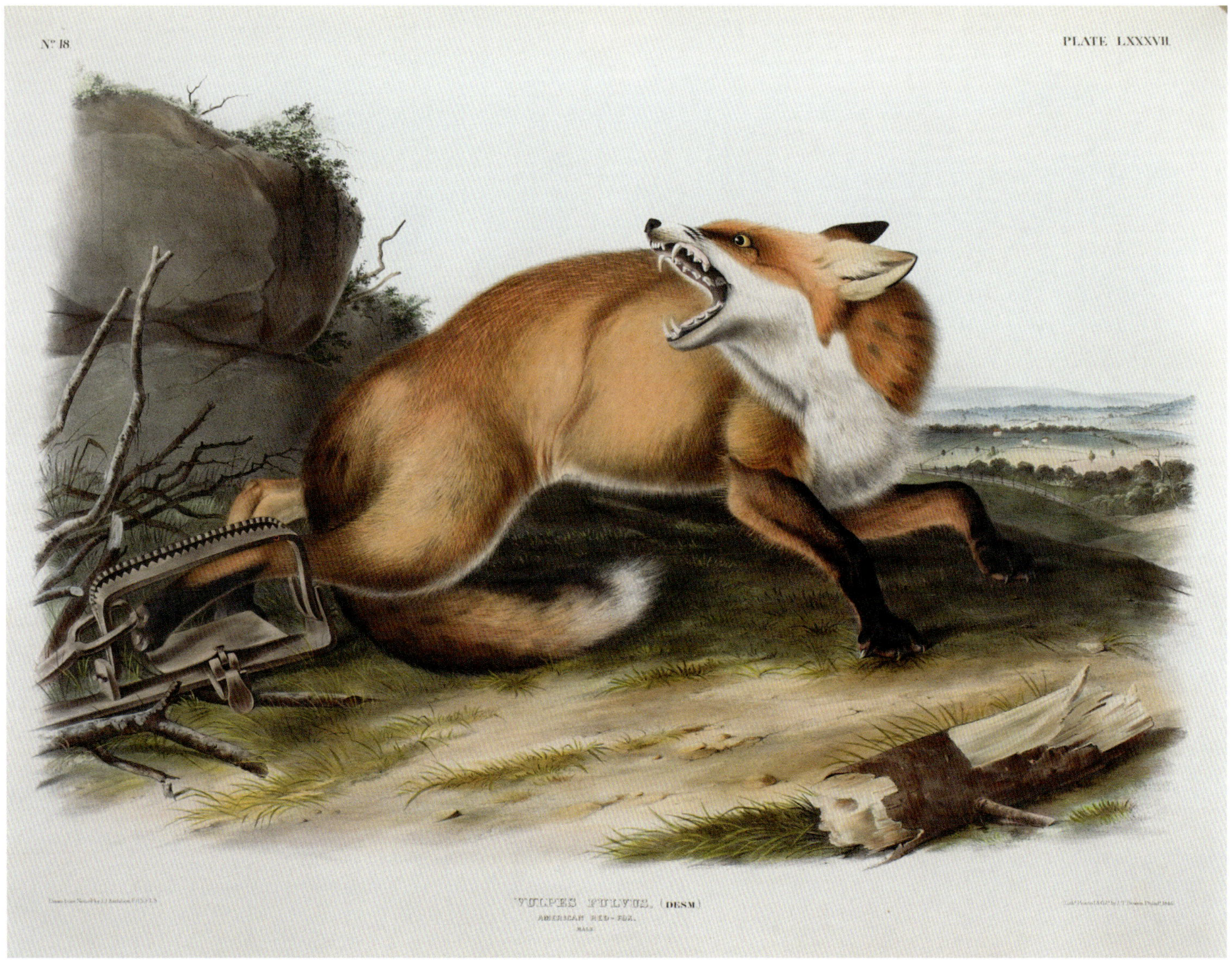

American Red-Fox, from John James Audubon, *The Viviparous Quadrupeds of North America* (New York: J. J. Audubon, 1845–48), plate LXXXVII. Printed by J. T. Bowen. Lithograph with hand-coloring. 55 × 71 cm (21 ¾ × 27 ¾ in.). LCP, **Am 1845, Aud 9241.F.

One of the problems Bowen faced was that he not only had to print and color an increasing number of plates for the growing subscription list but also had to reprint and color earlier plates so new subscribers could have complete sets. It was difficult for Bowen to keep up with all the work on the *Birds,* so in 1841 Audubon hired George Endicott, from New York City, to lithograph fifteen hundred impressions each of fifteen images (plates 136 to 150), which were colored by J. W. Childs, also from New York.[57] Bowen eventually overcame his problems and continued to produce the rest of the prints until the work was completed, in 1844. The success of the octavo *Birds* led to its republication six more times, from 1856 to 1871. In the later editions, most prints were simply reprinted from Bowen's original stones, though plates 136 to 150 now had the Bowen imprint, some stones were modified or redrawn, and, beginning with the second edition, tint stones were added to the images.

Overall, Audubon was certainly pleased with Bowen's work, for he turned to the lithographer again when he began work on his next project, *The Viviparous Quadrupeds of North America* (fig. 81), authored with the Reverend John Bachman, a friend and naturalist. This publication, using images painted by Audubon and his sons, in particular John Woodhouse Audubon, contained 150 imperial-folio hand-colored lithographs by Bowen, which were published between 1845 and 1848. Not as many impressions were made of these prints, with probably just over three hundred sets produced, but this was still a major project for Bowen, who once again received universal praise for his work. In 1844 Bachman wrote about Bowen's lithographs, "They are most beautiful and perfect specimens of the art. I doubt whether there is anything in the world of Natural History like them. I do not believe that there is any man living that can equal them."[58]

The text for the *Quadrupeds* was not finished until 1854, three years after John James Audubon died. It was Audubon's sons and Bachman who completed the work and also began, in 1848, an octavo edition of the *Quadrupeds,* which was completed in 1854, with reduced and modified versions of the folio images, plus the five extra plates that had been added to the text for the folio edition. It seems that at first Bowen had problems keeping up with the publishing demands for this work, for some of the plates from the first volume of the first edition were printed by the New York firm of Nagel and Weingaertner,[59] but the majority of the first-edition plates, and all those from the three subsequent editions (the last published in 1870), were printed and colored by the Bowen firm.

From 1839 on, Bowen was busy working on the production of the plates for these Audubon works. His business lithographed stones for 805 different Audubon images, some in multiple variations, and ran off hundreds to thousands of impressions, each hand-colored by Bowen's firm. As Wainwright noted, in this period Bowen's business was almost totally consumed by this work: "Bowen's absorption in works on natural history gradually removed him from the more conventional activity of a general lithographic business. . . . From the time in 1839 when he became the printer of Audubon's *Birds* until the day of his death, Bowen was more or less constantly employed by the naturalist or his sons Victor and John."[60]

Bowen did find some time, however, to work on other publications. Not only did he bring out the fourth edition of Wild's *Views of Philadelphia* in 1848, but he produced prints for Anne Hill's *Drawing Book of Flowers and Fruit* (1844) and for volume I of Henry R. Schoolcraft's *Historical and Statistical Information Respecting the History, Condition, and Prospects of the Indian Tribes of the United States* (1851), as well as another artist's copybook, *Studies of the Human Figure* (ca. 1854–55).

Even after he started working for Audubon, Bowen, of course, continued to produce the plates for McKenney's folio Indian volumes. The completion of that work in 1844 and the success of Audubon's octavo edition of the folio *Birds of America* seem to have inspired Bowen to embark on the publication of a reduced, octavo edition of the *History of the Indian Tribes of North America* (fig. 82). The first part of this work, "Sold to Subscribers only" for the price of $1.25, was published by J. T. Bowen in 1847, "To be Completed in Thirty Parts." The preface explained Bowen's motivation:

> The universal approval of the folio edition of the work, has induced the publisher of the present edition to alter the size to *royal octavo,* and thus place it within reach of the thousands, who with taste and learning equal to those of the patrons of the large edition, have no less capacity to appreciate its worth and beauties. . . . The publisher has the happiness to believe, that he is not forcing upon the public this edition of this truly national work, but that he is only responding to the universal demand for it, by those whose intelligence, and taste for the fine arts, enable them to appreciate its value. He also believes that the smaller edition will be preferred to the large, as it is better suited for a library.

When completed, this edition also contained 120 prints lithographed and hand-colored by the Bowen firm, most simply reduced versions of the folio portraits. However, two of the three frontispieces are completely different, with one being an image of "Prairie on Fire (The Escape)" and the other the octavo portrait of "Red Bird, A Winnebago," this portrait appearing for the first time. The publication of this book was soon taken over by D. Rice & A. N. Hart, who issued subsequent editions that included the Bowen lithographs. Later editions, published by Rice, Rutter & Co. beginning in 1865, used plates redrawn and lithographed by the new publisher.

By the early 1850s Bowen was recognized as the leading American lithographer for natural-history book plates, so it was not surprising that he was approached by John Cassin, a Philadelphia ornithologist, to produce prints for a work that Cassin intended as a supplement to Audubon's *Birds of America.* As Cassin wrote to his friend Assistant Secretary of the Smithsonian Institution Spencer F. Baird on May 21, 1852, "I had repeated conversations with him [Bowen] before I commenced my first Number . . . but he was so hurried. . . . [He] is overpowered with too much business, especially Audubon's quadrupeds which he says is work that does not pay."[61]

Cassin had to find another printmaker for his planned book, entitled *Illustrations of the Birds of California, Texas, and British and Russian America.* He commissioned Henry Louis Stephens to make the drawings, and Louis Rosenthal, another Philadelphia lithographer, was hired to do the plates. The first part was issued in 1852, priced at $1.25, or "To Subscribers, $1.00," with the claim that it was "To be Completed In Thirty Numbers, published Monthly." Cassin was not pleased with the resulting plates, and because of this and other problems only about fifty copies of this first part, with five plates, were produced before Cassin ceased publication.

Cassin did not give up, however; the following year he was able to convince J. T. Bowen to take over the work, and the first part of the "second edition" of *Illustrations of the Birds* was published by J. B. Lippincott & Co. in 1853. Cassin explained that now "it has become practical to engage the most accomplished and experienced Lithographic Artists, so far as relates to Natural History."[62] The drawings for the plates were done by George G. White and transferred to stone by Philadelphia lithographic artist William Hitchcock, but soon Cassin had Hitchcock draw the images directly onto stone (fig. 83). Cassin figured that he had to get 250 subscribers to be successful,[63] which he was unable to do, so in mid-1854 the project was aborted after only ten parts, containing a total of fifty plates. Lippincott & Co. did publish three editions of the complete work from 1856 to 1865, but the runs were small, and the work was not a financial success for Cassin.

Despite this setback, Cassin was enthused by the opportunities offered for making ornithological plates for publications and by the steady stream of contracts for lithographs to illustrate U.S. government reports, which began in the 1840s. He decided to get more involved with Bowen's production of natural-history plates. On May 29, 1855, he wrote Baird: "Bowen is too indecisive for a business man but I intend to push for him pretty strong in the Nat. Hist. plates—and have some idea of connecting myself with him in the Lithography business . . . though of the necessity of exertion to get contracts or how to get them he has no more idea than a child—he, rather foolishly as

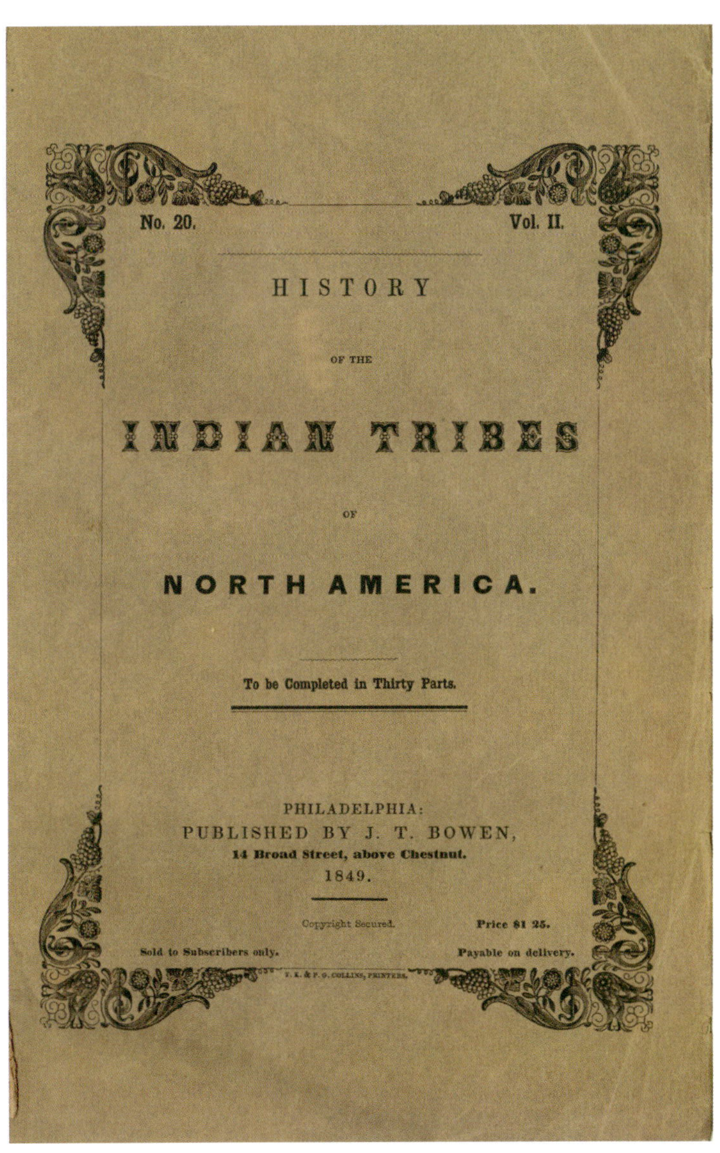

FIG. 82

Cover of part 20 of *History of the Indian Tribes of North America* (Philadelphia: J. T. Bowen, printed by T. K. & P. G. Collins, 1849). 28 × 18 cm (11 1/8 × 7 1/8 in.). Philadelphia Print Shop.

FIG.83

William E. Hitchcock, *The American Stone Chat,* from John Cassin, *Illustrations of the Birds of California, Texas, Oregon, British and Russian America,* 2nd ed. (Philadelphia: J. B. Lippincott & Co., 1856). Printed by J. T. Bowen. Lithograph with hand-coloring. 18 × 27 cm (7 1/8 × 10 5/8 in.). LCP, *Am 1856 Cass, 13929.O.

FIG.84

Tholeys, *Allied Cock of the Woods, Tetrao Urogalloides,* from D. G. Elliott, *A Monograph of the Tetraoninae, or Family of the Grouse* (New York: D. G. Elliott, 1865). Printed by Bowen & Co. Lithograph with hand-coloring. 44 × 59 cm (17 ½ ×23 ¼ in.). LCP, **Am 1865 Elli, Log1079.F.

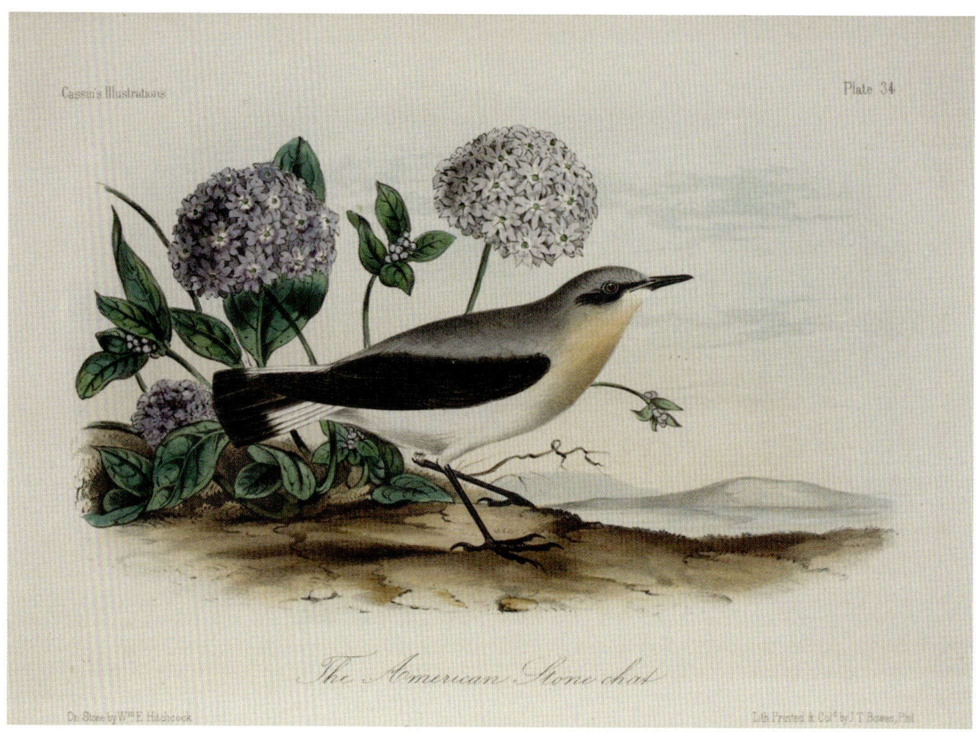

Cassin's Illustrations

Plate 34

The American Stone chat

On Stone by Wm E. Hitchcock

Lith Printed & Cold by J T Bowen, Phil

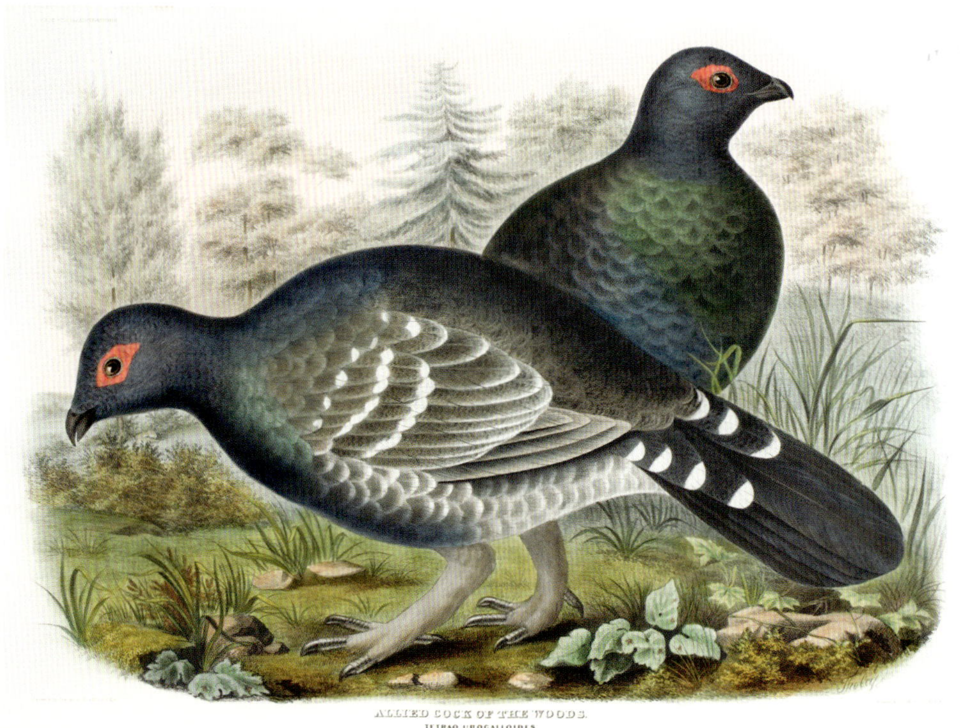

ALLIED COCK OF THE WOODS.
TETRAO UROGALLOIDES

time goes, relies on merit or superior ability."[64] It was not long after this that John T. Bowen died, and Cassin was soon heavily involved in the firm, in 1858 becoming the partner of the widow Lavinia Bowen in the renamed firm Bowen & Co.[65]

Bowen & Co. continued to produce lithographic plates for various publications, including later editions of the works of Audubon and McKenney, and they were able to gain some of the coveted government contracts. Bowen & Co. produced plates for a number of the government exploring expeditions, culminating in *The Birds of North America* by Cassin, Spencer F. Baird, and George Lawrence in 1860, which consisted mostly of plates previously issued in the government reports.

The final flourish of publication-plate production by the firm was in the later 1860s, when Bowen & Co. produced prints for the works of American ornithologist Daniel Giraud Elliot, a well-traveled ornithologist and skilled painter who produced a number of ornithological books with hand-colored lithographs by Bowen & Co. First was his *Monograph of the Tetraoninae, or Family of the Grouse* in 1865 (fig. 84), with twenty-seven plates, followed in 1867 by *A Monograph of the Pittidae, or Family of Ant Thrushes,* with thirty-one plates, and then by *The New and Heretofore Unfigured Species of the Birds of North America,* published in parts from 1866 to 1869 and containing seventy-two lithographs.

This was the final major work by the Bowen firm, which closed its doors in 1869. It marked the end of a long history of a lithographic business that came to dominate the production of hand-colored plates for publications in America. After the Civil War, plates in publications tended to be produced using chromolithography and steam-powered printing presses, with which it was easier to control the quality of the color and which was overall a more efficient and less expensive technology. However, while other fine plates for publications were produced in Philadelphia after the demise of the Bowen business, no American lithographer ever produced such a marvelous body of impressive publication plates as those of the Bowen firm between 1837 and 1869.

Although Bowen's was the Philadelphia firm most involved in the production of plates for publications, the business founded by Thomas Sinclair in 1838 was also heavily engaged in this aspect of the lithography trade. Sinclair was a Scotsman who had immigrated to Philadelphia at least by 1833, when he drew the print *Quadrille de Contredanses* for Kennedy & Lucas. In 1838 Sinclair acquired the press of John Collins and started his own firm. In 1854 he took on his eldest son, William B. Sinclair, as a partner in the firm Sinclair & Co., and then in 1871 his younger son John joined the business, thereafter known as T. Sinclair & Son. Thomas Sinclair died in 1881, but his younger son continued the business until it was acquired by Harris & Sons in 1889.[66]

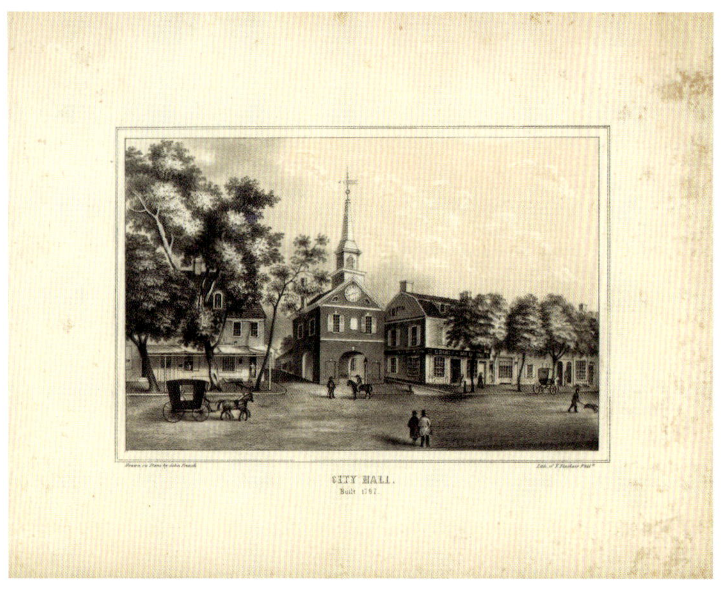

FIG. 85

John French after John Collins, *City Hall, Built 1797,* from *Views of the City of Burlington, New Jersey* (Burlington: Printed by T. Sinclair, 1847). Lithograph, tinted with one stone. 14 × 20 cm (5 3/8 × 7 7/8 in.). LCP, *Am 1847, Col 8212.F.

Sinclair's firm was a fairly typical lithographic business from the period, though particularly known for color lithography, being one of the first in Philadelphia to experiment with color printing. Sinclair made his first tinted lithograph in 1843 and was awarded a silver medal for color lithography from the Franklin Institute, with the citation "Mr. Sinclair has acquired a skill in this kind of printing which is doubtful if the best French artists can excel."[67] Sinclair produced many colorful advertisements and a large number of sheet music covers in the 1840s and 1850s, as well as portraits, certificates, fashion plates, views, images of important events, genre prints similar to those being published by the New York firm Currier & Ives, and, in the 1880s, theatrical advertisements.

From the beginning, however, a considerable majority of the output of the Sinclair firm appeared not as separate sheets but as plates in a wide variety of publications. As the Philadelphia historian Joseph Jackson said, Sinclair "did a great deal of illustrating for books, for New York and Philadelphia publishing houses."[68] In his first year in business, Sinclair printed a portrait of John Greenleaf Whittier by John Collins, from whom he had purchased his presses, which was included in *History of Pennsylvania Hall* (1838). The following year, Samuel George Morton's *Crania Americana* was issued with most of its plates by John Collins, but a number lithographed by Sinclair, including the frontispiece portrait of Ongpatonga based on a painting by J. Neagle.

In the following decades, Sinclair produced hundreds of lithographs for publications of all sorts. He produced maps and other illustrations for reports of various companies and institutions, and plates for magazines, gift books, histories, and natural histories,[69] as well as for view books like John Collins's *Views of the City of Burlington, New Jersey* (1847) (fig. 85). He produced plates for several books published by the American Sunday-School Union and illustrations and illustrated covers and title pages for many other children's publications.

The largest number of prints Sinclair made were those done for U.S. government publications (fig. 86). As discussed previously, beginning about the time Sinclair started his business, the government commissioned a vast number of plates for its reports. The *Pubic Ledger* reported on February 8, 1856: "the execution of work for the Government of the United States, in illustrating reports of expeditions, by Mr. Duval, and Mr. Sinclair, is an important branch of the Lithographic business in Philadelphia." We have seen that Duval, as well as the Bowen firm, worked on these

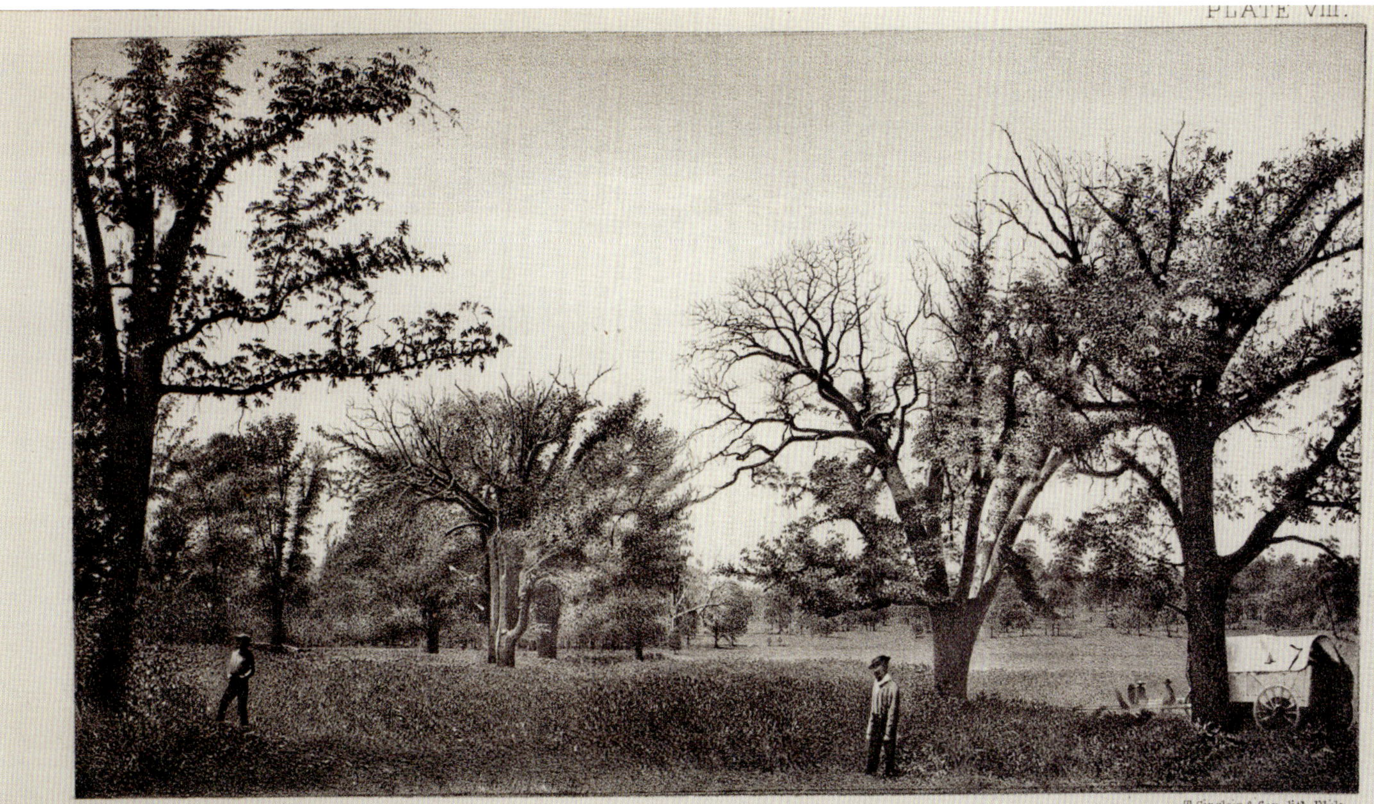

reports, but the Philadelphia business that benefited most from this work was that of Sinclair, who produced plates for about half a dozen government publications, including volumes II, III, and V of the *Pacific Railroad Surveys* (1855–56). It has been estimated that more than six million separate lithographic prints were produced for just these three *Pacific Railroad Survey* volumes,[70] and though Sinclair produced only a fraction of those, this gives some idea of the scope of the work his firm did for these government publications.

The records of R. G. Dun & Company include reports on Sinclair's business and provide an interesting footnote on the firm's work for the government. It is somewhat surprising to note that despite the fact that Sinclair & Co. had substantial contracts to produce lithographs for the U.S. government in the 1850s, the Dun investigator, on December 9, 1880, reported of Thomas Sinclair that "about the year 1860, he failed." However, the report continues with the note that Sinclair "settled up his old debts," and states that subsequent to taking his son into the firm, "they have . . . done well."[71]

FIG. 86

Oak Grove, White Mountain Range, Arizona, from George M. Wheeler, *Annual Report upon the Geographical and Geological Surveys and Explorations West of the 100th Meridian, in Nevada, Utah, Colorado, New Mexico, and Arizona* (Washington, D.C.: GPO, 1873), plate VIII. Printed by T. Sinclair & Son. Lithograph. 11 × 18 cm (4 ¼ × 7 ¼ in.). LCP, Am 1873 Geog Sur (bw), 53963.O .2.

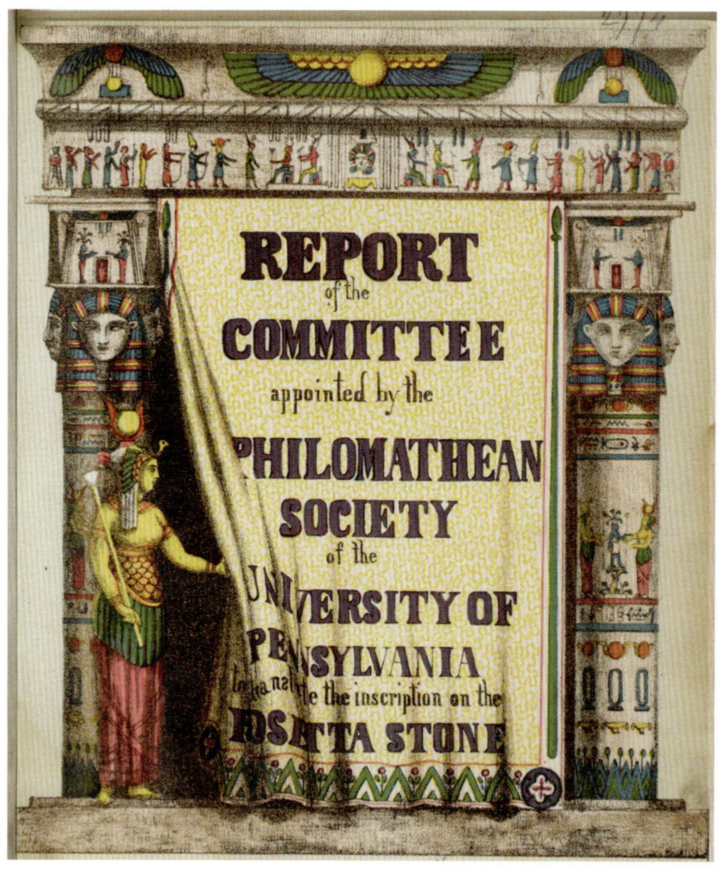

FIG. 87

Title page for Henry Morton, *Report of the Committee Appointed by the Philomathean Society of the University of Pennsylvania to Translate the Inscription on the Rosetta Stone* (Philadelphia: Printed by L. N. Rosenthal, 1858). Chromolithograph. 22 × 18 cm (8 ¾ × 7 1/8 in.). LCP, Am 1858 Pen Uni, 2774.Q.

Interestingly, this entry goes on to say that "they do a large amount of work for the U.S. Light House Board, Coast Survey, Maps, Charts, etc." In an entry for the following year, dated May 28, 1881, the report states: "They are doing considerable work for the US Govt., such as maps & charts, which pays them well."[72] Sinclair is known to have published a "Geological map of Virginia, Nev. and immediate vicinity" for the U.S. Geological Survey in 1882,[73] but other than this, no government maps from the 1880s with Sinclair's name on them have been found, so it is not clear whether the maps and charts he produced at this time were separately issued, though it is likely that most would have been illustrations for government reports.

On February 8, 1856, in the heyday of Philadelphia lithography, the *Public Ledger* ran a brief article titled "The Lithographic Business of Philadelphia": "The business of Lithographing has become an important branch of the arts in Philadelphia, giving employment to a large number of pressmen and artists, as well as extending the fame of our city to all parts of the country, by means of the beautiful lithographic pictures sent from the establishments now in operation. The principal lithographers in Philadelphia are P. S. Duval, Thos. Sinclair & Co., Wagner & McGuigan, and Rosenthal." We have already seen how the production of plates for books and periodicals was crucial to the first two establishments listed in this article, those of Duval and Sinclair, but the other two cited premier firms were also heavily involved in this aspect of lithography.

The Rosenthal firm was founded by brothers who had emigrated from Russian Poland and established their business in Philadelphia about 1851. Often identified as "L. N. Rosenthal," after Louis, who was the principal business manager, the Rosenthals made a wide range of lithographs until 1884. They produced both lithographs and chromolithographs, including views, music sheets, labels, advertising prints, and a series of Civil War battle scenes and encampments drawn by Louis's brother Max, the firm's principal artist.

An advertisement for the firm published in 1856 lists the many types of prints the Rosenthals were able to produce, among which were "Illuminated Frontispieces for Books" and "Illustrations of all kinds for Books and Magazines." As with the Sinclair firm, this publication-plate production was one of the most important and highly regarded parts of their business. Max Rosenthal's son, Albert, recalled:

When I came into my father's studio in my sixteenth year [1879], he was occupied in lithographing plates for the works of Professor Cope and Dr. Liedy [*sic*], and plates for the "Medical History of the Civil War" for the government. These were followed by colored plates of the Yellowstone Park, painted by Thomas Moran. The work that my father had great pride in was the plates for Dickinson's "American Numismatics," and he was guide, philosopher, and friend to Dr. Henry Morton in the book on the Rosetta Stone [fig. 87]. While none of these plates were signed by him, I recognize his technique in most of them and he himself told me that he had much to do with the plates in this book. Also to be added are Barclay's book on the Holy Land, and Sloan's "Architecture."[74]

Besides those mentioned by Albert Rosenthal,[75] the Rosenthal firm produced plates for a number of other publications in the 1850s. I have already mentioned the plates Rosenthal lithographed after drawings by Henry L. Stephens for the unsuccessful first edition of John Cassin's *Illustrations of the Birds of California, Texas, Oregon, British and Russian America* (1852). Cassin probably originally hired this pair because of the success of *The Comic Natural History of the Human Race* (1851), which also included plates by Rosenthal after drawings by Stephens (fig. 88).

In 1851 Charles W. Webber began a series of seven projected volumes entitled *The Hunter-Naturalist,* focusing on men like John James Audubon and Alexander Wilson, who were "Primitive Hunter and modern Field-Naturalist combined." Only two volumes, *Romance of Sporting, or Wild Scenes and Wild Hunters* (1851) and *Wild Scenes and Song-Birds* (1854), were published, both with plates by Rosenthal. Those in the first volume were chromolithographs based on drawings by Alfred J. Miller; Harry T. Peters states they "were among the first true chromos of importance and the first set of chromo book illustrations."[76] With all these publications, and others such as J. Franklin Reigart's *Life of Robert Fulton* (1856), clearly the Rosenthal firm was very "occupied in lithographing plates."

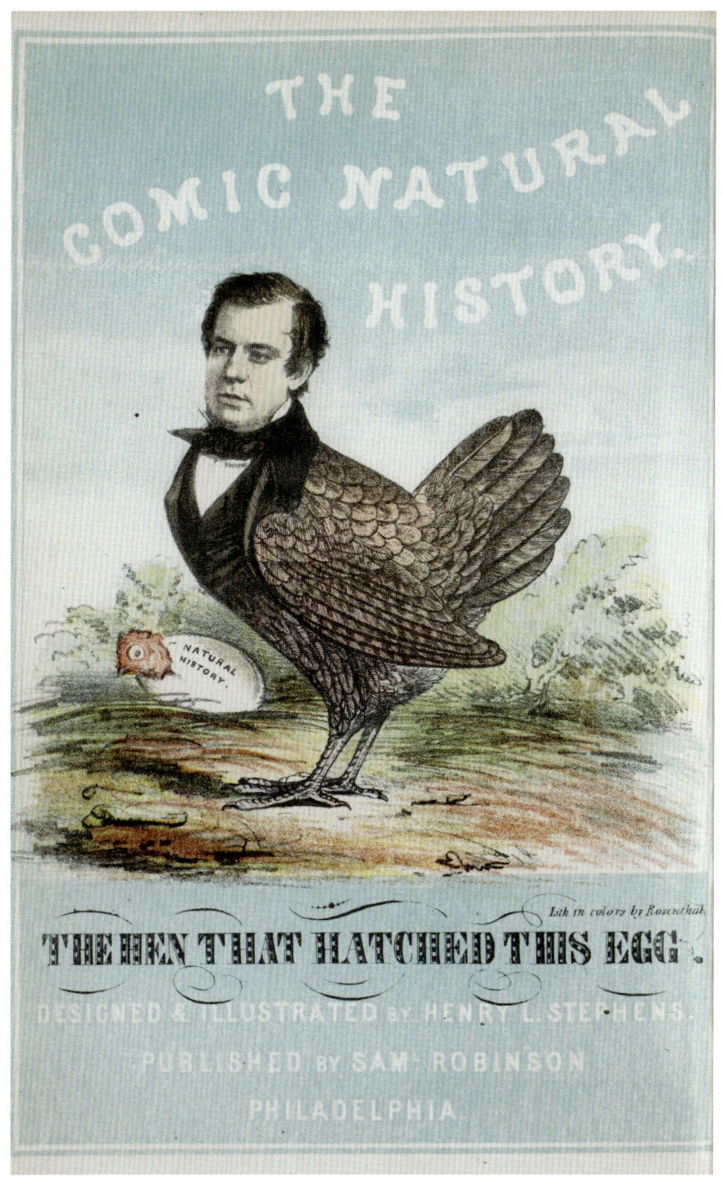

FIG. 88
Henry L. Stephens, *The Hen That Hatched This Egg,* from *The Comic Natural History of the Human Race* (Philadelphia: S. Robinson, 1851). Printed by L. Rosenthal. Chromolithograph. 26 × 16 cm (10 1/8 × 6 1/4 in.). LCP, Am 1851 Stephens, 13471.Q.

The last of the big four Philadelphia lithographic firms from around midcentury listed by the *Public Ledger* was Wagner & McGuigan. Plates for books and periodicals probably factored less in this firm's business than for any other major Philadelphia lithographer, their specialty being advertisements. In Wainwright's *Philadelphia in the Romantic Age of Lithography,* Wagner & McGuigan are credited with almost fifty advertisements showing business storefronts, as described in chapter 6, about twice as many as by any of their chief competitors in this field, Duval, Sinclair, and Frederick Kuhl. Wagner & McGuigan did, however, still produce an interesting body of plates for various publications.

Thomas S. Wagner, who initially worked for P. S. Duval, first became involved in producing such plates for his own *United States Ecclesiastical Gallery* (1841). In 1844 he joined with James McGuigan and E. J. Pinkerton to form Pinkerton, Wagner & McGuigan. Pinkerton, who had also previously worked with Duval, had set up his own press the year before, when he lithographed the title page for *Miss Leslie's Magazine.* Pinkerton, Wagner & McGuigan took advantage of contracts for producing plates for various publications, including the *Guide to Laurel Hill Cemetery, Near Philadelphia* (1844) and the magazines *Godey's Magazine and Lady's Book, The Ladies' Garland,* and *Ladies' National Magazine.*

In 1845 Pinkerton retired; Wagner and McGuigan continued until their building was destroyed by fire in 1857, after which they each set up on their own. Plates for publications did not make up a particularly large part of their business, but Wagner & McGuigan did continue to produce plates for a number of different books. Their ability to produce such plates was confirmed by George Spratt, editor of *Obstetric Tables* (1850) (figs. 89a–b). This work was copied from a London original, which included complex overlapping plates with up to five layers. As Spratt wrote, "It was so novel and so difficult a piece of work, that no lithographers liked to undertake it. . . . the Editor, however, having some similar work done by Messrs. Wagner & McGuigan, was convinced from what he saw of their skill, that it could be done by them fully equal to the original, and much cheaper."[77]

From this survey of plates for various publications by preeminent Philadelphia lithographers, it is clear that this type of work was a crucial component of their businesses. Plates for books and periodicals formed the majority of the output of Kennedy & Lucas, Wild & Chevalier, J. T. Bowen—who came to Philadelphia specifically for this type of work—Thomas Sinclair, and the Rosenthals. These prints also played a major role in the businesses of C. G. Childs, P. S. Duval, and to a lesser extent Wagner & McGuigan.

The crucial role that plates for publications played in the trade of Philadelphia lithographers is not surprising, as for much of the nineteenth century Philadelphia

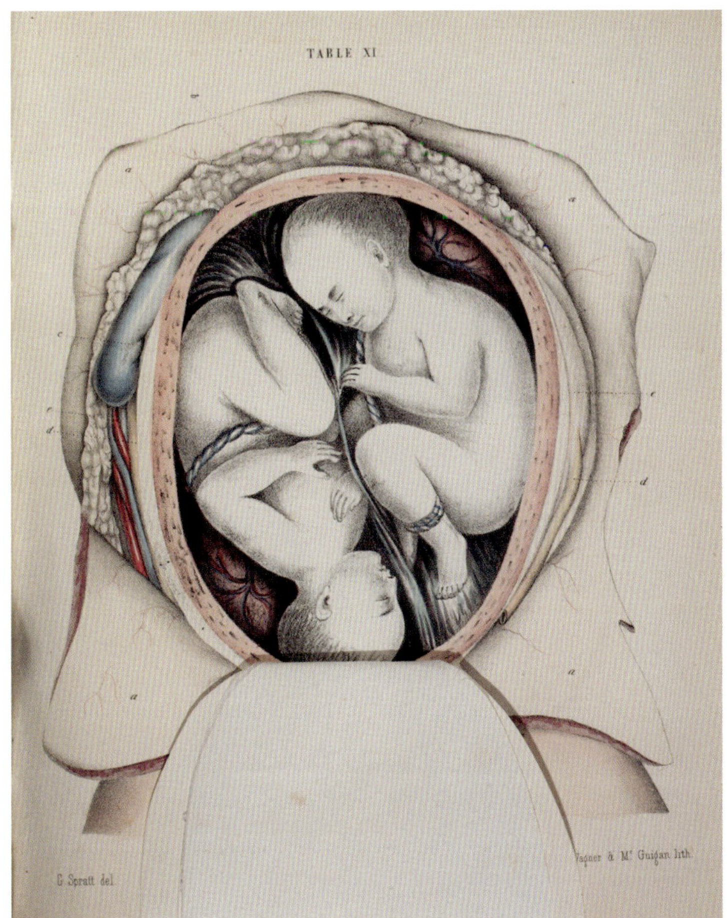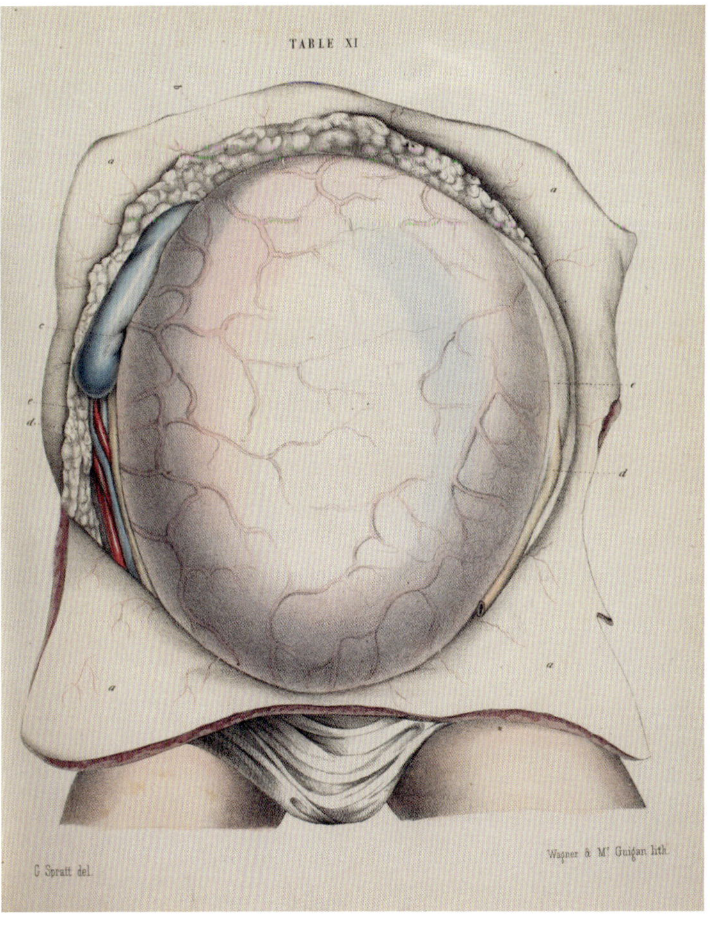

was the leading center of book and magazine publishing in America. With the growth in the popularity and expectation of lithographic plates in these publications, it was natural that many Philadelphia lithographers would take advantage of this opportunity. Once the government started publishing its illustrated reports using lithographs in the 1840s and 1850s, the work of producing these plates became more evenly divided among the cities on the East Coast, but before then the majority of publications with lithographic plates were made in Philadelphia. Although printmakers in New York, Boston, and Hartford overshadowed those from Philadelphia in producing separately issued, "frameable" lithographs, Philadelphia dominated in making lithographic plates for publications, a mainstay of its lithography trade in the nineteenth century.

FIG. 89 A–B
Table XI in G. Spratt, *Obstetric Tables* (Philadelphia: James A. Bill, 1850). Printed by Wagner & McGuigan. Lithograph with hand-coloring. 27 × 24 cm (10 ¾ × 8 ¼ in.). LCP, Am 1850 Spratt, 13034.Q.

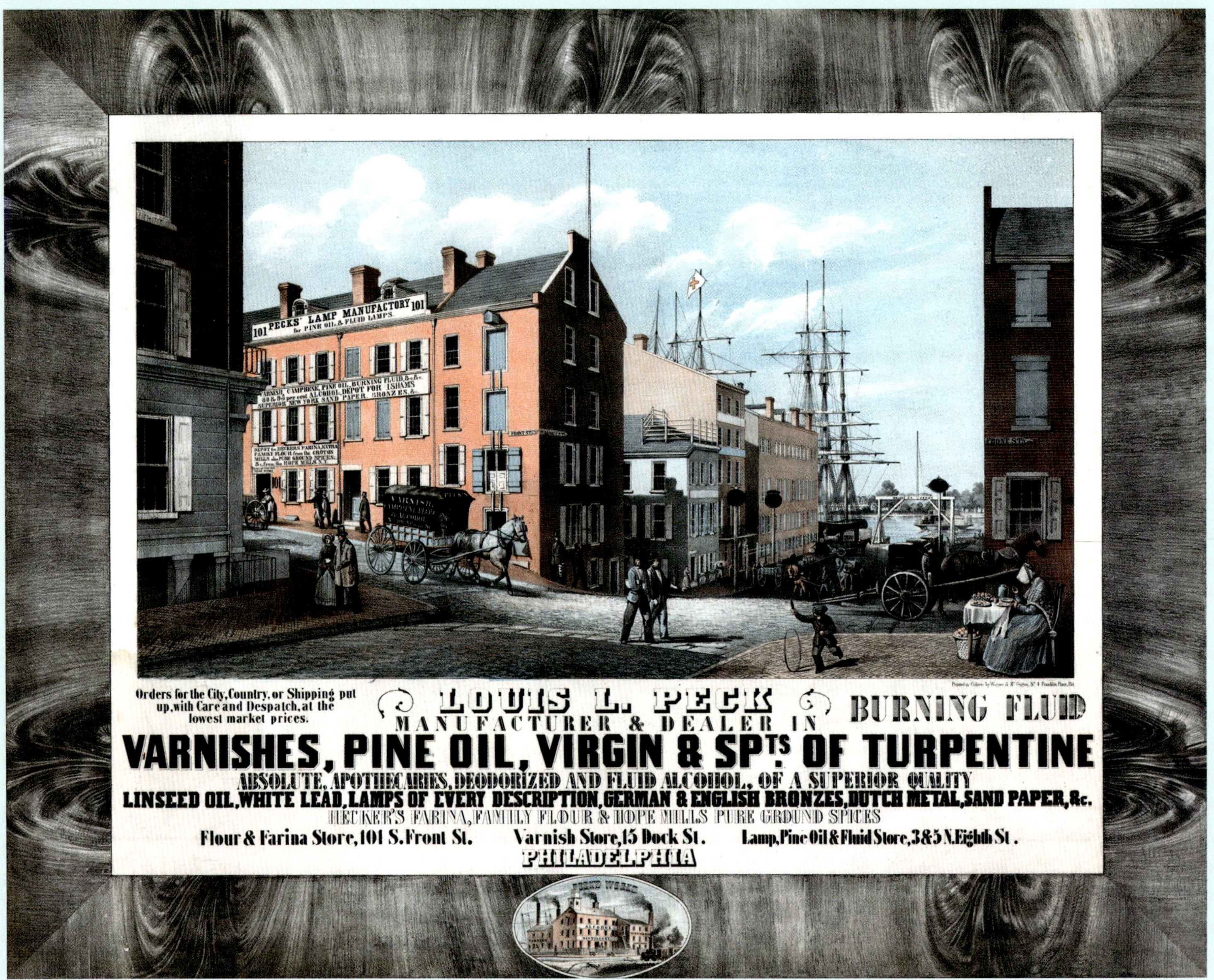
Orders for the City, Country, or Shipping put up, with Care and Despatch, at the lowest market prices.
LOUIS L. PECK
MANUFACTURER & DEALER IN
BURNING FLUID
VARNISHES, PINE OIL, VIRGIN & SPts. OF TURPENTINE
ABSOLUTE, APOTHECARIES, DEODORIZED AND FLUID ALCOHOL, OF A SUPERIOR QUALITY
LINSEED OIL, WHITE LEAD, LAMPS OF EVERY DESCRIPTION, GERMAN & ENGLISH BRONZES, DUTCH METAL, SAND PAPER, &c.
HECKER'S FARINA, FAMILY FLOUR & HOPE MILLS PURE GROUND SPICES
Flour & Farina Store, 101 S. Front St.
Varnish Store, 15 Dock St.
Lamp, Pine Oil & Fluid Store, 3 & 5 N. Eighth St.
PHILADELPHIA

COMMERCIAL ARCHITECTURE IN PHILADELPHIA LITHOGRAPHS

DELL UPTON

Philadelphia's commercial landscape was radically transformed in the first half of the nineteenth century. In post-Revolutionary Philadelphia, as in other American cities, home and work—commerce, artisanry, and domesticity—shared the same spaces. Men and women, whites and blacks, rich people and poor ones, practitioners of many trades and businesses—all lived and worked near one another in wooden shacks, cheap boardinghouses, warehouses, small commercial buildings, or large structures that combined elite residences, warehouses, and countinghouses. The headquarters of great firms of importing merchants stood next to shipbuilders' yards, sailmakers' lofts, ship chandlers' stores, auction houses, and groggeries, as well as the homes of people with no direct relationship to the sea or to importing, such as cutlers, fruiterers, and Hannah January, "layer-out of the dead." All these were crowded together "with the utmost care to prevent loss of space," as one nineteenth-century observer sardonically noted.[1]

Just as great merchants lived on the waterfront in or next to the buildings that housed their goods and the wharfs where their ships were moored, early shopkeepers and artisans worked in their houses. The Mutual Assurance Company for Insuring Homes from Loss by Fire policies of the 1780s and 1790s are full of such businesses. Brass founder Samuel Parker, for example, occupied a three-story house on the north side of Arch Street between Fourth and Fifth Streets that had two rooms on a floor, with the front room on the ground story "not plaistered and occupied for a workshop." The heirs of merchant John Allen insured a three-story house on the east side of

FIG. 90

Louis Peck Manufacturer & Dealer in Burning Fluid Varnishes, Pine Oil, Virgin & Sp[iri]ts of Turpentine (Philadelphia: Printed in colors by Wagner & McGuigan, [ca. 1855]). Double-tinted lithograph. 56 × 70 cm (22 × 27 ¼ in.). POS 444, LCP, P.2134.

Water Street with a "lower story store and parlor."[2] Such an "integrated house" might have a second front door leading to the owner's residence upstairs, and it might have a somewhat larger window opening into the shop.[3]

Late-eighteenth-century Philadelphians, like the residents of other northern ports, began to dismantle these hybrid spaces. As trade heated up in the early Republic years, urban waterfronts were repeatedly denounced as overcrowded and inadequate for the needs of contemporary commerce. Merchants began to think that waterfronts were too valuable to waste on their own residences or on housing and services for their lesser neighbors.[4] The 1808 demolition of the "shanties" of Samuel Saviel and of the widow Tinee Cranshaw, both African Americans and both fruiterers, for the construction of a large warehouse for the York and Lippincott firm of auctioneers was a story echoed repeatedly in the Quaker City during the first half of the nineteenth century.[5] Fear of epidemics impelled many among the well-to-do to move their homes away from the commercial wharves.[6] At the time of his death, on December 26, 1831, Stephen Girard, the richest man in Philadelphia and, some said, the richest man in the United States, resided in a mansion at 23 North Front Street, adjacent to his countinghouse. He was reputedly the last merchant living on the Quaker City's waterfront. Building by building, the mixed landscape of the eighteenth-century waterfront disappeared (fig. 90).

The meticulously rendered, often brightly colored lithographs of Philadelphia's commercial buildings, created to advertise the businesses they depict, are engrossing, visually delightful snapshots of the transition from the older, domestically based, commercial world to a new, larger-scale corporate economy. Most of the known prints were made in the 1840s, although not all of the buildings they picture were new in that decade. In the 1850s, as large-scale manufacturing played an ever-larger role in Philadelphia's economy, lithographers found more of their business coming from the owners of the new industrial enterprises that ringed the city to the north and west.

Around 1855 Wagner & McGuigan produced an advertisement for Louis L. Peck's varied businesses that offers a rare lithographic glimpse of the rapidly vanishing, hybrid commercial landscape of the early nineteenth century (fig. 90). Peck's store at 101 South Front Street, at the northeast corner of Walnut, occupies the center of an image that, uncharacteristic of the genre, depicts much of the surrounding neighborhood. Peck's store consists of two early-nineteenth-century dwelling houses converted to commercial use, with a purpose-built structure of the same size and shape added to the end of the row. This provides loading doors and a cathead (a projecting beam fitted with a pulley and rope) for raising goods to the upper levels. Peck's delivery wagon rolls down Front Street. In the left foreground one sees the corner of a substantial house with a marble ground story and an iron balcony projecting from its façade. Whether it is still used as an elite residence is unclear from the image. Visible at the right is the corner of another house, revealed in an 1849 map as one of a row of identical-sized structures filling the narrow band between Front and Water Streets and extending from Walnut to Dock Street.[7] The form of the shutters on the upper stories suggests that it might now be a commercial property. On the far side of Water Street, stretching down the hill behind Peck's establishment, are a three-story and a four-story house. One has a second-story iron balcony, and the canopy over its door is supported by elaborate console brackets. The tall circular signs at the curbside show that both were operated as hotels or inns, the only businesses that could legally erect such markers. The last building, the site of Thomas P. Cope's warehouse early in the century, is a four-story structure with four entries.[8] The closed shutters covering many of the windows mark it as a warehouse. Peck's neighborhood, then, retained much of the architecture of the old hybrid landscape, but the residences had for the most part been adapted to rougher commercial uses. At the right side of the scene is another reminder of an older Philadelphia: a huckster at her table, offering for resale the unwanted fruits and vegetables that she had bought cheaply at the closing of the previous day's market.

By calling this world "domestically based," I mean two things. First, most of the businesses depicted in the lithographs were organized like the older mercantile firms, as individual proprietorships and partnerships. Nearly all bear the names of one or two people: John Horn, Drugs; Jordan and Brother, Wholesale Grocers; Joseph Oat and Son, Coppersmiths (POS 411, POS 414, POS 417). And they operated from buildings that, like Peck's, were domestic in scale and shape. Many were repurposed houses. While earlier merchants and artisans had worked *in* their houses, these images show us the waning of this practice. Jordan and Brother's wholesale grocery firm on North Third Street occupied a building whose large lower-floor windows mark it as a dwelling-store combination that, as activity in the upper windows shows, had been entirely taken over by the business (POS 414). The same was true of James Lane's stove store at 218 North Third Street (POS 403) and of the building next to Piper and Andrews Warm Air Furnace Manufactory on North Sixth Street, which was a house converted to a factory of undeterminable purpose (fig. 91). More remarkably, to the right of Piper and Andrews's modern pier-front building is a low wooden structure whose wide front window is fitted with a falling shutter, hinged at the bottom edge and made to be fastened horizontally to serve as a counter. Falling shutters were the earliest kind of Euro-American shop front. They are illustrated in medieval market images, and surviving (or reconstructed) examples can be found on early modern English buildings and pre-Revolutionary American ones. Pioneering Philadelphia historian

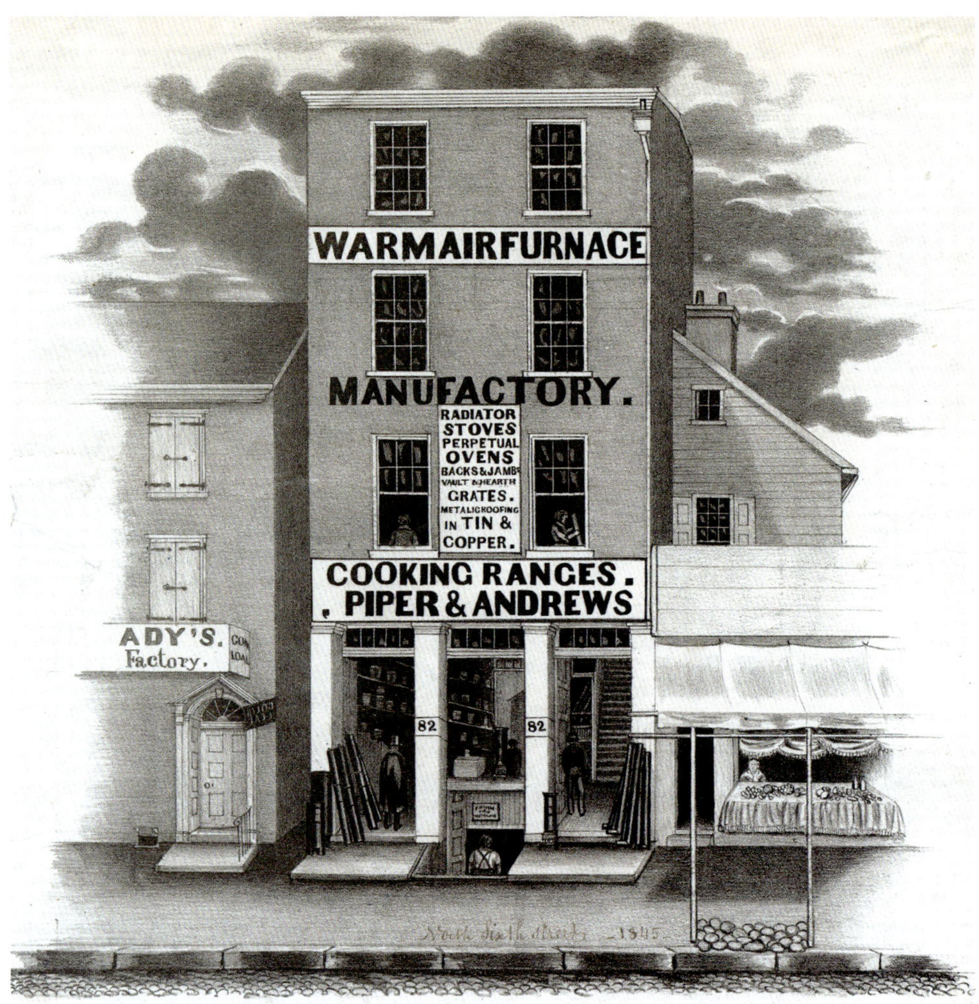

John Fanning Watson identified them as the oldest kind of commercial structure in Philadelphia.[9] In the lithograph a woman sits behind the cloth-draped shutter selling fruits and vegetables, shaded by an awning stretched over the sidewalk.

The appropriately named Loud and Brothers, builders of pianofortes, occupied a mid- to late-eighteenth-century house at 150 Chestnut Street (fig. 92). As depicted in one of the earliest surviving commercial lithographs, it still sported curtains in its upper-story windows, a sign of its continued use as a residence. The ground floor, however, had been refitted with an elaborate shop front in the French-inspired style of the 1820s. Two doors, one opening into the shop and one to stairs leading up to the residence, flank a broad bowed, or "bulk," window through which the firm's wares are visible.

The Loud and Brothers store as it stood in 1831 was the product of significant transformations of the architecture and geography of commerce in Philadelphia in the early Republic. This was a very fine structure. Its windows boasted eared and pedimented frames, and its façade was brick covered with roughcast stucco scored to imitate stone.[10] Its alteration to a shop was part of the westward movement of commerce so memorably described by Watson, who claimed that since the beginning of the nineteenth century, "houses . . . of grand dimensions were running up for dwellings above Fifth and Sixth streets even while stores were following close after from Fourth Street. In a little while the reputation for stands on High Street became so great and rapid, that the chief of the large dwellings were purchased, and their rich and beautiful walls were torn to pieces to mould them into stores."[11]

Shops such as Loud and Brothers also marked a general movement toward specialization at all levels of trade. In the late eighteenth century, merchants sold all sorts of imported and domestically manufactured goods to all sorts of customers. As the volume and variety of goods increased, it became easier to control a single line or a related line of goods. Specialization affected both "shipping merchants," or wholesale importers, and small shopkeepers. After 1800, too, many artisans' products were replaced by industrially produced goods whose manufacturers preferred to bypass traditional all-purpose merchants to sell to specialized wholesale merchants or occasionally directly to retail shopkeepers.[12] The career of Front Street merchant Nathan Trotter exemplified this change. He began his career as part of a firm of general traders, but once on his own he gradually dropped lines of merchandise until, by the 1820s, he was exclusively an importer of semimanufactured metals for the use of craftsmen and manufacturers.[13]

These lithographs vividly illustrate this change, as merchants moved from general selling to specialization. Most of the commercial prints advertise wholesale commodities such as groceries and hardware. Dealers in chemical products, who offered everything from paints to drugs under one roof, were the largest single category of firm represented in the surviving lithographs of the antebellum years.

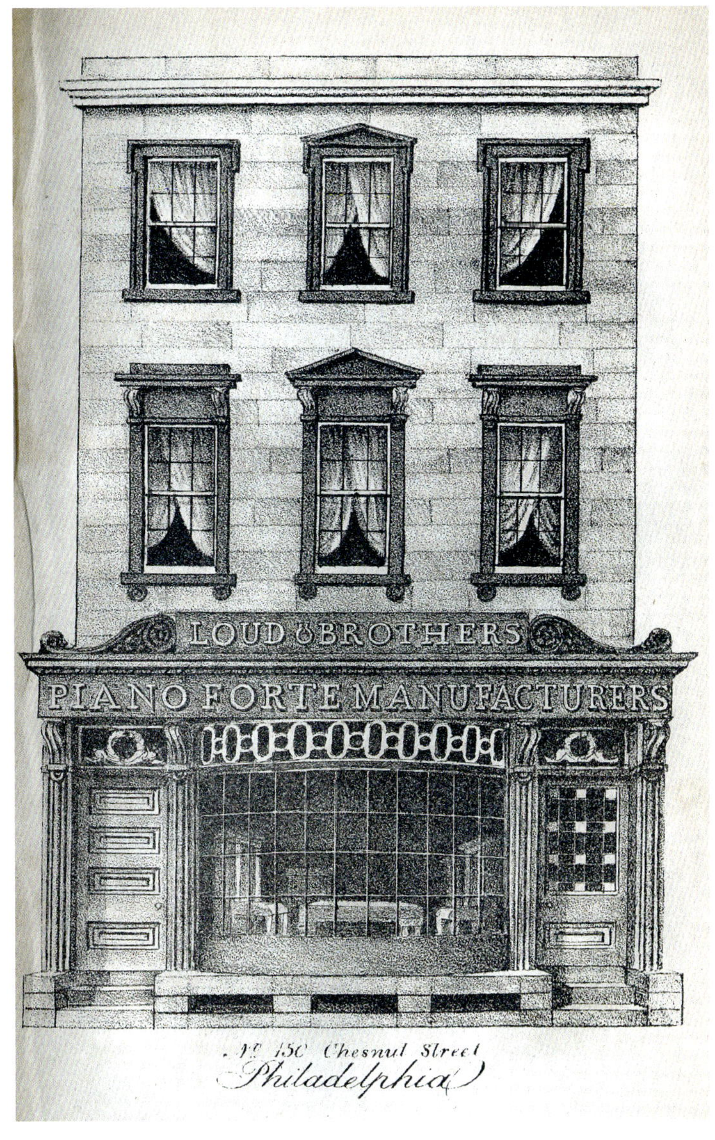

FIG. 92

William L. Breton, *No. 150 Chesnut Street Philadelphia,* from James Mease and Thomas Porter, *The Picture of Philadelphia from 1811 to 1831* (Philadelphia: Robert DeSilver, 1831). Printed by Kennedy and Lucas. Lithograph. 18 × 10 cm (7 × 4 in.). POS 509, LCP, Am 1831 Mease.

A significant minority of the lithographs tout retail sellers of fine goods such as jewelry, clothing, and particularly hats, for a second transformation heralded by the Loud and Brothers lithograph was the separation of wholesale and retail selling. The combination of mercantile specialization and the spread of genteel standards of behavior, which prompted those who aspired to respectability to isolate themselves from less refined people and spaces, led to the spatial separation of wholesale and retail trade and altered their architectural settings. According to Watson, this process began in Philadelphia just before the Revolution, when John Wallace began to sell imported worsted, satin, and brocade shoes for women. At the end of the eighteenth century, specialized shops were common and tended to cluster together. Milliners and sellers of women's shoes settled along Second Street between Dock and Spruce Streets, while men's shoe stores gathered on High Street.[14]

Watson described the business district in 1800 as limited largely to Front Street, backed by Second Street between Arch and Chestnut. By the mid–nineteenth century, Front, Second, Third, and Fourth Streets extending into the Northern Liberties were predominantly commercial thoroughfares, while other businesses extended west along Market Street and Chestnut Street. Chestnut was beginning to assume the role of genteel shopping district, while the more plebeian Market Street was home to the first of the great ready-made clothing stores. The surviving lithographs reflect this geography. Those businesses whose locations can be mapped form a T-shaped pattern, clustering most heavily along North Third Street and around Market and Chestnut Streets from Third to Seventh Streets.

The relatively informally organized shops and warehouses of the eighteenth century were rigorously reorganized internally and externally in the first half of the nineteenth century. Urban wholesale and retail businesses followed different strategies both in interior layout and in addressing the street, but they were organized by similar principles. Wholesale stores were arranged inside for maximum flexibility of use. Alfred Hoffy's view of William Newell's store at 3 South Water Street shows a large ground-floor room, which is open to the street through a granite-piered façade and in which the second story is supported by a thick central beam running front to back and reinforced in the middle by a square wooden post (fig. 93). In the second bay (opening) from the right a rope loop reveals the location of the hoist that conveyed goods to the upper stories, allowing them to be loaded directly from the street.[15] With a stair along one side wall and a counting room (office) partitioned off at the rear (probably indicated by the windows visible through the left bay of the façade), this was the standard organization for stores that handled bulk goods of all sorts.

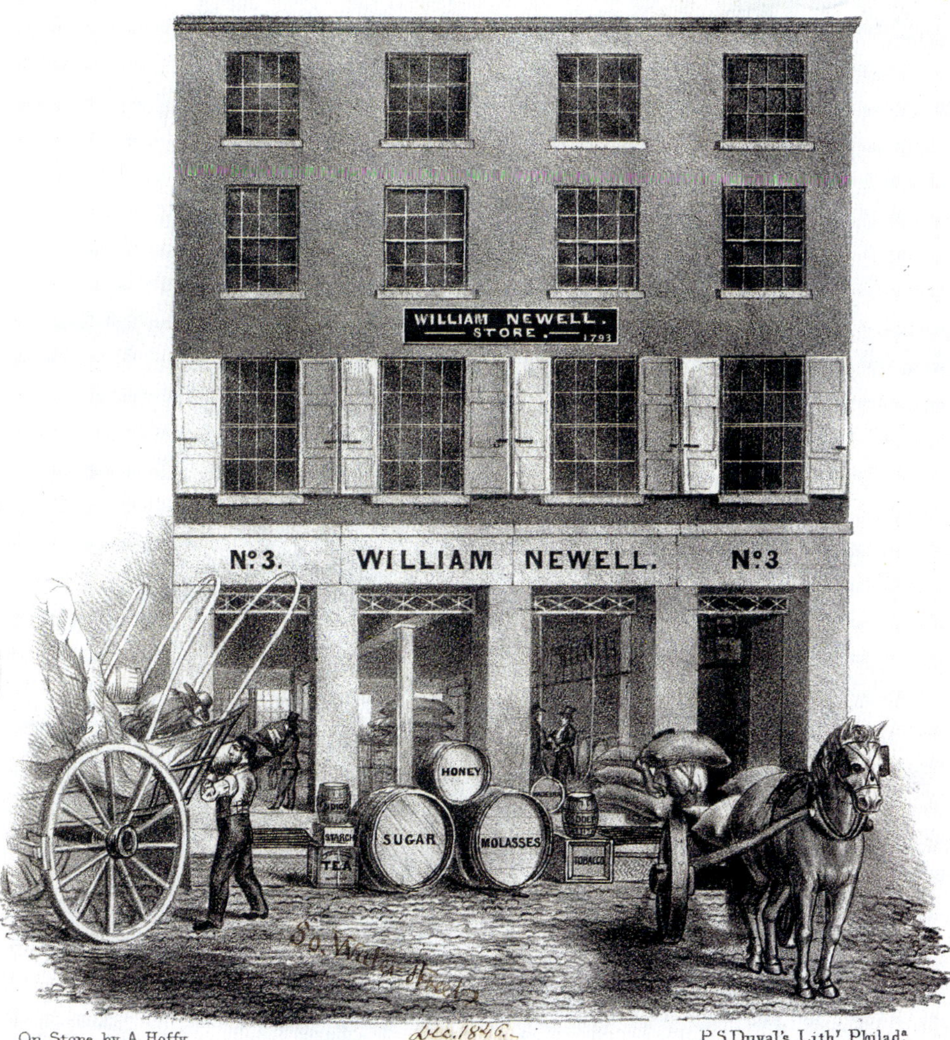

These kinds of wholesale stores were a staple of the practice of Thomas S. Stewart, a carpenter-architect who supplemented his relatively rare large-scale buildings with commercial structures, tenements, and residential alterations. His design of circa 1835 for the firm of Smith and Brown envisioned just this kind of store: the five-story brick structure, 23½ feet wide by 82 feet deep, had two "hoisting machines" and two "fireproofs" (brick chambers for safekeeping of records). All the windows were covered with shutters lined with iron, a standard fireproofing strategy but one that was some-times counterproductive. When two stores at 36 and 37 South Wharves caught fire in 1834, "as the roof of the building was slated, and the doors and window shutters completely covered with strong sheet iron," the firemen could not get to the fire before the buildings were destroyed. However, a daring man entered the fireproof in one counting room to save the account books.[16] Stewart's estimate for the Smith and Brown store included $450 for granite, evidence that the ground-floor façade would be supported on granite piers, as in William Newell's store. As urban buildings, the articulation of the public space and flow of traffic outside was as important to commercial architecture as its interior organization. The plane that separated the private interior of the shop from the public street received the most careful attention of any aspect of such architecture, and it was this feature that was transformed most dramatically in the first half of the nineteenth century.

As early as the second decade of that century, the owners of wholesale stores began to open up the ground-story façades of their establishments. George Justice offered to do this in 1812 at two of Stephen Girard's Front Street stores. Justice proposed "that two door Sills of Stone be procured of Sufficient length to accomodate Whole Sale Stores to be placed in or near the Centre of Each of the fronts & that four Windows for the two fronts be also made or procured that Shal Suit the hight of the now [?] Storys to fill up the Vacuom [?] or Spaces after Sufficient deduction for piers of brick for the Acomodation of sd fronts." In other words, Justice would cut away the front wall, leaving only brick piers to support the upper floors, and replace the demolished fabric with doors and windows.[17]

In the 1820s wholesale stores in American ports began to be built with ground floors opened up by continuous street-front arcades.[18] After 1830 trabeated (post-and-lintel) granite-piered shop fronts such as William Newell's and Smith and Brown's were standard. Their advantage was that they allowed the entire ground story to be filled with glazed doors or windows. The first ones were built in Boston in the mid-1820s. New York had adopted them by the end of that decade, despite the apparent instability of the thin supports, a perception reinforced by the collapse of one of New York's earliest examples, Phelps and Peck's wholesale store in 1832.[19] Rows of such buildings, virtually identical in size and appearance, replaced the more varied ranks of mercantile buildings that characterized the eighteenth- and early-nineteenth-century American waterfronts. The row of stores in the first block of North Front Street, built in 1830–31 for Stephen Girard, is one of the finest groups of such stores surviving in the United States.[20]

These trabeated shop fronts effectively broke the membrane between the store and the street. For dealers in bulk merchandise and for some retailers of coarse goods, the façade might consist entirely of glazed doors that could be opened to leave nothing but the piers between the interior and the exterior (figs. 91, 93). By midcentury, thin cast-iron piers allowed even greater transparency of the front wall. Merchants who sold smaller or more fragile goods, such as drugs and chemicals or textiles, often filled one or more bays with windows that could be used to display their goods in a more protected fashion (fig. 94).

Early-nineteenth-century urbanites were obsessed with ordering their unruly cities. The simple grid was adopted as the container in which "separation and classification" could be imposed on everything from personal relationships to the display of goods, and it was applied to everything from urban plans to commercial buildings to public institutions to desks.[21] In William Newell's store, the walls and openings implicitly extend the street grid to the interior. Piles of bulging sacks seem to define aisles aligned with the granite piers of the façade. A similar use of the bay system to organize the interior is apparent in the lithographs of Thomas Minford's Tea Ware House (POS 754), Foering & Thudium's Cheap Stove Ware-House (POS 266), and Lockwood & Smith's China, Glass and Queensware store (POS 441).

The porous façade also allowed the merchant to colonize the street. By the 1830s the line between the public and private domains in the wholesale districts had been thoroughly blurred. In cities from Boston to New Orleans, canvas awnings converted sidewalks into covered passages (POS 457.3).[22] These were fastened to the front of the building and attached at curbside to a standardized frame consisting of two round vertical posts linked by a pair of horizontal members joined to them just below the top (fig. 94).[23] Triangular side panels sometimes closed the ends of the awning and were treated as signs. While awnings shaded passersby, they also claimed the sidewalk as a quasi-private space that became increasingly important to urban businesses.[24] Would-be New Orleans merchant Richard Barry wrote to his landlord, "As to my doing any business in the grocery line without the awning [it] is totally out of the question."[25]

Goods were stacked at the curb at delivery and pickup, which was legal, but the sidewalk under the awning also became an extension of the display area, which was forbidden by multiple ordinances in both the city and the Northern Liberties.[26]

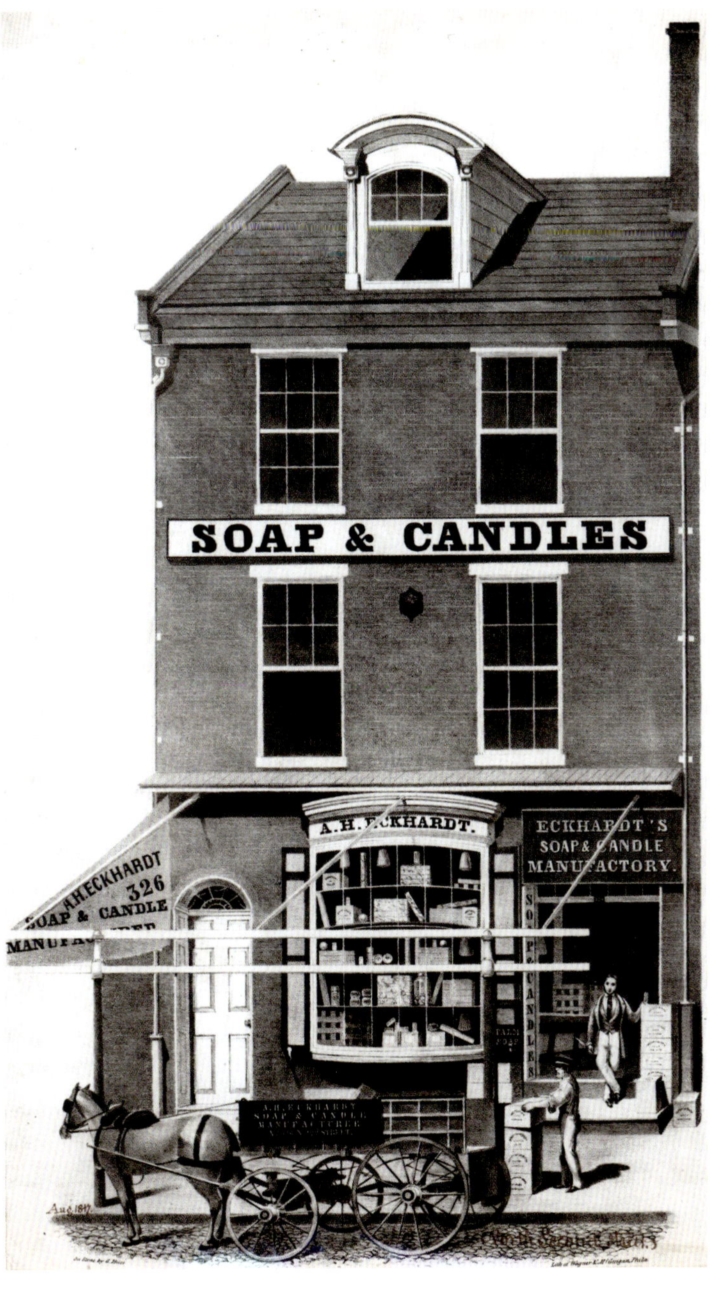

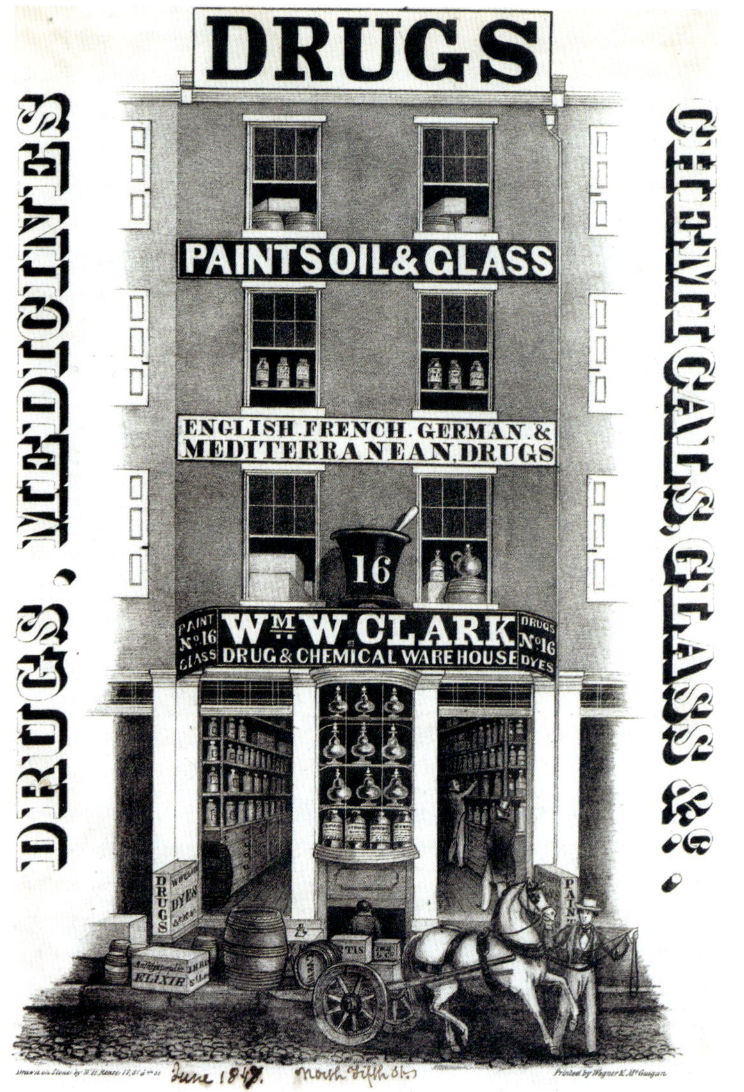

William H. Rease, [*Wm. W. Clark, Drug & Chemical Warehouse, 16 North Fifth Street, Philadelphia*] (Philadelphia: Printed by Wagner & McGuigan, 1847). Lithograph. 29 × 19 cm (11 3/8 × 7 1/2 in.). POS 862, LCP, P.2248.

At the very least platforms or vitrines were built beneath the windows, or pedestals against the piers, to show off the firm's wares. Larger, more durable merchandise covered the entire sidewalk in both the wholesale and the retail districts (POS 416, POS 345).[27] In Boston's retail district, visitor Alexander Mackay noted that the shops were "gorged with goods, so much so as literally to ooze out at doors and windows; and what a gaudy flaunting show they make! Piled in tempting masses on the hard brick pavement, you are ready to stumble over goods at every step you take, whilst from the upper windows stream whole pieces of flaring calicos and gaudy ribbons; the whole impressing one with the idea that business was making a holiday of it, and had donned, for the occasion, its most showy habiliments."[28] In New York's wholesale districts along Pearl and Wall streets, he reported,

> The narrow side-walk is covered with goods, whilst the thoroughfare, not many feet wide, is also here and there invaded, so that at some points you have no alternative, in proceeding, but to jump over boxes, or squeeze yourself, as best you can, between bales of merchandize. Nor is mid-air even free from the intrusion; for from many lofty cranes, heavy and bulky masses are dangling, in a way that makes you feel nervous for your head, whilst you are busy taking care of your feet.[29]

Sellers of goods that needed protection from the elements opened the fronts of their buildings with large windows, either filling the interstices between piers with full-height sash and glazed doors or piercing solid walls with "bulks," or projecting bay windows (fig. 95; see also POS 223).[30] Invented in London in the 1750s, bulk windows quickly made their way to Philadelphia. By 1769 the city council felt obliged to regulate the "late extraordinary encroachments" on the streets, including "jut-windows, bulks, and other incumbrances," and to levy a thirty-shilling fine on anyone whose bulk window obstructed foot traffic.[31] Nevertheless, bulks remained relatively rare until the end of the eighteenth century. Of thirty-four buildings used wholly or partially for commercial purposes and described in the surviving

Mutual Assurance Company surveys of 1784 to 1794, only one boasted bulk windows.[32]

The architectural evidence of the lithographs shows that bulk windows became common in the 1790s. The oldest bulk window John Fanning Watson's informants could recall was installed in an early-eighteenth-century tavern at Front and Market Streets to adapt it as a hardware store. It was a rectilinear shed-roofed affair that could be closed with wooden shutters.[33] The earliest bulk windows recorded in the lithographs and in early photographs of Philadelphia projected in a shallow segmental curve. Their muntins formed a natural grid within which goods could be displayed in an orderly but profuse array. The bulk in A. H. Eckhart's Soap and Candle Manufactory on North Second Street, a building of about 1820, was employed in this manner (fig. 94). Like others in the drug and chemical trade, William W. Clark filled the gridded bulk of his North Fifth Street store, a building of about 1840, with fancifully shaped bottles that would have contained brightly colored liquids (fig. 95). The light glinting off them in the daytime would catch the eye, and they would be even more striking at night, backlit from inside when the shop remained open after dark. On a walk in 1800, diarist Elizabeth Drinker and her son "stop'd to look at the col[er]ed bottles in an Apothecarys shop in third street near Chestnut street."[34]

By the 1840s some merchants had adopted flat windows made of large panes of newly available cheap plate glass (fig. 96).[35] These expansive windows filled most of the ground-floor façade, making the public-private membrane transparent, at least, even if it was not eradicated as in the trabeated wholesale storefronts. By midcentury important shopping streets were bounded by continuous walls of glass. A walk along Front Street and one along Chestnut Street would have offered a similar experience of visual flow between the sidewalk and the interiors (figs. 97, 98). In fact, in lower-class retail streets, shop fronts might have been as open as in wholesale districts (fig. 99; see also POS 439).[36] One visitor to the Bowery, New York's working-class shopping district, discovered that in the street's most commercial stretches "the sides of the streets appear to be all door, and the walls only separate the different concerns."[37]

Bulks and plate-glass shop windows (and the lithographs themselves) were part of a growing emphasis on aggressive selling that began in the early years of the new Republic. Whereas traditional merchants sold to those who came to buy specific items, new-style merchants, especially retail shopkeepers, sought to persuade customers to

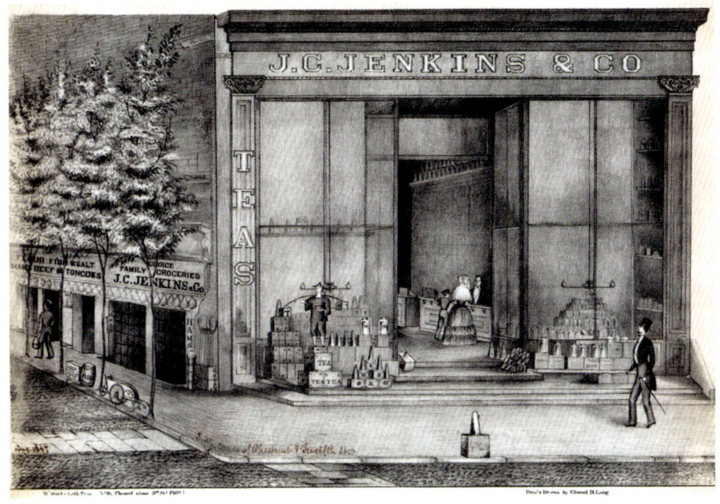

FIG. 96
Ellwood D. Long, [*J. C. Jenkins & Co. Grocery and Tea Store, S.W. Corner of Chestnut and 12th Streets, Philadelphia*] (Philadelphia: W. Stott's Lith. Press, 1847). Lithograph. 27 × 39 cm (10 ¾ × 15 ¼ in.). POS 394, LCP, P.2055.

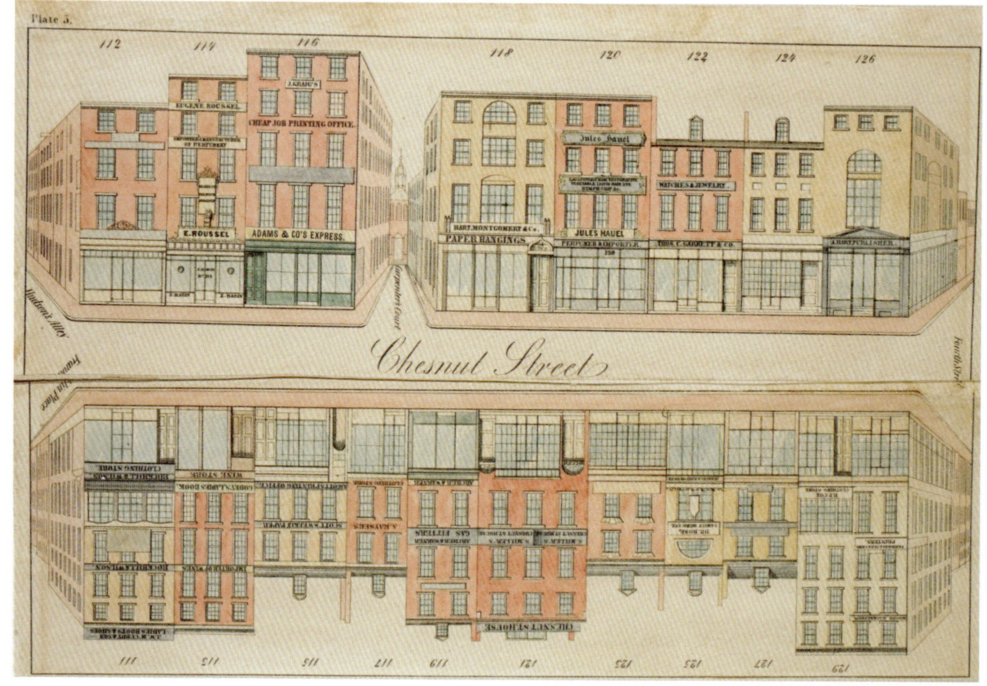

buy goods that they might not have intended to purchase. Jewelers, wallpaper merchants, hat makers, and saddlers all filled their windows with enticing displays of merchandise (fig. 100; see also POS 409, POS 831, POS 855).[38] By the 1830s consumers had responded to these enticements by inventing the now-familiar but then-new practice of shopping—and window shopping.

A New York editor found "a silent eloquence in shop windows." The window shopper

> pleases himself by indulging his curiosity, or by gratifying his taste, and he pleases the shopkeeper by the unartificial homage which he thus pays to the taste which arranged the articles, and by the promise which he thus holds out of the probability of his becoming a purchaser. If we could conceive of such an event, though, indeed, it is hardly a supposable case, that a spirited shopkeeper had expended several hundred dollars in fitting up his shop most magnificently, and in glazing his windows with acres of plate-glass, and in selecting the finest pieces of mahogany, and in purchasing the most splendid lamps and lustres; and after all this, if no one should stop and look admiringly on the shop, it would be almost enough to break the poor man's heart. It is, therefore, an act of humanity to look in at shop-windows. He that looks

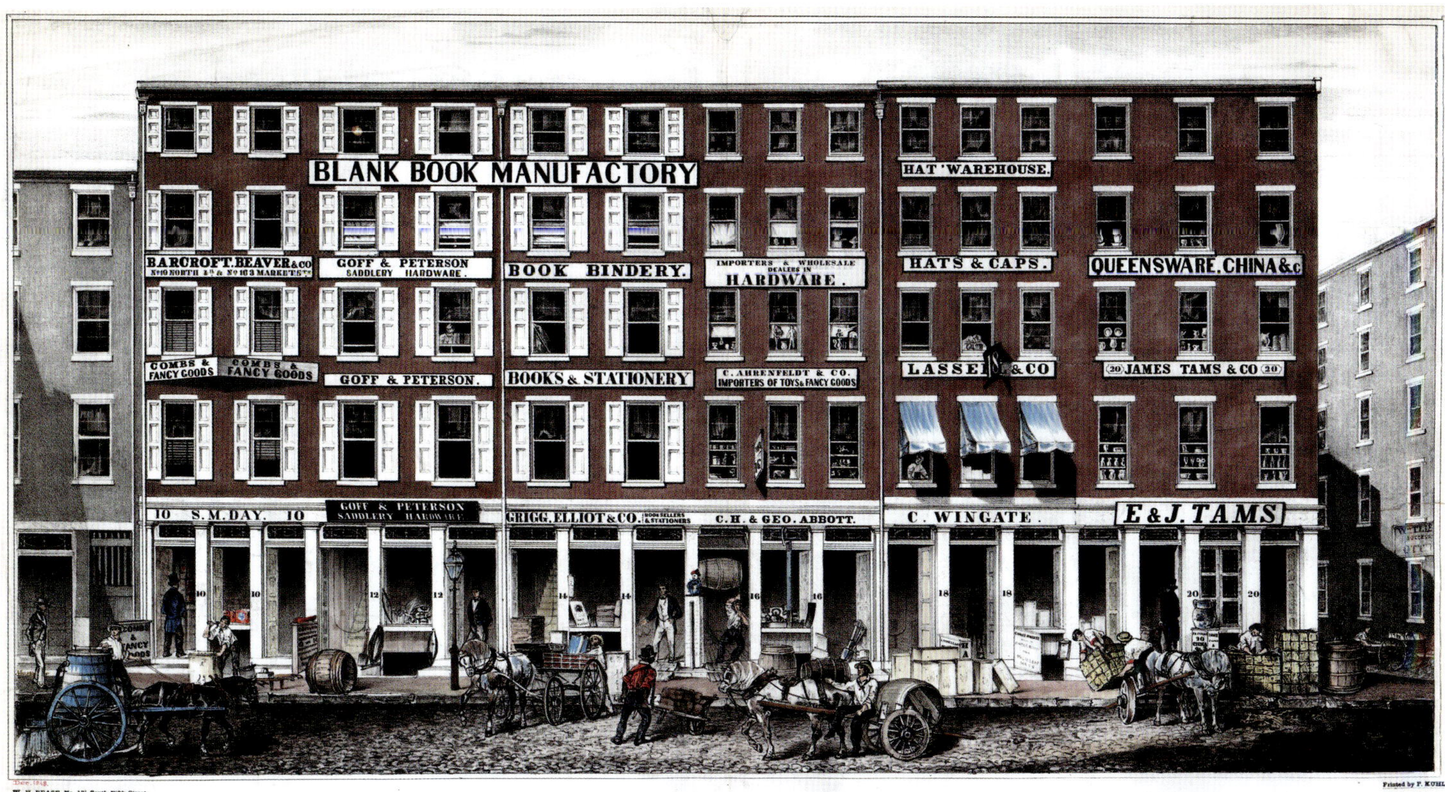

into a shop-window affords as much pleasure to the shop-keeper as the little fishes in the river, when they nibble the bait, afford to the juvenile indulgers in piscatorial propensities.[39]

Show windows were among the tamer ways to attract custom. The most striking aspect of the lithographs is not the windows they show but the signs that cover the exteriors of shops and warehouses. Even restrained buildings were marked by signs over the doors, lettering on the cornices of bulk windows, and signs on walls between the rows of windows. Wholesalers and lower-class retailers covered every available surface with lists of their wares, their names, their attractive terms of sale. Signs were attached to awnings and fastened to walls in ways that sometimes obstructed window openings. They thrust out over the sidewalk from façades. They stood on eaves. They were

FIG. 98
William H. Rease, *Grigg Block, North Fourth Street, Philadelphia* (Philadelphia: Printed by F. Kuhl, 1848). Lithograph with hand-coloring. 61 × 91 cm (23 ¾ × 36 in.). POS 331, LCP, P.2077.

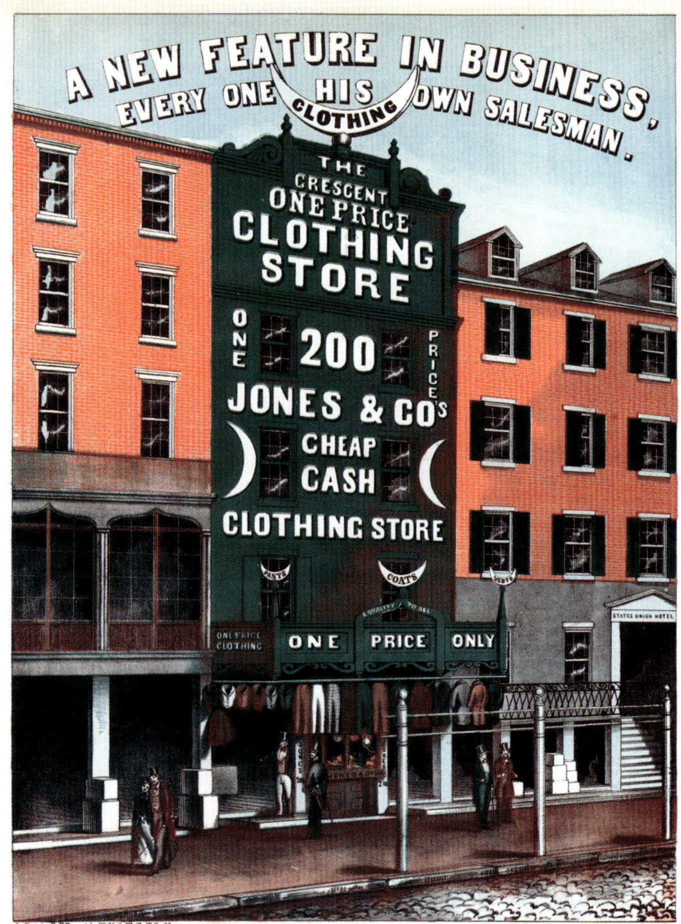

Robert F. Reynolds, *Jones & Co. of the Crescent One Price Clothing Store, No. 200 Market St[reet], Above 6th, Philada.* (Philadelphia: Printed by Wagner & McGuigan, ca. 1855). Chromolithograph. 57 × 42 cm (22 ¾ × 16 ½ in.). POS 413, LCP, P. 2142.

lettered in script of every size and font (figs. 99, 101). In the 1850s "flaring and intrusive signs and advertisements, which meet the eye at every turn," might be set off against luridly colored walls to make them even more visible.[40]

According to historian David Henkin, signs established the street as a realm of public encounter with competing propositions and demands as much as newspapers, religious and political tracts, or public speeches did. Insistent signs drew passersby into a discourse that forced them to evaluate claims and make choices. Like the advertising columns of a newspaper, with its blocks of text organized in a gridded matrix, each building on the commercial street was a kind of block advertisement set within a similar gridded matrix, waiting to be scanned by the viewer.[41] It is no accident that when these buildings were lithographed, the signs that allowed the building to be easily identified on the street and that added visual interest to the image also served as the lithograph's advertising copy. The world of the printed text and the world of the street intersected in the sign.

Sensory overload was central to retail sales in the antebellum decades. Not one button but a hundred, not one hat but a hundred, not one strip of wallpaper but a hundred, overwhelmed the shopper and made it appear as though everything one could possibly want was there for the buying. On the exterior, words on signs were combined with symbols, images, and sample goods to intimate the profusion that one would find inside. At T. Sharpless & Sons' textile ware room, for example, long pieces of cloth, hung like curtains on rods set between the building's piers, fluttered out onto the street (POS 736). Melloy & Ford ("Quick Sales & Small Profits") displayed tinware on pedestals on the balcony over their shop front, while Hartley & Knight's bedding warehouse featured mattresses thrust out the open windows on dollies (POS 465, POS 345). At a shop next to Charles Oat's lamp store on North Second Street a long string of hats and bonnets suspended from the cornice caught the breeze like Japanese lanterns (POS 104).

Gigantic objects—mortars and pestles, watches, coffee pots, oil cans, teapots, top hats—burst from façades or pierced the skyline, foreshadowing the roadside landscape of the next century (POS 291, POS 337, POS 397, POS 465, POS 673, POS 852).[42] Jones & Company painted the façade of their Crescent One Price Clothing Store on

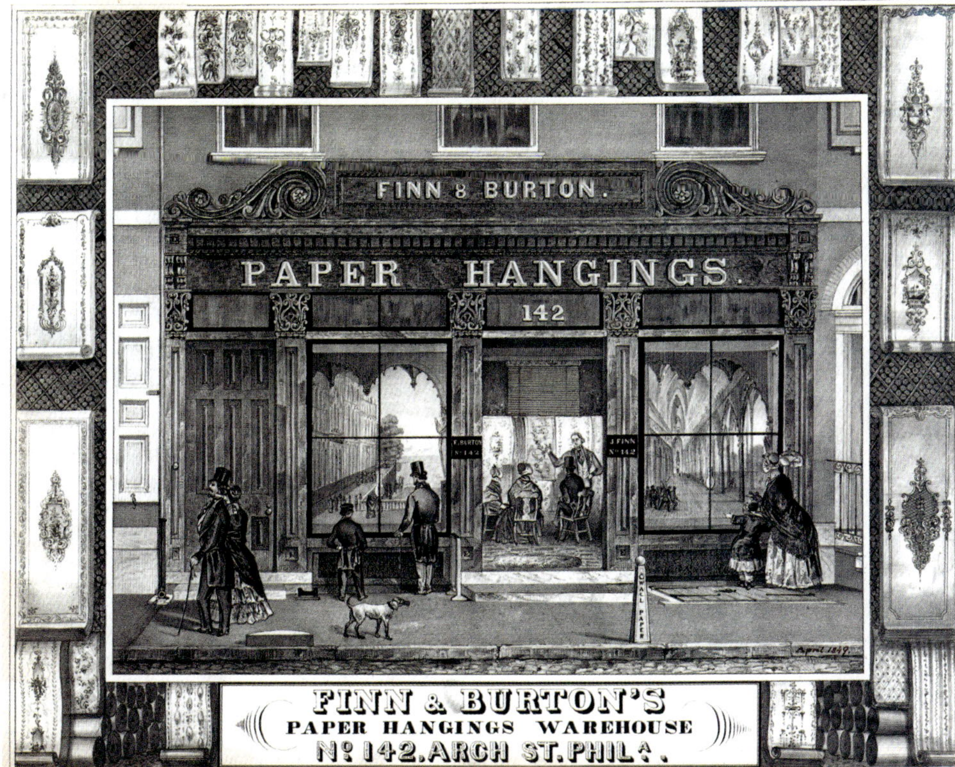

FIG. 100

William H. Rease, *Finn & Burton's Paper Hangings Warehouse No 142 Arch St. Phila.* (Philadelphia: F. Kuhl, 1849). Lithograph. 42 × 50 cm (16 ½ × 20 in.). POS 250, LCP, P.2082.

Market Street black to set it off from the brick buildings to either side and topped it off with a giant crescent. Their competitors J. M. Bennett and J. C. Umberger upped the ante to draw attention to their Tower Hall Clothing Bazaar, a block east of the Crescent Store (POS 35): They added a crenellated cornice, flanked by two small towers supporting statues and punctuated by a tall flagpole, to their four-story early-nineteenth-century building. By 1856 they had replaced this structure with a purpose-built six-story headquarters designed by the architectural firm of Sloan and Stewart. Now Tower Hall really had a tower, a two-stage castellated spire that capped an elaborate neo-Romanesque façade (POS 288).[43]

Retail stores were organized more formally than wholesale stores, with counters clearly separating the customer's from the clerk's spaces (fig. 96; see also POS 61).[44] Ranks of shelves, compartments, or drawers arrayed behind the counter allowed goods to be displayed in an orderly, categorized fashion that was also meant to overwhelm by the sheer numbers of similar items offered (figs. 95, 102; see also POS 291, POS 854, POS 862).[45] In this way, the logic of the urban grid permeated retail shops even more decisively than it did wholesale stores.

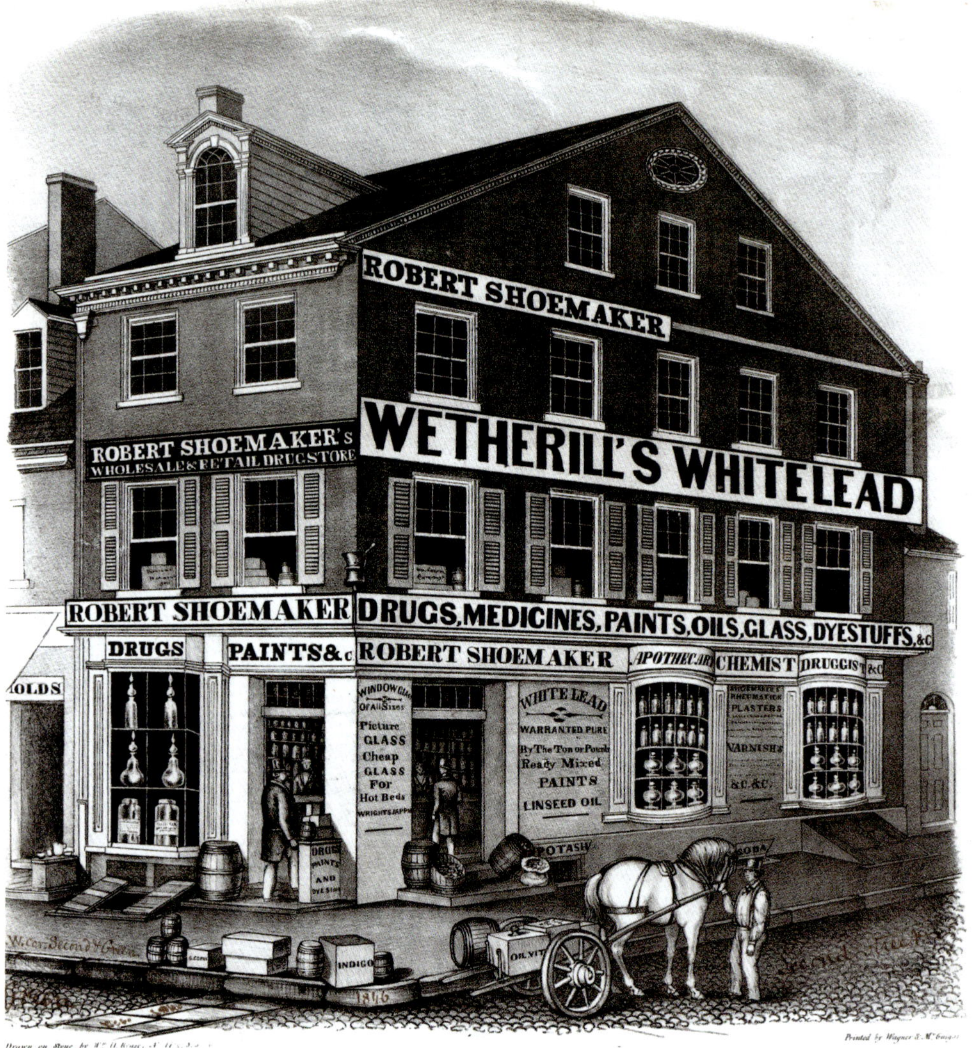

Even as the growing commercial economy generated the boisterous selling techniques and crowded sidewalks of the wholesale and cheap retail districts, some early
Philadelphians adopted modes of self-presentation that were conspicuously understated but authoritative, and they sought public and private spaces in which they might
exercise their taste away from the people and activities they believed inferior to them.
Historians have labeled this code of personal identity and public interaction gentility,
civility, or refinement.[46]

Enterprising shopkeepers in Philadelphia in the years after the Revolution adopted a pose of gentility as a way to attract such elite customers. They did so by selling
only select, luxury goods, by moving their businesses inland from the hurly-burly of

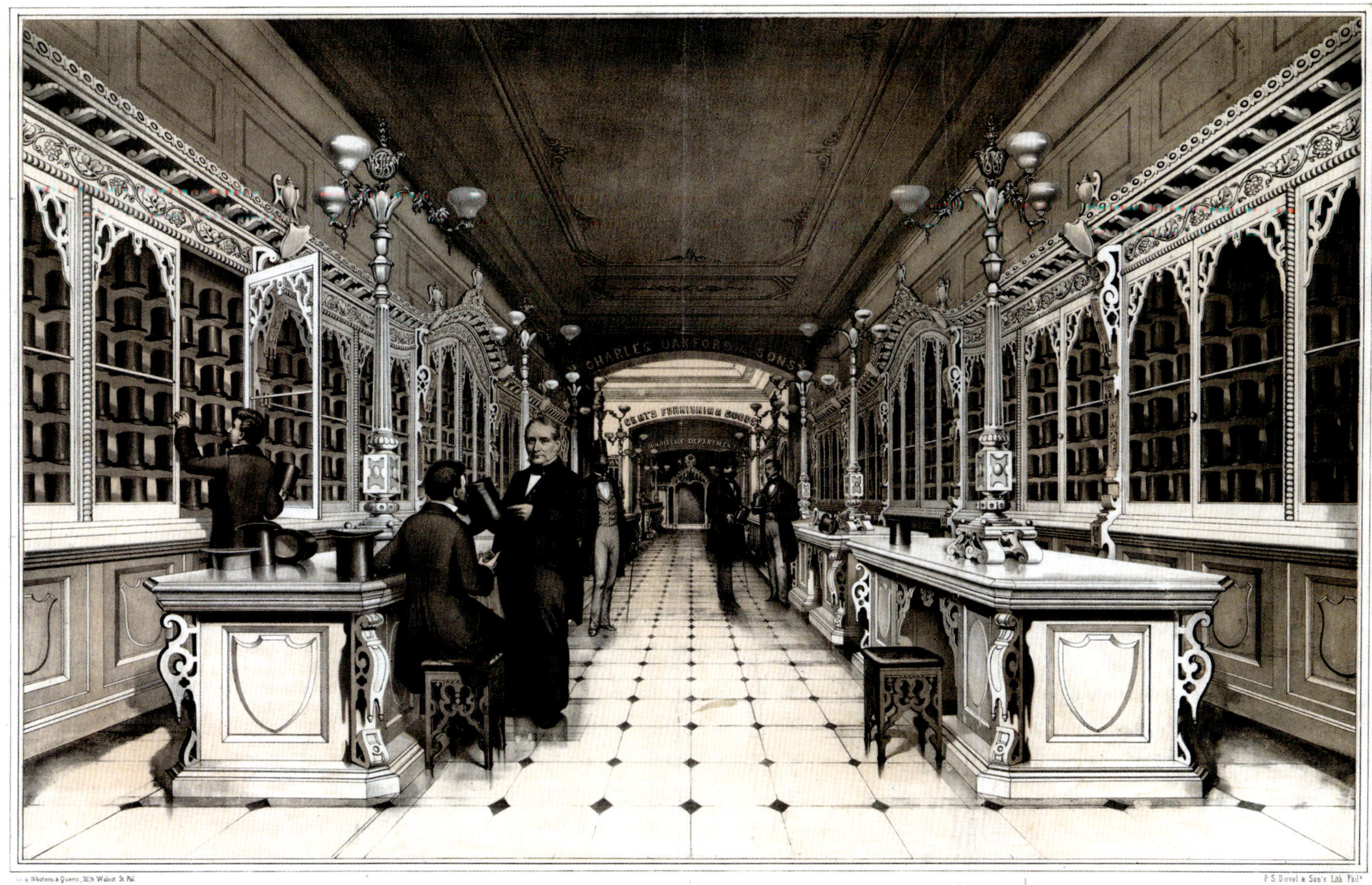

the wholesale district, and by implementing sales rituals adapted from aristocratic master-servant relationships. The first to do so, John Fanning Watson claimed, was Mr. Whitesides, a Londoner who opened a bulk-windowed shop at (old) 134 Market Street "in the true 'Bond-street style.' . . . The then uncommon sized lights in the two bulks, and the fine mull-mull and jaconet muslins, the chintses, and linens suspended in whole pieces, from the top to the bottom, and entwined together in puffs and festoons, (totally new,)" startled and eventually alienated Philadelphians. "The shopman, behind the counter, powdered, bowing and smiling, caused it to be 'all the stare' for the time. There being too much of the 'pouncet box' in the display, however, and the 'vile Jersey half-pence, with a horsehead thereon' being wrapped up, when given in

FIG. 102

Ibbotson & Queen, *Charles Oakford & Sons Model Hat Store Nos. 826 & 828 Chesnut Street, Continental Hotel, Philadelphia* (Philadelphia: P. S. Duval, ca. 1860). Lithograph, tinted with one stone. 39 × 60 cm (15 ½ × 24 in.). POS 106, LCP, P. 2029.

William Birch, *South East Corner of Third and Market Streets, Philadelphia* (Philadelphia: W. Birch & Son, 1799). Engraving with hand-coloring. 33 × 39 cm (12 ¾ × 15 ½ in.). LCP, P. 2276.14.

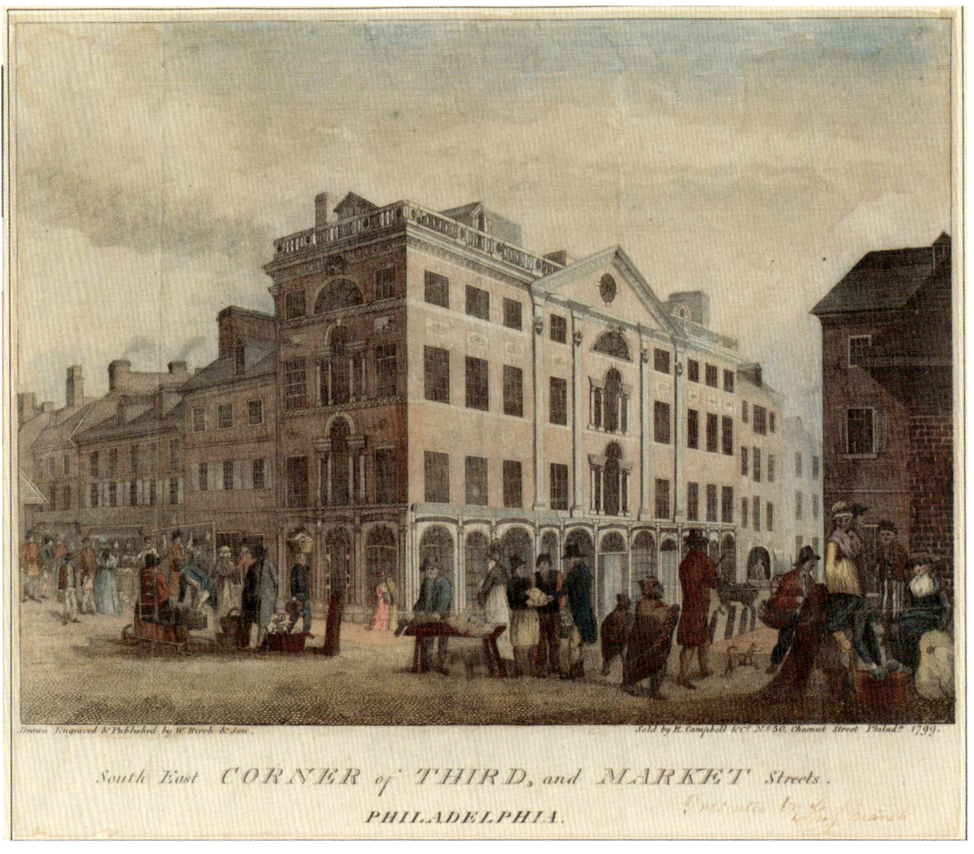

change in whitey brown paper, with a counter bow to the ladies, seeming rather too civil by half for the (as yet) primitive notions of our city folks."[47]

Architecture was essential in establishing the tone for genteel retailing. In 1793–94 Joseph Cook erected an eye-catching building at the southeastern corner of Third and High (Market) Streets (fig. 103). This four-story brick structure was only the width of an ordinary row house, but it extended quite far along Third Street. It was embellished in the new neoclassical manner, with its long side broken by a central pavilion defined by a pediment and four tall pilasters of attenuated proportions, giving the building a family resemblance to Robert Adam's fashionable new Adelphi development in London. The upper levels of the pavilion and the narrow end façade on Market Street were lighted by Palladian and semicircular windows. The entire ground floor was treated as a series of arcaded bays separated by thin pilasters. Three of these arches contained shop doors, and the others were probably fitted with bulk windows.[48] There were two levels of cellars underneath, the lower one devoted to kitchens and the upper to sitting rooms for the tenants of the stores above. These shops "presented a scene of magnificence not surpassed by any place of business on the globe, at that day," wrote James Mease and Thomas Porter in their reissued city guide, originally published in 1811.[49] William Birch made an engraving of the Shakespeare Buildings, as they were called, that depicted them in their heyday and emphasized their social and architectural novelty. The block is surrounded by smaller and more workaday buildings of an older type. As he was wont to do, Birch filled the foreground with figures meant to comment on the main subject of the picture. In contrast to the refined, protected commercial space inside the Shakespeare Buildings, the street is filled with hawkers, hucksters, and wheelbarrow men, male and female, white and black, mostly poor, as reminders of the rude underside of retailing. But like Mr. Whitesides and his bewigged clerks, the Shakespeare Buildings were a failure, nicknamed "Cooke's Folly." They were stripped of their ornaments, rented to plebeian businesses, including the ready-to-wear clothiers who became the hallmark of lower-class High Street retailing, and finally torn down after only a few decades' service.[50]

The first tenants of the Shakespeare Buildings were jewelers. We do not know what the interiors of their shops looked like, but we might take a hint from the "Goldsmith and Jewelers show shop" of Joseph Anthony Jr., which was surveyed by the Mutual Assurance Company in December, 1793, just as the Shakespeare Buildings were going up. Anthony's establishment stood on the south side of High Street only a few doors west of Cooke's Folly. It boasted a paneled counter with a mahogany top and a rear wall "all of compass work," meaning that it was fitted with arched niches. These had mahogany-framed sash above and solid mahogany doors below like the display cupboards in a wealthy person's parlor. The two bulk windows on the façade flanked a frontispiece, or classically framed door, trimmed with fluted pilasters.[51]

As in Anthony's store, the shelves, compartments, and counters of luxury stores offered a medium for the elaborate architectural decoration that signaled gentility. Counters topped with marble or mahogany and richly framed shelves served to move the process of buying from the come-one, come-all world of monetary exchange ("Cheap for Cash"; "Quick Sales & Small Profits") to the more private, more refined one of connoisseurship (POS 439; POS 465).[52] Architecturally ambitious interiors such as Anthony's were built throughout the first half of the nineteenth century. Bailey & Kitchen's jewelry store at 134 (now 428) Chestnut Street featured "washbds. & windows cased,—Groind-Arch Cieling, form'd with wood & plaister'd, Stucco cornice & mouldings on the ceiling. In front are 2 neat Circular end Bulk windows, Each 30 lights, Glass 14 × 20 in Shutters folding in boxes, Cover'd by Neat hanging pilasters." A Langenheim stereographic photograph of around 1860 shows that the Bailey firm eventually moved to even more lavishly decorated premises.[53]

Because lithographs were meant to inform potential customers of the location of a business, they tended not to record the interiors of genteel shops of this sort until the 1850s. But the few late lithographs that do so demonstrate that the architectural intent remained constant: to evoke the exclusive and refined air of elite residences.[54] In the 1840s, for example, the hatter Charles Oakford occupied a modest converted three-story house at (old) 104 Chestnut Street and conducted his business in a relatively conservative manner, as a James Queen lithograph of around 1843 reveals (POS 108).[55] By 1854 Oakford had moved farther out on Chestnut Street to number 158 (POS 109). Both walls of this long narrow space were lined with grids of shelves as usual, but these were topped by an elaborate cornice, while glazed doors in the neo-Gothic style protected the orderly rows of top hats inside. The counters were made in the same style and appear to have been topped with marble. The floor was marble paved, as well. Monumental gas-lighting fixtures that looked like miniature street lights stood on the counters. Small Gothic stools were provided for the customers' comfort. Six years later the firm, now Charles Oakford & Sons, had moved into the new Continental Hotel in the 800 block of Chestnut (fig. 102). The lithographer simply revised most of the earlier lithograph, including the two pairs of figures lounging against the counters, but changed the floor pattern and added an elaborately stenciled ceiling. At the rear a brightly illuminated light well with a tall mirror on the back wall made the space appear deeper than it was. A stereographic view taken in the same year confirms that Oakford had in fact moved the fittings of his second store to the new space. The counter is cluttered with textiles, and umbrellas hang from the light fixtures.[56]

If the gentrification of commercial interiors is infrequently documented in the lithographs, the refinement of exteriors is not. The façades of genteel businesses were organized as coordinated, architecturally ambitious compositions, as the lithograph of the Loud and Brothers shop illustrates (fig. 92). Doors and projecting or flat display windows were framed by heavy pilasters and cornices. Some shop fronts from the 1840s were depicted as though they were made of stone, but most likely they were wood marbleized or grained to imitate grander materials (fig. 100; see also POS 72, POS 298).[57] The pilastered façade of Finn & Burton's paper-hangings store at 142 Arch Street is treated in that manner. The firm's name stands atop the shop front's cornice as a blocking course flanked by elaborate carved brackets. Finn and Burton have hung scenic wallpapers in the display windows as though they were paintings. That in the left window shows a row of buildings on a quay, while the one at the right depicts the interior of a Gothic church. Both views are framed by similar Gothic-style borders, suggesting that they were part of a coordinated set of papers. Visible through the door, patrons are seated before three suspended rolls of wallpaper while a salesman explains their fine points like a lecturer in an art-history class.

What these exteriors lack most conspicuously are the rambunctious signs and emblems that enlivened the wholesale and lower-class retail districts. Among the genteel, "glaring allurements at windows, . . . over-reaching signs, [and] big bulk windows" were widely condemned.[58] One journalist, for example, was shocked to find the façade of New York's Astor House hotel "disfigured by the signs of the merchants and tradesmen who have leased the ground story. The bad taste of the occupants, in putting up signs without any uniformity of shape and size, is the subject of universal remark."[59] Critics attributed this practice to the effrontery of greed and unseemly competition: "A little impudence, well employed, will sometimes do wonders in the way of making money."[60] It is also possible to read the genteel aversion to commercial display as an expression of an aesthetic of visual uniformity and understated elegance also manifested by wealthy Philadelphians' habit of removing conspicuous eighteenth-century exterior ornaments from their houses. "A modern innovation, which some regard as defective in good taste, has been to tear down almost universally from the superior houses, all the ancient ornaments which were not conformed to the modern taste. . . . The old houses, too, had much relief work on the fronts of the houses,—but the taste now is to affect a general plainness combined with neatness."[61]

The Philadelphia Arcade (John Haviland, 1824–26) epitomized the genteel mercantile aesthetic (POS 572). In common with arcades in Europe and others in the United States (Philadelphia's was first), it was meant to constitute a self-contained exclusive shopping district. Its façade was coordinated with that of the Chestnut Street Theater a few doors down. The proprietors attempted to create a genteel environment by prohibiting exterior signs, which cost them several prospective tenants. The shop fronts on the interior "avenues" were uniform in appearance and almost certainly did not have goods standing in front of them or affixed to their exteriors.[62] Like the Shakespeare Buildings, its most renowned genteel commercial predecessor, the arcade quickly failed. In its declining years, before it was demolished in 1860, it became a hotel and a bath, and its façade was then covered with signs and bulk windows (POS 628).[63]

The commercial lithographs show us much about the architecture and business practices of one segment of mercantile Philadelphia in the mid–nineteenth century. The businesses they advertised concentrated most heavily along Chestnut and Market Streets between Second and Ninth Streets, and stretched north into the Northern Liberties along Third Street and south along Second Street to the Second Street Market. According to Alexander Mackay, who visited Philadelphia in the mid-1840s, Third Street was "the dividing line between the wholesale and retail business of the

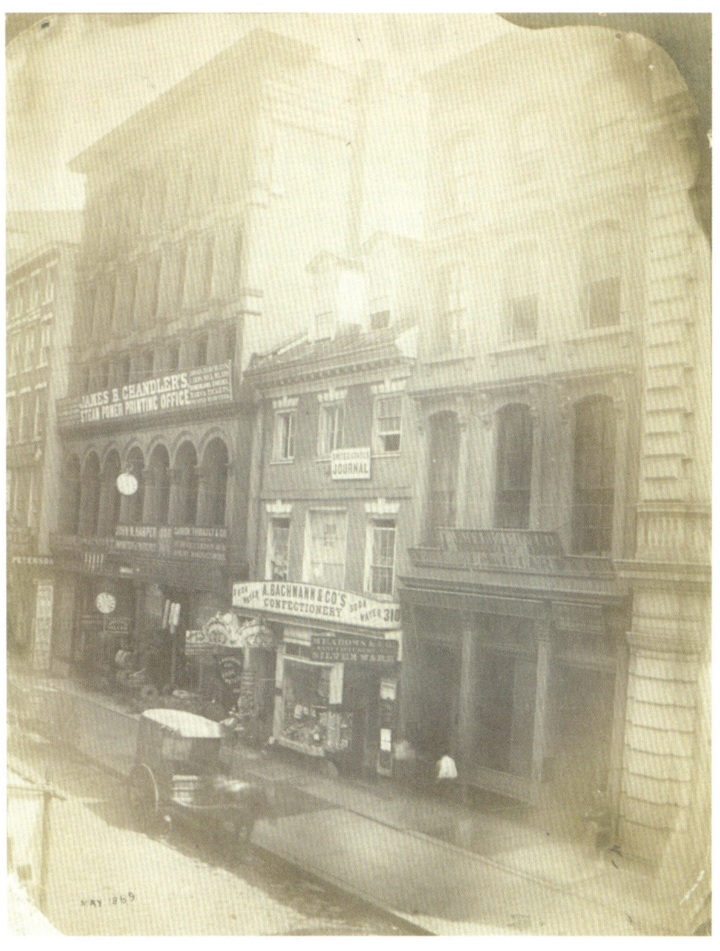

FIG. 104
Frederick De Bourg Richards, *The Poulson Mansion. Lately No. 106 Chestnut Street, Now No. 310,* May 1859. Salted paper print. 21 × 16 cm (8 ¼ × 6 ¼ in.). LCP, (3)2526.F.72.

town; partaking itself largely of both, with the exception of market-street, which is the great retail mart."[64] Early-twentieth-century memoirist William H. Jordan described North Third as the headquarters of the jobbing trade, including wholesale dry goods, notions, groceries, crockery, hardware, tobacco, and drugs.[65] Eventually dry-goods and notions stores moved to Market Street, laying the foundations for the cheap-clothing houses whose brightly painted buildings advertised "One Price Cash Clothing" (fig. 99; see also POS 337, POS 439).[66] These kinds of businesses attracted out-of-town shopkeepers and other visitors who could not be expected to keep abreast of day-to-day changes in the city's commercial landscape, particularly of businesses' peregrinations. Correlation of the directory information compiled by Nicholas Wainwright with the dates written on the LCP prints by collector Charles A. Poulson in the nineteenth century suggests that the lithographs of the 1840s and 1850s were often created when merchants opened new businesses or moved established ones. Absent directory assistance or the Internet, lithographs posted in steamboats or near points of debarkation may have served to apprise visitors of relocations.

This means that the lithographs depict a relatively narrow slice of Philadelphia commercial life on the whole. With the notable exception of the shop next to the Piper & Andrews Warm Air Furnace Manufactory (POS 603), they ignore small-scale shops and neighborhood merchants. While customers and workers in the businesses advertised often appear in the prints, only occasionally do the itinerant street sellers sneak into the controlled pictorial space of the lithographs. These are the vendors whom genteel Philadelphians found so vexing throughout the nineteenth century and who are depicted so conspicuously in William Birch's engraving of the Shakespeare Buildings: a newsboy here, a peddler there, a huckster at her table in another scene (fig. 103; see also POS 104, POS 321, POS 465).[67] The street life depicted in Philadelphia's commercial lithographs, then, is considerably tamer than that described in other sources.

More important, the commercial lithographs of the 1840s and 1850s downplay the radical transformation in scale and appearance of the developing city center during those decades. For the most part, the buildings in these prints were survivors of the domestically scaled commercial environment at a time when Philadelphia constituted *"a city building on the top of the former!"* in which "all is now self exalted and going upon stilts."[68] Business buildings ballooned, growing taller and more voluminous, and their scale—the height of their stories, the size and numbers of their architectural elements—increased commensurately. Façades were more ornately ornamented, often taking advantage of the cheap mass production in cast iron of otherwise costly architectural elements. Individual buildings or "blocks" often housed numerous businesses of a kind that would have had their own premises in former decades. Because the lithographs were commissioned by individual merchants, only rarely does one glimpse the remaking of the city in them. An exception relates to the progress of the hatter Charles Oakford's career. As we have seen, he began business in a converted house at 104 (now 308) Chestnut Street (POS 108). After constructing a larger manufactory in 1850, he was able to move to the elaborate store in Swaim's Block at 158 Chestnut (now in the 600 block, after street numbers were changed in 1856) (POS 109). Finally, in 1860, he became one of several tenants in the ground floor of the enormous new Continental Hotel in the 800 block of Chestnut. Meanwhile the site of Oakford's original store was redeveloped as the warehouse and offices of the Goodyear Rubber, Packing & Belting Company (POS 321). This seven-bay, five-story structure was constructed in the up-to-date neo-Romanesque style, apparently of brownstone. The ground floor accommodated two shops: Goodyear's own at 104 and Peterson's book establishment at 102, with the upper floors given over to a printer and office tenants.

The architectural history of Oakford's businesses encapsulates the transformation of central Philadelphia's commercial landscape in the mid–nineteenth century, otherwise missing from lithographs and other prints except for collective images such as the panoramic business directories published by DeWitt Clinton Baxter in the late 1850s. However, the transformation immediately strikes the viewer of photographs of the 1850s and 1860s. The small structures that captivate the eye in the commercial lithographs are nearly submerged beneath the new skyline growing up around them (fig. 104). The conditions in which the commercial lithographs of the 1840s flourished no longer pertained.

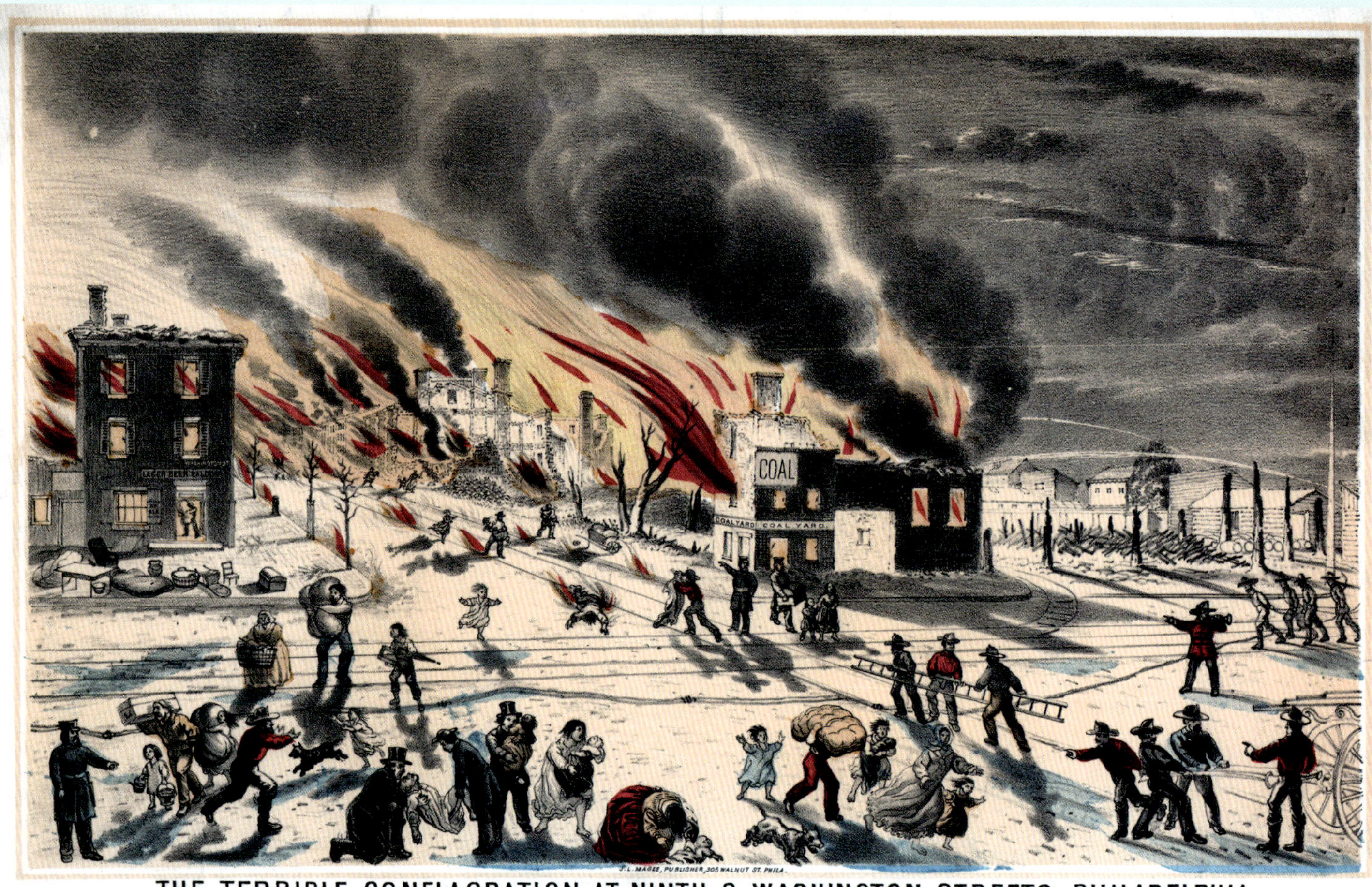

THE TERRIBLE CONFLAGRATION AT NINTH & WASHINGTON STREETS, PHILADELPHIA.

On the Morning of Wednesday February 8th 1865.

This disastrous conflagration commenced in the storage yard at Ninth & Washington Street. The material was bonded, and under the charge of a U.S. officer. At the time the terrible fire broke out, there were 1951 barrels of oil within the inclosure, of which 494 barrels remained unburnt. The amount of oil in gallons burnt foots up to 58,280. The entire loss in property will reach $400,000. Nine persons lost their lives, mostly the family of Capt. J.H. Ware. He was badly burnt, but will recover. His wife and 5 daughters were burnt. Two sons escaped badly burnt, they have since died. There also perished a fireman named Saml. Mc Menamin Fleetwood.

The Property destroyed.

Forty dwellings, two factories, seven stables, one wagon house, ten miscellaneous structures, twelve frame sheds, one brick office, one coal yard, one large coal shed, one coal oil storage shed, which, with outhouses &c., will make a total of about one hundred structures. — List of Dead and Missing. — Mrs. Barbara Ware, aged 43 years. Miss Annie Ware, 23 years. — Emma Ware, 20 years. — Helen Ware, 13 years. — Isabella Ware, 4 years. — Rebecca Ware. — Albert Ware, 17 years. — Clayton Ware, 10 years. — The Scott family is missing. — Samuel Mc Menamin Fleetwood.

ERIKA PIOLA

DRAWN ON THE SPOT

Philadelphia Sensational News-Event Lithographs

Before the advent of the news photograph, television, and the Internet, lithographs provided the citizens of Philadelphia with their first glimpse of local celebrations, exhibitions, and tragedies reported by the city's press. Due to the speed and efficiency of the print process, lithographs provided the optimal medium for pictorial journalism during the nineteenth century.[1] The prints (derived through the versatility of a planographic process) provided illustrations of the events reported in the newspapers, which the newspaper industry itself could not produce efficiently until the late nineteenth century. Engravings in illustrated weekly periodicals have long overshadowed lithographs in the study of graphic journalism. However, lithographs provide another, more immediate way of documenting the events and experiences of daily life. Philadelphia, as a city crucial to the history of American lithography, provides a case study of news-event prints and a focus for gaining a broader understanding of the motives behind their production and of the reception of lithographic journalism. This chapter, through an analysis of the origins, composition, and dissemination of a selection of these prints, explores the visual culture created by lithographs of public and newsworthy events in Philadelphia issued between the 1830s and 1870s.[2]

The visual dissemination of "news,"[3] once dependent upon print reproductions of fine-art paintings depicting events, had by the first decades of the nineteenth century, before photography, evolved to include lithographers' own conceptions of celebrations and tragedies.[4] This essay, like Bryan LeBeau's analysis of Currier & Ives lithographs as cultural artifacts, places news-event lithographs—defined as separately

issued prints contemporaneously documenting local newsworthy events—"in historical context, . . . to venture beneath the surface of literalness."[5] As virtually no records
exist to document how Philadelphia lithographers conceived of news events, examination of related histories of newspaper reporting and periodical illustrations provides
some theories for exploring the literal and visual construction of these graphics. By
comparing the content of the prints with corresponding newspaper accounts, analyz-
ing the captions printed with the images, contextualizing the artists' influences, and
deconstructing visual motifs, we can gain insight into the professional culture that
informed this niche genre of the Philadelphia lithographic market.

Within three years of its establishment, Childs & Inman,[6] the first premier commercial Philadelphia lithographic firm, issued the earliest known Philadelphia news-
event lithograph, *Skating. Scene on the River Delaware at Philadelphia. Febry. 12th 1831.*[7]
Although news-event lithographs never flooded the Philadelphia market and the New
York lithographic firm Currier & Ives dominated the field in the general publication
of this genre of print, a concentrated analysis of prints documenting the newsworthy
events of a single city provides a focus for a broader understanding of the motives in
the production and reception of lithographic journalism. Unlike many of the Currier
& Ives views, which documented events occurring across the nation and were based
only on newspaper or telegraph accounts, Philadelphia news-event lithographs, while
of more limited production, were based on the work of local artists who had the ability to be "on the spot."[8]

Despite the attention Currier & Ives receive as lithographers of news events, they
never issued a view of any of the Philadelphia events described in this chapter.[9] Perhaps because Philadelphia was a center for early lithography that rivaled New York,
Currier & Ives were discouraged from entering that market, or possibly Currier, out of
some latent respect for the city where he formerly practiced his profession, conceded
the few Philadelphia news-event views to Philadelphia lithographers.

The peak production period of Philadelphia news-event lithographs occurred in
1855–56, just before the rise in circulation of *Harper's Weekly* and *Frank Leslie's Illustrated Newspaper.* Given the popularity in the later 1850s of these illustrated weeklies, their wood engravings quickly overtook lithographs as the standard medium for
pictorial journalism.[10] The composition of the popular-periodical form of pictorial
journalism has been described by nineteenth-century popular-visual-media historians John Nerone, Kevin Barnhurst, and Joshua Brown as having a "telescoping" effect influenced by themes from genre painting, where a series of moments from the
event are condensed into a single scene. Although focused on periodical illustrations,
their analysis of the composition of these images as pictorial narratives that "invited

thorough perusal" holds true for lithographic pictorial journalism as well. In addition, lithographs still provided a more "instantaneous" view because they could be issued as quickly as two days after an event rather than the more usual week or two.

Several of the lithographs discussed below follow the description of Barnhurst and Nerone of images "composed by sketch artists who acted like correspondents. They gathered visual impressions as they walked around an event, to use them to construct a composite scene. . . . their depictions of events were temporally sequential, allowing for telescoping of a sequence of occurrences."[11] The news-event lithographs serve as an overlooked precursor in the study of graphic journalism. Despite previous visual-culture scholars' views of news lithographs as disseminating an "at a glance" message, analysis of the composition of these images proves the opposite.[12] Like the illustrations in the weeklies, lithographic pictorial journalism in Philadelphia delivered pictorial narratives that "invited thorough perusal" and at an even earlier date.

Given the small number extant and the lack of advertisements for these lithographs, many people probably noticed the prints while posted in printshop windows or purchased them from street hawkers.[13] The prints provided news while simultaneously promoting lithographers' work to the public. Unlike the illustrated weeklies, lithographs—as separately issued large-format prints—could be readily posted in the shop window or, if purchased, flattened out on a table, unfettered by pages of text. Individuals could stand in public or sit in private and scan an image slowly, from edge to edge, processing the visual details, without the textual distractions of a periodical. This format allowed for an even more intense form of "privileged subjectivity" in the viewer's interpretation of the narrative of an event.[14]

By the time of the Centennial Exhibition of 1876, the celebratory event of the century for Philadelphia, the aforementioned periodicals dominated the field of graphic journalism, and the lithographs issued during the exhibition did not really document the event so much as evoke it. By the turn of the century, the newspaper industry that had spurred the lithographic trade to issue sensational views had enthroned photomechanical reproductions as the primary medium for pictorial journalism.[15]

The premier lithographers of the early 1830s, Childs & Inman issued the earliest known lithograph documenting a Philadelphia news event. Drawn by Edward W. Clay, a caricaturist and cartoonist with an eye for human details, *Skating. Scene on the River Delaware at Philadelphia. Febry. 12th 1831* (fig. 105) documents the not so "Great Eclipse of 1831." Sensationalized in the newspapers as a potential doomsday, the astronomical event was barely noticeable by those who, as portrayed in the lithograph, gathered at public spaces such as the Delaware River. Although dark clouds fill the

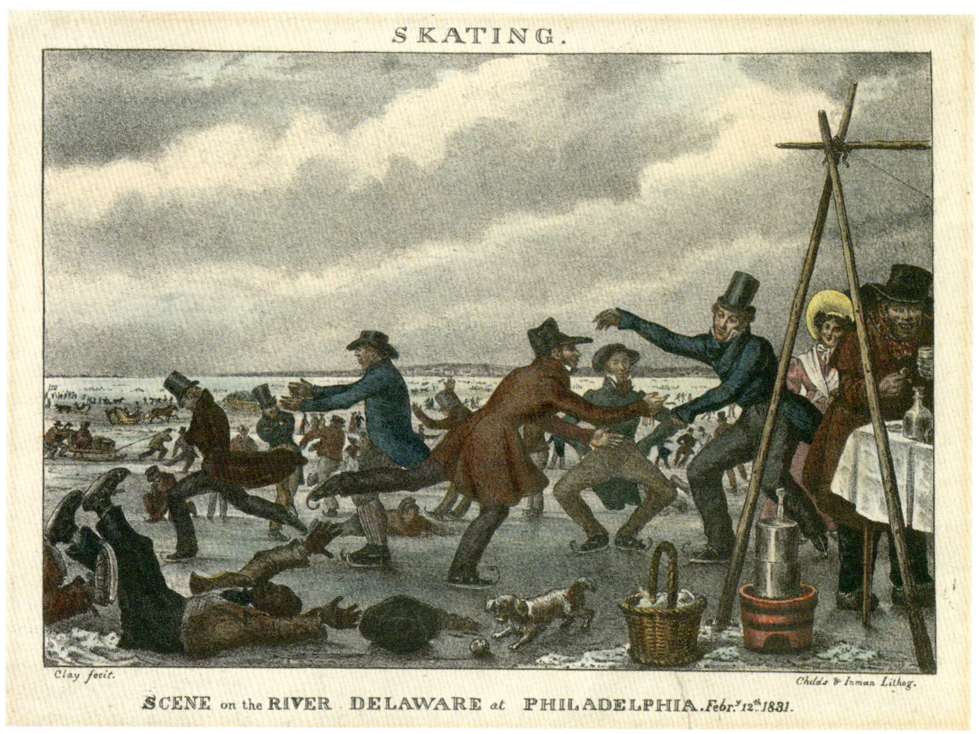

FIG. 105

Edward W. Clay, *Skating. Scene on the River Delaware at Philadelphia. Febry. 12th 1831* (Philadelphia: Childs & Inman lithog., 1831). Lithograph with hand-coloring. 21 × 27 cm (8 × 10 ½ in.). POS 696, Division of Home and Community Life, National Museum of American History, Smithsonian Institution, Harry T. Peters America on Stone Collection, DL *60.3655.

sky, the "fifteen thousand persons . . . amusing themselves by sliding and skating on the river, while the numerous booths . . . were observed to do a brisk business in hot punch," dominate the scene, as they did the newspaper account in the *Saturday Bulletin*.[16] Later audiences unaware of the significance of the date that produced a "foolish feeling of disappointment" would not even know that a solar eclipse was occurring in the view.[17]

The dubious nature of the event depicted in this print allowed artistic license to meld with reported facts to create a news view disguised as a genre scene, which it is most often understood to be.[18] For this dubious effect, akin to a wink to the viewer, Clay employs a comic African American character, a staple of many of his cartoons.[19] In addition, the title includes the date of the eclipse as a historical marker but does not mention its significance. Through the ambiguous title and focus on the ethos of an averted disaster, the artist and lithographers portrayed an intentional misdirection in the visual and textual messages, unregistered by the later viewer but understood with complicity by the contemporary audience. As a consequence, Childs & Inman could sell and the consumer could buy, absent a "foolish feeling," a print documenting a "historic" day in essence, if not in substance. Tacit understandings about the reality of news-event lithographs between the lithographer and the public, although

first exemplified by this Childs & Inman print, are evoked
by the composition of this entire genre of print. The relation,
whether corroborative or contradictory, between pictorial narratives and written accounts covering the same events necessarily influenced the conception and reception of lithographic
pictorial journalism.

Despite this earliest focus on a nonhorrific event, disaster and tragic views dominate the genre in Philadelphia and
therefore this chapter. The oblique composition and titling
of *Skating* is absent from *Destruction by Fire of Pennsylvania
Hall. On the Night of the 17th May, 1838* (fig. 106), issued by
English émigré lithographer John T. Bowen, presumably after the work of Swiss-born artist John C. Wild.[20] The earliest
known, separately issued lithograph of a tragic event shows
the horrific destruction, just three days after interracial dedica-
tion ceremonies, of the local meeting place for abolitionists at
Sixth and Haines Streets. A large crowd of cheering spectators looks on as firefighters
spray water on an unaffected adjoining building in a refusal to fight the actual blaze,
which would completely destroy the hall.[21] Within a few days, Bowen issued this print,
which was described in the *United States Gazette* as perpetuating "a remembrance of
which we have no reason to desire a long life."[22] As evident from the wording of his
advertisement, one of the few for this genre of lithograph, a sense of morality propelled Bowen to publish this shamefully tragic scene, a motive lacking from the prints
of tragedies soon to be issued within a society increasingly conditioned to the ubiquity
of sensational news.

Unlike Bowen's *Pennsylvania Hall,* morality played little part in the publication
of *An Accurate Sketch from Nature, of the Exterior and Interior of the House No. 39,
N[or]th Fourth St. Philadelphia, Where the Atrocious Murder of Mrs. Rademacher Was
Committed on the Night of the 23d, March 1848, Her Wounds, and Exact Position When
Discovered* (fig. 107). This unattributed print, found in the collection of scrapbooks
compiled by Philadelphia businessman Samuel Castner Jr. (1843–1929),[23] shows the
first sensationalized murder in Philadelphia since the birth of commercial lithography
in the city. The city was consumed by interest in the murder of twenty-three-year-old
Catherine Rademacher, the sister-in-law of Philadelphia lithographer Augustus Kollner, described as "such a butchery . . . never before committed in Philadelphia."[24]

The sensational portrayal of tragic events has had a long history in the United
States, beginning with ballads and broadsides about illicit crimes in the eighteenth

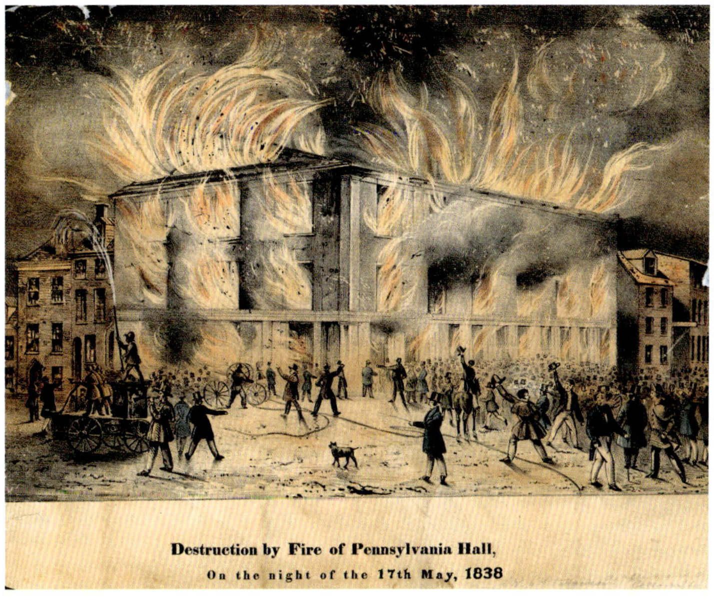

FIG. 106
John Caspar Wild, *Destruction by Fire
of Pennsylvania Hall. On the Night of the
17th May, 1838* (Philadelphia: J. T. Bowen,
1838). Lithograph with hand-coloring.
29 × 35 cm (8 × 11 in.). POS 179, LCP,
P.9057.27.

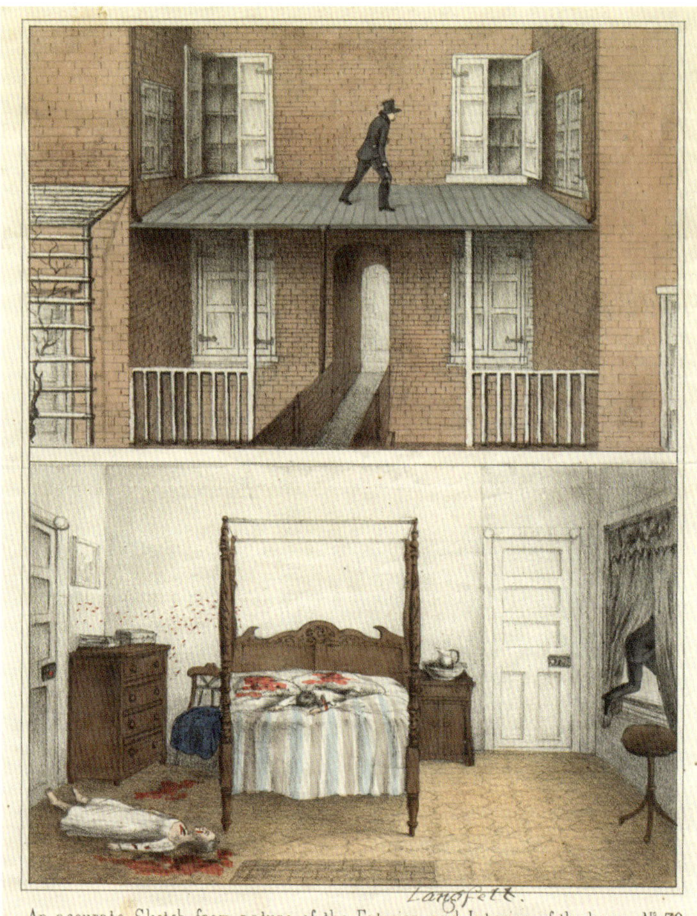

An accurate Sketch from nature, of the Exterior and Interior of the house N.º 39, N.º Fourth S.ª Philadelphia, where the atrocious murder of M.ªª **Rademacher**, was committed on the night of the 23.ª March, 1848, her wounds, and exact position when discovered.

century and continued and augmented by the penny press, dime novels, and other ephemera in the nineteenth century.[25] Cultural historian Isabelle Lehuu, in her work *Carnival on the Page,* examines this phenomenon of sensational news grounded in storytelling and argues that the popular press of the antebellum era caused a revolution in the temporal framework of, desire for, and acceptance of sensational news, transforming it into a daily expectation by the general public.[26]

The news lithographs played a part, although smaller, in this dissemination of the sensational to the mass public. The lithographs documenting the murder scenes of Catherine Rademacher in 1848 and, later, the Dearing family in 1866 formed a key segment of the panoply of song sheets, trial pamphlets, and dime novels that supplemented the news reports of sensational incidents. Lithographs, as separately issued prints illustrating such tragic events, allowed for more focus on the image, the visual narrative as conceived by the pictorial journalist, when unaccompanied by pages of printed words. Compared to newspaper accounts and trial pamphlets, the composition of the Rademacher and Dearing crime scenes highlights the artistic license taken in the form of supposition, telescoping, and dramatic effect.

The visual narrative of the Rademacher murder—designed as a composite of the before and after, and the outside and inside, of the crime scene—shows the bookstore and residence of homeopathic-medicine dealer Charles L. Rademacher. There on March 23, 1848, the Rademachers were awakened by an intruder searching their bedroom, who beat Mr. Rademacher senseless and slew his pregnant twenty-three-year-old wife. A broken knife, resembling a shoemaker's tool, was found at the scene. The next day, Charles Langfeldt, a German shoemaker recently released from Eastern State Penitentiary, was arrested for the crime. He was brought to the courthouse, swarmed by spectators, for his hearing a few days later, when it was reported that "nothing like it was ever before witnessed in Philadelphia."[27]

No doubt the sensational nature of the murder promoted the publication of the lithograph, but the trade of Augustus Kollner, brother-in-law to the murdered victim, also no doubt provided another impetus. Kollner, an artist and lithographer himself and a key witness of the crime scene, made a sketch of it for the coroner's inquest, later published in the illustrated pamphlet *Authentic Narrative of the Murder of Mrs. Rademacher: With Splendid Illustrations, Drawn and Engraved Expressly for This Work.* Also published in the newspapers[28] were his sketch and testimony, both likely models for the unsigned lithograph.

Unlike the pamphlet illustrations, the print contains subtleties taken for granted in the lithographic medium that add to the pictorial narrative. For instance, the arbor, easily perceived as incidental, actually signifies the "easiest approach" from the Rademacher's neighbor "Mr. Slade's yard," described in testimony by Kollner. The appearance of the assailant also follows witness John Frank's description of the suspect: "the man he saw in the alley had a hat on," and "the hat was worn low down his head or drawn down close over his eyes and face."[29]

The visual telescoping used to elicit the horror of the attack also affected the composition. The lithographer, in contrast to the written and visual testimony of Kollner,[30] portrays the blood-soaked bodies of Catherine and her severely wounded husband in altered positions in order to expose the hand-colored wounds and to depict the scene supposedly moments after the crime. As a consequence, the leg of the fleeing murderer extends into a transposed setting (a mirror image of the actual setting), with Catherine shown face up as opposed to face down and her husband unconscious on the bed as opposed to mobile. This transposition of the decor of the room implies the speed of production. In drawing on the stone, the artist did not bother to factor into account that the image would be reversed during printing, although the bloody pillows and doorknob as well as the position of the wounds on Catherine's body prove consistent with reports.

The print, shocking mainly due to the hand-colored blood, provides more of a "near accurate," rather than an "accurate," sketch of the scene as so described in the title. It was probably issued within a week of the murder, despite the lack of the murderer's name, since it included details from the testimony. Given the public intrigue over the murder, the lithograph provides a less exploitative scene than the text and visuals of the pamphlet (fig. 108), which included a Mr. Hyde–like caricature of the killer and the passage, "Another stab and another—and the warm life-blood leaps from the

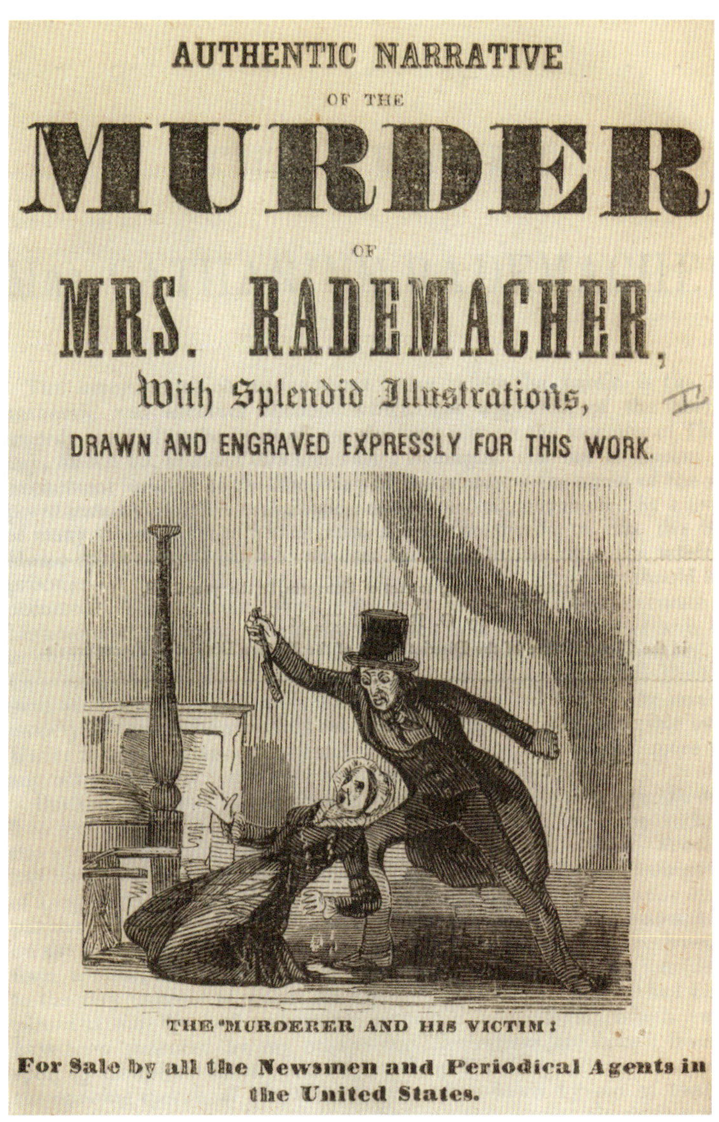

FIG. 108

Cover of *Authentic Narrative of the Murder of Mrs. Rademacher: With Splendid Illustrations, Drawn and Engraved Expressly for This Work* (Philadelphia: G. B. Zieber & Co., 1848). Wood engraving with letterpress. 22 × 15 cm (8 ¾ × 5 ¾ in.). LCP, Am 1848 Lan 51889.O.2.

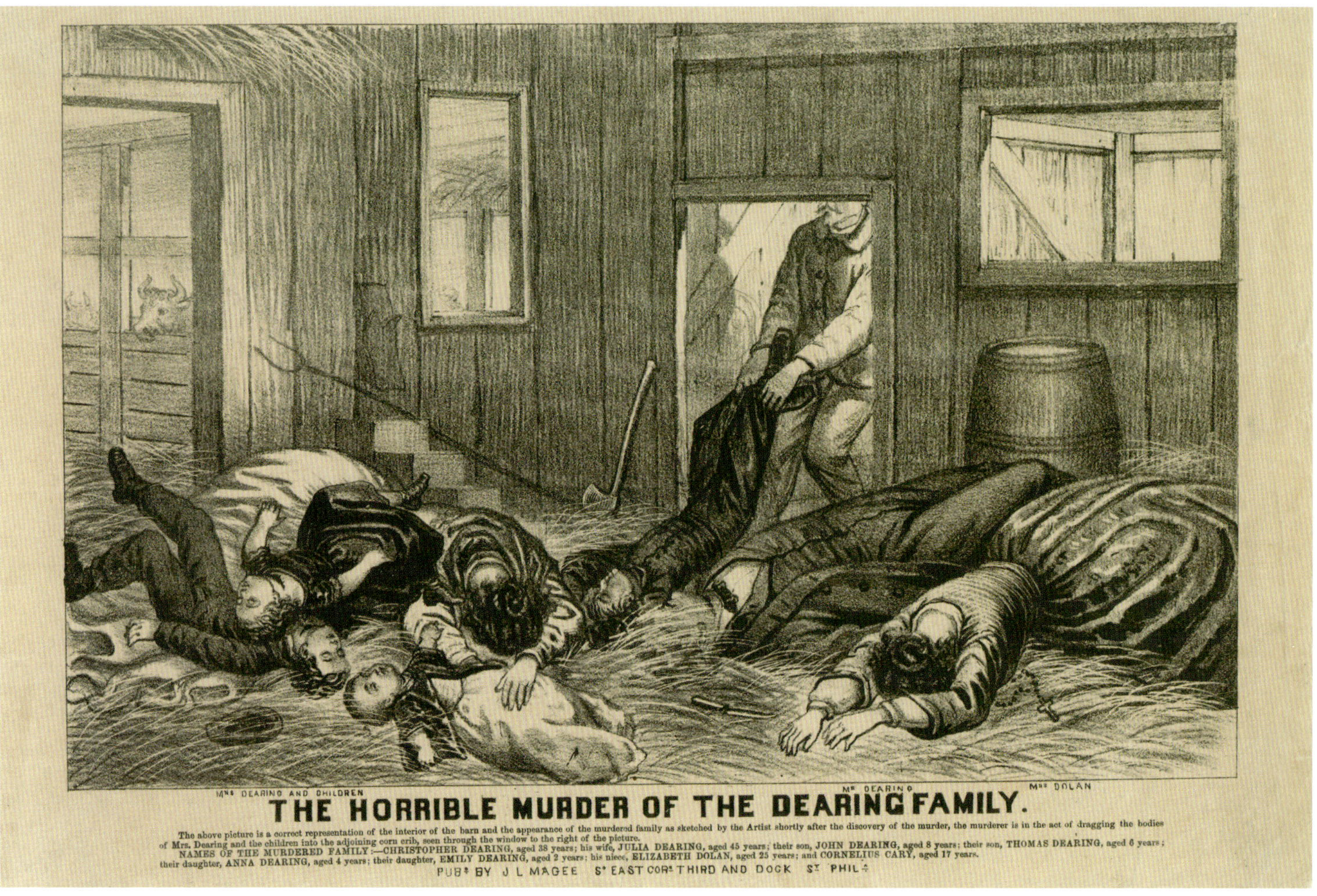

FIG. 109

The Horrible Murder of the Dearing Family
(Philadelphia: J. L. Magee, 1866). Lithograph. 26 × 36 cm (10 ¼ × 14 in.). POS 361, HSP, Bb 892 D 285.

FIG. 109

The Horrible Murder of the Dearing Family (Philadelphia: J. L. Magee, 1866). Lithograph. 26 × 36 cm (10 ¼ × 14 in.). POS 361, HSP, Bb 892 D 285.

palpitating veins . . . discoloring couch and wall with its gory murderous hue."[31] A voyeuristic yet somber tone infuses the print, executed in a somewhat unsophisticated manner. Perhaps the respect for Kollner as a fellow lithographer influenced the less ghoulish composition, or more likely, the lithographer was new to such a genre and issued the lithograph to profit from the public's desire for any and all documentation of a sensational murder story.

Nearly twenty years after the Rademacher incident, "one of the most horrible butcheries of human beings—more atrocious in its terrible details than the Langfeldt" murder—occurred with the killing of the entire Dearing family by their disgruntled farmhand Antoine Probst.[32] Probst, a German immigrant and swindler, was a recently rehired farmhand of the Dearings' who murdered the family, Cornelius Carey, another field hand, and Emily Dolan, a visiting relative, for, according to testimony, revenge and money. Days after his rehire, Probst lured all but one of the victims, the other field hand, into the barn. One by one, he clubbed each person in the head with a hammer before hacking each of their throats with an ax. He then dragged each body into a corncrib and covered them with hay, where neighbors discovered the corpses three days later.

Given the magnitude of the crime, the largest murder in Philadelphia's history at that time, not one, but two lithographs portraying the tragedy at the South Philadelphia farm could be purchased by those eager not only to read about but also see the murder. An eerie, sophisticated, and self-aware quality lacking in the earlier Rademacher murder scene permeates these lithographs, one published by the most prolific Philadelphia lithographer of sensational prints, John L. Magee, and the other unattributed, but possibly also by him. Whereas the Rademacher print shows the viewer the before and the after moments of the horrid crime, the Magee print *The Horrible Murder of the Dearing Family* (fig. 109) portrays the culminating moments of the killings. This print is complemented by *View of the Farm Where the Murder of the Deering [sic] Family Was Committed by the Fiend Antoine Probst on April 7th 1866* (fig. 110).

Although little is known of John L. Magee (born ca. 1820), his work dominates this chapter. The *Horrible Murder* is just one of several news-event lithographs produced by Magee's studio, which issued at least half of the dozen known news prints from the period discussed. A former apprentice of lithographer James Ackerman, Magee worked in New York as an artist, particularly a political cartoonist, as well as an illustrator of children's books from the early 1840s to 1850s. He also exhibited genre paintings at the National Academy of Design and the American Art Union. Magee was not unfamiliar with news-event lithography when he arrived in Philadelphia after 1852. James Baillie had published Magee's drawing *The Grand Washington Monument Procession,* "taken on the spot" in New York in 1847.[33] His focus on the human element dominates the foreground of this print, as it would his later work of this kind, but with an absence of the frenetic style for which he would later become known. Based on his skills as a cartoonist and genre painter, he created provocative figures, with detailed visages on the verge of caricatures, but empathetic rather than satiric. By the 1860s, Magee issued the only Philadelphia sensational-event lithographs in the city. In addition to these prints, he continued to work primarily as a political cartoonist but executed advertisements, church views, and portraits on occasion as well. He

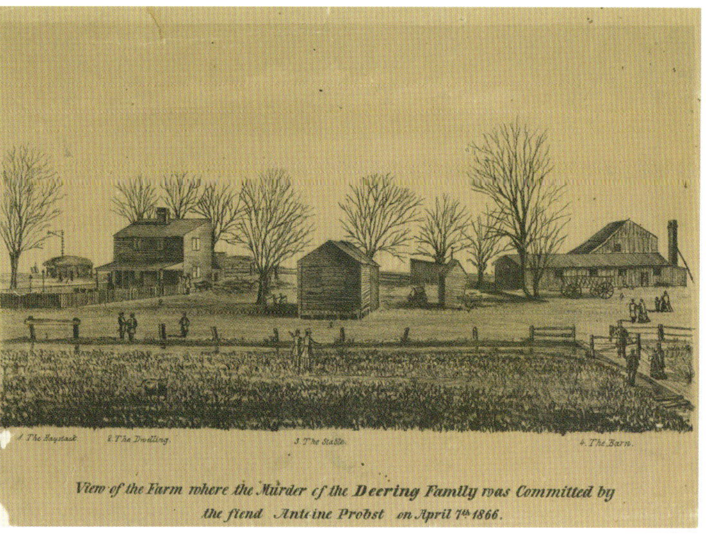

FIG. 110

View of the Farm Where the Murder of the Deering [sic] Family Was Committed by the Fiend Antoine Probst on April 7th 1866 (Philadelphia, 1866). Lithograph, tinted with one stone. 21 × 29 cm (8 ½ × 11 ½ in.). POS 799, Print and Picture Collection, FLP, Philadelphiana—Farms.

remained active in the Philadelphia trade until a few years after the issue of what was probably his last sensational news-event print of the Dearing murder in 1866.[34]

With the *Horrible Murder* print, Magee echoes and in turn transcends the Rademacher print in style, execution, and form. Unlike his disaster prints, soon to be discussed, the murder print exhibits a more refined drawing style and artistic license, gradually divulging information obtained from the confession of the assailant. As did the lithographer of the Rademacher print, Magee includes a statement about his composition of the murder, which was discovered by neighbors on April 11, 1866. He promotes "a correct representation" of the scene and appearance of the deceased and directs the viewer to the murderer, "dragging the bodies of Mrs. Dearing and the children into the adjoining corn crib." Since Probst is not mentioned by name in the title, Magee's additional claim of a sketch done shortly after the discovery of the murder makes sense. Probably like the news reporters, he conceived of the act and scene from talking with witnesses and the police at the farm within a day or so of the murder report[35] and before the capture and confession of Probst.[36]

To elicit the horror of the crime most effectively, Magee's composition (necessarily based on deduction) implies that the murderer killed the family together, despite the fact that Mr. Dearing and Emily Dolan were originally reported as found outside the barn.[37] He does, however, provide "a correct representation" by showing the slit throats, the probable murder instrument (the ax), and the bodies of Dearing and his cousin separate from those of his wife and children. This "separation" creates the additional emotional charge of a tragic maternal scene.

The power of the narrative rests on the portrayal of the children and the public's knowledge of the wounds. The children, depicted with angelic faces, unmarred by the reported "terribly mangled" head injuries, and with barely visible disfigured necks, envelop their mother, who lies face down in the hay. Her husband and relative (also portrayed with obscured visages) lie not far from her. By Mr. Dearing lies a knife, and by the corncrib rests an ax, the weapons that slashed the throats of the defenseless family. Although the audience knows the horrid physical state of those murdered, the lithograph proves sensational not through grotesque graphics but through understated visual details informed by the newspaper accounts, which connect the viewer to the family. The composition, although misleading, still compels an emotional response from the viewer by focusing on the most innocent of the victims.

Following the arrest and confession of Probst on April 14, the *View of the Farm* served as a virtual map to those who had read about the scene of the crime and understood the significance of "The Haystack," "The Dwelling," "The Stable," and "The Barn." The "knots of persons seen in all directions discovering the heart-rending event," reported mainly as women, knew the infamous facts associated with the structures.[38] The haystack had contained the headless body of the first murder victim, field hand Carey. The dwelling had been ransacked and later used by Probst to shave, change, nap, and eat. The stable held the animals he fed before his departure, and, of course, the barn served as his lure for the heinous crime.

Despite the great interest of the public that encouraged the creation of these sensational prints of murder, these graphics formed a small segment of the genre of news-event lithographs that fed Philadelphians' morbid curiosity. Disaster scenes formed the core. Invariably hand-colored and infused by a more garish style, these prints nonetheless act as a cultural lens on the lithographic profession despite their oft-criticized crude appearance.

Although Philadelphia news lithographs trickled into the market during much of the time period examined in this book, a confluence of the worst rail and steamboat accidents in 1855 and 1856 caused a near flood of the market in comparison. During these years, Philadelphia lithographers issued at least eight disaster prints of three tragic accidents on the Camden and Amboy Railroad,[39] the North Pennsylvania Railroad, and the Philadelphia and Camden Steamboat Company line.[40] Magee issued lithographs depicting the latter two tragedies. Ironically (or perhaps foretellingly), the largest number of Philadelphia news-event lithographs known in any single year since the successful establishment of the lithograph trade were issued about the time of the inception of *Frank Leslie's* and *Harper's Weekly.*[41]

For passengers of the steamboat *New Jersey* March 15, 1856, proved a very bad day when Captain Ebenezer Corson, in midvoyage to Camden from Philadelphia, attempted to return his burning vessel to the Arch Street Wharf in Philadelphia. Within thirty feet of the pier, the pilot house collapsed. Corson survived by leaping ashore, leaving the boat unmanned and out of control. The ship drifted back into the river, thus making this incident more infamous and sensational than the typical steamboat accident. Philadelphia lithographers Magee (with publisher Alfred Pharazyn) and George G. Heiss (with printers Wagner & McGuigan) issued five versions, indicative of a strong market for the views of the *New Jersey* disaster, in sets of three and two prints, respectively.

Working within blocks of the disaster, the team of Magee and Pharazyn issued the elaborately titled *Terrible Conflagration and Destruction of the Steamboat "New Jersey," on the Delaware River, Above Smith's Island, on the Night of March 15th, Between 8 and 9 o'Clock, in Which Dreadful Calamity Over 50 Lives Are Supposed to Have Been Lost* (fig. III) within about forty-eight hours of the accident, which continued to draw spectators to the Arch Street pier several days following the tragedy.[42] Magee, although only

FIG. 111

Terrible Conflagration and Destruction of the Steamboat "New Jersey," on the Delaware River, Above Smith's Island, on the Night of March 15th, Between 8 and 9 o'Clock, in Which Dreadful Calamity Over 50 Lives Are Supposed to Have Been Lost (Philadelphia: J. L. Magee and A. Pharazyn, 1856). Lithograph with hand-coloring. 22 × 34 cm (8 ½ × 13 ½ in.). POS 745, LCP, P.2202.

FIG. 112

Terrible Conflagration and Destruction of the Steam-Boat "New Jersey," on the River Delaware, Opposite Philadelphia, on the Night of Saturday, March 15th, 1856, Between 8 and 9 o'Clock, by Which Dreadful Calamity Sixty-One Lives Were Lost. Names of All on Board (Philadelphia: A. Pharazin, 1856). Lithograph with hand-coloring. 26 × 36 cm (10 ¼ × 14 in.). POS 744, LCP, P.2252.

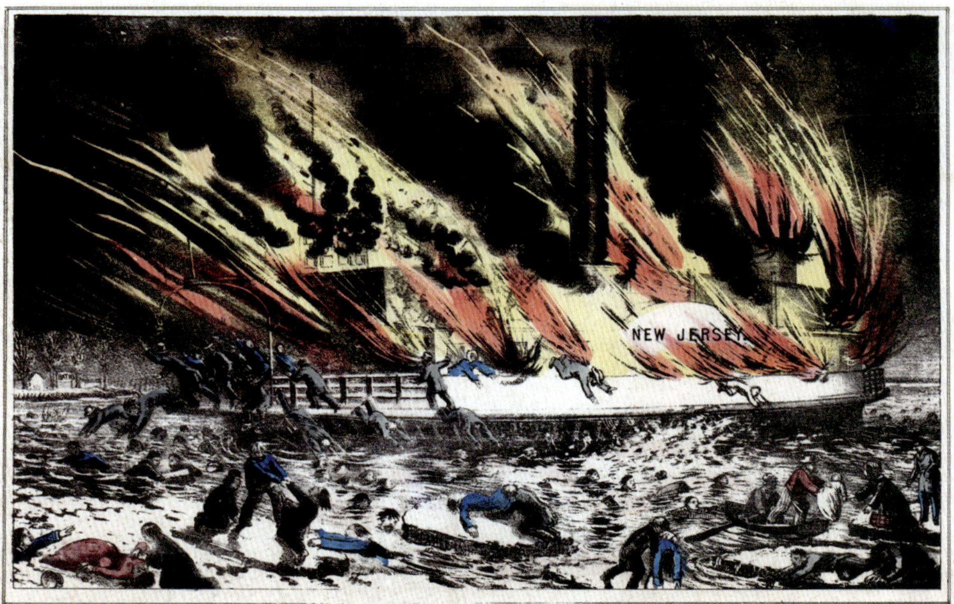
TERRIBLE CONFLAGRATION AND DESTRUCTION OF THE STEAMBOAT "NEW JERSEY,"
On the Delaware River, above Smith's Island, on the Night of March 15th, between 8 and 9 o'clock, in which dreadful calamity over 50 Lives are supposed to have been lost.
Published and for sale by J. L. Magee, 48 Passyunk Road and A. Pharazyn, 103 South Street

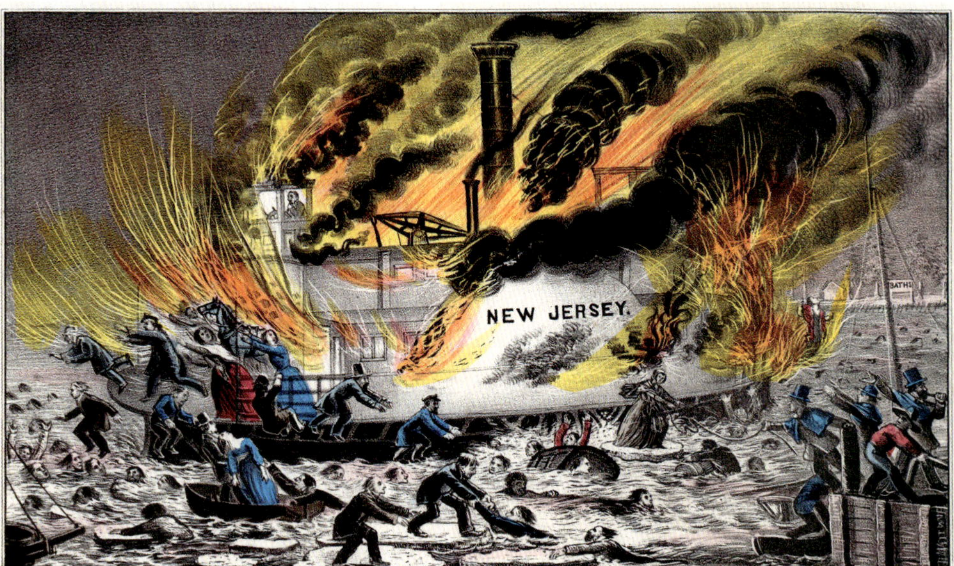
NEW JERSEY.

Published by A. Pharazin 103. South Street.
TERRIBLE CONFLAGRATION AND DESTRUCTION OF THE STEAM-BOAT "NEW-JERSEY,"
On the River Delaware, opposite Philadelphia, on the Night of Saturday, March 15th, 1856, between 8 and 9 o'clock, by which Dreadful Calamity Sixty-One Lives were lost. Names of all on Board.
The Dead.--Abm. Janney, John Little, James M. Shermer, John S Newton, Mrs. Shade, Alex. Claxton, James McCaffey, Francis Fitzpatrick, Francis Baird, Fredk. A. Thompson, Myer Reinbeck, Var. Nixon, Charles Weatherby, Henry Lelarge, Mary Massey, Charles Sharpe, Samuel Briggs, Asa Bullard. Thomas Smith, John Fidell. Colored—Emory Riley, Mary Ann Diggs, James Williams, Jacob Campbell, James A. Kennard, Morris Baily, Henry Johnson, Luther Oney, Elijah Hutchinson, B. H. Simons, Edw. Manorky.—Total 31.
The Missing.--Miss E. Fullerton, Thomas Allen, Miss Sally Carman, John T. Parsons, Edw. Merchamp, Charles Hollinshead, Charles Keyser. John Prince, Charles Beale, — Ehilean, Miss E. Jones, J. W. Wainwright, — Quinn, — Bachrack's German boy, — Riddle, Mrs Wagstaff, Ann Oakman, Saml. Gilberson's child, Miss Sarah Prescott, Mrs S. W. Gwinn, A. W. Foreman. Colored—Maj. Snively's boy, J. Wesley Stewart, — Snorden, — Smith, James Mitchell, Edward Simons, Peter Mosely.—Total 30. Entered According to Act of Congress in the District Court for Eastern District of Pa. by A. Pharazyn.
The Saved.--W. H. Yeaton, Jacob Earlin, Alfred Bradley, Miss Stow, Mrs. Nixon and child, Mr. Hewing, Mr Edwards, Mr. Crispin, Mr. Ferguson, Capt. Corson, Carney Carter, Edw. Hoopes, Chas. F. Dickson, Thos. Starns, F. Herring, Gotleib Eckhart, Alfred Brodnay, Mrs. Giberson, Mr. Shade, Capt. J. H. House, Wm. Copeland, Maj. Snively, — Patterson, T. H. Dudley, R. W. Mitchell, Mrs. Stearns, Miss Fidel, L. Newton, Mr. Nagel, Mr. Howard, David Jester, Wm. Young, John Springer, Wm. P. Wilson, James M. Steeling, Jas. Thompson, Wm. F. Agnew, Mr. Barton, Saml. Giberson, Godfrey Ostenhart, Mr. Hayward, Chas. Dixey, Restore Cressman, N. E. Chase, Chas. Keyser.—Total, 46.

listed as a publisher, presumably drew the scene for the original print and, given the style, the subsequent variants, though
these too are not attributed to him. Variations on one of the
later-issued lithographs included an updated, larger number
of the deceased in the title;[43] a caption listing the names of the
dead, missing, and saved; and a transposed view of the New
Jersey shoreline in the background (fig. 112).[44]

Heiss, who operated a studio located even closer to the
disaster than that of Magee and Pharazyn, designed in the
same short time *Conflagration of the Steam Boat New Jersey on
the Delaware River Opposite Philada. March 15th 1856 in Which
50 Persons Lost Their Lives* (fig. 113). Like Magee and Pharazyn,
Heiss issued a later variant print not only with an edited title
but in a larger format with an expanded vista (fig. 114). Heiss,
whose typical subject was firefighting equipment, found himself "on the spot."[45] He recorded, "Lithographed from a draw-
ing made on the wharf above Vine St." in the imprint. Apparently, given his proximity,
he felt compelled to depart from his typical genre to document the disaster and create
a news-event print with a tone dramatically different from that of Magee's work.

Unlike the Magee scenes, the Heiss prints show a view of the vessel after it
floated back out on the river, awaiting assistance from its sister steam ferry the *Dido*.
The Heiss prints, tinted with a deep grayish tone to represent the night sky, evoke a
sense of abandonment and lost hope for the drifting boat. The prints are literally and
figuratively dark and dull compared to the Magee prints. The Magee prints, vibrantly
hand-colored in yellow, blue, and red, capture the tragedy when the boat veers out of
control close to the shore and evoke the panic, terror, and sense of impending death
and destruction missing from the Heiss lithographs. A woman on an ice floe reaching
for her limp baby as it is being handed to her from a rescue boat, the restive horse
engulfed in flames near the pilot, still at the helm, and the fleeing passengers and
struggling victims in the water all portray more harrowing moments than the Heiss
views.

Magee, through depiction of an African American victim and separate listings in
the caption in the later variant, also acknowledges the significant African American
presence on the steamboat, as reported in the press. However, his portrayal of a single
African American falls short of accuracy, given that about half of the missing and
saved were African Americans. Although both lithographers presumably issued multiple prints to meet public demand, one cannot help but assume the staid Heiss prints

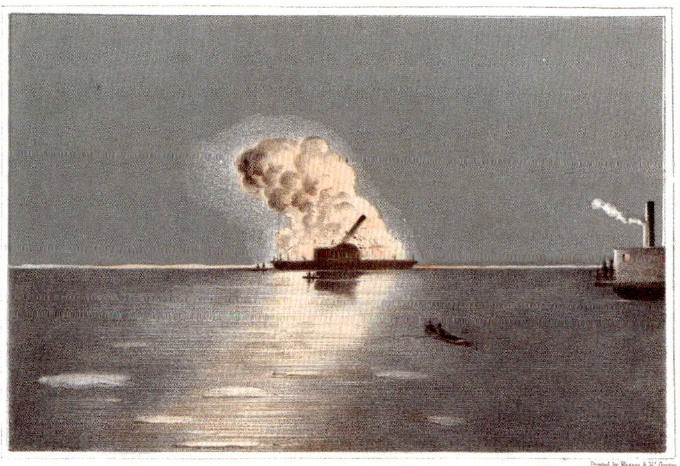

FIG. 113
George G. Heiss, *Conflagration of the
Steam Boat New Jersey on the Delaware
River Opposite Philada. March 15th 1856 in
Which 50 Persons Lost Their Lives* (Philadel-
phia: Published by the artist, printed by
Wagner & McGuigan, 1856). Lithograph
with hand-coloring and tinted with one
stone. 14 × 21 cm (5 3/8 × 8 in.). POS 155,
LCP, P.2026.

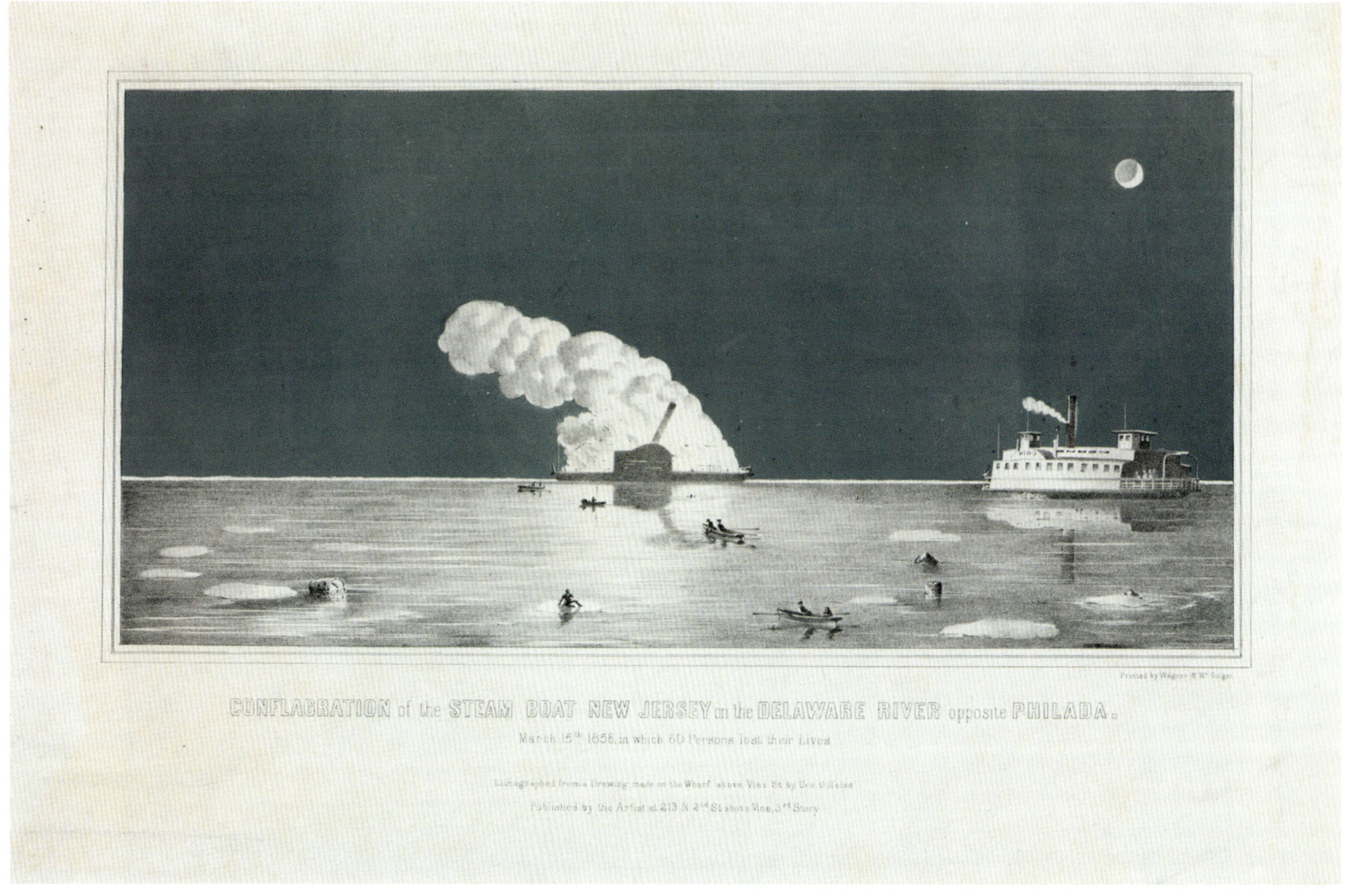

FIG. 114
George G. Heiss, *Conflagration of the Steam Boat New Jersey on the Delaware River Opposite Philada. March 15th 1856 in Which 60 Persons Lost Their Lives* (Philadelphia: Published by the artist, printed by Wagner & McGuigan 1856). Lithograph, tinted with one stone. 37 × 56 cm (14 ¼ × 22 in.). POS 154, HSP, Bc 83 N 548.

proved less commercially successful than those from the dynamic hand of Magee. Perhaps the collecting practices of the trustees of the Mutual Assurance Company for Insuring Homes from Loss by Fire can serve as the yardstick. Copies of all the Magee variants, rather than the Heiss prints, resided in their collections, known to contain a focus on popular graphics related to fires and firefighting.[46]

The year 1856 also bore witness to the worst rail accident at that time, infamously known as the "Picnic Train Tragedy," when on July 17 about sixty people died and nearly one hundred were injured, many of them children from St. Michael's Roman Catholic Church Sunday School in Philadelphia. Magee again put crayon to stone for a sensational event and issued one of the two prints showing the collision of the North Pennsylvania Railroad excursion trains *Shakamoxon* and *Aramingo* near Ambler, Pennsylvania.[47] City trains, handcars, and individuals on foot and "in every description of vehicle" traveled to the scene, including Magee and Simeon Boerum, to be "on the spot."[48]

As with the *New Jersey* prints, very differently composed news-event lithographs entered the print market for purchase by those curious about and heartbroken from an accident that "rendered railroad lines as bloody as battlefields."[49] Again Magee faced competition from a lithographer composing an image outside of his subject specialty. Magee, with his seemingly natural sense of the visually sensational, produced a work that overpowers that of his competitor Boerum, usually a wood engraver of advertising vignettes.[50] Drawn on stone by William H. Rease, (ironically) known for his attention to human detail, Boerum's *Awful Accident on the North Pennsylvania Rail Road on Thursday July 17th 1856* (fig. 115) epitomizes the roughshod appearance often associated with "rush" lithographs. By not employing the telescoping motif, Boerum portrays only the moment of impact from a reserved distance, almost in the style of a landscape view. The sticklike figures representing victims of the crash seem minuscule details, and the destruction to the vehicles garners much of the focus. The splotches of hand-coloring amplify the sense of a quickly drawn sketch.

In contrast, *The Dreadful Accident on the North Pennsylvania Rail-Road, About 14 Miles Above Philadelphia, on Thursday, July 17, 1856, at About 6 A.M., Which Resulted in the Death of Over Sixty, and Terribly Wounding About One Hundred Persons, Excursionists of St. Michael's R. C. Church, Kensington* (fig. 116) immediately draws the eye of the viewer. Magee, as with his *New Jersey* print, provides a close-up of the tragedy, with the foreground dominated by the victims, Good Samaritans, and rescue workers, and he employs a much more expansive title and caption than Boerum. Despite the immediacy of production, as evident from Magee's notice that "many of the wounded are in a very precarious condition, and the death of several is hourly looked for," this artist-reporter provides his audience with a better executed and gut-wrenching portrayal of the disaster by placing the focus on the human element.

The strategically hand-colored graphic uses the telescoping effect and shows the entangled, smoking, and burning locomotives as the backdrop to a pandemonium of persons ejected and jumping from the flaming wreck. In the foreground limbless and headless bodies lie on a mattress and on the ground, dead children are transported on a makeshift stretcher, women cry in disbelief and horror, and rescue workers carry buckets of water. The lithograph grasps the sentiment, without the ethnic bias, of the news account, which states, "As most of the victims, or greater portion, were Irish,

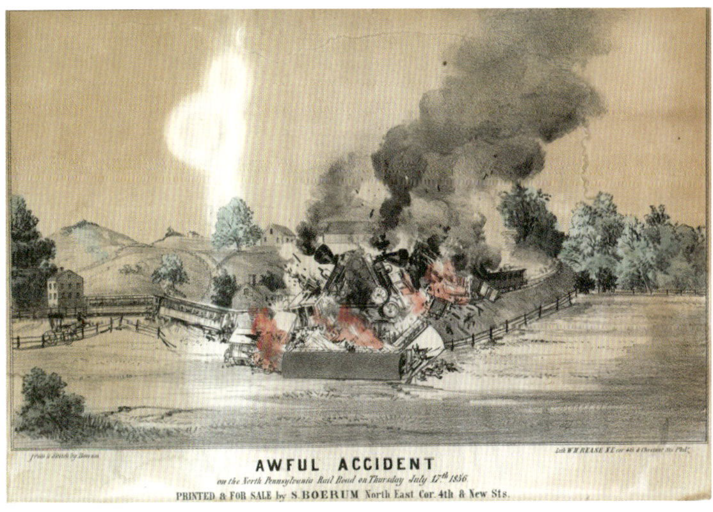

FIG. 115
William H. Rease after Simeon Boerum, *Awful Accident on the North Pennsylvania Rail Road on Thursday July 17th 1856* (Philadelphia: Printed by S. Boerum, 1856). Lithograph with hand-coloring. 26 × 36 cm (10 1/4 × 14 in.). POSP 12, LCP, Gift of David Doret, P.2007.21.13.

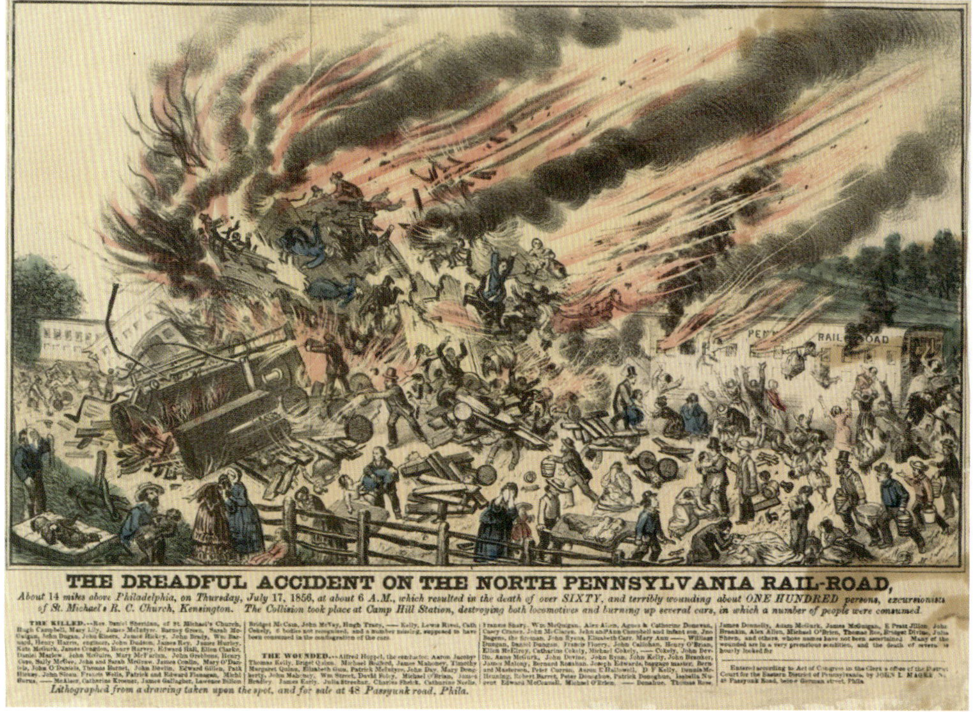

of course the demonstration of grief which met one's helpless ears [was] of the most violent character. They surpassed anything within the range of the reportorial experience."[51] Any member of the public who gazed upon the Magee print perceived the terror of the victims, the efforts of the rescue workers, and the despair of personal loss that words alone could not express.

From 1856, the year of these tragedies, until the Civil War, no known Philadelphia sensational-event prints appear to have been published in the city until Magee rekindled the genre. In 1862 and 1865 the lithographer with a propensity to illustrate the tragedies of life issued two similarly composed scenes of a factory explosion and the worst fire in the city in more than a decade. Conceived during the Civil War, the peak of the popularity of the illustrated weekly periodical and the early era of photography, the lithographs bear the influences of a visually literate society consumed with depictions of death.[52]

Although disaster lithographs by nature lend themselves to visual hyperbole, *Explosion and Burning of the Cartridge Factory, Cor. Tenth and Read, March 2[9]th 1862* (fig. 117) raises the bar. Given the nature of the catastrophe, the artist-reporter had the thematic tools to portray a most horrific scene. The rather staid and possibly preliminary title on this probable proof print, unlike those of earlier views of tragedies, belies

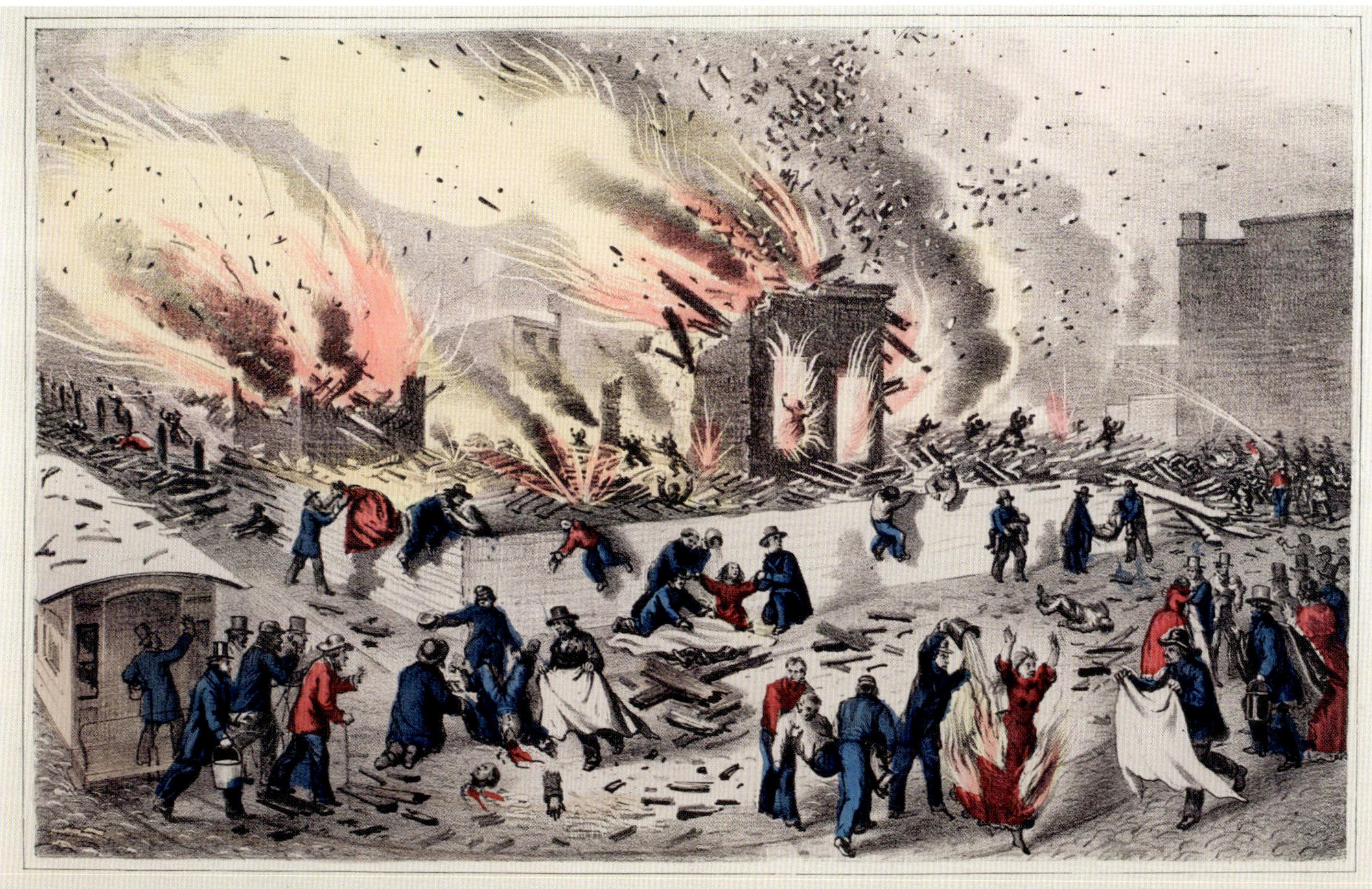

the horror of the event that created one of the most taxing emergencies for Pennsylvania Hospital up to that time.[53] As reported in the press, more than fifteen people, including the son of the proprietor, physician, and professor Samuel Jackson, perished in the explosion of the factory, which employed seventy-eight persons, mainly women and children, whose remains splattered blood on neighboring buildings, knocked pedestrians to the ground, and destroyed property.[54]

Although unattributed, the composition heavily suggests, through the drawing style and focus on the victims in the foreground, a Magee print. While the account in the *Philadelphia Inquirer* reports the facts in an almost farcical fashion—for example, "a human cheek was found sticking to the bricks on the front of a house"[55]—the lithograph portrays the horrifically bizarre aftermath in less exploitative but equally

FIG. 117

Attributed to John L. Magee, *Explosion and Burning of the Cartridge Factory, Cor. Tenth and Read [sic], March 2[9]th 1862* (Philadelphia, 1862). Lithograph with hand-coloring. 36 × 49 cm (14 × 19 ¼ in.). POS 215, HSP, Bb 83 C 328.

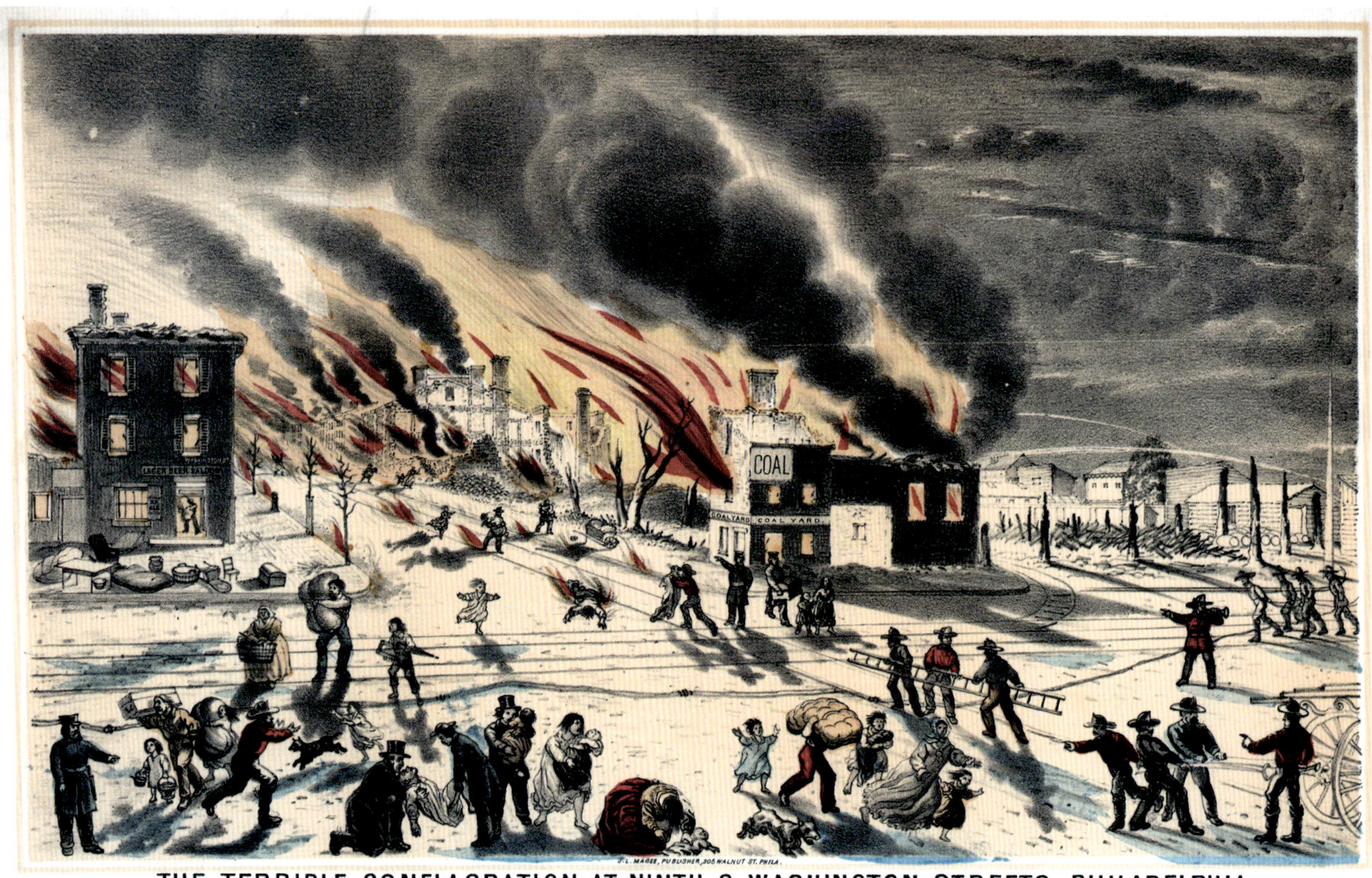

FIG. 118

The Terrible Conflagration at Ninth & Washington Streets, Philadelphia. On the Morning of Wednesday February 8th 1865 (Philadelphia: J. L. Magee, 1865). Lithograph with hand-coloring. 24 × 38 cm (9 ½ × 15 1/8 in.). POS 746, LCP, 6549.F.

extreme graphic terms. Through hand-coloring and a less cluttered composition than his previous disaster views, Magee again uses his usual themes of Good Samaritans and panicked victims but employs a variant telescopic effect that does not show the explosion itself, but rather the immediate aftermath. The lithograph depicts and highlights through hand-coloring a decapitated and dismembered figure, but one being shrouded, not propelled through the air, as well as female figures engulfed in flames, although they were men, according to written accounts.[56] Whereas the previously described prints include similar scenes of bodily mutilations, the hand-coloring and the central position of the decapitated body in the sight line of the burning woman direct the viewer to the most horrifically wounded figure. Had the mass-circulated photographic and engraved images of the brutality of the war, which seemed to feed the public's fascination with the gory details of death, forced Magee to be even more graphic in his depiction of this tragedy?

The public learned about battle casualties not only through the daily press accounts but also through the illustrated articles of the weekly periodicals *Harper's* and *Frank Leslie's* and the relatively new medium of paper photography, which provided eyewitness accounts of unromanticized death at a level never seen before. An estimated total of six thousand engravings of the conflict dominated the periodicals,[57] and hundreds of photographs, including postmortems epitomized by Timothy H. O'Sullivan's *Harvest of Death* (1863), infiltrated parlors and photographic salons to compound the realism of the horrors of war for an increasingly visually literate society. Magee appears to have used the versatility of lithography to his advantage in response to the war-induced heightened fascination and curiosity of the visually morbid. The print, through the hand-colored details, exhibits the realism associated with photography and yet as a nonphotographic medium allows for a telescopic pictorial narrative that oddly proves less irreverent than the newspaper accounts of the event, which focused more on body parts than on people. This illusion of realism thus heightens its emotional impact.

A little over three years later, the State House (now Independence Hall) fire-alarm bell alerted the city to the "most terrible conflagration that has occurred in Philadelphia since the great fire of July 1850," and prompted the creation of *The Terrible Conflagration at Ninth & Washington Streets, Philadelphia. On the Morning of Wednesday February 8th 1865* (fig. 118).[58] The alarm alerted not only the volunteer firemen shown in the print but also Magee, who worked from a studio at 305 Walnut Street, not far from the State House, and who had been absent from Philadelphia for the 1850 fire.

The fire began by arson, destroyed a square mile of property, and caused the deaths of the Ware family, reported as "roasted alive in the streets,"[59] and of the fireman Samuel Fleetwood, who had attempted to rescue them. The "terrible conflagration," which emanated from a barrel of coal oil at the Blackburn & Co. yard, sent swarms of displaced families onto the snow-covered streets shortly after 2:00 A.M. that wintery night in February.[60] Unfairly judged as "crude" and lacking depth, with "persons portrayed [to] appear [as] caricature," the hand-colored print deserves reevaluation based on a comparison of its explicative visual narrative with the newspaper accounts of the fire.[61]

Similar in composition to the cartridge-factory view, this Magee print amplifies the realism of his earlier works through more focused visual details of specific moments as opposed to a crowded view pictorially representative of the general tone of a news article. Magee's depiction reflects the passages that recorded "fathers and mothers in quest of children, children screaming after parents, younger portions of families set to watch goods that had been saved, wrapped in shawls to protect them from the cold and damp night air."[62] The role of the police officers and firemen receives its due as well.

Amid the commotion, police officers assist residents with their possessions, providing an "order to [the] scene," and direct firefighters, some "who make the air vocal with their energetic shouts," toward the blaze and burnt ruins of the coal yard and its surroundings.[63] The mother, in the central foreground, who stumbles and drops her baby as a dog flees past them on the snow-covered street, and Jim McManus, the tavern owner frantic to save his few possessions, also reflect and expand upon the newspaper accounts.[64] The heroism of the police officers and firefighters is secondary to the desperation of the fleeing families and tavern owner, who evoke empathy in the viewer of this crisis. Despite a journalist's reflection that "the scene at the place of the conflagration can only be imagined by reporters and those who have had business at such melancholy periods," Magee allowed the public not to imagine the scene but to witness it.[65]

To compensate for the absence of an eyewitness or newspaper account, news-event prints often included a detailed caption, providing supplementary information to the visual narrative. *Terrible Conflagration* contains the most extensive caption printed on a Magee news-event lithograph. The text includes the extent and cost of the damage, the names of the missing and dead, including Fleetwood, and provides additional information that allows one to infer a date for the publication as early as February 9, 1865.[66] No doubt the normative effect of the detailed daily newspaper accounts of death and destruction of the continuing Civil War required disaster prints to contain even more explanation to catch and keep the public eye. The popularity of the weeklies likely played a role as well.

The style of the caption reflects the "primacy of the pictures' representation," as described in Brown's studies of periodical illustrations.[67] Although the lack of pages of text allowed for a more personal interpretation by the viewer, the absence also spurred the need for a more detailed caption to provide the setting for the image. Nonetheless, unlike Magee's murder print, the caption does not explain any of the details depicted, but rather the cause and outcome of the pictorial narrative. The viewer perceives the scene based on his or her own assumptions of the accuracy versus the dramatic effect achieved by the lithographic artist-reporter in his rendering of the event.

Tragedies were not the only Philadelphia events attracting "knots of visitors." In 1876 spectators swarmed the city to attend the Centennial Exhibition. The international exhibition that celebrated the hundredth anniversary of the nation epitomized a sensational event through its social, economic, and historical magnitude.[68] Years in the making, the exhibition promoted the history and progress of nineteenth-century society through the nearly two hundred newly erected buildings containing exhibits showcasing the premier industries, art, and agriculture of the many participating states and nations. The dozens of lithographs, predominantly commemorative, panoramic, and bird's-eye views of the built environment of the fair, did the same.

Centennial lithographs mark the end of Philadelphia news-event lithography. Rather than issue a news-event print published within a day of an exhibition event, Philadelphia lithographer Thomas Hunter issued many of the color-printed lithographs during the planning stages of the Centennial, between 1874 and 1876. The views by Hunter and his colleagues focus on the layout of the fair and generally show the entire grounds or individual buildings, with fair visitors populating the scenes as small foreground figures for atmosphere or as an allegory of the international nature of the exhibition (fig. 119). These lithographs later served as advertisements as well as souvenirs for the fair participants.[69]

As stated earlier, by the time of the Centennial, illustrated periodicals and photography had assumed the throne of pictorial journalism, and news-event lithographs had all but disappeared from the Philadelphia print market. *Frank Leslie's* coverage of the daily activities and events at the fair was so complete that the periodical had enough material to publish a special edition of illustrated accounts the following year.[70] By the 1870s, lithography had transformed itself from a practical trade into a commercial enterprise focused on advertising. Trade cards, labels, and poster advertisements dominated the output of the lithographic factories that had evolved from the smaller studios of earlier in the century.[71] Lithographs depicting the Centennial Exhibition encompassed panoramic views, often stamped with the name of a business as a promotion, and numerous trade cards and circular advertisements. For major events like the international fair, the printing process that had been used to document news events had become more essential to the marketing of them.

In 1947 historian Joseph G. E. Hopkins, in response to an exhibition of picture journalism, stated "that in any of the pictures on display, be it a disaster, a political event, an exposé, there is as much honesty, and infinitely more interest, than in a letterpress story of the same date . . . the artist included without thought details of costume, expression, décor, which the writing man would have taken for granted."[72] Nearly thirty years later, graphics scholar Peter Marzio observed that "historians tend to ignore the artist as a news reporter" because historical truth may be subjected to artistic license, and he made a plea that scholars "pursue the more realistic, the more answerable question of purpose."[73] Through the work of Barnhurst, Nerone, Brown,

LeBeau, and most recently Elisabeth S. Hodermarsky,[74] analysis of illustrated news has come a long way from the days when these scholars made their pleas for more scholarly attention, and yet sensational news-event lithographs, unlike their "documentary" (i.e., military, political, and genre-scene) cousins, still remain in the shadows of nineteenth-century visual scholarship.

From the 1830s to 1870s, news lithographs formed a key segment of the printed sensational matter that increasingly pervaded society, together with the penny press, the illustrated weekly, and the burgeoning field of photojournalism. A genre of print dependent on heightened public interest produced by a trade dependent on commissions, news-event lithographs offer a unique opportunity to examine lithographers' artistic and commercial motives.

When Childs & Inman issued the first Philadelphia news-event lithograph in 1831, the publishers would probably have described the print as a genre scene, given the dubious nature of the sensational event portrayed (the Great Eclipse of 1831, which was barely noticeable) and its issuance before the concept of pictorial journalism had taken hold. In the decades that followed, as Currier & Ives became synonymous with news-event prints, a few Philadelphia lithographers endeavored to gain a foothold as occasional news artists in the local print market. Lithographs, more versatile as a visual medium, more quickly issued in a loose print format, and hand-colored for effect, exhibited visual effects that predated the artistic conventions associated mainly with wood engravings in periodicals.

Lithographers, like news reporters, learned of sensational news events through alarm bells, the telegraph, and eyewitnesses, and traveled by foot, coach, and rail to the scenes to create their "drawn on the spot" views. The more sensational the event, the more likely a print by a lithographer. The press reports of the shocking Dearing and Rademacher murders; the North Pennsylvania Railroad crash, with the largest death count of its time; and the 1865 Washington Street fire, the worst in the city in more than a decade, promoted the publication of prints expected to be profitable because of the public's fascination with such events. The location of the lithographic studio in relation to a disaster also affected who issued these prints. The Heiss and Pharazyn prints of the *New Jersey* steamboat tragedy might not have seen the light of day if not for the location of their studios so close to the disaster. The locations were not only convenient for the rendering of the lithograph but were also on the route of the several spectators, and possible print buyers, to the scene of the tragedy.

Although a number of Philadelphia lithographers issued disaster prints over the decades, Magee assumed control of this niche market by the 1850s, when he relocated to Philadelphia. As a lithographer of disaster prints, he surpassed his competitors

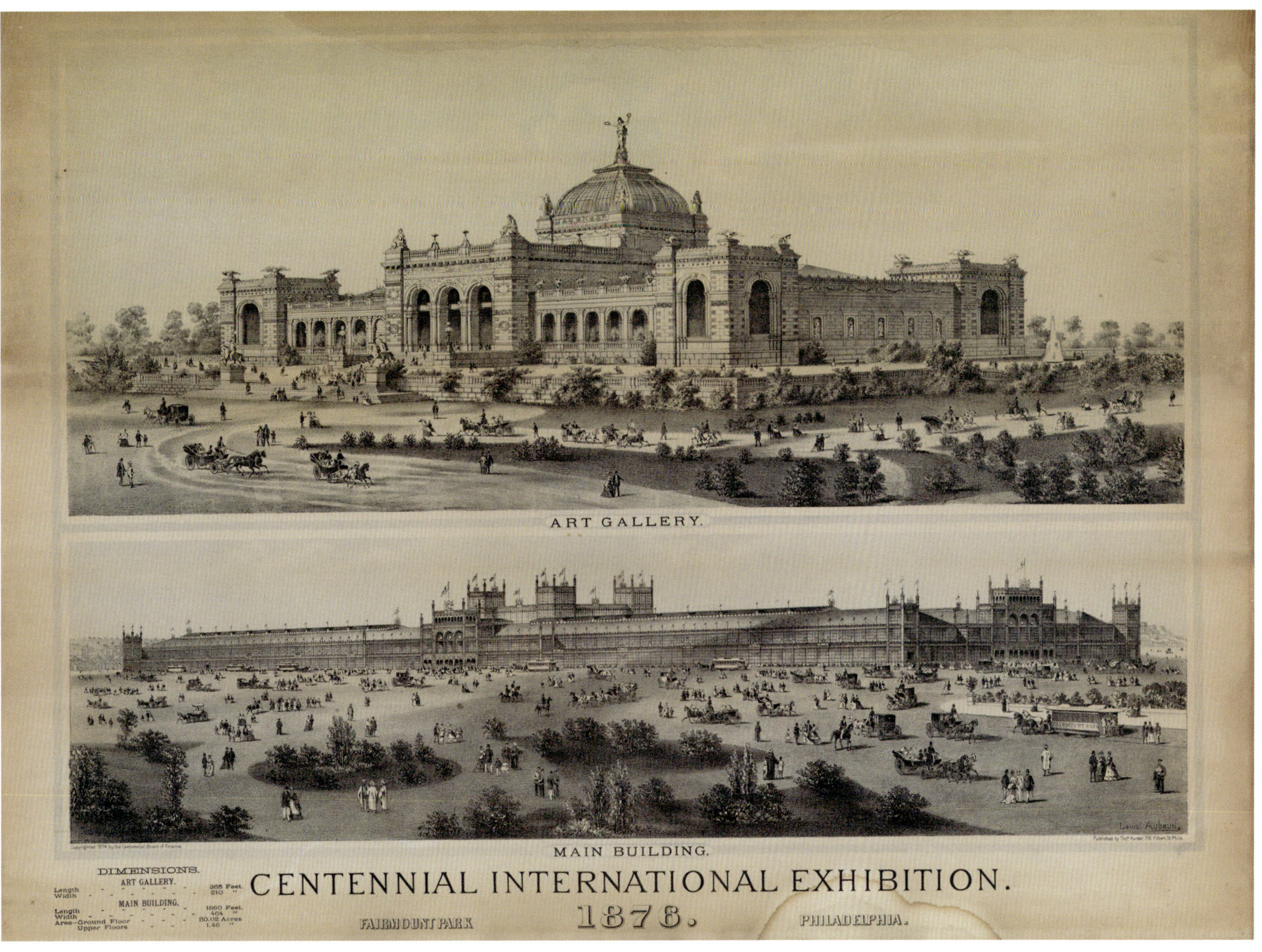

through a focus on the human element gained from his earlier work as a cartoonist. More of his news-event prints appear in institutional collections than those of any of the other lithographers documented in this essay.[75] His prints, which focused on the victims and provided lengthy captions, grabbed and held the attention of the viewer at a level unequaled by the prints of his professional colleagues, which more often focused on the mechanics of the accident. In addition, his 1866 Dearing-murder print highlights the evolution of the artist and the lithographic medium over the decades. Although disaster views rarely veered from the use of hand-coloring as an added dramatic effect, the murder print provides a scene inherently shocking despite the lack

FIG. 119

Louis Aubrun, *Art Gallery. Main Building. Centennial International Exhibition. 1876. Fairmount Park, Philadelphia* (Philadelphia: Thos. Hunter, 1874). Lithograph, tinted with one stone. 49 × 64 cm (19 × 25 in.). POS 26, LCP, Gift of David Doret, P.2006.28.7.

of color. Through a sophisticated composition of the dead family, Magee creates a pictorial scene based not on sensationally illustrated gore but on the inhumanity of the crime, a tragic maternal scene that "stirred the heart's depths of all with horror and indignation."[76]

This essay endeavors to answer, at least partially, the question of the "purpose" of news-event lithographs in the Philadelphia market. These lithographs act as a mirror that reflects not only the societal infatuation with the sensational but also the reality of life in Philadelphia, which included rail accidents, fires, and murder. Not only do the mundane details of that era's "costume, expression, and decor" infiltrate the imagery, but the visual composition and textual details provide a window into the purpose of the Philadelphia lithographer. Because these prints were often crude in appearance and small in number compared to other genres of lithographs, their importance has been overlooked in the study of Philadelphia lithographers and their reading of the public taste. Philadelphia news-event lithographs as a nonfacsimile print medium not only felt shockingly real but also reflected the many layers of spectatorship involved in their creation and interpretation.

Here is the paradox. Even though the Philadelphia artist-news reporter was "on the spot" to sketch the scene, drawing on the stone himself and issuing a print within two days, both the lithographer and his contemporary audience understood that the lithograph was a means to provide an informative pictorial narrative, not a facsimile, of the event. These lithographs are a kaleidoscope of the daily lives of the society portrayed within the prints, the public that procured them, and the lithographers who created them. As both an immediate process with an emotional impact, similar to photography, and yet still a representation of storytelling similar to periodical illustrations, sensational news-event lithographs represent an analytical bridge between print and photojournalism rich for the continuing study of visual culture.[77]

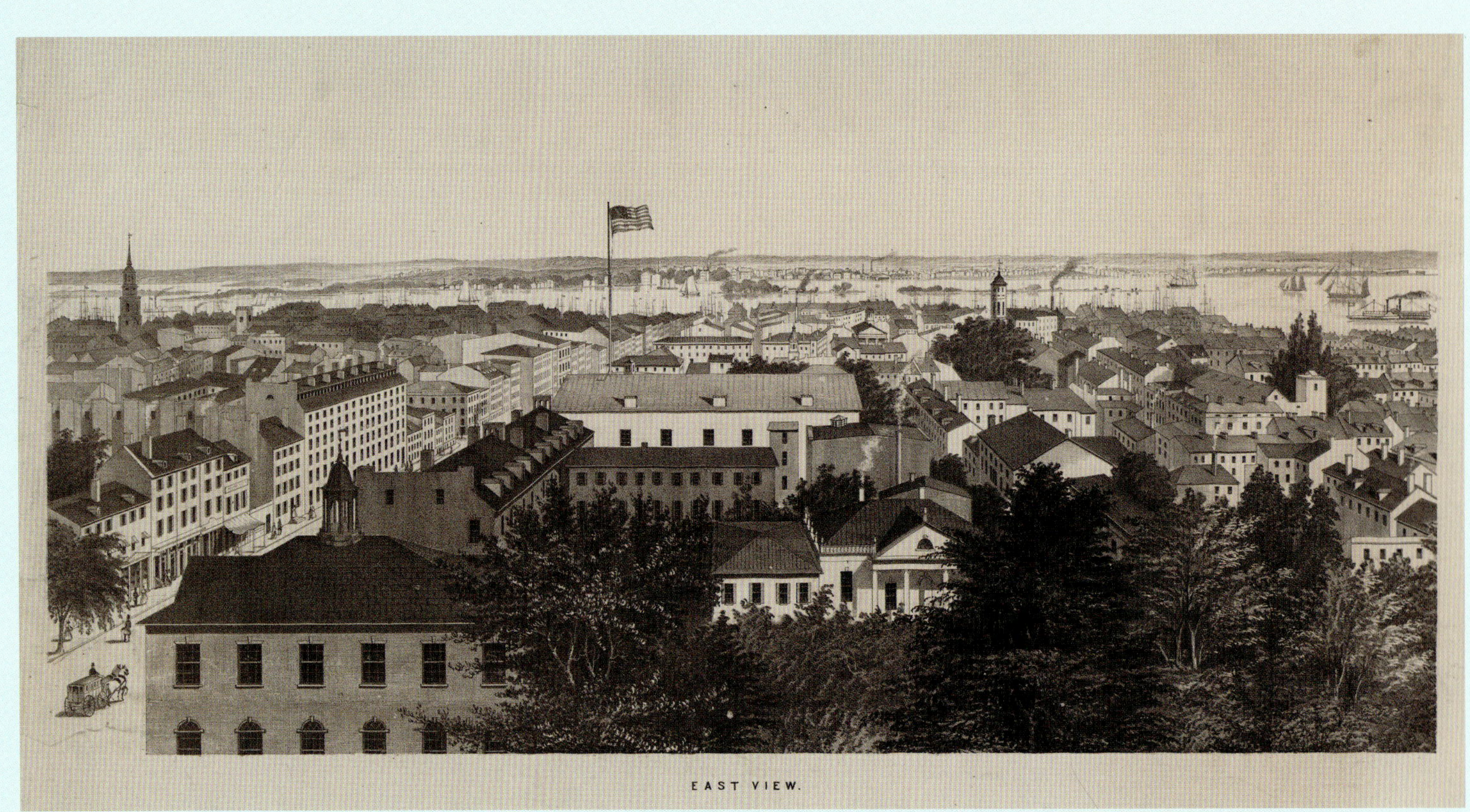

EAST VIEW.

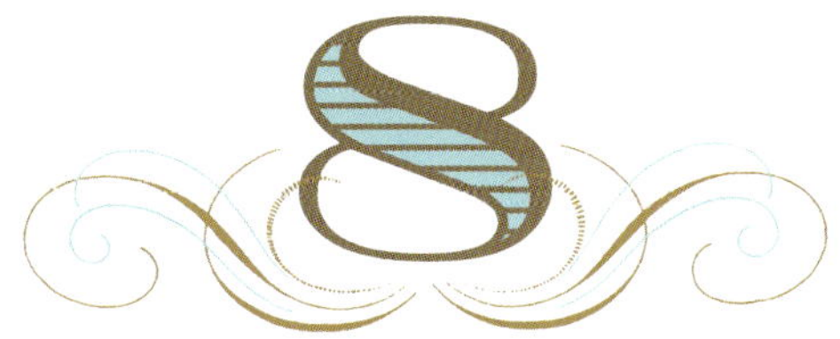

PHILADELPHIA LITHOGRAPHY AND AMERICAN LANDSCAPE

DONALD H. CRESSWELL

When portrait painter Bass Otis produced the first lithographed print in America for the July 1819 issue of the *Analectic Magazine* (see fig. 1), his creation of a landscape was neither casual nor accidental. The rapid expansion of American territory in the second decade of the century saw the admission of Louisiana (1812), Indiana (1816), Mississippi (1817), Illinois (1818), and Alabama (1819) as states of the Federal Union. In the very next year inclusion of the first state west of the Mississippi River would be solidified by the Missouri Compromise of 1820, which carved out the first new state from the lands explored by the Lewis and Clark Expedition.

Landscape, that is, pictures of land and the land beyond, was certainly on the minds of all Americans. The leading painters of the early nineteenth century were producing much more landscape work than previously. The great portraiture that was a feature of the seventeenth and eighteenth centuries was dwindling in proportion to other genres. Heroic depictions of great battles during the American Revolution were losing luster. Americans were weary of the War of 1812, which featured much senseless killing and destruction, as a sideshow to the Napoleonic conflicts in Europe. The more exciting and positive growth of America, and particularly western America, was favored by the new, young artists who, even in their portraits, placed landscapes as backgrounds suggesting progress to the lands beyond civilization.[1]

Before the ascendancy of Jacksonian political, social, and economic ideas in the 1820s and 1830s, Americans thought about art in terms provided by British and European theory as articulated in Joshua Reynolds's *Discourses,* Edmund Burke's *Ideas of the Sublime and Beautiful,* and Charles-Louis Clerisseau's descriptions of neoclassical architecture. In America the first long historical (and promotional) study of art was published in 1834 by William Dunlap in his *History of the Rise and Progress of the Arts of Design in the United States.* Although Dunlap's biographical approach to a history of art in America requires close reading to find aesthetic and moral judgments, they are perhaps adumbrated in the title, with the words "rise" and "progress."[2] Two years later the *American Monthly Magazine* of January 1836 published Hudson River School founder Thomas Cole's "Essay on American Scenery," which did provide a critical analysis.[3] Cole analyzed American landscapes with a focus on "a component of scenery, without which every landscape is defective—. . . water"—and discussed various renderings of lakes, waterfalls, and rivers. Here was a statement on how landscapes illustrated "the harmony of creation" and how American scenery, with its wildness, was just as good as European, with its "vestiges of antiquity." He concluded by stressing that American natural scenes were closer to God than Europe's artificial landscapes as inspirations for art.

Just as their British counterparts had celebrated travel to find the picturesque and record it in essays, poetry, paintings, and prints, Americans "trooped off to shudder deliciously at the height and force of Niagara Falls."[4] Print scholar Christopher Lane has produced an entire book on prints of Niagara Falls that documents the many artists who competed to capture the grandeur and beauty of that natural phenomenon.[5] As stated by literature scholar Elizabeth McKinstrey, "these artists' intentions were less documentary than artistic. They experimented increasingly with vantage points, compositional devices, and stylistic techniques to convey impressions and manipulate viewers' responses."[6] The artists who drew Niagara are a "who's who" of American art in the nineteenth century, including John Vanderlyn, John Trumbull, and William James Bennett, and printmakers rendered and made available those images through every medium, including lithography.

Prominent young American painters of the first two decades of the nineteenth century, including Vanderlyn, Washington Allston, Thomas Sully, John Wesley Jarvis, and Henry Inman, introduced landscapes (in the vein of Niagara Falls) into painting by providing subtle but beautiful backgrounds to their classical portraits.[7] Often details in the landscape told of the depicted subject's life or profession. An example of a portrait with this format is John Neagle's *Pat Lyon at the Forge* (1829), held in the collections of the Pennsylvania Academy of the Fine Arts.[8] It shows the wealthy and prominent Lyon as a workman at a forge doing the job that gave rise to his prosperity. Outside a window is a view of the Walnut Street Jail, where he was once imprisoned, an icon of the adversity that he overcame.[9]

Neagle and his fellow artists probably were aware of Bass Otis's lithograph of a landscape, but at that time lithography was a new technology. The resulting image on stone signified the success of a new printing process but not the creation of a work of art. As with most new inventions, "technicians" willing to experiment could be enticed to engage the new process, while traditionally trained artists and engravers proved more resistant. None, however, could deny that the ability to create shaded tones through lithography was superior to engraving, with its cross-hatching and stipple techniques. Consequently, within the decade after the establishment of the first commercial lithographic firm in Philadelphia in 1828, lithographed landscapes began to enter the local print market within portraiture, on sheet music covers, as parlor prints, and as advertisements.

No print was made based on Neagle's full-length portrait of Pat Lyon, but a similar American story is told by a portrait lithograph of Pennsylvania governor Joseph Ritner (1835–39), issued during the year of his reelection in 1838 and drawn by noted lithographic portrait artist Albert Newsam and printed by P. S. Duval (fig. 120).[10] The lithograph, one of the earliest to use landscape imagery with portraiture, reproduces John F. Francis's full-length portrait painting of Ritner, fashionably dressed, with his plow in front of a beautiful farm. Although in essence a portrait, the composition of the lithograph reads as a political campaign poster. The rural setting of the print alludes to Ritner as the "farmer of Washington County" who rose to the position of governor and, by extension, as the "People's Candidate." The plow, an image from the Pennsylvania state seal, and the Conestoga wagon in the background also suggest the print was a work of political propaganda.[11] The wagon traveling down the hillside road symbolizes not only the great western movement but also Pennsylvania industry and the thousands of those distinctive vehicles that were made in that state, and particularly in Philadelphia.[12] During the political campaign lithography allowed for the quick production of this idealized image, which not only served as a means of promoting the candidate but was also "well suited as a parlour ornament,"[13] virtues lacking in a printed, text-only handbill.

Lithographic landscapes also appeared in Philadelphia by the early 1830s on the covers of sheet music, an efficient and effective marketing device. Indeed, the ease

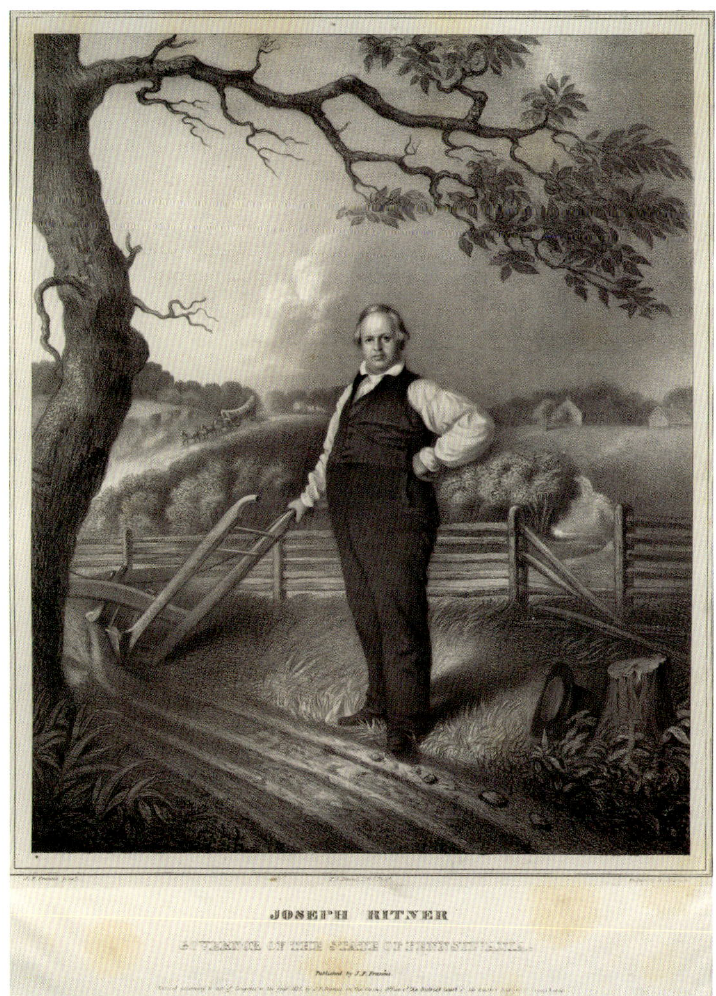

FIG. 120

Albert Newsam after John F. Francis, *Joseph Ritner Governor of the State of Pennsylvania* (Philadelphia: P. S. Duval, 1838). Lithograph. 36 × 30 cm (14 × 11 ½ in.). HSP, Albert Newsam Collection, V-100, Box 9, Folder 10.

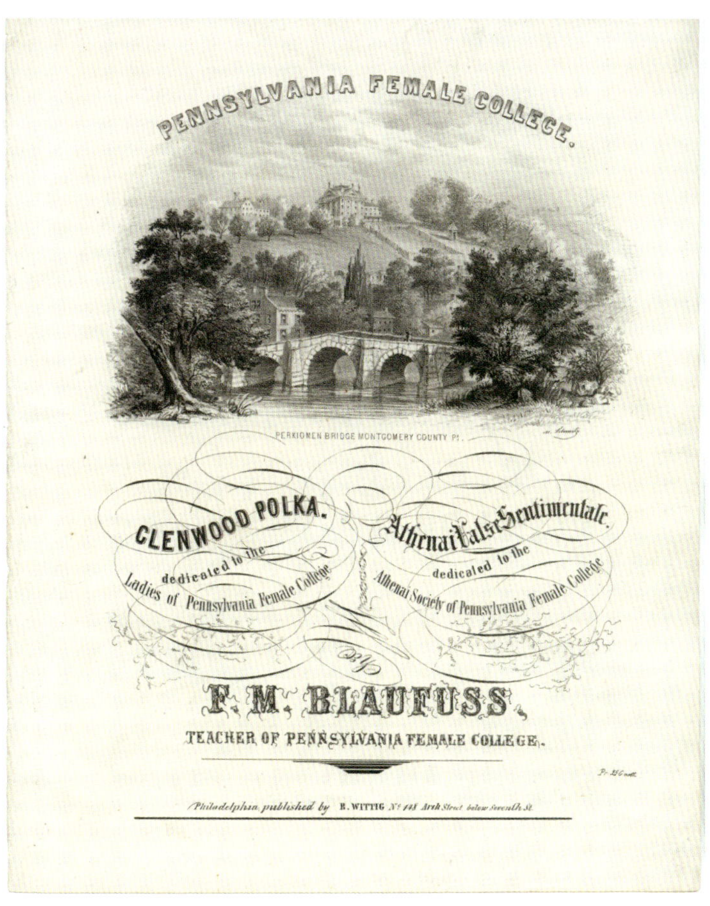

Mathieu Schmitz, *Glenwood Polka Dedicated to the Ladies of Pennsylvania Female College* (Philadelphia: R. Wittig, ca. 1865). Lithographed folio pictorial cover with three pages of music. 33 × 26 cm (13 × 10 in.). Philadelphia Print Shop.

with which scales and notes could be drawn on a stone provided an impetus for Alois Senefelder's invention, and the music-publishing field was therefore an early adopter of this technology.[14] A well-done landscape served as a perfect vehicle to catch a potential customer's eye and as a piece of art displayed on the music rack of the parlor piano. In 1832 Philadelphia music publisher G. E. Blake issued *Blake's Cabinet of Music [Grand March as Performed by the Philadelphia Band, Composed and Respectfully Dedicated to the Philadelphia Fire-Men by John M. Clemens]* with a cover containing a hand-colored view of the Fairmount Waterworks printed by Kennedy & Lucas (POS 58). The view on the sheet music of the *Glenwood Polka Dedicated to the Ladies of Pennsylvania Female College* (fig. 121), published in 1865, provides another fine example of this visual marketing. The scene drawn by Philadelphia artist and music professor Mathieu Schmitz depicts the Pennsylvania Female College in present-day Collegeville, Pennsylvania, on a high hill above the old and picturesque Perkiomen Bridge.[15] Although lithographers often included their imprint on sheet-music covers, as did Kennedy & Lucas, the printer of this one remains anonymous. It is known that Schmitz designed covers printed by both Thomas Sinclair and P. S. Duval. However, in this instance only music publisher R. Wittig receives the credit so richly deserved by the unknown Philadelphia lithographer for such a well-executed illustration and interior musical score.[16]

While Wittig's sheet music cover celebrated a road and an institution barely west of Philadelphia, other Philadelphia lithographers used landscape imagery to chronicle greater forces on a larger scale. By the mid–nineteenth century, some exquisite and colorful landscape prints captured the dramatic beauty of paintings from the Hudson River School.[17] When reproduced through the tonal properties of lithographs, enhanced by hand-coloring, or color-printed as chromolithographs, the symbolism and aesthetics of landscape paintings could be fully appreciated by all classes of people in their homes or in printshops. No longer was art available only in museums or private collections.[18] Emblematic of a lithograph's ability to present such a powerful portrayal for the masses is Herline & Hensel's[19] circa-1860 monumental *View of Pennsylvania Rail Road Bridge over the Susquehannah River 5 Miles Above Harrisburg* (fig. 122).[20] The one-track bridge, finished in 1849, is set

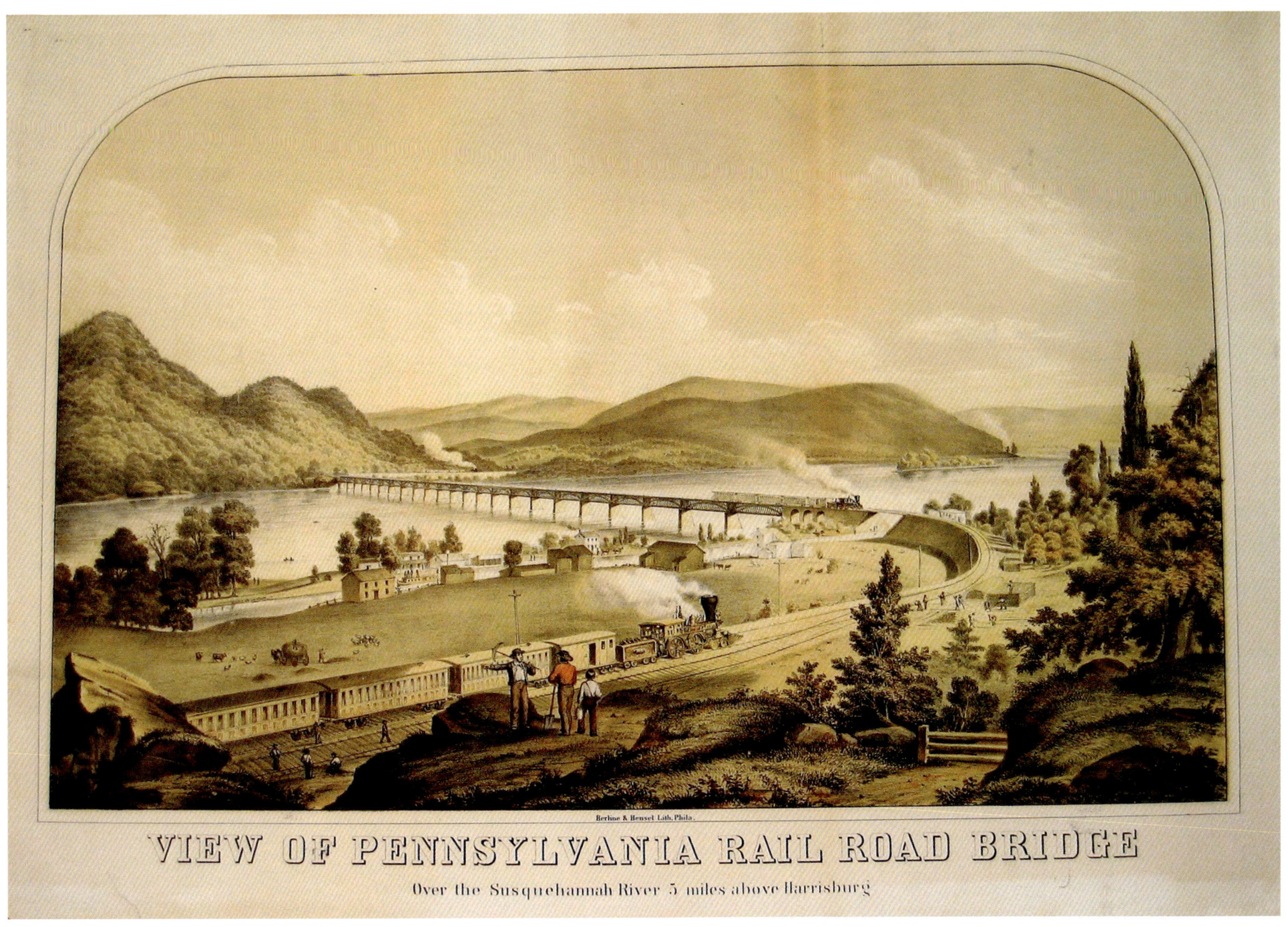

against a beautifully portrayed landscape of mountains, river, and fields, with details of farming, lumbering, and transportation, in the form of both canal and railroad. The lithographers not only depict the coexistence of the technological and natural worlds of the mid–nineteenth century but document the early state of a bridge that augurs a great future for transportation and industry in Pennsylvania. This site on the Pennsylvania Rail Road, which caused major concern during the Civil War when General Lee's Confederate Army thrust toward Harrisburg during the Gettysburg Campaign, was transformed in 1877 into a marvel of engineering, a two-track iron-truss bridge, which was replaced in 1902 by a four-track stone-arch bridge, the longest of its type in the world when finished.

FIG. 122
View of Pennsylvania Rail Road Bridge over the Susquehannah River 5 Miles Above Harrisburg (Philadelphia: Herline & Hensel, ca. 1860). Lithograph with hand-coloring. 40 × 61 cm (15 ½ × 24 in.). Philadelphia Print Shop.

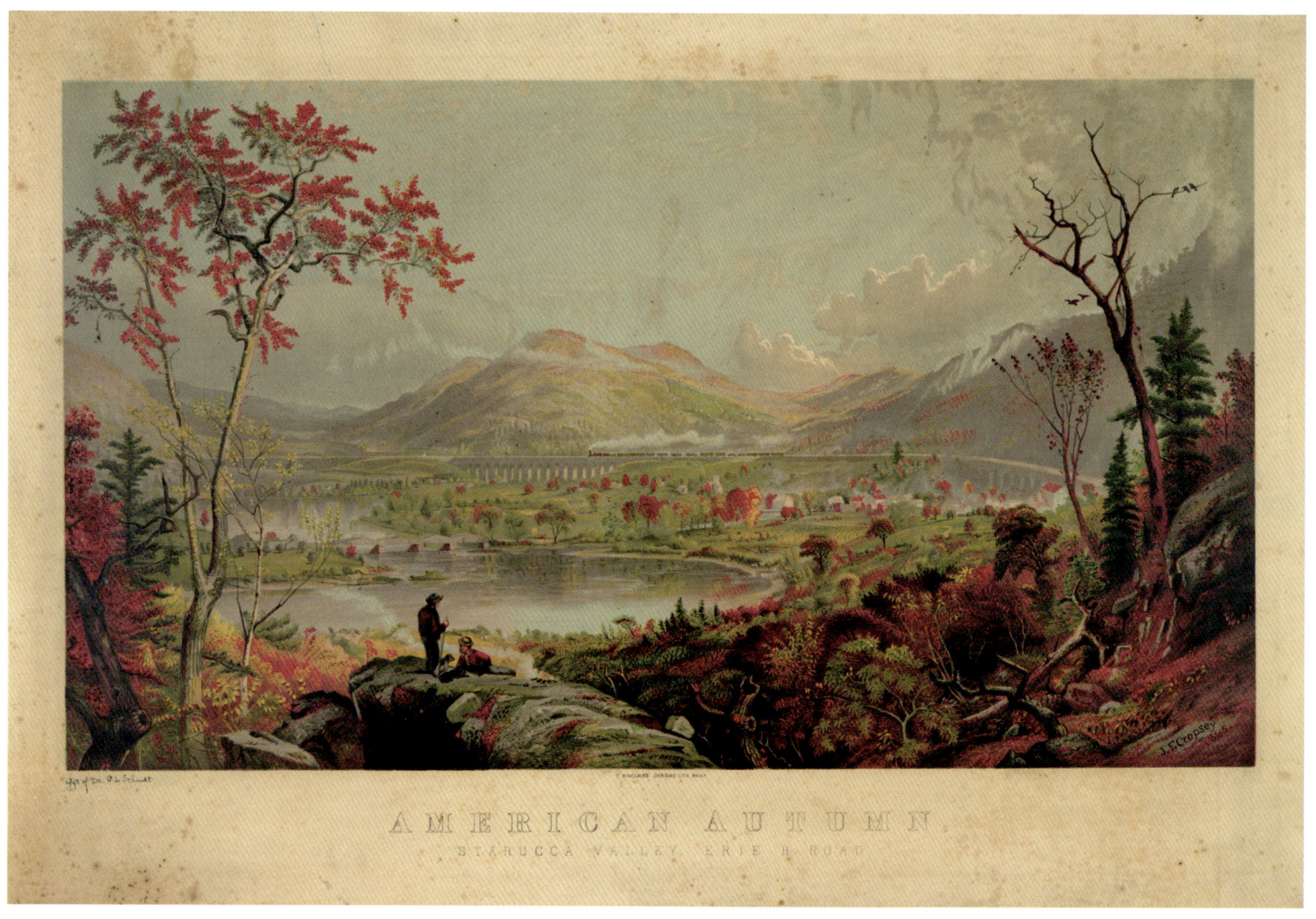

FIG. 123

William Dreser after Jasper Francis Cropsey, *American Autumn, Starucca Valley, Erie
R. Road* (Philadelphia: Thomas Sinclair,
1865). Chromolithograph. 56 × 79 cm (22
× 31 7/8 in.). LOC, PGA—Dreser–American autumn (D size) [P&P].

Another large landscape that saw wide circulation was a print of Hudson River painter Jasper F. Cropsey's monumental oil *Starucca Viaduct, Pennsylvania,* which was renamed *American Autumn, Starucca Valley, Erie R. Road* (fig. 123) when chromolithographed in Philadelphia by William Dreser[21] for Thomas Sinclair in 1865. While capitalizing on the artist's reputation for producing brilliant, colorful autumnal scenes, it also celebrated the engineering of the railroad viaduct, which crossed not only the Starucca Creek but also the entire valley near Lanesboro, Pennsylvania. While the print deserved a large circulation, its distribution received extra impetus when it was given to participants in a lottery that Uranus H. Crosby used to raise funds to save his opera house in Chicago.[22]

Along with western expansion during the early and mid–nineteenth century came the rise of great American cities. The appearance in the print market of grand urban prospects that celebrated and documented buildings within geometric plans paralleled this rise.[23] These prints, predominantly large-format lithographs often called panoramic or bird's-eye views because they were made from a theoretical elevated observation point, provided a stage to show powerful economic and social activity. During the nineteenth century this subgenre of landscape was very popular in America and can be seen as closely akin to maps, albeit the view was downward from an oblique angle rather than straight down. These views served as commercial promotions for cities and towns. They showed major features such as roads, railroads, public buildings, and some private businesses, and occasionally homes and other commercial buildings, especially if the owners paid the designers to include them.

John Reps, an urban planning scholar who has written extensively on the history of panoramic views, charts viewmakers by time period, years of activity, and volume of output.[24] The earliest producers, such as J. W. Hill, J. C. Wild, Augustus Kollner, Edwin Whitefield, and John Bachmann, all produced lithographic views that had landscape art as elements to be admired.[25]

An outstanding example of a raised perspective of this caliber was a popular view from Camden, *Bird's Eye View of Philadelphia,* which appeared about 1850 with a variety of imprints bearing the same title. The repeated appearance of these imprints, some credited to prominent publishers of views such as Bachmann or B. F. Smith Jr. and others to the lesser-known G. Matter, testifies to the commercial success of the print, and panoramic views in general, during the 1850s.[26] The hand-colored lithograph issued by John Bachmann portrays the expanse of central Philadelphia looking from above the northeast edge of Windmill Island and documents a city in transition (fig. 124). By this time a channel had been dredged through the island to accommodate ferry boats to and from Camden. A large and perhaps improbable amount of shipping plies the Delaware River, and it includes some of the newest, large paddlewheel steamers, as well as traditional sailing vessels. The major thoroughfare, Market Street, with its headhouse and six soon-to-be-removed market sheds, guides the eye through Centre Square (site of City Hall today) to the Schuylkill River.[27] The tree-named streets parallel Market Street and intersect the numbered streets. Throughout this marvel of city planning, famous buildings can be distinguished, including Christ Church, the First and Second Banks of the United States, the State House (Independence Hall), and Cramp Ship Yards. Off in the distance is Fair Mount, with its reservoir on top to provide the city with the "modern" convenience of plentiful fresh

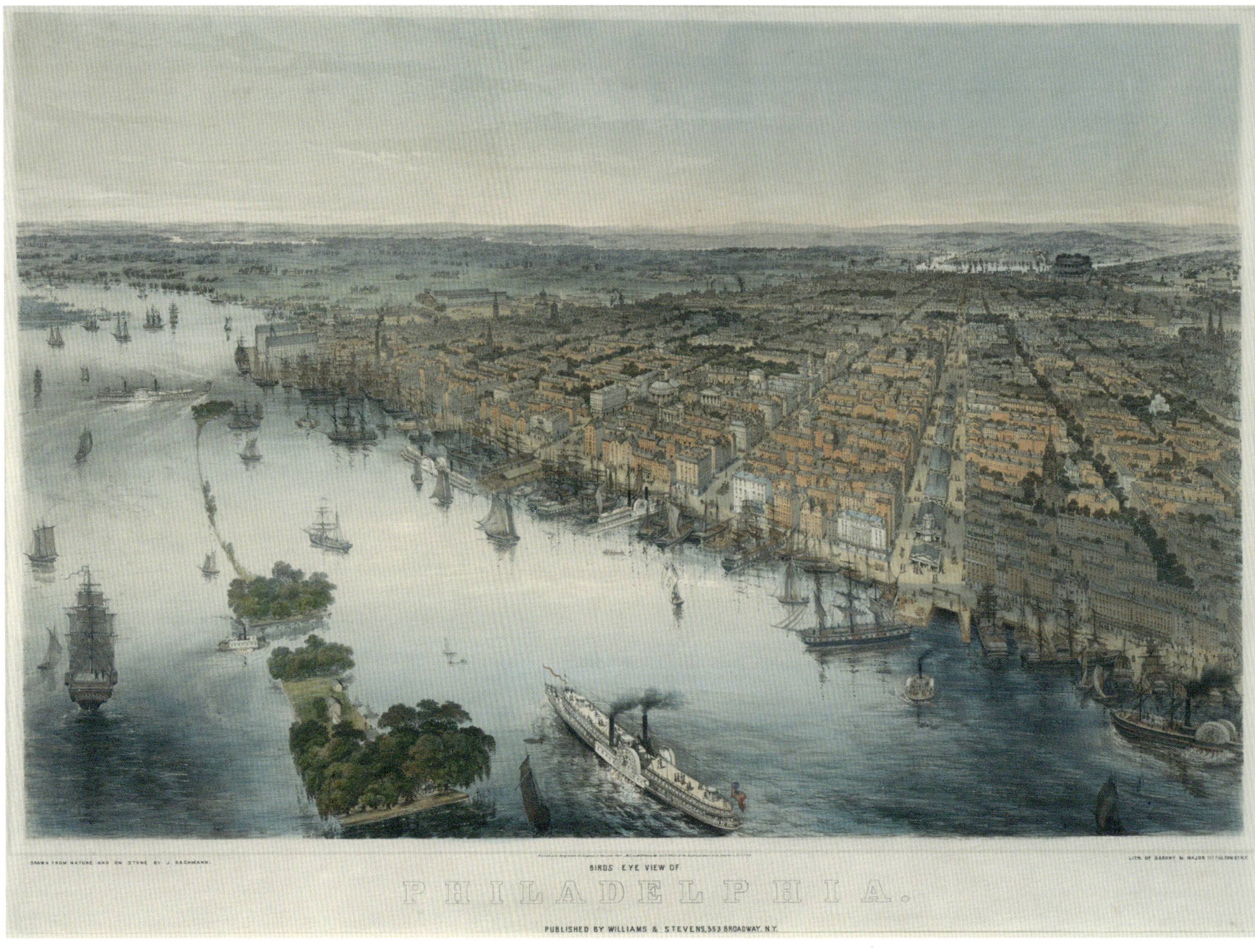

FIG. 124
John Bachmann, *Bird's Eye View of Philadelphia* (New York: Williams & Stevens, printed by Sarony & Major, 1850). Lithograph with hand-coloring. 47 × 69 cm (18 3/8 × 27 in.). POS 49a. Used by permission of the Rare Book Department, FLP.

water. Even a viewer not familiar with the city and its major features—both natural and man-made—can marvel at the powerful imagery of this panorama.

Another *Bird's Eye View of Philadelphia* issued by John Bachmann shows the city from the opposite vantage point (fig. 125).[28] Looking from the relatively recently developed area of West Philadelphia, the viewer sees at the bottom of the print the Fairmount Bridge, which led to the waterworks and the foot of the elevation that held the great reservoir. The burgeoning Fairmount Park is located at the western end of the Market Street Bridge, and factories are evident to the south along the Schuylkill River, as are the gasworks that supplied the comfortable homes and powerful factories, while

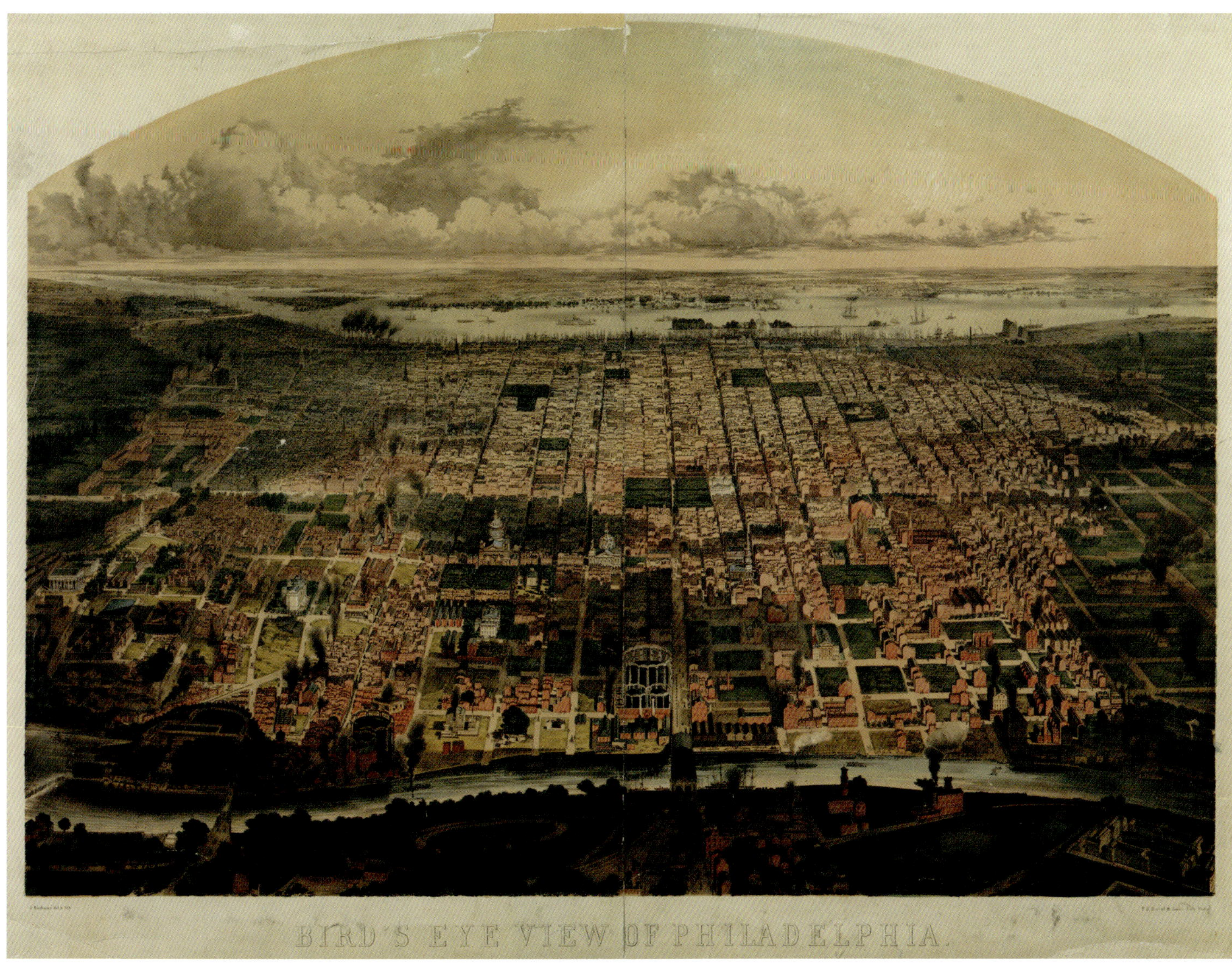

all five of the original bucolic squares are well delineated. The largest and most precisely drawn building is the Cathedral of Saints Peter and Paul, facing Logan Square. A viewer can distinguish the bold façade created by the architect Napoleon Le Brun. Along the top are the extensive wharves of Philadelphia, as well as the growing City of Camden.

Another type of landscape print is the panoramic view that portrays an entire city. Often issued before the Civil War as a set of four lithographs, each print shows a section of the city from a different point of the compass. In 1838, as discussed in chapter

FIG.125

John Bachmann, *Bird's Eye View of Philadelphia* (Philadelphia: John Weik, printed by P. S. Duval & Son, 1857). Chromolithograph. 68 × 96 cm (26 ½ × 35 ¾ in.). POS 49.1, HSP, Bc 865 B 124a.

5, John Caspar Wild issued a popular set of four views from the State House steeple as a supplement to his seminal *Views of Philadelphia and Its Vicinity* (POS 542a–d).[29] In 1853 the English immigrant Edwin Whitefield, working in Boston and New York as well as Philadelphia on landscapes and flower illustration, published a larger and more detailed set of four views from the same perspective titled *Panoramic Views of Philadelphia from the State House.*[30] Fifteen years after Wild's set, viewers continued to appreciate the novelty of the exacting execution of such imagery, as evident in this account by an anonymous writer for the *Public Ledger:*

> We have just seen some highly finished lithographic views of Philadelphia taken from the State House, and representing the north, south, east and west view of the city, as would be presented to a spectator looking from the steeple. The artist is Mr. E. Whitefield, and he has succeeded in giving an accurate and beautiful sketch in which all the principal streets, public buildings and objects of note in the city are distinctly traced. The field of view embraces several miles on either side, and it is a matter of surprise to the uninitiated, how so many objects can be brought so accurately within the limits of distinct representation upon a space occupying but a foot or two of paper. This is the mystery of the art, which to the artist is no mystery at all, but a plain matter of rule, as definitely fixed as geometry can make it. Mr. Whitefield deserves to meet with success in his effort, and our citizens will no doubt encourage him to further undertakings.[31]

The *East View. Looking Down Chestnut St. Across the Delaware. Camden N. J. in the Distance* (fig. 126) provides an "accurate and beautiful sketch" of the heart of the early city, depicting the steeple of Christ Church at midground and looking down to see the east wing of the State House. As in the 1850 Bachmann view from Camden, buildings of historic significance, such as Christ Church, the Merchants' Exchange, and the First and Second Banks, are prominently depicted in the panorama. Visual references to the flourishing economy of the growing city pervade the view as well. The rising smoke from several smokestacks, the sailing ships and steamers on both sides of Windmill Island in the Delaware River, and the growing city of Camden evoke the sense of Philadelphia as the "workshop of the world." However, the format, unlike bird's-eye views, also allows for a more focused depiction of the streetscape, as evident in the foreground and to a lesser degree the periphery. The statue of Benjamin Franklin in the alcove of the Library Company of Philadelphia cannot be overlooked, nor can the street and pedestrian traffic in front of the commercial and residential

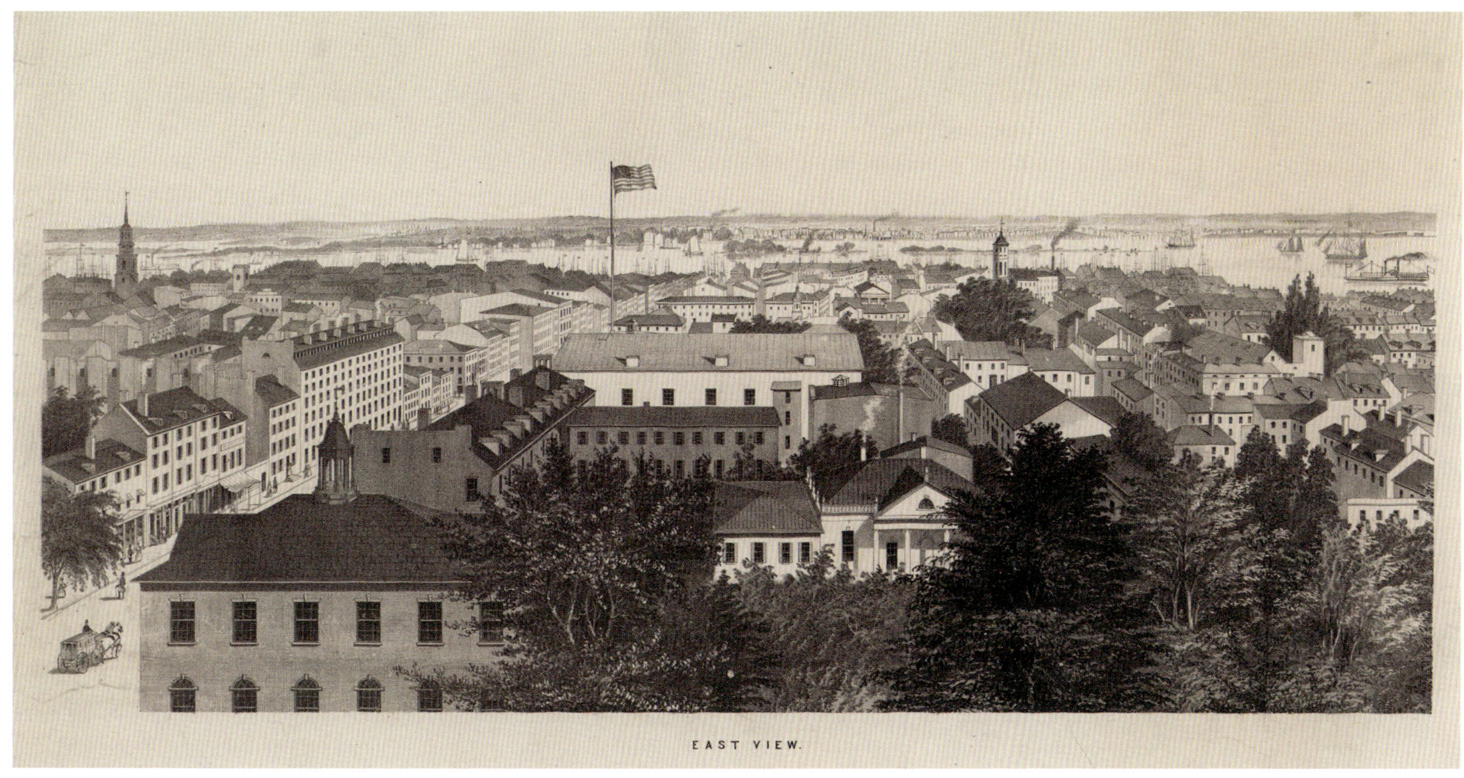

buildings along Chestnut Street. Whitefield's now-scarce and fascinating views were part of a nineteenth-century artistic and documentary tradition of artists, lithographers, other graphic artists, and printers working in many cities throughout the United States.

Philadelphia lithographers gravitated toward celebrating their own city not only in expansive landscapes but also through more concentrated views of monumental buildings often depicted as cityscapes. In 1838 Wild & Chevalier printed an idyllic and sophisticated view of Girard College. The cityscape celebrated the completion of the main building, designed by Thomas U. Walter, and served as a promotion for new subscribers to the *Saturday Courier* (fig. 127). Lithographed views proved ideal souvenirs by the late 1830s. No longer a novel printing process in the city, lithography provided a more cost-effective means than engraving for generating giveaways, many of which became keepsakes that are today's valuable ephemera. Newspaper proprietors could gain subscribers, while newspaper carriers could earn an extra penny. This promotional piece shows Founder's Hall from the southeast, its impressive size highlighted by the figures shown milling around its base and strolling the grounds. A small vignette in the title area shows the whole complex of buildings at the school, including

FIG.126
Edwin Whitefield, *East View. Looking Down Chestnut St. Across the Delaware. Camden N. J. in the Distance* (New York: Wm. Endicott & Co., 1850). Lithograph. 27 × 50 cm (10 ½ × 19 ½ in.). POS 544a, LOC, PGA—Endicott–Panoramic views (E size) [P&P].

John Caspar Wild, *Girard College. Pictorial Illustration to the Philadelphia Saturday Courier* (Philadelphia: Wild & Chevalier, 1838). Lithograph. First state. 23 × 33 cm (8 ¾ × 12 ¾ in.). POS 311.1, HSP, Bb 46 G 518c.

Laurent Deroy after Augustus Kollner, *Fairmount Water-Works* (New York and Paris: Goupil, Vibert & Co., printed by F. L. Cattier, 1848). Lithograph with hand-coloring. 23 × 31 cm (9 × 12 ¼ in.). POS 238, LCP, P.8970.3.

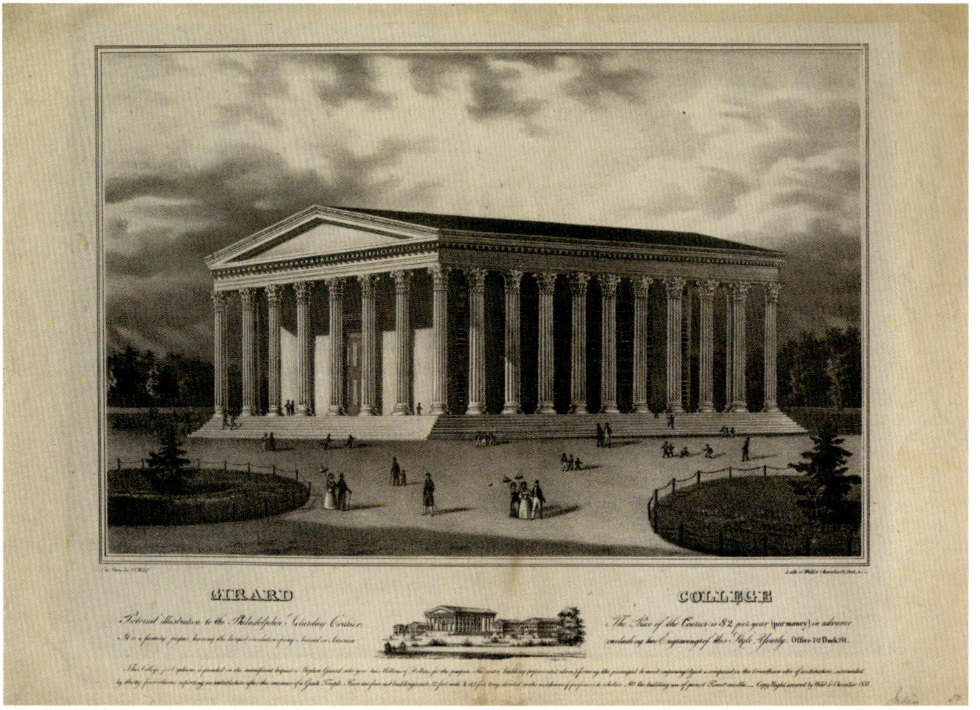

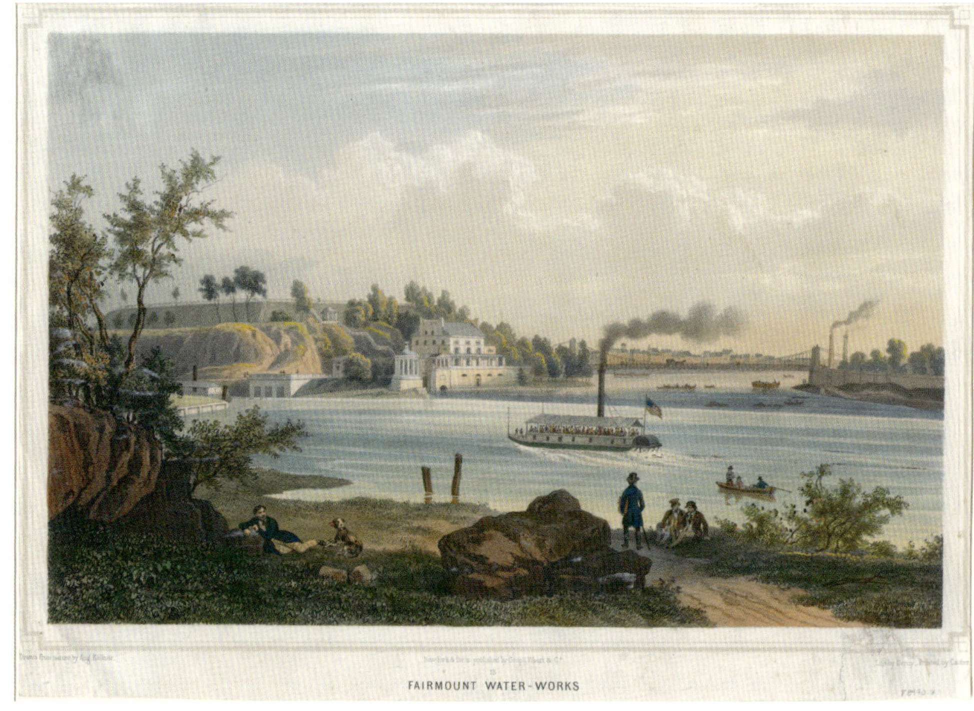

the ones still under construction, which were completed in 1847. Since the original plans were rigidly followed, this advance depiction of a great and famous Philadelphia landmark is accurate in detail and scale.

One of the most beautiful and accurate lithographs of a public building in Philadelphia is *Fairmount Water-Works* by artist and lithographer Augustus Kollner, published by Goupil, Vibert & Company in 1848 for *Views of American Cities* (1848–51) (fig. 128).[32] Kollner came to Philadelphia from Germany, where he studied art in Düsseldorf and lithography with Dorndorf in Frankfurt.[33] He was first recorded in Philadelphia city directories as a lithographer in 1844, and associated with printer John H. Camp from the late 1840s to early 1850s. The partnership produced maps as well as genre prints, portraits (especially animals), and landscapes. During the same period Kollner also produced his long-admired series of American scenes.

From the early years of commercial lithography in the city, the waterworks served as a favorite subject for landscape prints. Kollner's print for *American Cities* is one of the finest of this bucolically situated feat of architecture and engineering, itself one of the few American sites favorably judged by Mrs. Frances Trollope in her *Domestic Manners of the Americans* (London, 1832). Although the lithograph showcases the classically designed architecture of the pump house, it also includes small visual details of importance: the fence surrounding Fair Mount on the left is not incidental but was used to keep animals and children out of the water supply; the canal barge, fitted with a steam engine to take passengers and freight up the river to the Schuylkill canal, did not just provide foreground activity but represented Philadelphia's investment in western expansion. Like Herline & Hensel's *View of Pennsylvania Rail Road Bridge,* this Kollner lithograph uses landscape not to diminish but to enhance the beauty of mid-nineteenth-century technology.

The *Commissioners Hall, Northern Liberties, Phila.* drawn by Charles Conrad Kuchel after Thomas M. Scott's painting and lithographed by P. S. Duval shows a less bucolic but equally appealing cityscape (see fig. 67). This delightful winter scene, described in an article in the *Public Ledger* in July 1853, shows two delicately drawn and colored horse-drawn sleighs traveling through a snowy street in front of the dignified old stone building flying the American flag, depicted on February 22, 1852.[34] This building, located on the east side of Third Street between Buttonwood and Green Streets, had served in colonial times as a barracks for British army officers quartered in the city and was acquired by the commissioners in 1814. We are given an informative view of the governmental center of the Northern Liberties before the area was incorporated into the city of Philadelphia in 1854. The print documents Philadelphia society as well. Incidental figures in contemporary dress walk down the street, along

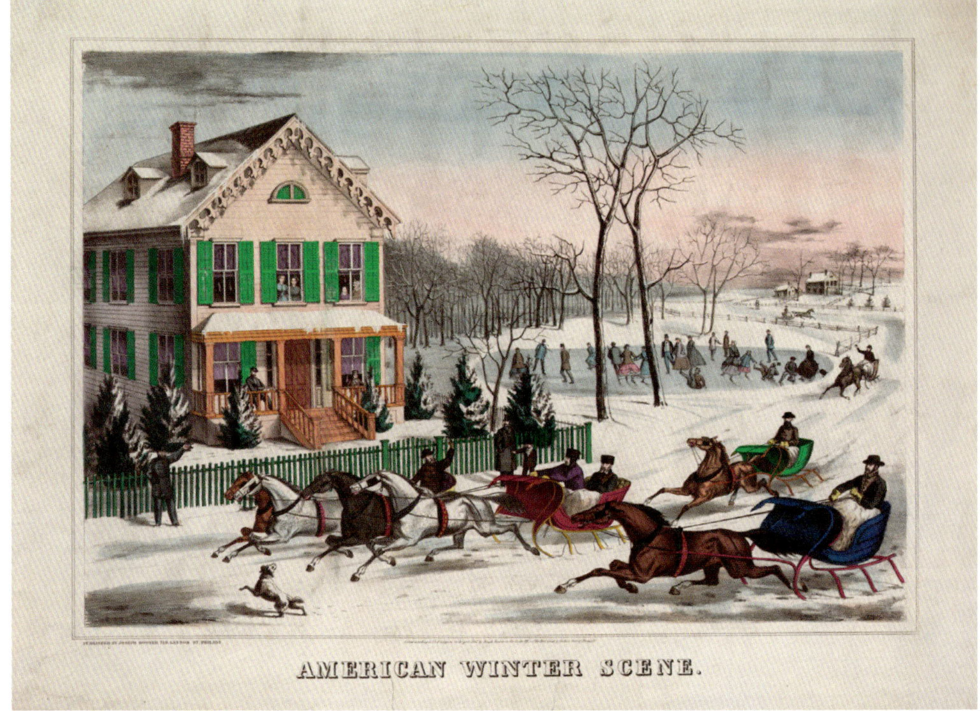

with romping dogs, snowball-throwing little boys, and a man hard at work shoveling the ankle-deep snow. All these carefully worked details add both immense charm and intriguing insights into winter life in Philadelphia. It is perhaps prescient (or ironic) that a newspaper article of 1853 referred to the building as an "object of interest as a relic," which became even more obsolete after consolidation with the city in 1854.

Stalwart lithographer Duval did not publish as many color-printed Philadelphia cityscape views as did other local firms in the midcentury. However, the few known views, including *Commissioners Hall,* that he did produce in the early 1850s reflect the high quality for which he was known. The similarly impressive views *Northern Liberties & Spring Garden Water Works* and *Tamany Fish House, on the Pea Shore* also exhibit the artistic talent and technical skill that helped to create Duval's commanding reputation (POS 512, POS 742).[35] Duval must have made limited print runs, for these prints are now among the rarest of all the wonderful nineteenth-century cityscape views of Philadelphia.

The most prolific Philadelphia publisher of chromolithographed parlor prints was Joseph Hoover. Originally trained as an architectural wood turner, Hoover first began his association with color lithography as a picture-frame maker. He established a wood-turning and framing establishment in the city in 1856, which by 1865 had

evolved into a wholesale print depot. By 1868 the "chromo
and print publisher" began to supervise the technical work
of Duval & Hunter and James Queen,[36] and established his
own printing plants by the mid-1870s. During the Centennial
Exhibition of 1876, Hoover won a medal for excellence for his
chromolithographs purportedly after James Queen's renderings, and by 1893 he partnered with his son Henry in the firm,
which produced between 600,000 and 700,000 chromolithographs annually.[37]

Although he is predominantly known for his chromolithographs, Hoover's hand-colored lithographs have considerable charm, as evidenced by the lovely and detailed *American
Winter Scene* (fig. 129). As might be expected in a time when
cities were choked with smoke and people crowded together,
more winter scenes portrayed life in the country than in the cities. Because throughout the nineteenth century fresh air was believed to be a curative, printmakers everywhere populated country scenes with healthy people and animals in the most aestheti-
cally pleasing settings possible. A typical winter day—when the air was clear, the sun
was bright and warm, and people had come out to play just after a snowfall—usually
served as the backdrop,[38] as it does in Hoover's 1867 lithograph *American Winter Scene*.
Men in sleds race by a tidy home, whose inhabitants gaze out at the scene. In the
middle distance a crowd of well-dressed men, women, and children enjoy skating on
a frozen pond. As in other landscape lithographs, the human presence provides an
added liveliness and interesting details representative of contemporary fashion. The
harnesses on the horses and especially the painted window shades in the house (fig.
130) provide a lens into the domestic history of the 1860s. Referring to painted window shades that were made in quantities of hundreds of thousands, Philadelphia antiquarian John Fanning Watson stated that the factory of George W. Blabon & Co.,
established around 1853, besides manufacturing a large variety of oil cloths, produced
painted window shades and was perhaps the largest in the country, "having the capacity for making 50,000 pairs a month."[39] Lithographers could also produce designs on
window shades, as did Duval, and on lampshades, as did Thomas S. Wagner, formerly
of the firm Wagner & McGuigan.[40] Due to the ephemeral nature of these paintings
and prints—victims of light exposure and changing tastes—these shades are seen no
more, but they can still be appreciated through this charming Hoover lithograph.

Landscape artists portrayed shifts in American demographics beyond only quaint
views of winter scenes in the country. The growth of suburbs between large cities and

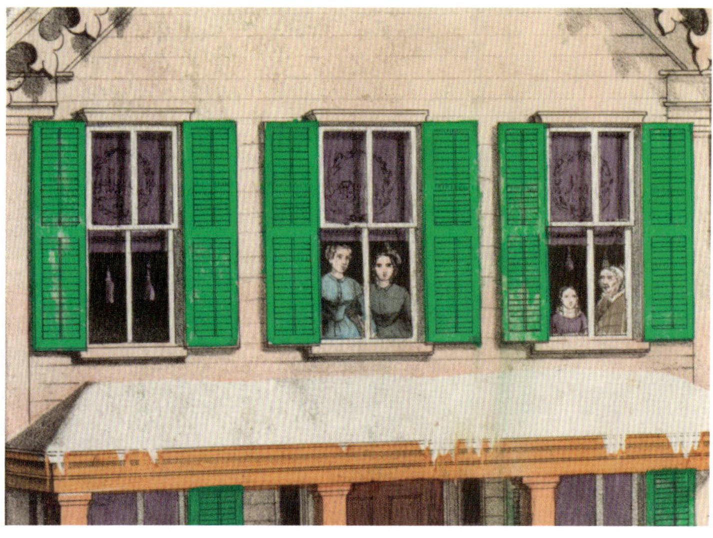

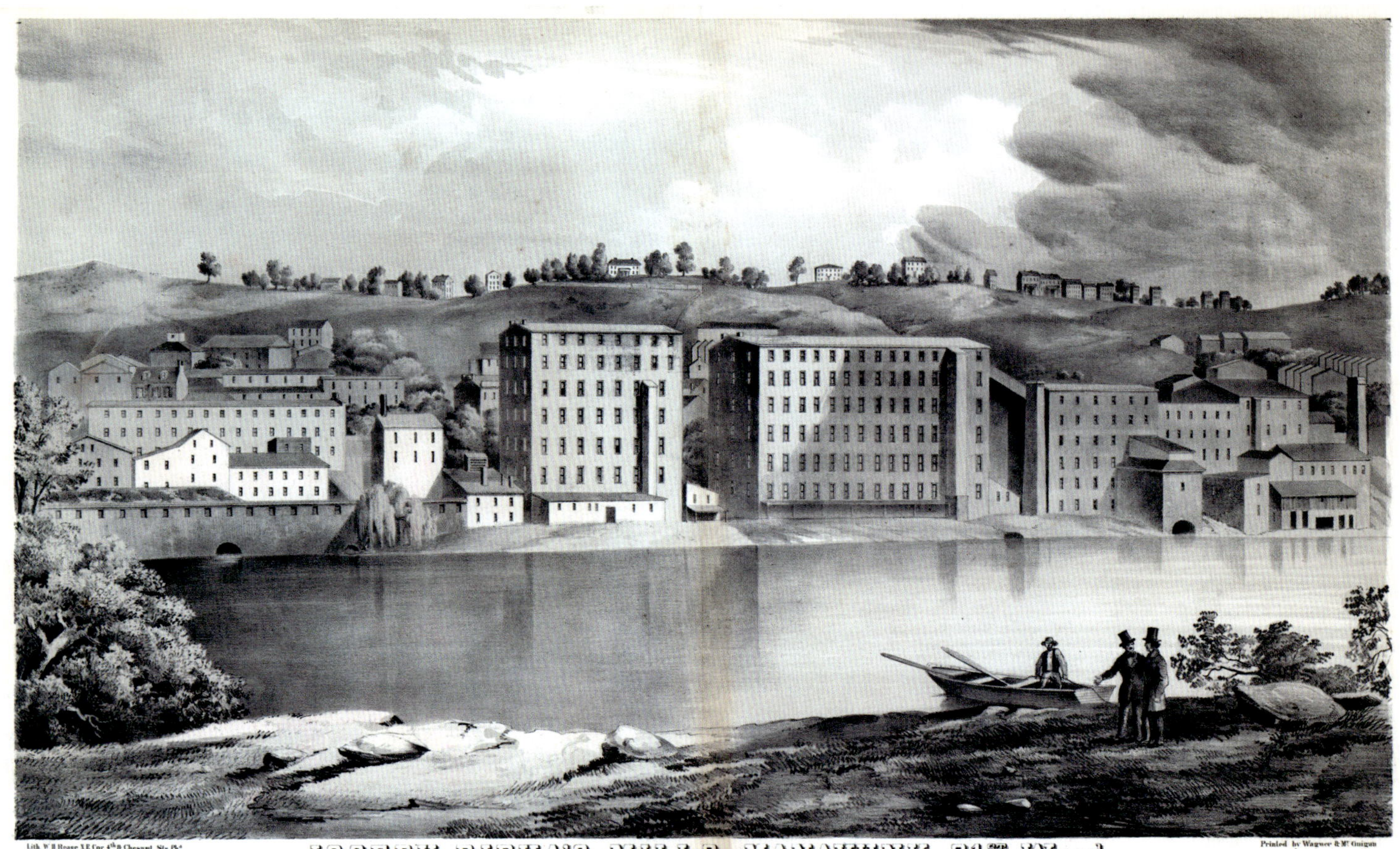

William H. Rease, *Joseph Ripka's Mills. Manayunk 21st Ward,* from J. H. Colton, *Atlas of America* (New York: J. H. Colton & Co., 1856). Printed by Wagner & McGuigan. Lithograph. 39 × 64 cm (15 ¼ × 25 ½ in.). POS 418, LCP, P. 2139.

the country accompanied industrial growth from the early decades of the nineteenth century.[41] When factories were built outside the center of Philadelphia on the upper banks of the Delaware or Schuylkill River, houses were constructed around them.[42] Philadelphia lithographers documented this shift not only through genre prints but through industrial landscape advertisements of the factories that caused the suburban growth. In 1856 Joseph H. Colton & Company issued in Philadelphia a commercial edition of the *Atlas of America* with some of the most interesting and decorative trade advertisements of the period, including a landscape view of Joseph Ripka's Mills in Manayunk, printed by Wagner & McGuigan.

In the mid-1850s the Colton Company of New York issued a series of these commercial atlases with engravings, maps, and lithographs customized to various cities, such as Philadelphia, New York, and Boston. Each book—a world atlas judging by

the inclusion of maps of every country of the world as well as the states of the Union—
also contained a profusion of advertisements for the businesses and industries of the
particular city for which it was published. The atlas, strategically placed in hotel lobbies and other venues where businessmen and their families gathered, garnered patrons for the businesses advertised but also served as a means for the mass dissemination of lithographic views of a city, such as *Joseph Ripka's Mills. Manayunk 21st Ward
Philadelphia. Manufacturer of All Descriptions of Plain & Fancy Cottonades for Men &
Boy's Clothing Warehouse 32 So. Front St.* (fig. 131).

In the mid–nineteenth century, Manayunk, which took its name from the Indian
word meaning "place of drinking," was a prosperous mill town. It had its origins in
the dam, canal, and locks built by the Schuylkill Navigation Company in 1821. The
regular use of this canal, the steady stream of water power, and the easy transportation
to Philadelphia and markets further afield created a good business climate for the mill
owners of Manayunk. Joseph Ripka had set up his mills in Manayunk in 1831 and by
the time of this lithograph was the largest cotton manufacturer in the United States.
His mills are depicted from a vantage point on the west bank of the Schuylkill, with
the growing town surrounding them. On top of the ridge behind the mills is shown
the then-small community of Roxborough, with the elegant residences of the owners
and managers and the plainer dormitory buildings of the workers.

Although Wagner & McGuigan printed *Ripka's Mills* in a black-and-white documentary manner by using one stone, other lithographers for Colton used multiple
stones to produce exquisite chromolithographs containing other industrial landscapes.
The chromolithograph advertisement printed by Herline & Co. for the Philadelphia
spice grinding company C. J. Fell & Brother, with a mill in Delaware (fig. 132), represents an outstanding example of American color printing. The fine execution and
registration of the colors of the pictorial details, lettering, and vignette create an ab-
solutely beautiful landscape that should be admired as fine art even though it was set
into the framework of a commercial poster. Although the design of the print renders
the landscape view of the Faulkland Spice Mill[43] as something of a detail, the industrial landscape is necessary to the context of this adverting print. The list of spices offered
and examples of plants that frame both sides, as well as the goddess and American
flags bordering the small vignette, have little marketing significance without the view
of the mill that produced the numerous high-quality American products cited.

Philadelphia lithographers' use of landscapes for promotion extended beyond
commercial advertisements to include views of city events, particularly fairs and exhibitions. One of the two most significant city fairs documented through lithography
occurred June 7–28, 1864, when the city mounted the Great Central Fair for the

benefit of the soldiers' relief organization, the U.S. Sanitary Commission. The fair of art, craft, and historical exhibits organized around contributions[44] was housed in temporary buildings erected on Logan Square. *Buildings of the Great Central Fair, in Aid of the U.S. Sanitary Commission* (fig. 133) depicts the vaulted main gallery, designed by Strickland Kneass, flanked by H. E. Wrigley's adjacent tented rotundas across from the Cathedral of Saints Peter and Paul. A deer and a turkey grazing in a pasture near the Horticultural Department rotunda add to the landscape feel. Designed by James Queen and printed in nine colors by P. S. Duval & Son, the chromolithograph sold for $2 as a souvenir and helped organizers raise more than $1,000,000 from the huge crowds drawn to the three-week event, especially when visited by President Lincoln.[45] Although the concept of a print as a fund-raising device was not new, the medium of the *Central Fair* print was.

Chromolithography was still perceived as a novel, imperfect art form in America at the time of the Civil War. During Philadelphia's Sanitary Fair, chromolithography gained a new level of interest when Duval attracted "the attention of every visitor" and daily printed and sold the souvenir chromolithograph on the central promenade of the main gallery. The print proved so popular that by June 23 the *Philadelphia Inquirer* reported "a numerous edition has been entirely exhausted and a new one is now ready." The combination of Queen's artistry and Duval's reputation no doubt promoted the purchase of the print, also issued in a smaller format as a souvenir card.[46]

The event in Philadelphia history that generated the most landscape art and documentation was the Centennial Exhibition of 1876. Every phase of the construction, the grand opening, and the swell of activity throughout Philadelphia was illustrated and published through wood engravings, line engravings, and lithography.[47] The ultimate souvenir would have been a fine colorful lithograph. Even before the exhibition opened, on May 10, 1876, the map- and view-printing establishment H. J. Toudy & Company published *Bird's Eye View, Centennial Buildings. 1876.* The lithograph, based on the plans and architectural drawings, showed the entire Centennial grounds from an elevated position over the Schuylkill River. The broad boulevards, fountains, and bridges are shown, and the impressive main buildings are depicted with fine detail and identified by a key under the image. A number of renderings of the smaller buildings are included. Mindful that print patrons would desire and expect an accurate view, Toudy issued a second version of the lithograph to reflect the changes to the grounds made soon after the opening of the exhibition (fig. 134). He redesigned the landscape view to show the three-mile fence that surrounded the grounds, and a tall observation tower can be seen just beyond where a large flag in the earlier print had been placed in the center distance. The Reading Railroad added a terminal for the exhibition just

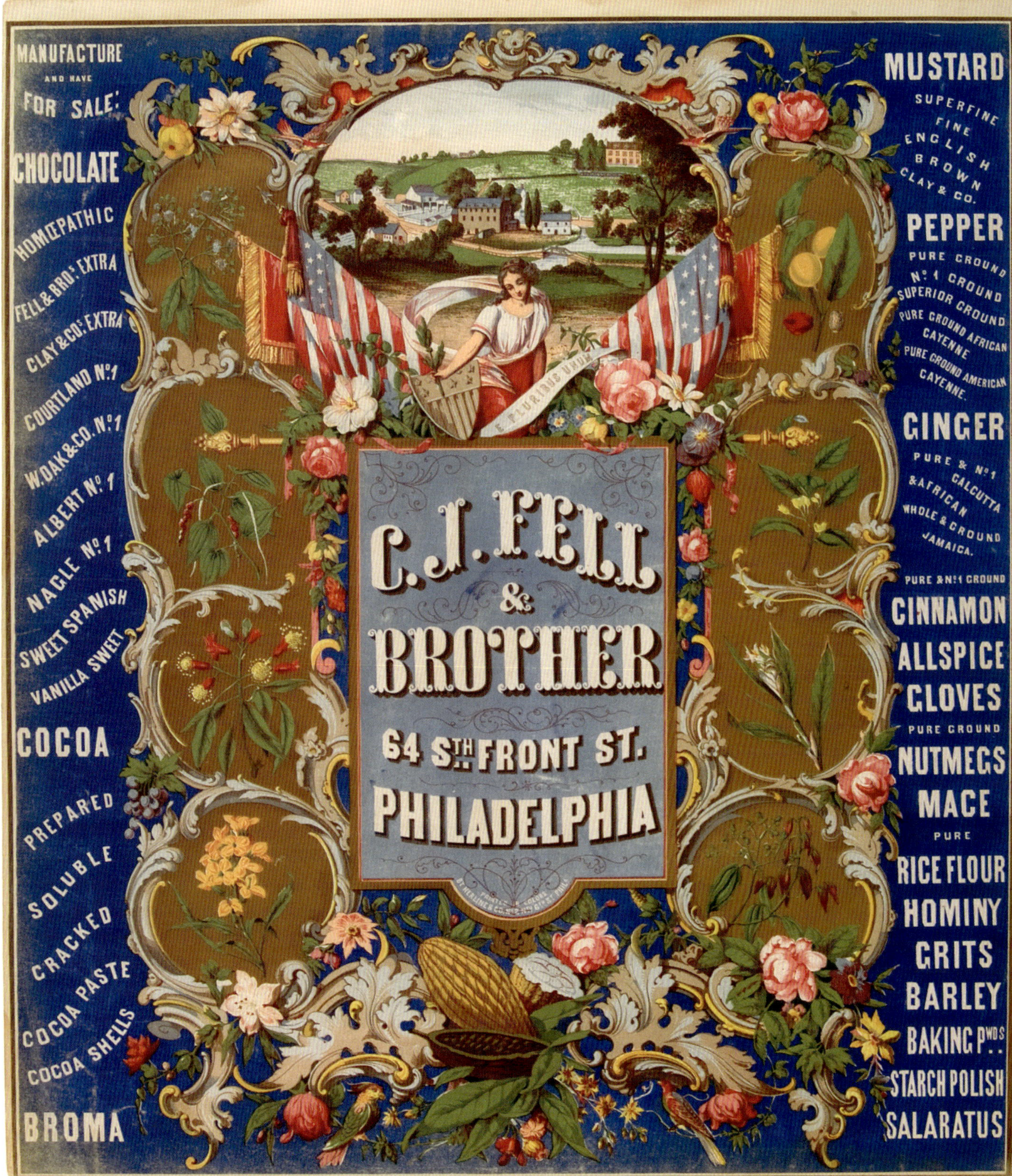

MANUFACTURE
AND HAVE
FOR SALE:
CHOCOLATE
HOMŒPATHIC
FELL & BROS EXTRA
CLAY & COS EXTRA
COURTLAND Nº1
W. OAK & CO. Nº1
ALBERT Nº 1
NAGLE Nº 1
SWEET SPANISH
VANILLA SWEET
COCOA
PREPARED
SOLUBLE
CRACKED
COCOA PASTE
COCOA SHELLS
BROMA
MUSTARD
SUPERFINE
FINE
ENGLISH
BROWN
CLAY & CO.
PEPPER
PURE GROUND
Nº 1 GROUND
SUPERIOR GROUND
PURE GROUND AFRICAN
CAYENNE
PURE GROUND AMERICAN
CAYENNE.
GINGER
PURE & Nº 1
CALCUTTA
& AFRICAN
WHOLE & GROUND
JAMAICA.
PURE & Nº 1 GROUND
CINNAMON
ALLSPICE
CLOVES
PURE GROUND
NUTMEGS
MACE
PURE
RICE FLOUR
HOMINY
GRITS
BARLEY
BAKING PWDS
STARCH POLISH
SALARATUS
C. J. FELL
&
BROTHER
64 STH FRONT ST.
PHILADELPHIA
E PLURIBUS UNUM

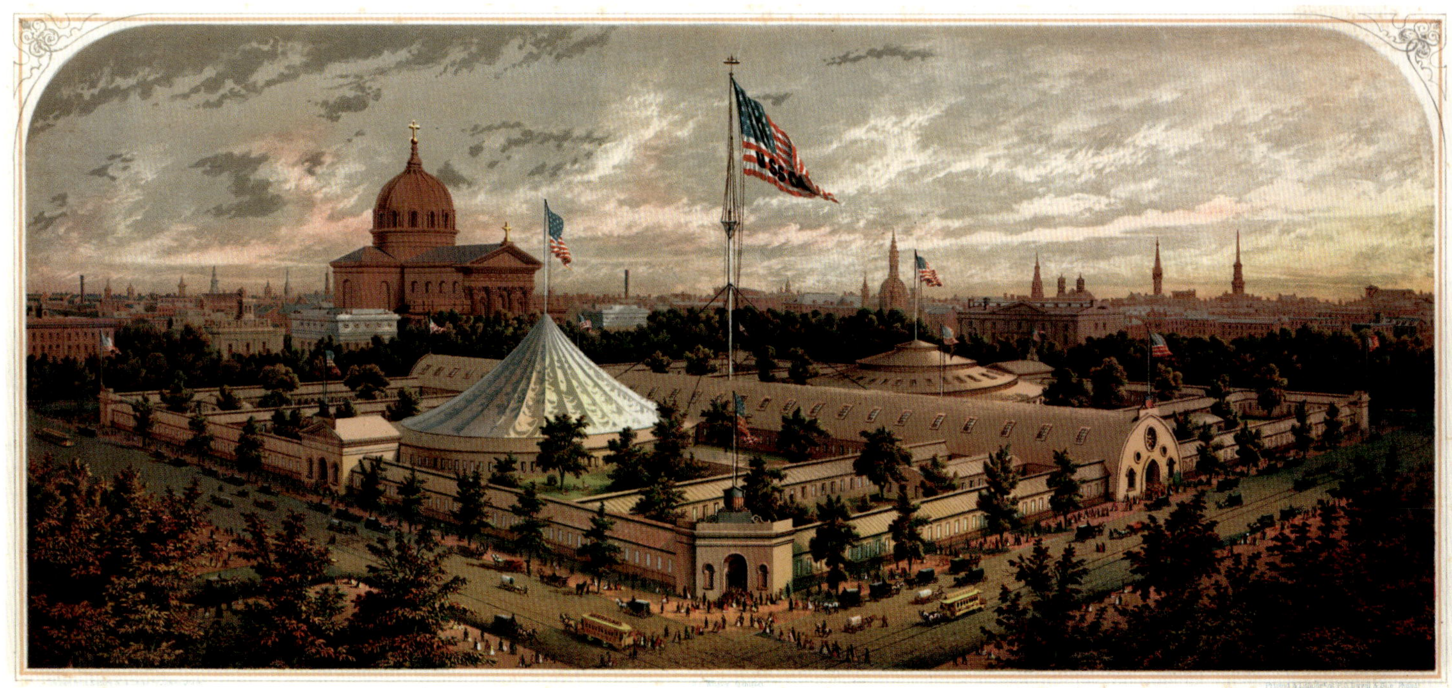

outside the grounds, and this detail is prominently depicted in the foreground, with a passenger train pulling into the station from the north. Two features of note are illustrations of the large temporary hotels that had been constructed just outside the grounds and a small sketch plan of the exhibition with the names of the buildings that appears in the bottom margin. While other prints of the Centennial Exposition may have been more finished in their artistic appeal, Toudy's lithographs were most similar to the small and grand bird's-eye views discussed earlier that promoted and later documented thousands of American cities and towns in the United States and Canada.[48]

By the last two decades of the nineteenth century, printing of landscapes was being replaced by new and revised technologies. Photography had come of age due to improvements in cameras and film. Creators of documentation that once would have been produced with lithography sought what was considered the truth of the lens. Flights of imagination and a search for ideal landscape were espoused by proponents of the etching revival. James McNeill Whistler and his disciples in western Europe and America captured landscapes using an economy of line that seemed "modern." In the

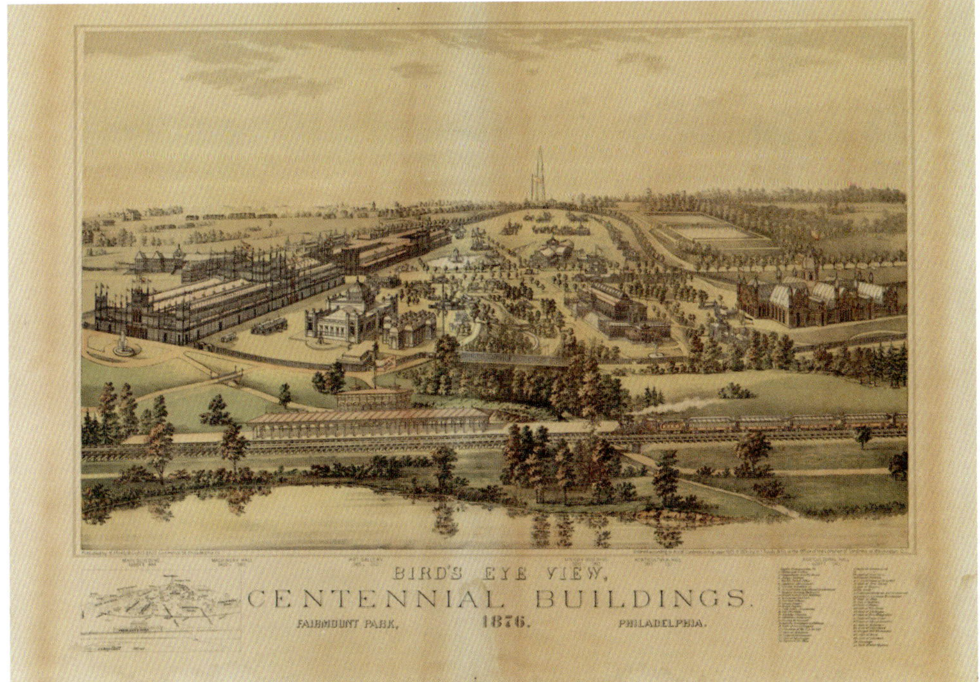

FIG. 134

Bird's Eye View, Centennial Buildings. 1876.
Fairmount Park. Philadelphia (Philadelphia: H. J. Toudy & Co., 1876). Chromolithograph, tinted. Second state. 54 × 69
cm (21 1/4 × 27 1/4 in.). POS 42, LCP, Gift
of David Doret, P.2002.49.2.

meantime lithography became synonymous with the "chromo," which was associated by some with advertising and sentimental art that used very garish colors.[49]

For approximately half a century the lithographers of Philadelphia produced land-scapes that told stories of many places, but with emphasis on their own area. When lithography was introduced to the United States, Philadelphia was one of the few places with the art resources and technology to use it. As lithographic establishments spread to the plains and the mountains and all the way to the Pacific Ocean, Philadelphia remained a center in the production of landscape lithographs. A wonderful and beautiful body of art remains.

CHAPTER I

1. "Lithography," *American Journal of Science* 1, no. 4 (1819): 439. For biographies of the artist, see John Carpenter McKee, "Bass Otis and His Critics" (master's thesis, University of Delaware, 1995); Thomas Knoles, *The Notebook of Bass Otis, Philadelphia Portrait Painter* (Worcester, Mass.: American Antiquarian Society, 1993); and Wayne Craven, *Bass Otis: Painter, Portraitist, and Engraver* (Wilmington: Historical Society of Delaware, 1976).

2. American Philosophical Society, *Early Proceedings of the American Philosophical Society for the Promotion of Useful Knowledge, Compiled . . . from Manuscript Minutes of Its Meetings from 1744 to 1838* (Philadelphia: McCalla & Stavely, 1884), 487 (entry for May 7, 1819).

3. Charles Alexandre Lesueur (1778–1846) was a French-born artist, naturalist, and early member of the Academy of Natural Sciences. In Philadelphia in 1821 he drew and printed lithographs after sketches of specimens he made while on scientific surveys of the northeastern United States. These lithographs illustrated a small number of the complete run of the October 1821 issue of the *Journal of the Academy of Natural Sciences of Philadelphia.* Philip J. Weimerskirch, "The Beginnings of Lithography in America," *Journal of the Printing Historical Society* 27 (1998): 50, 56.

4. For accounts of early American lithography, see Weimerskirch, "Beginnings of Lithography," and Philip J. Weimerskirch, "Lithographic Stone in America," *Printing History* 11, no. 1 (1989): 2–15.

5. Weimerskirch, "Beginnings of Lithography," 49–52.

6. *National Intelligencer and Washington Advisor,* January 8, 1808, as quoted in Peter C. Marzio, "American Lithographic Technology Before the Civil War," in *Prints in and of America to 1850,* ed. John D. Morse (Charlottesville: University Press of Virginia, 1970), 221.

7. *Analectic Magazine* 12 (November 1818): 430–31.

8. *American Journal of Science* 4 (October 1821): 169. Barnet & Doolittle "availed themselves in Paris of a regular course of practical instructions" and returned with "not only the skill but the peculiar materials and press necessary to the execution of the art."

9. "Account of the Art Now Practiced in Europe for Multiplying Copies of Drawings and Manuscripts, by Means of a Peculiar Stone and Ink, Lately Discovered," *Medical Repository* 5 (January 1808): 244–46.

10. Georgia B. Barnhill, "The Introduction and Early Use of Lithography in the United States" (paper presented at the 67th International Federation of Library Associations and Institutions Council and General Conference, Boston, Mass., August 16–25, 2001).

By June 1831 even the Philadelphia women's journal *Godey's Lady's Book* had described and promoted the process in an article titled "Lithography."

11. The short-lived firm of Barnet & Doolittle of New York, the first commercial lithographic firm in America, was founded in early 1821 and ceased operations by June of the following year. Henry Stone established a press in Washington, D.C., in 1822, Anthony Imbert began publishing lithographs in New York in 1825, and the Pendleton brothers, William and John, took up the trade in Boston in 1825. See Weimerskirch, "Beginnings of Lithography," 49–67.

12. In Philadelphia city directories David Kennedy was never listed as a lithographer. From 1803 to 1822 he was listed as having a glass and picture store and later as a carver and gilder. Between 1828, when he formed his partnership with Lucas, and 1833, when Lucas died, the firm was listed simply as a looking-glass store. Kennedy's family operated a looking-glass manufactory and a tavern during this period. Although William B. Lucas operated a lithographic press solely for a few months before partnering with David Kennedy, Kennedy & Lucas is commonly thought of as the first commercial lithographic establishment in the city.

13. The first public announcement of the partnership was published in the *National Gazette* on December 10, 1828.

14. At the time of his death, about 1850,

Brewster still maintained a lithographic press at his portrait-painting and daguerreotype studio. *Public Ledger,* April 5, 1850.

15. [P.S. Duval], "Lithography," in *American Encyclopaedia of Printing,* ed. J.L. Ringwalt (Philadelphia: Menamin & Ringwalt / J.B. Lippincott & Co., 1871), 279.

16. The names of the practicing lithographers were gathered from Harry T. Peters, *America on Stone: The Other Printmakers to the American People* (Garden City, N.Y.: Doubleday, 1931), and Philadelphia city and business directories, predominantly *DeSilver's Philadelphia Directory and Stranger's Guide* and *A. M'Elroy's Philadelphia Directory,* issued between 1825 and 1840. See also Wainwright, 1–45.

17. Edwin Freedley, *Leading Pursuits and Leading Men: A Treatise on the Principal Trades and Manufactures of the United States; Showing the Progress, State, and Prospects of Business; and Illustrated by Sketches of Distinguished Mercantile and Manufacturing Firms* (Philadelphia: Edward Young, 1856), 236. Blonde may be the "experienced Printer from France" that the firm announced in their newspaper advertisement in the *National Gazette,* October 5, 1829.

18. *United States Gazette,* February 14, 1832.

19. James Clonney (1812–1887), an English-born artist, drew lithographic plates printed by Childs & Inman for *The Cabinet of Natural History and American Rural Sports* between 1830 and 1833. His is one of a number of brief biographies of artists included in Charles C. Eldredge, *Tales from the Easel: American Narrative Paintings from Southeastern Museums, Circa 1800–1950* (Athens: University of Georgia Press, 2004), 104.

20. Henry Inman Letters, 1828–45, AAS. The bulk of the known letters of Henry Inman reside at this institution. See particularly the letters dated June 3, 1830; February 6, 1831; March 8, 1831; and March 19, 1831. See also Henry Inman to C.G. Childs, March 19, 1831, Society Collection, HSP.

21. *United States Gazette,* December 20, 1830, as quoted in Wainwright, 17. Although not mentioned in the notice, Blonde may have stayed on as their pressman.

22. In the nineteenth-century lithographic trade the term "draftsman" often referred to the artist who drew on the stone.

23. Freedley, *Leading Pursuits,* 237.

24. The twists and turns of these alliances were primarily documented in Philadelphia newspaper accounts published in the *United States Gazette* and the *National Gazette* and are described in the account of the lithographic industry 1828–34 in Wainwright, 6–29. See also "The Lithographic Business of Philadelphia," *Public Ledger,* February 8, 1856.

25. As quoted in Carl Malcolm Cochran, "James Fuller Queen—Artist and Lithographer" (master's thesis, University of Pittsburgh, 1954), 6. Carbon copy in the Carson Collection. By 1857 an apprentice in the Philadelphia lithographic trade could also enter the local union, as described in the 1857 constitution of the Lithographic Printers Union: "An apprentice in the last year of his time (providing he has received three years instruction at the time of application) expressing a desire to become a member of this Union, may do so." *Constitution and By-Laws of the Lithographic Printers Union of Philadelphia* (Philadelphia: Printed by F.W. Thomas, 1857), 11, in the collection of the Pennsylvania German Society, Philadelphia, Pa.

26. *Public Ledger,* October 3, 1845, and September 25, 1847.

27. See also Frederick Pilliner's advertisement as a wood engraver in *Public Ledger,* August 23, 1850.

28. *Pennsylvania Inquirer and Daily Courier,* February 26, 1842.

29. For a general overview of the transatlantic print trade, see E. McSherry Fowble, *Two Centuries of Prints in America, 1680–1880: A Selective Catalogue of the Winterthur Museum* (Charlottesville: Published for the Henry Francis du Pont Winterthur Museum by the University Press of Virginia, 1987), particularly 1–31, 271–85.

30. Wainwright, 9.

31. See the circa-1833 proof billhead for "Cardington Factory" printed and inscribed by Charles Fenderich in the collections of the Library of Congress, POS 82, PGA—Fenderich, no. 59 (A size) [P&P]; the billhead of P.S. Duval inscribed in 1839 in the collections of AAS; and E. Ketterlinus invoices dated October 27, 1862, June 26, 1862, and January 27, 1863, in Lithography, Vertical Box 1, Warshaw Collection.

32. Transfer work was an essential element of the trade from its inception, being a duplicative process that eliminated the need to design in reverse. An image was transferred to stone from a less durable wood block or copper plate through specially treated ink and paper. Given the large print runs possible with lithography, this was a particularly cost-effective operation. See [Duval],

"Lithography," 284–85, for a description of the process.

33. *Pennsylvania Inquirer and Daily Courier,* February 26, 1835.

34. Eight lithographs surveyed for the *Philadelphia on Stone* project contain a Watson imprint. Peters, *America on Stone,* 379, cites a map and book illustrations printed by Watson in his entry for the lithographer. In describing Watson as a historian, Peters conflates John Frampton Watson, the lithographer, with John Fanning Watson, the Philadelphia antiquarian.

35. See Wainwright, 10–58, where the author cites the majority of these promotional articles in the footnotes.

36. Copies of several advertisements from the Philadelphia newspapers for the sale of lithographs between 1828 and 1878 are held in the research files for the *Philadelphia on Stone* project. The average price of uncolored lithographs (less than 20 × 24 inches) remained around 25 cents for this period. In 1838 John T. Bowen advertised a hand-colored lithograph after John Trumbull's *Declaration of Independence* at a cost of $10. *Saturday Courier,* December 8, 1838.

37. *Girard College* (POS 311.1 and 2) and [*Fairmount Waterworks*] (POS 241.1 and 2). The publishers of the *Saturday Chronicle* offered a similar inducement. Subscribers, in return for the advance payment of a one-year subscription, would receive two lithographs by Alfred Hoffy, including one of the Falls of Schuylkill (copy not located during survey). *Pennsylvania Inquirer and Daily Courier,* February 29, 1840.

38. *National Gazette,* October 5, 1829.

39. Wainwright, 6–29. See also the Childs & Inman lithographs surveyed for *Philadelphia on Stone* and described in LCP's online catalog and the *Philadelphia on Stone* Digital Catalog.

40. Joseph O. Pyatt, *Memoir of Albert Newsam* (Philadelphia: Printed for the author, 1868), 147. See the Albert Newsam Collection, HSP, for the most comprehensive collection of lithographic portraits produced by Newsam. These holdings are listed in D.McN. Stauffer, "Lithographic Portraits of Albert Newsam," *PMHB* 24, no. 3 (1900): 267–89; 24, no. 4 (1900): 430–52; 25, no. 1 (1901): 109–13; 26, no. 3 (1902): 382–86.

41. *National Gazette,* April 15, 1830. In 1831 Inman quoted a similar fee of $25–$30 for the drawing and one hundred impressions of a portrait. See Henry Inman to C.G. Childs, January 5, 1831, Dreer Collection—Painters and Engravers, HSP.

42. Wainwright, 22.

43. An 1849 invoice from the firm of P.S. Duval lists the price of $2 for the paper and printing of twenty-five copies of a portrait, or about $8 for one hundred copies. Although the cost is based on paper and the labor of making the impressions, as opposed to drawing, the overall price for such work had obviously decreased for patrons. Lithography, Vertical Box 1, Warshaw Collection.

44. At least nine prints were issued as part of the series, of which one, the *Fourth Presbyterian Church,* has recently been discovered and is held in the private collection of David Doret.

45. The lithographs surveyed for the *Philadelphia on Stone* project are described in LCP's online catalog and the *Philadelphia on Stone* Digital Catalog.

46. "J.T. Bowen, Lithographer & Print Colourer, No. 94 Walnut Street, Philadelphia," published in J.R. Savage, *The Philadelphia Circulating Business Directory: For 1838* (Philadelphia: Published at Morris's Xylographic Press, 1838), 107 (POSA 41).

47. Although the Fairmount Waterworks often served as the subject of lithographs, including the 1838 views by John T. Bowen, the Castle of the State in Schuylkill (Schuylkill Fishing Company), the Belmont Incline, and the Robert Morris Hotel also served as subjects. For these lithographs after the work of Moses Swett, George Lehman, and John C. Wild, respectively, see the *Philadelphia on Stone* Digital Catalog.

48. Primary evidence describing the day-to-day operations of American firms during the earlier period of the trade exists from few sources, with the diary of New York lithographer Charles Hart (active from the late 1830s), in the Manuscript Division of the New York Public Library, most often used. Most additional knowledge about the internal workings of lithographic establishments must be inferred from the lithography manuals, lithographs, and the small amount of extant documentation related to European firms. See Georgia Brady Bumgardner, "George and William Endicott, Commercial Lithography in New York, 1831–1851," in *Prints and Printmakers of New York, 1825–1840,* ed. David Tatham (Syracuse: Syracuse University Press, 1986), 43–66; David Tatham, "The Lithographic Workshop, 1825–1850," in *The Cultivation of Artists in Nineteenth-Century America,* ed. Georgia Brady Barnhill, Diana Korzenik, and Caroline F. Sloat (Worcester, Mass.: American Antiquarian Society, 1997), 45–54; and

Michael Twyman, *Breaking the Mould: The First Hundred Years of Lithography,* Panizzi Lectures 2000 (London: British Library, 2001), particularly lecture 1.

49. All of the equipment owned by Kennedy & Lucas was sold at auction after Lucas died. The sale, with a listing of the equipment, was announced in the *United States Gazette,* March 1, 1834.

50. For more in-depth descriptions of the tasks that would have been undertaken by shop workers and apprentices by the 1830s, see [Duval], "Lithography"; *Democratic Art,* chap. 5; Alois Senefelder, *The Invention of Lithography,* translated from the original German by J.W. Muller (New York: Fuchs & Lang Manufacturing Co., 1911); and W.D. Richmond, *The Grammar of Lithography: A Practical Guide for the Artist and Printer in Commercial & Artistic Lithography, & Chromolithography, Zincography, Photo-Lithography, and Lithographic Machine Printing* (London: Wyman & Sons, 1880).

51. See *Democratic Art,* 65–67, and Weimerskirch, "Lithographic Stone in America," for an overall discussion of this aspect of the trade.

52. *Public Ledger,* December 9, 1847.

53. *Pennsylvania Inquirer,* August 26, 1852. The advertisement ran through November 1852.

54. This figure is extrapolated from the appraisal of lithographic stones in the estate of Thomas Wagner. Thomas Wagner, Year 1863, Will 51, Vol. 436, Register of Wills, City Hall, Philadelphia. Medium stones (16–26 inches) and small stones (less than 16 inches) were appraised at 6 cents and 2 cents per pound, respectively.

55. Before 1860 lithographers often included notice of their retention and reuse of stones on their invoices. See the invoice of P.S. Duval, dated 1839, AAS, Graphic Arts Lithf Duva Prob Duva, and *Democratic Art,* 67. An invoice from Augustus Kollner dated December 15, 1852, held in the private collection of David Doret, contains the caveat, "N.B. The stone is not included in this bill."

56. [Duval], "Lithography," 286, and *Pennsylvania Inquirer and Daily Courier,* January 1, 1841.

57. See *Democratic Art,* 78, for paperweight figures. See the R.G. Dun & Co. Collection for credit reports: Pennsylvania, vol. 35, p. 39; vol. 135, p. 320w; vol. 141, p. 23.

58. See *75 Years of Lithography, 1882–1947* (New York: Amalgamated Lithographers of America, 1957), 11, for the 1850 figure. The figure for 1840 was compiled from the listings for lithographers in *M'Elroy's Philadelphia Directory for 1840.*

59. Edwin Freedley, *Philadelphia and Its Manufactures: A Hand-Book Exhibiting the Development, Variety, and Statistics of the Manufacturing Industry of Philadelphia in 1857* (Philadelphia: Edward Young, 1858), 183–85.

60. Figure extrapolated from trade listings in *M'Elroy's Philadelphia Directory for 1860; Public Ledger,* February 8 and 11, 1856; and Lorin Blodget, *The Industries of Philadelphia as Shown by the Manufacturing Census of 1870, Compared with 1860 and Estimates for 1875* (Philadelphia: Collins, printer, 1876).

61. Edwin Freedley, *Philadelphia and Its Manufactures: A Hand-Book of the Great Manufactories and Representative Mercantile Houses of Philadelphia in 1867* (Philadelphia: Edward Young & Co., 1867), 539–40, 547.

62. For census results, see Theodore Hershberg, ed., *Philadelphia: Work, Space, Family, and Group Experience in the Nineteenth Century* (New York: Oxford University Press, 1981), 65. In 1850 there were ninety-three printing and publishing firms in Philadelphia.

63. In chapter 2 of this volume Michael Twyman discusses the types and mechanics of the lithographic presses used by Philadelphia lithographers. By 1831 Adam Ramage advertised his sale of "lithographic presses at least equal to those imported from England or France, which could be seen in use in the offices of Messrs. Childs & Inman and M.E.D. Brown of this city." In 1835 Philadelphia printing-press manufacturer Sheldon Graves advertised he "intended" to manufacture lithographic presses, and in 1845 Charles Massey, also of Philadelphia, advertised his lithographic presses. Besides these advertisements, no further evidence of their presses has been found. In 1851 R. Hoe & Co. of New York, the major nineteenth-century printing-press manufacturer, advertised lithographic handpresses at prices ranging from $150 for the smallest bed (19 × 24 inches) to $350 for the largest bed (28 × 48 inches). *Saturday Evening Post,* December 10, 1831; *Pennsylvania Inquirer and Daily Courier,* September 3, 1835; Peter C. Marzio, "Lithography as a Democratic Art: A Reappraisal," *Leonardo* 4 (Winter 1971): 37–48; *R. Hoe & Co. Manufacturers of Single and Double Cylinder, and Type Revolving Printing Machines, Washington and Smith Hand Presses, Self Inking Machines, etc.* (New York: William Van Norden, printer, 1851), 27.

64. Duval promoted his operation of

several presses in the *Public Ledger,* April 12, 1856, two years after Wagner & McGuigan had advertised that they had "upwards of forty presses" in the *Catalogue of the Twenty-Fourth Exhibition of American Manufactures* (Philadelphia: William S. Young, printer, 1854), 39. Variants of the Wagner & McGuigan advertisement were also published in *The Philadelphia Merchants' & Manufacturers' Business Directory for 1856–57* (Philadelphia: Griswold & Co., [1856]), [15], front ad section, and *McElroy's Philadelphia Directory, for 1856* (Philadelphia: Edward C. & John Biddle, printed by Henry B. Ashmead, 1856), 10, front ad section.

65. "The Lithographic Business of Philadelphia," *Public Ledger,* February 8, 1856.

66. Figure quoted in Jennifer Ambrose, "Picturing Factories and Storefronts: Mid-19th Century Advertising Lithographs" (paper presented at "Impressions of Philadelphia," North American Print Conference 2007, Philadelphia, September 28, 2007).

67. While working in the trade, Hoffy also exhibited portrait paintings at the Artists Fund Society and Pennsylvania Academy of the Fine Arts between 1840 and 1848. Peter Hastings Falk, ed., *The Annual Exhibition Record of the Pennsylvania Academy of the Fine Arts,* vol. 1, *1807–1870,* reprint with revisions of the 1955 edition of Anna Wells Rutledge's *Cummulative [sic] Record of Exhibition Catalogues* (Madison, Conn.: Sound View Press, 1988), 100.

68. See *McElroy's Philadelphia Directory* for the years 1848 to 1851 and the *Philadelphia on Stone* Biographical Dictionary.

69. These deductions are made from city directory listings of identified lithog-

raphers and imprints on lithographs surveyed for *Philadelphia on Stone* and included in LCP's online catalog and the *Philadelphia on Stone* Digital Catalog.

70. *North American,* December 17 and 18, 1852.

71. *Public Ledger,* August 13, 1861. Pilliner worked as an engraver before he entered the lithographic trade about 1855.

72. "The Lithographic Business of Philadelphia," *Public Ledger,* February 8, 1856, with a correction published February 11, 1856.

73. Freedley, *Leading Pursuits,* 237–38.

74. "The Lithographic Business of Philadelphia," *Public Ledger,* February 8, 1856, with a correction published February 11, 1856.

75. These firms may have controlled as much as 65 percent of the trade. Out of the estimated 177 presses, Duval was operating thirty-four and Wagner & McGuigan about forty. Unfortunately, the actual sizes of Sinclair's and Rosenthal's establishments are currently unknown. However, Frederick Bourquin, a lithographic map publisher, had about twenty presses in 1856. If Rosenthal and Sinclair were larger than Bourquin, then presumably they each had more than twenty presses in operation.

76. See note 64 above and the circa-1847 advertisement *Wagner & McGuigan's Lithographic Establishment for Drawing Lettering & Printing No. 116 Chesnut St. Philadelphia,* POSA 113, Harry T. Peters America on Stone Collection, Division of Home and Community Life, Smithsonian (DL *60.3081).

77. *Democratic Art,* 3. Marzio reports that in 1860 there were approximately sixty lithographic firms in America, employing eight hundred people. This averages to about thirteen employees

per firm, making this author's estimates for Philadelphia much higher than the national average. Using this national average from 1860, Philadelphia lithographers would have employed around 213 people.

78. *The Industries of Philadelphia* (Philadelphia: Richard Edwards, 1881), 140.

79. Freedley, *Philadelphia and Its Manufactures* (1858), 183–84, and *Gopsill's Philadelphia City Directory for 1870* (Philadelphia: James Gopsill, 1870).

80. Figure compiled from the checklist included in Cochran, "James Fuller Queen," and Queen's lithographs surveyed and cataloged for the *Philadelphia on Stone* project.

81. Of the samples analyzed, the Pennsylvania-born lithographers made up 36 percent of lithographers in 1840, 33 percent in 1850, and 37 percent in 1860.

82. *Democratic Art,* 171.

83. For statistics on German immigrants in the city of Philadelphia, see Hershberg, *Philadelphia: Work, Space,* 180. Hershberg uses the postconsolidation boundaries of Philadelphia in compiling the data.

84. Ibid. The percentage grew to 7.5 in 1860.

85. *Constitution and By-Laws of the Lithographic Printers Union.*

86. Ibid., article VI.

87. About twenty listings for meetings were found during research for the project.

88. *Philadelphia Inquirer,* December 1, 1862. The article also states that "in some shops, when the men have constant work, a greater amount is realized."

89. George D. Shubert Diary, 1866, Special Collections, Paley Library, Temple University, insertion.

90. *Philadelphia Inquirer,* November 24, 1862.

91. *Public Ledger,* June 21, 1866.

92. Entry for June 1, 1866, George D. Shubert Diary.

93. The illustrated invitation for this ball, the *Second Grand Ball of the Lithographic Printers Union. On Monday Ev'g, May 18th 1863 at the Musical Fund Hall,* lists organizers and committee members. POSP 205, LCP, P.9343.277.

94. About 12 percent of the identified lithographers served in benevolent, civic, and ethnic organizations, based on a sampling of 259 lithographers. The evidence for their involvement was most often gathered from obituaries; the numbers of lithographers involved in benevolent and fraternal organizations could be much higher given the subjective nature of these announcements.

95. Matthias S. Weaver Diaries, 1840–43, Ohio Historical Society, Columbus, Ohio.

96. Savage, *Philadelphia Circulating Business Directory: For 1838,* 106.

97. *The Mercantile Register, or Business Man's Guide* (Philadelphia: H. Orr, 1846), 198.

98. The advertising text reads: "He continues to execute portraits from life and on stone, landscapes from nature, anatomical and architectural drawings, machinery, music titles, maps, plans, circulars, checks, bill heads, bills of lading, price currents, fac-similes, labels, commercial blank &c., transferring from copper plates, steel plates, wood cuts and manuscripts."

99. James Queen, *Duval, Williams & Duval late P.S. Duval & Son lithographers, 22 & 24 South 5th St., ab. Chestnut Philada.* (Philadelphia: Duval, Williams & Duval, ca. 1860), POSA 16, HSP, Ba 61 D 956a.

100. Max Rosenthal, *L.N. Rosenthal. Lithographic office, removed to N.W. cor. of Fifth & Chestnut Sts. Philadelphia* (Philadelphia: L.N. Rosenthal, 1856), POSA 51, LCP, (5) 2526.F.b.

101. *A. Koellner, Painter, No. 74 Corner of Chestnut and Exchange Streets, Philadelphia* (Philadelphia: P.S. Duval, 1840), POSA 2, LCP, 8115.F.1.

102. The Ketterlinus firm was nationally known for its manufacturers' labels. Judges of their display at the 1858 Exhibition of American Manufacturers at the Franklin Institute noted, "Much of this fanciful work was imported from England and France, but Ketterlinus can now supply the demand with an article just as good." As quoted in *Democratic Art,* 27.

103. *E. Ketterlinus & Co., Letter-Press and Lithographic Printers, No. 40 North Fourth St., First Door Above the Merchant's Hotel, Philadelphia. Counting House Almanac for 1854* (Philadelphia: E. Ketterlinus & Co., ca. 1853), POSA 19, HSP, Ba 614 K 512b, and "E. Ketterlinus, Steam Power Letter-press and Lithographic Printing House, N.W. Cor. Arch & 4th Sts.," published in *Gopsill's Philadelphia City Directory for 1870,* opp. 854 (verso) (POSA 23).

104. Maps were excluded from the scope of the *Philadelphia on Stone* project. However, a survey of maps printed by Philadelphia mapmakers, including the collections at LCP, by Jefferson M. Moak of the National Archives is currently in progress. See the previous map studies by Moak, *Atlases of Pennsylvania: A Preliminary Checklist of County, City, and Subject Atlases of Pennsylvania* (Philadelphia: Jefferson Moak, 1976) and "Louis H. Everts: American Atlas Publisher and Entrepreneur," *Coordinates,* ser. B, no. 11, 2009: http://sunysb.edu/libmap/coordinates/seriesb/no11/b11.htm.

105. Walter Ristow, "The Map Publishing Career of Robert Pearsall Smith," *Quarterly Journal of the Library of Congress* 26 (July 1969): 170–96.

106. *Industries of Philadelphia* (1881), 140.

107. *Public Ledger,* February 26, 1849. Duval exhibited window shades "on which are portrayed the battles of Lexington and Bunker Hill" at the Franklin Institute Exhibition of American Manufacturers in 1849 (*Philadelphia Inquirer,* October 22, 1849). Evidence that Duval was still in the shade business in 1852 comes from the *Public Ledger,* November 13, 1852: "Another branch of this establishment is the manufacture of window-shades."

108. Thomas Wagner, Year 1863, Will 51, Vol. 436, Register of Wills, City Hall, Philadelphia.

109. Names gathered from listings in McElroy's and Gopsill's Philadelphia city directories between 1856 and 1874. For the lithographers cited, see in particular the 1864 McElroy edition for Wagner, the 1868 Gopsill edition for V. Quarre, and the 1872 Gopsill edition for E.P. & L. Restein.

110. Anne Williams, *Cutting a Fine Figure: The Art of the Jigsaw Puzzle* (Lexington, Mass.: Museum of Our National Heritage, 1996), 6.

111. *The Great American Centennial Exhibition Puzzle Blocks, in Sectional Parts* (New York: Manufactured by George H. Chinnock, ca. 1875), POS 327a–e, LCP, P.2007.21.12a–k.

112. *Internal Revenue Assessment Lists for Pennsylvania, 1862–1866* (National

Archives Microfilm Publication M787, Roll 7); *Records of the Internal Revenue Service,* Record Group 58, National Archives, Washington, D.C.; Pennsylvania, vol. 142, p. 18, R.G. Dun & Co. Collection; *Philadelphia Inquirer,* August 21, 28, September 11, and December 23, 1873; and *Gopsill's Philadelphia City Directory for 1890.*

113. John T. Bowen, Administration 397, Recorder of Wills, City Hall, Philadelphia, and Pennsylvania, vol. 11, p. 316, R.G. Dun & Co. Collection.

114. John Cassin, *United States Exploring Expedition, During the Years 1838, 1839, 1840, 1841, 1842, Under the Command of Charles Wilkes,* vol. 8, *Mammalogy and Ornithology, with a Folio Atlas* (Philadelphia: J.B. Lippincott, 1858), vi, and *Proceedings of the Academy of Natural Sciences of Philadelphia,* vol. 10 (Philadelphia: Printed for the Academy, 1859), 178. The bird is *Calliste laviniae,* now normalized to *Tangara lavinia,* a South American tanager.

115. Wainwright, 58.

116. Women received training in lithography at the School of Design possibly as early as the school's inception, in 1844. See Elizabeth Mosimann, "'The Useful and Beautiful': 19th-Century Botanical Lithography in Philadelphia," *Imprint: Journal of the American Historical Print Collectors Society* 12 (Autumn 1987): 17–18.

117. *Report of the Twenty-Second Exhibition of American Manufactures: Held in the City of Philadelphia, from the 19th to the 30th of October, 1852, by the Franklin Institute, of the State of Pennsylvania, for the Promotion of the Mechanic Arts; With the Address of the Hon. Judge Kelly* (Philadelphia, 1852), 20, 23.

118. These genres account for about one-third of the nine hundred lithographs for this period surveyed and cataloged for *Philadelphia on Stone.*

119. Of the 480 lithographs for this period described by Wainwright, 215, or about 45 percent, are separately issued pictorial advertisements. These numbers omit eight important early commercial views published as illustrations in *Picture of Philadelphia from 1811 to 1831,* printed by Kennedy & Lucas in 1831.

120. We use the term "pictorial advertisement" or "advertising poster," as opposed to "trade card," to describe this genre of lithograph. Wainwright and other print scholars have referred to this format of print as a trade card, in keeping with its precursor—a smaller, eighteenth-century engraved advertisement. As the term "trade card," by contemporary standards, most often denotes a mass-produced small-format "multicolored collectible giveaway" of the later nineteenth century, we have delineated the terms to avoid confusion. See also Jennifer Ambrose, "Nineteenth-Century Philadelphia Advertising Prints," in "The Library Company of Philadelphia," special issue, *Antiques,* 170, no. 2 (August 2006): 100 n. 2.

121. Of the 215 separately issued pictorial advertisements described by Wainwright, Rease was responsible for 94. By comparison, Robert F. Reynolds, Philadelphia's second most prolific advertising artist in this period, drew 13 advertisements.

122. After several race riots in the 1840s, the African American population in the city was at about 5 percent in 1850, dropping to about 3 percent by 1860, with the predominant occupations being domestic servant and laborer. Statistics were compiled from figures quoted in W.E. Burghardt DuBois, *The Philadelphia Negro: A Social Study* ([Philadelphia]: Published for the University of Pennsylvania, 1899), 36.

123. A German lithographer, Kuhl established his shop in Philadelphia about 1840 or 1841 and left the city for San Francisco around 1854. He formed a partnership with George Kuhl, probably his younger brother, 1842–46. Kuhl also worked with John Childs at the Walnut Street address between 1848 and 1854.

124. See Ambrose, "Nineteenth-Century Philadelphia Advertising Prints," 94–101, and "Picturing Factories and Storefronts."

125. *The Philadelphia Fashions & Tailors' Archetypes* (Philadelphia: Samuel A. Ward & Asahel F. Ward, July, 1849).

126. More than thirty large-format fashion plates have been located. A very early plate, depicting London fashions for men, was issued by Childs & Inman in *William's Reports of London Fashions* for June 1832, LCP, P.9177.38. Known examples for fashion publishers S.A. & A.F. Ward were printed between 1842 and 1856. Lithographic artist Matthias S. Weaver describes working on plates for the Wards in his diaries of 1841 and 1842 (Matthias S. Weaver Diaries, 1840–43), although copies of these images have not been found. F. Mahan published plates between 1852 and 1867, and examples of John R. Shankland plates, many in the collections of the Library of Congress, exist for the years between 1849 and 1854. See the *Philadelphia on Stone* Digital Catalog.

127. *Catalogue of the Eighteenth Exhibition of American Manufactures, Held in Philadelphia, 1848* (Philadelphia: William S. Young, printer, 1848), 6.

128. Entry for October 12, 1842, Matthias S. Weaver Diary.

129. Undated entry after that of October 3, 1843, Matthias S. Weaver Diary: "Account of all the work done by me, when finished, and the price I received." For a full account of Weaver's career, see Sarah Weatherwax, "Matthias Weaver: The Reluctant Lithographer" (paper presented at "Impressions of Philadelphia," North American Print Conference 2007, Philadelphia, September 28, 2007).

130. *Public Ledger,* September 17, 1851.

131. Volunteer-fire-company certificates issued between about 1865 and 1873 constitute about 20 percent of the more than one hundred certificates surveyed for the project and about half of the certificates issued from the mid-1860s to the early 1870s. Detailed lithographic views of the companies' fire engines drawn and printed by Philadelphia lithographer George Heiss (surveyed for the project) during the 1850s preceded the issuance of these certificates. The appearance and popularity of these two genres of prints coincided with the growing civic push to create a paid professional fire department under the administration of the city government.

132. See Mark E. Neely Jr. and Harold Holzer, *The Union Image: Popular Prints of the Civil War North* (Chapel Hill: University of North Carolina Press, 2000), for an overview of the influence of the war on the print market. For an overview of the effect of the war on the social climate of Philadelphia, see J. Matthew Gallman, *Mastering Wartime: A Social History of Philadelphia During the Civil War* (Philadelphia: University of Pennsylvania Press, 2000), and par-

ticularly chap. 5 for the economic effect of the war on the city's tradesmen.

133. Ancestry.com, *U.S. IRS Tax Assessment Lists, 1862–1918* [online database].

134. Sinclair charged different rates for his printing of the lithograph between 1863 and 1865, as follows: 1863 (second printing)—460 impressions at 30 cents; 1864—235 impressions at 39 cents; 1864—468 impressions at 45 cents; and August 1865 (final)—700 impressions at 40 cents. Samuel B. Fales Collection, Correspondence, Box 2, Folder 7, HSP.

135. *Pubic Ledger,* December 18–21, 1861.

136. Henry S. Morais, *The Jews of Philadelphia: Their History from the Earliest Settlements to the Present Time; A Record of Events and Institutions, and of Leading Members of the Jewish Community in Every Sphere of Activity* (Philadelphia: Levytype Co., 1894), 368. Several of these prints are held in the collections of LCP and are cataloged in the online catalog WolfPac, http://pacscl.exlibrisgroup.com:48992/F.

137. The trade card and calendar are included in the specimens album, LCP, P.9349. See Jay T. Last, *The Color Explosion: Nineteenth-Century American Lithography* (Santa Ana, Calif.: Hillcrest Press, 2005), 128, for a reproduction of the later-printed Ketterlinus card.

138. Peter Duval to Albert Newsam, August 30, 1864, Albert Newsam Papers, Box 1, Folder 4, HSP.

139. Gallman, *Mastering Wartime,* 35, and Russell F. Weigley et al., *Philadelphia: A 300-Year History* (New York: W.W. Norton, 1982), 395–96.

140. Articles about the printing of the lithograph appeared in the *Philadelphia Inquirer,* June 15 and 23, 1864, and in *Our Daily Fare,* no. 11, June 20, 1864.

Although the articles did not specify whether a steam press was used, given the large numbers purportedly issued, it most likely was. LCP holds three copies of the print as part of the John A. McAllister Collection compiled by the Philadelphia antiquarian during the Civil War, providing further evidence of the large numbers in circulation at the time.

141. Joseph Jackson, "Some Notes Towards a History of Lithography in Philadelphia," in *The Official Reference Book of the Lithographers International Protective and Beneficial Association, S.A. No. 14 of the United States: 1899* (Philadelphia, 1900), 19, claims without providing a date that John H. Camp operated the first steam lithographic printing press in Philadelphia. No evidence has been found to substantiate this claim.

142. See the notice signed by P.S. Duval and attached to the cover of *Military Magazine and Record of the Volunteers of the City and County* 1 (1839), which notifies subscribers of the price differentials between individual plain and colored plates, with plain at 25 cents and colored at 50 cents each. The price difference for a "number," that is, a set of plates, was $5 for plain and $10 for colored.

143. Freedley, *Leading Pursuits,* 237.

144. Freedley, *Philadelphia and Its Manufactures* (1858), 183.

145. Jeweler Alfred Pharazyn operated a dry-goods store with a print-coloring establishment above. A credit report dated October 25, 1856, describes his "principal" business as "coloring pictures for the publishers," for which it "employs 20 to 30 girls." Pennsylvania, vol. 136, p. 387, R.G. Dun & Co. Collection.

146. Virginia Penny, *Five Hundred Employments Adapted to Women: With the Average Rate of Pay of Each* (Philadelphia: John E. Porter & Co., 1868), 70. Penny discretely identifies the lithographer simply as "B., lithographer, Philadelphia." There are several possibilities, including Lavinia Bowen.

147. See ads placed in the *Public Ledger* by lithographer Alfred Hoffy on October 4, 1845, and colorist Alfred Pharazyn on September 27, 1852.

148. Penny, *Five Hundred Employments*, 69. Little information is available about the rates of pay for colorists. Penny gives the rate of pay for girls ten to twelve years old working for Nathaniel Currier in New York in 1868 as $3–$7 per week. Helena Wright, *With Pen & Graver: Women Graphic Artists Before 1900* (Washington, D.C.: National Museum of American History, 1995), 4, writes that at midcentury young women could earn about 3–10 cents per print, or about $2.50 to $5 a week, at the better establishments.

149. See *Democratic Art* for the most comprehensive work on the history of American chromolithography.

150. Max Rosenthal, *L.N. Rosenthal. Lithographic office, removed to N.W. Cor. of Fifth & Chestnut Sts. Philadelphia* (Philadelphia: L.N. Rosenthal, 1856), POSA 51, LCP, (5) 2526.F.b.

151. Christian Schussele, *P.S. Duval's Colour Printing & Lithographic Establish[ment]. P.S. Duval & Co. Artisan Building Ranstead Place, West from 26 South 4th St. Philadelphia* (Philadelphia: Lith. of P.S. Duval & Co., ca. 1849), POSA 75, Philadelphiana—Lithographers, FLP.

152. The *Philadelphia on Stone* project surveyed 684 lithographs printed between 1850 and 1870—139 of these were chromolithographs (20 percent). In the 1850-to-1860 period, 82 out of 480 prints surveyed were chromolithographs (17 percent). Between 1861 and 1870, 57 out of 204 prints were chromolithographs (28 percent).

153. *Public Ledger*, February 26, 1849. This article, entitled "Improvements in Lithography," gives an account of a dinner held at Duval's lithographic establishment at Ranstead Place for his workers and friends to celebrate the incorporation of steam power in their operations.

154. Freedley, *Leading Pursuits*, 237.

155. [Duval], "Lithography," 278.

156. Michael Twyman, *Printing, 1770–1970: An Illustrated History of Its Development and Uses in England* (London: Eyre & Spottiswoode, 1970), 57.

157. Freedley, *Philadelphia and Its Manufactures* (1867), 547.

158. [Duval], "Lithography," 278, and Blodget, *Industries of Philadelphia*, 23.

159. For census results, see Hershberg, *Philadelphia: Work, Space*, 65. In 1850 there were ninety-three printing and publishing firms in Philadelphia. Lorin Blodget and Edwin T. Freedley, *Philadelphia and Its Industries: A Descriptive Review* (Philadelphia: Press of John D. Avil & Co., 1885). In 1882 there were 263 printing and publishing firms, twenty-nine of which were lithographic establishments.

160. *Public Ledger*, May 8, 1872.

161. In 1878 the Resteins operated from Seventh and Dickinson Streets, having relocated from the 700 block of Federal Street. Jackson, "Notes Towards a History of Lithography," 21.

162. *Philadelphia Inquirer*, January 3, 1866; *Public Ledger*, November 24, 1870; *Philadelphia Inquirer*, September 16, 1872; *North American*, November 1, 1877; and *Philadelphia Inquirer*, March 26–27, 1878.

163. Pennsylvania, vol. 133, p. 275, R.G. Dun & Co. Collection. According to Ketterlinus's 1871–72 credit reports, he owned $250,000–$500,000 in real estate.

164. *Philadelphia Inquirer*, March 26, 1878. Toudy maintained only $20,000 worth of insurance for a lithographic business that specialized in large-format work and operated Hoe steam presses, as advertised on their trade cards issued for the Centennial Exhibition of 1876. In 1876 the average price for a R. Hoe & Co. patent lithographic printing machine with a stone bed of 36 × 52 inches was about $6,200. Large stones cost 12 cents per pound, with an average large stone (32 × 24 × 4 inches) weighing about three hundred pounds. Given the nature of their work and the cost to reequip and rebuild the business, it is no surprise the firm dissolved. See *H.J. Toudy & Co. Practical Lithographers and Publishers, Hoe & Co., Steam Lith. Press,* trade card, 1876, AAS, Graphics Collection; *R. Hoe & Co., Printing Press, Machine & Saw Manufacturers* (New York: R. Hoe & Co., 1876), 17; Theodore Low De Vinne, *The Printers' Price List: A Manual for the Use of Clerks and Book-Keepers in Job Printing Offices* (New York: F. Hart & Co., 1871), 452; and Michael Twyman, "Lithographic Stone and the Printing Trade in the Nineteenth Century," *Journal of the Printing Historical Society* 8 (1972): 35.

165. All of these businesses received good credit reports from R.G. Dun & Co. during the latter 1860s and 1870s, tes-

tifying to their preeminent standing in the trade. Pennsylvania, vol. 141, p. 23; vol. 152, p. 318; vol. 131, p. 284; and vol. 143, p. 295—R.G. Dun & Co. Collection.

166. As reported in the *New York Times,* November 11, 1873, "Blacksmiths, painters . . . lithographers, engravers, and patternmakers are all suffering severely by the falling off in work." Five years later, an article by an unnamed lithographer in the *Printers' Circular* claimed conditions had not much improved: as, "to a large extent, the services of the lithographers were entirely dispensed with, the work of the printer went on, he was the necessity and the lithographer the luxury." *Printers' Circular* 13, no. 3 (May 1878): 51–52.

167. By the early 1880s, Goldsmith's Hall was also tenanted by the stationery and printing firm E.C. Markley & Co. on the fifth and sixth floors, law offices on the first floor, and the chamois-leather business of Haehnlen's son, E.G. Haehnlen & Co., in the basement.

168. *Philadelphia Inquirer,* December 12, 1882, and January 26 and 28, 1886. The value of the equipment and products of the firm was reported as $150,000 and $100,000, respectively, attesting to the financial stability of a partnership able to recover from two high-priced disasters in a short period of time. See also Pennsylvania, vol. 151, p. 188, R.G. Dun & Co. Collection.

169. *Philadelphia Inquirer,* June 9–10, 1874, and Pennsylvania, vol. 133, p. 297, R.G. Dun & Co. Collection. Despite these notices and credit reports as well as billheads with Reyenthaler's name in the Warshaw Collection, the few biographies about Ketterlinus and the

history of the firm do not record Reyenthaler's brief proprietorship of the firm between 1874 and 1876. All known accounts report that John L. Ketterlinus assumed operations of the business in 1875–76 following the retirement of his father.

170. *Report of the Twenty-Seventh Exhibition of American Manufactures: Held in the City of Philadelphia, from October 6th, to November 12th, 1874, by the Franklin Institute, of the State of Pennsylvania, for the Promotion of the Mechanic Arts, 1874* (Philadelphia: Barnard & Jones, printers, 1874), 89.

171. Wainwright, 74. S.C. Duval started his own establishment about 1877 and remained in the trade, including management of lithographer A.L. Weise, until about 1879 at 401 Ranstead Place, and later at 834 Arch Street. HSP holds a trade card for the short-lived firm of Duval. See *Of the Old Firm of P.S. Duval & Son, and Late of Duval & Hunter, S.C. Duval, Lithographer, 401 Ranstead Place, Above Chestnut Street, Philadelphia* (Philadelphia: S.C. Duval, ca. 1877), POSA 66, Trade Card Collection—D, HSP.

172. Pennsylvania, vol. 149, p. 267, R.G. Dun & Co. Collection; Jackson, "Notes Towards a History of Lithography," 21; and Freedley, *Philadelphia and Its Manufactures* (1867), opp. p. 134.

173. "Otto Martin & Co.," in *Industries of Philadelphia* (1881), 65.

174. As overall prices for supplies decreased somewhat, the cost of labor did not. Listings in the 1868 and 1878 editions of *Printers' Circular* show that the average price for plate paper had dropped from about 32 cents per pound in 1866 to 15 cents per pound in 1876 during an era of depression for the industry.

Printers' Circular 13, no. 3 (May 1878): 51–52, and *Democratic Art,* 90–93.

175. De Vinne, *Printers' Price List,* 72.

176. Ibid., 426, and *Philadelphia Inquirer,* December 1, 1862.

177. *Public Ledger,* March 16, 1871.

178. See Penny, *Five Hundred Employments.*

179. *Philadelphia Inquirer,* November 6, 1871.

180. U.S. Bureau of the Census, "Tenth Census of the United States, 1880: Philadelphia, Pennsylvania"; Roll: T9_1167, www.ancestry.com.

181. *McElroy's Philadelphia Directory for 1863.* Godver's listing as "colored" in the city directory may be a misprint. Other genealogical documentation reports Godver as "white," but he resided in a predominantly African American neighborhood during the 1860s.

182. See the lithograph by James S. Reider, *Pennsylvania Institution for the Deaf and Dumb,* copyrighted in 1880 and containing a vignette entitled "The Lithographic Room," LCP, P.8970.24. According to H. Van Allen, *A Brief History of the Pennsylvania Institution for the Deaf and Dumb* (Philadelphia: W.R. Cullingworth, 1893), 32, the first annual report for the school, in 1823, noted that provisions were made for teaching pupils industrial arts. Although such courses received less attention in subsequent years, such training was "never disregarded and the school offered instruction in printing for the past ten years," that is, since 1883. Albert Newsam received training under artist George Caitlin at the institution in the late 1820s, but it is unclear if the school had a formal training program for lithography during that period.

183. Demographic data compiled from a sampling of about three hundred of the

five hundred lithographers identified during the project and the residential addresses of lithographers listed in the Philadelphia business and city directories for the year 1875 served as the sources for this analysis.

184. De Vinne, *Printers' Price List,* 426.

185. Ibid. Although trade journals, such as the *Printers' Circular,* criticized the poor skills of those advancing in the profession, because they were devoid of the proper training, successful lithographers like Louis Prang advocated trade schools as the more appropriate training given the increased mechanization of jobs, such as grinding and wetting stones, which in the past had been performed by apprentices (*Democratic Art,* 170–71). See also Walter Licht, *Getting Work: Philadelphia, 1840–1950* (Cambridge: Harvard University Press, 1992), 99–140, particularly 99–109.

186. *Printers' Circular* 1, no. 8 (October 1866): 103, and no. 10 (December 1866): 131.

187. "Specimens of Printing," *Printers' Circular* 7, no. 10 (August 1872): 213; no. 13 (May 1873): 92; 8, no. 11 (January 1874): 386; 11, no. 12 (February 1877): 330; 12, no. 11 (January 1878): 251; "Degener & Weiler's 'Liberty' Card and Job Presses," *Printers' Circular* 2, no. 10 (December 1867): 350; "Godfrey's Improved India Rubber Roller Compound," *Printers' Circular* 3, no. 4 (June 1868): 120; "The Bronstrup Lithographic Hand Press," *Printers' Circular* 11, no. 4 (June 1876): 107. Product endorsements included Eugene Ketterlinus for Degener, Jacob Haehnlen and George S. Harris for Godfrey, and Thomas Hunter and Geo. S. Harris & Son for Bronstrup.

188. Thomas S. Sinclair to Rice, Goddard & Co., billhead, May 16, 1867, AAS, Graphic Arts Collection; Billheads, Lithography, Vertical Boxes 1, 2, and 4, and Printers & Printing, Vertical Box 11, Warshaw Collection. Boell's financial success during the 1860s can also be gleaned from his 1870s credit reports. See Pennsylvania, vol. 152, p. 92, R.G. Dun & Co. Collection.

189. De Vinne, *Printers' Price List,* 415.

190. The specimens album (LCP, P.9349), cited in note 137 above, demonstrates the massive output of this Jewish firm, established about 1859. The album, probably compiled by a printer once associated with Stein & Jones, contains hundreds of circa-1860s trade-card, banknote, and certificate designs with their imprint, in addition to a calendar issued by the firm, portraits of the lithographers, and several commercial lithographed specimens printed by Philadelphia and Cincinnati firms active during the 1860s, including Haehnlen and Ehrgott & Fohrbriger.

191. Letterheads, Lithography, Vertical Boxes 1, 2, and 4, and Printers & Printing, Vertical Box 11, Warshaw Collection.

192. Ketterlinus Printing House to Riehle Bros., November 8, 1876, Lithography, Vertical Box 1, Warshaw Collection.

193. William Boell to Riehle Bros., Oct. 25, 1879, ibid.

194. Theodore Leonhardt to John M. Miller, June 16, 1877, Lithography, Vertical Box 2, Warshaw Collection.

195. Theodore Leonhardt to John M. Miller, February 4, 1880, ibid.

196. Surveys of the holdings of the collaborating institutions yielded about 350 lithographs for 1866–78 and about 650 for 1851–65.

197. These genres of lithographs, often described as jobbing prints and ephemera, were not surveyed for the project, unless advertisements for Philadelphia lithographers. LCP holds a collection of more than one thousand trade cards predominantly advertising Philadelphia firms that informed the research about the trade during this period.

198. See the advertisement sections of the *Public Ledger,* September 12, 1868; *North American,* September 7, 1869, and May 30, 1870; and *Philadelphia Inquirer,* August 3, 1872. See also "Prominent Lithographers of the United States: John D. Avil," *Lithographers' Journal* 4, no. 3 (March 1893): 52–53. The Geddes firm remained in the lithographic trade until at least 1945, and the Christy and Avil firms until at least the turn of the century.

199. See Stuart Ewen, *Captains of Consciousness: Advertising and the Social Roots of the Consumer Culture* (New York: McGraw-Hill, 1976); Pamela Walker Laird, *Advertising Progress: American Business and the Rise of Consumer Marketing* (Baltimore: Johns Hopkins University Press, 2001); T.J. Jackson Lears, *Fables of Abundance: A Cultural History of Advertising in America* (New York: Basic Books, 1994); and Susan Strasser, *Satisfaction Guaranteed: The Making of the American Mass Market* (New York: Pantheon, 1989).

200. "Art-Lithographers of the United States: Joseph Hoover," *Lithographers' Journal* 5, no. 3 (September 1893): 52–53, and *Democratic Art,* 39–40. According to the *Lithographers Journal,* he issued 600,000–700,000 chromolithographs a year.

201. Edgar Williams, "A History of the Inquirer," *Philadelphia Inquirer,* June 30, 2003. Between 1868 and 1878, James

S. Earle & Sons ran advertisements almost weekly in the *North American* and the *Philadelphia Inquirer.* Although Earle was the most aggressive, a number of looking-glass and frame stores also advertised, including Wilson, Hood & Co.; George C. Reukaff; C.F. Haseltine; and G.W. Pitcher.

202. See *Democratic Art,* 116–29.

203. The National Chromo Company was established in June 1875 by *Christian Voice* proprietor James M. Munyon and in 1876 distributed most of the Resteins' chromolithographs. The unincorporated firm led a financially unstable existence and was acquired by J. Latham & Co. of Boston in 1879. Pennsylvania, vol. 148, p. 410, R.G. Dun & Co. Collection.

204. *Duval & Hunter's Catalogue of Oleograph Publications for the Season 1873–4* (Philadelphia, 1873), Graphic Arts Division, Smithsonian; *National Chromo Co., 927 Chestnut St. Philadelphia, Pa.* (Philadelphia, 1876), Printers & Printing, Vertical Box 1, Warshaw Collection.

205. *North American,* April 10, 1874, and *Wall Street Daily News,* December 1, 1880.

206. Despite the rise of chromolithography, however, separately issued uncolored and tinted lithographs produced between 1866 and 1878 still remained a branch of the Philadelphia industry and outnumbered by about four to one the chromolithographs surveyed. This was no doubt an effect of the Panic and of commercial patrons' requesting cost-cutting measures, that is, less color printing for larger-format prints in the mid-1870s.

207. See note 120 above.

208. Several texts have been written about nineteenth-century advertising in the United States, and the following are just a few that address the effect of lithography on the advertising trade. Nathaniel C. Fowler, *About Advertising and Printing: A Concise, Practical, and Original Manual on the Art of Local Advertising* (Boston: A.M. Thayer & Co., 1889); Robert Jay, *The Trade Card in Nineteenth-Century America* (Columbia: University of Missouri Press, 1987); Last, *Color Explosion;* Lears, *Fables of Abundance;* and Luna Lambert Levison, "Images That Sell: Color Advertising and Boston Printmakers, 1850–1900," in *Aspects of American Printmaking, 1800–1950,* ed. James F. O'Gorman (Syracuse, N.Y.: Syracuse University Press, 1988), 83–103.

209. HSP's trade-card collection includes circa-1885 bookmark and trade-card advertisements for Edward Stern & Co. (established in 1871) that advertise "bookmarkers" and "floral cards" (POSA 26 and 27).

210. Haehnlen advertisements of this nature appeared in *Philadelphia Southern Steamship Manufacturers and Mercantile Register* (Philadelphia: M'Laughlin Brothers, 1866) (POSA 48) and Freedley's *Philadelphia and Its Manufactures* (1867), 546 (POSA 47). Ketterlinus issued a circa-1865 trade card depicting the exterior of his establishment (POSA 21, LCP, P.9349.142f), and Breuker & Kessler commissioned Wenderoth, Taylor, and Brown to photograph their multistory building for inclusion in their advertisement album for hotel lobbies issued about 1871. Wenderoth, Taylor, and Brown album, LCP, P.9059.13.

211. De Vinne, *Printers' Price List,* 205.

212. The Philadelphia Archdiocesan Research Center holds more than twenty circa-1880 Packard & Butler lithographs of exteriors and interiors of Catholic churches. According to an 1882 Dun credit report, the company was established about 1877, employed five artists, received "all the orders they [could] readily fill," had excellent credit, and was valued at $15,000–$18,000. The firm operated until 1885. Pennsylvania, vol. 158, p. 327, R.G. Dun & Co. Collection.

213. *Philadelphia Inquirer,* October 2, 1873.

214. Although lithographers often "borrowed" popular designs from one another, copyright became important for the prints issued for the Centennial. Toudy & Co. filed and prevailed in a copyright infringement case against Breuker & Kessler over a print based on a drawing by exhibition architect Hermann J. Schwarzmann, copyrighted by Toudy in March 1875. U.S. Circuit Court, Eastern District of Pennsylvania, Equity Case File # 49, April Sessions, 1875.

215. Hunter operated twenty-one Bronstrup handpresses in 1876 and was advertised as one of the largest establishments in Philadelphia. *Printers Circular* 11, no. 4 (June 1876): 107. It was said of his work for the Centennial: "no more interesting and imperishable *souvenirs* of the Centennial Exhibition than these pictures will be secured . . . there will be a rush for them in 1876; and the lapse of years must add greatly to their intrinsic value." "Centennial Pictures," *Printers' Circular* 10, no. 6 (August 1875): 155.

216. By 1886, Harris had four hundred employees and capital assets valued at $400,000. In less than ten years, he had added another two hundred em-

ployees, including those of T. Sinclair and Son, purchased in 1889. At the time of his death, in 1893, his estate was worth nearly $440,000. Last, *Color Explosion,* 92–95, 287; Jackson, "Notes Towards a History of Lithography," 21.

217. "International Jury Awards," *Philadelphia Inquirer,* September 28, 1876; "Made Public at Last: The Awards Decreed by the United States Centennial Commission on the Recommendation of the Committee on Appeals—Successful Philadelphia Exhibitors—The State and Vicinity," *Philadelphia Inquirer,* December 4, 1876.

218. *Theo. Leonhardt & Son. Commercial lithography. 324 Chestnut St. Philadelphia.* (Philadelphia: Theo. Leonhardt & Son, May 1, 1876), POSA 98, HSP, Trade Card Collection—L.

219. With the four-volume set advertised at a price of $3,000, or about $250 a print, Kollner considered the lithographs to be fine-art prints. Unfortunately, Kollner misjudged the contemporary market, and the prints were not profitable. See Nicholas B. Wainwright, "Augustus Kollner, Artist," *PMHB* 84 (July 1960): 344.

CHAPTER 2

1. For a discussion of the methods used for drawing on stone in the first half of the nineteenth century, see Michael Twyman, *Lithography, 1800–1850: The Techniques of Drawing on Stone in England and France and Their Application in Works of Topography* (London: Oxford University Press, 1970).

2. Godefroy Engelmann cites an analysis of a piece of lithographic stone in his *Traité théorique et pratique de litho-graphie* (Mulhouse, [1840]). Made by the chemist Henri Schlumberger, it reads: calcium carbonate 97.22%, silica 1.90%, alumina 0.28%, iron oxide 0.46%, waste 0.14%.

3. For a general account of lithographic stone, see Michael Twyman, "Lithographic Stone and the Printing Trade in the Nineteenth Century," *Journal of the Printing Historical Society* 8 (1972): 1–41; and for the development of the stone quarries at Solnhofen, Maria L. Müller-Burger, *Die Solnhofer Plattenkalk-Industrie in Vergangenheit und Gegenwart.* Wirtschafts- und Verwaltungsstudien mit besonderer Berücksichtigung Bayerns 70 (Leipzig: Scholl, 1926).

4. W.E. Swinton, *Fossil Birds,* 2nd ed. (London: British Museum [Natural History], 1965), 13, 17–29, 51.

5. The chemical basis of lithography is thoroughly described in Garo Z. Antreasian and Clinton Adams, eds., *The Tamarind Book of Lithography: Art & Techniques* (Los Angeles: Tamarind Lithography Workshop; New York: Harry N. Abrams, 1971), 255–80.

6. See Philip J. Weimerskirch, "The Beginnings of Lithography in America," *Journal of the Printing Historical Society* 27 (1998): 49–67, particularly 50–56.

7. Twyman, *Lithography,* chap. 6.

8. Ibid., chaps. 7 and 8, for a discussion of the earliest lithographic treatises.

9. A copy of the first edition of Charles Hullmandel's *The Art of Drawing on Stone* (London: C. Hullmandel & R. Ackermann, 1824) must have been in Philadelphia shortly after publication, since it is listed in the 1825 edition of the catalog of LCP.

10. In the early years of the process in Europe it was claimed that as many as ten to twenty thousand impressions could be taken from an ink-drawn stone. See Twyman, *Lithography,* 76–77, 78.

11. For Kollner (1813–1906), see Nicholas B. Wainwright, "Augustus Kollner, Artist," *PMHB* 84 (July 1960): 325–51.

12. For a more detailed discussion of these techniques, see Twyman, *Lithography,* chap. 9.

13. T.H. Fielding, *On the Theory of Painting: To Which Is Added, an Introduction to Painting in Water-Colours* (London: Published for the author by Ackermann & Co., 1842), 136–37; Twyman, *Lithography,* 219–20, 222.

14. John W. Reps, *John Caspar Wild: Painter and Printmaker of Nineteenth-Century Urban America* (St. Louis: Missouri Historical Society Press, 2006), 29–51.

15. Twyman, *Lithography,* 124–27.

16. Ibid., 128–29, 135–38.

17. Exceptionally strong and thin paper made of plant fibers with origins in Asia.

18. See, for example, a note by George Cumberland (Senior) in his *Scenes Chiefly Italian by G. Cumberland* (1821), Yale Center for British Art, Fol A D20, and a note to J.S. Paterson, *Sketches of Scenery in Angus and Mearns* (ca. 1824), Yale Center for British Art, S 497, both of which are quoted extensively in Michael Twyman, "Charles Joseph Hullmandel: Lithographic Printer Extraordinary," in *Lasting Impressions: Lithography as Art,* ed. Pat Gilmour (Canberra: Australian National Gallery, 1988), 69, 70.

19. Charles Hullmandel to Matthew Gregson, December 4, 1820, Gregson Correspondence, Liverpool Record Office, 920 GRE 2/50, quoted in Twyman, "Hullmandel," 63.

20. *Gentleman's Magazine* 92 (November 1822): 398. See also Twyman, "Hullmandel," 70, 72, 365–66 n. 142.

21. Wainwright, 50.

22. Michael Twyman, "The Tinted Lithograph," *Journal of the Printing Historical Society* 1 (1965): 39–56.

23. Ibid., 40, 43–44.

24. Wolfgang Wegner, "'Les Oeuvres Lithographiques' und ihre Entstehungsgeschichte: Ein Beitrag zur Erforschung der Inkunabelzeit der Münchner Lithographie," *Oberbayerisches Archiv* 87 (1965): 139–92.

25. Twyman, "Tinted Lithograph," 46–53; Twyman, *Lithography,* chap. 14.

26. *Charles Oakford & Sons, No. 834 & 836 Chestnut St., Philadelphia. 1866. Wholesale and Retail Dealers and Manufacturers of Hats, Caps & Furs* (Philadelphia: J. Haehnlen, 1866), POSP 25, LCP, P.9465, and *Exterior View of the Tabernacle of the Alexander Presbyterian Church, Rev. Alfred Nevin. D.D. Pastor. N.E. Corner of Nineteenth and Green Streets. Philadelphia.* (Philadelphia: L.N. Rosenthal's lith., ca. 1858), POS 218, HSP, Bb136, A374.

27. Twyman, "Tinted Lithograph," 53–54.

28. For example, many of the plates in D.T. Valentine's *Manual of the Corporation of the City of New York* of the 1850s.

29. For American chromolithography, see *Democratic Art* and Jay T. Last, *The Color Explosion: Nineteenth-Century American Lithography* (Santa Ana, Calif.: Hillcrest Press, 2005).

30. POSP 155.2, LCP, P.9210.11. Print included in the *Philadelphia on Stone* Digital Catalog.

31. See Michael Twyman, *Images en couleur: Godefroy Engelmann, Charles Hullmandel et les débuts de la chromolithographie* (Lyon: Musée de l'imprimerie; Paris: Panama musées, 2007), 34–52, 54, 89, 90.

32. Godefroy Engelmann, *Album chromolithographique, ou Recueil d'essais du nouveau procédé d'impression lithographique en couleurs inventé par Engelmann père & fils à Mulhouse* (Paris: Risler fils; Leipzig: Del Vecchio, 1837).

33. For very early accounts of "engraving on stone," see Twyman, *Lithography,* 77, 91, 101–2, 104–5, 130–31. For later accounts, see Engelmann, *Traité théorique,* 286–90; Alfred Lemercier, *La lithographie française de 1796 à 1896* (Paris: Ch. Lorilleux, [1898]), 127–34; and W.D. Richmond, *The Grammar of Lithography: A Practical Guide for the Artist and Printer in Commercial & Artistic Lithography, & Chromolithography, Zincography, Photo-Lithography, and Lithographic Machine Printing* (London: Wyman & Sons, 1878), 131–39.

34. For a discussion of such views as advertising, see Jennifer Ambrose, "Nineteenth-Century Philadelphia Advertising Prints," in "The Library Company of Philadelphia," special issue, *Antiques,* 170, no. 2 (August 2006): 94–101. The use of lithographically drawn trompe l'oeil frames around several of the larger prints (e.g., figs. 32 and 39) suggests that they were designed to be displayed as surrogates for pictures on walls.

35. Photographs of Philadelphia buildings taken at much the same time as many of the lithographs discussed here reveal the copious use of painted lettering to advertise stores and their products, with some letterforms almost identical to those in William Rease's lithographs. See in particular *Delaware Avenue & Spruce Street,* ca. 1859, from the album "Views of Old Philadelphia Collected by Joseph Y. Jeanes" (reproduced under item 327 in *Jay T. Snider Collection, Featuring the History of Philadelphia and Important Americana* [New York: Bloomsbury Auctions, 2008]).

36. D.M. Henkin, *City Reading: Written Words and Public Spaces in Antebellum New York* (New York: Columbia University Press, 1998).

37. See Nicolete Gray, *Nineteenth Century Ornamented Typefaces,* new ed. with a chapter on ornamented types in America by Ray Nash (London: Faber & Faber, 1976), and Rob Roy Kelly, *American Wood Type, 1828–1900* (1969; repr., New York: Da Capo Press, 1977).

38. The lithographic artist and letterer Matthias Weaver (1816–47) is known to have lettered some stones for Rease and the printer Thomas Sinclair in the early 1840s. Entries in Weaver's diaries suggest that Rease did not normally do his own lettering, at least at this stage: "spent the rest of the day lettering for Rease" (October 2, 1843) and "Lettered Rease's Stone for him" (October 3, 1843). Matthias S. Weaver Diaries, 1840–43, Ohio Historical Society, Columbus, Ohio. Information kindly supplied by Sarah Weatherwax, LCP.

39. Warshaw Collection. One set of documents relates to a consignment of 32 stones in 11 cases, to the value of 1,710.64 marks, which was supplied by Jacob & Wilhelm Arauner of Solnhofen to A. Hirsch of Philadelphia in 1886. Another relates to a shipment of 264 stones in 43 cases, to the value of 2,962.70 marks, and weighing about ten thousand kilograms gross, supplied by C. Daeschler of Munich to A.J. Uffenheimer & Co. of Philadelphia in 1885–86. Details of the sizes and quali-

ties of the stones are given by Twyman, "Lithographic Stone," 39 n. 2.

40. The idea of using metal plates as a substitute for stone was proposed initially by Senefelder in his English patent specification of 1801 (2518). He used them in Paris from around 1818, as did other printers from time to time, particularly from the 1840s. Zinc was the preferred metal at the time, but it was used for maps, music, and similar line work rather than quality crayon drawing.

41. Wainwright, 26.

42. For sizes of large stones, see Twyman, "Lithographic Stone," 35–36; and for "American quality" stones, ibid., 38 n. 4.

43. Philip J. Weimerskirch, "Lithographic Stone in America," *Printing History* 11, no. 1 (1989): 2–15.

44. *Democratic Art,* 65.

45. Ibid., 91.

46. For a survey of lithographic hand-presses, see Michael Twyman, "The Lithographic Hand Press, 1796–1850," *Journal of the Printing Historical Society* 3 (1967): 3–50.

47. See ibid., 41–44, for a discussion of the output of such presses.

48. For example, as illustrated on a bill-head of the F.F. Oakley Lithographic Company of Boston in the late 1850s (*Democratic Art,* fig. 10); in the *Lithographers' Journal* 1, no. 2 (October 1891) (*Democratic Art,* fig. 15); and on trade advertisements of P.S. Duval of 1858 (POSA 70, LCP, Dir Phila 1858 [63] 10840.O.frontispiece) and Wagner & McGuigan, ca. 1855 (POSA 115.1, LOC, Unprocessed in PR 13 CN 1997:105).

49. Advertisement of Wagner & Mc-Guigan, *Wagner & McGuigan's Lithographic Establishment for Drawing Lettering & Printing No. 116 Chesnut [sic] St. Philadelphia,* ca. 1847, POSA 113, Harry T. Peters America on Stone Collection, Division of Home and Community Life, Smithsonian (DL *60 3081), illustrated in *Democratic Art,* fig. 5.

50. There is some evidence that French wooden presses were in the United States in the early days of lithography. Charles Hart, an Englishman who was apprenticed as a lithographer to George and William Endicott in New York from 1839 to 1844 and later had his own lithographic business, included a drawing of a wooden press in his manuscript memoirs ("Lithography, Its Theory and Practice, Including a Series of Short Sketches of the Earliest Lithographic Artists, Engravers, and Printers of New York," Lithographic Records, Manuscript Division, New York Public Library). He described it as an "old French Star wheel press," on which he printed D'Avignon's portrait of Henry Clay in 1844. What is almost certainly the oldest surviving wooden lithographic press of this kind anywhere was brought to Mexico from Europe by the Italian artist Claudio Linati in 1825. It was still in use for demonstration purposes in the early 1970s. See Michael Twyman, *Early Lithographed Music* (London: Farrand Press, 1996), pl. 56. The press belongs to the Fundación Armando Birlain and until May 2010 was on display in the Museo Cultural de Artes Gráficas, Mexico City.

51. Twyman, "Lithographic Hand Press," 35–37, fig. 45.

52. Alois Senefelder, *Vollständiges Lehrbuch der Steindruckerey* (Munich: Thienemann; Vienna: Gerold, 1818), 225; Senefelder, *A Complete Course of Lithography: Containing Clear and Explicit Instructions in All the Different Branches and Manners of That Art* (London: R. Ackerman, 1819), 180; Senefelder, *The Invention of Lithography,* trans. J.W. Muller from the 1821 edition of *Vollständiges Lehrbuch der Steindruckerey* (New York: Fuchs & Lang Manufacturing Co., 1911), 154.

53. Twyman, "Lithographic Hand Press," 46–49.

54. Ibid., 49.

55. Maclure, Macdonald & Macgregor of London were referred to as using a self-acting machine from Vienna, which ran at 800 impressions an hour (Robert Hunt, "Lithography, and Other Novelties in Printing," *Art-Journal* [1854]: 2), and in February 1854 the firm placed an advertisement in the *Journal of the Society of Arts* (three insertions) claiming they were "lithographers by steam-power." Sigl's steam-powered machines were mentioned specifically in another publication of the same year (J. Timbs, *The Year-Book of Facts in Science and Art* [London: David Bogue, 1854], 113–14). They were described as "now successfully worked in England by Messrs. Maclure, Macdonald & Co." and as being run at 800 to 1,000 impressions an hour (about 700 for large folio formats) by the Imperial Printing Office in Vienna.

56. [P.S. Duval], "Lithography," in *American Encyclopaedia of Printing,* ed. J.L. Ringwalt (Philadelphia: Menamin & Ringwalt / J.B. Lippincott, 1871), 279. See also note 153 to chapter 1 above.

57. A notice in the *Public Ledger,* February 21, 1850, confirms that Wagner & McGuigan were using steam power to drive their presses at about the same

time as Duval, and possibly earlier: "Lithographic Printing by steam—We have received from Messrs. Wagner & McGuigan, Lithographers, a copy of a print of the Lord's Supper, which has been executed by the first lithographic steam power printing machine ever successfully invented. All the operations of printing are performed by the machine, a feed-boy only being required. It will accomplish more work in one day than a dozen handpresses would, and do it well, as the print before us is a proof. Measures have been taken to secure a patent for the machine." No patent seems to have been secured, possibly because it was not as described in the *Public Ledger.* It is almost as though this account was based on one of the presses illustrated (middle right) on Wagner & McGuigan's advertisement, which shows a boy feeding a power-assisted press but does not indicate the means of dampening and inking the stone, either by hand or machine. *Wagner & McGuigan's Steam Lithographic Printing Establishment, No. 4 Athenian Buildings Franklin Place Philadelphia,* ca. 1855 (POSA 115.1, LOC, Unprocessed in PR 13 CN 1997:105).

58. U.S. patents 22,519 (January 4, 1859), 42,125 (March 29, 1864).

59. U.S. patent 32,372 (July 2, 1861).

60. U.S. patent 43,796 (August 9, 1864).

61. [Duval], "Lithography," 278. Duval refers to Huguet as "Eugues," which suggests that his source was spoken language. Huguet & Vaté were granted a French patent (9262, April 26, 1853), and Huguet (represented by Mathieu) another for improvements to lithographic presses (French patent 45571, June 12, 1860). Vaté had already taken

out a patent for a cylinder press that could be steam driven (French patent 1895, February 23, 1846).

62. *Democratic Art,* 84.

63. Ibid., 84–87.

64. [Duval], "Lithography," 278.

65. *La typologie Tucker* I (1876): 681.

66. The process involved drawing on stone with washes of lithographic ink in varying strengths and had been patented by the English printer Charles Hullmandel (English patent 8683, November 5, 1840). The lithotint referred to in the text, the first to be produced in the United States, was drawn by John H. Richard and printed by P.S. Duval in Philadelphia. It was published as *Grandpapa's Pet* in *Miss Leslie's Magazine* 7 (April 1843): 113 (POSP 99, LCP, P.2005.18.39) along with an article "The New Art of Lithotint" (see fig. 63). See *Democratic Art,* 126, 252–53; and for the process, Twyman, *Lithography,* 145–53.

67. See note 32 to chapter 1.

CHAPTER 3

1. "Summary," *New York Observer and Chronicle,* January 31, 1856, 39.

2. Unless otherwise noted, all works illustrated or discussed in this essay are by James Queen, from his archive in the Carson Collection, Prints & Photographs Division, LOC. Also listed in the captions are the item numbers in the catalogue raisonné in Carl Malcolm Cochran, "James Fuller Queen—Artist and Lithographer" (master's thesis, University of Pittsburgh, 1954; hand-annotated carbon copy in the Carson Collection). Lithographs first referenced by Wainwright are marked with their updated POS item numbers

in parentheses in the text and captions. Updated Wainwright information can also be found online at http://www.librarycompany.org/pos/index.htm.

3. Cochran, "Queen," 5. See also Carl Malcolm Cochran, "James Queen: Philadelphia Lithographer," *PMHB* 82 (April 1958): 139–75, which is based on the author's master's thesis. All Cochran references are to the thesis rather than the article.

4. James Queen after Anthonie Jacobus van Wyngaerdt, *Home Sweet Home* (Philadelphia: Duval & Hunter, 1871), PGA—Duval—Home Sweet Home (C size), LC-USZC4-2056. James Queen, *Baltimore Convention, Old Tippecanoe, A Patriotic Song* ([Philadelphia?]: Leopold Meignen & Co. Publishers & Importers of Music, 1840). Printed by P.S. Duval. M1665.W4 O c-MUSIC, LC-USZ62-91863. See also fig. 57.

5. The majority of the drawings and prints in the Carson Collection are undated, but a range of dates has been established based on Queen's use of particular papers, media, and styles. No items from the post–Civil War era have been found in the Carson Collection.

6. Interview with Marian Carson, September 16, 1996, cited in Harry Katz, "Prints and Drawings," in *Gathering History: The Marian S. Carson Collection of Americana,* ed. Sara Day (Washington, D.C.: Library of Congress, 1999), 85, 95.

7. Day, *Gathering History,* vi–vii; Cochran, "Queen," 1; Carson Collection Case File, Prints and Photographs Division, LOC.

8. James Queen, Year 1886, Will 102, Register of Wills, City Hall, Philadelphia. In 1886 Queen bequeathed six books to his sister Henrietta Andrews. LCP

holds the complete transcription of the Queen will in the *Philadelphia on Stone* lithographer research files.

9. Cochran, "Queen," 4–5. Francis Queen claimed to have been self-educated, but given his rise in the publishing world, that claim may not have been entirely true. See *Dictionary of Literary Biography,* s.v. "Queen, Frank," http://www.bookrags.com/biography/frank-queen-dlb/5.html.

10. According to the 1850 Population Census for Pennsylvania, Southwark, 2nd Ward, John, James, and Francis were all married.

11. *Dictionary of Literary Biography,* s.v. "Queen, Frank."

12. Bruce Laurie, *Working People of Philadelphia, 1800–1850* (Philadelphia: Temple University Press, 1980); Laurie, "Fire Companies and Gangs in Southwark, the 1840s," in *The Peoples of Philadelphia: A History of Ethnic Groups and Lower-Class Life, 1790–1940,* ed. Allen F. Davis and Mark H. Haller (Philadelphia: Temple University Press [1973]), 71–87; Susan G. Davis, "'Making Night Hideous': Christmas Revelry and Public Order in Nineteenth-Century Philadelphia," *American Quarterly* 34 (Summer 1982): 185–99.

13. 1860 Population Census, Pennsylvania, Philadelphia, 8th Ward, 1st Precinct; 1864 U.S. IRS Tax Assessment Lists, District 2, Pennsylvania. Exceptional personal property, including watches, pianos, horse-drawn carriages, and silver, required an additional tax payment. Queen's only exceptional personal property was his watch.

14. Laurie, "Fire Companies and Gangs," 75, 78–80. The two groups had formed the same company until 1842, when disagreements over temperance led to an internal dispute that divided it into two.

15. John Rubens Smith, a British-born artist who worked for a number of years in Philadelphia, created a certificate for the Philadelphia Association for the Relief of Disabled Firemen between 1830 and 1840. PR 13 CN 1996:023, no. 3. Currier & Ives created two series of nonsatirical firefighting prints, *The American Fireman* (1858) and *The Life of a Fireman* (1854–66), Prints and Photographs Division, LOC. Sara W. Duke, "'Always Ready': The American Fireman as Historic and Cultural Icon," *Library of Congress Information Bulletin* 61 (Sept. 2002), http://www.loc.gov/loc/lcib/0209/firemen.html.

16. The Carson Collection does not have the final lithograph. The print is held by HSP, Bc72 Q3A, and LCP, Wainwright Collection, Prints & Photographs Department *P.2189. http://www.librarycompany.org/pos/index.htm.

17. James Queen and his family had friends at the Navy Yard, one of whom, Bernard Fitzsimons, a merchant, signed the consent for Queen's apprenticeship to Lehman & Duval. When Queen married, in 1843, his brother Francis sent him a letter in the care of Fitzsimons at the Navy Yard. Cochran, "Queen," 6–8.

18. "Fall of a Wharf in Philadelphia," *New York Daily Times,* July 3, 1856, 8.

19. Wainwright, 38, 73–74; Peter Duval to Albert Newsam, August 30, 1864, LCP, cited in Wainwright, 73.

20. I. Schmolze and J. Queen, [*Diploma of the Philadelphia Society for Promoting Agriculture . . . at the Annual Exhibition Held at Powelton, Philada. Sept. 1860*], lithograph, 1860.

21. P.S. Duval & Son, *P.S. Duval & Son's Lithographic Establishment, S.W. Corner of 5th & Minor Sts. (near Chestnut.) Philadelphia* (Philadelphia: P.S. Duval & Son, ca. 1861), POSA 121, LCP, BW—Advertisements—D (2)5786.F.121a. My thanks to Erika Piola for bringing this lithograph and its reference to Queen to my attention.

22. Cochran, "Queen," 4, 104. Cochran interviewed Queen's granddaughter Mary Queen Davis, who provided him with most of the information on Queen's family history and personal goals.

23. *Entrance of Delaware Water Gap* (graphite on cream paper), 1850; *Delaware Water Gap* (graphite on cream paper), 1850; *Delaware Water Gap* (chromolithograph, published in Philadelphia by Ibbotson & Queen, [ca. 1856], PGA—Ibbotson & Queen–Delaware Water Gap (C size), LC-DIG-pga-03859 (digital file from original print).

24. Although Queen had created military work before the Civil War, especially his 1840 lithograph *Camp Wayne, Pennsylvania Volunteer Encampment on the Paoli Battle Ground, Sept. 19th, 20th, 21st, 22nd 1840* (*U.S. Military Magazine,* vol. 1, P.S. Duval Lith. Philada. [Philadelphia: Huddy & Duval, ca. 1840]), his Civil War work is based on personal experience.

25. Biographical/Historical Notes, Civil War Volunteer Saloons and Hospitals Ephemera Collection Finding Aid, McA 5778.F, LCP, May 2006, 5–6; Russell F. Weigley, et al., *Philadelphia: A 300-Year History* (New York: W.W. Norton & Co., 1982), 399; *Ladies' Repository* 36 (1876): 312.

26. *Citizens Volunteer Hospital, Corner of Broad St. and Washington Avenue,* chromolithograph, ca. 1863. Printed in colors by P.S. Duval & Son. This example is filled out and dated March 2, 1863. LC-DIG-ppmsca-19649.

27. *Citizens Volunteer Hospital Association of Philadelphia, Instituted September 5, 1862, Erected September 5th 1862, for Temporary Relief of Sick and Wounded Soldiers, Arriving in and Passing through Philadelphia. Closed, August 9th, 1865,* lithograph, ca. 1865, printed by P.S. Duval & Son, lith., Phila. LC-DIG-ppmsca-19653. http://www.librarycompany.org/pos/index.htm.

28. *Lookout Mountain, Tenn.,* chromolithograph mounted on gray wove paper, ca. 1863; *John Clem: A Drummer Boy of 12 Years of Age Who Shot a Rebel Colonel upon the Battle Field of Chickamauga, Ga., Sept. 20, 1863,* lithograph, from the series Album Sketches of the Great Southern Campaign (Philadelphia: P.S. Duval & Son, ca. 1863), Cochran 504; [*Ulysses S. Grant in Uniform*], chromolithograph, proof before letters, n.d., Cochran 924; *Champions of Liberty,* lithograph with tint stones (Philadelphia: P.S. Duval & Son, 1865), Cochran 506.

29. *Old John Brown's Career Illustrated,* F.J. Pilliner, n.d., chromolithograph, presented to the yearly subscribers of the *Philadelphia Weekly* (all over the land) by E.S. Dean, publisher and proprietor, 337 Chestnut St., Philadelphia, Pa., Cochran 441; *The Volunteers in Defence of the Government Against Usurpation 1861,* chromolithograph (Philadelphia: P.S. Duval & Son, 1861), Cochran 317; *Great Central Fair for the United States Sanitary Commission, Philadelphia, June 1864,* lithograph

with tint stones, printed by P.S. Duval & Son; *The Story of Gettysburg,* watercolor drawing on white wove paper, [ca. 1863], Cochran 113.

30. *War Roll for the Weccacoe Fire Company, Always Useful—Fireman in Peace—Soldiers in War,* graphite, [1862 or 1863?], LC-DIG-ppmsca-19648.

31. Peter Duval to Albert Newsam, August 30, 1864, LCP, cited in Wainwright, 73.

32. *Done Up,* lithograph, n.d. [but between 1845 and 1863], Cochran 307.

33. James Queen after H.L. Stephens, [*The Adventures of a Conscript as Told by Himself*] ([Philadelphia], 1863), copyrighted by William A. Stephens, Cochran 1002, unprocessed in PR 13 CN 1997:105 [item]; James Queen after H.L. Stephens (?), [*Sheet of Birds, Perhaps Trading Cards, Uncut, 25 Birds in All, but Numbers up to 30*] ([Philadelphia?], ca. 1860s?), Cochran 1004; James Queen after H.L. Stephens, [*Journey of a Slave from the Plantation to the Battlefield*] ([Philadelphia], ca. 1863), PGA—Queen–Journey of a slave (B size), LC-DIG-ppmsca-05453; James Queen after H.L. Stephens, *Stephens's Album Drolleries No. 1.: Our Relations at Home and Abroad* (Philadelphia: W.A. Stephens, 1863), LCP, Print Department, Henry Lewis Stephens Collection [5780 .F.55a-l].

34. 1860 Population Census, Pennsylvania, Philadelphia, 1st Ward, 8th Precinct, June 22. The document records James F. Queen as a designer living with his wife, Sarah (Sally), and children Emma, Mary, and Elizabeth, as well as Elizabeth Harvey and Albert Henry. Cochran, "Queen," 8. Cochran states that Sally took in two nephews when her sister and her sister's husband died within a year of each other, but only

one nephew is listed in the 1860 census. Another of Sally's sisters, Elizabeth, remained with the family for her entire life. Queen's income was sufficient for him to own a home worth $1,800 and personal property worth $400 that year.

35. [*Interior Domestic Scene, with a Woman Ironing*], charcoal and ink wash drawing on paper pressed with metal plate, December 11, 1857, LC-DIG-ppmsca-19638.

36. 1870 Population Census, Pennsylvania, Philadelphia, 3rd Division, June 21. The government record lists James F. Queen as a lithographic artist, living with children Emma, a teacher, and Lizzie, as well as Elizabeth Harvey, housekeeper.

37. 1880 Population Census, Pennsylvania, Philadelphia, 7th Ward, June 2: James F. Queen is recorded as a chromo artist, living with children Emma, a teacher, and Elizabeth, a piano teacher, as well as Elizabeth Harvey and an African American servant, Barbarie Denney. 1880 Population Census, Philadelphia, 11 June: Peter Duval is listed as a boarder living with Joseph Breece and his wife, Harriet, and their daughters Ellen and Lizzie. It is clear from the will of James Queen that he had loaned his former employers money and that his estate had the resources to cancel the debt.

38. Cochran, "Queen," 5; "City and Surburban News," *New York Times,* November 26, 1882, 7.

39. James Queen, Year 1886, Will 102, Register of Wills, City Hall, Philadelphia; *Gopsill's Philadelphia City Directory for 1890* (Philadelphia: James Gopsill's Sons, 1890). Even Rebecca Queen, widow of Francis Queen, had

moved in with her brother-in-law after the death of her husband: 1890 United States Census, Pennsylvania, Philadelphia, 1st Ward.

40. The latest work LOC has attributed to James Queen is *Knights of Pythias Knightly Brother Certificate* (Philadelphia: T. Hunter, 1875), copyrighted by S.S. Davis, PAGA 7, no. 1983 (E size), although publisher Joseph Hoover's award-winning chromolithographs of the Centennial Exhibition of 1876 are also attributed to Queen. Cited in *Democratic Art*, 39. Hoover published the prints without an attribution, and Queen did not sign the stone, but as Hoover was not an artist himself, it is likely that Queen created the images.

41. 1880 Population Census, Pennsylvania, Philadelphia, 7th Ward, June 2, 1880.

42. James Queen, *The Baptism of Christ* (Philadelphia: Duval & Hunter, 1873), PGA—Queen, James–Baptism of Christ (C size), LC-DIG-pga-04060 (digital file from original print).

43. James Queen, *Home Sweet Home* (Philadelphia: Duval & Hunter, 1871), PGA—Duval–Home Sweet Home (C size), LC-DIG-pga-03675 (digital file from original print).

44. *Democratic Art*, 176.

45. Cochran, "Queen," 5 and 9–10, describes the cause of death as "cerebro-spinal sclerosis," now known as multiple sclerosis.

CHAPTER 4

1. Until the publication of this work, Wainwright contained the most extensive biography of Peter S. Duval. See Wainwright, 30–45 and 61–74.

2. [P.S. Duval], "Lithography," in *American Encyclopaedia of Printing*, ed. J.L. Ringwalt (Philadelphia: Menamin & Ringwalt / J.B. Lippincott & Co., 1871), 282.

3. City of Philadelphia, Department of Records, City Archives, RG 130.3 Mayor's Court, Naturalization Declaration Docket, 1814–38.

4. See chapter 1 in this book.

5. *National Gazette,* September 13, 1832.

6. John McAllister Papers, 001, Box 2, Folder 165. HSP.

7. Ibid.

8. *Pennsylvania Inquirer and Daily Courier,* November 7, 1837.

9. See chapter 5 in this book for a discussion of lithographic plates in books, including the work done by Lehman & Duval for these publications.

10. Approximately 15 percent of a sample of three hundred lithographers identified through the *Philadelphia on Stone* survey were associated with Duval at some point in their careers.

11. See chapter 3 in this book for a discussion of Queen's life and career.

12. See Georgia Brady Bumgardner, "George and William Endicott: Commercial Lithography in New York, 1831–51," in *Prints and Printmakers of New York State, 1825–1940,* ed. David Tatham (Syracuse: Syracuse University Press, 1986), 47, for a discussion of the division of labor in a lithographic shop. Queen's promotion to superintendent was announced in a Duval advertisement now in the collection of LCP (BW—Advertisements—D (2)5786.F.121a).

13. See Nicholas B. Wainwright, "The Age of Nicholas Biddle, 1825–1841," in *Philadelphia: A 300-Year History,* by Russell Frank Weigley et al. (New York: W.W. Norton & Co., 1982), particularly 301–6, for an overview of how the economic turmoil affected Philadelphia.

14. Naturalization Declaration Docket, 1814–38. Duval became a naturalized U.S. citizen on May 29, 1841 (www.ancestry.com).

15. For a general introduction to the topic of Philadelphia's French community, see Francis James Dallett, "The French in Philadelphia: The French Benevolent Society of Philadelphia," in *Invisible Philadelphia: Community Through Voluntary Organizations,* ed. Jean Barth Toll and Mildred S. Gillam (Philadelphia: Atwater Kent Museum, 1995), 78–82.

16. Francis James Dallett Papers, Series 3, Box 17, Folders 1 and 2. HSP.

17. Ibid., Folder 1.

18. Ibid.

19. Ibid., Folder 19. While most of the names appearing on the membership rolls of both of these organizations are clearly French, a few names, including "G. Lehman" (which may indicate Duval's partner, George Lehman), indicate that membership was not limited to only those of French descent.

20. "Liberty for Europe—Immense Demonstration," *Public Ledger,* April 25, 1848.

21. "Reception to M. De Lesseps," *Philadelphia Inquirer,* March 8, 1880.

22. Grand Lodge of Free and Accepted Masons of Pennsylvania, Grand Secretary, Membership Book 2-1, p. 183.

23. See "Odd Fellows Certificate," *Public Ledger,* August 25, 1857, for a description of the certificate printed by Duval. HSP's collection includes an invitation to an I.O.O.F. ball (Ba 61 D 956c).

24. Thomas Phenix, *Masonic Memorial* (Philadelphia: s.n., 1860).

25. "Murder and Suicide," *Public Ledger,* June 3, 1844.

26. In 1853 Eugene Roussel was listed on the ballot as the sole candidate for treasurer of the society. Dallett Papers, Series 3, Box 17, Folder 1.

27. Ibid.

28. Jayne K. Kribbs, comp. and ed., *An Annotated Bibliography of American Literary Periodicals, 1741–1850* (Boston: G.K. Hall, 1977), 131. A digital copy of the *Parlour Review* in the collection of Harvard is available on Google Books.

29. *Orchardist's Companion* 1 (April 1841): unpaginated prefatory remarks. For general information about botanical lithography, see Elizabeth Mosimann, "'The Useful and Beautiful': 19th-Century Botanical Lithography in Philadelphia," *Imprint: Journal of the American Historical Print Collectors Society* 12 (Autumn 1987): 12–20.

30. *Pennsylvania Inquirer and Daily Courier,* September 10, 1841.

31. *Military Magazine and Record of the Volunteers of the City and County* 1 (March 1839): preface.

32. Undated letter attached to LCP's copy of vol. 1 of *Military Magazine and Record of the Volunteers of the City and County.* This letter provides pricing information different from that appearing in the periodical itself. According to the letter, a year's subscription containing colored prints cost $10, while one with black-and-white illustrations cost half that price. Separately issued colored plates cost 50 cents each; black-and-white 25 cents.

33. Cadwalader Family Papers, Series VII: General George Cadwalader, Box 22, "Financial papers, receipted bills, 1842–1847." HSP.

34. Twelfth Census of the United States, 1900.

35. *The Mercantile Register, or Business Man's Guide* (Philadelphia: H. Orr, 1846), 198.

36. Fourteen advertisements for Duval's business were among the prints surveyed in the *Philadelphia on Stone* project, the largest number of advertisements for any Philadelphia lithographer. The longevity of Duval's career probably accounts for the large number.

37. A view of the exterior of Duval's shop appears on a piece of early 1840s pictorial stationery in LCP's collection. See note 32 above.

38. Peter S. Duval to Levi Morris, billhead, October 9, 1839, AAS, Graphic Arts Collection. For examples of textual references, see *Mercantile Register,* and the lithograph, *Girard College. Main Building.* in LCP's collection (P.2057).

39. *Public Ledger,* July 29, 1840.

40. *Public Ledger,* July 25, 26, and 27, 1842.

41. "To Be Let," *Public Ledger,* April 6, 10, 11, and 12, 1848.

42. "Improvements in Lithography," *Public Ledger,* February 26, 1849.

43. "Lithography and Zincography," *Public Ledger,* June 21, 1849. Frederick Bourquin is identified as Duval's partner from about 1852 to 1857 in court documents regarding Duval's 1859 insolvency hearing. See City of Philadelphia, Department of Records, City Archives, RG 20, Insolvency Petitions of the Common Pleas Court, Philadelphia County, Box A-175, Peter S. Duval, 1859.

44. "Improvements in Lithography," *Public Ledger,* February 26, 1849.

45. See chapter 2 in this book.

46. [Duval], "Lithography," 282–83.

47. "The Art Union," *Public Ledger,* October 8, 1852.

48. [Duval], "Lithography," 283.

49. Wainwright, 42.

50. In 1850 everyone living with Peter Duval shared the last name Orr, with the exception of two young adults who were probably servants. Stephen Orr, listed as an eighteen-year-old lithographer, is most likely Stephen C. Duval. Searches through Philadelphia directories and later censuses failed to find any additional references to any of the Orr family members (including Stephen Orr). In 1860 Peter and Stephen Duval were living with a Dr. Addinell Hewson, the Hewson family, and a few servants. No information could be found about Duval's wife or any other surviving children. 1850 Population Census, Pennsylvania, Philadelphia, South Ward, and 1860 Population Census, Pennsylvania, Philadelphia, 8th Ward.

51. "Fine Winter Scene," *Public Ledger,* July 1, 1853.

52. "The City News," *Saturday Courier,* April 30, 1842.

53. Harry T. Peters, *America on Stone: The Other Printmakers to the American People* (Garden City, N.Y.: Doubleday, 1931), 131. No primary source has been found to corroborate this information.

54. "Destructive Conflagration—Great Loss—Firemen Injured, &c," *Daily Pennsylvanian,* April 12, 1856.

55. Rembrandt Peale to Anna Atwood, August 24, 1859, Charles Coleman Sellers Files, APS.

56. Ibid.

57. Ibid. Three years later Peale may still have owed money from this transaction with Duval, since he is listed in Duval's 1859 insolvency court documents as owing Duval $17.90. See Insolvency Petitions, Duval, 1859.

58. *North American,* June 28, 1856.

59. Wainwright, 70, states that Stephen Duval had served an apprenticeship with his father and had spent three years in Paris studying the lithographic trade before becoming his father's partner, but offers no source for this information.

60. Insolvency Petitions, Duval, 1859. I want to express my gratitude to historian Donna Rilling and Jefferson Moak, former archivist at the Philadelphia City Archives, who brought this material to my attention.

61. Ibid. The role of agents in distributing Duval prints deserves additional research. The late Thomas Beckman, registrar of the Historical Society of Delaware, found evidence that Louisville, Kentucky, engraver and lithographer Henry Miller acted as Duval's authorized agent by 1857, but the source of that information is unclear. An H. Miller & Co. of Louisville is listed in the court documents as owing Duval $261.34, a separate listing from the money owed by the unspecified "Agents."

62. In 1859 $25 had the equivalent purchasing power of $676 in 2010; $10 had purchasing power of $271. See http://measuringworth.com/ppowerus/result.php.

63. These men were Cornelius Dinneen, L[ouis] Leitz, V[ictor] Lowenberg, H[enry] Charbonnier, and William Kelly. In the middle of this list were the names of two other men, F[rancis] Lawton and H[enry] Morris, also identified as lithographers, who probably were also owed wages. Insolvency Petitions, Duval, 1859.

64. Ibid. Other lithographic artists listed as creditors included A[lphonse] Bigot, W[illiam] H. Rease, and Christian Schussele.

65. Insolvency Petitions, Duval, 1859.

66. See *Democratic Art,* 28–31, for a discussion of the Schoolcraft project and the failure of the chromolithographs to please the author, the artist, or the publisher.

67. *Accounts of the Late Superintendent of Public Printing,* 35th Cong., 2nd Sess., H.R. Report No. 189, February 28, 1859.

68. Joseph O. Pyatt, *Memoir of Albert Newsam* (Philadelphia: Printed for the author, 1868), 147.

69. "Mr. Nott tells me this morning that you wanted to rent a room in his house," wrote Duval. "I have no objection if this is agreeable to you but I think it is against your interest both in point of expenses and in the employment of your time. . . . This is my opinion as a friend that wishes your interest to be guarded but if you desire in tacking [*sic*] the room I will let you do as you please and send the stones [there?]." Note on verso of P.2005.2.16, *Portrait Prints, LCP.

70. Albert Newsam to Peter Duval, March 22, 1864, John McAllister Papers, 003, Box 1, Folder 4, and Albert Newsam to Peter Duval, November 11, 1862, John McAllister Papers, 001, Box 2, Folder 165, LCP on deposit at HSP.

71. Peter Duval to Albert Newsam, August 30, 1864, Albert Newsam Papers, Box 1, Folder 4, LCP on deposit at HSP.

72. Ibid.

73. May 7, 1860, billhead for Duval, Williams & Duval, private collection of David Doret.

74. Peter Duval to Albert Newsam, August 30, 1864, Albert Newsam Papers, Box 1, Folder 4, LCP on deposit at HSP.

75. *Philadelphia Inquirer,* June 21, 1864.

76. Articles about the printing and sale of the lithograph appeared in the *Philadelphia Inquirer,* June 2, 15, and 23, 1864, and in *Our Daily Fare,* no. 11, June 20, 1864.

77. Entry dated July 19, 1861, Pennsylvania, vol. 135, p. 320w, R.G. Dun & Co. Collection.

78. "The Japanese Embassy—Visit to the Custom House Stores, Glass Works &c," *Public Ledger,* June 16, 1860. Perhaps some embassy delegates were familiar with Duval's printing of the illustrations for the U.S. government reports on Commodore Matthew Perry's 1853 trip to Japan. All of that work was destroyed in the 1856 fire.

79. *Public Ledger,* February 11, 1856, and Lorin Blodget, *The Industries of Philadelphia as Shown by the Manufacturing Census of 1870, Compared with 1860 and Estimates for 1875* (Philadelphia: Collins, printer, 1876), 23. [Duval], "Lithography," 278.

80. One-third of the Duval lithographs surveyed for 1859–69 were certificates. See chapter 1 in this book.

81. *Description of the Print Entitled Washington's Triumphal Entry, New York, Nov. 25th, 1783* (Philadelphia: J.B. Chandler, printer, 1861), 3.

82. Nobody with the last name Swander is listed in Philadelphia directories during this time period. There are too many Williamses listed, none of whom is identified as a lithographer, to be able conclusively to identify the Williams involved with the Duval firm.

83. Pennsylvania, vol. 135, p. 320w, R.G. Dun & Co. Collection.

84. "Centennial of Senefelder," *Philadelphia Inquirer,* August 18, 1871, and November 7, 1871.

85. See *Duval & Hunter's Catalogue of Oleograph Publications for the Season 1873–4* (Philadelphia, 1873), Graphic Arts Division, Smithsonian.

86. Entry dated September 18, 1874, Pennsylvania, vol. 152, p. 318, R.G. Dun & Co. Collection.

87. The entry dated July 23, 1874, ibid., reports the dissolution of Duval & Hunter and says that Duval "talks of going to Richmond Va." Stephen Duval is not listed in Philadelphia city directories for either 1875 or 1876.

88. 1900 Population Census, Borough of Manhattan and Duval Family Group Record, on www.ancestory.com.

89. Philadelphia City Death Certificates, 1803–1915 (www.familysearch.org). http://pilot.familysearch.org/record-search/start.html#p=recordResults;giveNname=peter%20s.;searchType=standard;surname=duval;deathYear=1886.

90. *Articles of Association of the Monument Cemetery of Philadelphia* (Philadelphia: Printed by J. Thompson, 1837). Lehman & Duval's plan accompanied a pamphlet entitled *The Monument Cemetery of Philadelphia (Late Pere la Chaise)* (Philadelphia: [J.A. Elkington]; Rackliff and King, printers, 1837).

91. Thomas H. Keels, *Philadelphia Graveyards and Cemeteries* (Charleston, S.C.: Arcadia Publishing, 2003), 118–19.

CHAPTER 5

1. The term "lithographer" in this essay is used for the person or firm that as a business produced lithographs. In the early days of lithography, such a lithographer often wore other hats, serving, for example, as the craftsman who actually drew the image onto the stone or as the publisher of the print or of the book or magazine in which the print appeared. The focus of this essay is on the businesses that produced lithographs.

2. The client might be a private individual or a publisher or even the lithographer himself, for a speculative publication.

3. It was easier and faster to create an image on a stone than to engrave a metal plate or wood block, and more lithographic images could be run off without a loss of image quality. On November 12, 1821, Arthur J. Stansbury tried to convince Mathew Carey to hire him to make lithographs for some of Carey's publications. "The advantage to the publisher presented by this species of engraving [i.e., lithography] consists chiefly in two particulars,—very important ones, rapidity and economy. The specimens I send you were executed in less than half the time they would have required on metal of any kind—and they can be afforded at half the price demanded by the engravers." Quoted by Philip J. Weimerskirch, "The Beginnings of Lithography in America," *Journal of the Printing Historical Society* 27 (1998): 62.

4. The term "publication" is used in this essay to refer to a book, portfolio, pamphlet, or periodical.

5. "Lithography," *Analectic Magazine* 14 (July 1819): 73.

6. Sally Pierce, *Early American Lithography: Images to 1830* (Boston: Boston Athenaeum, 1997), 10. For a thorough analysis of the conception and production of nineteenth-century natural-history illustrations, including lithographed plates, see Ann Shelby Blum, *Picturing Nature: American Nineteenth-Century Zoological Illustration* (Princeton: Princeton University Press, 1993).

7. Lithography is a planographic process, whereas wood engraving is a relief process, so the latter could be printed from the same press and on the same page as letterpress type.

8. That is, on a separate sheet of paper, not on a text page.

9. For general information on American colorplate books, see William S. Reese, *Stamped with a National Character: Nineteenth Century American Color Plate Books* (New York: Grolier Club, 1999), and James N. Green, "Colorplate Books in the Collection," in "The Library Company of Philadelphia," special issue, *Antiques* 170, no. 2 (August 2006): 72–79.

10. For the publication history of the *City of Philadelphia,* see Martin P. Snyder, "William Birch: His Philadelphia Views," *PMHB* 73 (July 1949): 271–315; Snyder, *City of Independence: Views of Philadelphia Before 1800* (New York: Praeger Publishers, 1975); and S. Robert Teitelman, *Birch's Views of Philadelphia: A Reduced Facsimile of the City of Philadelphia,* rev. ed. (Philadelphia: Free Library of Philadelphia, 2000).

11. John Tebbel and Mary Ellen Zuckerman, *The Magazine in America, 1741–1990* (New York: Oxford University Press, 1991), 10–13.

12. Frank Luther Mott, *A History of American Magazines,* vol. 1, *1741–1850* (Cambridge: Harvard University Press, 1938), 337, 341–42, and Tebbel and Zuckerman, *Magazine in America,* 10–11.

13. For more on Kennedy & Lucas, see Harry T. Peters, *America on Stone: The Other Printmakers to the American People* (Garden City, N.Y.: Doubleday,

1931), 249, and Wainwright, 9–10, 25–26.

14. For more on William L. Breton, see Martin P. Snyder, "William L. Breton, Nineteenth-Century Philadelphia Artist," *PMHB* 85 (April 1961): 178–209. See also note 44 to chapter 1 above.

15. George A. Seibel, *300 Years Since Hennepin: Niagara Falls in Art, 1678–1978* [Niagara Falls, Ont.: Niagara Falls Heritage Foundation, 1978], 12, 62.

16. A caveat concerning the comments in this chapter about the number and types of prints produced by different Philadelphia lithographers: The author's surveys of prints were based on personal experience, published sources, and the catalogs of major American institutions. There will certainly be prints by these firms that were not included in these surveys, and some specific types of prints will inevitably have been underrecorded. Ephemeral, job-order prints (such as labels, billheads, and tickets) and prints that were produced by artists and amateurs for their personal use are two examples. However, these types of prints would generally have been made in small runs, and they likely had significantly less financial impact on the lithographic firms than publication prints, which tended to have larger runs. On a more general note, separately issued prints as a whole are less likely to survive and be recorded than prints issued in a publication. However, the conclusions in this chapter based on the author's surveys are quite general and use only figures that would not be invalidated even by a generous assumption of missing nonpublication prints.

17. The best general source on Wild and his work is John W. Reps, *John Caspar Wild: Painter and Printmaker of Nineteenth-Century Urban America* (St. Louis: Missouri Historical Society Press, 2006).

18. In the August 1, 1835, issue of the *Saturday Courier*, Wild was said to have left because he was "discouraged by the coldness of his reception in our city and anxious to advance his fortunes." Quoted in John Francis McDermott, "John Caspar Wild: Some New Facts and a Query," *PMHB* 83 (October 1959): 452.

19. Ibid., 453. He was encouraged in this by Nicholas Longworth, a wealthy Cincinnati attorney and supporter of the arts, who wrote in a letter in November 1835 that Wild had "taken some views of our Town. . . . He will probably, at my suggestion, publish a series of views (lithographic)."

20. Cited by Martin P. Snyder, "J.C. Wild and His Philadelphia Views," *PMHB* 77 (January 1953): 33.

21. Andrew M'Makin is cited as the author of an 1835 editorial in the *Saturday Courier* that lauded Wild as an artist, lithographer, and colorist. McDermott, "Wild: New Facts," 452.

22. Snyder, "Wild and His Philadelphia Views," 34.

23. Ibid., 35.

24. The prints in the first three parts were printed by John Collins, but beginning in April, when part four was issued, the prints were printed by Wild & Chevalier.

25. Snyder, "Wild and His Philadelphia Views," 38.

26. *Views of St. Louis* and *The Valley of the Mississippi Illustrated*.

27. Approximately 71 of the 114 prints by Wild listed in Reps, *Wild,* 126–45, 136–39.

28. Snyder, "Wild and His Philadelphia Views," 47.

29. For more information on Childs, see Peters, *America on Stone,* 136–39, and Wainwright, 10–29.

30. Martin P. Snyder, *Mirror of America: The Developing Life of Philadelphia Seen in Engravings, 1801–1876* (Gladwyne, Pa.: M.P. Snyder, 1996), 60–62.

31. For more information on Newsam, see D. McN. Stauffer, "Lithographic Portraits of Albert Newsam," *PMHB* 24 (1900): 267–89, 430–52; 25 (1901): 109–13; 26 (1902): 382–86; and Wendy Wick Reaves, "Portraits for Every Parlor: Albert Newsam and American Portrait Lithography," in *American Portrait Prints,* ed. Wendy Wick Reaves (Charlottesville: Published for the National Portrait Gallery, Smithsonian Institution, by the University Press of Virginia, 1984), 83–134.

32. There is much information on the business relationship of Inman and Childs in the Henry Inman Letters, AAS.

33. "We have once referred to a growing custom among our citizens of submitting to Mr. Childs a likeness, for which he may make faithful lithographic copy one hundred of which reduced to any desired size, may be furnished for about forty dollars—A pleasing mode of gratifying distant friends or of multiplying memorials of the departed." *United States Gazette,* August 13, 1830.

34. Quotation from the back of the paper covers for the first part of volume 3 (1833). John and Thomas Doughty, brothers from Philadelphia, jointly published the work until May 1832, when Thomas moved to Boston to paint full time, John continuing on as sole publisher. It was Thomas, who

listed himself as "landscape artist" as early as 1820 and is considered one of the founders of the Hudson River School of artists, who provided twenty-four images for *The Cabinet of Natural History*. For more information, see Robert F. Looney, "Thomas Doughty, Printmaker," *Imprint: Journal of the American Historical Print Collectors Society* 4 (Autumn 1979): 2–10.

35. John Doughty advertised on the part covers that he intended to include thirteen parts in the third volume, but only four were produced. This abrupt halt and the scarcity of the text and plates of the third volume seem to indicate that subscriptions for *The Cabinet of Natural History* in 1833 were not sufficient to cover Doughty's costs.

36. The most detailed discussion of the lithographs in this work is Christopher W. Lane, "A History of McKenney and Hall's *History of the Indian Tribes of North America*," *Imprint: Journal of the American Historical Print Collectors Society* 27 (Autumn 2002): 2–15.

37. By April 1833 Childs & Inman had produced four hundred impressions of a dozen different portraits. See Herman J. Viola, *The Indian Legacy of Charles Bird King* (Washington, D.C.: Smithsonian Institution Press, 1976), 74.

38. Bradford had been able to sign up only 104 subscribers. See Ron Tyler, *Prints of the West* (Golden, Colo.: Fulcrum Pub., 1994), 40.

39. In a letter to Childs, Inman "obliges" Childs to obtain from the gentlemen connected with the "Indian Gallery of Portraits" the contracted remuneration to which he is entitled, being "a certain sum for every 5 that are finished. There is now due a considerable amt." Henry Inman to Col. C.G. Childs, October 25, 1833, Henry Inman Letters, AAS.

40. Wainwright, 26.

41. It is impossible to say whether the crudeness of the images is owing to Lewis's original drawings (McKenney did not use Lewis's original paintings but instead copies made by Charles Bird King) or to the lack of skill of J. Barincou (also spelled "Barinsou"), who drew the Lewis images onto stone. Barincou, a Philadelphia portrait artist, is not recorded as doing any other lithographic work, so perhaps it was he who was to blame for the somewhat awkward appearance of these prints. For the prints done for McKenney's *History,* Lehman & Duval used Albert Newsam, who had remained with the firm after Childs left and who was very skilled at rendering portraits on stone.

42. Edwin Freedley, *Leading Pursuits and Leading Men* (Philadelphia: Edward Young, 1856), 237.

43. Alfred A. Hoffy, artist, lithographer, and publisher, was born in England in 1796, immigrated to the United States by 1835, and moved to Philadelphia about 1838. See the *Philadelphia on Stone* Biographical Dictionary of Lithographers.

44. Quoted in Wainwright, 62.

45. Freedley, *Leading Pursuits,* 237.

46. Ron Tyler, "Illustrated Government Publications Related to the American West, 1843–1863," in *Surveying the Record: North American Scientific Exploration to 1930,* ed. Edward C. Carter II (Philadelphia: American Philosophical Society, 1999), 147–72.

47. Duval's name does not appear on any of these maps, but in November 1848 his firm received the Third Premium Award from the Franklin Institute for his work on a "Universal Atlas in folio, a most beautiful specimen of the art of transferring and lithographic printing, from the press of P.S. Duval, Philadelphia, transferred by [Frederick] Bourquin." Documented by the David Rumsey Collection (http://www.lunacommons.org/luna/servlet/detail/RUMSEY~8~1~35700~1200926:North-America-Philadelphia,-Publis), which owns the actual atlas submitted by Duval to the Franklin Institute to be considered for the award.

48. Freedley, *Leading Pursuits,* 237.

49. Opportunities for publishers of books grew tremendously in the middle two quarters of the nineteenth century. As Michael Winship writes, "The establishment of a national market for books . . . was a major development of this period" ("Distribution and the Trade," in *The Industrial Book, 1840–80,* A History of the Book in America, vol. 3 [Chapel Hill: Published in association with the American Antiquarian Society by the University of North Carolina Press, 2007], 122). However, it was also a period when publishers of various publications were constantly fighting not only to find subscribers but to get those already subscribed to continue making their payments (Mott, *History of American Magazines,* 1:513–14).

50. Peters, *America on Stone,* 103.

51. The first known work by Hoffy was a print of the great fire in New York City on December 16, 1835, which he drew on stone and which was printed and colored by J.T. Bowen. See I.N. Phelps Stokes, *The Iconography of Manhattan Island, 1498–1909* (New York: Robert H. Dodd, 1925), 3:618–19.

52. From part 17 on, Bowen used the name

"Lithographic & Print Coloring Establishment" for his work on these prints.

53. *Public Ledger,* March 3, 1838.

54. Audubon and lithographer J.B. Chevalier acted as the publishers for the first five volumes of the edition.

55. Ron Tyler, *Audubon's Great National Work* (Austin: University of Texas Press, 1993), 74.

56. Ibid., 80.

57. Ibid., 81.

58. Alice Ford, comp and ed., *Audubon's Animals: The Quadrupeds of North America* (New York: Studio Publications in association with Crowell, [1951]), 59.

59. The number of Nagel and Weingaertner prints varies in different examples of the first edition, from as few as seventeen to as many as thirty-one. See Bill Steiner, *Audubon Art Prints: A Collector's Guide to Every Edition* (Columbia: University of South Carolina Press, 2003), 153.

60. Wainwright, 57.

61. Quoted by Robert M. Peck, in the introduction to John Cassin, *Illustrations of Birds of California, Texas, Oregon, British and Russian America.* (1856; Austin: Texas State Historical Association, 1991), 17.

62. Ibid., 18.

63. Ibid., 13.

64. Quoted in ibid., 28.

65. It has been suggested that Cassin's involvement with Lavinia Bowen went beyond this, that he married her. However, this has been clearly established as incorrect. After 1858 Lavinia continued to be listed as Bowen in city directories, with an address different from Cassin's. Also, Cassin married Hannah Wright in 1837, and she survived him by almost two decades. When Hannah died, on June 23, 1888, she was buried in Laurcl Hill Cemetery, Philadelphia, right next to John's grave, with the inscription "Wife of John Cassin" on her gravestone. This research, and much else, can be found in material about John Cassin by Bert Filemyr and Jeff Holt at www.dvoc.org/History/Cassin-John/CassinJohn.htm. See chapter 1 for further discussion of Lavinia Bowen's career.

66. Peter Hastings Falk et al., eds., *Who Was Who in American Art, 1564–1975: 400 Years of Artists in America* (Madison, Conn.: Soundview Press, 1999), 3:3044, and Jay T. Last, *The Color Explosion: Nineteenth-Century American Lithography* (Santa Ana, Calif.: Hillcrest Press, 2005), 149.

67. Last, *Color Explosion,* 149.

68. Joseph Jackson, "Some Notes Towards a History of Lithography in Philadelphia," in *The Official Reference Book of the Lithographers International Protective and Beneficial Association, S.A. No. 14 of the United States: 1899* (Philadelphia, 1900), 19.

69. See Blum, *Picturing Nature,* chap. 5, for discussions about the working relationship between Sinclair and Stephen F. Baird, editor of the Smithsonian Institution's scientific publications.

70. Tyler, "Illustrated Government Publications," 170.

71. Pennsylvania, vol. 144, p. 485., R.G. Dun & Co. Collection.

72. Ibid.

73. Thanks to Jefferson Moak for this and other information on Sinclair's work with maps.

74. Recorded by Peters, *America on Stone,* 345–46.

75. The publications mentioned in this quote are papers by Edward Drinker Cope and Joseph Leidy that appeared in scientific journals in the 1870s; *The Medical and Surgical History of the War of the Rebellion* (1870–88); the report for Ferdinand V. Hayden's 1871 geological-survey expedition to Yellowstone; M.W. Dickeson's *American Numismatic Manual* (1860); Charles Reuben Hale, S. Huntington Jones, and Henry Morton's *Report of the Committee Appointed by the Philomathean Society of the University of Pennsylvania to Translate the Inscription on the Rosetta Stone* (1858); J.T. Barclay's *City of the Great King* (1858); and Samuel Sloan's *Model Architect* (1852), *City and Suburban Architecture* (1859), *Constructive Architecture* (1859), *American Houses* (1861), and *Homestead Architecture* (1861).

76. Peters, *America on Stone,* 344.

77. George Spratt, *Obstetric Tables: Comprising Graphic Illustrations, with Descriptions and Practical Remarks; Exhibiting on Dissected Plates Many Important Subjects in Midwifery* (Philadelphia: James A. Bill, 1850), preface.

CHAPTER 6

1. Abraham Ritter, *Philadelphia and Her Merchants, as Constituted Fifty @ Seventy Years Ago* (Philadelphia: Published by the author, 1860), 24, 46, 72–73, 133, 142, 149; John L. Cotter, Daniel G. Roberts, and Michael Parrington, *The Buried Past: An Archaeological History of Philadelphia* (Philadelphia: University of Pennsylvania Press, 1992), 216–38; Elizabeth Blackmar, *Manhattan for Rent, 1785–1850* (Ithaca: Cornell University Press, 1989), 48, 82–86; Joan H. Geismar, "Patterns of Development in

the Late-Eighteenth and Nineteenth-Century American Seaport: A Suggested Model for Recognizing Increasing Commercialism and Urbanization," *American Archeology* 5 (1985): 175–84; Anne-Marie Cantwell and Diana diZerega Wall, *Unearthing Gotham: The Archaeology of New York City* (New Haven: Yale University Press, 2001), 224–41; [Robert Waln Jr.], *The Hermit in America on a Visit to Philadelphia: Containing Some Account of the Beaux and Belles, Dandies and Coquettes, Cotillion Parties, Supper Parties, Tea Parties, &c. &c. of That Famous City,* ed. Peter Atall (Philadelphia: M. Thomas, 1819), 69. Ritter's book is a valuable lot-by-lot tour of the early-nineteenth-century Philadelphia waterfront, keyed to a series of detailed maps.

2. Mutual Assurance Company policy no. 122 (October 25, 1785) and policy nos. 168, 169 (March 14, 1787), in Anthony N.B. Garvan et al., eds., *The Architectural Surveys, 1784–1794,* Mutual Assurance Company Papers (Philadelphia: Mutual Assurance Co., 1976), 1:92–93, 121–22.

3. The phrase "integrated house" is Elizabeth Blackmar's (*Manhattan for Rent,* 11).

4. Jacques-Pierre Brissot de Warville, *New Travels in the United States of America: Performed in 1788* (Dublin: Printed by W. Corbet, for P. Byrne, A. Grueber, et al., 1792), 316; David M. Scobey, *Empire City: The Making and Meaning of the New York City Landscape* (Philadelphia: Temple University Press, 2002), 134, 136.

5. Ritter, *Philadelphia and Her Merchants,* 142.

6. Blackmar, *Manhattan for Rent,* 84, 86; Richard C. McKay, *South Street:*

A Maritime History of New York (1934; repr., New York: Haskell House, 1971), 137; John F. Watson, *Annals of Philadelphia and Pennsylvania in the Olden Time* (Philadelphia: J.B. Lippincott, 1868), 1:225. All subsequent references are to this edition, except as noted.

7. Map of eastern Center City, ca. 1849, HSP, online at http://www.brynmawr.edu/iconog/1849rps/1849ph.html, accessed January 21, 2009.

8. The site is identified as Cope's in Ritter, *Philadelphia and Her Merchants,* map facing p. 37.

9. Watson, *Annals of Philadelphia,* 1:221.

10. Franklin Fire Insurance Company of Philadelphia, survey of Thomas, John, and Philologus Loud piano works, 150 Chestnut Street, January 26, 1831. Copy in Philadelphia Historical Commission files.

11. Ibid., 1:226.

12. Ibid., 1:226–27; Glenn Porter and Harold C. Livesay, *Merchants and Manufacturers: Studies in the Changing Structure of Nineteenth-Century Marketing* (Baltimore: Johns Hopkins University Press, 1971), 4–9.

13. Elva Tooker, *Nathan Trotter, Philadelphia Merchant, 1787–1853* (Cambridge: Harvard University Press, 1955), 112–13. Trotter's career exemplifies those of other old-style Philadelphia merchants, many of whom, like Trotter, were bewildered by the new trade patterns.

14. Watson, *Annals of Philadelphia,* 1:226, 239. On the appearance of genteel shops elsewhere, see Richard L. Bushman, *The Refinement of America: Persons, Houses, Cities* (New York: Knopf, 1992), 359–60. Although Watson's successors disputed the details of his account, the general pattern and relative chronology he offers is reliable.

See Willis P. Hazard's corrections of Watson in John F. Watson, *Annals of Philadelphia and Pennsylvania in the Olden Time* (Philadelphia: Edwin S. Stuart, 1905), 3:149.

15. For hoists in use, see William H. Rease, *John Hibler, Importer & Wholesale Dealer in Foreign & American Wines & Liquors. No. 56, North Third Street, (second door above Arch,) Philadelphia* (Philadelphia: Printed by F. Kuhl, [1844]), POS 410, and William L. Breton, [*Wine & Liquor Store. Charles Egner 10 North Third Street, Philadelphia*] (Philadelphia: Lehman & Duval Lithrs. Philada. [ca. 1837]), POS 845.

16. Thomas S. Stewart Ledger, 1829–, Athenaeum of Philadelphia; "Destructive Fire," *Register of Pennsylvania* 13, no. 2 (January 11, 1834): 32.

17. George Justice to Stephen Girard, 1812, Real Estate in General, 1810; Real Estate Accounts, 1810–31, Stephen Girard Papers, ser. 11, reel 216 (microfilm, APS). This may have been "Nugent's store," for which a workman's wage receipt from May 27, 1812, survives in the same group of papers.

18. Ellen Fletcher Rosebrock, *Counting-House Days in South Street: New York's Early Brick Seaport Buildings* (New York: South Street Seaport Museum, 1975), 27. A number of early-nineteenth-century arcade-fronted mercantile stores survive along Decatur Street in New Orleans, for example.

19. Ibid., 32–33; [Asa Greene], *A Glance at New York: Embracing the City Government, Theatres, Hotels, Churches, Mobs, Monopolies, Learned Professions, Newspapers, Rogues, Dandies, Fires and Firemen, Water and Other Liquids, &c. &c.* (New York: A. Greene, 1837), 7–8, 10; James T. Mease and Thomas Porter,

The Picture of Philadelphia (Philadelphia: Robert DeSilver, 1831), 2:vii; "City Rambles," *New-York Mirror* 9 (May 12, 1832): 358–59.

20. John R. Griffiths, "To Slating his five new Stores West side of Front street betwixt High and Mulberry Streets," October 22, 1830, Real Estate Accounts, 1817–25, Stephen Girard Papers, 1973 227mf ser. 11, reel 217 (microfilm, APS).

21. For more on the grid and the quest for urban order, see Dell Upton, *Another City: Urban Life and Urban Spaces in the New American Republic* (New Haven: Yale University Press, 2008), 133–44.

22. John Caspar Wild, *Market Street, from Front St.* (Philadelphia: J.T. Bowen, ca. 1840, 1848). For photographic confirmation of this practice, see Frederick De Bourg Richards, *Hart's Building, North Side of Chestnut East from Sixth St.,* 1861, LCP, (6)1322.F.83b, and Henry B. Odiorne, [*S.E. Corner of South and Second Streets*], May 1860, LCP, (7)1322.F.69a.

23. A 1790 ordinance set the minimum height of the lower rails of awning frames at six feet four inches. A Northern Liberties ordinance of 1815 established the same standard. An 1846 Philadelphia law added a requirement that the side panels be at least seven feet six inches above the sidewalk. (Charles A. Poulson, John Trucks, and Saunders Lewis, comps., *Ordinances of the Corporation of, and Acts of Assembly Relating to the City of Philadelphia* [Philadelphia: Crissy & Markley, 1851], 53, 299; James Goodman, *A Digest of Acts of Assembly Relating to the Incorporated District of the Northern Liberties; and of the Ordinances for the Government of the District* [Philadelphia: F.

Pierson, 1853], 114.) Blacksmith Henry Beagle's lithograph advertised awning frames (POS 348).

24. James Stuart, *Three Years in North America,* 3rd, rev. ed. (Edinburgh: Robert Cadell, 1833), 1:32.

25. Richard Barry to John McDonogh, October 2, 1846, John McDonogh Papers, box 12, folder 15, Tulane University Library.

26. See Poulson, Trucks, and Lewis, *Ordinances,* 54 (1790), 143 (1824), 299 (1846); Goodman, *Digest,* 115 (1815). The possibility that this sidewalk display was a convention of the lithographs to illustrate a merchant's wares is denied by contemporary photographs, which illustrate the same practice. See, for example, Frederick De Bourg Richards, [*Warnick, Chadwick & Bro. Stove Factory and Iron Founders*], March 1859 or 1860, LCP, P.9808.1; *Perkins & McFarland Standard Heaters Ranges and Stoves,* ca. 1860, LCP, P.9153.3.

27. William H. Rease, [*Joseph Feinour & Son Stove Store and Joseph Feinour's Tin, Copper Brass & Iron Ware House 213–215 South Front Street, Philadelphia*] (Philadelphia: Printed by Wagner & McGuigan Lithrs. 100 Chesnut [*sic*] St., [1846]); [*Hartley & Knight's Bedding Warehouse, 148 South Second Street, Philadelphia*] [Philadelphia, 1846].

28. Alexander Mackay, *The Western World, or Travels in the United States in 1846–47: Exhibiting Them in Their Latest Development, Social, Political, and Industrial; Including a Chapter on California,* 2nd ed. (London: Richard Bentley, 1849), 1:25.

29. Ibid., 1:87.

30. [*F. Leaming & Co. Hardware, Nail, Steel, Hollow-ware & Looking Glass Store. No. 215 Market Street*] (Philadelphia: Childs & Inman Press, [ca. 1831]).

31. Poulson, Trucks, and Lewis, *Ordinances,* 20.

32. Mutual Assurance Company policy nos. 388, 389 (December 11, 1793), in Garvan et al., *Architectural Surveys,* 1:252–53.

33. Watson, *Annals of Philadelphia,* 1:222. I am assuming that the bulk window shown in McClees & Germon's photograph of the building is, or reproduces the form of, the original (McClees & Germon, [*Old London Coffee House, Front and Market Streets, Philadelphia*], ca. 1854, LCP, 8339.F.16.).

34. *The Diary of Elizabeth Drinker,* ed. Elaine Forman Crane (Boston: Northeastern University Press, 1991), 2:1337 (September 3, 1800).

35. Kenneth M. Wilson, "Window Glass in America," in *Building Early America: Contributions Toward the History of a Great Industry,* ed. Charles E. Peterson (Radnor, Pa.: Chilton Book Co., 1976), 161–63.

36. Robert F. Reynolds, *Lippincott & Co. South West Corner of Fourth & Market St Philadelphia* (Philadelphia: Wagner & McGuigan's Steam Press, [1858]).

37. [William M. Bobo], *Glimpses of New-York City: By a South Carolinian (Who Had Nothing Else to Do)* (Charleston, S.C.: J.J. McCarter, 1852), 163.

38. *John C. Farr & Co. Importers of Watches, Watchmakers Tools. Silver & Plated Ware, Musical Boxes, etc. No. 112, Chestnut St. Between 3rd & 4th St. Philada.* (Philadelphia: Printed in colors at P.S. Duval's Estabt., [ca. 1850]); William H. Rease, [*Western Paper Hangings Establishment, 501 Market Street, Philadelphia.*] [Philadelphia: Bryson & Cooper,

1847]; Rease & Schell, *Wm. D. Rogers' Coach and Light Carriage Manufactory, Corner of 6th & Master Streets, Philadelphia* (Philadelphia: Printed by Wagner & McGuigan, [ca. 1854]).

39. "Shop Windows," *New-York Mirror* 6 (September 27, 1828): 93.

40. Watson, *Annals of Philadelphia,* 1:240. Watson was thinking particularly of lottery brokers' signs, but his phrase sums up the objections of refined urbanites to signs.

41. David M. Henkin, *City Reading: Written Words and Public Spaces in Antebellum New York* (New York: Columbia University Press, 1998), 5, 10–13, 50–61.

42. William H. Rease, [*Garden & Brown, Silk & Fur Hat Manufactory, 196 Market Street, Philadelphia*] (Philadelphia: Printed by Wagner & McGuigan, [1847]); Robert F. Reynolds, *H.B. McCalla, Successor to the Late Andrew McCalla, No. 252 Market St. First Hat & Cap Store Below 8th St. South Side, Philadelphia* (Philadelphia: Printed in colors by Wagner & McGuigan, [ca. 1852]); Matthias S. Weaver, [*J. & J. Reakirt, Wholesale Druggists and Importers of Drugs, Chemicals, Paints, Dye-stuffs, &c. &c. S.E. Cor. of Third & Callowhill Sts., Philada.*] (Philadelphia: Sinclair's Lith., [1846]); William H. Rease, *Melloy & Ford, Wholesale Tin Ware Manufacturers* ([Philadelphia]: Printed by F. Kuhl, [1849]); [*Samuel Powell & Co. Ship & House Work in Tin, Copper, Brass and Iron*] [Philadelphia, 1847]; John L. Magee, *Wm. B. Eltonhead, Dealer in All Kinds of Watches, and Manufacturer of All Kinds of Jewelry and Silver Ware, 184 South Second Street, (between Pine & Union Streets, west side,) Philadelphia* (Philadelphia: T. Sinclair's Lith., [ca. 1855]).

43. This was certainly the building Watson had in mind when he denounced the overshadowing of venerable institutional buildings by "*towering* business houses and hotels" in his "Final Appendix of the Year 1856" (Watson, *Annals of Philadelphia,* 2:591).

44. William L. Breton, *Bowlby & Weaver's Hardware Store No. 77 Market Street Philadelphia* (Philadelphia: Kennedy & Lucas, [1831]).

45. Rease, [*Garden & Brown*]; [*Wm D. Parrish, Book Bindery, Paper & Rag Warehouse, Paper Books and Stationery, 4 North Fifth Street, Philadelphia*] [Philadelphia, 1847]; William H. Rease, [*Wm. W. Clark, Drug & Chemical Warehouse, 16 North Fifth Street, Philadelphia*]: *Drugs, Medicines, Chemicals, Glass &c..* (Philadelphia: Printed by Wagner & McGuigan, 1847]).

46. The key historical texts are John Kasson, *Rudeness and Civility: Manners in Nineteenth-Century Urban America* (New York: Hill & Wang, 1990); Bushman, *Refinement of America;* and Cary Carson, "The Consumer Revolution in Colonial British America: Why Demand?" in *Of Consuming Interests: The Style of Life in the Eighteenth Century,* ed. Cary Carson, Ronald Hoffman, and Peter J. Albert (Charlottesville: University Press of Virginia for the United States Capitol Historical Society, 1994), 483–697. For a more extended treatment of gentility in retailing, see Upton, *Another City,* 147–79.

47. Watson, *Annals of Philadelphia,* 1:222.

48. William Birch's 1799 engraving is ambiguous, but the muntins are rendered as curves, suggesting that he was trying to indicate the swelling curve of bulk windows.

49. Mease and Porter, *Picture of Philadelphia,* 2:92.

50. Watson, *Annals of Philadelphia,* 1:240; J. Thomas Scharf and Thompson Westcott, *History of Philadelphia, 1609–1884* (Philadelphia: L.H. Everts, 1884), 1:487.

51. Mutual Assurance Company policy nos. 388, 389, in Garvan et al., *Architectural Surveys,* 1:252.

52. Reynolds, *Lippincott & Co.;* Rease, *Melloy & Ford.*

53. Franklin Fire Insurance Company survey 1534, 1834, copy in Philadelphia Historical Commission archives; W. and F. Langenheim, *Bailey & Co.'s Jewelry Store,* ca. 1860, LCP, (8)1322.F.31g.

54. On commercial interiors as imitations of, and models for, genteel domestic spaces, see Katherine C. Grier, *Culture and Comfort: People, Parlors, and Upholstery, 1850–1930* (Rochester, N.Y.: Strong Museum, 1988).

55. On Oakford's earlier shop and his mode of operation, see Upton, *Another City,* 335. The appearance of Oakford's stores is confirmed by Julio H. Rae, *Rae's Philadelphia Pictorial Directory and Panoramic Advertiser* (Philadelphia, 1851), pls. 4, 10, online at www .brynmawr.edu/iconog/panos/r6sw11. jpg, accessed February 7, 2009.

56. W. & F. Langenheim, [*Interior View of Charles Oakford & Sons Hat Store, Continental Hotel, 826–28 Chestnut Street, Philadelphia*], ca. 1860, LCP, (8)1322.F.33c.

57. Robert F. Reynolds, [*C.F. Mansfield. Paper Hangings. Wholesale and Retail, 275 South Second Street, Philadelphia*] (Philadelphia: Printed by F. Kuhl, [1848]); William H. Rease, [*George Mecke Cabinet Maker and Upholsterer, No 355, North 2nd St. Nearly Opposite*

Tammany St. Philadelphia.] [Philadelphia: Wagner & McGuigan, 1846].

58. John F. Watson, *Annals and Occurrences of New York City and State in the Olden Time* (Philadelphia: Henry F. Anners, 1846), 205.

59. "The Astor House," *New-York Mirror* 13 (June 25, 1836): 414.

60. "Mercantile Drumming," *Atkinson's Casket* 8 (September 1833): 405.

61. Watson, *Annals of Philadelphia,* 1:220–21.

62. The managers of the New York Arcade (1826), another Haviland-designed building, ordered individual shopkeepers to keep their stores "free of every nuisance or thing whatsoever, that would be unsightly, and . . . not [to] place or hang up any goods outside of said store or counter at any time during business hours" ("Explanations, Rules, and Regulations of the New York Arcade and Free Halls of Exhibition," *Frank Leslie's Illustrated Newspaper* 3, no. 55 [December 27, 1856]: 63).

63. William H. Rease, *Public Baths. Thos. E.J. Kerrison's Arcade-Baths* [Philadelphia, 1847]. For a more detailed account of the vicissitudes of the Philadelphia Arcade, see Upton, *Another City,* 145–79. For a photograph of the arcade in its last state, see Frederick De Bourg Richards, *North Side of Chestnut Street, West of Sixth Street,* January 1858, LCP, (3)2526.F.39 (Poulson).

64. Mackay, *Western World,* 1:140.

65. William H. Jordan, *North Third Street, Philadelphia, Forty-Five Years Ago* (Philadelphia: Philadelphia Press of the New Era Printing Co., 1905), 3.

66. Reynolds, *H.B. McCalla;* Reynolds, *Lippincott & Co.* On the rise of the ready-made clothing trade, in which Philadelphia was an important player,

see Michael Zakim, *Ready-Made Democracy: A History of Men's Dress in the American Republic, 1760–1860* (Chicago: University of Chicago Press, 2003).

67. William H. Rease, *Charles C. Oat's Lamp Store No. 32 North Second St. Philadelphia.* [Philadelphia: Wagner & McGuigan?, ca. 1848]; E. Luders, *Goodyears Rubber, Packing & Belting Company: Warehouse 104 Chestnut St. Philada. Factory Newtown, Connecticut. Belting, Packing, Hose, Clothing, Druggist-Articles, etc.* [Philadelphia: Lithy. of A. Kollner, ca. 1856]; Rease, *Melloy & Ford.*

68. Watson, *Annals of Philadelphia,* 2:591, 589.

CHAPTER 7

1. Peter C. Marzio, "Illustrated News in Early American Prints," in *American Printmaking Before 1876: Fact, Fiction and Fantasy* (Washington, D.C.: Library of Congress, 1975), 53–54.

2. Due to the interdisciplinary nature of the study of visual culture, the term has had many definitions. For my purposes, I subscribe to the view of Vanessa R. Schwartz and Jeannene M. Przyblyski that visual culture is defined by "its objects of study, which are examined not for their aesthetic value per se but for their meaning as modes of making images and defining visual experience in particular historical contexts." "Visual Culture's History: Twenty-First Century Interdisciplinarity and Its Nineteenth-Century Objects," in *The Nineteenth-Century Visual Culture Reader,* ed. Vanessa R. Schwartz and Jeannene M. Przyblyski (New York: Routledge, 2004), 6–7.

3. Several works have been published that discuss the realism of various nineteenth-century print and photographic processes, including Walter Benjamin, "The Work of Art in the Age of Mechanical Reproduction (1936)," in Schwartz and Przyblyski, *Visual Culture Reader,* 63–70; William Mills Ivins, *Prints and Visual Communication* (Cambridge: Harvard University Press, 1953); and Alan Trachtenberg, *Reading American Photographs* (New York: Hill & Wang, 1989). See also B.E. Maidment, *Reading Popular Prints* (New York: St. Martin's Press, 1996); Gillen D'Arcy Wood, *The Shock of the Real: Romanticism and Visual Culture, 1760–1860* (New York: Palgrave, 2001); and Mason Jackson, *The Pictorial Press: Its Origin and Progress* (London: Hurst & Blackett, 1885). Although the latter volumes focus on the visual culture of Great Britain, they provide perceptive commentary on the philosophical debates and cultural influences in the creation, dissemination, and reception of popular visual media depicting everyday life.

4. See Beatrice Farwell, *French Popular Lithographic Imagery, 1815–1870,* vol. 8, *Contemporary Events and Caricature* (Chicago: University of Chicago, 1988), 1; Bryan F. LeBeau, *Currier & Ives: America Imagined* (Washington, D.C.: Smithsonian Institution Press, 2001), 1–7; Marzio, "Illustrated News," 53–60; Neil Harris, "Pictorial Perils: The Rise of American Illustration," in *The American Illustrated Book in the Nineteenth Century,* ed. Gerald W.R. Ward (Charlottesville: University Press of Virginia, 1987), 3–19; Ulrich Keller, "Photojournalism Around 1900: The Institutionalization of a Mass

Medium," in *Shadow and Substance: Essays in the History of Photography,* ed. Kathleen Collins (Bloomfield Hills, Mich.: Amorphous Institute Press, 1990), 283–303; and Clement Shorter, "Illustrated Journalism: Its Past and Its Future," *Contemporary Review* 75 (1899): 481–95.

5. LeBeau, *Currier & Ives,* 4. I will not investigate the broad genre of "documentary prints," which can include military, political, and genre scenes and events of more national importance.

6. Wainwright, 17–25.

7. According to LeBeau, Currier & Ives published more than fifty steamboat-disaster prints alone, including, in 1840, the seminal *Awful Conflagration of the Steamboat Lexington* print, which is often misidentified as the first news lithograph. Currier actually published his first news lithograph in 1835, four years after the first Philadelphia-issued news-event print. (LeBeau, *Currier & Ives,* 19.)

8. See Menaheim Blondheim, *News over the Wires: The Telegraph and the Flow of Public Information in America, 1844–1897* (Cambridge: Harvard University Press, 1994), and Daniel Czitrom, *Media and the American Mind: From Morse to McLuhan* (Chapel Hill: University of North Carolina Press, 1982), 1–29.

9. Gale Research Group, *Currier & Ives: A Catalogue Raisonné* (Detroit: Gale Research, 1983).

10. Joshua Brown, *Beyond the Lines: Pictorial Reporting, Everyday Life, and the Crisis of Gilded Age America* (Berkeley: University of California Press, 2002), provides the most recent and comprehensive scholarship discussing the evolution of nineteenth-century pictorial journalism. The work focuses on the history of *Frank Leslie's Illustrated Newspaper* in the context of the periodical as reflecting the race, class, and gender tensions of the Progressive Era. See particularly chaps. 1–3, which provide an overview of the conception, production, and dissemination of this form of graphic news. See also Kevin G. Barnhurst and John Nerone, "Civic Picturing vs. Realist Photojournalism: The Regime of Illustrated News, 1856–1901," *Design Issues* 16 (Spring 2000): 59–79 (to which my citations refer), revised and republished as chap. 4 in Kevin G. Barnhurst and John Nerone, *The Form of News: A History* (New York: Guilford Press, 2001), 111–39, and Frank Luther Mott, *A History of American Magazines,* vol. 2, *1850–1865* (Cambridge: Harvard University Press, 1938), 192–93, 452–67, and 469–87.

11. Barnhurst and Nerone, "Civic Picturing," 71, and Brown, *Beyond the Lines,* 33, 68.

12. Beatrice Farwell, *The Cult of Images: Baudelaire and the 19th-Century Media Explosion* (Santa Barbara: University of California, 1977), 9, and Brown, *Beyond the Lines,* 68.

13. John Collins advertised his "disaster" lithograph of the Camden-Amboy Railroad accident of August 29, 1855, in the *Trenton State Gazette,* September 15, 1855, as being sold by "the flying stationers," that is, street peddlers.

14. Barnhurst and Nerone, "Civic Picturing," 71.

15. Brown, *Beyond the Lines,* 233–42, and Barnhurst and Nerone, *Form of News,* 111–49. See also Dan Schiller, *Objectivity and the News: The Public and the Rise of Commercial Journalism* (Philadelphia: University of Pennsylvania Press, 1981); William David Sloan, *Perspectives on Mass Communication History* (New York: Routledge, 1991), particularly chap. 9; and Mitchell Stephens, *A History of News* (Philadelphia: Harcourt Brace & Co., 1997).

16. *Saturday Bulletin,* February 12, 1831.

17. As quoted in Louis Masur, *1831: Year of Eclipse* (New York: Hill & Wang, 2001), 5–6.

18. Martin Snyder, for example, cites the print in an essay about the preponderance of human activity in nineteenth-century Philadelphia prints and does not mention the eclipse. Martin P. Snyder, "Liveliness: A Quality in Prints of Philadelphia," in *Philadelphia Printmaking: American Prints Before 1860,* ed. Robert F. Looney (West Chester, Pa.: Tinicum Press, 1977), 119.

19. Nancy Davison, "E.W. Clay: American Political Caricaturist of the Jacksonian Era" (Ph.D. diss., University of Michigan, 1980), is the most definitive biography of Clay to date. The work includes a lengthy entry about Clay's *Life in Philadelphia* series, originally issued 1828–30, which employed racist, satiric portrayals of members of middle-class African American Philadelphia society. LCP also holds several political cartoons by Clay that contain comic African American figures, portrayed as shoe shiners, chimney sweeps, and gravediggers.

20. John W. Reps, *John Caspar Wild: Painter and Printmaker of Nineteenth-Century Urban America* (St. Louis: Missouri Historical Society Press, 2006), 43–44, 157 nn. 26–28.

21. See Samuel Webb, *History of Pennsylvania Hall* (Philadelphia: Printed by Merrihew & Gun, 1838), for a detailed description of the event. The pamphlet

is illustrated with lithographic and engraved plates, excluding the cited print. The illustrations are advertised on the last page of the pamphlet as for sale in a limited supply of larger frameable versions at the Philadelphia Anti-Slavery Office. See also Henry Mayer, *All on Fire: William Lloyd Garrison and the Abolition of Slavery* (New York: St. Martin's Press, 1998), 241–48.

22. *United States Gazette,* May 23, 1838, and "Published This Day," *Public Ledger,* May 28, 1838.

23. Castner, a proprietor of Castner Stereograph Transparencies, prominent Philadelphia merchant, amateur photographer, and active member of the American Catholic Historical Society, assembled a collection of more than twenty scrapbooks of prints, photographs, and newspaper clippings of Philadelphia history. The collection was given to the Free Library of Philadelphia in 1947.

24. "Reported for the North American and U.S. Gazette: Examination of Charles Langfeldt, the Supposed Murderer of Mrs. Rademacher," *North American,* March 28, 1848.

25. Isabelle Lehuu, *Carnival on the Page: Popular Print Media in Antebellum America* (Chapel Hill: University of North Carolina Press, 2000), 51–57; Marzio, "Illustrated News," 54–60; Stephens, *History of News,* 189–94; James N. Green and Wendy Woloson, "From the Bottom Up: Popular Reading and Writing in the Michael Zinman Collection of Early American Imprints," online exhibition, http://www.librarycompany.org/zinman; and David Anthony, "The Helen Jewett Panic: Tabloids, Men, and the Sensational Public Sphere in Antebellum New York," *American Literature* 69 (September 1997): 487–514.

26. Lehuu, *Carnival on the Page,* 37–58. See also Stephens, *History of News;* Schiller, *Objectivity and the News;* and Barnhurst and Nerone, *Form of News.*

27. "Examination of Charles Langfeldt," *North American,* March 28, 1848.

28. Ibid. and "Further Particulars of the Murder," *Pennsylvanian,* March 28, 1848.

29. "Examination of Charles Langfeldt," *North American,* March 28, 1848.

30. *Authentic Narrative of the Murder of Mrs. Rademacher: With Splendid Illustrations, Drawn and Engraved Expressly for This Publication* (Philadelphia: G. Zeiber, 1848), 5.

31. Ibid.

32. "Murder: The First Ward the Scene of a Horrible Butchery," *Press,* April 12, 1866.

33. See I.N. Phelps Stokes, *The Iconography of Manhattan Island, 1498–1909* (New York: Robert H. Dodd, 1925), 3:882, pl. A-26-C.

34. 1860 Population Census, Pennsylvania, Philadelphia, 1st Ward, 2nd Division; 1870 Population Census, Pennsylvania, Philadelphia, 26th Ward, District 84; George C. Groce and David H. Wallace, *The New-York Historical Society Dictionary of Artists in America* (New Haven: Yale University Press, 1957), 418; Peter Hastings Falk et al., eds., *Who Was Who in American Art, 1564–1975: 400 Years of Artists in America* (Madison, Conn.: Soundview Press, 1999), 2:2158; and E. McSherry Fowble, *Two Centuries of Prints in America, 1680–1880: A Selective Catalogue of the Winterthur Museum Collection* (Charlottesville: Published for the Henry Francis du Pont Winterthur Museum by the University Press of Virginia, 1987), 481. See also the online catalogs of AAS, LOC, and LCP, which contain numerous records describing the lithographs drawn and issued by Magee.

35. "The Murder: The Body of the Missing Boy Found in the Hay Stack," *Press,* April 13, 1866.

36. Magee also published a portrait of the murderer titled *Antoine Probst: The Murderer of the Dearing Family.* A copy dated 1866 resides in the collections of the AAS, Graphic Arts Lithf Mage Prob.

37. "Murder: The First Ward the Scene of a Horrible Butchery," *Press,* April 12, 1866.

38. Ibid. and "The Great Tragedy," *Philadelphia Inquirer,* April 16, 1866.

39. Transplanted Philadelphia lithographer John Collins executed a lithograph of the tragedy, "drawn on the spot," titled *Accident on the Camden and Amboy Railroad, Near Burlington, N.J. Aug. 29th 1855. 21 Persons Killed, 75 Wounded.* Printed by Thomas Sinclair, the print most closely resembles Magee's compositions that focused on the victims, but in a less garish style, with muted hand-coloring. A copy of the print resides in the collections of HSP, Bb 674 C14 (POSP 4). The pencil-and-wash study for the lithograph resides in the collections of AAS, Drawings Collection, Box 9, Folder 7.

40. See Mark Aldrich, *Death Rode the Rails: American Railroad Accidents and Safety, 1828–1965* (Baltimore: Johns Hopkins University Press, 2006); R. John Brockman, *Accident Investigation Reports, 1822–1879* (Amityville, N.Y.: Baywood Pub. Co., 2005); and Edgar A. Haine, *Railroad Wrecks* (New York: Cornwell Books, 1993).

41. Brown, *Beyond the Lines,* 22-26.

42. As reported in the *Daily Pennsylvanian:* "Terrible Calamity on the Delaware," March 17, 1856; "City Matters: The Late Disaster; Recovery of More Bodies," March 18, 1856; "City Matters: The Disaster Upon the Delaware," March 19, 1856; and "The Burning of the Steamboat New Jersey," March 20, 1856.

43. An article in the *Patriot* indicated "some sixty persons, men, women, and children perished" ("Terrible Disaster," March 19, 1865).

44. A second variant print containing the phrase "Over 60 lives lost" in its title is cited in Anthony N.B. Garvan and Carol A. Wojtowicz, *Catalogue of the Green Tree Collection* (Philadelphia: Mutual Assurance Co., 1977), 145.

45. Wainwright, 78.

46. Garvan and Wojtowicz, *Green Tree Collection,* 145.

47. "The Disaster on the North Pennsylvania Railroad," *Bulletin,* July 18, 1856; *Daily Pennsylvanian,* July 18 and 19, 1856; and, from the *North American,* "The Railroad Disaster," July 18, 1856, and "Railroad Disaster and the Preventatives," July 19, 1856.

48. "The Disaster on the North Pennsylvania Railroad," *Bulletin,* July 18, 1856.

49. "Railroad Disaster and the Preventatives," *North American,* July 19, 1856.

50. Boerum was an engraver, lithographer, die sinker, and printer who worked in Philadelphia and New Jersey. An advertisement for his business at 310 Chestnut Street is included in *Ladies Philadelphia Shopping Guide & Housekeeper's Companion: For 1859* (Philadelphia: Published by the author, 1859). He possibly served in the New Jersey Cavalry during the Civil War.

51. "The Disaster on the North Pennsylvania Railroad," *Bulletin,* July 18, 1856.

52. Brown, *Beyond the Lines,* 46–67; William P. Campbell, *The Civil War: A Centennial Exhibition of Eyewitness Drawings* (Washington, D.C.: National Gallery of Art, 1961); Pat Hodgson, *The War Illustrators* (New York: Macmillan, 1977); W. Fletcher Thompson Jr., *The Image of War: The Pictorial Reporting of the American Civil War* (New York: T. Yoseloff, 1960); and Trachtenberg, *Reading American Photographs,* 71–118.

53. "Local Intelligence: A Terrible Explosion," *Philadelphia Inquirer,* March 31, 1862, and Thomas G. Morton, M.D., and Frank Woodbury, A.M., M.D., *History of Pennsylvania Hospital, 1751–1895* (Philadelphia: Times Printing House, 1897), 106.

54. "Local Intelligence: A Terrible Explosion," *Philadelphia Inquirer,* March 31, 1862.

55. Ibid.

56. Ibid.

57. Brown, *Beyond the Lines,* 49.

58. "Frightful Calamity," *Patriot,* February 16, 1865. Although no known Philadelphia lithographer issued a print of the great fire of 1850, to which the 1865 fire was compared, New York lithographer G.E. Leefe published a view of the earlier tragedy titled *The Great Conflagration in Philadelphia on Tuesday July 9th 1850* (POS 329), which is held in the collections of HSP, Bb 83 P 544.

59. "Frightful Calamity," *Patriot,* February 16, 1865, and "Awful Conflagration: Destruction of a Coal Oil Warehouse," *Philadelphia Inquirer,* February 9, 1865.

60. "Frightful Calamity" and "Awful Conflagration."

61. Garvan and Wojtowicz, *Green Tree Collection,* 148.

62. "Awful Conflagration: Destruction of a Coal Oil Warehouse," *Philadelphia Inquirer,* February 9, 1865.

63. Ibid.

64. "Frightful Calamity," *Patriot,* February 16, 1865.

65. Ibid.

66. One of the families listed as missing on the print was the Scotts, who are reported as unharmed in "City Intelligence: The Late Conflagration," *Philadelphia Inquirer,* February 11, 1865.

67. Brown, *Beyond the Lines,* 71.

68. See Bruno Giberti, *Designing the Centennial: A History of the International Exhibition in Philadelphia* (Lexington: University Press of Kentucky, 2002).

69. Christopher W. Lane and Don Cresswell, *Prints of Philadelphia at the Philadelphia Print Shop, Featuring the Wohl Collection* (Philadelphia: Philadelphia Print Shop, 1990), 110–12. See also Theresa R. Snyder, "Better Than Fair: Ephemera and the Centennial Exhibition," *Popular Culture in Libraries* 4 (July 1996): 21–62, particularly 43–47.

70. *Frank Leslie's Historical Register of the United States Centennial Exposition, 1876: Embellished with Nearly Eight Hundred Illustrations . . . by the Most Eminent Artists in America; Including Illustrations and Descriptions of All Previous International Exhibitions,* ed. Frank H. Norton (New York: Frank Leslie's Pub. House, 1877).

71. See *Democratic Art,* and Jay T. Last, *The Color Explosion: Nineteenth-Century American Lithography* (Santa Ana, Calif.: Hillcrest Press, 2005).

72. Joseph G.E. Hopkins, "Plain Talk in Pictures," *New-York Historical Society Quarterly* 31 (April 1947): 105.

73. Marzio, "Illustrated News," 60.

74. See Elisabeth Hodermarsky, "The Kel-

logg Brothers' Images of the Mexican War and the Birth of Modern-Day News," in *Picturing Victorian America: Prints by the Kellogg Brothers of Hartford, Connecticut, 1830–1880,* ed. Nancy Finlay (Hartford: Connecticut Historical Society, 2009), 73–84.

75. Copies of Magee's sensational prints described in the (now-dispersed) Green Tree Collection are held in the Harry T. Peters and Cigna Collections, both at the Smithsonian, and LCP, AAS, FLP, and HSP.

76. "The Great Tragedy," *Philadelphia Inquirer,* April 16, 1866.

77. Barnhurst and Nerone, "Civic Picturing," 78–79.

CHAPTER 8

1. See David M. Lubin, "Art in the Age of National Expansion: Genre and Landscape Painting," in *Art in America: 300 Years of Innovation,* ed. Susan Davidson (New York: Guggenheim Museum, 2007), 94–139.

2. William Dunlap, *A History of the Rise and Progress of the Arts of Design in the United States,* 2 vols. in 3 (1834; repr., New York: Dover Publications, [1969]).

3. Thomas Cole, "Essay on American Scenery," *American Monthly Magazine* 1 (January 1836): 1–12.

4. Richard McLanathan, *The American Tradition in the Arts* (New York: Harcourt, Brace & World, 1968), 165.

5. Christopher W. Lane, *Impressions of Niagara: The Charles Rand Penney Collection* (Philadelphia: Philadelphia Print Shop, 1993).

6. Quoted in ibid., 37.

7. John Wilmerding, *American Art* (New York: Penguin Books, 1976), 61–82.

8. Ibid., 70.

9. Through a window in the background peeks a small cupola. Although the cupola is usually assumed to belong to the Walnut Street Jail, where Lyon was imprisoned, it is more likely the top of Carpenters' Hall, where the Bank of Pennsylvania was housed at the time of its robbery, of which Lyon was accused. Mantle Fielding, *Catalogue of an Exhibition of Portraits by John Neagle* (Philadelphia: Pennsylvania Academy of the Fine Arts, 1925), 10.

10. See Wainwright, 34.

11. See Roger Butterfield, "The Folklore of Politics," *PMHB* 74 (April 1950): 167. Butterfield suggests the portrait lithograph was the first to use the icon of an American politician at his plow.

12. The Conestoga wagon was developed around 1750 in the Conestoga Valley of Pennsylvania. By the mid–nineteenth century, Philadelphia had become a manufacturing center of carriages and wagons. See Edwin Freedley, *Philadelphia and Its Manufactures: A Hand-Book Exhibiting the Development, Variety, and Statistics of the Manufacturing Industry of Philadelphia in 1857* (Philadelphia: Edward Young, 1858), 394, 443–49.

13. Quoted in Wainwright, 34.

14. The Keffer Collection, held by the University of Pennsylvania Library, contains hundreds of examples of sheet-music covers printed by Philadelphia lithographers. A digital catalog of the collection can be accessed at http://www.library.upenn.edu/collections/rbm/keffer/.

15. The site is northwest of Philadelphia, in Montgomery County, and the music was composed by F.M. Blaufuss, a teacher at the college. The college

closed in 1881, and the ladies were accepted at the present-day Ursinus College.

16. For further discussions about the importance of lithography for the publication of sheet music, see Donald William Krummel and Stanley Sadie, *Music Printing and Publishing* (New York: W.W. Norton, 1990); Harry Dichter and Elliott Shapiro, *Handbook of Early American Sheet Music, 1768–1889* (New York: Dover, 1977); Jay T. Last, *The Color Explosion: Nineteenth-Century American Lithography* (Santa Ana, Calif.: Hillcrest Press, 2005), 261; and Lester Levy, *Picture the Songs: Lithographs from the Sheet Music of Nineteenth-Century America* (Baltimore: Johns Hopkins University Press, 1976).

17. See *American Paradise: The World of the Hudson River School,* introduction by John K. Howat (New York: Metropolitan Museum of Art, 1987), for a comprehensive overview of this art movement.

18. See *Democratic Art.*

19. Herline & Hensel was the partnership between Philadelphia lithographers Edward Herline (1835–1902) and Daniel Hensel (1830–1919). Established in 1857, the business known for its chromolithographs and bird's-eye-view prints operated from 630 Chestnut Street until about 1866, when the partnership dissolved.

20. An earlier version of the view after Benjamin F. Smith Jr. was printed by P.S. Duval about 1850. See Stephanie Munsing, *Made in America: Printmaking, 1760–1860; An Exhibition of Original Prints from the Collections of the Library Company of Philadelphia and the Historical Society of Pennsyl-*

vania, April–June, 1973 (Philadelphia: Library Company of Philadelphia, 1973), 49–50.

21. William Dreser, born May 31, 1818, in Hesse-Homburg, Germany, was a lithographer active in Philadelphia ca. 1847–ca. 1860 and ca. 1870–72. Dreser maintained a working relationship with Thomas Sinclair from the 1850s to 1860s. He delineated lithographs for Sinclair beginning around 1850, including advertisements and ornithological book plates, in addition to *American Autumn, Starucca Valley, Erie R. Road.*

22. See E. McSherry Fowble, *Two Centuries of Prints in America, 1680–1880: A Selective Catalogue of the Winterthur Museum* (Charlottesville: Published for the Henry Francis du Pont Winterthur Museum by the University Press of Virginia, 1987), 399, and *Democratic Art,* 33.

23. See Gloria-Gilda Deák, *Picturing America, 1497–1899: Prints, Maps, and Drawings Bearing on the New World Discoveries and on the Development of the Territory That Is Now the United States,* 2 vols. (Princeton: Princeton University Press, 1988); Fowble, *Two Centuries of Prints,* 271–85, 369–99; and John Ramsay, "The American Scene in Lithograph," *Antiques* 61 (September 1951): 180–83.

24. John W. Reps, *Views and Viewmakers of Urban America* (Columbia: University of Missouri Press, 1984), provides the most comprehensive overview of the history of bird's-eye and panoramic views, including discussions of the effect of lithography in the promotion of this genre of print, of which Reps lists 4,480 titles. See also his *Making of Urban America* (Princeton: Princeton University Press, 1965) and *Town Plan-*

ning in Frontier America (Princeton: Princeton University Press, 1969).

25. Reps, *Views and Viewmakers,* 3–16.

26. Ibid., entries 3576–78 and 3585. Christopher W. Lane and Don Cresswell, *Prints of Philadelphia at the Philadelphia Print Shop, Featuring the Wohl Collection* (Philadelphia: Philadelphia Print Shop, 1990), item 168, illus. on p. 82.

27. The market sheds were removed by city ordinance in 1859.

28. For an overview of the career of John Bachmann, see Nat Case, "John Bachmann and the American Bird's Eye View Print," *Imprint: Journal of the American Historical Print Collectors Society* 33 (Autumn 2008): 19–35.

29. See Reps, *Views and Viewmakers,* items 3565–72; John W. Reps, *John Caspar Wild: Painter and Printmaker of Nineteenth-Century Urban America* (St. Louis: Missouri Historical Society Press, 2006), 47–50; Lane and Cresswell, *Prints of Philadelphia,* item 138, illus. on p. 60.

30. See Bettina A. Norton, *Edwin Whitefield—Nineteenth-Century North American Scenery* (Barre, Mass.: Barre Publishing, 1977), 132, illus. on pp. 84–87. See also Reps, *Views and Viewmakers,* items 3580–83.

31. *Public Ledger,* Philadelphia, July 1, 1853.

32. Deák, *Picturing America,* 377–78. The author includes a complete list of the prints published by Goupil, Vibert & Company as *Views of American Cities* (1848–51).

33. Harry T. Peters, *America on Stone: The Other Printmakers to the American People* (Garden City, N.Y.: Doubleday, 1931), 254–55.

34. "Fine Winter Scene," *Public Ledger,* July 1, 1853.

35. Lane and Cresswell, *Prints of Philadelphia,* 85–86; Peters, *America on Stone,* 166–67.

36. According to Hoover's biography in "Art-Lithographers of the United States: Joseph Hoover," *Lithographers' Journal* (September 1893): 53, the "technical execution was by Duvall [*sic*] & Hunter, but the entire supervision as to color, details and proofs, was by Mr. Hoover, who thus made himself personally responsible for the success of the final result."

37. Ibid., 52–53; Last, *Color Explosion,* 196; *Democratic Art,* 39–40.

38. Although the prolific New York firm Currier & Ives produced many of these views from the mid–nineteenth century and beyond, other major firms, including Joseph Hoover in Philadelphia, Strobridge & Co. in Cincinnati, the Endicotts of New York, and J.H. Bufford and Haskell & Allen of Boston, issued such prints as well. The online catalogs of LOC and AAS list several of these lithographs. See also Bryan F. LeBeau, *Currier & Ives: America Imagined* (Washington, D.C.: Smithsonian Institution Press, 2001), particularly 176–77.

39. John F. Watson, *Annals of Philadelphia and Pennsylvania in the Olden Times* (Philadelphia: Edwin S. Stuart, 1891), 3:127–28.

40. Peters, *America on Stone,* 393–95.

41. A number of works discuss the political, economic, and social influences on the development of nineteenth-century suburbs. The following represent a small segment of this scholarship: Delores Hayden, *Building Suburbia: Green Fields and Urban Growth, 1820–2000* (New York: Vintage Books, 2004), and Robert Lewis, ed., *Manufacturing*

Suburbs: Building Work and Home on the Metropolitan Fringe (Philadelphia: Temple University Press, 2004).

42. See Cynthia J. Shelton, *The Mills of Manayunk: Industrialization and Social Conflict in the Philadelphia Region, 1787–1837* (Baltimore: Johns Hopkins University Press, 1986), and Russell F. Weigley et al., *Philadelphia: A 300-Year History* (New York: W.W. Norton & Co., 1982), 477–79.

43. Jonathan Fell purchased this Brandywine Springs, Delaware, mill in 1828 to grind spices. Before that purchase the spices were ground in Philadelphia, but that facility was then turned into offices and warehouses. Fell's spices had a broad reputation and were distributed to major cities around the world. The Brandywine Springs mill, last operated by his sons, burned in 1867 but was rebuilt.

44. Prominent lithographers Duval, Sinclair, and McGuigan contributed lithographs and cash as cited in the *Philadelphia Inquirer,* June 21, 1864.

45. For fuller descriptions of the fair, see J. Matthew Gallman, *Mastering Wartime: A Social History of Philadelphia During the Civil War* (Philadelphia: University of Pennsylvania Press, 2000), chap. 6, and J. Thomas Scharf and Thompson Westcott, *History of Philadelphia, 1609–1884* (Philadelphia: L.H. Everts & Co., 1884), 1:815–16.

46. A copy of the card is held in the Print and Photograph Department, LCP.

47. The best overall documentary description is *Frank Leslie's Illustrated Historical Register of the Centennial Exposition, 1876,* ed. Frank H. Norton (New York: Frank Leslie's Publishing House, 1876), which has appeared in a facsimile edition with an introduction by Richard Kenin (New York: Paddington Press, 1974). See also Gloria-Gilda Deák, *American Views: Prospects and Vistas* (New York: Viking Press, 1976), 122–25.

48. John Reps points out many other creators of "views" from the second half of the century, such as Albert Ruger, Augustus Koch, Oakley H. Baily, and Thaddeus Mortimer Fowler. While their productions are fascinating as documents with abundant information, they are not landscape fine art. Reps, *Views and Viewmakers,* 3–16.

49. *Democratic Art,* chaps. 11–12.

NOTE ABOUT SOURCES

The following entries represent the sources consulted while researching this book and the surveys for the *Philadelphia on Stone* project. Periodicals, newspapers, and directories listed in the bibliography primarily indicate the items and issues cited in the text of the essays or the notes and do not necessarily reflect all of the titles or the complete runs examined for the project. Although not listed, the genealogical websites ancestry.com, footnote.com, and GenealogyBank.com also informed the content of this book. Please consult the bibliography compiled for the *Philadelphia on Stone* Biographical Dictionary of Lithographers (http://www.librarycompany.org/pos/bibliography.htm) for additional listings of the sources surveyed.

ARCHIVES AND MANUSCRIPTS

Beyond Wainwright Collection. Print and Photograph Department, LCP.

Cadwalader Family Papers. Series VII: General George Cadwalader. HSP.

Castner, Samuel. Collection. Prints & Picture Department, FLP.

Cigna Collection. Division of Home and Community Life, Smithsonian.

City of Philadelphia, Department of Records, City Archives, RG 130.3 Mayor's Court, Naturalization Declaration Docket, 1814–38 (Peter S. Duval), and RG 20, Insolvency Petitions of the Common Pleas Court, Philadelphia County, Box A-175, Peter S. Duval, 1859.

Dallett, Francis James. Papers. HSP.

Doret, David. Collection of Centennial Ephemera. LCP.

Doret, David. Private collection.

Dreer Collection—Painters and Engravers. HSP.

Dun, R. G., & Co. Collection. Pennsylvania. Microfilm, Manuscript Division, Hagley Museum and Library.

Duval & Hunter's Catalogue of Oleograph Publications for the Season 1873–4. Philadelphia, 1873. Graphic Arts Division, Smithsonian.

Fales, Samuel B. Collection, Correspondence. HSP.

General Prints Collection. Athenaeum of Philadelphia.

Girard, Stephen. Papers. Real Estate Accounts, 1810–31 and 1817–25. Girard College. Microfilm, APS.

Graphic Arts Collections. Division of Information Technology and Communications. Smithsonian.

Graphics Collections. HSP.

Hart, Charles. "Lithography, Its Theory and Practice, Including a Series of Short Sketches of the Earliest Lithographic Artists, Engravers, and Printers of New York," Lithographic Records, Manuscript Division, New York Public Library.

Inman, Henry. Letters. AAS.

Inman, Henry. Letters. Society Collection. HSP.

Kollner, Augustus. Collection. Prints & Picture Department, FLP.

Lithography Collection. Graphic Arts Department, AAS.

McAllister, John. Papers. HSP.

McDonogh, John. Papers. Tulane University Library, New Orleans, Louisiana.

Newsam, Albert. Print Collection. HSP.

Newsam, Albert. Papers. LCP.

Peters, Harry T. America on Stone Collection. Division of Home and Community Life, Smithsonian.

Philadelphiana Collection. Prints & Picture Department, FLP.

Philadelphia Wills: 1682–1900. Register of Wills. City Hall, Philadelphia.

Popular Graphic Arts Collections. Prints & Photographs, LOC.

Prints Collection. The Philadelphia History Museum at Atwater Kent.

Queen, James. Archive. Carson Collection. LOC.

Queen, James. Year 1886, Will 102, Register of Wills, City Hall, Philadelphia.

Records of the U.S. Customs Service, 1745–1997 (RG 36), National Archives and Records Administration, Philadelphia.

Richards, Frederick DeBourg. Collection. Print and Photograph Department, LCP.

Sellers, Charles Coleman. Papers. APS.

Shubert, George D. Diary, 1866. Special Collections, Paley Library, Temple University, Philadelphia.

Stephens, Henry Lewis. Collection. Print and Photograph Department, LCP.

Stewart, Thomas S. Ledger, 1829–. Athenaeum of Philadelphia.

Wagner, Thomas. Year 1863, Will 51, Vol. 436, Register of Wills, City Hall, Philadelphia.

Wainwright Collection. Print and Photograph Department, LCP.

Waite, Emma Forbes. [Notes on American Lithography]. AAS.

Warshaw Collection of Business Ephemera. Archives Center, Smithsonian.

Weaver, Matthias. Diaries, 1840–43. Ohio Historical Society, Columbus.

CONTEMPORARY NEWSPAPERS AND TRADE JOURNALS

American Lithographer & Printer (New York)
Daily Pennsylvanian (Philadelphia)
Franklin Journal, and American Mechanics' Magazine; Devoted to the Useful Arts, Internal Improvements, and General Science (original and new series) (Philadelphia)
Lithographer's Journal (Philadelphia)
National Lithographer (Jersey City)
National Gazette (Philadelphia)
The Pennsylvanian (subsequently *Daily Pennsylvanian*)
New York Times
North American (Philadelphia)
Philadelphia Inquirer (previously *Pennsylvania Inquirer and Daily Courier, Pennsylvania Inquirer and National Gazette,* and *Pennsylvania Inquirer*)
The Press (Philadelphia)
Printers' Circular (Philadelphia)
Public Ledger (Philadelphia)
Saturday Courier (Philadelphia)
Saturday Evening Post (Philadelphia)
United States Gazette (Philadelphia)

PRIMARY AND SECONDARY PUBLISHED SOURCES

"Account of the Art Now Practiced in Europe for Multiplying Copies of Drawings and Manuscripts, by Means of a Peculiar Stone and Ink, Lately Discovered." *Medical Repository* 5 (January 1808): 244–46.

Accounts of the Late Superintendent of Public Printing. 35th Cong., 2nd Sess. H.R. Rep. No. 189. February 28, 1859.

Aldrich, Mark. *Death Rode the Rails: American Railroad Accidents and Safety, 1828–1965.* Baltimore: Johns Hopkins University Press, 2006.

Ambrose, Jennifer. "Nineteenth-Century Philadelphia Advertising Prints." In "The Library Company of Philadelphia," special issue, *Antiques* 170, no. 2 (August 2006): 94–101.

———. "Picturing Factories and Storefronts: Mid-19th Century Advertising Lithographs." Paper presented at "Impressions of Philadelphia," North American Print Conference 2007, Philadelphia, September 28, 2007.

American Paradise: The World of the Hudson River School. Introduction by John K. Howat. New York: Metropolitan Museum of Art, 1987. Distributed by Harry N. Abrams.

American Philosophical Society. *Early Proceedings of the American Philosophical Society for the Promotion of Useful Knowledge, Compiled . . . from Manuscript Minutes of Its Meetings from 1744 to 1838.* Philadelphia: McCalla & Stavely, 1884.

Anthony, David. "The Helen Jewett Panic: Tabloids, Men, and the Sensational Public Sphere in Antebellum New York." *American Literature* 69 (September 1997): 487–514.

Antreasian, Garo Z., and Clinton Adams, eds. *The Tamarind Book of Lithography: Art & Techniques.* Los Angeles: Tamarind Lithography Workshop; New York: Harry N. Abrams, 1971.

Appleton's Dictionary of Machines, Mechanics, Engine Work & Engraving. New York: D. Appleton & Co., 1851.

Arnold, Grant. *Creative Lithography.* New York: Harper Bros., 1941.

Art & Commerce: American Prints of the Nineteenth Century; Proceedings of a Conference Held in Boston, May 8–10, 1975, Museum of Fine Arts, Boston, Massachusetts. Charlottesville: University Press of Virginia, 1978.

Authentic Narrative of the Murder of Mrs. Rademacher: With Splendid Illustrations, Drawn and Engraved Expressly for This Publication. Philadelphia: G. Zeiber, 1848.

Barnhill, Georgia B. *Bibliography on American Prints of the Seventeenth Through the Nineteenth Centuries.* New Castle, Del.: Oak Knoll Press, 2006.

———. "The Introduction and Early Use of Lithography in the United States." Paper presented at the 67th International Federation of Library Associations and Institutions Council and General Conference, Boston, Mass., August 16–25, 2001.

———. "The Publication of Illustrated Natural Histories in Philadelphia, 1800–1850." In *The American Illustrated Books in the Nineteenth Century,* edited by Gerald W. R. Ward, 53–88. Charlottesville: University Press of Virginia, 1987.

Barnhurst, Kevin G., and John Nerone. "Civic Picturing vs. Realist Photojournalism: The Regime of Illustrated News, 1856–1901." *Design Issues* 16 (Spring 2000): 59–79.

———. *The Form of News: A History.* New York: Guilford Press, 2001.

Beall, Karen F. "The Interdependency of Printer & Printmaker in Early 19th-Century Lithography." *Art Journal* (Spring 1980): 195–201.

Benjamin, Walter. "The Work of Art in the Age of Mechanical Reproduction (1936)." In *The Nineteenth-Century Visual Culture Reader,* edited by Vanessa R. Schwartz and Jeannene M. Przyblyski, 63–70. New York: Routledge, 2004.

Bennett, Whitman. *A Practical Guide to American Nineteenth Century Color Plate Books.* New York: Bennett Book Studios, 1949.

The Bicentennial of Lithography: A Keepsake for the Members of the Book Club of California. San Francisco: Book Club of California, 1999.

Bishop, J. Leander. *A History of American Manufactures from 1608 to 1860: Exhibiting the Origin and Growth of the Principal Mechanic Arts and Manufactures, from the Earliest Colonial Period to the Adoption of the Constitution and Comprising Annals of the Industry of the United States in Machinery, Manufactures, and Useful Arts, with a Notice of the Important Inventions, Tariffs, and the Results of Each Decennial Census.* Vol. 1. Philadelphia: Edward Young & Co., 1861.

Black, Mary. *American Advertising Posters of the Nineteenth Century: From the Bella C. Landauer Collection of the New-York Historical Society.* New York: Dover Publications, 1976.

Blackmar, Elizabeth. *Manhattan for Rent, 1785–1850.* Ithaca: Cornell University Press, 1989.

Blodget, Lorin. *The Industries of Philadelphia as Shown by the Manufacturing Census of 1870, Compared with 1860 and Estimates for 1875.* Philadelphia: Collins, printer, 1876.

Blodget, Lorin, and Edwin T. Freedley. *Philadelphia and Its Industries: A Descriptive Review.* Philadelphia: Press of John D. Avil & Co., 1885.

Blondheim, Menaheim. *News over the Wires: The Telegraph and the Flow of Public Information in America, 1844–1897.* Cambridge: Harvard University Press, 1994.

Blum, Ann Shelby. *Picturing Nature: American Nineteenth-Century Zoological Illustration.* Princeton: Princeton University Press, 1993.

[Bobo, William M.]. *Glimpses of New-York City: By a South Carolinian (Who Had Nothing Else to Do).* Charleston, S.C.: J. J. McCarter, 1852.

Bridson, Gavin D. R., and Geoffrey Wakeman. *Printmaking and Picture Printing.* Williamsburg, Va.: Bookpress, 1984.

Brissot de Warville, Jacques-Pierre. *New Travels in the United States of America: Performed in 1788.* Dublin: Printed by W. Corbet, for P. Byrne, A. Grueber, et al., 1792.

Brockman, R. John. *Accident Investigation Reports, 1822–1879.* Amityville, N.Y.: Baywood Pub. Co., 2005.

Brown, Bolton. *Lithography.* New York: F. Carrington, 1923.

———. *Lithography for Artists: A Complete Account of How to Grind, Draw upon, Etch, and Print from the Stone, Together with Instructions for Making Crayon, Transferring, etc.* Chicago: Published for the Art Institute of Chicago by the University of Chicago, 1930.

Brown, Joshua. *Beyond the Lines: Pictorial Reporting, Everyday Life, and the Crisis of Gilded Age America.* Berkeley: University of California Press, 2002.

Brown University, Department of Art. *Early Lithography, 1800–1840.* Providence, R.I.: Annmary Brown Memorial Library, 1968.

Bumgardner, Georgia Brady. "George and William Endicott: Commercial Lithography in New York, 1831–1851." In *Prints and Printmakers of New York State, 1825–1940,* edited by David Tatham, 43–66. Syracuse: Syracuse University Press, 1986.

Bushman, Richard L. *The Refinement of America: Persons, Houses, Cities.* New York: Knopf, 1992.

Butterfield, Roger. "The Folklore of Politics." *PMHB* 74 (April 1950): 164–77.

Campbell, William P. *The Civil War: A Centennial Exhibition of Eyewitness Drawings.* Washington, D.C.: National Gallery of Art, 1961.

Cantwell, Anne-Marie, and Diana diZerega Wall. *Unearthing Gotham: The Archaeology of New York City.* New Haven: Yale University Press, 2001.

Carey, John T. "The American Lithograph from Its Inception to 1865." Ph.D. diss., Ohio State University, 1954.

Carson, Cary. "The Consumer Revolution in Colonial British America: Why Demand?" In *Of Consuming Interests: The Style of Life in the Eighteenth Century,* edited by Cary Carson, Ronald Hoffman, and Peter J. Albert, 483–697. Charlottesville: University Press of Virginia for the United States Capitol Historical Society, 1994.

Carter, Edward C., II, ed. *Surveying the Record: North American Scientific*

Exploration to 1930. Philadelphia: American Philosophical Society, 1999.

Casper, Scott E., Jeffrey D. Groves, Stephen W. Nissenbaum, and Michael Winship, eds. *The Industrial Book, 1840–1880.* A History of the Book in America, vol. 3. Chapel Hill: Published in association with the American Antiquarian Society by the University of North Carolina Press, 2007.

Catalogue of an Exhibition Illustrative of a Centenary of Artistic Lithography, 1796–1896. New York: Grolier Club, 1896.

Catalogue of the Eighteenth Exhibition of American Manufactures, Held in Philadelphia, 1848. Philadelphia: William S. Young, printer, 1848.

Catalogue of the Twenty-Fourth Exhibition of American Manufactures, Held in the City of Philadelphia, by the Franklin Institute, of the State of Pennsylvania, for the Promotion of the Mechanic Arts, from the 14th Day of Nov., to the 2d Day of Dec., 1854. Philadelphia: William S. Young, printer, 1854.

Centennial Exhibition (1876: Philadelphia, Pa.). *Official Catalogue.* 2nd and rev. ed. Philadelphia: J. R. Nagle & Co., 1876.

"Chromolithography." *Philadelphia Photographer* 3 (August 1866): 233–34.

Cochran, Carl Malcolm. "James Fuller Queen—Artist and Lithographer." Master's thesis, University of Pittsburgh, 1954.

———. "James Queen: Philadelphia Lithographer." *PMHB* 82 (April 1958): 139–75.

Cohn, Majorie, and Claire I. Rogan. *Touchstone: 200 Years of Artist's Lithographs.* Cambridge: Harvard University Art Museums, 1998.

Cole, Thomas. "Essay on American Scenery." *American Monthly Magazine* 1 (January 1836): 1–12.

Comstock, Helen. *American Lithographs of the Nineteenth Century.* New York: M. Barrows & Co., 1950.

Constitution and By-Laws of the Lithographic Printers Union of Philadelphia. Philadelphia: Printed by F. W. Thomas, 1857.

Cotter, John L., Daniel G. Roberts, and Michael Parrington. *The Buried Past: An Archaeological History of Philadelphia.* Philadelphia: University of Pennsylvania Press, 1992.

Courtney, Rosemary. "M. E. D. Brown (1810–1896): American Lithographer and Painter." *American Art Journal* 12 (Autumn 1980): 66–67.

Craven, Wayne. *Bass Otis: Painter, Portraitist, and Engraver.* Wilmington: Historical Society of Delaware, 1976.

Cutbush, James. *The American Artist's Manual and Dictionary of Practical Knowledge in the Application of Philosophy to the Arts and Manufacturers.* Vol. 1. Philadelphia: Johnson & Warner, and R. Fisher; W. Brown, printer, 1814.

Czitrom, Daniel. *Media and the American Mind: From Morse to McLuhan.* Chapel Hill: University of North Carolina Press, 1982.

Dallett, Francis James. "The French in Philadelphia: The French Benevolent Society of Philadelphia." In *Invisible Philadelphia: Community Through Voluntary Organizations,* edited by Jean Barth Toll and Mildred S. Gillam, 78–82. Philadelphia: Atwater Kent Museum, 1995.

Davis, Susan G. "'Making Night Hideous': Christmas Revelry and Public Order in Nineteenth-Century Philadelphia." *American Quarterly* 34 (Summer 1982): 185–99.

Davison, Nancy. "E. W. Clay: American Political Caricaturist of the Jacksonian Era." Ph.D. diss., University of Michigan, 1980.

Day, Sara, ed. *Gathering History: The Marian S. Carson Collection of Americana.* Washington, D.C.: Library of Congress, 1999.

Deák, Gloria-Gilda. *American Views: Prospects and Vistas.* New York: Viking Press, 1976.

———. *Picturing America, 1497–1899: Prints, Maps, and Drawings Bearing on the New World Discoveries and on the Development of the Territory That Is Now the United States.* 2 vols. Princeton: Princeton University Press, 1988.

Description of the Print Entitled Washington's Triumphal Entry, New York, Nov. 25th, 1783. Philadelphia: J. B. Chandler, printer, 1861.

De Vinne, Theodore Low. *The Printers' Price List: A Manual for the Use of Clerks and Book-Keepers in Job Printing Offices.* New York: F. Hart & Co., 1871.

Dichter, Harry, and Elliott Shapiro. *Handbook of Early American Sheet Music, 1768–1889.* New York: Dover, 1977.

Dictionary of Literary Biography. Detroit, Mich.: Gale Research Co., 1978–.

Drepperd, Carl W. "Why Only Currier & Ives?" *Antiques* 11 (February 1927): 108–12.

Drinker, Elizabeth. *The Diary of Elizabeth Drinker.* Edited by Elaine Forman Crane. 3 vols. Boston: Northeastern University Press, 1991.

Duke, Sara W. "'Always Ready': The American Fireman as Historic and Cultural Icon." *Library of Congress Information Bulletin* 61 (September 2002). http://www.loc.gov/loc/lcib/0209/firemen.html.

Dunlap, William. *A History of the Rise and Progress of the Arts of Design in the United States.* 2 vols. in 3. 1834. Reprint, New York: Dover Publications, [1969].

[Duval, P. S.]. "Lithography." In *American Encyclopaedia of Printing,* edited by J. L. Ringwalt, 276–86. Philadelphia: Menamin & Ringwalt / J. B. Lippincott & Co., 1871.

Eckhardt, George. "Early Lithography in Philadelphia." *Antiques* 28 (December 1935): 249–52.

Eighty Years Progress of the United States. New York: L. Stebbins, 1861.

Eldredge, Charles C. *Tales from the Easel: American Narrative Paintings from Southeastern Museums, Circa 1800–1950.* Athens: University of Georgia Press, 2004.

Encyclopaedia Americana: A Popular Dictionary of Arts, Sciences, Literature, History, Politics, and Biography. Boston: Sanborn, Carter & Bazin, 1856.

Engelmann, Godefroy. *Album chromolithographique, ou recueil d'essais du nouveau procédé d'impression lithographique en couleurs inventé par Engelmann père & fils à Mulhouse.* Paris: Risler fils; Leipzig: Del Vecchio, 1837.

———. *Traité théorique et pratique de lithographie.* Mulhouse, [1840].

Every Man His Own Printer, or Lithography Made Easy: Being an Essay upon Lithography in All Its Branches, Showing More Particularly the Advantages of the "Patent Autographic Press." London: Waterlow & Sons, 1854.

Ewen, Stuart. *Captains of Consciousness: Advertising and the Social Roots of the Consumer Culture.* New York: McGraw-Hill, 1976.

Falk, Peter Hastings, ed. *The Annual Exhibition Record of the Pennsylvania Academy of the Fine Arts.* Vol. 1, *1807–1870.* Reprint with revisions of the 1955 edition of Anna Wells Rutledge's *Cummulative [sic] Record of Exhibition Catalogues.* Madison, Conn.: Sound View Press, 1988.

———, ed. *Who Was Who in American Art.* Madison, Conn.: Sound View Press, 1985.

Falk, Peter Hastings, Audrey Lewis, Georgia Kuchen, and Veronika Roessler, eds. *Who Was Who in American Art, 1564–1975: 400 Years of Artists in America.* 3 vols. Madison, Conn.: Sound View Press, 1999.

Farwell, Beatrice. *The Cult of Images: Baudelaire and the 19th-Century Media Explosion.* Santa Barbara: University of California, 1977.

———. *French Popular Lithographic Imagery, 1815–1870.* 12 vols. Chicago: University of Chicago Press, 1988.

Fielding, Mantle. *Catalogue of an Exhibition of Portraits by John Neagle.* Philadelphia: Pennsylvania Academy of the Fine Arts, 1925.

———. *Dictionary of American Painters, Sculptors, and Engravers.* Poughkeepsie, N.Y.: Apollo Books, 1983.

Fielding, T. H. *On the Theory of Painting: To Which Is Added, an Introduction to Painting in Water-Colours.* London: Published for the author by Ackermann & Co., 1842.

"Fine Arts: Stump-Lithography and Zincography." *Museum of Foreign Literature and Science* 26 (January–June 1835): 473–74.

Finlay, Nancy, ed. *Picturing Victorian America: Prints by the Kellogg Brothers of Hartford, Connecticut, 1830–1880.* Hartford: Connecticut Historical Society, 2009.

Ford, Alice, comp. and ed. *Audubon's Animals: The Quadrupeds of North America.* New York: Studio Publications in Association with Crowell, [1951].

———, ed. *John James Audubon.* Norman: University of Oklahoma Press, [1964].

Fowble, E. McSherry. *Two Centuries of Prints in America, 1680–1880: A Selective Catalogue of the Winterthur Museum Collection.* Charlottesville: Published for the Henry Francis du Pont Winterthur Museum by the University Press of Virginia, 1987.

Fowler, Nathaniel C. *About Advertising and Printing: A Concise, Practical, and Original Manual on the Art of Local Advertising.* Boston: A. M. Thayer & Co., 1889.

Frank Leslie's Historical Register of the United States Centennial Exposition, 1876: Embellished with Nearly Eight Hundred Illustrations . . . by the Most Eminent Artists in America; Including Illustrations and Descriptions of All Previous International Exhibitions. Edited by Frank H. Norton. New York: Frank Leslie's Publishing House, 1877.

Frank Leslie's Illustrated Historical Register of the Centennial Exposition, 1876. Edited by Frank H. Norton. New York: Frank Leslie's Publishing House, 1876. Facsimile with an introduction by Richard Kenin. New York: Paddington Press, 1974.

Freedley, Edwin. *Leading Pursuits and Leading Men: A Treatise on the Principal Trades and Manufactures of the United States; Showing the Progress, State, and Prospects of Business; and Illustrated by Sketches of Distinguished Mercantile and Manufacturing Firms.* Philadelphia: Edward Young, 1856.

———. *Philadelphia and Its Manufactures: A Hand-Book Exhibiting the Development, Variety, and Statistics of the Manufacturing Industry of Philadelphia in 1857.* Philadelphia: Edward Young, 1858.

———. *Philadelphia and Its Manufactures: A Hand-Book of the Great Manufactories and Representative Mercantile Houses of Philadelphia in 1867.* Philadelphia: Edward Young & Co., 1867.

Gale Research Group. *Currier & Ives: A Catalogue Raisonné.* Detroit: Gale Research, 1983.

Gallman, J. Matthew. *Mastering Wartime: A Social History of Philadelphia During the Civil War.* Philadelphia: University of Pennsylvania Press, 2000.

Gandy, Lewis Cass. "The Story of Lithography." *Supplement to the Lithographers Journal* 24 (February 1940): 1–16.

Garvan, Anthony N. B., et al., eds. *The Architectural Surveys, 1784–1794.* Vol. 1. Philadelphia: Mutual Assurance Co., 1976.

Garvan, Anthony N. B., and Peter C. Welsh. *Victorian American Lithographs from the Harry T. Peters America on Stone Collection.* Washington, D.C.: Smithsonian Institution, 1961.

Garvan, Anthony N. B., and Carol A. Wojtowicz. *Catalogue of the Green Tree Collection.* Philadelphia: Mutual Assurance Co., 1977.

Gascoigne, Bamber. *Milestones in Colour Printing, 1457–1859.* Cambridge: Cambridge University Press, 1997.

Geismar, Joan H. "Patterns of Development in the Late-Eighteenth and Nineteenth-Century American Seaport: A Suggested Model for Recognizing Increasing Commercialism and Urbanization." *American Archeology* 5 (1985): 175–84.

Giberti, Bruno. *Designing the Centennial: A History of the International Exhibition in Philadelphia.* Lexington: University Press of Kentucky, 2002.

Gilmour, Pat, ed. *Lasting Impressions: Lithography as Art.* Philadelphia: University of Pennsylvania Press, 1988.

Golden, Jack. "Posters, Past and Present." *Imprint: Journal of the American Historical Print Collectors Society* 2 (November 1977): 6–8.

Goodman, James. *A Digest of Acts of Assembly Relating to the Incorporated District of the Northern Liberties; and of the Ordinances for the Government of the District.* Philadelphia: F. Pierson, 1853.

Gopsill's Philadelphia City Directory for 1870. Philadelphia: James Gopsill, 1870.

Gopsill's Philadelphia City Directory for 1890. Philadelphia: James Gopsill's Sons, 1890.

Gray, Nicolete. *Nineteenth Century Ornamented Typefaces.* New edition with a chapter on ornamented typefaces in America by Ray Nash. London: Faber & Faber, 1976.

Green, James N. "Colorplate Books in the Collection." In "The Library Company of Philadelphia," special issue, *Antiques* 170, no. 2 (August 2006): 72–79.

Green, James N., and Wendy Woloson. "From the Bottom Up: Popular Reading and Writing in the Michael Zinman Collection of Early American Imprints." Online exhibition. http://www.library-company.org/zinman.

[Greene, Asa]. *A Glance at New York: Embracing the City Government, Theatres, Hotels, Churches, Mobs, Monopolies, Learned Professions, Newspapers, Rogues, Dandies, Fires and Firemen, Water and Other Liquids, &c. &c.* New York: A. Greene, 1837.

Grier, Katherine C. *Culture and Comfort: People, Parlors, and Upholstery, 1850–1930.* Rochester, N.Y.: Strong Museum, 1988.

Groce, George C., and David H. Wallace. *The New-York Historical Society Dictionary of Artists in America.* New Haven: Yale University Press, 1957.

Haine, Edgar A. *Railroad Wrecks.* New York: Cornwell Books, 1993.

Harris, Neil. "Pictorial Perils: The Rise of American Illustration." In *The American Illustrated Book in the Nineteenth Century,* edited by Gerald W. R. Ward, 3–19. Charlottesville: University Press of Virginia, 1987.

Hayden, Delores. *Building Suburbia: Green Fields and Urban Growth, 1820–2000.* New York: Vintage Books, 2004.

Hazen, Edward. *The Panorama of Professions and Trades, or Every Man's Book.* Philadelphia: Uriah Hunt, 1837.

Heck, J. G. *Iconographic Encyclopaedia of Science, Literature, and Art Systematically Arranged by J. G. Heck.* Edited by Spencer F. Baird. Vol.

4. New York: Rudolph Garrigue, 1852.

Henkin, David M. *City Reading: Written Words and Public Spaces in Antebellum New York.* New York: Columbia University Press, 1998.

Hershberg, Theodore, ed. *Philadelphia: Work, Space, Family, and Group Experience in the Nineteenth Century.* New York: Oxford University Press, 1981.

Hodermarsky, Elisabeth. "The Kellogg Brothers' Images of the Mexican War and the Birth of Modern-Day News." In *Picturing Victorian America: Prints by the Kellogg Brothers of Hartford, Connecticut, 1830–1880,* edited by Nancy Finlay, 73–84. Hartford: Connecticut Historical Society, 2009.

Hodgson, Pat. *The War Illustrators.* New York: Macmillan, 1977.

Hopkins, Joseph G. E. "Plain Talk in Pictures." *New-York Historical Society Quarterly* 31 (April 1947): 97–105.

Hornung, Clarence P. *Handbook of Early American Advertising Art.* New York: Dover Publications, 1947.

Howe, Kathleen Stewart. *Intersections: Lithography, Photography, and the Traditions of Printmaking.* Albuquerque: University of New Mexico Press, 1998.

Hudson, Graham. *The Design & Printing of Ephemera in Britain & America, 1720–1920.* London: British Library; New Castle, Del.: Oak Knoll Press, 2008.

Hullmandel, Charles. *The Art of Drawing on Stone.* London: C. Hullmandel & R. Ackermann, 1824.

Hunt, Robert. "Lithography, and Other Novelties in Printing." *Art-Journal* (1854): 1–3.

The Industries of Philadelphia. Philadelphia: Richard Edwards, 1881.

Ivins, William Mills. *Prints and Visual Communication.* Cambridge: Harvard University Press, 1953.

Jackson, Joseph. "Bass Otis, America's First Lithographer." *PMHB* 37 (October 1913): 385–94.

———. "Lithography." In *Encyclopedia of Philadelphia,* vol. 4. Philadelphia, 1933.

———. "Some Notes Towards a History of Lithography in Philadelphia." In *The Official Reference Book of the Lithographers International Protective and Beneficial Association, S. A. No. 14 of the United States: 1899.* Philadelphia, 1900.

Jackson, Mason. *The Pictorial Press: Its Origin and Progress.* London: Hurst & Blackett, 1885.

Jay, Robert. *The Trade Card in Nineteenth-Century America.* Columbia: University of Missouri Press, 1987.

Jay T. Snider Collection, Featuring the History of Philadelphia and Important Americana. New York: Bloomsbury Auctions, 2008.

Jordan, William H. *North Third Street, Philadelphia, Forty-Five Years Ago.* Philadelphia: Philadelphia Press of the New Era Printing Co., 1905.

Kasson, John. *Rudeness and Civility: Manners in Nineteenth-Century Urban America.* New York: Hill & Wang, 1990.

Katz, Harry. "Prints and Drawings." In *Gathering History: The Marian S. Carson Collection of Americana,* edited by Sara Day, 73–96. Washington, D.C.: Library of Congress, 1999.

Keller, Ulrich. "Photojournalism Around 1900: The Institutionalization of a Mass Medium." In *Shadow and Substance: Essays in the History of Photography,* edited by Kathleen Collins, 283–303. Bloomfield Hills, Mich.: Amorphous Institute Press, 1990.

Kelly, Rob Roy. *American Wood Type, 1828–1900.* New York: Da Capo Press, 1977. First published 1969 by Nostrand Reinhold Co.

Knoles, Thomas. *The Notebook of Bass Otis, Philadelphia Portrait Painter.* Worcester, Mass.: American Antiquarian Society, 1993.

Kribbs, Jayne K., comp. and ed. *An Annotated Bibliography of American Literary Periodicals, 1741–1850.* Boston: G. K. Hall, 1977.

Krummel, Donald William, and Stanley Sadie. *Music Printing and Publishing.* New York: W. W. Norton, 1990.

Ladies Philadelphia Shopping Guide & Housekeeper's Companion: For 1859. Philadelphia: Published by the author, 1859.

Laird, Pamela Walker. *Advertising Progress: American Business and the Rise of Consumer Marketing.* Baltimore: Johns Hopkins University Press, 2001.

Lambert, Luna Frances. "The Seasonal Trade: Gift Cards and Chromolithography in America, 1874–1910." Ph.D. diss., George Washington University, 1980.

Lane, Christopher W. "A History of McKenney and Hall's *History of the Indian Tribes of North America.*" *Imprint: Journal of the American Historical Print Collectors Society* 27 (Autumn 2002): 2–15.

———. *Impressions of Niagara: Addendum.* Philadelphia: Philadelphia Print Shop, 2002.

———. *Impressions of Niagara: The Charles*

Rand Penney Collection. Philadelphia: Philadelphia Print Shop, 1993.

Lane, Christopher W., and Don Cresswell. *Prints of Philadelphia at the Philadelphia Print Shop, Featuring the Wohl Collection.* Philadelphia: Philadelphia Print Shop, 1990.

Last, Jay T. *The Color Explosion: Nineteenth-Century American Lithography.* Santa Ana, Calif.: Hillcrest Press, 2005.

———. "Trade Card Lithographers." *Advertising Trade Card Quarterly* 1 (1994): 18–19.

Laurie, Bruce. "Fire Companies and Gangs in Southwark, the 1840s." In *The Peoples of Philadelphia: A History of Ethnic Groups and Lower-Class Life, 1790–1940,* edited by Allen F. Davis and Mark H. Haller, 71–87. Philadelphia: Temple University Press, [1973].

———. *Working People of Philadelphia, 1800–1850.* Philadelphia: Temple University Press, 1980.

Lears, T. J. Jackson. *Fables of Abundance: A Cultural History of Advertising in America.* New York: Basic Books, 1994.

LeBeau, Bryan F. *Currier & Ives: America Imagined.* Washington, D.C.: Smithsonian Institution Press, 2001.

Lehuu, Isabelle. *Carnival on the Page: Popular Print Media in Antebellum America.* Chapel Hill: University of North Carolina Press, 2000.

Lemercier, Alfred. *La lithographie française de 1796 à 1896.* Paris: Ch. Lorilleux, [1898].

Levison, Luna Lambert. "Images That Sell: Color Advertising and Boston Printmakers, 1850–1900." In *Aspects of American Printmak-ing, 1800–1950,* edited by James F. O'Gorman, 83–103. Syracuse: Syracuse University Press, 1988.

Levy, Lester. *Picture the Songs: Lithographs from the Sheet Music of Nineteenth-Century America.* Baltimore: Johns Hopkins University Press, 1976.

Lewis, Robert, ed. *Manufacturing Suburbs: Building Work and Home on the Metropolitan Fringe.* Philadelphia: Temple University Press, 2004.

Licht, Walter. *Getting Work: Philadelphia, 1840–1950.* Cambridge: Harvard University Press, 1992.

"Lithography." *American Journal of Science* 1, no. 4 (1819): 439.

"Lithography." *Analectic Magazine* 12 (November 1818): 430–31; 14 (July 1819): 67–73.

"Lithography." In *Bibliography on American Prints of the Seventeenth Through the Nineteenth Centuries,* edited by Georgia Barnhill, 138–44. New Castle, Del.: Oak Knoll Press, 2006.

"Lithography." *Boston Monthly Magazine* 1, no. 7 (December 1825): 378–84.

"Lithography." *Scientific American* 7, no. 45 (July 25, 1852): 357.

"Lithography." *United States Literary Gazette* 4 (June 15, 1828): 226.

"Lithography." *Western Review* 1, no. 1 (August 1819): 59–60.

Looney, Robert F. "Thomas Doughty, Printmaker." *Imprint: Journal of the American Historical Print Collectors Society* 4 (Autumn 1979): 2–10.

Lubin, David M. "Art in the Age of National Expansion: Genre and Landscape Painting." In *Art in America: 300 Years of Innovation,* edited by Susan Davidson, 94–139. New York: Guggenheim Museum, 2007.

MacKay, Alexander. *The Western World, or Travels in the United States in 1846–47: Exhibiting Them in Their Latest Development, Social, Political, and Industrial; Including a Chapter on California.* 3 vols. 2nd ed. London: Richard Bentley, 1849.

Maidment, B. E. *Reading Popular Prints.* New York: St. Martin's Press, 1996.

Mann, Maybelle. "Augustus Kollner." *Imprint: Journal of the American Historical Print Collectors Society* 6 (Spring 1981): 19–22.

Manual of the Corporation of the City of New York. Compiled by D. T. Valentine. For the Years 1850–59, vols. 10–19. New York: Common Council, 1850–59.

Marzio, Peter C. "American Lithographic Technology Before the Civil War." In *Prints in and of America to 1850,* edited by John D. Morse, 215–56. Charlottesville: University Press of Virginia, 1970.

———. *The Art Crusade: An Analysis of American Drawing Manuals, 1820–1860.* Smithsonian Studies in History and Technology, no. 34. Washington, D.C.: Smithsonian Institution Press, 1976.

———. "The Democratic Art of Chromolithography in America: An Overview." In *Art and Commerce: American Prints of the Nineteenth Century,* 76–102. [Boston]: Museum of Fine Arts, 1978.

———. *The Democratic Art: Pictures for a 19th-Century America; Chromolithography, 1840–1900.* Boston: D. R. Godine; Fort Worth: Amon Carter Museum of Western Art, 1979.

———. "Illustrated News in Early American Prints." In *American Printmaking Before 1876: Fact, Fiction, and*

Fantasy, 53–60. Washington, D.C.: Library of Congress, 1975.

——— . "Lithography as a Democratic Art: A Reappraisal." *Leonardo* 4 (Winter 1971): 37–48.

Marzio, Peter C., and Milton Kaplan. "Lithographs as Historical Documents." *Antiques* 102 (October 1971): 669–74.

Masur, Louis. *1831: Year of Eclipse.* New York: Hill & Wang, 2001.

Mayer, Henry. *All on Fire: William Lloyd Garrison and the Abolition of Slavery.* New York: St. Martin's Press, 1998.

McDermott, John Francis. "John Caspar Wild: Some New Facts and a Query." *PMHB* 83 (October 1959): 452–55.

McElroy's Philadelphia Directory, for 1856: Containing the Names of the Inhabitants of the Consolidated City, Their Occupations, Places of Business, and Dwelling Houses; A Business Directory, a List of the Streets, Lanes, Alleys, the City Offices, Public Institutions, Banks, &c. Philadelphia: Edward C. & John Biddle, printed by Henry B. Ashmead, 1856.

McGrath, Daniel F. "American Colorplate Books, 1800–1900." Ph.D. diss., University of Michigan, 1966.

McKay, Richard C. *South Street: A Maritime History of New York.* 1934. Reprint, New York: Haskell House, 1971.

McKee, John Carpenter. "Bass Otis and His Critics." Master's thesis, University of Delaware, 1995.

McLanathan, Richard. *The American Tradition in the Arts.* New York: Harcourt, Brace & World, 1968.

Mease, James T., and Thomas Porter. *The Picture of Philadelphia.* 2 vols. Philadelphia: Robert DeSilver, 1831.

M'Elroy's Philadelphia Directory for 1840: Containing the Names of the Inhabitants, Their Occupations, Places of Business, and Dwelling-Houses. Philadelphia: A. M'Elroy, 1840.

The Mercantile Register, or Business Man's Guide: Containing a List of the Principal Business Establishments, Including Hotels, and Public Institutions in Philadelphia. Philadelphia: H. Orr, 1846.

Merrill, Peter C. *German Immigrant Artists in America: A Biographical Dictionary.* Lanham, Md.: Scarecrow Press, 1997.

Merten, John W. *Stone by Stone Along a Hundred Years with the House of Strobridge.* Cincinnati: Historical and Philosophical Society of Ohio, 1950.

Military Magazine and Record of the Volunteers of the City and County (Philadelphia) 1 (1839).

Moak, Jefferson. *Atlases of Pennsylvania: A Preliminary Checklist of County, City, and Subject Atlases of Pennsylvania.* Philadelphia: Jefferson Moak, 1976.

———. "Louis H. Everts: American Atlas Publisher and Entrepreneur." *Coordinates,* ser. B, no. 11 (2009). http://www.stonybrook.edu/libmap/coordinates/seriesb/no11/b11.pdf.

The Monument Cemetery of Philadelphia (Late Père la Chaise). Philadelphia: [J. A. Elkington]; Rackliff & King, printers, 1837.

Morais, Henry S. *The Jews of Philadelphia: Their History from the Earliest Settlements to the Present Time; A Record of Events and Institutions, and of Leading Members of the Jewish Community in Every Sphere of Activity.* Philadelphia: Levytype Co., 1894.

Morton, Thomas G., M.D., and Frank Woodbury, A.M., M.D. *The History of Pennsylvania Hospital, 1751–1895.* Philadelphia: Times Printing House, 1897.

Mosimann, Elizabeth. "'The Useful and Beautiful': 19th-Century Botanical Lithography in Philadelphia." *Imprint: Journal of the American Historical Print Collectors Society* 12 (Autumn 1987): 12–20.

Mott, Frank Luther. *A History of American Magazines.* Vol. 1, *1741–1850;* Vol. 2, *1850–1865.* Cambridge: Harvard University Press, 1938.

Müller-Burger, Maria L. *Die Solnhofer Plattenkalk-Industrie in Vergangenheit und Gegenwart.* Wirtschafts- und Verwaltungsstudien mit besonderer Berücksichtigung Bayerns 70. Leipzig: Scholl, 1926.

Munsing, Stephanie. *Made in America: Printmaking, 1760–1860; An Exhibition of Original Prints from the Collections of the Library Company of Philadelphia and the Historical Society of Pennsylvania, April–June, 1973.* Philadelphia: Library Company of Philadelphia, 1973.

Munson, Fred C. *History of the Lithographers' Union.* Cambridge, Mass.: Amalgamated Lithographers of America, 1963.

Neely, Mark E., Jr., and Harold Holzer. *The Union Image: Popular Prints of the Civil War North.* Chapel Hill: University of North Carolina Press, 2000.

The New American Cyclopaedia. New York: D. Appleton & Co., 1860–63.

"The New Art of Lithotint." *Miss Leslie's Magazine* 7 (April 1843): 113–14.

New-York Historical Society. *Dictionary of Artists in America.* New Haven: Yale University Press, 1957.

Nipps, Karen. *Naturally Fond of Pictures: American Illustration of the 1840s and 1850s.* Philadelphia: Library Company of Philadelphia, 1989. An exhibition catalog.

Norton, Bettina A. *Edwin Whitefield—Nineteenth-Century North American Scenery.* Barre, Mass.: Barre Publishing, 1977.

"Notice of the Lithographic Art, or the Art of Multiplying Designs by Substituting Stone for Copper Plate, with Introductory Remarks by the Editor." *American Journal of Science* 4, no. 1 (October 1821): 169–71.

The Orchardist's Companion 1 (April 1841): preface.

Ormsbee, Thomas Hamilton. "Advertising Prints: A Phase of American Lithography." *American Collector* 3 (July 1938): 8–9, 20.

Parton, James. "Popularizing Art." *Atlantic Monthly* 23 (March 1869): 348–57.

Peck, Robert McCracken. Introduction to *Illustrations of Birds of California, Texas, Oregon, British and Russian America,* by John Cassin, 3–38. Austin: Texas State Historical Association, 1991. Originally published in Philadelphia by J. B. Lippincott, 1856.

Pennell, Elizabeth Robbins, and Joseph Pennell. *Lithography and Lithographers: Some Chapters in the History of the Art.* New York: Macmillan, 1915.

Pennell, Joseph. "Lithography." *Print Collectors Quarterly* 2 (December 1912): 459–82.

Penny, Virginia. *Five Hundred Employments Adapted to Women: With the Average Rate of Pay of Each.* Philadelphia: John E. Porter & Co., 1868.

Peters, Harry T. *America on Stone: The Other Printmakers to the American People.* Garden City, N.Y.: Doubleday, 1931.

———. "The Little-Known American Lithograph." *Prints* 3 (March 1933): 1–13.

Pettit, James S. *Modern Reproductive Graphic Processes.* New York: D. Van Nostrand, 1884.

Phenix, Thomas. *Masonic Memorial.* Philadelphia, 1860.

The Philadelphia Fashions & Tailors' Archetypes. Philadelphia: Samuel A. Ward & Asahel F. Ward, July, 1849.

Pierce, Sally, and Catharina Slautterback. *Boston Lithography, 1825–1880.* Boston: Boston Athenaeum, 1991.

Pierce, Sally, with Catharina Slautterback and Georgia Brady Barnhill. *Early American Lithography: Images to 1830.* Boston: Boston Athenaeum, 1997.

Porter, Glenn, and Harold C. Livesay. *Merchants and Manufacturers: Studies in the Changing Structure of Nineteenth-Century Marketing.* Baltimore: Johns Hopkins University Press, 1971.

Porzio, Domenico, ed. *Lithography: 200 Years of Art, History & Technique.* New York: Abrams, 1983.

Poulson, Charles A., John Trucks, and Saunders Lewis, comps. *Ordinances of the Corporation of, and Acts of Assembly Relating to the City of Philadelphia.* Philadelphia: Crissy & Markley, 1851.

Pyatt, Joseph O. *Memoir of Albert Newsam.* Philadelphia: Printed for the author, 1868.

Rae, Julio H. *Rae's Philadelphia Pictorial Directory and Panoramic Advertiser.* Philadelphia, 1851.

Ramsay, John. "The American Scene in Lithograph." *Antiques* 61 (September 1951): 180–83.

Reaves, Wendy Wick. "Portraits for Every Parlor: Albert Newsam and American Portrait Lithography." In *American Portrait Prints,* edited by Wendy Wick Reaves, 83–134. Charlottesville: Published for the National Portrait Gallery, Smithsonian Institution, by the University Press of Virginia, 1984.

Reese, William S. *Stamped with a National Character: Nineteenth Century American Color Plate Books.* New York: Grolier Club, 1999.

Report of the Twenty-Second Exhibition of American Manufactures: Held in the City of Philadelphia, from the 19th to the 30th of October, 1852, by the Franklin Institute, of the State of Pennsylvania, for the Promotion of the Mechanic Arts; With the Address of the Hon. Judge Kelly. Philadelphia, 1852.

Report of the Twenty-Seventh Exhibition of American Manufactures: Held in the City of Philadelphia, from October 6th, to November 12th, 1874, by the Franklin Institute, of the State of Pennsylvania, for the Promotion of the Mechanic Arts, 1874. Philadelphia: Barnard & Jones, printers, 1874.

Reps, John W. *John Caspar Wild: Painter and Printmaker of Nineteenth-Century Urban America.* St. Louis: Missouri Historical Society Press, 2006.

———. *The Making of Urban America.* Princeton: Princeton University Press, 1965.

———. *Town Planning in Frontier America.* Princeton: Princeton University Press, 1969.

———. *Views and Viewmakers of Urban America.* Columbia: University of Missouri Press, 1984.

R. Hoe & Co. *R. Hoe & Co., Printing Press, Machine & Saw Manufacturers.* New York: [R. Hoe & Co., 1876].

R. Hoe & Co. *Manufacturers of Single and Double Cylinder, and Type Revolving Printing Machines, Washington and Smith Hand Presses, Self Inking Machines, etc.* New York: William Van Norden, printer, 1851.

Richmond, W. D. *The Grammar of Lithography: A Practical Guide for the Artist and Printer in Commercial & Artistic Lithography, & Chromolithography, Zincography, Photo-Lithography, and Lithographic Machine Printing.* London: Wyman & Sons, 1880.

Rickards, Maurice. *The Encyclopedia of Ephemera: A Guide to the Fragmentary Documents of Everyday Life for the Collector, Curator, and Historian.* Edited and completed by Michael Twyman with the assistance of Sally de Beaumont and Amoret Tanner. New York: Routledge, 2000.

Ristow, Walter. *American Maps and Mapmakers: Commercial Cartography in the Nineteenth Century.* Detroit: Wayne State University Press, 1985.

———. "Lithography and Maps, 1796–1850." In *Five Centuries of Map Printing,* edited by David Woodward, 77–112. Chicago: University of Chicago Press, 1975.

———. "The Map Publishing Career of Robert Pearsall Smith." *Quarterly Journal of the Library of Congress* 26 (July 1969): 170–96.

Ritter, Abraham. *Philadelphia and Her Merchants, as Constituted Fifty @ Seventy Years Ago, Illustrated by Diagrams of the River Front, and Portraits of Some of Its Prominent Occupants, Together with Sketches of Character and Incidents and Anecdotes of the Day.* Philadelphia: Published by the author, 1860.

Rosebrock, Ellen Fletcher. *Counting-House Days in South Street: New York's Early Brick Seaport Buildings.* New York: South Street Seaport Museum, 1975.

Rudge, William Edwin. *Early American Trade Cards: From the Collection of Bella C. Landauer.* New York: W. E. Rudge, 1927.

Sartain, John. *The Reminiscences of a Very Old Man, 1808–1897.* New York: D. Appleton & Co., 1899.

Scharf, J. Thomas, and Thompson Westcott. *History of Philadelphia, 1609–1884.* 3 vols. Philadelphia: L. H. Everts & Co., 1884.

Schein, R. H. "Representing Urban America: 19th-Century Views of Landscape, Space, and Power." *Environment & Planning D: Society & Space* 11 (1993): 7–21.

Schiller, Dan. *Objectivity and the News: The Public and the Rise of Commercial Journalism.* Philadelphia: University of Pennsylvania Press, 1981.

Schwartz, Vanessa R., and Jeannene M. Przyblyski. "Visual Culture's History: Twenty-First Century Interdisciplinarity and Its Nineteenth-Century Objects." In *The Nineteenth-Century Visual Culture Reader,* edited by Vanessa R. Schwartz and Jeannene M. Przyblyski, 3–36. New York: Routledge, 2004.

Scobey, David M. *Empire City: The Making and Meaning of the New York City Landscape.* Philadelphia: Temple University Press, 2002.

Seavey, Charles A. "Government Graphics: The Development of Illustration in U.S. Federal Publications, 1817–1861." In *A History of Book Illustration: 29 Points of View,* edited by Bill Katz, 514–47. Metuchen, N.J.: Scarecrow Press 1994.

Seibel, George A. *300 Years Since Hennepin: Niagara Falls in Art, 1678–1978.* [Niagara Falls, Ont.: Niagara Falls Heritage Foundation, 1978].

Senefelder, Alois. *A Complete Course of Lithography: Containing Clear and Explicit Instructions in All the Different Branches and Manners of That Art.* Preface by Frederic von Schlichtegroll. Translated from the original German by A. S. London: R. Ackerman, 1819.

———. *The Invention of Lithography.* Translated from the 1821 edition of the German text by J. W. Muller. New York: Fuchs & Lang Manufacturing Co., 1911.

———. *Vollständiges Lehrbuch der Steindruckerey.* Munich: Thienemann; Vienna: Gerold, 1818.

75 Years of Lithography, 1882–1947. New York: Amalgamated Lithographers of America, 1957.

Shelton, Cynthia J. *The Mills of Manayunk: Industrialization and Social Conflict in the Philadelphia Region, 1787–1837.* Baltimore: Johns Hopkins University Press, 1986.

Shorter, Clement. "Illustrated Journalism: Its Past and Its Future." *Contemporary Review* 75 (1899): 481–95.

Sloan, William David. *Perspectives on Mass Communication History.* New York: Routledge, 1991.

Smith, R. A. *Philadelphia as It Is in 1852.* Philadelphia: Lindsay & Blakeston, 1852.

Snyder, Martin P. *City of Independence: Views of Philadelphia Before 1800.* New York: Praeger Publishers, 1975.

———. "J. C. Wild and His Philadelphia Views." *PMHB* 77 (1953): 32–75.

———. "Liveliness: A Quality in Prints of Philadelphia." In *Philadelphia Printmaking: American Prints Before 1860,* edited by Robert F. Looney, 111–29. West Chester, Pa.: Tinicum Press, 1977.

———. *Mirror of America: The Developing Life of Philadelphia Seen in Engravings, 1801–1876.* Gladwyne, Pa: M. P. Snyder, 1996.

———. "William Birch: His Philadelphia Views." *PMHB* 73 (July 1949): 271–315.

———. "William L. Breton, Nineteenth-Century Philadelphia Artist." *PMHB* 85 (April 1961): 178–209.

Snyder, Theresa R. "Better than Fair: Ephemera and the Centennial Exhibition." *Popular Culture in Libraries* 4 (July 1996): 21–62.

Stauffer, D. McN. "Lithographic Portraits of Albert Newsam." *PMHB* 24 (1900): 267–89, 430–52; 25 (1901): 109–13; 26 (1902): 382–86.

Steiner, Bill. *Audubon Art Prints: A Collector's Guide to Every Edition.* Columbia: University of South Carolina Press, 2003.

Stephens, Mitchell. *A History of News.* Philadelphia: Harcourt Brace & Co., 1997.

Stokes, I. N. Phelps. *The Iconography of Manhattan Island, 1498–1909.* Vol. 3. New York: Robert H. Dodd, 1925.

Stokes, I. N. Phelps, and D. C. Haskell. *American Historical Prints, Early Views of American Cities.* New York: New York Public Library, 1932.

Strasser, Susan. *Satisfaction Guaranteed: The Making of the American Mass Market.* New York: Pantheon, 1989.

Stuart, James. *Three Years in North America.* 3rd, rev. ed. Vol. 1. Edinburgh: Robert Cadell, 1833.

Tatham, David. "The Lithographic Workshop, 1825–1850." In *The Cultivation of Artists in Nineteenth-Century America,* edited by Georgia Brady Barnhill, Diana Korzenik, and Caroline F. Sloat, 45–54. Worcester, Mass.: American Antiquarian Society, 1997.

Taylor, Charles H. "Some Notes on Early American Lithography." *Proceedings of the American Antiquarian Society* 32 (April 1922): 68–80.

Tebbel, John, and Mary Ellen Zuckerman. *The Magazine in America, 1741–1990.* New York: Oxford University Press, 1991.

Teitelman, S. Robert. *Birch's Views of Philadelphia: A Reduced Facsimile of the City of Philadelphia.* Rev. ed. Philadelphia: Free Library of Philadelphia, 2000.

Thompson, W. Fletcher, Jr. *The Image of War: The Pictorial Reporting of the American Civil War.* New York: T. Yoseloff, 1960.

Timbs, J. *The Year-Book of Facts in Science and Art.* London: David Bogue, 1854.

Tooker, Elva. *Nathan Trotter, Philadelphia Merchant, 1787–1853.* Cambridge: Harvard University Press, 1955.

Trachtenberg, Alan. *Reading American Photographs.* New York: Hill & Wang, 1989.

Tuckerman, Henry T. *Book of the Artists.* New York: G. P. Putnam & Sons; London: Sampson Low & Co., 1867.

Twyman, Michael. *Breaking the Mould: The First Hundred Years of Lithography.* Panizzi Lectures 2000. London: British Library, 2001.

———. "Charles Joseph Hullmandel: Lithographic Printer Extraordinary." In *Lasting Impressions: Lithography as Art,* edited by Pat Gilmour, 42–90. Canberra: Australian National Gallery, 1988.

———. *Images en couleur: Godefroy Engelmann, Charles Hullmandel et les débuts de la chromolithographie.* Lyon: Musée de l'imprimerie; Paris: Panama Musées, 2007.

———. "The Lithographic Hand Press, 1796–1850." *Journal of the Printing Historical Society* 3 (1967): 3–50.

———. "Lithographic Stone and the Printing Trade in the Nineteenth Century." *Journal of the Printing Historical Society* 8 (1972): 1–41.

———. *Lithography, 1800–1850: The Techniques of Drawing on Stone in England and France and Their Application in Works of Topography.* London: Oxford University Press, 1970.

———. *Printing, 1770–1970: An Illustrated History of Its Development and Uses in England.* London: Eyre & Spottiswoode, 1970.

———. "The Tinted Lithograph." *Journal of the Printing Historical Society* 1 (1965): 39–56.

Tyler, Ron. *Audubon's Great National Work.* Austin: University of Texas Press, 1993.

———. "Illustrated Government Publications Related to the American West, 1843–1863." In *Surveying the Record: North American Scientific Exploration to 1930,* edited by Edward C. Carter II, 147–72. Philadelphia: American Philosophical Society, 1999.

———. *Prints of the West.* Golden, Colo.: Fulcrum Pub., 1994.

United States. Patent Office. *Annual Report of Commissioner of Patents: Report of the Commissioner of Patents, for the Year . . .* Washington, D.C.: Patent Office.

Upton, Dell. *Another City: Urban Life and Urban Spaces in the New American Republic.* New Haven: Yale University Press, 2008.

Viola, Herman J. *The Indian Legacy of Charles Bird King.* Washington, D.C.: Smithsonian Institution Press, 1976.

Wainwright, Nicholas B. "The Age of Nicholas Biddle, 1825–1841." In *Philadelphia: A 300-Year History,* by Russell Frank Weigley et al., 258–306. New York: W. W. Norton & Co., 1982.

———. "Augustus Kollner, Artist." *PMHB* 84 (July 1960): 325–51.

———. "Lithographic Note." *PMHB* 84 (October 1959): 455–56.

———. *Philadelphia in the Romantic Age of Lithography: An Illustrated History of Early Lithography in Philadelphia, with a Descriptive List of Philadelphia Scenes Made by Philadelphia Lithographers Before 1866.* Philadelphia: Historical Society of Pennsylvania, 1958.

[Waln, Robert, Jr.]. *The Hermit in America on a Visit to Philadelphia: Containing Some Account of the Beaux and Belles, Dandies and Coquettes, Cotillion Parties, Supper Parties, Tea Parties, &c. &c. of That Famous City.* Edited by Peter Atall. Philadelphia: M. Thomas, 1819.

Watson, John F. *Annals and Occurrences of New York City and State in the Olden Time.* Philadelphia: Henry F. Anners, 1846.

———. *Annals of Philadelphia and Pennsylvania in the Olden Time.* 2 vols. Philadelphia: J. B. Lippincott, 1868.

———. *Annals of Philadelphia and Pennsylvania in the Olden Time.* Enlarged with many revisions and additions by Willis P. Hazard. 3 vols. Philadelphia: Edwin S. Stuart, 1905.

———. *Annals of Philadelphia and Pennsylvania in the Olden Times.* 3 vols. Philadelphia: Edwin S. Stuart, 1891.

Watt, Alexander. *Mechanical Industries Explained: Showing How Many Useful Arts Are Practised.* London: W. & A. K. Johnston, 1881.

Weatherwax, Sarah. "Matthias Weaver: The Reluctant Lithographer." Paper presented at "Impressions of Philadelphia," North American Print Conference 2007, Philadelphia, September 28, 2007. Copy at LCP.

Webb, Samuel. *History of Pennsylvania Hall.* Philadelphia: Printed by Merrihew & Gun, 1838.

Weber, Wilhelm. *A History of Lithography.* London: Thames & Hudson, 1966.

Wegner, Wolfgang. "'Les Oeuvres Lithographiques' und ihre Entstehungsgeschichte: Ein Beitrag zur Erforschung der Inkunabelzeit der Münchner Lithographie." *Oberbayerisches Archiv* 87 (1965): 139–92.

Weigley, Russell Frank, et al. *Philadelphia: A 300-Year History.* New York: W. W. Norton & Co., 1982.

Weimerskirch, Philip J. "The Beginnings of Lithography in America." *Journal of the Printing Historical Society* 27 (1998): 49–67.

———. "Lithographic Stone in America." *Printing History* 11, no. 1 (1989): 2–15.

Weitenkampf, Frank. "Lithographs." In *The Concise Encyclopedia of American Antiques,* edited by Helen Comstock, 371–75. New York: Hawthorn Books, 1958.

———. "Painter-Lithography in the United States." *Scribners Magazine* 30 (May 1903): 537–50.

Welsh, Peter C. "The Lithograph: A Mirror of Victorian Taste." *Antiques* 80 (September 1980): 240–43.

Williams, Anne. *Cutting a Fine Figure: The Art of the Jigsaw Puzzle.* Lexington, Mass.: Museum of Our National Heritage, 1996.

Wilmerding, John. *American Art.* New York: Penguin Books, 1976.

Wilson, Kenneth M. "Window Glass in America." In *Building Early America: Contributions Toward the History of a Great Industry,* edited by Charles E. Peterson, 150–64. Radnor, Pa.: Chilton Book Co., 1976.

Wood, Charles B., III. "Prints and Scientific Illustration in America." In *Prints in and of America to 1850,* edited by John D. Morse, 161–92. Charlottesville: University Press of Virginia, 1970.

Wood, Gillen D'Arcy. *The Shock of the Real: Romanticism and Visual Culture, 1760–1860.* New York: Palgrave, 2001.

Wright, Helena E. "The Image Makers: The Role of the Graphic Arts in Industrialization." *IA: The Journal of the Society for Industrial Archeology* 12 (1986): 5–18.

———. *With Pen & Graver: Women Graphic Artists Before 1900.* Wash-

ington, D.C.: National Museum of
American History, 1995.

Young, William, ed. *A Dictionary of American Artists, Sculptors, and Engravers.* Cambridge, Mass.: William Young & Co., 1968.

Zakim, Michael. *Ready-Made Democracy: A History of Men's Dress in the American Republic, 1760–1860.* Chicago: University of Chicago Press, 2003.

JENNIFER AMBROSE, photo archivist, National Baseball Hall of Fame & Museum, worked in the Print and Photograph Department of the Library Company of Philadelphia from 1994 to 2008, serving as associate curator 2000–2008. She served as project director of *Philadelphia on Stone* 2007–8. Before coming to the Library Company, she worked with a wide variety of historical and museum collections. Ambrose received her B.A. from Marlboro College in Vermont and her M.A. in American history from the State University of New York at Albany.

DONALD H. CRESSWELL, Ph.D., has been co-owner of the Philadelphia Print Shop for twenty-five years, before which he worked for ten years as an academic librarian and teacher. Throughout his career he has written books, essays, and book reviews while also giving public addresses for conferences and making guest appearances, including as a print expert on PBS's *Antiques Roadshow.* His works include *The American Revolution in Drawings and Prints: A Checklist of 1765–1790 Graphics in the Library of Congress* (Library of Congress, 1975), *Prints of Philadelphia,* coauthored with Christopher W. Lane (Philadelphia Print Shop, 1990), and contributions and essays in *Treasures of State* (H. N. Abrams, 1991) and *Virginia in Maps* (Library of Virginia, 2000).

SARA W. DUKE, curator of popular and applied graphic art, has worked in the Print & Photograph Division of the Library of Congress since 1991 and was promoted to her current position in 2003. Dr. Duke received her B.A. from Bennington College, her M.L.S. from the University of Maryland at College Park, and her Ph.D. in European history from the State University of New York at Stony Brook. She has published numerous articles on the graphic collections at the Library of Congress, primarily focusing on cartooning and satire.

CHRISTOPHER W. LANE is co-owner of the Philadelphia Print Shop. He received his B.A. from Trinity College, Hartford, in philosophy and an M.A. from Oxford University in philosophy, politics, and economics. He is the author of numerous articles on, and guides to, collecting historic prints and maps, including *Prints of Philadelphia,* coauthored with Donald H. Cresswell (Philadelphia Print Shop, 1990), *Impressions of Niagara* (Philadelphia Print Shop, 1993), and *Panorama of Pittsburgh* (The Frick, 2008). In addition, he curated the exhibitions "Impressions des Chutes du Niagara" at the Castellani Art Museum of Niagara University in 2002 and "Panorama of Pittsburgh" at the Frick Art & Historical Center in 2008. Since 1997 he has served as a print and map expert on PBS's *Antiques Roadshow.*

ERIKA PIOLA, associate curator and codirector, Visual Culture Program, has worked in the Print and Photograph Department at the Library Company of Philadelphia since 1997 and served as the project director of *Philadelphia on Stone* 2008–10. She received her B.A. from Haverford College and her M.A. in history from the University of Pennsylvania. She is a coauthor of *Center City Philadelphia in the Nineteenth Century* (Arcadia, 2006) and has published essays in *Encyclopedia of Nineteenth-Century Photography* (Routledge, 2007), *Imprint: Journal of the American Historical Print Collectors Society, Art Documentation,* and the *Journal of the Ephemera Society of America.*

MICHAEL TWYMAN is emeritus professor of typography and graphic communication at the University of Reading (U.K.), where he has taught for half a century. He is currently director of the Centre for Ephemera Studies at the university. He is the author of many books and articles on printing history and graphic design, including *Printing, 1770–1970* (Eyre & Spottiswoode, 1970), *Lithography, 1800–1850* (Oxford University Press, 1970), *Early Lithographed Books* (Farrand Press, 1990), *Early Lithographed Music* (Farrand Press, 1996), *Breaking the Mould: The First Hundred Years of Lithography* (British Library, 2001), and has been working on a wide-ranging book on chromolithography.

DELL UPTON, professor of architectural history and chair of the Department of Art History at the University of California, Los Angeles, is the author of *Another City: Urban Life and Urban Spaces in the New American Republic* (Yale University Press, 2008), as well as *Architecture in the United States* (Oxford University Press, 1998), *Holy Things and Profane: Anglican Parish Churches in Colonial Virginia* (Architectural History Foundation / MIT Press, 1986), and *Madaline: Love and Survival in Antebellum New Orleans* (University of Georgia Press, 1996). In addition, he served as a consultant and chief catalog essayist for "Art and the Empire City: New York, 1825–1861," an exhibition held at the Metropolitan Museum of Art in the fall of 2000. Upton was formerly professor of architectural history at the University of California, Berkeley, and Shea Professor of Art History at the University of Virginia.

SARAH J. WEATHERWAX has worked at the Library Company of Philadelphia since 1993, serving as curator of prints and photographs since 1996. Previously she held curatorial positions at the State Museum of Pennsylvania and the Brooklyn Historical Society. She has published articles in *Antiques; Imprint: Journal of the American Historical Print Collectors Society; Daguerreian Annual;* and *Stereo World* and was a coauthor of *Center City Philadelphia in the Nineteenth Century* (Arcadia, 2006). Weatherwax holds a B.A. in history from the College of Wooster (Ohio) and an M.A. in history from the College of William and Mary.